TO STAND ASIDE
OR STAND ALONE

JEWS AND JUDAISM: HISTORY AND CULTURE

SERIES EDITORS
Mark K. Bauman
Adam D. Mendelsohn

FOUNDING EDITOR
Leon J. Weinberger

ADVISORY BOARD
Tobias Brinkmann
Ellen Eisenberg
David Feldman
Kirsten Fermaglich
Jeffrey S. Gurock
Nahum Karlinsky
Richard Menkis
Riv-Ellen Prell
Raanan Rein
Jonathan Schorsch
Stephen J. Whitfield
Marcin Wodzinski

TO STAND ASIDE
OR STAND ALONE

SOUTHERN REFORM RABBIS
and the CIVIL RIGHTS MOVEMENT

P. ALLEN KRAUSE

EDITED BY MARK K. BAUMAN
WITH STEPHEN KRAUSE

The University of Alabama Press
Tuscaloosa

The University of Alabama Press
Tuscaloosa, Alabama 35487-0380
uapress.ua.edu

Typeface: Garamond and Arial

Manufactured in the United States of America
Cover image: From left to right: Rev. Dr. Martin Luther King, Jr., unknown man, Dr. Benjamin
E. Mays, Rabbi Jacob Rothschild (in foreground with four-peaked handkerchief in pocket),
unknown man (head partly obscured), unknown woman, *Atlanta Constitution* editor Ralph
McGill, and Archbishop Paul Hallinan at the dinner honoring Dr. King after he won the
Nobel Peace Prize, National Council of Christians and Jews, Dinkler Hotel, Atlanta, Georgia,
January 27, 1965. Mays, Rothschild, McGill, and Hallinan cochaired this event, which was the
first integrated formal dinner in Atlanta. LBSCB12-120g, Lane Brothers Collection, Special
Collection and Archives, Georgia State University Library.
Used by permission of Georgia State University Library.
Cover design: Michele Myatt Quinn

∞

Publication made possible in part through the generous support of the Southern Jewish
Historical Society, www.jewishsouth.org.

Library of Congress Cataloging-in-Publication Data

Names: Krause, P. Allen, 1939– author. | Bauman, Mark K., 1946– editor. | Krause, Stephen
(Stephen K.), editor.
Title: To stand aside or stand alone : Southern Reform rabbis and the civil rights movement / P.
Allen Krause ; edited by Mark K. Bauman with Stephen Krause.
Other titles: Jews and Judaism (Tuscaloosa, Ala.)
Description: Tuscaloosa : University of Alabama Press, [2016] | Series: Jews and Judaism : history
and culture | Includes bibliographical references and index.
Identifiers: LCCN 2016014719| ISBN 9780817319243 (cloth : alk. paper) | ISBN 9780817390211
(e book)
Subjects: LCSH: Rabbis—Southern States—Interviews. | Rabbis—Political activity—Southern
States. | Reform Judaism—Southern States. | African Americans—Civil rights. | Civil rights—
Religious aspects—Judaism.
Classification: LCC BM750 .K69 2016 | DDC 323.1196/0730088296—dc23
LC record available at https://lccn.loc.gov/2016014719

We dedicate this book to our children,
Stephen, Gavriella, and Roger,
whose love makes all things possible.
—Allen and Sherri Hofmann Krause

Contents

Figures

Acknowledgments

This work could not have been written were it not for the continual assistance of many individuals. Of key importance were the writer's informants—rabbinic and lay alike—who gave so generously of their time and knowledge. Above all, I wish to express appreciation to Dr. Stanley F. Chyet, associate director of the American Jewish Archives. The rabbis of old surely had men like Dr. Chyet in mind when they advised struggling researchers like myself: "Take for yourself a teacher." For his constant guidance and constructive criticism, I am truly grateful.
—P. Allen Krause

⸝

My husband did not live to see the publication of this book. This volume is based on the interviews and research he conducted during the 1960s, but goes far beyond that work. By including his original introduction, he and I honor Dr. Chyet and the individuals willing to be interviewed. Because this work transcends the original, I add the following. I would like to acknowledge the encouragement of Dr. John Hope Franklin, who worked closely with Allen over several decades on both the research and the book manuscript. Dr. Franklin's thoughtful comments to Allen about the importance of this work, as Allen was working to complete the manuscript while on sabbatical at Harvard, gave him the courage to push through the myriad of challenges that this book presented.

I would also like to acknowledge Dr. Mark Bauman's discovery of and early enthusiasm for Allen's research, and subsequent articles, before he had even met Allen. The two finally connected at a meeting of the Southern Jewish Historical Society in 2004. Dr. Bauman approached Allen and asked, "Are you the real Allen Krause? I have been looking for you for a long time."

This chance connection began a long-term collaboration that would ultimately welcome Allen into the world of serious academia and help him realize his dream of publishing this book. Thank you, Mark, for suggesting, editing, nudging, and encouraging—sometimes all at the same time. Without Dr. Bauman's loving hand, this book would not have seen the light of day.

I am grateful to our son, Stephen, for his many hours of work editing and clarifying the language of the manuscript. Allen and I are both very proud and grateful for his willingness to share his skills in this venture.

—Sherri Hofmann Krause

Preface

Besides ordination and earning a master's degree at Hebrew Union College–Jewish Institute of Religion, Allen Krause earned an undergraduate history degree at the University of California, Los Angeles, and pursued graduate studies at the University of Chicago and the University of California, Berkeley. He studied at Harvard as a Daniel Jeremy Silver Fellow and HUC-JIR further awarded him a doctor of divinity degree.

When I began studying southern Jewish history during the late 1970s, Allen's article derived from this research was among the first works I read. It had been reprinted in the first anthology in the field.[1] As I indicated in the introduction to an anthology on the subject that I coedited, Allen's research provided the basis for the study of the topic for virtually every study thereafter.[2] Yet Allen's research was never published, and he did not pursue further publication of the materials for over three decades.

During this period he pursued a full-time career as a pulpit rabbi and a part-time career as an adjunct professor. Beginning with his student days as a Congress of Racial Equality (CORE) volunteer, he applied his Judaism to social activism. He served a congregation in Fremont, California, before moving to Temple Beth El of South Orange County in 1984, where Allen filled the pulpit until receiving emeritus status. He inaugurated Jewish day schools in both locations. During the 1970s he worked on behalf of the Save Soviet Jewry movement and traveled to the Soviet Union in 1986 in support of refusenik families. A founder of the Ad Hoc Rabbinic Committee to Rescue Ethiopian Jewry, he led a national petition campaign that pressed for United States government action. He also assisted the Reform synagogue in Ra'anana, Israel. In 1994 he organized a local interfaith conference that brought people together for workshops and speakers for fifteen years and cofounded the South County Interfaith Clergy. After 9/11 he expanded his ties to the Muslim community with the creation of Living Room Dialogues at the Orange County Islamic Foundation Mosque in Mission Viejo, California. Allen presided over the Orange County Board of Rabbis and the Pacific Association of Reform Rabbis, beside serving on the executive board of the Central Conference of American Rabbis (CCAR) and chairing the CCAR Task Force on Rabbi/Cantor Relations. In 2011, the Orange County Human Relations

Committee granted Allen the Community Leader Award. He was the first rabbi to receive the award in forty years.[3] He lived the life of the social activist rabbi that drew his attention as a rabbinical student and historian.

In 2007 Allen submitted a proposal for a presentation at the Southern Jewish Historical Society (SJHS) conference to take place in Washington, DC. I co-chaired the program committee with Stephen J. Whitfield of Brandeis University. The program committee approved the proposal, and Allen's presentation was a highlight of the conference.

In my role as editor of the SJHS-sponsored journal, *Southern Jewish History*, I had already begun a correspondence with Allen concerning the submission of a revised version of the article for publication. Thus began our collaboration and friendship.

Initially, Allen was extremely hesitant to submit an article for publication. He just did not trust editors. Extremely meticulous in his writing and research, he was concerned that an editor would muddle his words. I, an editor nicknamed "the Slasher," had to prove myself. After two reviewers recommended publication, I returned his manuscript for revision covered with red ink and with suggestions for a legion of substantive changes. As I often comment, I am only as good an editor as an author is willing to exert the extra effort. And Allen was more than willing and able to do so.

The result was a highly revisionist article on Rabbi Burton Padoll of Charleston, South Carolina. The prevailing literature emphasized conflicts between rabbis and congregations over civil rights. Allen stressed Padoll's difficult personality and the fact that he did not first establish himself in the Jewish and secular communities. Padoll left under duress, but his position in favor of civil rights became a symptom of underlying issues rather than a root cause in itself.[4] Allen's article also fills a geographic void in that it treats a rabbi in South Carolina, the one Deep South state not included in this volume.

Allen continued to conduct research and give presentations at SJHS conferences. His next published article again derived from a presentation and revised previous notions. Benjamin Schultz had thus far been the only rabbi in the South identified as openly favoring segregation and opposing the civil rights movement. Segregationists widely praised and quoted his writings and statements. Although serving a congregation in Mississippi, Schultz hailed from Brooklyn, New York. Allen traced Schultz's long career in northern congregations and his anticommunist crusade during the Cold War. Schultz turned out to be a strident McCarthyite. When he was hounded out of the North for his views, he readily agreed with his newfound southern friends that communists led the civil rights movement. The threat that the communist menace posed to the United States far exceeded racism in Schultz's calculations. Far from exonerating Schultz's behavior, Allen placed Schultz's position in the broader context of the rabbi's warped thought process.[5]

In his original findings, Allen Krause had concluded that few rabbis had spoken out in behalf of black rights and that their congregations had attempted to curtail their activities and, in some cases, had forced them out. This was a logical perception from the vantage of the mid-1960s. I believe that his years in the pulpit and working with congregation boards as an activist rabbi influenced Allen's later interpretation. It had become clear to him that rabbis had to earn respect and standing in their communities to become effective and accepted spokespeople. An acerbic individual who failed in other ways as a pulpit rabbi could hardly expect the support of congregants when they perceived that the rabbi's actions placed them in jeopardy. Further research, reflection, and recent secondary publications also indicated that far more rabbis in the South acted on the positive side of the civil rights movement than had previously been counted. Oftentimes these unsung heroes worked quietly in their local communities behind the scenes. Several of the individuals highlighted in this book exemplify this. P. Irving Bloom, Alfred Goodman, Nathaniel Shore, and William Silverman hitherto have largely gone unnoticed.

Allen retired from his pulpit in 2008 and enjoyed a marvelous dinner and tributes in his honor. Allen, his wife, Sherri, Stephen Whitfield, Michael Cohen of Tulane, my wife, Sandy, and I enjoyed dinner together while attending the 2009 SJHS conference in New Orleans. Allen and I discussed possible scenarios for a book project based on his original interviews. He had further discussions with Gary P. Zola, director of the Jacob R. Marcus Center of the American Jewish Archives (AJA) and professor at Hebrew Union College–Jewish Institute of Religion. Gary, AJA archivist Kevin Proffitt, and the staff subsequently provided major assistance on the project that ensued. Allen's original research and substantial additional material are available at AJA.

In October 2011, the SJHS met in Columbia, South Carolina, and Allen gave his last presentation. Having battled cancer for years, he sat in a wheelchair and new medications took their toll. Allen's was perhaps the most courageous and determined performance anyone in the audience had ever witnessed. He received a standing ovation. Allen, his devoted son Stephen, Ellen Umansky of Fairfield University, Lee Shai Weissbach of the University of Louisville, Sandy, and I met for dinner. Allen asked me to finish his project if he was unable to do so, and I agreed. During the next agonizing months, he continued to work and give me status reports before he finally succumbed on March 3, 2012. Sherri and Steve asked me to fulfill my promise, and Steve provided the various files.

Steve reviewed my original edits of the manuscript and provided numerous important changes. After giving an outstanding presentation at the SJHS conference in Nashville in 2015 based on his father's interview with Rabbi William B. Silverman, he realized that he could decipher many words and phrases that the original transcriber missed besides correcting errors in the transcription. Steve's work in this regard has greatly enhanced the integrity of the interviews.

I accepted the task of editing this manuscript out of the highest respect for a truly remarkable individual and in memory of a dear friendship cut all too short. Given Allen's distrust of editors, I have used my track change "red ink" cautiously, although I add analysis throughout and appropriate secondary works to citations without qualms. In a very few places, I have also deleted some of the unnecessary wording in Allen's questions or the rabbis' replies, indicating as such with ellipses. Certain issues like italicizing words unnecessarily and eliminating hyphens for "African American" have been corrected without indication of doing so since these alter the transcript and not the original oral interview tape recording. Punctuation, spelling, and italicized emphasis have been changed from the transcript without indication of the changes since these reflected the opinion of the transcriber rather than what was actually spoken. In no case have I altered the substance of any interviews. That Allen Krause was not a professional historian is apparent from some of the sources he cited and, in some places, the paucity of citations. Although I have attempted to remedy this by updating Internet addresses, deleting untrustworthy websites, and adding sources, retracing his steps is not always possible. Yet his introductions were never intended to be definitive histories of the local communities but rather to give context. This is the way they should be read.

Steve reviewed and revised, and then I provided a final edit. We benefited greatly from the insights of peer reviewers supplied by the University of Alabama Press. One reviewer remains anonymous but Gary P. Zola allowed his identity to be disclosed. Adam Mendelsohn, with whom I coedit the press's series Jews and Judaism: History and Culture, graciously agreed to include the volume in the series and provided important feedback and support, as did the press's editor in chief, Daniel Waterman. I also greatly appreciate the prodigious efforts of project editor Joanna Jacobs and copyeditor Jennifer Manley Rogers. Rachel Heimovics Braun provided tremendous assistance formatting the materials and giving additional feedback.

Allen did not have time to introduce the interviews or compose conclusions. I have provided these. Although Allen was unable to compile the background information on either rabbis Milton Grafman or Jacob Rothschild, the extensive literature on both allow the addition of his annotated transcripts without that information.

I greatly appreciate and acknowledge the assistance of the following individuals and organizations in identifying and/or providing illustrations: Archivists Catherine Kahn and Paula Fortier, Touro Infirmary Archives; Sean Benjamin and

Samantha Bruner, Louisiana Research Collection, Howard-Tilton Memorial Library, Tulane University; Janet Bordelon, the former history department director at the Goldring/Woldenberg Institute of Southern Jewish Life; President Edward G. Kaufman and Archivist Heather Hammond at Ohef Sholom Temple, Norfolk, Virginia; Rabbi Robert Loewy, Gates of Prayer, Metairie, Louisiana; Rabbi Edward Cohen, Temple Sinai, New Orleans; Rabbi P. Irving Bloom, Archivist Susan Thomas, and Secretary Susie Broos, Congregation Sha'arai Shomayim/ Spring Hill Avenue Temple, Mobile, Alabama; Dr. Anne Landau and Barbara Levingston, Adath Israel, Cleveland, Mississippi; Rabbi Martin Hinchin and Archivist Jacque Caplan, Congregation Gemiluth Chassodim, Alexandria, Louisiana; Rayna Goodman and Deborah Anderson, Temple Israel, Columbus, Georgia; Executive Director Mark Freedman and Annette Levy Ratkin, Annette Levy Ratkin Jewish Community Archives for the Jewish Federation of Nashville and Middle Tennessee, Nashville, Tennessee; Archivist Leona Fleisher and Secretary Mitzi Russell, Ohavai Sholom/Vine Street Synagogue, Nashville, Tennessee; Ellen Johnston, the Special Collections and Archives, Georgia State University Library; Myra Evans and photo editor Bita Honarvar, the *Atlanta Journal-Constitution*; and curators and archivists Gerald Chaudron, Sharon L. Banker, Brigitte Billeaudeaux, and James Cushing, Preservation and Special Collections, University Libraries, University of Memphis.

Phyllis Leffler and her grants committee generously provided a grant for the publication of this volume on behalf of the Southern Jewish Historical Society. I greatly appreciate the thoughtfulness of the committee and society in helping make this book possible.

—Mark K. Bauman

For my entire life, I knew my father as a beloved pulpit rabbi—first at several congregations in Northern California and then for the last twenty-five years of his life as the senior rabbi at Temple Beth El in South Orange County, California. I was only vaguely aware of the other work my father was doing in his spare time: uncounted hours spent transcribing and annotating interviews that he had taken in 1966, when he was just a young rabbinic student with an interest in the response of southern rabbis to the civil rights movement.

My father worked on this manuscript for many years. It was his pride and joy—his entrée into an academic world that he valued deeply. His intention following his retirement in the summer of 2008 was to devote himself full-time to completing the book, and then to move on to new academic and post-rabbinic endeavors. Unfortunately, my father was diagnosed with an incurable cancer just three months following retirement.

The next four years saw my father spend thousands of hours completing the histories and annotations you see before you. When it became clear that his illness would not allow him to live to see his book in print, he approached Mark Bauman and I with a very special request: to review the various chapters of his book upon his death and do whatever needed to be done in order to complete the editing process and see the book through to publication.

The time I have spent editing these chapters has brought me closer to my father. I now see how his life and his rabbinate were indelibly shaped by the lessons he learned from interviewing these southern rabbis: to work for justice, for the weakest among us, despite great personal and professional risk. My father embodied these lessons throughout his life.

I am honored to have been a part of this project. I am immeasurably grateful to Mark Bauman for his efforts shepherding this manuscript from inception to completion; to the University of Alabama Press, which was always my father's first choice of publisher; to my mother, who spent many hours with me discussing my edits and brainstorming titles for the book; and to all the members of the Southern Jewish Historical Society whom I have had the pleasure of meeting over the past few years while attending your conferences. Thank you all for giving me the opportunity to work with you in pursuit of such a worthy goal. And thank you to my dad, who I wish was here in person to see his dream come true.

—Stephen Krause

TO STAND ASIDE
OR STAND ALONE

Author's Introduction

I entered the University of California, Los Angeles, in 1957, within days of the Soviet Union's successful launch of Sputnik, a rather significant jolt during the general sanguinity of the Eisenhower era. My four undergraduate years proved to be both troubling and exhilarating. For the first time, my image of America as "land of the free and home of the brave" was challenged by a growing awareness that we Americans were not always the good guys in white hats. Those "Cowboys and Indians" movies I had watched religiously as a child became a metaphor for my failure of nerve, a growing awareness that the Indians were not the ones who were the savages.[1] This shift affected the way that I viewed the civil rights struggle that was playing itself out across the country during the early 1960s, and while at UCLA I became active in the movement in a number of ways including volunteering for the local chapter of the Congress of Racial Equality.[2] I was part of the disillusioned college youth of the 1960s bent on making this country and the world a better place.

After graduating from UCLA with a degree in American history, I was fortunate to study at the Cincinnati branch of the Hebrew Union College–Jewish Institute of Religion. There, I found myself drawn to an aspect of the civil rights movement that had, to that point, remained largely unexplored by historians: what was the role of rabbis in the South in relation to the civil rights movement? Fortunately the American Jewish Archives housed at Hebrew Union College contained very valuable materials, which Dr. Stanley Chyet, the associate director of the archives, brought to my attention: newspaper clippings, sermons, speeches, correspondence of rabbis serving southern congregations, and other unpublished documents. To supplement this material, I developed a questionnaire that I then sent to over seventy rabbis—every rabbi who had been serving in a southern pulpit for at least five years. Approximately one-third of these responded. Subsequently, fourteen men (there were no female rabbis in the United States at the time) agreed to let me interview them at the upcoming June 1966 Central Conference of American Rabbis (CCAR) in Toronto, Canada.

I hitched a ride to the convention with a classmate, armed only with a nineteen-dollar tape recorder and cassette tapes that I had purchased for ten for a dollar.[3] I met with each of the fourteen rabbis during the course of the convention. As a balance to the rabbis' testimonies, while at the convention I also interviewed officials then serving in the Anti-Defamation League (ADL), the Southern Regional Council, and the Religious Action Center of the Union of American Hebrew Congregations (UAHC; now called the Union for Reform Judaism [URJ]), as well as the Rev. Fred Shuttlesworth.[4]

Little did I know then that some of the rabbis who granted me interviews would deserve to be viewed favorably by history for their role in the struggle for black civil rights. Unfortunately, even today their names are little known. When asked by the curious about the topic of my research, although I answer that I am writing about the role southern rabbis played in the civil rights movement in the South, invariably they respond by naming someone such as Abraham Joshua Heschel, a northern rabbi who flew to the South to march alongside Rev. Martin Luther King Jr. A few might recall Jacob Rothschild, whose Atlanta synagogue was bombed in 1958, but otherwise the rabbis who are recalled and praised are ones from Cleveland, San Francisco, New York City, Boston, or their hometown synagogue, who went south to march for a day or two before returning home to a hero's welcome. These rabbis from the North faced risks and demonstrated courage and commitment but so did Perry Nussbaum and Charles Mantinband living in the Deep South, and, to a lesser extent, rabbis such as P. Irving Bloom, Julian Feibelman, Alfred Goodman, William Silverman, and Malcolm Stern in more moderate communities. They faced these risks daily, and their stories deserve to be told and remembered.

Of course, not all rabbis in the South opted to follow the same path. As some stood up against the evils of the separate and unequal system, others made peace with it or found reasons to justify inaction. Somewhat surprisingly, some of the latter also volunteered to be interviewed and, when interviewed, shared their thought processes and the reasons they remained relatively silent. Even some rabbis in congregations in less difficult settings still opted to be more circumspect and avoid making waves. The transcriptions of the interviews that follow make it clear who fell into each category.

Eli Evans, author of a classic book on southern Jewish history, expressed surprise at the candor of this group's responses to my queries.[5] The perspective of time makes it possible to suggest why these men felt it important to sit down and speak the truth to a young seminary student whom they had never met. I think it was because they knew that they were living through a pivotal moment in history, and they wanted their stories told. But for many, their candor came only with the promise that their stories would not be made public for at least twenty-five years. Thus I wrote two sections: section one (276 pages) told each rabbi's story anonymously (for example, a discussion with "Rabbi H" in community "M"), while section two (fifty-six pages), to which access was restricted to selected members of the archives, provided a key to the names and places, and contained brief chapters that were too sensitive to be made part of the public domain at that time. Over the last fifteen years, a number of scholars of southern Jewish history, including Melissa Fay Greene, Marc Dollinger, and several of the authors of chapters in the anthology edited by Mark K. Bauman and Berkley Kalin, have used the materials contained in the restricted section while writing about this explosive period of American Jewish history. But none has yet had access to the original tapes and interviews.[6] As I write this, all but two of the rabbis interviewed have long since died. As those interviewed wished over four decades ago, their voices can finally be heard.

Geographical Boundary

"Why pick on the South?" one of the interviewees tossed out for my consideration. "Since when does the South have a monopoly on racism?" Or, as another southern rabbi put it: "Integration is not a regional issue, but a national problem." When asked much the same question in the early 1960s, Langston Hughes responded: "Not that the North is perfect. Not that New York is paradise. But compared to some of our deep South cities, Manhattan is Heaven."[7] Needing to narrow my focus to make the work manageable, Hughes's logic seemed compelling. Moreover, Supreme Court decisions relating to race relations after 1954 affected the South disproportionately, because in this region prejudice against African Americans was entrenched in the legal system, and the court singled out the region for attention.[8] In the years following the 1954 Supreme Court decision in *Brown v. Board of Education of Topeka, Kansas,* the South became a cauldron of activity, stirred by thousands of militant integrationists who descended on it and shook its foundations to the core.

Since this book is based on my 1966 interviews, the geographic scope of the work is limited to those states in which the rabbis I interviewed were serving: Alabama, Georgia, Louisiana, Mississippi, Tennessee, and Virginia. With the exceptions of Tennessee and Virginia, each of the other states may be described as part of the Deep South. According to government census data for 1960, Mississippi, Louisiana, South Carolina, Alabama, and Georgia had the highest percentage of African American residents of any of the states that had been part of the former Confederacy.[9] These states were also the most dependent on plantation-type agriculture during the antebellum period. One hundred years later, these states still comprised the part of the South that remained most hostile to integration and the most supportive of a racist philosophy.

Temporal Boundary: From *Brown* to the Kerner Commission

In addition to geographic parameters, I set a temporal limit for this study. This was not difficult, since the interviewees almost unanimously believed that the most important date in modern southern history was May 17, 1954, the day the

Brown decision was rendered by the US Supreme Court. That decision ignited civil rights activities unlike anything the South had witnessed since Reconstruction. Although the agitation for change hit different communities at different times, in the South as a whole 1954 was the year that marked the beginning of the end of the old order. In some instances, cities and towns were not shaken until years after the Supreme Court decision, a few as late as the Freedom Rider years in the early 1960s. Yet from the mid-1950s on, tension tinged the air throughout the South. Things were no longer business as usual. A sense of unease nestled into the minds of black and white alike, and not even citizens of the deepest portions of the Deep South could pay it no heed.

This book concerns itself, then, with the role of the Reform congregational rabbi in the South from 1954 through 1967, a period that takes us a few years past the end of the Freedom Rides and the Freedom Summer through the appointment of the Kerner Commission.[10]

A Word on Sources

As noted earlier, not all rabbis who served in the South during those years are represented in this study. Rather, only a sampling of those affiliated with Reform synagogues are included. Inadequate information was available on the Conservative and Orthodox rabbinate in the South, and none of the rabbis in those movements responded to my questionnaire or agreed to be interviewed. The information that I was able to accumulate about their activities was mostly furnished by their Reform colleagues, and thus might be perceived as subjective. Finally, there simply were very few Conservative and Orthodox rabbis in the South during these years. In fact, only one Orthodox congregation in the entire state of Mississippi employed a full-time, ordained rabbi.[11]

In terms of the Reform rabbis, the interviewees include less than 10 percent of those serving in the South during the years under consideration. No rabbis from North Carolina, South Carolina, or Florida appear. To some degree, by agreeing to be interviewed, the rabbis included were self-selecting. They also attended one particular CCAR convention, another self-selective factor.

These caveats notwithstanding, the experiences of those rabbis studied proved to be highly representative. They served in the land of the somewhat possible and the land of the almost impossible, in small towns and large cities, in the Deep South and the Upper South.[12] Their actions ran the gamut from the most active and courageous to the meekest and most accepting of the status quo. Their responses to critical questions document general agreement concerning certain issues and wide variations on others. If more or even all the Reform rabbis had been included, important details would have been added, but the basic findings, I believe, would remain.

In addition to the primary materials culled from the American Jewish Archives and other special collections identified in the citations, numerous books and periodicals provided important background and context for the interviews. These sources, including W. J. Cash's *The Mind of the South*, provided insights into the stage on which the rabbis acted. On occasion authors might turn to the Jewish community as a whole and mention the rabbis in passing, so that their findings proved of limited value when seeking specifics.

In recent years many additional sources have become available, particularly Mark K. Bauman and Berkley Kalin's *The Quiet Voices* and Clive Webb's *Fight against Fear*. In addition, excellent studies of particular communities appeared (*But for Birmingham* by Glenn T. Eskew is one fine example) as well as rabbinic papers now available in various university archives.[13] Finally, I interviewed some members of the Jewish communities that these rabbis served who retained vivid memories of those troubled times. All of the transcripts in this volume are from the interviews I conducted at the CCAR convention held in Toronto, Canada, in June 1966.

All statements and information set forth in this book, although obviously the sole responsibility of the author, are, at least indirectly traceable to these sources.

—P. Allen Krause, December 2012

Editor's Introduction

Rabbi P. Allen Krause interviewed the rabbis in this book at a specific moment in time. Their responses to his questions reflected their previous experiences and current activities and perceptions unvarnished by what with hindsight we know came later. President John F. Kennedy was assassinated just three years before the interviews. Malcolm X had only recently been assassinated. The Rev. Martin Luther King Jr. and Robert Kennedy were not martyred until two years later. Protesters marched from Memphis, Tennessee, to Jackson, Mississippi, as the interviews were being conducted. President Kennedy's successor, Lyndon B. Johnson, under pressure from such actions, was pressing Congress to pass the critical civil rights laws. In fact, one of the most significant civil rights acts had come into law only one year before the interviews. The major impact it would exert on voting and elections could hardly be imagined. The interview with James Wax preceded the signature event in Memphis that came to mark his position. At the convention where these interviews took place, the Central Conference of American Rabbis (CCAR) passed a resolution opposing the Vietnam War. The war, and opposition to it, took attention away from the civil rights movement, and resolutions by the CCAR and similar organizations as well as King's later opposition to the war entwined and complicated the issues. The Black Power phase of the civil right era was in its infancy. Violence in Watts had broken out during the summer of 1965. Conflicts over affirmative action, Andrew Young's United Nations ambassadorship, the UN resolution branding Zionism as racism, comments made by Jesse Jackson during his unsuccessful run for the Democratic nomination for the presidency, the Brownsville/Crown Heights incident, and other divisive events had not yet dug a deep chasm between members of the black and Jewish communities and their organizations. The civil rights movement had not yet moved its center to targets in the North. The marches, demonstrations, and boycotts, federal court decisions and acts passed by Congress notwithstanding, the actual results—the actual changes in the country and in people's lives—only unfolded in the ensuing decades. Would the passing of time and exposure to what came later have influenced the rabbis' opinions? This question speaks to the strengths of the interviews as primary sources but also their limitations.

The first generation of historians who chronicled the modern civil rights era tended to research the subject from the top down, concentrating as they did on the national leaders and organizations and the actions of the three branches of the federal government. Only later did attention shift to the local leaders, organizations, and forces. From this perspective, Krause was a pioneer. He concentrated on the rabbis in the local communities and on local initiatives. He also chose to interview the southeastern representatives of national organizations rather than their New York or Washington directors.

Nonetheless, Krause's focus and questions also reflected a moment in time. Later historians would ask more about the influences on the rabbis' actions and their motivation. Were they impacted by the influence of the Pittsburg Platform of 1885 and Prophetic Judaism on the definition of Reform Judaism and the role of the rabbi? What about Holocaust consciousness and the Adolf Eichmann trial that had taken place earlier in the decade? Some interviewees allude to their motivations while others fail to do so. Because Krause limited his questions to the South, the rabbis fail to comment on the violence/insurrections in northern cities except in passing.

Krause interviewed only a small group of rabbis. However, the group he interviewed was highly representative of the Reform rabbinate in the South in several ways. They served in small and large communities, in Deep South and Upper South/Old South and New South cities, and in locations that illustrated a variety of responses to the civil rights movement. More significantly, the rabbis displayed a full spectrum of ideas and actions.

These provisos notwithstanding, because of the illustrative nature of the interviews and the amazing insights and information that they provide, the historian can draw conclusions from the many patterns that the interviews and background information disclose. Certain factors tend to be relatively uniform while others run along a spectrum.

In his article and research, Krause makes distinctions between rabbis in the Deep South, what he termed the "land of the almost impossible," and in more moderate environs, his "land of the almost possible." He also identifies differences in the size and make-up of the Jewish communities and in the paths the rabbis followed. These factors remain critical.

The rabbis were born between 1895 and 1931. Yet this spread is somewhat misleading. Besides Charles Mantinband and Julian Feibelman, the two oldest, and P. Irving Bloom, the youngest, everyone else was born between 1907 and 1919, a span of only twelve years. In 1954, the pivotal year of the *Brown v. Board of Education* decision, this cohort's ages ranged from thirty-five to forty-seven. These were relatively young men in the prime of their careers, all with experience in the rabbinate behind them. They felt confident in their positions as rabbis.

With the exceptions of Perry Nussbaum (Ontario), Nathaniel Share (Montreal),[1] and Moses Landau (Vienna), all were born in the United States. Bloom and Julian Feibelman were born in Mississippi and James Wax in the border state Missouri, while the others were born in the North. Yet this is somewhat misleading. Mantinband was raised in Virginia, and most had prior experience in the South. They were no strangers to southern mores or congregations.

Ten of the thirteen rabbis received ordination from Hebrew Union College (HUC), and two others were ordained at the Jewish Institute of Religion (JIR), which merged with HUC in 1950. Landau, the only exception to this educational pattern, was born, raised, and educated in Europe. All also obtained college degrees and most received graduate degrees. Again with the exception of the two oldest and youngest, they graduated from the Reform seminary between 1932 and 1946. They largely fit the profile of the typical American Reform rabbinate of their generation. However, their educational levels possibly placed them above many of their Protestant counterparts.

Although the Old World background of all of the rabbis could not be determined, either one or both parents of at least six hailed from Eastern Europe. Again this typified HUC graduates and a growing percentage of the Reform rabbinate of the period. Unlike those of the previous classical Reform generation, these rabbis espoused Zionism and increasing traditionalism, including the use of more Hebrew in religious services and education. Sometimes these innovations created as much conflict between rabbis and congregants as their civil right activities, or even more.

The rabbis grew up through the Great Depression and World War II. Their experiences influenced their outlooks. They participated in social justice activities including social work, counseling, and assistance to those with physical or mental challenges. Most served as military chaplains (Bloom and Hinchin during the Korean conflict and most others during World War II) with the exceptions of Julian Feibelman, Moses Landau, and James Wax. Wax had been turned down for the chaplaincy for medical reasons, and Landau, who only arrived in the United States in December 1938, then spoke little English. World War II became a war against Nazi racist persecution, something that surprisingly largely goes unmentioned in the interviews. Little is also said about their military service. Perry Nussbaum, for example, mentions only that it provided him entrée into the American Legion and thereby offered legitimacy. Although unnoted in his interview, in 1946 Jacob Rothschild referred to his experience on Guadalcanal in his first sermon on bigotry, asserting that black and white soldiers had bled the same color blood fighting and dying for their country.

Krause did not press the question of motivation, yet virtually all of the interviewees provided insights on the issue. Many were exposed to activist rabbis who served as role models as they grew up, in college, or when they served as assistant rabbis. The veneration with which most held Charles Mantinband suggests that he served a similar function. A few also pointed to specific biblical prophets that they admired and, seemingly to some extent, sought to emulate. Overwhelmingly, they defined their activism through their roles as rabbis. This is what a Reform rabbi stood for and did, and they acted through their positions as rabbis. This is why most insisted on freedom of the pulpit and the right to speak out without synagogue-board approval. They spoke of support for civil rights as applied Judaism. Only Milton Grafman insisted that he acted solely as a human being. Conversely, for Nussbaum, civil rights activities largely defined any successes he achieved as a rabbi.

These interviews greatly reinforce and expand on the growing literature on the activist rabbis. Yet almost nothing beyond the superficial has appeared previously concerning the rationale, thought processes, and actions of the gradualist rabbis. In these interviews these rabbis clearly articulate their perceptions and positions and describe their actions. Among the most important and insightful findings of this book is how much they agreed with each other.

Given the opinions expressed by the interviewed rabbis, it may be appropriate to view the gradualist and activist positions as two schools of thought. Partly based on the differences in these ideological underpinnings, the two groups varied in how far they were willing or believed wise to go. Clear dividing lines do appear, for examples, on having Martin Luther King Jr. speak at a CCAR convention, on the wording of a CCAR resolution supportive of African American civil rights, on direct interaction with local African American leaders, or on actual treatment of northern Jews who traveled south to march and demonstrate. Nonetheless, both activists and gradualists did work behind the scenes for social justice and peaceful desegregation, and their communities honored both as voices of reason and positive action. The term "gradualist" should not be taken to mean that the rabbis in this school stood aside or failed to act.

Surprisingly, few of the rabbis mention their empathy for black rights because of persecution of and prejudice against Jews. None indicated that they fought for Jewish rights by fighting for the rights of another minority. They recognized that anti-Semitism tended to increase with massive resistance to the civil rights movement. Both black and white Christians tended to assume that Jews supported black rights, and many racists believed that Jews, often equated with communists, instigated and led the civil rights movement.

Virtually all of their congregations were established either before or shortly after the Civil War. Those begun as traditional transitioned to Reform during the last decades of the nineteenth century. Jews lived in each community for some time before creating an official congregation. Jews rose into the middle and upper classes especially through mercantile pursuits, typically moving from clothing and dry goods stores to department stores during the nineteenth century. Although a small minority, they held civic offices and contributed disproportionately to their communities.

From the 1880s into the 1920s the original Jews mostly from the German states and Alsace-Lorraine were gradually overwhelmed in number by Jews from Eastern Europe. The new immigrants followed a similar economic trajectory as their predecessors although they tended to belong to either Orthodox or Conservative congregations during the modern civil rights era.

By the 1950s some Jews in each community traced their local roots back generations. The Jewish populations dramatically expanded during and after World War II with migrants from elsewhere in the United States, particularly from the North. Although Nussbaum and Jacob Rothschild suggested that newcomers tended to be more racist and pro-segregation than the old timers for economic reasons, generally the transplants were more open to desegregation.

Virtually all of the communities were located on waterways, the key to early trade. They expanded with the growth of railroads. The early agricultural-based economy yielded to greater diversity by the mid-twentieth century. Local colleges, universities, medical schools, and military bases established and expanded during the two world wars proved to be especially important. The education and medical institutions brought Jewish professionals to the cities and tended to nurture moderate to liberal opinions. Particularly was this true of African American institutions. Communities tended to moderate their positions and limit violence in order to retain the military facilities. The disproportionate number of military facilities in the South can be attributed to the long tenures of southern members of Congress. Seniority led to committee chairs, power, and influence. The politicians owed their longevity to obtaining federal resources but also to their staunchly segregationist positions. Ironically, the local communities' desires to retain military spending counteracted southern congressional support for massive resistance.

Leadership, or the lack thereof, greatly influenced the unfolding of events. In some communities, rabid racists created a climate of opinion tuned to violence. Moderates or pragmatists had the ability to lessen their impact. The latter could support segregation but recognize the inevitability of change and fear the loss of business brought about by violence. They supported the upholding of court edict on economic rather than moral grounds. In almost every community, rabbis worked with Catholic and a few Protestant (usually Episcopalian or Presbyterian) clergy. Yet the rabbis abhorred the role of the majority of Protestant ministers who either supported the status quo or remained silent. They also recognized that many who did speak out consequently lost their positions. The chances of a Catholic cleric or rabbi losing his position because of support for civil rights was minute in strong contrast with their Protestant peers.

Leadership from within and outside the African American community proved to be equally pivotal. Nashville, Atlanta, and a few other cities profited from the presence of presidents, professors, and students at black colleges and universities, as well as respected clergy and substantial black middle classes. These individuals often worked with moderate whites to secure change with little violence. Where white leaders resisted, these same individuals organized effective means of protest. National organizational leadership chose local situations in which they hoped to gain the greatest publicity and thereby impact the national stage. In the most recalcitrant locations and in locations with weak local black leadership, they pushed progress forward to a greater degree than had local people prevailed. Yet they also tended to go in and out of communities within a short period of time. The local leaders remained responsible for the consequences of the confrontations and long-term progress.

Rabbis and lay Jews in the North and national Jewish organizations often viewed their southern counterparts in a condescending fashion. They could not understand how Jews in the South would not or could not march and demonstrate openly for black civil rights. When southern Jews protested the statements and actions of national organizations or the participation of northern Jews in southern protest, northern Jews sometimes questioned whether southern Jews lived up to Jewish values. Historians including Cheryl Greenberg have tended to support the national perception.[2]

For their part, rabbis in the South expressed mixed feelings concerning their northern brethren and the national agencies. Most indicated that the national Jewish organizations had either no or negative impact on their communities. Yet several maintained that they had received helpful information and counsel especially from regional representatives of these organizations. A few supported the pro-civil rights resolutions passed by the national bodies while others either opposed these or believed they had no impact.

Their analysis is significant for understanding the local/national dynamic. The majority of the rabbis interviewed maintained that the national Jewish organizations and their northern members did not understand the region or the local situation and furthermore did not care about the position of southern Jews. Alfred Goodman, who favored the pro-civil rights resolutions passed by the national organizations, still insisted that those who sponsored them failed to understand the precarious situation in which southern Jews found themselves. Martin Hinchin, who argued that the resolutions hurt fund-raising in the South, agreed with others that the resolutions contributed to a climate of confrontation. Since the southern-based rabbis supported local, behind-the-scenes diplomacy, many believed that confrontation made their jobs more difficult because it hardened the opposition.[3] Even Nussbaum claimed that northern organizations and individuals did not listen, understand, or even care. Southern Jews represented such a small demographic with limited financial resources that they were easily dismissed as inconsequential. Malcolm Stern added that southern Jews served as sacrificial offerings. Wax stated that the Anti-Defamation League (ADL), for example, in its lack of knowledge and, implicitly, its patronizing attitude, wanted to send materials to the Memphis police chief who was already training his officers and acting positively. Rothschild fought the ADL when it attempted to control the flow of news after his temple had been bombed. Southern rabbis challenged the motivations of the national Jewish organizations. The organizations acted to gain credit and as a tool for fund raising. They failed to attack racism and segregation in the North where such actions could affect their relationships with their northern constituents.

Although those northern Jews and especially rabbis who ventured south to march and demonstrate were and have been perceived as heroes by northerners, most southern Jews and their rabbis abhorred such people's actions. To them, the interloping rabbis often failed to extend the courtesy of contacting the local rabbis. Nussbaum used Israel Dresner as an example of northern Jews who spoke down to their southern brethren. Dresner, once named, "the most arrested rabbi in America," was one of the three rabbis closest to Dr. Martin Luther King Jr. and the first rabbi arrested during an interfaith clergy freedom ride in 1961. He was deeply involved in marches and demonstrations in St. Augustine, Florida, and other hot spots. Nussbaum supported those with a true commitment but not the rabbis who demonstrated to make a gesture and then flew home to praise from their congregants. Grafman accused northern rabbis of hypocrisy. If they were so concerned with black rights, why did they not leave their lucrative northern pulpits and accept positions in the smaller and less prestigious southern congregations? Most significant to southern rabbis, the northern Jews who marched in the South and then quickly departed jeopardized the safety and economic viability of local Jews and exacerbated the situation. Paralleling the criticism of national civil rights leaders, southern rabbis recognized that local people had to deal with the fallout and antagonism created by the headline seekers.

Southern criticism of outside marchers and demonstrators begs the question of efficacy. Every southern rabbi interviewed believed in behind-the-scenes negotiations as the most effective means of progress. They rejected publicity and confrontation, even criticizing Rabbi Emmet Frank (1925–1987) of Alexandria, one of their own, for castigating Senator Harry F. Byrd, a massive resistance leader, in a personal attack. In this the date they give for the beginning of the civil rights movement is insightful. When Krause asked his interviewees about when they believed the civil rights movement began in their community, the immediate response from most of them was 1954, the year of the *Brown v. Board of Education* decision. The next immediate response was the year civil rights activity escalated in their immediate vicinity. Almost inevitably this date coincided with court-ordered integration or the beginning of major marches and demonstrations. The publicity the latter generated greatly contributed to the passage of important civil rights legislation and executive action. On further consideration, several rabbis indicated a much earlier time frame, to the mid-1940s or early 1950s, typically identifying local desegregation activities prior to court orders and demonstrations. African Americans could vote in several of the communities, and facilities, police forces, and ministerial associations were desegregated with little fanfare.

This mixture of experience fostered a quandary in the minds of most of these men. One wonders how much their mind-sets differed from the majority of black clergy in their time and place. Even the most moderately active recognized the pivotal impact of court decisions and orders, congressional acts, and presidential support for civil rights. Yet they also witnessed the process of gradual change on the local scene that they believed was jeopardized and made more difficult by agitation. Would civil rights have proceeded with local action fostered by federal court fiat? Their positive answer is likely correct. Nonetheless and just as likely, progress would have been slower, less complete, and dramatically varied from place to place. The marches, demonstrations, boycotts, and even violent confrontations that these engendered were essential to the passage of the federal laws and presidential actions without which substantial, sustained, and long-term change would have been problematic.

Krause asked the rabbis if they thought their actions made any difference. Most responded humbly indicating small victories and limited personal influence. Would the civil rights movement have progressed without their efforts? Undoubtedly it would have. They represented a small minority, and other actors and factors clearly exerted greater influence on the movement and on history. Nonetheless like southern white editors and other progressives, they disproportionately influenced public opinion and local actions. The rabbi activists fit within the pantheon of community heroes.

It has now been six decades since Krause asked how they thought historians would evaluate them a half-century later. The answer today is as mixed as their actions and beliefs. One finds little sympathy for those who equivocated and limited their activities to random sermons and minor changes in the status quo. Fears for themselves and their congregants were real, but unrealistic alternatives and self-serving explanations failed to sit well even with their more activist southern colleagues. A few of the rabbis apparently had little or no direct interaction with African Americans, including black clergy, beyond their relationship with domestic and menial workers or the poor. These rabbis argued that African Americans had to rise economically and educationally to earn a position at the table and benefit from desegregation. One such rabbi actually recognized the parallels between this position and that of Germanic leaders of the nineteenth century who demanded that Jews had to rise culturally and educationally in order to earn citizenship. These rabbis promoted up-lift programs but failed to recognize that without structural changes even educated middle- and upper-class African Americans would suffer from lack of opportunity, rights, and influence.

On the other hand, the interviews disclose that even these rabbis worked for desegregation albeit in a limited fashion. Furthermore, more Reform rabbis in the South stood out as moderates and progressive in terms of the civil rights movement then enumerated by previous historians. Most did so quietly and consistently while some acted more dramatically confronting mayors, ministering to demonstrators incarcerated in Parchman Penitentiary, appearing in the national media, and sponsoring interracial events. Many received threats and were subjected to violence. Their actions stood out especially in relation to those of many of their Protestant counterparts. The civil rights movement was highly complex. It resulted from multiple forces and actors on several levels. For the least active, Krause's original conclusion holds true: "the southern rabbi has done a great deal, but he could do so much more."[4] The activist rabbis deserve to be recorded among those who made a difference.

—Mark K. Bauman

I
In the Land
of the Almost Possible

1
P. Irving Bloom

Mobile, Alabama, and Its Jewish Community

First settled by the French in 1699, Mobile quickly became the capital of French Louisiana. England took the city in 1763 only to be supplanted by Spain seventeen years later, which relinquished it to the United States in 1813. It became part of Alabama, the twenty-second state, six years hence.

Throughout the first half of the nineteenth century, the city served as a key distribution site for the cotton and slave trades. Following the Civil War, it remained a busy hub for cotton brokers to the Gulf of Mexico. World War I brought steel factories and shipbuilding to Mobile, while the Second World War witnessed the influx of almost one hundred thousand people to meet the needs of the shipyards and Brookley Army Air Field, a major supply base. Pulp and paper industries substantially offset the economic upheaval caused by the closure of the airfield in the mid-1960s.

Regardless of its cosmopolitan influences, to some extent Mobile remained a southern city in relation to racial segregation. The first desegregation case filed in Mobile County did not come until nine years after the Supreme Court decision in *Brown v. Board of Education* ordering the end of "separate but equal" schools. The matter went before the United States District Court in March 1963 after the school board rejected a petition presented five months earlier to begin the desegregation process.[1] District Judge Daniel H. Thomas granted the school board fifteen months to implement the *Brown* ruling, but in July the Court of Appeals overruled him and called for integration to begin at the start of the 1963–1964 school year. Additional litigation delayed the process further, even though city commissioner Joseph Langan, a former state senator and five-time mayor of Mobile, advised that it was everyone's responsibility to abide by the rulings of the courts. Langan's opinion drew a hostile salvo from Governor George Wallace who reminded Langan that "it behooves any state or local official to use all his ingenuity and ability to prevent integration rather than to bring it about."[2]

Mobile's White Citizens' Council, focusing on preventing or at least delaying school desegregation, distributed flyers and leaflets attesting to the "intellectual inferiority of the Negro," the "Communist manipulation of the civil rights movement," the "unconstitutionality of the rulings of the courts," and the role that Jews were playing in the effort to enforce "mongrelization." To support their cause, the council brought in segregationist luminaries including Eugene "Bull" Connor from Birmingham, Leander Perez from New Orleans, and Governor Ross Barnett of Mississippi.

The city's two newspapers, the *Birmingham (AL) Register* and the *Birmingham (AL) Press*, owned by the same corporation, spoke with one voice regarding the evils of integration. The *Register* editorialized that "if this nation is to escape dictatorship, it will be necessary to bring an end to usurpation of power by the executive and judicial branches of the federal government."[3] Six weeks earlier the *Press* had warned, "It is clear that there has been a major conspiracy involving highest government officials, members of the Congress and myriad left-wing pressure groups . . . to create a national police state as powerful as ever existed in this world."[4]

Despite the concerted efforts of Mobile's White Citizens' Council, press, school board, and the state government, two African Americans, Henry Hobdy and Dorothy Davis, entered Murphy High School on the morning of September 10, 1963, and remained part of the student body, in defiance of harassment by students, parents, and other racists. Nonetheless, according to Rabbi Bloom, "Murphy ended its first week of desegregation with 'relative calm' prevailing and with attendance near normal."[5]

The traumatic nature of school desegregation was somewhat out of character for Mobile, in that it had already quietly integrated its public parks, libraries, transportation, and lunch counters without demonstrations, sit-ins, or great public angst in comparison with other Alabama cities. Mobile was able to do this in a relatively painless way because of its cosmopolitan atmosphere and the influx of northerners who manned the steel mills, shipyards, and army airfield. These factors, coupled with a mayor who outspokenly opposed massive resistance and who had open channels of communication with the African American community, made Mobile a city where it was relatively easier and less dangerous to integrate than in Birmingham, Alabama, or Jackson, Mississippi, and to openly accept the inevitability and possibly even the desirability of racial equality.[6]

The oldest such enclave in Alabama, Mobile's Jewish community traces its origins to physician Solomon Mordecai's arrival in 1823. Seven years later Solomon and Israel Jones relocated from New Orleans. The Jones brothers subsequently held seats on the city council, and Israel briefly served as acting mayor. Jacob Cohen won election as city marshal only two years after his arrival in 1839. Philip Phillips, an 1835 transplant from South Carolina, won a seat in the state legislature, became chairperson of the State Convention, and was sent to Washington in 1852 as a member of the House of Representatives. Jews of Mobile, although few in number, were thus quickly accepted into civic life.[7]

By June 22, 1841, Mobile's Jewish population had reached sufficient size to purchase land for a cemetery. Three years later, Congregation Sha'arai Shomayim (The Gates of Heaven) was formed. Two years after that it engaged its first rabbi, Dutch-born Benjamin da Silva, and purchased its first building.

The influx of Jews from Eastern Europe beginning in the early 1880s led to the creation of an Orthodox synagogue, Congregation Ahavas Chesed (Love of Kindness) in 1894. When its members gathered to lay the cornerstone for their new building in 1911, the mayor of Mobile, Lazarus Schwarz (who was Jewish) spoke at the ceremony. Forty years later, reflecting the acculturation of the children of its founders, the congregation affiliated with the Conservative movement.

By 1912, approximately 1,400 Jews lived in Mobile. Their presence was obvious when one read the names of the downtown retail stores along Dauphin and Government Streets. With Eastern European immigration continuing into the early 1920s, the Jewish population swelled to 2,200. As the decades passed, however, these numbers dropped, ultimately stabilizing at approximately 1,200 to 1,500 individuals. Thus in 1960, Jews comprised about seven tenths of 1 percent of the city's estimated 191,000 total. Beginning in the 1940s, they steadily migrated to the western suburbs followed by the Jewish communal institutions including the synagogues and what became the Jewish Community Center. With its move to the suburbs, Sha'arai Shomayim became known as the Springhill (Spring Hill) Avenue Temple. In 1960, five years after their new facility in the suburbs had been dedicated, P. Irving Bloom came to Mobile to serve as the congregation's new rabbi.

P. Irving Bloom

Paul Irving Bloom was born on November 30, 1931, in Hattiesburg, Mississippi. His father, Herman David Bloom, had emigrated from Lithuania to Hattiesburg when he was eighteen or nineteen. His mother, Florence Kaplan Bloom, arrived in Hattiesburg from Poland as an infant. Shortly after Irving's birth, the family relocated to Thomasville, Georgia, where Herman Bloom served several communities as shochet (ritual slaughterer) and Hebrew teacher, and performed other rabbinic roles as a kol bo, or Jewish master of many trades. In the early 1940s the family moved to Vidalia, Georgia, where his parents took over a small dry goods store that his maternal grandparents were no longer able to run effectively.

Irving spent his childhood and teen years in Vidalia, where he felt comfortable and never experienced anti-Semitism. Although Irving grew up in a community with only half-a-dozen Jewish families and feeling at home, when he crossed the threshold of his house he found himself in "extra-territorial Lithuania," a place infused with Jewish culture and religion. Irving and his older brother, Samuel, were instructed by their father on the Torah (the first five books of Hebrew Scriptures), a little Mishnah and Gemara, and Rashi's popular eleventh-century chumash commentaries, as well as how to translate Hebrew into Yiddish.[8] It was thus a natural transition for Samuel and Irving to enter Jewish seminaries and become rabbis. After graduating from Vidalia High School in 1948 and attending the University of Georgia for one year, Bloom moved to Cincinnati where he continued to pursue his college degree at the University of Cincinnati while beginning rabbinic studies at Hebrew Union College.

Bloom received his BA with honors with a major in political science from the University of Cincinnati in 1952, then continued until his ordination at the Hebrew Union College–Jewish Institute of Religion four years later. While a student he served small congregations in Charleroi, Pennsylvania (1952, 1955–1956) and Anniston, Alabama (1953–1955), receiving valuable congregational experience in the process. Bloom married Patricia Frankel in August 1955, and the next fall, fresh from the seminary, entered the Air Force Chaplaincy School at Lackland Air Force Base in San Antonio. Upon completion of the two-month course, Chaplain Bloom received assignment to the 12th Air Force headquarters in Ramstein, Germany, where he remained until July 1958.

Next, Bloom served as the assistant to Rabbi Julian Feibelman at Temple Sinai in New Orleans. Feibelman became a life-long friend. While in New Orleans Bloom and his wife welcomed their first child, Jonathan, born in 1958. He also pursued a master's degree in political science, graduating from the University of Cincinnati in 1964. After fulfilling his two-year commitment in New Orleans, Bloom accepted an invitation to become the rabbi of Spring Hill Avenue Temple in Mobile, where his second child, Judith, was born in 1960. During his thirteen-year tenure, he served on the boards of a number of civic organizations and was active in dialogue with members of the African American community. In 1973 the Blooms moved to Temple Israel, a larger synagogue, in Dayton, Ohio, where he spent the next twenty-four years until retiring as Temple Israel's emeritus senior rabbi in 1997. Upon retirement he and his wife relocated to Fairhope, Alabama, across the bay from Mobile. Living in Atlanta as of this writing, Bloom conducts monthly services at his one-time student pulpit, Temple Beth El in Anniston, and at Temple Beth Israel in Gadsden, Alabama.[9]

Editor's Introduction to the Interview

In the following transcript, Rabbi P. Irving Bloom paints a picture of Mobile as a relatively progressive southern city able to integrate early and peacefully so long as Alabama's segregationist governors did not interfere. A port city with a substantial Catholic minority, Mobile benefited from forward-looking leadership that gradually integrated the city without fanfare and that kept lines of communications open with the local African American community. Neither the Ku

1. Rabbi P. Irving Bloom, c. 1970s (Bloom private collection). Used by permission of Rabbi P. Irving Bloom.

Klux Klan nor the White Citizens' Council established a secure presence in the city. Still, some Protestant clergy who spoke out in behalf of civil rights shortly before Bloom's arrival lost their pulpits, and he usually worked with only a select few ministers to achieve peaceful integration. Bloom acted through organizations, several of which he helped found, and behind the scenes to keep the schools open and promote gradual integration. Yet when the occasion warranted it, as was the case with the murder of the Rev. James J. Reeb, the rabbi stood out as a voice of courage. He neither sought nor received much assistance from national Jewish organizations and viewed their resolutions in favor of civil rights as appropriate but ineffective.

Most rabbis worked through ministerial associations, although in Mobile this organization failed to accomplish much. As Bloom indicates, the name was changed from Protestant to ministerial shortly before he arrived so that rabbis could join. He joined as the only Jewish member and quickly became president. The selection of the Reform rabbis to such a position was typical, as will be illustrated by most of the rabbis interviewed. In Mobile, Jews were accepted before Catholic priests and African American ministers. Yet three ministerial associations existed: one white, one black, and a third attempting to integrate. The latter, although avowedly against discrimination, had to reach out to African American ministers to secure their membership and participation.

The story of Mobile and its Reform rabbi suggests that gradual integration was possible in the Deep South, given the right circumstance. Nonetheless, federal court cases, executive orders, and congressional legislation almost certainly forced more change that would not have taken place otherwise for the foreseeable future.

Historians have been virtually unaware of some of the rabbis, including P. Irving Bloom, who Allen Krause interviewed. These profiles, along with others gradually coming to light, provide evidence that the involvement of southern-based rabbis in the civil rights movement was far more extensive than previously understood. Their tendency to work quietly behind the scenes probably contributed to their anonymity in historical annals.

In numerous cases these rabbis witnessed gradual, positive change, albeit often sparked by the forces of the federal judiciary, Congress, and African American pressure. Because they witnessed relatively peaceful change in a region in which violent confrontation was viewed as the norm, they tended to perceive their communities—New Orleans, Louisiana, Mobile, Alabama, Columbus and Atlanta, Georgia—as unique. Yet these experiences proved to be perhaps as normative as the violent confrontations. This point reinforces the argument against a monolithic regional paradigm. There were many Souths as well as many types of southerners in each location.

—Mark K. Bauman

P. Irving Bloom Interview

June 23, 1966

P. Allen Krause: In what period did you see a marked change in the amount of civil rights activity in your community?

P. Irving Bloom: Oh, I would say the fall of 1964 actually would mark an intensification in Mobile of this type of activity.

PAK: What about the Supreme Court decision of 1954? Did that have any major effect on your community?

PIB: Not until 1964. It took that long a period, you see. The attitude of Alabama and Georgia and Mississippi and a few other states as you know after the Supreme Court decision of '54 was one of total rejection, was one of *never*. That this is the law of the case, and not the law of the land. This is the argument, and technically I suppose it has some merit. Each decision of the Supreme Court is the law of the case, based on the particular facts upon which the case had been adjudicated. But, of course, the '54 decision was a very broad, general one: one which certainly was applicable to all of the states of the Deep South, which maintained a distinctly segregated two-fold school system, one for Negroes and one for whites. But there was no real activity; the Negro community did not push any requests for actual implementation of the Supreme Court decision of '54. It sort of, it was just there, and nothing was done about it.

PAK: What was it in 1964 that started this moving again?

PIB: It was earlier than '64—I think it was about '60 or '61—a suit was filed in the United States District Court for the Southern District of Alabama, which sits in Mobile.[10] A suit was filed asking for an order of the court to desegregate the school system in Mobile County. That suit bounced around in the courts in the United States District Court for the southern part of Alabama for a couple of years and was finally adjudicated and desegregation of the twelfth grade was ordered, effective the fall of 1964. I believe it was 1964; it might have been 1963; I'm not sure.

PAK: What was the response on the part of the non-Jewish white community of Mobile to the Supreme Court decision and the civil rights activism in 1963–64?

PIB: Well throughout the period it was simply a refusal to accept as law the decision of the Court. The political leadership of the state insisted it was not the law and we would not have to comply with it. In fact I wrote, and you may be interested in this, a paper about two years ago going over the legislative acts and the reaction of Alabama to the decision of the Court as seen through resolutions and laws passed by the legislature, and about other influences of the governor and so on during that ten-year period. It was submitted to the University of Cincinnati as a thesis to fulfill the requirement for an MA in political science there.[11] The laws passed by the legislature during this period and the resolutions which it passed indicate very clearly the attitude of total opposition, total antagonism, and a total refusal to accept.

PAK: Was there any kind of visible minority that spoke up with a more moderate approach?

PIB: No.

PAK: There wasn't any?

PIB: No, none in Alabama.

PAK: What about the press and the mass media in Mobile? Are they also in this completely segregationist approach?

PIB: The press in Mobile is our biggest obstacle to accomplishment—to progress. In fact I know fairly well the United States Attorney for the Southern District of Alabama, who is in Mobile.[12] It is interesting to note that after the president was assassinated, ten days or so later, the attorney general

[Robert F. Kennedy] wired all of the United States attorneys in the South, asking them for their opinion as to the one most significant change in community climate within the first two or three weeks following the president's assassination. The United States Attorney for the Southern district of Alabama, after thinking about it for a while, wired back that the most significant change, in his opinion, was that the press, which had heretofore been pretty bad, had gone completely radical right. In fact it took three or four days for the Mobile press to come up with a futile kind of editorial comment on the president's assassination.

PAK: What about the television and radio in your community?

PIB: The television and radio did not engage in too much editorial comment. One of the television stations is partially owned by the newspaper, so there is an interlocking kind of relationship between one of the stations. The other station is now controlled from outside the city, and we were hoping for better things from it, but it simply has not engaged in this area of work at all. It is now owned by a New Orleans syndicate, which is Jewishly controlled by the way, which owns the television station in New Orleans—by a very prominent, very philanthropic, and very liberal family. The station is not a rightist station but it is not a liberal station either. I mean it simply does not engage in editorial comments at all.

PAK: Regarding your Jewish community, how long has your congregation been in existence in Mobile?

PIB: Our congregation is the oldest congregation in the state of Alabama, chartered in 1844.

PAK: And the Jewish community [has] been in Mobile for how long?

PIB: Well, the Jewish community dates back from before the creation of the congregation. There were probably Jews when Mobile was chartered; when Bienville and d'Iberville, the two French men who started the area, landed in Mobile Bay some two hundred and fifty or so years ago.

PAK: Is there any significant percentage of your congregation who can trace their roots in the South back for more than one or two generations?

PIB: Yes, there are quite a few. I would say that we would have maybe twenty-five to thirty families out of two hundred whose roots would go back more than two generations in Mobile. Some as far back as six or seven generations.

PAK: What percentage of your congregation is post–World War II South?

PIB: I would say about 50 percent today.

PAK: What brings them into Mobile from the North?

PIB: The majority who came in came immediately post–World War II, between 1946 and 1949, when large numbers of men were discharged from the service and were looking for a place to earn a living. At that time Mobile was a growing community, and a great many found their way here because of the business or professional opportunities that Mobile seemed to offer.

PAK: What is the mood of your congregation and the Jewish community in Mobile? If I were to take the Jewish community in Mobile and place them beside the non-Jewish community, would there be any significant difference with regard to their outlook on race and civil rights?

PIB: On average yes, there would be a significant difference in their point of view. This is not to say that you would not find individuals within the Jewish community whose views would very closely approximate the views of the average non-Jewish segregationist. You would find such individuals within the Jewish community, but if you compared the total Jewish community, let's say if you compared the membership of the congregation, the views of the members of my congregation with the views, let us say, of the members of the Episcopal Church across the street—of that congregation—you would find that although in some cases individual views would approximate each other, that the overall view of my congregation would be far more liberal in these matters.

PAK: How many members of your congregation would you consider to be real segregationists?

PIB: Very few. No more than 10 percent.

PAK: How many other rabbis are there in your community?

PIB: One.

PAK: What denomination?

PIB: Conservative.

PAK: When this intense civil rights activity began, how did the ministers of your community react to the Supreme Court decision and to any civil rights activity?

PIB: Well let me say this: my relationship with Mobile begins in 1960. I think that is an important factor, too. Prior to my coming to Mobile there apparently was an attempt by a group of ministers to effect some sort of transportation desegregation, and apparently they all got their fingers burned— with one or two exceptions they all left Mobile within a year or two thereafter. So there was no organized ministerial involvement as such. I served as president a year or two ago of the Mobile Ministerial Association, and during my administration we changed the constitution so as to make it possible for Negro clergy and Catholic clergy to become members of the Mobile Ministerial Association. Prior to that, they were constitutionally excluded—it was an organization to which Catholics and Negroes were not invited. Now there are still no Catholic or Negro members of the Mobile Ministerial Association, but it is now constitutionally possible.

PAK: Why aren't there?

PIB: Because, as far as the Catholics are concerned, they don't believe the Bishop would permit it; and as far as the Negroes are concerned, no effort has been made to bring them in. That's the next step. The first step is to make it possible, but the next step is to go out actively seeking, which we have not done.

PAK: **When was it changed from a Protestant pastors group to a ministers association, so that you could join?**

PIB: Prior to my coming, not too long ago though. It is interesting that a Jew, that a rabbi could serve as president of that group.

PAK: **Was your predecessor in your pulpit active in any way in the civil rights movement?**

PIB: I really don't know, and I'll tell you why: because by the time this thing became any way acute, my predecessor died—in 1960—and he had been seriously ill for two or three years prior to that. So during the period when this would have become an important issue, I think that his physical condition was such that he just wasn't functioning sufficiently to be a part of that or really anything else. He died of Parkinson's in the summer of '60, and for about three years before that he had been functioning in a limited capacity.[13]

PAK: **What is the tenor of the ministers association now in terms of the civil rights issue?**

PIB: They ignore it.

PAK: **Was the liberal element [of the local clergy] replaced with a more conservative element after these people left?**

PIB: No, they weren't replaced with a more conservative element. I would say that their successors simply did not want to go out on a limb, which would result in the same thing that had happened to their predecessors.

PAK: **In the time that you have been in Mobile, what has your response been to or involvement in civil rights activity in specific instances?**

PIB: Well I have to answer that by telling you a little bit about Mobile. . . . You see, Mobile is a different community than many communities in the South. In fact, as far as I know and I think this is accurate, Mobile is the only city of any size in either Georgia, Alabama, or Mississippi about which you have not read in the papers of a demonstration, a march, a sit-in—anything of this sort we have not had in Mobile. There are a number of reasons for it. For one thing many of the goals that were fought for in the streets in Birmingham, just two years ago, have been commonplace in Mobile for ten years or twelve years. For example Negroes on the police force—they were fighting about in Birmingham in 1964. I think the first Negro was appointed to the police force of Birmingham within the last six months or so. Negroes have been on the police force in Mobile since 1952—since before the Supreme Court decision on schools. Public areas had been desegregated in Mobile long before the 1960s, the parks, the playgrounds, things of this sort. Why? It's hard to put your finger on it. The main influence lies in one individual who has been mayor and city commissioner over the years, who is a liberal individual and who has maintained lines of communication through the years with the Negro community.[14] So the Negro community has felt that it could accomplish more by direct negotiations with the political structure, which it could not approach, you see, in most other southern communities. There were no lines of communication in Birmingham between the Negro leadership and the mayor two years ago, three years ago. Or in Albany, Georgia. Or in Jackson, Mississippi. Or in Montgomery, Alabama.

PAK: Do you understand how a mayor with liberal inclinations like this could be elected in a community as you described Mobile to be?

PIB: It's an anomaly, but he has been able to do these things without inflaming the populace. He has been able to work quietly, with little public attention and simply been able to do these things. I think that the general climate of Mobile, while reflecting the same basic feelings as the rest of Alabama in terms of a desire to maintain segregation and old traditional attitudes and so on, has nonetheless not had the active impulse to fight against these things. They were against them, but if the leadership would move in these directions they would not be totally opposed by the populous. This is the key, because I think it is the leadership of Alabama and the other communities that has aroused the public feeling by their constant reiteration of never, saying "This is not the law of the land," "It will never happen," "It's a bunch of Communists, leftists, crackpots in Washington," et cetera—as our governor has said on many occasions. Now this type of political inflammatory leadership you did not have on the local level in Mobile, ever.

PAK: Is the Klan active in Mobile?

PIB: No.

PAK: What about the White Citizens' Council?

PIB: They were active for a time. Their influence has diminished considerably. The Klan has not been active in Mobile. The National States Rights Party has tried to get a foothold in Mobile and has not succeeded. I think this is the reason that there is a different political climate in Mobile than existed elsewhere in the state and has made some quiet progress possible. Now, you asked for rabbinic involvement. My involvement is as a member of the Interfaith Ministerial Association. Now this is not the regular one. There is a white ministerial association and a Negro ministerial association. The

Interfaith Ministerial Association is a third group formed by a small group of ministers, both white and Negro, who wanted an integrated group.

PAK: When was this formed?

PIB: This was formed about 1961 or '62. It has not been terribly active. It has been largely a paper organization with occasional meetings, but it does exist.

PAK: Do you know where the original idea was?

PIB: Yes, the impetus for that came from a Presbyterian minister, a Methodist minister, and myself.

PAK: Was this at an informal meeting of the three of you? Was there anything structured about this in any way?

PIB: No, the three of us were quite friendly and we got talking about it and decided we ought to have such a thing. So we approached a few men in the Negro community and got one going. As simple as that. Never did very much. Frankly, I don't consider it a great accomplishment. Frankly, it's hard to differentiate between involvement as a rabbi and involvement as an individual. It's hard to say in what capacity one involves one's self.

I would say that my own involvement is as a part of every group in town that is working in this area. The Mobile Council on Human Relations, which is headed interestingly enough by a white Episcopal priest serving a Negro church in Mobile. Also I was one of the founders of a group that we called ABLE [Alabamians Behind Local Education] back in 1963. Incidentally, the first desegregation that came to schools in Mobile was in '63.

PAK: 1963.

PIB: Right the fall of '63. In the spring of '63 a number of people were beginning to be concerned, particularly with the governor's agitation, that we might come to a situation where we'd find ourselves having closed schools in the fall, rather than admit the Negro students who had been ordered admitted by the United States District Court. So we tried to form an organization, and did form an organization that we wanted to be local in nature, so as not to give rise to the charge of outsiders, et cetera, which would try to skirt as much as possible the segregation-integration issue and whose theme song would be "open schools." An organization, in other words, which would not come out either for or against integration, but in effect would be for, since its theme song would be "education is important" and "come what may we must have open schools." So we formed such an organization. We called it ABLE.

PAK: Could you specify whom you mean by "we"?

PIB: "We" is the same small circle of people who were interested in this: A Methodist minister, a few laymen, a few Jewish laymen and a few Christian laymen who got together in informal talks and decided to try to form this organization. We got some help from the Southern Regional Council Atlanta office—a man by the name of Paul Anthony came down and helped us organize. We took the name ABLE, Alabamians Behind Local Education. You can see the impact of the name. We began to write letters to the editor, again, always skirting. Anything that said we ought to integrate the schools would have drawn immediate public condemnation and would have not been effective at all. The work of our organization was geared to saying that we are a lawful group. Whatever the law is, it is, but, whatever it is, our schools must remain open and educate our children. We got all this material from what had happened in other communities when school systems closed and violence had been stirred up. We used Southern Regional Council stuff, ADL [Anti-Defamation League] stuff, all of this kind of material. And yet despite all the caution we got smeared in the end. The governor appointed a special committee in the legislature to investigate alleged communist influence in ABLE in Mobile. Pamphlets were distributed listing the names of the people who were involved in ABLE as being communist sympathizers and so on.

PAK: Were you included in this?

PIB: Yes. I wouldn't have wanted to be left out. It was a mark of distinction, as it were. All of our names were included. They had the membership list; they knew who had been active in ABLE. But it blew over. The president of ABLE at that time was a woman, Mrs. Hollis Wiseman,[15] who is not Jewish, although she has a name that could be taken for Jewish. We had some contacts in Montgomery and through the efforts of the attorney general, Richmond Flowers, the investigation was quashed a little bit. It all made headlines in the Mobile press for a while and that was it—no great *tzimmis* [Yiddish for no big deal/no trouble]. When school desegregation came that fall, our community was fairly well prepared for it. Had it not been for the governor it would have come off without incident. The governor decided to send the state police into Mobile and to surround the school and not permit the Negro students to enter. So the first day, the law enforcement was taken out of the hands of the Mobile city police and also the Mobile County sheriff's office, who were well prepared to cope with it—and completely taken out of their hands, taken over by captain or major lingo and the state police. For a couple of days the schools were closed. Then as mysteriously as they appeared, they disappeared; the governor withdrew the state police. City and county law enforcement took over, and Negro students began, without further incident, attending Murphy High School.

PAK: Have you or your group had any other activity in this area other than school integration?

PIB: No not really. ABLE is virtually nonexistent today because the purpose for which it was created was served. Namely peaceful integration and open schools.

PAK: Were there any other areas that you can think of in which you were involved in civil rights activities?

PIB: Well, of course it's hard to define really what "civil rights" is. I mean, for example, we've had numerous meetings of committees appointed by the city, discussing areas of open employment and things of this sort, with the bankers and the industrial people. All of this sort of thing I have been involved in over the last four or five years. Again, you see, Mobile is a little bit unique as far as overt activity goes—there hasn't been a sit-in, a demonstration, a march of any kind in the city of Mobile.

PAK: Have you ever as a member of a group or as an individual tried to exert pressure on the power structure through a phone call or a visit or a talk with somebody in your community?

PIB: Yes, but I'm not sure it would be directly civil rights matters. It depends on how narrowly or broadly you define civil rights. For example, we had a question in the community just recently, within the last two months, where the school board turned down Title One funds for a summer school program.[16] It is going to have to be an integrated program and there are almost two million dollars involved. And the school board turned it down by a vote of two to one, with three commissioners. And again a number of us, including myself, were terribly concerned about this, feeling that this educational program was a must, and we, all of us who were interested, Jews and non-Jews, did what we could to get the action reversed. On my part, this included contacting the one school commissioner who was the swing man of the three, and contacting friends of mine who knew him, urging them to contact him and urge him to reverse his position. Now is this a civil rights matter? I don't really look at it as such, although it had certain ramifications in the segregation-desegregation issue, since that is the main reason the commission killed it. But I really would not classify this as a civil rights matter.

PAK: Did you know this commissioner?

PIB: I had met him. I did not know him well. I knew him by name and he knew me by name. And there were a number of people whom I knew well who knew him well.

PAK: Has there been any attempt in Mobile to integrate transportation or public facilities or to make voting easier for Negroes?

PIB: Voting has not been a problem in Mobile for fifteen years. Negroes have freely registered in Mobile County for, I would say, since the early fifties, about 1952.[17] Transportation has been integrated in Mobile for at least eight years. Public accommodations did not integrate in Mobile until passage of the Civil Rights Act of '64, which made it mandatory on public accommodations, but since that date public accommodations have been fully integrated in Mobile.

PAK: Other than what we have been talking about, what else have you done which you think might touch upon civil rights?

PIB: I would say, action within groups, and, of course, pulpit preachment to the congregation. I have not chosen to address the Rotary Club or the Downtown "this, that, or the other," on a civil rights issue—that would be a little too volatile to handle. But this hesitancy does not apply in preaching to my own congregation, where all of these issues have been fully explored and discussed.

PAK: From the very beginning of your time in Mobile?

PIB: I would say from about the second year on.

PAK: Did you make any agreement with your congregation when you went in with regards to the pulpit?

PIB: No. They of course asked about this, and I told them what my feelings were. I also told them that, having been born and reared in the South, that I felt I understood the problem, and that I felt as far as they were concerned, in inviting a rabbi, they would have to invite a rabbi in whose discretion and wisdom and good judgment they could have confidence. [But I also told them] that they could not tie any man to an agreement to talk about this, to do that, not to talk about this. They ought to search for a man in whose judgment they had confidence, and if they didn't have this confidence in a man's judgment then they should not take him as their rabbi.

PAK: Was there ever a time when you were quoted in the newspapers or in some publication in the South because of a statement you made on civil rights or due to a sermon or any other involvement?

PIB: No.

PAK: But your name was listed with the . . .

PIB: My name *was* listed with the ABLE list, and also it was listed in the newspaper—this occasioned a good deal of comment in the community—[but] not as much as I had feared. I was rather proud of my people on that one. You recall when the Reverend Reeb, the Unitarian minister was brutally assaulted and killed?[18] The local NAACP [National Association for the Advancement of Colored People] had a memorial service for Reeb in a Negro church, a service at which I delivered the invocation, and the service was reported in the press and my participation in it was reported. This occasioned a little reaction from some of the non-Jewish white community, and a little bit from my own congregation, but I was pleased with the fact that it did not elicit as much negative reaction from my congregation as I anticipated. I knew there would be some; in fact I anticipated more than actually came about.

PAK: What was the reaction from the non-Jewish community?

PIB: That this was a Negro thing and that no white man should have any part in it. That Reeb got what was coming to him, and it's not necessary to glorify him, and deify him, and make a martyr out of him, and participate in any kind of activity of this sort.

PAK: How were you made aware of this feeling?

PIB: Letters, phone calls.

PAK: And with regard to the congregation?

PIB: Phone calls, letters. The same thing. Some anonymous. Some signed.

PAK: Did this, or any other concern about your civil rights activity, ever come to the board for discussion there? Have you ever been approached by official representatives of the congregation?

PIB: No. I have been approached by board members and even by officers of the congregation as individuals, voicing their personal feelings. But I would draw a distinction—I don't think you are asking me that—I think you are asking me whether there was ever any official board action to discuss this, and no, there hasn't been.

PAK: Have you ever felt that it was possible that this might happen?

PIB: Not really, no. I suppose it would remotely be possible—I never thought it would happen though, because we've had a fairly good understanding that they may disagree with me, but that I'm nonetheless free to pursue the activities that I think to be right and proper.

PAK: Was there any communication at all between yourself and any of the so-called Negro activists groups, and by this I even include the NAACP, which is not in the same activist category as, for example, SNCC [Student Nonviolent Coordinating Committee]?

PIB: Not a great deal. There is occasional contact. It has been largely through an intermediary, through the Methodist District Superintendent of Mobile, who has really served as the intermediary between Negro leadership and members of the white community whom they had wanted to reach.[19] They have really not approached me directly, except on the Reeb business, when they asked me if I would come and deliver the invocation, and that was really not a question of the invocation—it was a question of physical presence demonstrating support for their activity and their cause.

PAK: Was this attended by any other rabbi?

PIB: No.

PAK: By a large number of white ministers?

PIB: No, they had a white Protestant and a white Catholic and myself.

PAK: How do you see your role in order to best accomplish the goals which you have for civil rights in your community?

PIB: The role is to work within organizations that seek to improve the situation and to stay out of the newspaper as much as possible, because publicity does not help us at all. Publicity hurts the goal that we are trying to achieve. When the new auditorium was built—we have a new eight-, nine-million-dollar auditorium, which is fully integrated—every effort was made, and successfully made, to keep the newspapers from indicating to the general public that this facility was integrated.[20] This is not news. I mean if you come there, you see it. You don't need an article in the paper to show you that the new auditorium that is going to open is integrated. In fact we were so successful with that that the Citizens' Council took an ad in the paper which said that the new auditorium is integrated, don't go there, don't support it. It was not reported by the press.

PAK: I keep harping on the "we." . . . I want to understand who the "we" is in this case.

PIB: In a community of this sort the "we" is a couple of dozen of interested individuals—rabbis, a Protestant minister or two, Father [Albert S.] Foley, who is the Jesuit sociology professor at Spring Hill College,[21] a few people from the League of Women Voters, a few people who are former ABLE people.

PAK: How were you involved in the opening of the auditorium?

PIB: The involvement there again was with a couple of other clergymen who felt that we should talk to the newspaper. Just on our own. No organization—we felt that we just should point out to the newspaper the desirability of omitting this item from the publicity.

PAK: Who made the decision that the auditorium was going to be integrated in the first place?

PIB: Well the city. It's the city auditorium . . .

PAK: The city . . . ?

PIB: There was no problem about that. I mean there was no fight necessary to obtain the integrated auditorium. The City Commission built the auditorium, and it was clear from the beginning that this was a public facility, built by tax funds, and it would have to be integrated. There was no necessity for liberal-minded people to persuade the City Commission of this— there was no thought of doing this any other way.

PAK: Rabbi, what role do you think that the national Jewish organizations have played in the civil rights movement and activity in your area of Mobile?

PIB: Virtually none.

PAK: Have they attempted to play a role?

PIB: You mean by sending people in on the scene or by national resolutions? Well, the national resolutions make the front pages. When the Union [of American Hebrew Congregations] or ADL or AJC [American Jewish Committee] or anybody passes a resolution, this hits the press, but this has no real effect one way or the other. There are of course many Jews who are terribly upset about it, who don't like the idea of Union resolutions or ADL resolutions on the subject of civil rights, but I'm convinced that it makes very little difference one way or the other—its effect is not harmful, it's not helpful, it's just not, period. ADL has an office in Alabama now that serves only Alabama. Previously we have been served by their southeast regional office in Atlanta. Now ADL will send a man in every now and then. He'll come in and he'll talk to Father Foley at Spring Hill College, he'll talk to the half a dozen people who are interested and whom he knows to be liberals and see if he can send them some material, or work in any way as far as the Jewish angle is concerned. He is more interested in anti-Semitism than in Negro civil rights activity—[he's more interested in] an anti-Semitic reaction, what the Council is doing, what the Klan is doing, what the National States Rights party is doing, this kind of thing. So I would say that as far as national Jewish organizations are concerned, as far as the effect in Mobile, that it's nil.

PAK: **Do you see any role that they could be playing which they aren't playing, which might be helpful to you?**

PIB: No I really don't. I have no objection to national resolutions. I think we should have them. I think we should have these positions as a religious body, nationally; I certainly think we ought to have them. But as far as helping in a Mobile situation, they would not help.

PAK: **Could you list, in the order of importance according to your experience in Mobile, the people or forces that have been most influential in bringing about some sort of progress in the field of civil rights in your city?**

PIB: I would say the top of the list—and I think we have a very good record in Mobile compared to other southern cities—the number one on the list is the man who is now the mayor of Mobile and who has been either commissioner or mayor for the last twelve years.[22] This is the top of the list. The political structure has been in constant communication with the Negro community. The Negro community has had a place to go and an ear to talk to politically. Now this has not been true of the industrial, of the economic power structure, and one must distinguish between the two. The economic power structure has lent itself to this thing and given an open ear, if it is in fact open today, only very recently—it's only within the last year or so. This is the big problem today. It's not the political structure in the city [that is a problem], [but] the political structure in the state has an effect. Secondly, the fact that Mobile is a port city gives it a little more liberal atmosphere. People of different nationalities and different types [live here]. Thirdly, Mobile is one of the few cities in the South with a significant percentage of Catholic population, and when the Catholic form a big enough minority, not the majority, but when they form at least 15, 20, 25 percent of the population, they tend to be a liberalizing influence. . . . The Interfaith Ministerial Association is a third group formed by a small group of ministers, both white and Negro, who wanted an integrated group.

PAK: When was this formed?

PIB: This was formed about 1961 or '62. It has not been terribly active. It has been largely a paper organization with occasional meetings, but it does exist.

PAK: Do you know where the original idea for it came from?

PIB: Yes, the impetus came from a Presbyterian minister, a Methodist minister, and myself. The Mobile Council on Human Relations, which is headed interestingly enough by a white Episcopal priest serving a Negro church.

2
Julian B. Feibelman

New Orleans, Louisiana, and Its Jewish Community

The Mississippi River where it meets the Gulf of Mexico is one of the most strategically desirable locations in North America for the exchange of goods within the United States and overseas. Yet the area also presents serious challenges: tropical weather, frequent hurricanes, flooding, and swampland that offer a breeding ground for mosquitoes that in the past bore a variety of deadly diseases.

Despite the drawbacks, by 1718 Jean Baptiste La Moyne, Sieur de Bienville, established New Orleans as the capital of the Louisiana territory and fortress that controlled access to the wealth of the continent's interior. Nonetheless, New Orleans languished as a result of the paucity of settlers and insufficient support from Versailles. The future of the Crescent City lay in the land-grant concessions along the Mississippi River. By 1740, indigo, tobacco, and lumber shipped through the city provided the lifeblood of its economy.

In the 1763 treaty that marked its defeat in the Seven Years War, France transferred title to its Louisiana lands to Spain. However, by 1772 it reverted back to French sovereignty. Beginning with the American Revolution, an increasing number of Americans moved into the Mississippi Valley and produced important staples, including wheat, flour, corn, beef, and pork. The 1803 Louisiana Purchase removed the remaining political barriers to the development of New Orleans's economic and tactical potential, and consequently the city's population exploded from 8,000 in 1803 to nearly 170,000 in 1861. By 1810 New Orleans had mushroomed into the fifth largest city in the United States.[1] Like Mobile, its neighbor along the Gulf coast, the diverse nature of its origins contributed to a cosmopolitan ethos that helped define the city.

Eli Whitney's improved cotton gin, James Hargreaves's spinning jenny, and Robert Fulton's steamboat transformed the South and thereby facilitated New Orleans's prosperity. "King Cotton" supported a new plantation oligarchy that also produced tobacco and sugar on the backs of their slave laborers, and profits filled the coffers of the wealthy merchants, brokers, bankers, and shipowners who controlled trade at the mouth of the Mississippi.

Yet, the port city did not require chattel labor to produce cash crops within its borders. On the eve of the Civil War, slaves comprised only 8 percent of the population. Most slaves worked in domestic capacities or practiced trades that eventually allowed some to purchase their freedom. Because the city served as a melting pot of people who traced their origins to France, Germany, Ireland, Africa, and the Caribbean, a unique ambience emerged particularly in relation to music, food, and ethnic and racial interaction. This, plus its great need for merchants, made it one of the most attractive cities in the country for Jewish settlers.[2]

However, antebellum prosperity was constructed on a fragile foundation. The postbellum abolition of slavery and the opening of overseas competition for cotton production rendered the plantation crops less profitable, and railroad expansion elsewhere undercut the economic advantages offered by the Mississippi River. In the decade prior to the war, J. D. B. De Bow warned New Orleans's leaders that as the river became less valuable as a transportation corridor, the only way to ensure New Orleans's economic future was through railroad construction.[3] Although De Bow took the lead in the pages of his newspaper, *DeBow's Review*, he did so with the support of others including Judah P. Benjamin. In 1852 Benjamin, a prominent Jewish New Orleans attorney, merchant/plantation owner, United States senator, and, ultimately, holder of three Confederate Cabinet posts, argued that only if New Orleans established a direct rail to California would it benefit from trade with Asia.[4]

The failure to build a railroad was not entirely the fault of nearsighted plantation owners. The cost to lay tracks on the marshland and bayous of southeastern Louisiana would have been enormous. By 1860 New Orleans was falling inexorably behind in the national grain trade, indicative of its decreasing importance as an export center. Chicago, meanwhile, which had previously sent goods downriver, emerged as a national trading hub through its utilization of the railroad network. One city could flourish and another stagnate based on good or poor access to the rails. New Orleans had 168,675 inhabitants in 1860, as compared to Chicago's 112,172. By 1900, Chicago's population had skyrocketed to 1,698,575 while New Orleans's had reached only 267,104.[5]

Yellow fever also repeatedly undermined the city's growth, with thousands dying from the disease during epidemics that continued throughout the nineteenth century, causing the city to earn an unenviable reputation as one of the nation's unhealthiest environments. In 1901 Walter Reed discovered that mosquitoes spawning in still waters carried the disease. Four years and 452 additional deaths later, the city finally improved its drainage, sewage, and water supply systems, effectively eliminating the scourge of yellow fever in the city.

Following World War I, New Orleans made a concerted effort to attract tourists and conventions. Both industries quickly became second only to the port in economic significance as the city emerged as an entertainment capital.[6] The tourist trade suffered during the Great Depression and the country's entry into

World War II, but the financial impact was ameliorated by the growth of war-related industries. New Orleans native Andrew Jackson Higgins designed a landing craft for vehicles and personnel (Higgins LCVP) that was ultimately used in Operation Overlord on D-Day, Operation Torch in North Africa, and in several Pacific campaigns. Higgins's company expanded to eight plants and employed over twenty thousand workers at its peak. In July 1943, it produced more landing crafts than all of the other shipyards in the nation combined.[7] The petrochemical industry also grew exponentially in response to war demand. Companies like Alexander Shipyard and Arthur Levy Enterprises prospered, supplying submersible rigs and various ocean craft to meet the needs of oil company giants including Shell and Gulf.[8] During the years when the civil rights movement occupied center stage, the port, the petrochemical industry, and the influx of post-war tourists and conventions served as the foundation of the local economy. They supported a cosmopolitan atmosphere and, in the case of tourism and the convention trade, could be dramatically impacted by positive and negative publicity and their national image, factors potentially impacting on responses to desegregation.

The Jewish presence in New Orleans goes back to the colonial era. By 1960 the majority of Jews in New Orleans had a medium annual family income over $10,000 and could therefore be classified as members of the upper middle class. According to one survey, 83 percent of employed Jews either owned businesses or worked as professionals, in management, as clerks, or as salespeople (less than twenty percent fit the latter category). The remaining seventeen percent held less prestigious jobs. Forty-one percent had been born there; twenty-four percent had lived in the city for at least thirty years and an additional ten percent for at least ten years. Over ninety percent of New Orleans's Jews affiliated with at least one of the eight area synagogues. Although most of the influential synagogues traced their history to before the Civil War, the largest and equally prestigious, Temple Sinai, was founded in 1870.

Jews were a highly respected element of New Orleans's population.[9] Yet the overwhelming majority feared any type of involvement that might make Jews too conspicuous, particularly if that involvement could be interpreted as contrary to the prevalent white position. Rabbi Nathaniel Share ultimately judged the local Jewish population as being mostly "sympathetic to the Negro" in thought, if not in deed; while in Rabbi Julian Feibelman's eyes New Orleans Jews differed hardly at all on racial issues from Protestants of a comparable socioeconomic level. Sociologist Leonard Reissman saw it this way: "To be sure, some typically Southern values have been assimilated by Jewish families who have lived as Southerners for generations. . . . Hence, one encounters a loyalty to the city and the region that is hardly the mark of a 'luftmensch.' . . . Attitudes towards race are not unrestrainedly equalitarian but sometimes are hedged by some of the elaborate rationale that Southerners of conscience have evolved to justify segregation. . . . But the Southern tradition has been tempered by a Jewish tradition which has prevented a complete acceptance of that strange orientation mystically called 'the Southern way of life.' The Jew is not an average white Southerner in his general attitudes toward race, aristocracy, or the Civil War."[10]

Although Feibelman and Share could identify only a few congregants who vocally supported desegregation, they could also point to few who outspokenly opposed it. Alfred O. Hero reinforced this analysis: "Although a relatively large number of New Orleanians who identify themselves as Jews have been paternalist segregationists by preference and uncomfortable with changing race relations in their city, virtually none have agreed publicly with the intransigent position of the Citizens Council."[11]

If the vast majority of Jews in New Orleans were not outwardly supportive of the methods and extremism of the White Citizens' Councils (if not with their goals), they remained, according to these two New Orleans rabbis, very sensitive to *mah yomru hagoyim* ("What will the non-Jews say?"). Being highly concentrated in retail businesses, Jews felt substantial concern for their livelihood. Equally important, they feared that appearing to demur from the traditional southern views on segregation would result in social ostracism and anti-Semitism. These realities formed part of the milieu in which the rabbis operated in the Crescent City. Rabbis Julian Fiebelman and Nathaniel Share noted the fears in their interviews, and each was impacted by these realities in their congregations. Nonetheless, the Temple Sinai board and membership reacted in a positive fashion to Fiebelman's invitation to Ralph Bunche. Actions and reactions apparently varied in relation to time and circumstance.

Other aspects of the local environment further influenced events. By the 1960s Catholics comprised almost 50 percent of New Orleans's population of 627,000. This gave the city a unique position in the South, albeit one again similar to Mobile. Its cosmopolitan nature, the result of a port-based economy with an ethnically and religiously diverse population, mitigated its southern provincialism. In comparison with other southern cities, New Orleans could be labeled moderate in its approach to racial issues. Rabbi Share claimed, "New Orleans is not the South, it's a different kind of city." This would have been true to an even greater degree, if not for several regional characteristics. Confrontation over school desegregation came as a major shock to the city partly because integration had already been taking place, slowly and quietly for years, prior to 1954. New Orleans, like many southern communities, had an active White Citizens' Council, federal marshals to escort African American children to school, and so forth. Although the city's power structure generally did not express vocal defiance to the Supreme Court's *Brown* decision, one analyst classified it as, at best, "neutral" in this matter. Louis Lomax averred, "Time and time again, they refused to speak out, despite the fact that certain other responsible citizens urged them to do so."[12] Also typically southern, very few Protestant ministers could be counted among these "responsible citizens." Feibelman and Share both expressed disappointment in their Protestant peers. Local Catholic priests, however, could often be counted on to provide a vocal, liberal response.

The presence of a strong anti-integration voice in the area provides another regional characteristic. Leander Perez, a hard-core racist who served as a Louisiana state judge and the undisputed political boss of Plaquemines Parish, acted from a stronghold less than fifteen miles from the city proper. In 1965, Perez summarized his racial views thusly: "Animals right out of the jungle. Passion. Welfare. Easy life. That's the Negro." Perez used his considerable power to keep the county's large black population from voting, obtaining decent housing, attending integrated schools, or using any public facilities patronized by whites. When Archbishop Joseph F. Rummel moved to integrate the Catholic school system in the area, Perez arranged for the picketing of his residence and organized boycotts to cut off donations to the church. Perez's supporters burned a cross on the Archbishop's lawn, torched one Catholic school, and drained a school bus's brake fluid at another. Rummel excommunicated Perez on April 16, 1962.[13]

Julian B. Feibelman

Julian Beck Feibelman was born in Jackson, Mississippi, on March 23, 1897, to Abraham and Eva (Beck) Feibelman. He spent his childhood in Jackson, the city of his mother's birth, a childhood in which he never had the sense "of being different in any way whatsoever."[14] Feibelman earned a bachelor of arts degree from Millsaps College in 1918, even though he left school early in order to enlist in the army. Remaining close to home, he served fifteen months at Camp Shelby, in Hattiesburg, Mississippi, during World War I.

Feibelman entered the University of Mississippi Law School following his military service, but shortly thereafter decided to become a rabbi. In 1920, he transferred to the Hebrew Union College in Cincinnati. Given his Mississippi upbringing, the move provided quite a challenge. Jackson's Jewish community was so small during his youth that he rarely saw a rabbi and had no formal Jewish education. His family was so assimilated that "aside from eating these required crackers called matzos on Passover . . . and fasting on the Day of Atonement . . . that was the only [Jewish] thing we did."[15] The seminary seemed like a foreign world to the young man, filled with boys from New York's lower east side and less exotic northerners. "The professors," he reminisced, "were for the most part old German pedagogues with their old world manners expecting the students to rise when you come in the room."[16] This was certainly a far cry from Millsaps. Nevertheless, Feibelman persevered and received ordination in 1926.

After a series of student congregational experiences, his first rabbinic position was at Philadelphia's historic Reform Congregation Keneseth Israel, where he served as William Fineshriber's assistant.[17] Feibelman remained in Philadelphia for ten years in what he later called "a position of no great responsibility."[18] During this period, nine black men were accused of rape in Alabama—the so-called "Scottsboro Nine." Feibelman was so appalled at the miscarriage of justice in the case that he participated in meetings and letter-writing campaigns, and gave talks on the subject. Although nothing came of his and others' efforts, he consoled himself "with the thought that I was living my faith and upholding the prophetic admonition to 'set free the prisoners.'"[19] While working at Knesseth Israel, Feibelman earned a master of arts degree from the University of Pennsylvania in 1929 and began work on a doctorate, which he received three years after he left for the South. While at Penn, Feibelman struck up a friendship with a "fair-skinned Negro young lady," whom he met for lunch in the university commons each Monday. "We were friends and classmates," Feibelman wrote. "Not once did I think I was sitting and sharing a meal with a Negro girl. I never saw her outside the classroom or the dining room. Nor did I remind myself that I had come 'a long way from my Mississippi upbringing.'"[20]

In September 1936, Feibelman ventured to New Orleans to become Temple Sinai's rabbi. Two years into his tenure, Feibelman defended a group of fourteen Tulane professors accused of being communist sympathizers. When he announced his Friday night sermon topic, "The Dangers of Red Baiting," the president of his temple's board of trustees warned him to "stick to religion," but the rabbi refused to comply, asserting his independence. He subsequently received support from some prominent members of his synagogue. This mixed pattern of confrontation, support, and independence continued as the rabbi spoke out on behalf of civil rights. In his second year in New Orleans, Feibelman married Mary Anna Fellman, a fifth-generation New Orleanian from a long line of Temple Sinai members.

Feibelman immersed himself in community affairs. During World War II he served as chairman of the Home Service Committee and the Camp and Hospital Committee of the New Orleans Red Cross, and volunteered as Field Director for the Red Cross in New Orleans military camps. He also served as president of many organizations including the Louisiana Society for Mental Health, the Louisiana Association for Mental Hygiene, the Family Service Society, the Rotary Club, the New Orleans Urban League (of which he was a charter member), the Boy Scouts of America, the Foreign Policy Association, the Veterans Information Center, the Jewish Federation, and the Jewish Community Center. Feibelman lectured at Tulane University on world religion and acted as religious director of the southwestern division of the National Conference of Christians and Jews.

Beyond his synagogue and community responsibilities, Feibelman found time

2. Rabbi Julian B. Feibelman, date unknown
(Temple Sinai, New Orleans). Used by permission of
Rabbi Edward Cohn, Temple Sinai. Photographer:
Fred Kahn; photograph used by permission of
Catherine Kahn.

to edit the *New Orleans (LA) Jewish Ledger* (1940–1944) and to publish his
memoirs. He received numerous awards during his lifetime including the Loving Cup Award (1968). The *New Orleans (LA) Times-Picayune* granted this
high honor to "citizens who have worked unselfishly for the community without expectation of public acclaim or material reward."[21] Feibelman retired with
emeritus status in 1967 and died in New Orleans on October 10, 1980, at the
age of 83. In his autobiography, *The Making of a Rabbi*, published the year of his
death, Feibelman comments on his views concerning integration.[22] But the interview provides his position at a date much closer to the pivotal events.

Editor's Introduction to the Interview

Like Mobile, the Crescent City served as home to a diverse and cosmopolitan
population including a substantial Catholic presence. Coupled with an economy
sensitive to negative publicity, these factors translated into an environment of
the almost possible. As in many places in the South, gradual peaceful change
occurred in New Orleans even before widespread federal action and extensive
black protest. This did not preclude violence, confrontation, and resistance once

the broader forces for change entered into the equation. This duality tended to shock moderate whites who expected better of their community.

Jews comprised a very tiny percentage of the population in each southern community. Partly because of this relative isolation, they tended to have high rates of synagogue affiliation. In New Orleans during the early 1960s, for example, such affiliation was estimated at 90 percent. Although this did not necessarily translate into regular attendance at services, it may have reflected and contributed to a sense of group belonging. Even congregants who only attended synagogue during the annual High Holiday services might also feel a sense of association with their rabbi. These identifying factors possibly contributed to the rabbis' moral suasion.

Feibelman wrote a history of his community and a memoir. Several other rabbis compiled histories of the civil rights movement in their southern communities as well. Implicitly they were conscious of history and the era in which they lived as a key historical moment. This awareness possibly provided part of their calling to do what they perceived to be the right thing.

Feibelman, like P. Irving Bloom, was born in Mississippi. Several other rabbis with pulpits in the South also had southern birthplaces. This facilitated their understanding of their environment and the people in it, albeit without mitigating their frustration with both.

Many of these interviews include issues not typically considered. Here Feibelman recounts how he and a US Marshal accompanied a white girl to a school undergoing integration that was being boycotted by other white students. Although his presence was intended primarily to reassure and possibly help protect a white child, his action supported the civil rights struggle. The rabbi and his congregation also became involved as early as 1949 with the invitation to Ralph Bunche and by providing a venue for other integrated meetings. Seemingly simple requests as studying the implications of the *Brown* decision resulted in threats and harassment for rabbis like Feibelman. Even in a place like New Orleans, dissenters lived with well-founded fear.

—Mark K. Bauman

Julian B. Feibelman Interview

June 22, 1966

P. Allen Krause: What date in your community marked the beginning of more intense civil rights activity than in any prior period?

Julian B. Feibelman: I would go back to December 1954. I think the Supreme Court decision was in May, wasn't it?[23] Nothing had been done in New Orleans about this at all in integrating the schools. Some of us met and thought that we ought to approach the school board, which we did. We framed this statement and a lady and myself appeared before the school board, at one of its regular meetings on a Monday evening. This was in the month of December, if I remember correctly, that year, '54.[24] The statement outlined the situation and said that we felt that some recognition would have to be made of such a decision in a metropolitan school system, and we concluded by asking the school board to survey the situation, look into it in light of the required changes, and see what could be presented to the community. That was, I thought, a very innocent approach. Before I was awake the next morning I got a telephone call, in fact I got several telephone calls blasting the living daylights out of me, calling me all sorts of names and this, that, and the other.[25] I didn't know what it was all about until we went out to pick up the morning paper to discover there was a two-column headline on the front page saying that the rabbi had asked the schools in New Orleans to integrate, which I did not do.

PAK: It just said "the Rabbi"?

JBF: The Rabbi. It said "Rabbi Asks," so from then on things began to pop. I was called up by friend and foe alike, and I simply repeated that we only asked that they study the situation, see what they were going to do in the light of the required federal decision.

PAK: Were you not just one of a group that had asked this?

JBF: I was only one of two who appeared before the school board. A group had assisted in helping to frame the statement. This group, incidentally, was the old Southern Conference of Human Welfare, only it had changed its name to . . . the Southern Conference for Education. [Its Executive Director was] a man whose name you probably will come across, by the name of James Dombrowski.[26] I was called up by the most adamant of the school board members to ask if that group had anything to do with the framing of this statement. I told them that the only thing they did was mimeograph our sheet for us, that they did not meet with us, and so forth. The fact that that group was even identified with it damned the whole situation. This man [Dombrowski] was so persona non grata that anything he touched was ruined before it ever got to light.

PAK: Who was the other gentleman that was with you?

JBF: It was a lady by the name of Mrs. Charles Keller. She happened to come from a very fine family; she was a very liberal spirit and lovely woman. She, I am sure, softened somewhat the blow by virtue of the fact that her family stood for what it was. She's one of those exceptional liberals in a family of very great conservatives. I would say that was the beginning, as far as I was concerned, of any participation whatsoever in the civil rights movement.

Now I don't know if you want to use this or not, but in 1949, when things were not [inaudible] and there was no disturbance of any kind at all, there was the request made to me to open Temple Sinai on an integrated basis, because Ralph Bunche had consented to speak in New Orleans and could not find an auditorium.[27] The civic auditorium was closed to him; the university [Tulane] told the group, "don't embarrass us, we can't help you and it only makes it worse by asking." They came to me. I said I would take it up with my board, I don't consider the temple my property, and the board at its regular meeting, this was several months in advance, passed it but not unanimously. And that night, which was I think December 14th, was a very rainy, cold night in '49. . . . it had been advertised extensively. I got a telephone call by 7:30 that evening saying that the beautiful stained glass windows in Temple Sinai were going to be smashed that night.[28] There was some talk on the part of the board they would like to have policemen around; I said, "No, we want no policemen; we want no identification that we are apprehensive; we just don't want anything like that." The Negroes got there much earlier than the whites. And the place was three-quarters filled with Negroes downstairs and upstairs—that auditorium takes care of almost 1,400. We had to open up the extra auditorium in the adjoining building, which took care of about 300 to 350 more. I spent the two hours of the time of this meeting just walking around to see that the exits were clear, because people were sitting on the floor, Negroes were sitting all around the wall, and I said, "Don't close this exit. Any fire marshal could come in anytime and stop this meeting if we have violated the law that the fire exits are closed." Well the meeting went off beautifully, nothing happened, and this is in 1949. We had had a policy in Temple Sinai for years where integrated meetings were held on a smaller scale of about 200 to 250. We never had any problems of any kind; it was one of the few places where such meetings could be held. So we were more or less known as a Temple where all people were welcome.

PAK: **What was the nature of some of these meetings?**

JBF: The Family Service Society always held an annual meeting there to which all people came, and [there were] smaller groups, and Negro ministers had been coming frequently to other types of meetings for clergy groups and things like that.

PAK: **Did these start after World War II?**

JBF: I don't know whether they preceded my stay there or not, but since I was there in 1936 there's never been any question about integrated meetings. I had a telephone call occasionally in the olden days when a man would call up in a very angry manner and say, "My daughter attended a meeting at your place, did you know that Nigras were there?" I said, "Yes I knew it." He said, "Well don't you know there is a law forbidding Nigras and whites to meet in the same building?" I said, "But that doesn't apply to churches."

I didn't know whether it did or not. In fact I'm almost sure it [did] apply, but I said it to him anyway, and he said, "Oh, I didn't know that." I said, "Well that's the reason we have them because it doesn't apply to churches." So he was mollified.

PAK: I want to go into this further a little later, but did you find more opposition to such action before 1954 than you found after?

JBF: Frankly in our temple I didn't find any action opposed to it either before or after.

PAK: What about from the non-Jewish community?

JBF: Nobody bothered about it. We had always had people; in fact, at confirmation exercises, I would say to people who came to me and [would] tell me that Daisy had been their child's nurse ever since she had been born, they wanted to let her come to the ceremony, and I said, "On one condition"; they said, "Oh yes, that'll be all right, she'll sit in the balcony." I said, "Oh no she won't! That's the condition; she sits with you. She's coming as a member of your family; she's going to sit with you." And for a while that was startling to them, but that happened and I've never heard anything about it, oh yes, except recently. I had a group from Dillard University. They'd been to the temple twice; the first [group] was about ten [students], and then the teacher studying religion said that he'd like to bring the whole freshman class. I said that it would be all right so one Friday night we had over one hundred Negro students there, recently this spring. Now I didn't notice anything, and I didn't hear anything, but the ushers told me that one woman got up and walked out and handed the prayer book back and said, "This is the end of my days in Temple Sinai. I'm not going to worship here." But I didn't see it; I didn't hear it; and I've heard nothing about anybody who might have resigned or anything else. So, with that little exception, I don't recall any unpleasant moment. When we had these very large church visitations of Operation Understanding . . . we had hundreds of Negroes there. They drank coffee and ate cookies just like everybody else. We had not only Negro priests and Negro ministers but we also had Negro nuns, and I've never experienced in my temple anything of an unpleasant nature except maybe a voice or two that would tell me, "Be careful don't expose yourself too much in this field. It can't do us any good." But that's after the issue was drawn.[29]

PAK: Has this whole topic ever come up in a discussion at a board meeting where the board seriously discussed a stand or a position that you had taken?

JBF: No, but I'll tell you what did happen one night. . . . One Rosh Hashanah, I think it was right after that 1954 decision, the following year I noticed on

New Year's Eve a policeman standing in the back of the Temple, and I said at the time, "What's the matter with that damn fool? He ought to be out in front watching the traffic." We always had a policeman to watch the traffic so we could have a place to park. And the president finally admitted to me that they'd asked for a policeman. He said, "You never can tell when some crackpot may want to take a shot at you." I said, "Well what could that fellow do in the back if somebody wanted to take a shot at me?"... I told them at that time that must never happen again.

PAK: Why did your congregants or some of your congregants believe that this was necessary?

JBF: That was the time when the phone calls were being directed to everybody, and I guess they felt that maybe if something might happen they better have some protection. It only happened that once; it didn't happen again. Now after the integration did actually get started at these three schools down in a neighborhood that I had never even seen before, I went with the United States Marshal on the last day that . . . this white child went to that school, which was boycotted by other white children. The last day that she went without her parents; in other words marshals took her and I rode along. It just happened to be that day that I went down just to see what it was like. Things had been fairly quiet with me and my home. Particularly up to that time, it was more or less an uninteresting ride. We approached these schools, the streets for blocks away were guarded by policemen, and two blocks away they had barriers up, and even the United States Marshal who knew the policeman on the corner had to show his identification before they'd let this car through. Now we rode through and came to a side door of this school. I got out of the car simply to let this little child out, and I don't suppose I could have been out of the car a whole minute. I don't know how in the name of God anybody knew that I was there, but I hadn't gotten back to my office by one o'clock that afternoon before I began to get phone calls telling me to stay away from that neighborhood, don't come back again. I don't know who it was. I didn't take it seriously. The only thing I can suspect is that this marshal, a young fellow in his thirties who drove the car, was so sullen, so mean and sinister, that I imagine he was performing a duty that was very distasteful to him, and it may have been a leak through him, although I couldn't prove it, and that he alerted somebody to get back at me for doing this.[30]

PAK: What was the response of the non-Jewish community of your city to the intensification of civil rights activity in your area?

JBF: That's hard to say because it was divided. It's an old city with old traditions, and I suppose with a great deal of conservatism in it, and you'll hear a lot of people that would say, "I don't want to deprive anybody of anything they justly should have, but I just can't associate with them." That was the general attitude of, I would say, the older group.

PAK: What about the hard-core segregationists in the ilk of [John] Kasper,[31] or the Ku Klux Klan, the [White] Citizens' Councils? How active were they in your community?

JBF: Of course the Citizens' Council was extremely active, and we had one in-famous personality who lives in New Orleans, but he is sort of a czar and a dictator of an adjoining parish, called Plaquemines Parish.[32] He led the Citizen's Council and he . . . publicly blasted anybody who stepped out of line according to his lines of restriction. I never came into personal contact with the man—we'd been together in meetings but I didn't notice him and he probably didn't notice me. However he knew who I was as I knew who he was.[33] He was one of the last of the little "sawdust Caesars," you know. Ruling his parish with such a fist that he actually put up a concentration camp with wire around it on a piece of land that either he owned or could use in that parish, and this isn't more than maybe fifteen miles from New Orleans, and he defied freedom marchers to come into his parish, and he was going to put them in that camp immediately and just lock them in, and he said, "the mosquitoes will do the rest. They're welcome to come into my parish." That's the way he said it.

PAK: Did he have much support in the general community?

JBF: In his community he is of such importance that no man, so I hear . . . can even get a job unless he approves it. . . . He's held office, his son holds office for many, many years. He gets sent to the state legislature, he's head of one of the Democratic parties there, and he's already this year set up a stricture in the Democratic committee in Louisiana so that [Lyndon B.] Johnson's name would not appear on the ballot. That's the type of man he is.

PAK: What about in New Orleans itself?

JBF: Generally speaking, in New Orleans he has no standing at all, except as a lawyer—he's regarded as a very shrewd, smart lawyer.

PAK: Was there a visible, progressive element in New Orleans?

JBF: Yes. There always was a progressive element—not large, not organized, not vocal—but there was an element. I had a part of it in my congregation. In fact, I got more approval from a small nucleus in my congregation then I got opposition from anybody. And while I say it was not large, it joined us . . . now we had a group in New Orleans, which was called SOS, "Save Our Schools."[34] We were organized, we paid minimum dues, we had meetings, we issued statements and things like that. . . . I didn't attend their meetings but they knew they had my support, and we conferred on a great many matters and in emergencies we worked quickly.[35]

PAK: What about the press and the mass media? What attitude did they take to this whole thing?

JBF: More or less negatively neutral. They did not come out blatantly as segregationists but you could tell they were, I suppose, compelled by adversaries. We only have one paper in New Orleans, that is one in the afternoon, one in the evening [the *New Orleans Times-Picayune* and the *New Orleans Daily Picayune* respectively], but it's the same management, same building, two staffs but one ownership. They never came out with anything that I would call liberal in anything.

PAK: Were you personally ever attacked by name in the mass media?

JBF: I think so. In fact there were some handbills pasted on an empty store front that I stopped to examine one day, because I was told about them, and I saw myself named there as a communist who wants to wreck the democratic system and things like that. My name was in two or three of these leaflets that were handed out.

PAK: Were you ever quoted—you said there was this one big headline that involved you—were you ever quoted [in the press]?

JBF: They used that constantly. They referred to it, and I was referred to as wanting to infiltrate communists into the country by means of protecting the Negroes. It wasn't the press so much as it was this handbill issued by the Citizens' Council.

PAK: I'd like to ask a few questions about your Jewish community. How long has your congregation been in existence?

JBF: Ninety-five years.

PAK: The Jewish community in New Orleans has been there quite a long time?

JBF: Oh yes, longer than that. The Jewish community dates itself from about 1828, because that's when the first records were known, but there were Jews there before then.

PAK: What is the economic standing and the source of income of the members of your congregation?

JBF: Mine happens to be on a very high economic level. I suppose that they would be considered a rich congregation. We have some very modest people too like all metropolitan congregations, but for the most part it's a very affluent congregation, and I have some very unusually rich members.

PAK: What's their source of income?

JBF: The leading person is the daughter of [Julius] Rosenwald of Sears Roebuck, another was [Samuel] Zemurray who was the head of the United Fruit Company for years.[36] Without those two families I don't think anything in New Orleans would have ever gotten off the ground as far as cultural benefits are concerned and many beneficiary agencies like Child

Guidance and things like that. Most of [the congregants] are professional
men, businessmen, old families, and the generations that go back originally
to peddlers but now they are substantial citizens. They've been very, very
philanthropic and helped a great deal in many civic ways.

PAK: **How susceptible are they to economic pressure put on by the non-
Jewish community?**

JBF: They're very sensitive to it. I don't know whether they're susceptible to
any pressure. They're almost too independent for that, but they're sensitive
to criticism, very sensitive.

PAK: **If I were to compare your congregants to a comparable non-Jewish
congregation, if there is one, would there be a difference in their attitude
toward Negroes and civil rights?**

JBF: I don't think so. I think there would be the same liberal element, and I
think that there would be a majority of conservatives, same pattern. I don't
think there would be much difference. They seem very fortunate on account of [this being] an old established community with a great deal of social mingling in New Orleans between Christians and Jews on the highest
social level. It only stops one time a year and that's when Mardi Gras balls
take place. The rest of the time it's almost on a par and equal.

PAK: **How large an element of vocal segregationists do you have in your
congregation?**

JBF: I wouldn't say that I have any [who are] vocal. I suspect that I have had
a few members who were actually members of the Citizen's Council, but
I can't put my finger on and say this is true, but I suspect it. I would say
they're in the vast minority if I have them at all.[37]

PAK: **Would you say that the majority would be happier if the status quo
was kept?**

JBF: Yes.

PAK: **Even if they could accomplish more progressive change without any
endangering of their own economic position?**

JBF: I think unquestionably they would. I want to tell you about one incident
and you can use it or leave it out as you see fit. I had a man who was very
well off; we have a little community across what we call "the Lake" over on
the Mississippi Gulf Coast, and they had a summer cottage there. But in
this particular climate and locality you can use these things all through the
year, like you can indulge in sports every morning. They had difficulty getting servants to keep that cottage and they had to sell it. It turned them
against Negroes in almost a vicious manner. And so much so that this man
who was a very representative citizen and a fine gentleman, he went so far
as to tell me once that [Theodore] Bilbo[38] was the only man after all who
represented him and his point of view in the Senate of the United States.

And I said to him, "How in the name of God can you say a thing like that?" and he said, "Well it's the truth." This stems from the fact that you can't get a servant anymore. And it warped his whole attitude. He's still a decent citizen, no question about that, but we just can't discuss this question anymore.[39]

PAK: **How many rabbis do you have in your community?**

JBF: We have seven congregations—one at the moment doesn't have a rabbi, but usually we have seven active rabbis and a Hillel director [at Tulane University], and formerly we had two or three emeritus rabbis, so we had nine or ten at one time. At the moment we have about seven.

PAK: **When there was an intensification of efforts to bring about better conditions . . . for the Negroes in New Orleans from a civil rights perspective, what reaction did the ministers of the community have to it?**

JBF: At one time we had a group called an Interfaith Group of Ministers. This group prepared that statement for the day that the streetcars and buses were to be integrated.[40] I would not say that it was a very effective group; I wouldn't say it was a group that I would be proud of, but the only thing I tried always to do was to get all of the ministers to act together. After this first experience of mine with the Supreme Court decision, I didn't feel individually that I could be effective. I felt that I could be enormously strengthened if I could get Catholics and Protestants into this group and such a group was formed. I was instrumental in bringing it together. I can't remember any more actually who formed it. But I was instrumental in it, and I certainly was leaned upon very heavily while it was working. It petered out. My big disappointment was that the Protestant ministry as a whole was not only lukewarm[41] but with one or two exceptions it was absolutely negative. The Catholics, of course, have such a variety of types in their parish that their priest representatives are usually picked, and liberals were picked. The Catholics were far more outstanding I would say.

PAK: **Did you find support from the Catholic clergy?**

JBF: Yes I did. Yes, much more support. The largest, I don't want to use the actual denomination, one of the largest Protestant churches where I felt it could have been a tremendous power to help this matter happened to have a man who was absolutely adamant in his negativism. In fact, he was one of those who met a group of what they call "kneel-ins"—you know, church-attending Negroes—and met them at the door and absolutely refused to let them enter his church, and told them, "Why don't you go where you would be wanted." Now his church backed him up. On the other hand, there was another Baptist church up in my neighborhood where the minister is virtually the reverse. He's liberal; he's broadminded; and he really is I would say an intellectual. So the Baptists have a variety too today, but this [other one] was the church where the influence would have been very positive had the pastor been of a different frame of mind. I always felt and I still feel today that the crux of this matter weighed on the religious bodies more than anything else. I'm not talking about courts; I'm talking about social groups or integrated groups in the community, which could have fostered progress in it, and that religion could have done so much to help this but it did not.

PAK: **I've been told on more than one occasion that integration isn't a religious matter but a sociological matter or an economic matter. You seem to take issue with that.**

JBF: Well did you hear the statement the other night [referring to one of the talks at the CCAR conference] that "all values are of the genus spiritual"? That's the way I look at the church. I feel that it is impossible to separate the social from the religious or the spiritual, and that the example should have been set by the religious group but was not.

PAK: **What about the Orthodox and Conservative rabbinate in your city? What was their response to this?**

JBF: They were, I would say, negative; not negative, neutral. They didn't do anything. I think one or two may have been really in favor of it, but they didn't do anything, nothing that I know of.

PAK: **I don't want to mention names, and if the question is out of order, please regard it as such, but was the Reform rabbinate active? How did they respond?**

JBF: The Reform rabbis, the three of us, were always present in these group meetings.[42] I would say the three Reform rabbis were of a most positive nature. We did not, I suppose, step out too far, but at least our position was known in our congregations and outside.

PAK: **You don't think this was the case in the Conservative and Orthodox congregations?**

JBF: I wouldn't know. I just don't know. In fact I know nothing that I could tell you about from their point of view. I think they would have stood with us but I can't recall anything.

PAK: **You spoke in detail about your participation in one or two specific instances of civil rights activity. Can you recall any other ones or can you give me an idea of . . . your methodology—how you went about accomplishing what your goals were? What involvement you had in certain pushes and drives in your community, et cetera?**

JBF: I don't know that I could tell you anything of specific interest beyond the general position that I tried to take and that I made it known to my congregation on more than one occasion in the pulpit. I felt they had a right to know where I stood and I think they knew it without any question or doubt.

PAK: **Did you ever speak on a specific topic, not on equality [in general] . . . but on "we should do this one thing in our community" or "we should vote for this person" or something like that?**

JBF: I don't think I recall anything that I did along those lines. I think, generally speaking, I tried to reach certain people personally by telephone or meeting and urge them to do certain things in an election or [to vote] for certain candidates on the school board and things like that.

PAK: **Can you remember a specific instance when you did something like this?**

JBF: Well I know we were very anxious to get rid of two particular men on the school board and bring in two more who were liberal and who had a bit more open-minded attitude. And I would in a quiet way speak to as many people as I could. I didn't make any big [to-do] about the thing and I didn't do anything publicly on a platform. Incidentally, we did succeed in getting those men in. You see, there came a time, after the federal courts began to act. All along I said I know that you cannot change people's morals and attitudes but you can change their ways by court action. When I came to that conclusion, and the courts were beginning to say, "This has got to be done, this has got to be done," and it was done—I felt we had reached at least a peak in the way upward and in so doing I felt that the work was being accomplished. I became more and more convinced that it had to be done that way. We've suffered a great deal, from some people's point of view, in New Orleans in sports, because we couldn't bring teams there into the Sugar Bowl if you had Negro players. I and a few others relish the thing. They thought that would help this movement along, and it has. Now we have Negro players on visiting teams and in Sugar Bowl Games. But we had a bad incident happen that you probably read about where two of the national football clubs that are playing in New Orleans, one of them picked up and left because they were already in a hotel. Now the hotels are completely open—the dining rooms are completely open—and there were two testimonial banquets [held] this year in honor of Negroes with a mixed group at both in the finest hotels. I think that was a very fine thing.

PAK: **Have you ever made a phone call or had talks with people that we would consider to be in the power structure of the community in order to influence action of some sort?**

JBF: Well I've made a visit to the mayor[43] with a committee on more than one occasion, asking him to help certain things along. I've visited the mayor with a group of ministers to ask him to set up an interracial committee, which he would not do. We didn't get it. We never had one. The new government has set one up on a state basis, and we haven't anything in the city because this mayor simply won't do it. He says we don't need it. Of course a great many people are blind to what's needed and what isn't, and he, in that particular case, is blind.

PAK: What was your response to things like the Freedom Rides?

JBF: They never got to my city. I had mixed emotions about them, and when one of the rabbis got hurt in one of these rides[44] I called up his hospital room and spoke to his nurse, offered to do anything that I could, asked him if he needed anything and so forth. But personally I thought he was actually going out of his way looking for things that maybe he could capitalize on. I happen to know a particular one, I don't want to mention any names, but take for instance this particular march through Mississippi right now. See, I'm a native Mississippian; I was born in Jackson, Mississippi, and I lived there until after the First World War when I got out of the army and eventually went to college in Cincinnati.

I don't think it's helping things any. I think that progress is a gradual process and this [the Freedom Rides and marches] only strengthens resistance and makes it a little more difficult. We have made enormous strides in New Orleans. We've got a far way to go, but at least we've made progress. This is all from the top down. It's the influential group that sets the example. The hardest group is going to be the bottom group that has to be moved upward, the white group . . . and it's going to take a long time. A condition like this is so integrated both in tradition and in mores that you just can't expect it to change overnight. And that's the reason I think in the rural neighborhoods where the progress is slowest of all, these marches frankly only upset the situation and probably [even] delay it.

PAK: What do you see as your role in the civil rights movement in the years to come?

JBF: As a rabbi?

PAK: Yes, as a rabbi in New Orleans.

JBF: Well I'm pretty sure that my position is known that I favor this, and that all I can do is to just keep on. At first I noticed there was a little pulling away in certain circles in the community from myself personally, but that's changed. I can't say that I've noticed any restraints or any weakening of friendships or things like that. At one time one of the socialites was quoted in the paper as saying I was nothing but a do-gooder. He took particular pains to come to me and tell me, "I didn't say that." He said, "You know I don't like the things you're standing for but I don't criticize you." Well I don't feel that my position is any different today than before. I simply don't feel I'm as active as I was say, ten years ago, because I feel the thing is in the only channel it can be in for effectiveness and that's the courts.

PAK: Did you ever join any groups—civil rights or non-civil rights groups—in order to further your goals in this area?

JBF: Only at one time . . . [when I joined] the Southern Conference of Human Welfare.

PAK: What about Rotary and groups like that?

JBF: Well I'm in Rotary. I'm past president of Rotary and I have spoken, I would say, not directly but at least with enough emphasis to let them know where I was, but that is a very conservative group. They are mostly businessmen. They've come along, I would say, remarkably well in the larger picture. They certainly have been as wonderfully kind to me as they could be.

PAK: Do you think it's valuable for a rabbi in a city such as yours to join such groups?

JBF: I think it is absolutely essential if a rabbi can get in it. It puts him in contact with the citizens of the first rank whether you like them or not, be they conservative—they're [certainly] no radicals. But at the same time, they get to see you, they invite you to speak at least once a year, you can talk along liberal lines. I had a talk I gave once to them, and I also gave it in Dallas for the Rotary club there, called "We Couldn't Do It Today," in which I said we could not pass a Bill of Rights today. I doubt if we could even pass the Constitution today. There was a Negro member of the Board of Aldermen in Jackson, Mississippi, at the turn of the century, and I remember his name, in which they said that he always knew how to keep his place, but he was a fine man. I used that in this talk before those clubs that we couldn't do it today. We couldn't elect a Negro to the City Council today. Sometime that's going to happen too.[45]

PAK: What's your feeling about national Jewish organizations? Do you think that they have in any way been helpful in helping you reach your goals in civil rights?

JBF: They haven't helped me any. I have mingled feelings about them. I think they must exist. I think they largely do good work. I know they have embarrassed certain communities by sending their representatives in without notifying even the local people and that has caused some resentment and some embarrassment. They have not done that in New Orleans, but we have a local office of the Anti-Defamation League, and we've been fortunate to have a series of very fine young men who are outstanding in their liberalism [and] in their activity, and they have won the respect of Catholics and Protestants all over. They are not accepted, naturally, by the reactionary groups, but at the same time they stand out as something that is very potent and very fine. That is the Anti-Defamation League; that is the only one I know anything about.

PAK: Do you think they have helped the cause of civil rights in New Orleans?

JBF: I'm sure they have.

PAK: If the history of your community was to be written, say, fifty years from now, would you think that the rabbis in your community would have played an important role in the advancement of the civil rights movement?

JBF: I would say that they represented the rabbinate in at least a forthright manner. I don't think we've done anything remarkable. One of our rabbis got himself into an awful brawl with this leader from that adjoining parish [Leander] Perez, but I don't want to talk about him.[46]

PAK: What about the South as a whole? Do you think the rabbinate will have played an important role in the advancement of the civil rights movement?

JBF: I think that the southern rabbinate as a whole would at least have some outstanding personalities. I think the most remarkable one of all is Charles Mantinband. Here was a terrific community—small, integrated in the sense of the old tradition and conservatism; and he absolutely stood out.

PAK: Did he make any changes? Did any changes come out of his work?

JBF: I can't say that he made any changes. I don't know. At least his community seemed to back him, and I've often said if I had lived in the Mississippi Delta instead of New Orleans, which is a metropolitan city, that I doubt very much whether I would even have tried to stand out, because I think that it might have brought economic ruin frankly to the congregation or community. And I know I have to thank God I didn't have to face it. I don't know if I would have the right to endanger them to that extent and that would at least have been a very vital consideration to me. However, I didn't have to face anything like that. I have some diehards in my temple, but they didn't do anything in the other direction and at least I was trying in one direction and I'd say very moderately. I was never a crusader and I was probably too old to enter the lists at that time. But by and large, speaking of the rabbinate, I would say it was commendable. I'm rather proud of the rabbinate. At least people knew who they were and what they were, whether they did anything or not. They didn't belong to the wrong group.

3
Alfred L. Goodman

Columbus, Georgia, and Its Jewish Community

The Georgia legislature established the city of Columbus in 1828. One of the few planned cities of the era in the United States, it benefited from the Chattahoochee River's access to the Gulf of Mexico. The river carried the area's most valuable crop, cotton, to Europe. Soon the city housed several cotton mills, textile factories, and warehouses. The arrival of the railroad facilitated the city's emergence as one of the most important industrial centers in the South, and Columbus gained the nickname "the Lowell of the South" in reference to the famous industrial city in Massachusetts.

During the Civil War, Columbus served as a major shipyard for the Confederacy, and its many ironworks manufactured swords and other materiel for the Confederate war machine. Ironically, the city did not experience the wrath of the enemy until Easter Sunday, 1865, when Union soldiers lead by General James Wilson, who had not yet learned of Robert E. Lee's surrender a week earlier, attacked the city and burned many of its factories to the ground.

After the war, cotton and textile exports brought renewed wealth. In 1918, on the eve of America's entry into World War I, the army established a fort named for local Confederate hero Brigadier General Henry L. Benning on the southeast edge of the city. Fort Benning provided basic training for army personnel being sent to Europe. After the war the fort closed until World War II, when it became home to the Infantry School commanded by General George C. Marshall. The 2nd Armored Division was formed there. Fort Benning also served as home to the 555th Parachute Infantry Battalion, which included African American soldiers. Thus, aside from a brief hiatus between the world wars, the military exerted a major impact on the local economy, bringing as many as 100,000 soldiers to the area.[1]

Jewish traders likely could be found in Columbus prior to the town's founding. Thirty years later, twenty Jewish families drawn by the growing number of textile mills and sawmills made the fledgling city their home. They ultimately established businesses that typically provided their neighbors with dry goods and clothing. In 1844, thirty-three-year-old Jacob I. Moses won election as Columbus's first Jewish mayor.

Many of the Jewish men of Columbus served in the Confederate army and nearly every Jewish family was touched either by the death of a loved one or by financial woes by the end of the conflict. Raphael J. Moses, a major during the war, earned the friendship of General Robert E. Lee and the trust of President Jefferson Davis. He won election to the Georgia legislature during Reconstruction and is credited with introducing the commercial production of peaches in the state.[2]

Jews established their first synagogue in the city in 1854. Congregation B'nai Israel (Children of Israel) rented space until 1859 when the congregants purchased a house and converted it into a place of worship. Although lacking rabbinic leadership, B'nai Israel provided traditional Jewish services and religious school education until 1875 when it became one of the founding synagogues of the Union of American Hebrew Congregations (UAHC), a move symbolic of gradually changing its identity from Orthodox to Reform. Reflecting the growing prosperity of its members and the assistance of many non-Jews, the congregation built an impressive Byzantine-style synagogue that they dedicated with great pomp and ceremony in September 1887. The congregation and its members had followed very typical trajectories of development and achievement. They came into their own and felt sufficiently comfortable to trumpet their positions with a conspicuous and distinctive structure.

Developments in Russia and Poland portended dramatic changes in the composition of the Jewish community. Fleeing pogroms, economic privation, and discrimination, millions of Jews fled Eastern Europe from 1881 to the 1920s, with most making their way to America. Columbus's central European Jews, most of whom had acculturated and become prominent merchants, had little in common with the newcomers who made their way to this small southern city. The refugees shared this discomfort and consequently, in 1892, organized congregation Sharis Israel (the Remnant of Israel), where they could feel at home with an Eastern European-style Orthodox service and people from a similar background. By 1915 the forty members of Sharis Israel dedicated their first synagogue building, optimistically built to seat 500.

Over the first half of the twentieth century, Jews of Columbus earned esteem not only as the result of their prominent economic presence on Main Street but also due to their civic mindedness and philanthropy. The Schwob family endowed the School of Music at Columbus State College (now Columbus State University). Laura Rosenberg won recognition as the most outstanding citizen in Columbus by the Lion's Club in 1931. Judge Aaron Cohn turned almost five decades on the bench into a crusade on behalf of troubled children. Maurice Rothschild's years on the Columbus school board resulted in a junior high school bearing his name. Frank Rosenthal, B'nai Israel's rabbi from 1907 to 1940, actively participated in several service groups.[3]

In 1952 the Orthodox Sharis Israel transformed itself into the Conservative

synagogue Shearith Israel. It erected a new building and achieved a peak membership of about 150 families. B'nai Israel, now known as Temple Israel and with a
membership of approximately 120 families when the decade began, also dedicated a new facility. During the 1980s the membership rose to over 180 families. Much of the vitality of Columbus's lone Reform synagogue resulted from
the long and effective tenure of Rabbi Alfred Goodman.[4]

In the June 1966 interview, Goodman spoke of the tremendous progress that
Columbus had made in the years following the *Brown v. Board of Education* decision of 1954. The progress he identified reflected dramatic changes from the
city's ugly history. In the early 1900s it had the reputation as the lynching mecca
of the South. Indeed, like many Deep South cities, the mayor and police chief en-
dorsed the Ku Klux Klan (KKK), and the community took violence for granted.[5]
The celebrated author Carson McCullers, who grew up in Columbus during the
1930s and '40s, later called the city "an intolerable place to live," a comment re-
flective of the prevalent racism.[6]

Ezra Johnston, who called himself "Parson Jack," acted as a key force of bigotry
in Georgia. He founded the Baptist Tabernacle in Columbus in 1931, broadcasted
a weekly radio show, and published two statewide newspapers, one of which had
more subscribers than either Columbus daily. Johnston used these media and
pulpit to relentlessly attack unions and "race mixing," and was very influential
in the local Klan Klavern. Johnston and the KKK often marched in full regalia
down the streets of the main business district. One such march was connected
to a September 8, 1939, citywide meeting that took place in Memorial Stadium,
during which the speakers openly threatened the homes and families of two black
activists, Dr. James Grant and Dr. Thomas Brewer, founders of the local National Association for the Advancement of Colored People (NAACP) chapter.

Brewer orchestrated a challenge to the state's white primary system, arranging for Primus E. King, a Columbus barber and minister, to attempt to vote in
the 1944 primary election at the courthouse in Muscogee County. During this
era of the "Solid South" when Republicans did not stand a chance of winning a
general election, a victory in the primary was tantamount to being elected, which
accounts for Brewer's strategy. King was, as expected, denied the right to vote
even though his name appeared on the registered voters' rolls. A white attorney,
Oscar D. Smith Sr., filed a lawsuit against the county Democratic Party Executive
Committee, requesting injunctive relief and $5,000 in damages. When Federal
Judge Hoyt Davis asked King whether he wanted the right to vote or the $5,000,
King eschewed the money in favor of the franchise. On October 12, 1945, the
court ruled in King's favor. When the local Democratic Party appealed the deci-
sion to the US Circuit Court of Appeals in New Orleans, Judge Samuel H. Sib-
ley, a Georgia native, denied the appeal, and on April 1, 1946, the US Supreme
Court denied certiorari. A decade later when a Columbus merchant gunned

down Thomas Brewer, the KKK staged a victory march down First Avenue a few days later and, to no one's surprise, the assailant was not convicted of the crime.[7]

Institutionalized and publicly sanctioned bigotry did not die easily. The *Columbus (GA) Enquirer* regularly printed the cartoon "Sunflower Seed." Written in black dialect, the characters depicted in the comic fit the negative stereotypes of African Americans.[8] Both major Columbus newspapers frequently used the "n-word."[9] Even the black soldiers based at Fort Benning were routinely subjected to embarrassment and acts of intimidation. Colin Powell, who later served as head of the Joint Chiefs of Staff and Secretary of State, recounts in his autobiography how, just prior to the passage of the 1964 Civil Rights Act, he went into a local hamburger joint and was admonished by the waitress: "You're a Negro. You'll have to go to the back door." Four other soldiers, two white and two black, were on a shopping trip in civilian clothes when police accosted and handcuffed them, then drove them in a paddy wagon to court. The presiding judge used a form of logic then common to the South when he proclaimed: "You're two white guys and two black guys walking together. That's disturbing the peace. Guilty." In 1941, a black soldier was found hanged in a wooded area at the fort. That same year, an MP was acquitted after shooting a black soldier whose great sin was talking back to a white telephone operator.[10]

Yet the old system began to come under attack in 1939 with the establishment of the Columbus branch of the NAACP and continued into the 1940s under the leadership of Grant, Brewer, King, and others. In 1952 Dr. Robert McNeill arrived to serve the prestigious 1,200-member First Presbyterian Church. The thirty-seven-year-old white pastor, a native of Birmingham, Alabama, had graduated from the Union Theological Seminary in Richmond, Virginia. Two years earlier, he had presented a report to the Alabama synod of the Presbyterian Church criticizing racial discrimination. A few years after his move to Columbus, he helped found a new black Presbyterian Church, to which he assigned a white minister. This stirred up so much controversy that *Look* magazine asked him to write an article about his work. In the article, published in the May 28, 1957, edition, he wrote, "As for the klansmen and their threats of violence, we do not fear them, we only pity them. God pity anyone who has to spread fear to be rid of fear, whose self esteem is so low that he has to flatten someone else to feel that he is upright. . . . Our greatest concern is with good citizens who create the climate of opinion, in their service clubs, in their coffee-break talks, in business transactions, in political decisions, in church affairs, in the management of the home. The heavy pressure we ministers feel comes from them . . . as though we were the real disturbers of the peace. There is little indignation expressed over the klan or racial violence, just silence, cold sweaty silence. The klan is the impassioned tip of the community's refined prejudice."

Besides the KKK, many members of his church responded negatively to their pastor's remarks. "Parson Jack" vehemently attacked McNeill through the pulpit and press, labeling him a communist and supporter of the NAACP. Rather than being cowed, McNeill called Ezra Johnston "the dirty linen of Columbus" who "spewed bigotry in every way he could think of." In December 1958, the Presbytery of Southwest Georgia appointed a commission headed by the Rev. Frank King of Valdosta to run McNeill's church while they sought to "resolve its internal problems." Although newspapers across the country reported that he had been fired because of his article and his position regarding integration, Frank King, who had removed McNeill, insisted, "The major problem in that church is not the racial issue. The present difficulty is deep and involved and has a history of several years standing. The racial issue has merely been used to trigger the explosion."

In June 1959, the presbytery formally dismissed McNeill. In his final sermon, "So That You May Have Integrity," McNeill described the differences between what he called an "Organization Church" and a "Proclaiming Church." In the former, its members substituted a "manager for a minister" and a "reporter for a preacher," measuring its success in terms of numbers of parishioners and contributions. McNeill implied that the First Presbyterian Church had become an Organization Church, one in which "the caliber of its gospel depends upon the satisfaction of its clientele." McNeill's was one of the voices that contributed to the end of the Jim Crow system that occurred within a decade of his departure.[11]

The death knell of the old system that began in earnest in 1946 with the abolition of the white primaries continued with the integration of the city's police force in 1952. Nine years later, the "black section" on buses was eliminated. Lunch counter desegregation followed in 1962. In the fall of 1963 John Townsend became the first African American admitted to Columbus College. Two years later, the city's school system began to integrate slowly. Albert Thompson, a black man, was elected to the Georgia House of Representatives in 1965, and in 1967 James Grant was rewarded for his decades of leadership with a seat on the school board. The vast majority of the white community opposed each of these changes. They resulted from increasing pressure from the city's black community, growing support from liberal whites, and a sense that integration was inevitable and continued resistance was pointless. Some Jews, including the young rabbi of Temple Israel, joined the progressive white voices that helped move the city toward integration.[12]

Alfred L. Goodman

Alfred Louis Goodman, born on August 16, 1918, in Cleveland, Ohio, earned his bachelor of arts degree at Western Reserve University before enrolling in the Jewish Institute of Religion in New York. After completing his religious stud-

3. Chaplain Alfred Goodman, Yokohama, Japan, 1946. (Goodman private collection). Used by permission of Rayna F. Goodman.

ies and receiving ordination in 1944, Goodman obtained his first rabbinic position at Temple Beth Israel in Lima, Ohio. One year later he entered the Army Air Corps and served as a chaplain in Japan. He then returned to Temple Beth Israel where he remained until 1950, when he answered the call at Temple Israel in Columbus, Georgia, a post he held until his retirement thirty-three years later.

Goodman, an excellent preacher and exemplar of Jewish values, was well suited to the congregational rabbinate. His obituary, printed in the *Columbus (GA) Ledger,* praised his intellect and warmth and noted that his congregants "genuinely loved him." Goodman quickly became known and admired in the general community as well and earned the respect of his peers as a speaker who consistently advocated for justice and tolerance. A resolution adopted by the synagogue's Jewish Ladies Aid Society notes that he was as beloved "as any individual in this community." The resolution also says that "he was a rabbi who meant what he said and said what he meant in all circumstances, and that his greatest sermon was expressed best by his own personal example."[13]

Shortly after his arrival in the city, Goodman helped establish the Columbus Council on Human Relations, the first integrated group in the city. Along with his friend the Rev. Robert McNeill, he became an outspoken advocate of equal rights and opportunities for the city's African Americans. Goodman actively participated in the state Council on Human Relations, served as president of the Columbus–Phenix City Ministerial Association, and as a board member of the Columbus Family Counseling Center. The synagogue tribute book published after his death indicates that during the earliest days of the civil rights movement, he "boldly and courageously supported the call for racial desegregation and, as a result of his efforts and the efforts of those like him, the City of Columbus passed through that turbulent period . . . without experiencing the violence and the deep hatred which ripped other communities apart."[14] On the national level Goodman's rabbinic colleagues recognized his qualities by electing him to the board of the Central Conference of American Rabbis and to the National Commission of Rabbinical Congregational Relationships.

Two and a half years after his retirement, a *Columbus Enquirer* writer headed a column "'Awesome': That's Rabbi Goodman." When he died of a viral infection on September 1, 1986, at the age of sixty-eight, the *Columbus Ledger* spoke for many in the city when it ended his obituary with the words, "We shall not see Alfred Goodman's like again soon."[15]

Editor's Introduction to the Interview

Patterns begin with this interview to emerge although each also brings new insights. Goodman, like Bloom and others, served as a chaplain, although for Goodman the location was Japan. They likely perceived World War II as a just enterprise against a madman, Adolf Hitler, who based his policies and appeals on racism. The war ended with the defeat of Hitler, but the liberation of the Nazi concentration camps again disclosed the results of racism and evil—realities that required continued vigilance to keep at bay. Curiously, the interviewees do not make this connection. As was the case with Goodman and Bloom, they stress their image of Jewish values and their roles as rabbis.

Like Mobile and many of the other locations where these rabbis filled pulpits, Columbus boasted a diverse economy anchored by a nearby military base. The presence of the military proved to be very important in relation to the success of the civil rights movement. Local boosters feared the removal of the bases and the jobs and money they brought if confrontation with the federal government over desegregation went too far. Goodman acknowledges an interesting point concerning his congregation's experiences with integration. He notes that Jewish soldiers brought their African American comrades in arms to services without incident. Goodman estimated that only a small percentage of his congregants supported segregation. None did so vociferously, and even these recognized the moral failing of their position.

4. (Left to right) Unidentified man (seated), Columbus, Georgia, Mayor J. R. Allen (standing in background), Rabbi Alfred Goodman (standing at desk, addressing a Columbus city council meeting), unidentified man (standing), and Assistant Mayor A. J. McClung (seated on the far right), 1960s. (Goodman private collection.) Used by permission of Rayna F. Goodman.

As in almost every locale, Jews traced their presence to Columbus's early history. They had risen economically into the middle and upper-middle classes largely as merchants, participated actively in civic affairs, and otherwise contributed to society. Yet they were neither part of the local power structure nor (although many interviewees do not mention this) welcomed into gentile society. They perceived that their positions remained tenuous. The Jewish communities in which these rabbis functioned were far from monolithic. Divisions existed between those descended from earlier nineteenth-century immigrants from Central Europe and those from Eastern Europe arriving between 1881 and the 1920s, after which Congress largely closed America's doors to certain immigrants. The variations in background included differences in worship and observance, although by the 1950s and '60s these lines began to blur. Symptomatic of the acculturation process especially of the second generation was the movement of many Orthodox congregations to Conservative affiliation shortly before and then after World War II.

One of the major questions to be considered concerns the impact made by the rabbis. Spokespeople for a very tiny minority, often less than one percent of a community's population, what differences could they possibly make? The majority of the Protestant clergy in these communities either remained silent or openly opposed desegregation. Those Protestant clergy outspoken in favor of change typically lost their positions. The Reform rabbis worked with a very few colleagues through ministerial associations and human relations councils. Since they were often perceived as symbolic representatives of all of the Jews in the community, including those from different backgrounds and with different religious practices, they frequently helped organize and won election as president of the ministerial groups. As Jews, they were viewed as valued aliens, a status that in some ways facilitated their work. Beyond the rabble rousers, the local community expected them to speak in behalf of social justice and tended to accept—if not act on—their pronouncements and activities.

Goodman helps explain a key factor affecting the influence a rabbi could exert on various elements of his Jewish community. A minority within their congregations who were typically more acculturated and traced their residency back generations tended to accept southern racial mores. The rabbi notes that even these members within his congregation recognized the moral failure of their position. His civil rights preaching and activism led them to be less outspoken than they would have been otherwise. He contrasts his experience in Columbus with that of the Reform congregation in Albany, Georgia, where the rabbi repeatedly considered resignation yet remained while supplying no such voice or leadership. From another perspective, Columbus fits Allen Krause's definition of a city in the land of the almost possible, whereas Albany, the battleground city within the same state identified with the Albany Movement and effective opposition to desegregation, falls in the category of a city in the land of the almost impossible.

Still another important issue was the relationship between the white power structure, white moderates, and African American leaders. When white moderates pressured the Columbus school board to develop a desegregation plan, they received silence as a response. Yet the school board quietly developed such a plan that it put into effect virtually immediately once the court ordered it to do so. White moderates worked with the school board for peaceful integration of the libraries, but both failed to communicate with black leaders. Consequently, demonstrations and confrontation took place unnecessarily. Different groups in Columbus, as elsewhere, feared black and white boycotts and demonstrations, violence and threats, confrontation, loss of political office, adverse publicity, outside involvement, change (or the lack thereof), and the unknown, among other things. A variety of fears and misunderstandings thus pervaded even the almost possible arenas.

—Mark K. Bauman

Alfred L. Goodman Interview

June 22, 1966

P. Allen Krause: Rabbi Goodman, what would you define as a legitimate regional scope of a [work] such as this?

Alfred L. Goodman: I would imagine that you would deal with the problem of segregation, the civil rights issue, in the area which we normally call about those states which lie south of the Mason-Dixon Line. The entire broad expanse of the southern states, about twenty of them.

PAK: Would you include also lower Florida and the entire state of Texas?

ALG: It is very difficult, you know, to define the South, because there is no one South. For instance, Georgia can certainly not be put into the same category as Alabama or Mississippi or Louisiana, or even South Carolina, in some respects. Nor is there even one Georgia. My community happens to be a rather advanced community because of the impact of Fort Benning, which lies just ten miles away and is a major economic factor in the growth of the community. So we are quite a cosmopolitan area.

PAK: What aspects of the civil rights movement have touched your community within recent years?

ALG: Well, all of the aspects, with the exception of civil rights freedom marches or open demonstrations. The only demonstrations that we have had were two instances: one in relation to bus desegregation, where we did have a couple of arrests and young people involved in breaking the segregation law, and the second in the desegregation of the public parks, where we had a couple of rough days. Aside from that everything has gone rather smoothly, and in my judgment rather rapidly, really, from what I thought it would be.

PAK: When was this? Would you say that there was a certain year or maybe a two- or three-year period which marked the starting point of intense civil rights activity?

ALG: Oh I don't think that there is any question but that the whole momentum began with the civil, with the school desegregation decision in 1954. I have only been in the South since 1950, so I can't guess prior to that time.

PAK: Have you seen any—then you have seen changes in your community since that date?

ALG: I have seen tremendous changes. Our entire community is now desegregated, with the exception of a few grades of the public schools which will be desegregated next year. I don't think that there should be any confusion in anybody's minds, however, mind [you], in the use of this term "desegregation"—there is no wholesale mixing of the races.

PAK: **What has been the response of the non-Jewish community here?—number one. Number two, what roles have the ministers played in this?**

ALG: This is a rather disturbing question, because, with the exception of one or two of the Christian ministers in my community, the minister really hasn't played a role in this whole area. The church has been rather backward in taking a stand. The national church organizations, as you know, have been very positive in their stand on civil rights. On the local level, the pastors and the ministers have been very reluctant to stick their necks out. I, and another minister in town, a local Presbyterian minister, were the only two white members of the Human Relations Council of Columbus, Georgia. The Presbyterian minister subsequently lost his job.[16]

PAK: **When did you become affiliated with this?**

ALG: As soon as it was reactivated in our city.

PAK: **What year was that?**

ALG: About 1955 or ['56], when the need for this kind of a group became quite evident.

PAK: **Did the non-Jewish community react violently in any way to the changes that were taking place, and . . . what was their reaction?**

ALG: There was no real violence. There were some tempers that flared, and when our human relations council became active, and when I and this Presbyterian minister became active in the human relations council, for instance, a telephone threat was made to a member of the board of trustees of my congregation saying that if I continued my activity in the human relations council that what had happened to the Presbyterian minister, who by that time was already gone from the community, would be peanuts. However this matter was taken up with our board of trustees, because they were concerned for me, not because they objected to my activities, but because they were concerned, and I had made it quite clear to them at that time that what I did in this area I did as a matter of conscience, and that it was not a board concern.

PAK: **Did you make such arrangements in advance of taking a position with this congregation?**

ALG: Oh no, no this had nothing to do with the temple board of trustees. This was, I was acting in my role as a rabbi.

PAK: **Did you come to an understanding with these people before you took the job that you would be able to have some sort of freedom of the pulpit or something like this . . .?**

ALG: With which people? With my own congregation? There has never been any question of the freedom of the pulpit—never.

PAK: **Regarding the Jewish community, how long has the congregation been in existence, and how long has the community been in existence?**

ALG: The congregation is now a hundred and twelve years old. The community existed from prerevolutionary days. There was a Jewish community when Columbus was just a trading post on the Chattahoochee River.

PAK: **What is the approximate size of the Jewish community?**

ALG: We have about 250 families in a community of a hundred and twenty thousand. So we are a very small percentage of the group.

PAK: **What percentage of this Jewish community of 250 [families] is affiliated with the congregation?**

ALG: With my congregation?

PAK: **No, with any Jewish congregation.**

ALG: Well, all of them are affiliated with one synagogue or the other.

PAK: **What is the economic standing and involvement of Jews in the city? . . . Where do they get their source of income?**

ALG: Well most of them are merchants, which incidentally makes them very vulnerable to pressure from the community. I am quite proud of them because, despite their vulnerability, they were the leaders in much of the desegregation movement. Now, I would not go so far as to say that they always did it for the right reason.

PAK: **Would you say then that, according to your experience, is there any difference in the orientation of the Jews toward civil rights activity and problems in comparison with the non-Jewish community in your period at Columbus?**

ALG: Yes, but I think that this is a result of their having been sensitized by preachment from the pulpit and by the actions of their rabbi.

PAK: **Are they mainly a southern type of community? . . . Have most of them been there for many years?**

ALG: The core of the community is deeply southern, yes. They have been there at least, most of them, for three generations.

PAK: **What percentage of your people . . . have views with regard to the segregation issue which you would . . . say are comparable to the non-Jews that we hear about so often?**

ALG: I would say there is a small proportion of the Jewish community of Columbus which has become completely acculturated, and therefore they feel about this problem the same way as their non-Jewish neighbors. But to give them their due credit, they have not been vocal about this; and there is not one of them who will not admit that morally they are wrong.

PAK: **Are there any other rabbis in the community?**

ALG: Yes, there is an Ortho—a Conservative rabbi as well.

PAK: **Has he in any way done anything in the area of civil rights activity?**

ALG: Well the Conservative rabbi who is there now has only been there a year, but, over this whole period of time that I have been there, the Conservative rabbi has never been active in the field.[17]

PAK: **Could you tell me, Rabbi, what has been your response to and involvement in specific civil rights activities in your area, any of them that you might think of?**

ALG: Well, as I say, I have been active in the revitalization of the human relations council in the area, which, incidentally, is the only biracial, was the only biracial group in the city up until about two years ago when the city commission officially established a biracial commission. I have been active in the program that looked toward the desegregation of the public schools, and when the Sibley Commission toured the state of Georgia, sounding out the feelings of the various communities on whether or not Georgia should comply with the school desegregation decision, I was active in seeing that people came to the commission hearings, and I was at the commission hearings myself along with a number of other ministers in town who were active in this particular area.[18] In the bus desegregation problem I happened to be out of the country when this came to a head, so I was not involved; but I was involved in the theatre desegregation, and I have been involved in talks with the board of education and the superintendent of education about the program for school desegregation, and I was active in the problems which arose when our playgrounds and libraries were desegregated. This was perhaps one of the most volatile situations that our city faced because, unfortunately, as is true throughout the South, the white power structure makes plans for desegregation without consultation with the Negro community. Our board of education had planned to desegregate the library, but they had not informed the Negro community about this. Therefore the Negroes picketed the library and invaded the library . . .

PAK: **Not realizing that it was being desegregated . . . ?**

ALG: Not realizing that within a period of two or three weeks the library would be desegregated, and we had some incidents of violence. As a matter of fact things got so hot that the newspapers called upon ministers to write a series of editorials in the paper about this, and I was one of those who was called upon to do so.

PAK: **What, what are those goals? If you had people—consider yourself, what are the goals in the civil rights movement in your area in the South?**

ALG: Well my goal would be, hopefully, to bring the community to a position where every man would be judged by what he is rather than by the color of his skin, which is, of course, the traditional Jewish attitude toward the relationship between the races.

PAK: **In your involvement in these various activities, what methodology have you used in order to accomplish these goals?**

ALG: Well, I have preached, both in my own congregation and in other congregations as well. I have used the method of persuasion and discussion. I have not become involved in freedom marches or in demonstrations, because, frankly, [and] this is a personal feeling of mine, this is not the way in which this problem can be solved. This can, of course, highlight a particular situation in which, where everything else has failed, where every other means of persuasion has failed, this can be brought to the fore, but it happens to be a personal predilection of mine not to get involved in these things. If I understand your question correctly, I would point out that, when, on a couple of occasions I have been called to Christian churches to speak in the area of religion and civil rights, I have always been very blunt about outlining the religious imperative that lies behind the civil rights movement, although Christians find it hard sometimes to follow the rules.

PAK: Who would invite you to . . .?

ALG: The Episcopalians—the Episcopal Church has invited me twice.

PAK: Is that because they have more liberal thought in this area, do you know?

ALG: This is an interesting question, I'm not sure. The Episcopal Church as a whole has been more liberal than any church in the South. The Episcopal Church in my community was the first church to desegregate, and, incidentally, let me make it quite clear at this point that the temple has always been desegregated, that there has never been segregation in our congregation. If Negroes came to worship, they were seated along with everybody else.

PAK: Did this in fact happen? Have Negroes in fact come to services?

ALG: Oh yes, for years they have come to services. They come from the post [Fort Benning], many of them come from the post along with their buddies, and they are always seated with other members of the congregation.

PAK: Has this ever brought about any kind of problem in the congregation?

ALG: Never, never. Now, to get back to the Episcopal Church, it was the first one that was desegregated. This does not mean that the congregation as a whole is extremely liberal, because they are not, but their minister there, their rector, and their bishop are, and this was the policy that was established by the ecclesiastical hierarchy. The people are rather reluctant to go along, and I think therefore are, have been anxious to seek guidance both from within their church and from without. This explains why they have asked me. In addition to which, they are aware of my involvement in the civil rights movement, too.

PAK: Is this basically the reason that you think you were invited to speak there, because of your involvement?

ALG: I think so, yes.

PAK: What about in the area of desegregation in the schools? What methodology did you use in working in this area?

ALG: Mostly a methodology of consultation with the power structure, persuasion of those who were responsible for the administration of the city and for the safety of its citizens—the police department, the sheriff, the

city commission, the county commissioners, and the school board of education. That the only thing they could do was to bow to the power of the law;
to follow the law, to open the parks and the schools. They were very reluctant to do this, as you can well understand. They did it—I won't always
say gracefully—but they did it, and having done it they insisted that there
would be no disturbance, and have lived up to this pledge. Our schools
have been peacefully desegregated, although I think it should be pointed
out, too, that this past year some of the primary grades of the school were
desegregated under a plan whereby anybody could apply for admission to
a school other than the one in his immediate neighborhood. There were
really very few applications for admission to white schools on the part of
Negroes in the primary grades. This disturbed me a great deal, and I consulted with some of my Negro friends in the human relations council about
it, and it was explained to me that this probably had to do with the fact
that little children have to be taken to school—they have to be walked to
school by their mother, or an older sister or brother, and it was easier for
them to go to the school that is close to their homes, rather than to another one.

PAK: **As a rabbi of a small congregation, and it was a very small number of
people compared to the non-Jewish community, what kind of weight do
you carry with the power structure in the community?**

ALG: Well, really not a great deal of weight, and this is one of the tragedies
of the South. That, outside of a city like Atlanta, where the power structure
has lined up solidly behind the civil rights movement, the people who have
been active in the civil rights movement are not those people who have
been, who belong to the power structure. However, if enough people group
themselves together and go to visit the board of education and the city
commission, the county commission and so forth, you can exercise some
pressure which will at least let them know that not everybody is opposed to
this process.

PAK: **Could you be very definite and sort of relay the, let's say, the school
integration thing—who is it that you would contact and . . . what was
your approach to get somebody to present your position for you or to
speak directly to the people involved?**

ALG: The first thing that happened was that we had a meeting of our human
relations council with the state director of that council about the school decision. Our school board hopefully was going to offer a plan to desegregate
the schools voluntarily, without a court order. Unfortunately it didn't work
out that way. I think here again that you have almost to live in the South to
understand the reasoning of these people. Since many of them are elected
officials or appointed by elected officials, the future, their future in these

important positions was at stake and therefore they—it was their feeling that they would not move in this direction until they were ordered to do so by a federal court. We met on the level of our human relations council and then a delegation composed of members of both the white and the Negro community waited upon the superintendent of education and consulted with him.

PAK: **Were you involved in this committee?**

ALG: Yes, I was involved in this, and then a smaller group, with which I was not involved, subsequently met with the board of education as well. When the court case was heard and a decision was rendered, the board already had immediately available a plan for desegregation. So, you see, they had been planning very carefully for this eventuality; very quietly, undercover, without letting any of us know what was going on, so that immediately when the decision was handed down, their plan was available for the court, and the court approved it. It has been tested twice. Both in the local—the district federal court, and in the court of appeals it has been approved.

PAK: **Did you as an individual, as an individual clergyman, make any statements that were reported in the press or anything like this?**

ALG: It occurs to me that I did, but I can't remember now the exact statement—this was now twelve years ago.[19]

PAK: **In this instance were there in any way repercussions on the part of your own congregation?**

ALG: No, no there has never been on the part of my own congregation any repercussions. This would not, don't misunderstand me, this would not indicate that there are not . . . [break in tape].

PAK: **Rabbi, what role did national Jewish organizations play in the civil rights movement in the South and in your area of the South?**

ALG: I think that everybody is pretty well aware of the role, the general role that the national organizations have played in the civil rights area in the South. The ADL particularly; the American Jewish Congress [AJCongress] to a certain extent, although they, we don't have any local chapters of this group in our area. The ADL has been helpful, in a way, although their entrance into the school situation elicited many unfavorable comments on the part of the local community. Now how have they been helpful? They have given the local rabbis and the local community leaders advice as to how to proceed when faced with particular situations. The regional director of the Anti-Defamation League came into Columbus and met with our human relations council and advised us as to the best policies to follow, both in regards to the school desegregation and the parks and the library problem.[20] The ADL made available to our school board all of its facilities and know-how about preparing the community, particularly the teachers, for the impact of desegregation. I must confess that the local school board did not take advantage of this offer; they felt that they could handle it on their own, and, as matters worked out, they did handle it successfully, although I think they could have learned something from the national Jewish organizations. And they have alerted us to possible pockets of trouble. They keep their, the ADL keeps its finger pretty closely on the activities of the rabble rousers in our area and, if they are coming into our community or if they are active in the immediate area, they let us know so that we can be on the lookout for them.

PAK: Have they in any way been detrimental to your goals and the accomplishments in any situation there?

ALG: I would not say so.

PAK: What about, for example, a situation like, I believe it was 1963, when the UAHC [Union of American Hebrew Congregations] gave Martin Luther King, had him as a keynote speaker in a conference. What was your response to that?

ALG: My response, or my congregation's?

PAK: Right, your response.

ALG: Well, I was at the banquet in which Martin Luther King was the speaker, and delegates from my congregation were there as well, because they wanted to hear what Martin Luther King had to say. I could not honestly say that every member of my congregation felt that this was the politic thing to do, but there was much more resentment, for instance, in my congregation over the recent biennial resolution on the war in Vietnam than there has been about any of the racial activities of the Union.[21]

PAK: I think the rabbis in Mississippi were quite vocal in their opposition to this. This was not the case in your state?

ALG: I don't know of any of the rabbis in the state of Georgia who have ever taken a position against this. That does not, of course, mean to say that there are not many laymen who might have done so.

PAK: What do you feel about the resolutions then of the CCAR [Central Conference of American Rabbis] in regards to civil rights in the South? Have they been, what is your response to them?

ALG: I think morally every one of these resolutions is justified, of course. My only reservation is that these resolutions generally are passed by men who are not really aware of all of the implications of the resolutions, nor do they come to the South to live with the situation and to solve the problems that they find there. This is my main objection incidentally, to Freedom Riders, who come down and agitate and then go back home again.

PAK: Do you think they are helpful in any way to the accomplishment of your goals?

ALG: Who?

PAK: **The Freedom Riders or the rabbis who come from the north and . . .**

ALG: Well they have never been in my community so I can't honestly answer that question.

PAK: **The response of your congregation, then, on the whole, has been one that would not be of any concern to you in your activities, in terms that they have not been detrimental in any way.**

ALG: Not at all, not at all. Now there is a congregation in our area, which shall remain nameless, where the response has been quite the opposite of that of my own congregation.

PAK: **What is the reason for that?**

ALG: It has been. Well it's a smaller community. It is a community which is much less cosmopolitan than the community of Columbus, and really, I find it very difficult to understand the attitudes of this Jewish congregation in this whole area.

PAK: **Have they had a frequent change of rabbis or anything like that?**

ALG: No, they have not. The rabbi has been with them now for a number of years. He has on several occasions attempted to leave the congregation but he comes back again.[22]

PAK: **What would you say—in more or less summation—would be the role that the rabbis played in your state, or, if that is too broad, in specific areas in your state, and then overall in the South in general, in the area of civil rights activity?**

ALG: Well I think I can speak for the state of Georgia, and pretty well for the whole South, because we have a Southeastern Association of Rabbis, so I am acquainted with what is going on in at least five states of the southeast region. I think the first responsibility, of course, of a rabbi in the civil rights area is in his immediate community. He has to sensitize people to the moral imperatives of Judaism, and this means beginning, of course, with his own congregation. They have to be made aware of what Judaism demands of them as human beings in their relations to other human beings. If he fails in this, of course, then his congregation is going to respond obviously with the same kind of prejudice that has been inbred in the southern community for a number of generations. Then he has to extend his activities beyond his immediate community to the larger local community in which he resides; he has to participate in as many kinds of civil rights activities as he feels can legitimately and purposefully accomplish the goals which he has set for himself.

PAK: **Have you ever felt the need to become involved in other groups and activities, non-civil rights, in order to lay the ground work for being effective in your community?**

ALG: Such as?

PAK: Such as patriotic organizations or community service groups?

ALG: Well, I am a member of the Rotary Club, and of course I am a lone voice crying in the wilderness, really, in the Rotary Club. There are only a very few people who believe as I do there, but, again there I have not hesitated to make my position quite clear, and those who differ with me differ on a very gentlemanly basis, and I could only hope that eventually I would be able to convert them, if I can use that term, to my way of thinking.

PAK: Did this whole idea of being able to speak more securely as an individual enter into your joining—let's say, for example, the Rotary Club—or was this just a thing that a rabbi would do in the community?

ALG: Well, I had been a member of the Rotary Club even before I came to Columbus and so I simply—my membership was simply moved. I think the rabbi has to feel that he is a part of other organizations in the community. Now I'm not a member of the American Legion or the AmVets or anything of this nature, by choice. I take an active role in the ministerial alliance, I'm a past president of that, and I don't try to restrict my activities in any sense just to the Jewish community. I feel I have a wide commission as well. On the state level I have served on the state board of the Georgia Council on Human Relations. I am a member of, a participating member of the Southern Regional, what's it called, I can't even remember the name now, Southern Regional Council—something of this nature—of which the human relations council used to be a subsidiary, but is no longer, and, on a personal basis, of course, I think that my own influence has been more or less restricted to a radius, let's say, of about forty miles around Columbus. I have not gone beyond that. I have not stumped the state, in other words, in this area, because I think that there are people in the local—the local leaders must carry the brunt of, the burden of this, the solution of this problem.

PAK: As a rabbi do you think that when the total picture is looked at, will the rabbis have played any kind of an important role? I realize that they represent a very small number of people.

ALG: I think that in the light of history it will appear that they have played a considerable role, yes, because I think the voice of the synagogue will be one of those that will be shown to have cried the loudest in this whole, in the solution of this whole problem. Because as I said at the very beginning, the national church organizations have taken very strong stands in this problem, but on the local level the Christian churches have been sadly lacking in leadership. I really cannot explain why. For instance, just this past couple of weeks the South Georgia Conference of the Methodist Church turned down a resolution that would have merged the Negro jurisdiction with the white jurisdiction of the church conference. This had nothing to do even with admitting Negroes to their churches on a local level. It was merely merging the ministers and the bishops, you know, into one organization and they turned it down. Who can explain why they did it, where Alabama and Florida accepted it. It is really very difficult to understand the reasoning of some of these folks.

PAK: Is there any of this material that you would want restricted only to use in the Archives?

ALG: I can't think of any that needs to be restricted. Everybody knows what I think and how I feel.

4
Martin I. Hinchin

Alexandria, Louisiana, and Its Jewish Community

Alexandria began in 1711 as a trade and mercantile supply center for an adjacent Spanish outpost. In 1785 the first organized settlement appeared on part of a land grant made by Spain to Alexander Fulton, a Pennsylvania businessman. The town was incorporated thirty-three years later.[1]

The area around the town was blessed with an abundance of pine and various hardwoods. Indigo, cotton, and sugar cane plantations dotted its immediate hinterland, and Alexandria served as a natural distribution point along the Red River between Shreveport and Baton Rouge. On the eve of the Civil War the town was home to 1,461 inhabitants, 481 of whom were African American. Alexandria played an important role in the industries most crucial to Louisiana, which at the time provided one-third of all US cotton exports and grew a third of the sugar consumed in the country.[2]

Jews comprised a small number of Alexandria's inhabitants. They may have arrived as early as 1810, but the first official record of Jewish presence dates to 1830 when Henry Michael Hyams came north from New Orleans. Hyams had already played an important role in the Reformed Society of Israelites in Charleston, South Carolina. A cousin of Judah P. Benjamin (Benjamin represented Louisiana in the United States Senate and served in the Confederate Cabinet), Hyams spent years with an Alexandria law firm and operated a plantation prior to returning to the big city. He ultimately served as a state senator and then as lieutenant governor of Louisiana.[3]

A small number of Jews from central Europe immigrated to Alexandria during the 1830s and '40s. In 1854, according to Elliot Ashkenazi, there were "about twenty Jewish peddlers 'roaming about' Alexandria."[4] Some of these settled in the town and opened stores. Thus, prior to the Civil War, the town claimed a few dozen Jewish inhabitants. However, the war's end brought a new influx of Jews, so that by 1870 an estimated 157 Jews lived in Alexandria.[5] Even before the war, this small group began creating Jewish institutions. In 1854 they purchased land for a cemetery and five years later established a traditional congregation,

Gemiluth Chassodim—the name, translated as "Acts of Loving Kindness," also indicated charitable functions.[6]

Jews contributed significantly to Alexandria's growth. A. Klotz established the first Jewish-owned warehouse for cotton and lumber, while Hecht & Co. was one of the first men's and ladies' apparel stores. Julius Levin opened successful mercantile and warehouse businesses after he returned from the Civil War. Jonas Rosenthal emigrated from Alsace in 1860 and, in partnership with his brothers Isaac, Mires, and Moses, founded one of the city's most important grocery stores. Mires Rosenthal used money from his grocery business to open a cotton brokerage company. Other Jewish merchants of note included E. Schmanliski, who had a music store, Carl August Schnack, who sold jewelry, and David Caplan, who arrived in Alexandria in 1891 and opened what became the city's most popular men's clothing store. By the turn of the century, the approximately six hundred Jews owned the majority of the city's businesses including its largest department store.

Jews also held important civic and political positions. Julius Levin served on the city council and presided over the school board for many years. Jonas Rosenthal sat on the executive committee of the Rapides Parish Democratic Party, won election to the city council, and served so many years as president of the school board that the city named an elementary school in his honor. Mires Rosenthal worked for the US Circuit Court for Rapides Parish from 1889 until his death, while Moses Rosenthal worked as federal Supervisor and Election Commissioner for Alexandria in 1876 and won election as city treasurer in 1878. In the following decades other Jews followed in these footsteps.

Initially the Jewish community consisted almost entirely of central European immigrants, but the eastern European Jewish exodus of 1881–1921 changed the composition and religious orientation of the city's Jewry, as it did throughout the country. Although most Jews remained in the now-Reform Gemiluth Chassodim, in 1913 the recent immigrants formed Orthodox congregation B'nai Israel (Children of Israel).

World War II brought important changes to the city. In 1942 the federal government took over the new Alexandria Municipal Airport and renamed it Alexandria Army Air Base. The facility was used as a training school for B-17 and B-29 bomber crews. After the war, the base reverted back to the city for use as a commercial airport. During the Korean War, the base was reactivated and assigned to the Tactical Air Command. Nine years later the facility was officially renamed England Air Force Base. Other nearby military bases included Camp Livingston, Camp Beauregard, Camp Claiborne, and Fort Polk. When functioning at full capacity, these bases infused capital to the local economy and brought many nonsoutherners including Jews to the area. Over the long run, however,

Alexandria remained dependent on timber and forestry products, and on cotton, sugar cane, and other crops.[7]

Although the city had a functioning branch of the National Association for the Advancement of Colored People (NAACP), civil rights activism came relatively late, partly as a result of a relative lack of hardcore racism. Thus Adam Fairclough opted to pay little attention to Alexandria in his book *Race and Democracy: The Civil Rights Struggle in Louisiana, 1915–1972*, because he had "the impression that Alexandria was a rather 'moderate' city compared to e.g. Shreveport and Monroe."[8] Although Alexandria may have been comparatively moderate in relation to other cities in Louisiana, its local newspaper, the *Town Talk*, could hardly be confused with the liberal *Atlanta Constitution* or the *Delta (MS) Democrat-Times*. One incident recorded by Odette Hines is instructive. When Clarence Forcia, an African American physician, died of a heart attack while treating a patient, the loss devastated the local African American community. Mrs. Hines and a friend went to the office of *Town Talk* to report Forcia's death, so that it could be noted in the next issue of the paper. When they explained their purpose, they "were informed that the paper didn't carry 'nigger news,' it only carried 'nigger crime.'"[9]

Odette Hines, wife of another local black physician, played a key role in ensuing events. In January 1964, the Louisiana office of the Congress of Racial Equality (CORE) asked people at the city's black community center to start a voter registration drive during what became known as Freedom Summer. The director of the center, however, who owed his position to Mayor W. George Bowden, told Hines that she and others in the community should "not even think about housing" the CORE people who were preparing to come to Alexandria. The timing could not have been worse from the director's perspective. The bodies of civil rights workers James Chaney, Andrew Goodman, and Michael Schwerner had been found just a few weeks before the CORE project was to begin in Alexandria, and tensions ran high. Although Hines was fearful for her life and the lives of her children, she welcomed three Freedom Summer workers who ultimately stayed with her for ten months. CORE included the local NAACP chapter in an umbrella group called Total Community Action that registered voters and taught classes on how to complete the registration form. The local Freedom Summer campaign proved only modestly successful since the local voter registrar engaged in lengthy conversations with each applicant in order to use up so much time that he could only see a few people each day.

Integration in Alexandria came grudgingly, but generally without violence. In the wake of the Supreme Court decisions of the late 1950s and early '60s, Alexandria began to integrate its public schools. In September 1964, twelve African American seniors were admitted to formerly all-white high schools without the violence that had accompanied such breakthroughs in many other cities. Following the passage of the Civil Rights Act of 1964, a group of local black leaders pushed for black employment in the city's all-white businesses. The business community responded tepidly at best. The manager of the city's Sears-Roebuck store provided the only positive response to the protestors. He immediately hired an African American accountant and a few sales people. In the words of Odette Hines, "They were the *only* cooperative white business" in the city.[10] Integration of restaurants came the next year also without major incidents.

Several key factors contributed to the lack of violence. The military bases and their personnel played an important part in moderating opinion. The city's business leaders, conscious of Alexandria's role as the port that supplied the rest of the country with timber, cotton, and food crops, were not eager to earn a reputation for confrontation similar to those of Birmingham, Selma, or Jackson. Also by 1963, eighty-five thousand Catholics resided in the Alexandria diocese, a large number of them in the city proper. Generally, as in New Orleans, members of the Catholic community were less militant than other Christian groups in their opposition to desegregation, and their religious leaders took a more positive approach in contrast to the majority of their Protestant counterparts. In early August 1963, Bishop Charles P. Grego issued a pastoral letter that was read at every mass held that Sunday in the Diocese of Alexandria. The letter noted, "We earnestly appeal to our people to accept the inevitable with understanding and restraint, with true Christian charity and with an awakened sense of justice, with good grace and characteristic American fairness."[11]

When Rabbi Martin Hinchin arrived in Alexandria in 1958, he found a community that was far less confrontational than other cities in the South and far more willing to implement the decisions of the courts than the Georgia community he left behind.[12]

Martin I. Hinchin

Martin Isaiah Hinchin was born on January 30, 1919, in Philadelphia, Pennsylvania. His parents, Aaron and Dora Povolosky Hinchin, had immigrated to Philadelphia from a town near Kiev in the Ukraine during the 1890s. Hinchin grew up in a kosher home supervised by his mother, whom he described as "fairly religious." His father, a ladies' dress designer who eventually manufactured ladies' dresses in his factory, was a chiropractor who never pursued this profession in the United States. Hinchin recalled that his father was "well-educated but not religious." Hinchin graduated from Philadelphia's Overbrook High School in 1936. He then earned a bachelor of arts degree from Yeshiva University in four years with majors in philosophy, psychology, and education. Although his upbringing likely influenced his decision to go to a Jewish university, his rabbi at Conserva-

5. Rabbi Martin Hinchin, 1988—the year
of his retirement. (Congregation Gemiluth
Chassodim Archives) Used by permission of
Rabbi Martin Hinchin.

tive congregation Har Zion, Simon Greenberg, also provided a role model and
encouragement to enter the rabbinate. Greenberg was a prolific author, a professor at the Jewish Theological Seminary, and one of the founders of what became the University of Judaism. Greenberg's tenure as the first president of this
fledgling seminary extended from 1947 to 1963.[13]

In spite of his Conservative background, Hinchin opted to enter the rabbinic
program at the Reform movement's Hebrew Union College [HUC] in Cincinnati. Following the school's practice, while a student he conducted High Holy
Day services in congregations in Logan, West Virginia, and Hamilton, Ohio.
World War II brought a more intense opportunity to develop his rabbinic skills.
In 1944 HUC President Julian Morgenstern sent Hinchin to Sioux City, Iowa,
to fill in for Rabbi Al Goldstein, who had taken a leave of absence from Mt. Sinai
Temple to become an army chaplain. After a year at Mt. Sinai, Hinchin returned
to Cincinnati to complete his studies. While in Sioux City he met Blossom Kalin,
whom he married on December 10, 1944.

After his ordination Hinchin was hired by Temple Emanu-El in Dothan,
Alabama. He served simultaneously as Emanu-El's rabbi and as director of the
Southeast Region of the Union of American Hebrew Congregations. In 1948,

after two years in Dothan, he moved to Temple B'nai Israel in Albany, Georgia. At the onset of the Korean War, Hinchin enlisted in the National Guard. Although never called to active duty, he attained the rank of lieutenant commander in the Naval Reserve. After a decade in Albany, Hinchin was offered and accepted the rabbinic post in a larger congregation, Gemiluth Chassodim, in Alexandria, Louisiana. In 1984, he published a history of Alexandria's Jewish community. Hinchin remained at Gemiluth Chassodim until the death of his first wife in 1988, at which point he retired and moved to Memphis, where his younger daughter lived. Carol, his second wife, died in 2001, twelve years after they got married. Reflecting on his career, Hinchin found the most enjoyable part of his rabbinate to be pastoral work. In his words, "I loved working with people and was involved with counseling and solving marital problems." In addition to serving as a congregational rabbi for forty-two years, Hinchin served as president of the Albany Ministerial Association (1953–1954) and the Rapides County Ministerial Association (1961–1962). He also served on the executive board of the Central Conference of American Rabbis as the founding chairman of the Committee on Contracts and Finance. On January 30, 2016, Rabbi Hinchin celebrated his ninety-fifth birthday.

Editor's Introduction to the Interview

Martin I. Hinchin served Gemiluth Chassodim for thirty years. Most other rabbis under consideration also benefited from long tenure. They endeared themselves to their congregants through pastoral and counseling services. Often as the only or most visible rabbi in their location, they immersed themselves in community affairs and benefited from stature and prestige. These factors cemented their positions almost regardless of their involvement in civil rights activities.

Many interviewees served in other southern congregations before obtaining more permanent positions. Hinchin, for example, had held pulpits in Dothan, Alabama, and Albany, Georgia, for a dozen years before his arrival in Alexandria. Although born, raised, and educated in the North, he came to Louisiana familiar with the region and its mores. Such past experiences helped prepare him and the other rabbis for the challenges they faced with desegregation.

In Hinchin's case, it apparently also engendered his acculturation. He viewed local white clergy in a positive fashion. From his perspective and theirs, change had and would come gradually. For them, the issue of black civil rights was neither religious nor moral but rather sociological. African Americans had to pull themselves up educationally and economically in order to earn full rights and equality. Hinchin worked with black and white conservatives to improve conditions, but believed that the marches and demonstrations taking place around him hindered progress. In Hinchin's view, conditions for African Americans in most of the South were not that bad; in fact, they were better off than their northern counterparts. Distancing himself, he defined the issue as Protestant and not Jewish.

Inherent contradictions appear. Hinchin depicts the general community as conservative and reasonable, seemingly totally apart from the fray and the deplorable racist conditions around it. His views on behalf of equal rights, he believed, were well known in the community, but he made it clear that he refrained from speaking out in sermons to his congregation or making public statements on civil rights issues because of fear of potential consequent harm to the Jewish community. Yet he maintained that Alexandria's Jews neither had to fear economic reprisals nor acquiesce to southern racial mores.

One wonders if Hinchin coded the messages in his interview because of fear of being quoted. He indicated that he did not preach about civil rights, but then qualified his statement by indicating that he discussed prophetic Judaism in a fashion that people understood referred to it. He refused to endanger his congregants, but he worked quietly behind the scenes for peaceful integration of the schools, and his daughter attended an integrated school. He appears to be more concerned with explaining the Central Congress of American Rabbis (CCAR) resolution condemning the Vietnam War than with the conflict surrounding his attendance at the previous CCAR banquet featuring Martin Luther King Jr. as the speaker. These dualities and contradictions coupled with the relatively positive environment in which he functioned make Hinchin's one of the more enigmatic interviews.

—Mark K. Bauman

Martin I. Hinchin Interview

June 22, 1966

P. Allen Krause: [What] would you say is "the South" with regard to civil rights? Would you include, for example, all of Florida and all of Texas?
Martin I. Hinchin: I would include all of the South, sure.
PAK: You would also include all of Texas?
MIH: Sure, yes.
PAK: What date . . . marks the beginning of intense civil rights activity in your area?
MIH: I was in Georgia in 1948, now I'm in Louisiana. I was in Georgia in 1948, from 1948 to 1958. Then I was in Louisiana from '58 to the present day. So I spent all my rabbinical life actually in the South. A few years in Alabama, too, before that. I would say that the actual intense movement started, of course, with the Supreme Court decision in 1948, but I think, from my observation, that a great deal of it had been done or was being

done for the Negro before 1948. Probably you would say maybe in anticipation perhaps of . . .

PAK: Now we're talking about the '54 decision, *Brown* versus . . . ?

MIH: No I think '48, before that.[14]

PAK: So you'd go back as far as '48?

MIH: I'd go back as far as '48—but the '54 decision, I think, had far more sweeping results.

PAK: So you noticed a change in intensity in the community you were in after '48?

MIH: After '48, yes. However there has always been some groundwork happening, I think with the community leaders much prior to that. The situation of the Negro has become a lot better since 1946 or even before '46. The authority [influence?] that Negroes have had on the civil rights movement came out of World War II, etcetera.

PAK: In '54 you were in Louisiana?

MIH: No in '54 I was in Georgia—Albany, Georgia.

PAK: What was the response to the new civil rights push on the part of the non-Jewish white population in the cities you were in during this period?

MIH: I think most of them sat and just waited until, perhaps, they were forced into some type of action. Even though in Georgia there were fine Negro-white relationships even prior to the civil rights decision of the Supreme Court. There were fine Negro-white relationships. I think perhaps these relationships were harmed in some respects even though the Negro was to gain a great deal from the decision. Yet, we've seen some ill will in the white community.

PAK: What about the ministers in the community you were in? What was their response to the civil rights activity?

MIH: Most of the ministers wouldn't touch it with a ten-foot pole. They didn't want to touch it, because it was part of their own traditions in their own congregation basically. Then again I think there was the problem of somebody who actually lives in the South knowing the situation as it was— knowing what was being done in the background, slowly but surely. Now it's not as quickly, of course, as the implementation the Supreme Court decision had urged upon them.

PAK: Do you think that they were in accord with the civil rights movement?

MIH: I think many of the ministers, yes. I think many of the ministers felt there had to be some impetus, but nevertheless they didn't like the way it was being implemented. Let me put it this way. I think that it was not so much a question of religion, of religious principles, as it was a sociological outlook. They felt that, sociologically, the Negro had to pull himself up by his own bootstraps with a little bit of help. This is not a religious cause as far as they were concerned.[15]

PAK: **They didn't speak about the moral problem at all?**

MIH: Nothing about the moral problem at all, no.

PAK: **How long was the congregation in existence in each one of the communities that you served?**

MIH: Well now, the Albany Jewish congregation was quite old. I mean it went back perhaps to the Civil War. The community in Alexandria, Louisiana, went back to before the Civil War.[16]

PAK: **Are these two communities similar in terms of size and outlook?**

MIH: They are similar in size but not in outlook, not in outlook, no. Now if you were to be speaking, for example, with someone from Atlanta as opposed to Albany, Georgia, you would find an entirely different outlook.

PAK: **What is the economic standing and involvement of the Jewish community in the city that you are in now and in the city where you were before?**

MIH: Well, most of them are merchants of some sort—very few in the professions in Albany, Georgia. Whereas [in Alexandria] I find a good number of my people in the professions, college graduates, and then, of course, with [the influx from] out-of-state it's turned into a sixty-forty proposition now as far as business versus professional. There is about, let's say, 35, 40 percent in the professions—lawyers, doctors, dentists, and the rest in business.

PAK: **How susceptible was your community and is your community now to economic pressures?**

MIH: I don't think that in Albany and then in Alexandria that you have economic pressure at all. They are not worried about economic pressure at all.

PAK: **You don't believe that in either place that they worry or are concerned about that?**

MIH: No, there's always a lunatic fringe element in the Negro population as well as in the white population as far as adverse relations is concerned.

PAK: **What about in Albany?**

MIH: Well now, I haven't been in Albany for years so I really can't say now. You know they have Martin Luther King down there and they had some civil rights marches there and so forth;[17] they had none in Alexandria at all to speak of. They had SNCC [Student Nonviolent Coordinating Committee] and a few other organizations, but they were quiet. There was no picketing.

PAK: **So you never felt that the people in your congregation in Albany were concerned with regard to their economic standing in the community because of this issue?**

MIH: I think that in Albany they took a strictly southern point of view, whereas in Alexandria they don't have to take that particular point of view. I think there is a difference here of southern outlook. Actually there is a poverty program of which I am a member of the board on which the conservative Negroes and whites work together amicably.[18]

PAK: **Did the Freedom Riders ever come down to your area?**

MIH: No, thank goodness.

PAK: **So your response would be a negative response to them?**

MIH: Right. The Freedom Riders never came down to Alexandria; pretty close, but not to Alexandria.[19]

PAK: **Could you comment on the response to demonstrations like the march that is going on right now in Mississippi?[20]**

MIH: Well my honest opinion is I don't think it accomplishes much, in spite of the fact that many may disagree with me. I have lived in the South for twenty years now. Twenty years of my adult life in the South, and I feel that the people here are going to have to solve their own problems, and they're solving them, even if they had to be prodded through legislation to do so, they're still doing it, nonetheless. And to add salt to the wounds is not helping the situation one bit. I think that these marches, when the rabbis come down and militants and so forth—I think it really sets the movement back to a certain degree, because the people have already oriented themselves, are beginning to orient themselves to the fact they are going to have to do something. And when these northerners come in, who know nothing of the southern background whatsoever, and don't tend to their own backyard, these people [the southerners] are kind of irate.

PAK: **What would your goal be for your community with regard to the civil rights movement in the South?**

MIH: First of all, I don't quite understand your question—could you clarify it?

PAK: **What kind of way would you like to proceed with the civil rights movement, and what would you like the results of it to be?**

MIH: I don't know; I've never really thought about the question, to tell you the truth. I would like to see, of course, the Negro to have better treatment in all respects, but my opinion is that he is going to have to earn it to a certain degree himself. We're going to have to help him—I think most of the white Protestant groups in the South realize it themselves. It's a real problem for them, and they are having to cope with the problem. I think it is more a problem for them than it is for Jews in the South. They are the ones that are going to really have to cope with the situation, and they are coping really, to a greater or lesser extent. But, nevertheless, they are going to cope with it, and I think and they think it's not going to happen overnight, even with legislation, because you can't legislate sociology. The background of the Negro is such that he is going to have to prove himself—through education, through his own morals, lift himself by his own bootstraps, which he will do, but it's going to take time, and I think that rushing these things through with freedom marches and all kinds of picketing and strikes—this is not going to do it—it's only going to create ill will.

PAK: What has been your approach in terms of methodology in order to accomplish what you think would be the goals?

MIH: Well, I don't preach to my congregation what to do with regards to this. I have my own ideas on civil rights which I don't foist upon my own congregation. They know what I think, because in private groups we discuss these matters. From the pulpit I very rarely discuss it, because I don't want to harm the Jewish community in any way, shape, or form. They know my point of view. I know their points of view. There are varying points of view within the community itself.

PAK: Do you generally find that your congregation does not like your point of view?

MIH: Now some of them do and some of them don't. There are varying groups of people in the congregation who realize that something has to be done. I think most of them really do, but they do not want to take the initiative with regards to the civil rights movement at all. And they resent other Jews who don't live in the community who try to force their ideas upon them.

PAK: So you don't use the sermon very much?

MIH: No.

PAK: You said that you use small discussion . . . ?

MIH: I use a better technique when I meet with a smaller group, because first of all you never know who is going to misquote you in whatever you said and they don't ask for your prepared text if you have one. They may take statements outside of context. Nevertheless, working in the community with the various organizations, you have a chance from time to time—many times, more than from time to time—to share your own opinion.

PAK: Can you give a specific instance?

MIH: Well, for example, in the Rotary Club. Every once in a while something would come up with regards to the civil rights movement when several of us would sit at a table, and we would discuss this problem very briefly, and every once in a while you would get a chance to put your ideas in—without arguing about the situation. If you're argumentative about the situation, you're lost.

PAK: Have you ever called up anybody in the power structure within your community in order to discuss Freedom Rides or . . . ?

MIH: Only so far as in the ministerial association we had several problems which Negroes had with their own Negro community, which they felt it might take a white committee to go to the mayor and the police commissioner with regard to these problems. We went to the police commissioner and spoke to him about many things with regards to police protection, with regards to the police maybe being a little unfair at certain times with regards to traffic regulations, things like that. All of this was done in committee, we never publicized [it]; it was always in the background.

PAK: It was never in the newspaper?

MIH: No.

PAK: Are there ministers who would not go with you?

MIH: Oh yes. There are several ministers, among the Baptists in particular. I don't think I want to be quoted on this, because I think the Baptists, who are the majority in my particular community, are very hesitant to put themselves on record with regard to civil rights. Most of my work, Allen, has been undercover work—it's been behind the scenes. Not undercover in the sense of surreptitious work but rather in the sense that it is under cover. We talk to people. It's quiet. It's done quietly. I believe you can do a lot of these good deeds without any fanfare, without any publicity. You can do more and influence more people than if you come out with a clipping in the newspaper or are quoted on TV.

PAK: Have you ever found yourself quoted in the newspaper on this issue?

MIH: No, no, never because the newspaper has a very careful policy not to be too controversial on this particular situation. They try to present the facts fairly, as they see it, and sometimes they get results that [are] anti-South, but nevertheless nothing that's too controversial.

PAK: I've been told by one southern rabbi that his methodology to get things done is to put a Christian out in front of you as a spokesman and you stay in the background, and that's the way you accomplish things. Do you agree with that?

MIH: This may be true, because sometimes a Christian minister can get more done than I can because of the fact that usually he has a larger congregation and he has more influence in the community than I do. Not influence ministerial-wise but more influence membership-wise than I would have because he has a larger congregation.

PAK: Have you personally used this approach?

MIH: Very rarely. Most of our work has been done by the ministerial association itself or in meetings at private homes.

PAK: What are the results of the actions then that you have performed within the civil rights area individually and as a member of this ministerial group?

MIH: Well, of course, the integration of the schools without difficulties, as a result of New Orleans[21] and Little Rock and other places; we participated. We also advocated the integration of schools in the best manner we knew how without creating any strife in the community, and there was no strife. There was very little comment. There were some comments sure; there were some snide remarks made with regards to Negros in the schools, but after the first few days all went well with no problems. My own daughter went to public high school when this was done.

PAK: **Do you think that you as a rabbi or you as a member of the ministerial association have been influential in bringing about change in your community?**

MIH: Oh, I definitely feel this way, but of course you can't put your finger on it and say this is what I have done, this is what I have done. I think through our contacts throughout the years, even in the pulpit—I remember saying before that I never preached about civil rights. Indirectly I think many of us preach about civil rights and our congregation understands it quite well, but it doesn't come out that way. When you talk about the prophetic views, let's say, we talk about the Negro situation—coding it—but the congregation knows exactly what you mean. If you generalize the terms rather than specific things, and if you handle it that way, there is no objection. What I am saying is: if you hit them square between the eyes, they will run.

PAK: **And you actually think that this is accomplishing something?**

MIH: Well, let's say it this way: if you're scratching your left ear with your right hand by way of the back of your head, you are still scratching your ear. It may be a long way to get there, but you are still scratching, nonetheless.

PAK: **What role have national Jewish organizations played in the civil rights movement in the South and specifically in your areas of the South?**

MIH: In my opinion I think they have done a great deal of harm. This goes for the Union [of American Hebrew Congregations], it goes for the B'nai B'rith, even for the Central Conference of Reform Rabbis[22] unfortunately. When they come out with civil rights statements, because a lot of these people have never lived in the South and they don't know the situation. They don't know it firsthand, like we do.

PAK: **How did they do harm?**

MIH: Well, number one I think our congregants would say it hurts our national fundraising campaign [for the UAHC], a great deal. We have to overcome it by saying that there are only a few of these rabbis who are very radically inclined, who feel this way; many of us are more moderate in our approach. Like it was this morning on the Vietnam problem. There were many more moderates on the Vietnam problem than there were radicals,

even though the statement went through. I have to go home now and explain the conference point of view. It was a majority vote, that's all.[23]

PAK: **So, the conference probably represented their own conscience but in
a personal relationship it doesn't help when a rabbi . . .**

MIH: It doesn't help that the national organizations are coming out with
these broad statements.

PAK: **Have any of the national organizations been detrimental to the progress of civil rights activity in your area?**

MIH: I think so. I mean, I think I made the statement before that when you
have a march or you have sit-ins and so forth, I think the white population
just becomes adamant towards them, and it becomes a yelling proposition,
and before you know it you have violence. If you can avoid these things and
do it calmly I think you would be better off.

PAK: **What was your response to the 1963 UAHC convention when Martin
Luther King was slated to speak?**

MIH: Many of my congregants were definitely opposed to it, as many of
the southern communities were. Many of the rabbis I think were asked
[by their congregational leaders] when they went to the UAHC convention to oppose it strenuously. I know of some rabbis who even avoided going to the banquet. I did not avoid going to the banquet. As a matter of
fact, when my congregation sent me to Chicago to that convention, I was
not sent with instructions. My congregation was a lot more liberal, I think,
than many of them. But some of the congregations did instruct their rabbi.
Some of them were sent with instructions on how to vote on the civil rights
question. My congregation let me use my good judgment, because I would
never embarrass them in any way, shape, or form with this question.

PAK: **Are there any discrepancies between your response to and/or participation in civil rights activities and that of your congregants? Have you
ever been criticized by the board or by any individuals because of your
actions?**

MIH: No, because I told my congregation when I came there; they knew
how I felt. I told them exactly how I felt about the civil rights problem,
but I told them this: That I would never embarrass them publicly with my
own particular views. That I would work very quietly, in my own way, for
the betterment of the Negro as I saw fit, and that I would never embarrass
them doing any public statements or any public embarrassment.

PAK: **So you have never run into any problems since you have come to your
congregation?**

MIH: Never run into one problem at all. Never; they respect my opinion and
I respect their opinion.

PAK: Have you ever had anybody in the congregation who felt that you don't do enough in the area of civil rights?

MIH: No, because actually I think that thing is up to me. I mean they don't tell me what to do, [and] I don't tell them how to run their business.

PAK: If a history was written fifty years from now, do you think, in terms of civil rights in the South, that the rabbis, considering the small number of Jews in the South, would have any kind of significance in terms of progress in civil rights?

MIH: Yes I do. I think the rabbis have done a good deal. Some of the rabbis have done a good deal to preserve the image of the Jew [and] at the same time to push the civil rights movement. But I will say this, this may be only my opinion and you may disagree with me, which is your privilege, but there are many of my colleagues who would agree with me that the whole question of the Negro is a sociological problem, not a religious problem. I think that people need to solve the problem sociologically better than they can religiously. I think that as religious leaders we can do a great deal towards aiding the cause with less publicity and by doing things behind the scene.

PAK: So you mean we should leave it more to the politicians than to the religious leaders?

MIH: Well this has been difficult. I wouldn't say politicians. I would say that there has to be something that has to be done in order to improve the lot of the Negros in the South. Then again I would say that the lot of the Negro isn't really that bad in the South. If you were to live here you would see for yourself what we are talking about, because the lot of the Negro up north is a heck of a lot worse, in my opinion, than the Negro's condition in the South.

PAK: Are you making a blanket statement for the whole South?

MIH: Oh, I imagine there are some black spots in the South in particular that I can't speak for, but I would say as a general rule the lot of Negroes is much, much better than ever it was, and even the liberal who settles in the South would say that I am not wrong. In the larger cities like Detroit, St. Louis, Chicago, Philadelphia, New York, and Los Angeles [it is worse than in the South]. Many Negroes who left the South, from Georgia and from Louisiana, are coming back. I am amazed by those who have left. Some of them may have worked in my own home, who left and went out to California, and they are coming back. They want their jobs back. So the grass is always greener in somebody else's pasture.

5
Jacob M. Rothschild

Atlanta, Georgia, and Its Jewish Community

During the era of the civil rights movement, Atlanta was perceived and portrayed as different from other cities in the South, as "the city too busy to hate"—one of the most moderate in terms of race relations. The progressive positions of Mayor William B. Hartsfield, *Atlanta Constitution* editor Ralph McGill, and Coca-Cola chief Robert Woodruff helped smooth the transition to desegregation. The ground had been prepared decades earlier with the active participation of established black leaders from historically black colleges including Morehouse College's President Benjamin E. Mays, prestigious black ministers including Martin Luther King Sr., and businesspeople like Jesse Hill of Atlanta Life. That said, the transition to integration in Atlanta was not easy. Many Atlantans desegregated not because they felt it was morally right but because they viewed it as economically expedient. Atlanta served as home to the modern Ku Klux Klan and Lester Maddox, and marches and demonstrations were required to press the issue.

On his arrival in 1947, Jacob M. Rothschild (1911–1973) came to the fore as the new rabbi of the historic Hebrew Benevolent Congregation, better known as the Temple.[1] With 1,200 family memberships, his was by far the largest congregation served by the rabbis interviewed by Allen Krause. Rothschild was deeply committed to the civil rights movement on both moral and religious bases and was fortunate to have perhaps the most progressive environment in which to work of all of the rabbis in the South. He became intimately involved in the struggle for civil rights and worked to achieve integration through a variety of means.

Consequently, the Temple was bombed on October 12, 1958. This event created great consternation and impacted the subsequent actions of other rabbis, especially Perry Nussbaum. If it could happen in Atlanta, it could happen anywhere; so one might as well speak out. Rothschild attributed the motives of the bombers more to anti-Semitism than to anti-black racism. However, he argued that the racist rhetoric emanating from the governor of Georgia and preachers in white churches created an environment in which anti-Semites felt encouraged to act out their hatreds. Ultimately, the Atlanta community's response to

6. Bomb damage to the Hebrew Benevolent Congregation
(The Temple) following a racially motivated bombing,
1958. Photographer Charles Vaughn, AJCNS1958–10-00v,
Atlanta Journal-Constitution Photographic Archives, Special
Collections and Archives, Georgia State University Library.
Used by permission of Photo Editor Bita Honarvar, *Atlanta
Journal-Constitution*. Image courtesy of Georgia State
University Library.

the bombing opened the floodgates to others in Atlanta and elsewhere in the
South to denounce the forces of hatred and discrimination.

Ralph McGill, winner of a Pulitzer Prize for his editorial "A Church, a School"
on the bombings of the Sixteenth Street Baptist in Birmingham and the Atlanta Temple, was the acknowledged "Pappy" of progressive southern journalists,[2] a role Rothschild filled to some degree within the rabbinate. How much
did public opinion figures like editors and clergy influence events? Clearly those
who acted as racist rabble-rousers gave massive resistance legitimacy and fostered
a negative environment and even violence. Conversely, progressive voices hastened the acceptance of law and court decision and opened the door for others to challenge the status quo. Perhaps the marches, demonstrations, and court
cases would have still brought about effective change, but these other voices, at
the least, eased the way.

Like many of his rabbinic colleagues in the South, Rothschild believed that his congregants and southern Jews generally were more liberal than their Christian counterparts. He provided a surprising and insightful explanation for one aspect of this: integration ultimately involved houses of worship, and since few African Americans were Jews, integration of synagogues posed a lesser challenge than desegregation of Protestant churches that would involve far more people.[3]

Few of the other interviewees touch on changes in the civil rights movement to the same extent as Rothschild. He alluded to the growing Black Power movement, a direction with which he disagreed, and expressed his belief that the strategy should change from the drama created by the Freedom Riders, something necessary and helpful in its time, to less dramatic forms of confrontation. He clearly disapproved of the move of the Southern Christian Leadership Conference (SCLC) into Black Power ranks. To his thinking, Atlanta had done well with a combination of local black leadership and white pragmatists. One can only conjecture about any sense of loss or lack of appreciation someone like Rothschild might have felt as he and other white liberals perceived themselves as being relegated from the movement.

Rothschild's comments concerning Martin Luther King Jr.'s reluctance to participate in Atlanta civil rights activities, the nature and depth of black leadership in the city and his direct interaction with it, and conflict between old and new leadership expand the importance of this interview beyond the actions of the Jewish community and the key Jewish community leader.

In 1965 Rothschild helped spearhead and plan the dinner honoring King on his return from receiving the Nobel Peace Prize. The Atlanta business community did not want to support the dinner until, at a meeting concerning the dinner held at the Piedmont Driving Club (a club that excluded African Americans and Jews), the head of Coca-Cola, J. Paul Austin, laid down an ultimatum to the city's elite: "We are an international business. The Coca-Cola Company does not need Atlanta. You all have to decide whether Atlanta needs the Coca-Cola Company." Within hours, the event tickets sold out. The dinner at the Dinkler Plaza Hotel was the first interracial banquet in Atlanta's history and served as a turning point for positive race relations and the integration of the city.

Rothschild remained deeply involved in the civil rights movement. When King was assassinated in 1968, Rothschild gave the eulogy at the memorial service held at the Episcopal Cathedral of St. Philip, the most prominent of the memorial services. Rothschild suffered a heart attack and died suddenly on New Year's Eve, 1973. Rabbi Maurice Eisendrath, president of the Union of American Hebrew Congregations (UAHC), Governor and Mrs. Jimmy Carter, Mayor Maynard Jackson, Congressman Andrew Young, Coretta Scott King, the Rev. Martin Luther King Sr., and other dignitaries attended his funeral on January 2, 1974.

—Mark K. Bauman

Jacob M. Rothschild Interview

June 23, 1966

P. Allen Krause: Rabbi Rothschild, when would you say would be the date that an intense civil rights activity began in your community of Atlanta?

Jacob M. Rothschild: Well I suppose that the first real breakthrough came after the 1954 decision, the Supreme Court decision, although Atlanta was involved in the Negro civil rights question [and had a] fairly advanced liberal status before that. The first time that I preached on it was in 1947, I think, immediately after I came to Atlanta. It was, as a matter of fact, more acceptable then because you were only talking theory; you were only talking abstraction. After the 1954 decision it became more difficult because the community was more aroused, was more resistant to the change. Then also you have to remember that Atlanta is a university community. It's the largest Negro university center, aside from Howard University in Washington—we have five or six Negro colleges there.[4] Negroes always had the vote in Atlanta, and we have a very wealthy Negro community in Atlanta.

PAK: Compared to other Negro communities in the South?

JMR: No, all over the country.

PAK: Wealthy in comparison to Negroes or in comparison to the whites too?

JMR: No, in comparison to the whites too. Not all of them, of course; we have slums and poorer-class Negroes too. As a matter of fact this is one of the problems that has arisen more recently with the upsurge of the lower-class Negro to power that [leads to] this whole problem that we are confronting now. Because there was a leadership in Atlanta in the Negro community, but it's a leadership that is no longer accepted by the Negro masses at the moment. They are considered to be "Uncle Toms." But they did have political power you see, and they did have wealth. They had their own businesses, own banks, own insurance companies. They participated by invitation to a great extent then in the municipal government. And they had power, because they had the vote and they had money. So Atlanta came into this a little differently than most southern communities where there was a sharp line of demarcation and no communication between the two, the whites and the Negro community, at all. The real conflict came after the 1954 decision.

PAK: What was the response on the part of the non-Jewish white population of Atlanta post-1954?

JMR: Foot dragging, reluctance, resistance, as little as the law demanded and as slowly as you could get away with it.

PAK: Was there any vocal ultra-segregationist element there?

JMR: There was, although Atlanta never had a White Citizens' Council.

PAK: What about the Klan?

JMR: The Klan is really inconsequential in Atlanta, although the headquarters
of two of the Klans is in Atlanta. But oddly enough, interestingly enough, a
few years ago the head of one of the Klans ran for public office in an area of
poor southern whites, lower-class whites, and [he] was roundly defeated.

**PAK: On the other hand, was there a visible, what we would consider a
more liberal element in Atlanta?**

JMR: Well this is one of the things that we were fortunate in having in
Atlanta, one of the things I think that made Atlanta different from other
southern communities. After 1954, Atlanta went through the same throes
of reaction that all of us in the southern communities did. That is the moderates abdicated; they didn't say anything and they turned over their power,
which they really had, to the extremists. This happened all over the South.
There was a feeling that, well, if we don't touch it, it will go away, maybe.
Atlanta is a part of Georgia, and therefore they were involved with the state
politicians who were much more reactionary than the Atlanta politicians,
but Atlanta had three or four things going for it. They had an enlightened
mayor[5] who had already had contact with the Negro community and had
been in office then about seventeen years and had good relationships with
the Negro community. They had a liberal press, headed by Ralph McGill,
whom you have heard of. They had a fine police chief,[6] who is still the chief
of police. And they had a nucleus of a courageous clergy. Among these four
they were able to get some liberal spokesmen. Now, Atlanta didn't integrate
its schools until 1961, I guess, later than that maybe, and it went through
the same business of "Never," or "We are going to close our schools rather
than integrate."[7] We then created an organization which we called HOPE,
which stands for Help Our Public Education. HOPE was influential, was
instrumental in creating a kind of public opinion that would make integration possible. Now the governor appointed a commission that went around
the state holding open meetings to have people express themselves, which
was a good thing, because it showed the state and the people in the state;
what they needed was the knowledge that they weren't alone. This helped
considerably in holding up their hands, giving the feeling that they weren't
isolated. After this commission[8] met it put in a majority and minority report. The majority report urged keeping the schools open. Then I think one
of the great traumatic events that got us over the line was the bombing of
the Temple.

**PAK: Can I wait on that for a second? You mentioned a nucleus of liberal
ministers. How many ministers do you have in Atlanta?**

JMR: Oh I guess we have got five, six, seven hundred.

PAK: Is there a completely integrated ministerial association?

JMR: There's no ministerial association in Atlanta. There is what they call the Atlanta Council of Churches, which theoretically is an organization of laymen and ministers, but only ministers belong. It is integrated. I'm not sure how many Negroes attend. But it's such an inconsequential organization anyway that it has really no—we didn't do things through the Atlanta, it was then called the Atlanta Christian Council.

PAK: So what was the group that was instrumental as a ministerial association?

JMR: This was a group of people acting as individuals.

PAK: You mean there is no set group that they work through as their tool?

JMR: None, no. We had our own meetings, went to see men on our own.

PAK: But you never even had a quasi group?

JMR: We organized ourselves. Not into a formal group, but you see Atlanta really isn't that big a city that you don't know everybody, that the clergy aren't aware of who is on their side, who thinks like they do. We enlisted the support and the aid of the men whom we knew would feel as we did. Then we went out and invited everybody to join in and those who did, did, that's all.

PAK: What would be the numbers and the influence on their own people of the liberal elements in the ministerial group in Atlanta?

JMR: You mean their influence among their own congregation?

PAK: Right. How large a percentage of the ministers would you include in this group?

JMR: Well in the first manifesto, so-called "Ministers' Manifesto," we only got eighty signatures.

PAK: And that was in which year?

JMR: That was 1959, I believe. I'm not quite sure.[9]

PAK: The second one, I think, was 1958.

JMR: Then the first one must have been 1957 or '56. It didn't say anything revolutionary incidentally. Largely it was concerned with the right to speak out and the religious—specifically Christian—attitude towards equality and human dignity and so forth. Now you ask, how influential were these men? Well, so far as their position was concerned, they were not by and large the ministers of the largest churches. The Baptists never signed and the couple who did are no longer in Atlanta. One of the leaders was the minister of a large Methodist church, but he's no longer in Atlanta.

PAK: Is there a relationship?

JMR: I would think so, although it's hard to prove. Now how much influence did they have among their own members? It's hard to say. I would think that they did not express the viewpoint of the majority of their members.

PAK: What about rabbis? How many rabbis are there in your community?

JMR: Not counting emeriti and assistants, there are five of us.

PAK: What denominations do they represent?

JMR: There is only one Reform temple and there is one Orthodox—no, one Conservative and there are three Orthodox.[10]

PAK: Have the Conservative and Orthodox rabbis in any way participated in civil rights activity?

JMR: Not to any great extent but not because they think differently, not because they are opposed to it. I think that really I sort of preempted their participation, because I was always so involved and the general community always came to me, looked to me, got me involved, that there wasn't much room for them, although they have signed all of these things.

PAK: Did they?

JMR: Yes, and I'm sure they preached in their congregation.

PAK: How long has your congregation been in existence?

JMR: We are celebrating our centennial next year.

PAK: How long has the Jewish community actually been there?

JMR: Not too long before then. Atlanta is comparatively a new southern city, and of course it was burned down during the war.

PAK: What is the size of your congregation?

JMR: Not quite twelve hundred families.

PAK: What percentage of your congregants would you say can trace, let's say, two generations back in the South and in Atlanta?

JMR: Well I can't answer that now, but if you ask me a month from now I could give you the exact figures, because my wife has just finished writing a history of the congregation for the centennial.[11] We sent out a questionnaire and one of the things in the questionnaire was to find out the answer exactly for this question. How many newcomers? How many first generation, second generation, third generation? So if you are really interested in those statistics . . .

PAK: How many members of your congregation represent an influx from the North and therefore northern approaches to the problem of . . .

JMR: I think that you will have to reevaluate your own thinking on this matter, because very often the northerners who come down out-southern the southerners in their attitudes. The idea that a northerner is liberal is for the birds. They aren't, as reflected now in their attitudes towards this 1966 civil rights bill where it affected them and their neighborhoods and their housing. Sometimes we found exactly the opposite, that they, in order to prove that they are good citizens of the South, are much more reactionary than southerners.

PAK: If I was to take your congregation and put it next to a similar-size

congregation of Protestants (not Baptists), would there be any appreciable difference in outlook on civil rights?

JMR: Yes. You may find something about that in some of the stuff I gave you. I'm not sure that I included it in one of those speeches or not, but I think that it is definitely and significantly and provably true that Jewish communities, at least my Jewish community, is much more liberal on the subject of civil rights than a comparable non-Jewish congregation.

PAK: **What would you attribute that to?**

JMR: Well, there are a lot of things you can attribute it to. First of all Judaism has always been involved in life in this world, and our attitudes towards social justice, whereas Christianity has emphasized the saving of the individual soul. They are dealing with heaven; we are dealing with life in this world. The whole concept of the Social Gospel is new to Christians; they haven't been taught this. It hasn't been a part of their religious experience. So it came as a shock to them that they were supposed to believe this. They were interested in saving their own individual souls, not in creating a better society, not in applying the principles of Christian faith to the society, only to themselves. That's one reason. The second reason is, I think, because integration involved them more specifically than it did Jews. We don't have any Jewish Negroes, in the South anyway, and not many anyway. They were confronted with the problem, [you] see their church is a social institution, and to open the doors of the church for them changed a whole way of life, not just a religious philosophy. Their—what do they call them—women's circles, ladies' circles, their Sunday schools—this is all social for them. One of the great problems that we had in the South was the problem of these people, even the more liberal of them, urging open accommodations, for example, restaurants, hotels, but not open churches.

PAK: **What is the economic standing of the Jews in your congregation? What is their source of income?**

JMR: Well, Atlanta, as you probably know, is a great regional center. All major businesses have regional offices in Atlanta. There are very few factories in Atlanta. It is the center for disinfectants, for that manufacturing company, Jordan Chemical Company. Oh, there are dozens of them. They all do very well by the way. The Atlanta [Jewish] community is pretty middle class. We don't have any cab drivers or waiters or this sort of thing.

PAK: **What would you say their source of income is?**

JMR: They are mostly merchant salesmen.

PAK: **Are they very susceptible to economic pressure put on them by the non-Jewish community?**

JMR: Yes, but not as susceptible as they would be in a small town.

PAK: **Do you think that this amounts to any significant amount of pressure?**

JMR: Never did in Atlanta, I'm sure. The largest department store is owned by Jews—Rich's. His resistance [to desegregation] was based on something entirely different. He was never afraid, I don't think, of a boycott.

PAK: **What percentage of the Jews in Atlanta are affiliated with some sort of a congregation?**

JMR: Oh about ninety-nine. We don't have a large unaffiliated population at all.

PAK: **Rabbi, what was your personal response and involvement in specific civil rights activities in your area?**

JMR: Well, that's a hard question because I was involved in practically everything that happened in Atlanta, and besides 1954 is a long time ago. But as I mentioned before, I began preaching on this subject long before the 1954 decision. So they weren't surprised when I showed up on the liberal side of the question. I think this is a good thing, because the congregation had been prepared before the confrontation itself, before the climactic event. They already knew something about what Judaism had to say on this subject.

PAK: **Did you start in vague generalities or did you start with specifics when you started preaching?**

JMR: I don't remember, really, but I always felt that it was the rabbi's obligation to teach Jews what Judaism had to say on all subjects, on all aspects of life. It was equally important for me to tell them what Judaism and Reform Judaism said about immortality, and also it was important for me to tell them what Judaism, Reform Judaism had to say about equal rights and so forth and so on. So this was always intertwined in my teaching and my preaching. As early, well again I can't remember dates, but our Sisterhood had a program at which we invited the Negro president of a Negro college to speak, and he brought his wife with him—it was a luncheon meeting—and there was some objection on the part of certain members of the congregation to this.

PAK: **Would you say this was before the 1954 [decision]?**

JMR: This was before. I simply said to one of the people that called me, "Well I don't know what you are complaining about. It's going to be a segregated lunch." He said, "It is?" And I said, "Yeah. Dr. Mays[12] and his wife are going to sit in the middle of the head table, and all the white people are going to be segregated around them." You know I had this sort of thing all the time. Now, when the Supreme Court decision came out, then we began to organize a little formally in the community. As I mentioned before I was a part of the ministerial group that was instrumental in having meetings and getting statements made and so forth. Our own congregation held meetings preparing them for school integration through our community affairs committee. The summer before the schools were to be opened we had a series of seminars at which the chief of police spoke [and] the superintendent of schools. Then we had the series of four Sunday morning seminars, more theoretical seminars on the responsibility of the community and Jews and so forth.

PAK: **Meaning mainly [a] congregational-family type of thing?**

JMR: Yes, for our congregation. When the public accommodations thing got hot in Atlanta, before that aspect of the civil rights bill was passed, the mayor had a meeting with hotel owners and restaurant owners and invited some of us to attend, and asked me to speak to them. When Martin Luther King received the Nobel Prize we decided he ought to have a dinner in Atlanta. I don't know whether you have ever heard this story of this business or not, but *Time* magazine, *Life* magazine had a good spread on it, a pretty accurate one. We couldn't get the power structure to go along, and we decided that we were going to have it whether they came or not. As a result we forced their hand. They could not not appear. And, what looked for a while to be a meeting of a few hundred people, turned out to be an overflow dinner with some sixteen hundred with a thousand people turned away, with national coverage.

PAK: **What role did you play in this?**

JMR: I was the chairman of the whole business and I also was the chairman of the meeting.

PAK: **You also introduced, if I remember correctly, Martin Luther King when he spoke at the UAHC convention.**

JMR: The biennial there in Chicago.

PAK: **I would appreciate you commenting on that. I know from my research so far that there was a good deal of dissent on the part of many of the southern rabbis as to whether or not King should have been . . .**

JMR: Southern communities, not southern rabbis?

PAK: **Well, the Mississippi rabbis almost unanimously, I think, wrote a letter to whomever it was in the UAHC saying that they were against doing this. Now I know that the rabbis possibly might have had [different] feelings, but they felt the pressure from their congregations sufficiently to say that they thought this was an unwise decision on the part of the UAHC, but you obviously did not.**[13]

JMR: Well, I didn't, but it wouldn't have made any difference whether I did or not, because I always felt free to act as my conscience dictated. I was never circumscribed either outwardly by the congregation or inwardly by the opposition—which of course there was. My congregation wasn't any different really than other congregations, and not everybody agreed with what I was doing, but . . .

PAK: **You felt that it was a good thing that he was the keynote speaker?**

JMR: I think that it was, sure it was wonderful that he spoke. He's a good friend of mine, and I was delighted with the invitation to introduce him. It didn't create any stir in my congregation. As a matter of fact I commented to them when I got back that either they didn't know what was going on, or I had accomplished more than I thought I had, because all these southern communities, some of them got up and walked out, some of them didn't come to the meeting. And I said, "You people didn't react at all. You didn't tell me it was good, it was nice, you didn't tell me it wasn't nice." They just accepted it. I think this is the result of long years of working and digging at the same subject, and it becomes acceptable.

PAK: You say voting has never been a problem in Atlanta?

JMR: Never.

PAK: What about employment?

JR: Well employment is an area in which I really haven't been too greatly involved. I happen to know the director now, the new one, [of the] government employment [agency], "Open Employment" [or] whatever they call the thing.[14] Don Hollowell, who is a lawyer, a Negro lawyer. Atlanta has Lockheed, which has signed the pledge and has equal opportunity and gradually now Negroes are being employed as equals. The problem now is largely getting Negroes who are qualified.

PAK: You personally have not been involved specifically in this area?

JMR: No.

PAK: What about other areas, transportation or the integration of public facilities?

JMR: I was involved in the Open Occupancy thing.[15] Actually whatever took place in Atlanta, I was at one point or another involved in, because there was a small group of us that were determined that Atlanta was going to be different than the rest of the South. Now I must say, and I told them this on many occasions, "them" meaning the people in Atlanta—none of them in my congregation—but the community, restaurant owners, hotel owners. Atlanta has not done anything because it was right; they have gone along because it was expedient. They don't want to destroy the image of Atlanta, and they don't want to do anything to endanger the tremendous economic growth of Atlanta. They are willing to go along. But there are very few of us who are willing to say that we are doing this because it's moral, because it's right. Of course this is the impasse that the whole civil rights movement finds itself in now. The foot dragging, the reluctance, the "as little as the law will allow," is all an expression of the fact that the hearts of men haven't been changed.

PAK: You mentioned the bombing of the synagogue. Can you take me backwards through it and just follow through in detail on what you

think is the specific cause of this incident, and how you handled it, and your reactions to it et cetera, et cetera?

JMR: Well the bombing was really, I guess, one of the most traumatic experiences not only for our congregation but for Atlanta, because Atlanta always prided itself on being a very enlightened community. This happened at the time when there was a whole spate of bombings, when the so-called Confederate Underground was active. They bombed a community center in Miami and I think one in Nashville, and there was a whole series of these things.[16] Atlantans thought themselves superior to this whole thing. When the temple was bombed it came as a tremendous shock to the Atlanta community. It was given international publicity; it was on the front pages not only of American newspapers, but all over the world. I have a scrapbook of headlines from all over the world. So it created worldwide attention.

PAK: When exactly was it?

JMR: It was October the twelfth, 1958. Now you ask, why? I suppose that part of it, at least, was because I was so obviously identified with the civil rights movement. This must have been one of the reasons why the temple was selected. But no member of my congregation ever said to me, "We told you so. You see." For which I give them great credit by the way. I think that it had nothing whatever to do with the integration question. What happened was that there was a small group of so-called Nazis who took advantage of an atmosphere of violence and urging on the part of government officials, city and state officials. The governor of our state said, for example, "We will fight at every crossroad, at every gas station." He didn't mean that— he wasn't going to fire a rifle—but there are people who will take advantage of the opening for lawlessness which it gives. They believed that the psychology of the people was prepared for this, for an act of violence, and they were willing to take advantage of it. They didn't bomb Negro churches; that wasn't their interest. They used the atmosphere to bomb a synagogue because they were specifically anti-Semitic. They were anti-Negro too, but this wasn't their major concern. Now what happened was, and this was the great value of it, if such a thing has a value, they misread the attitudes of the community in which they lived. Because the bombing of the temple created a reaction, a response of such horror, of such outrage, that it backfired, and as a result of the bombing of the temple, it now, for perhaps the first time in Atlanta, became possible to speak out. I'm firmly convinced that it was this episode that prevented Atlanta from becoming the same kind of closed society that Birmingham became or Mississippi became, because when the mayor, the very morning of the bombing, said over TV, "This is the harvest reaped by our politicians and elected officials who have encouraged this kind of action." Now once you say this then you make it possible for anyone to speak. So the bombing really was quite valuable in the ongoing story of Atlanta and the whole civil rights movement.

PAK: I want to find out your methodology of how you go about influencing people to do things in the direction that you want them to go. Can you think of any more specific event?

JMR: Well, the King dinner.

PAK: Okay, so how did you go about it? I want to know what the channels are that you used. Not specific persons, but techniques for accomplishing your purposes.

JMR: A few of us decided that Atlanta's first Nobel Peace Prize winner ought to have some recognition from his home town. Now it happened that our Nobel Peace Prize winner was a controversial figure and a Negro. I must confess that when we first met I didn't visualize opposition. I thought that it would be perfectly acceptable to the Atlanta community that, yes, we [as a city have] a Nobel Peace Prize winner. But, it didn't turn out that way. We had a meeting, oh a half a dozen of us. From there we went to the mayor[17] and enlisted his support, and he was anxious to cooperate. But he is the victim, the prey, at the mercy of the power structure too. So he went to certain people in the community and came back to us and said, "They won't go along," at which point both the power structure and the mayor thought that this was the end of the matter, because nothing happens in Atlanta without certain banks, Coca-Cola, and so forth. But we weren't willing to give up. So, without saying anything further to anyone—there was nothing we could do on this score—we simply went ahead and continued to plan the meeting. We were a bunch of amateurs, but we enlisted the aid of a public relations person, who volunteered her services; she was very helpful, and rented the Dinkler Plaza Hotel for the occasion, and just went on as though nothing had happened. We figured we would get—well, if we got five hundred people this would be a nice dinner, and it would honor King and so forth. At this point the power structure got wind of the fact that there was going to be a dinner. They had assumed there wasn't going to be one because they had already said, "No we won't do it." They called a meeting, a secret meeting, to which I was not invited, to decide what they were going to do. One of them, the most powerful one of all, said, "I had planned to be in Africa or in Europe or some place, but I will come back for this dinner, because I'm convinced that it's right." Well, when he said this, then the whole thing turned around.[18] Then the thing snowballed, and we got more reservations than we knew what to do with, and so forth.

Now let me backtrack for a minute because I think this is important and interesting. The Southern Christian Leadership Conference [SCLC] was obviously involved in the dinner, in the plans for the dinner, and they tried to take over—they wanted to do it their way and they even said that King himself wanted certain things, and there were some of these things that I didn't like. I'm a very stubborn individual, as you will know if you ever come to conferences and hear me on the floor. I don't have to agree with the majority if I think they are wrong, and I balked at some of the things that they wanted. Let me see if I can think of some of the specific things. Oh, certain people who were going to participate. This kind of thing.

PAK: Such as?

JMR: Well I didn't want it to be an SCLC dinner, and I didn't like some of the plans that they had for it, and then King said that he doesn't appear at meetings unless there is a fundraising for the SCLC. They wanted to sell tickets, you know, for twenty-five, fifty dollars. And I said, "If Dr. King doesn't want to appear, let him tell us now. He really doesn't have any choice. We are inviting him to be honored; if he doesn't want to be honored, let him tell us, and we'll call the whole thing off. It's not going to be a money raising experience. We are honoring a man, not raising money for him." Well, we had a big fight about it, but we won.

PAK: How direct is your contact with Dr. King?

JMR: I know him very well. He has been to our home; his wife and my wife are very good friends.

PAK: During this whole thing were you ever in direct contact with him instead of going through the SCLC?

JMR: Nobody is in direct contact with Dr. King anymore.

PAK: Why? What exactly is the line of communication? How do you reach him?

JMR: Well I reach him because I have my wife call his wife [*laughing*]. We have his private phone number, but he is never in Atlanta anymore. He is really outside the local sphere altogether. Where we used to see each other, and he'd come over to the house for dinner and we visited, we don't see them anymore at all. So our line of communication is through [Ralph] Abernathy and his public relations person, whose name I forget. Anyway, we had this dinner and it was a tremendous success, and I still believe that it was the only time in the history of the South that an audience of over sixteen hundred people, from all walks of life—bankers, professional men, scrub women, white, black—closed the meeting by standing up and singing "We Shall Overcome." I'll bet this is the first time it ever happened in the South, and this meeting was absolutely the most moving significant meeting that Atlanta ever had. Everybody said so.

PAK: What was your relationship with King prior to his becoming a national figure?

JMR: We were much closer then because we saw each other.

PAK: Did you work together or did you help him out in any way in certain activities in Atlanta?

JMR: No, because King was never involved in Atlanta.

PAK: He went straight to Montgomery, is that what he did?

JMR: He came to Atlanta from Montgomery, but this was one of the interesting things about this dinner by the way: King—and you can't use this in your [work]—but, King is afraid of Atlanta. He was afraid of his reception in Atlanta. He was afraid of the Atlanta Negro community. He wasn't comfortable in Atlanta, because Atlanta had its own leadership, you see, and King was never involved in anything in Atlanta except in a very superficial way.

PAK: So then, other than your personal relationship with King, has there been any real importance with regard to the civil rights scene in Atlanta or the South in your involvement with King and being friendly with him? Has this rubbed off on the civil rights scene in any way?

JMR: Well, only that King represents the civil rights leader, leader of the nonviolent movement all over and in Atlanta too, but my work in Atlanta was not with King. King was never in Atlanta.

PAK: Has your friendship with him in any way opened up channels for your work in Atlanta? Has it affected your work in Atlanta in any way?

JMR: No. My relationship with King is largely social, and we believe in the same thing. But my work in Atlanta was largely in conjunction with Ben Mays, who is the president of Morehouse College; with Rufus Clement, who is the president of Atlanta University and a member of the Board of Education; with Sam Williams, who is the president of the NAACP and a very good friend of mine. These are the people with whom we work in Atlanta. King was not involved in the Atlanta civil rights struggle at all.

PAK: What is your relationship with the Negro civil rights groups in Atlanta?

JMR: I have no contact whatsoever with SNCC.

PAK: Out of choice?

JMR: Partly; I'm not particularly enamored of their position. And until recently when this whole common man uprising in the Negro community came about, they didn't have any real authority in Atlanta.[19] They did conduct some of the picketing and the sit-ins, but the Atlanta Negro community is a very different community than others. They didn't have to have outside leaders come in. They had their leaders, and they have an overall organization of the Negro community, which I forget what they call it, which deals with the problems on the highest levels of government and on the planning stages of sit-ins, picketing, and so forth and so on. This is a little different than in other communities.

PAK: This is the group of leaders which is more or less being rejected by the SNCC element now?

JMR: To a certain extent yes, and this is one of the problems that they have. Although they still have the overall organization, and they are still, theoretically at least, cooperating groups.

PAK: Has the SCLC played an important role in Atlanta? If so what is your relationship with them?

JMR: Well the SCLC is one of these groups, but its activity is coordinated with and subordinated to the total Negro community activity. They have an organization—I'm going to put in here, if I didn't I meant to [*said while Rothschild is shuffling through papers, looking for something*]—I haven't been very clear I guess in explaining this to you. You see, when something happens in Birmingham, the Birmingham Negroes have neither the strength, nor the capacity, nor the leadership, nor really the courage to do it themselves. The same thing in Mississippi. They have got to bring in outsiders. When the outsiders leave, they are left high and dry. They are, again, prey to the situation. Now this is not true in Atlanta. Atlanta had its own leaders. They didn't need anybody from outside.

PAK: But when you want to contact the Negro community, have you ever had the time when you wanted to get in touch with them?

JMR: Oh sure.

PAK: Okay, now when you want to do that, how do you go about it?

JMR: I call Sam Williams, the president of the NAACP, a professor of philosophy at Morehouse College, a minister of the Friendship Baptist Church, and a very good friend of mine.

PAK: Is he the channel to the Negro community for you?

JMR: One of them.

PAK: What are the others? You mentioned one or two others I think.

JMR: I don't need a channel when I go to them.

PAK: Why?

JMR: They call me.

PAK: Who calls you? The heads of the organizations or the leaders of the . . .

JMR: Oh Ben Mays will call me when he wants something or when I can help with something. Rufus Clement will call me for something.

PAK: And he is?

JMR: He is the president of Atlanta University. I don't have to seek a channel into the Negro community; I'm kind of a part of this whole thing.

PAK: But if you have an idea that you want to get pushed, let's say at a meeting or something like that, and you want to take the initiative of contacting somebody—you would contact Williams or . . .

JMR: Or Ben Mays . . .

PAK: **Or have you had the opportunity to just call a Negro minister?**

JMR: Well, Sam Williams of course is a Negro minister, but they call me—I
have spoken in their churches—we are on a first name basis.

PAK: **What do they call you for? In the past few years what are the kind of
things that you have been called upon to do by members of the Negro
community?**

JMR: Well of course they called me for the King dinner right away. I was the
one that they contacted when they had the idea. Actually I had the idea. I
contacted them—"I think we ought to do this." We work very closely with
the director of the National Conference of Christians and Jews, who is an
extremely liberal person, and who has done a great deal in Atlanta, with
panels on rearing children of good will, and seminars on the police, and
so forth. . . . So we had these contacts. You see, you don't have to look for
somebody to plant a seed, or to—I don't know, we just do it.

PAK: **Well, what are some of the things that they ask you to do? I'm still
trying to exactly determine what you do. They call upon you to make
speeches and things?**

JMR: Well that is, I guess every rabbi . . .

PAK: **I think some of these things are too commonplace for you so that you
don't think . . .**

JMR: Yeah I guess so, because I really can't think of anything. Anything that
happens, anything that we have done in Atlanta. The Jewish community
wanted me to present the position of the Jewish community at these hearings on open schools, for example. They called me to make the presentation
for them.

PAK: **Who do you mean by the Jewish community?**

JMR: The total Jewish community.

PAK: **I mean who is it that . . .**

JMR: We have an Atlanta Community Council, Jewish Community Council.

PAK: **Have you had the support of the Jewish Community Council?**

JMR: Yes. I guess this is of really no consequence, but it's interesting. When there
was a certain judge in Atlanta, you may have heard of, Judge [Durwood T.]
Pye, who took the sit-in cases into his court and threw the book at all of
the participants, including a white college student from Connecticut College who was attending school at Spelman on an exchange year program.
Spelman is a Negro girls' school, like Goucher.[20] This girl, Mardon Walker,
was tried and eventually convicted, although she never served. I got a call
about six thirty one evening from a Mrs. Drimmer, and she said, "My husband is in jail. My husband is Professor Drimmer at Spelman College and
he is in jail. Can you do anything?" I said, "Why did you call me?" She

said, "Well I'm Jewish." She was white and her husband was white. I never heard of the man. So I said, "Well let's see what happened. Why is he in jail?" She said, "He's in jail for contempt of court." So I went down to the jail, and this guy testified as a character witness for Mardon Walker. Made a stupid statement on the stand, which most judges would have overlooked, but not Pye, and Pye gave him twenty days. Well, Pye also throws you into jail for contempt of court if you are a minute late into his courtroom; I mean he's this kind of a person and particularly on the matter of integration. He is rabid on the subject, and with white people involved in integration it is even worse. So I said, "Well, I don't know what I can do but I'll call Don Hollowell." Don Hollowell is a lawyer who is now head of this employment thing for the government. He was taking charge of all the civil rights matters. This is ten o'clock at night so I called Don and I said, "I'll come see you." He said, "Yeah I know what you want, you better come over." So I hurried over to his office, and he said, "I can't get this guy out of jail. First of all he is in contempt of court. In the second place we can file an appeal, but by the time the appeal is filed he will have served his twenty days." So I thought about it, and I said, "Well, what if I went to Judge Pye, on a personal basis, and asked him to reconsider?" He said, "Well, I don't know—you'll probably wind up in jail; you can't tell with this guy." I said, "Would Drimmer get more than twenty days?" He said, "No, it can't affect Drimmer." I said, "Well, I'll go see Pye." So the next morning before court opened I went into Judge Pye's chambers, and before I went in I went to the City Solicitor I also knew, and I told him I was going to see Pye, and I said, "Incidentally I may need your help. I may wind up in jail with him. Can you get me out?" He said, "I can't get you out, but I'll bring you food." So anyway I went to see Pye, and Pye said, "Would you appear in open court this afternoon on behalf of Professor Drimmer?" I said, "Well if you want me to I will." So I came down to court. He got Drimmer out of the jug, and I made my pitch for Drimmer.

PAK: As what, a character witness?

JMR: No, I was his lawyer. I was his counsel.

PAK: What did you say?

JMR: I said, "Your Honor, you know that I have the greatest respect for your court and all courts of law. Without law the country would fall into anarchy, and I'm not questioning your action in sentencing Professor Drimmer. I am sure that it was a carrying out of that which was just, and justice is your department, but Your Honor, I'm not a judge, I'm a rabbi, and just as justice is your department so mercy is my department. So I'm going to speak to you on the basis of mercy." Then I went on to say that his wife was pregnant, and they had a little kid and—he was the judge in one of the first trials of the Temple bombing—I recalled for him that I had been on the witness stand, and I am accustomed to public speaking, and even so, I was nervous and I may have said things that, on sober reflection, I might not have said, and that this affects all citizens that way, and that Professor Drimmer was eager to apologize for the statement that he made, and I would hope that he would accept his apology. He listened to Drimmer, and he said to the clerk, "Take an order; I'm dismissing the charges." It was really very funny, because after he left the courtroom the City Solicitor came up to me and he said, "Do you want to be on my staff?" He said, "It's the first case that the Negroes have won in this court since the [*laughter, which makes his next words inaudible*]." Don Hollowell looked at me, and he said, "Boy did you miss your calling! That is the first case I've won in this court in ten years." Anyway it worked out, but this is the sort of thing that they know I'm willing to do. This was just a dramatic kind of thing. The result is, of course, that I wish my own congregation held me in as high esteem as the Negro community does.

PAK: **What use have you made of the press to accomplish your goals? Have you often been quoted as an individual in the press?**

JMR: Yes, I have and I have written—I didn't bring that either—I wrote an article for the newspaper on the prophetic tradition on the subject of civil rights, and I've been on the radio and television, and I'm constantly—not so much anymore because things are sort of quieted down now—but I was constantly in the public eye on this subject. The result was that we had the usual harassing telephone calls, threats, and so forth and so on.

PAK: **Did you initiate sending these press releases to them?**

JMR: No, they came to me.

PAK: **Have you ever sent sermons, parts of sermons. . . ?**

JMR: No, never. We don't do that in Atlanta.

PAK: **The other thing, have you joined any organizations? I'm not talking about civil rights organizations now or organizations specifically aimed toward that direction. Have you joined any other organizations in order to make contacts, or to make your own position secure so that when you do get involved in civil rights you will have a stronger . . . ?**

JMR: You mean like civic organizations?

PAK: **Yeah, things like this.**

JMR: No, I was a member of Kiwanis for a while but it was so deadly that I just had to quit. I'm not a joiner.

PAK: **One rabbi said this, "It was very important to join patriotic organizations. It establishes patriotism and then . . . "**

JMR: [*interrupts*] Nah, I don't even belong to the Jewish War Veterans.

PAK: With regards to your congregation then, is there any discrepancy between your response to or participation in civil rights activity and that of your congregants? . . . Have you ever been criticized by the board or by an official synagogue representative?

JMR: I have never been criticized by the board. The board of the temple has been exemplary and most praiseworthy in this whole business. They have been very patient, very understanding, and have really been, I think, most praiseworthy in their attitudes. I have complete freedom of the pulpit. They have never in any way tried to stop me from either saying anything in the pulpit or taking an active part in the whole struggle. Perhaps the best example I can give you—now this of course wasn't true of the entire congregation nor even of the entire board—they didn't always agree with me, but they gave me the right to speak and act. Some few years ago a member of our congregation saw my daughter at a public restaurant with a Negro girl. [It] happened just by accident that my wife was in the same restaurant eating lunch, and I came over and spoke with her. That's how that person knew it was my daughter—I don't think otherwise she would have known. The next morning, first thing, this woman called my wife and voiced her very strenuous protest. Now my wife is a fourth generation southerner, and she can out southern talk any southerner in the world when she wants to. She sweet-talked this woman so that she didn't know her throat was cut, and that was the end of that conversation. But at the next board meeting a letter was submitted from this individual resigning from the congregation, because they couldn't belong to a congregation who permitted its rabbi's daughter to eat in public with a Negro. What would happen when we would get letters of resignation? Somebody says, "I move that it be accepted with regret," and somebody says "I second it," and that's the end, which is what happened—"I move that we accept it with regret" and "I second the motion." But then some guy said, "Wait a minute. Why should we accept it with regret? Let's say what we really believe." So they said, "We accept your resignation. We feel that you are absolutely right, because obviously your membership in the congregation has not taught you what Judaism really believes, and therefore your payment of dues is a waste of time." Which I thought was wonderful.

PAK: Have you ever felt that there might [be] a significant, a large enough number like this woman to start a break-off congregation or to go to another congregation?

JMR: They had no place else to go.

PAK: They could start a break-off congregation.

JMR: No.

PAK: **Because you have a large congregation there?**

JMR: No, I don't think so at all. It has never been even a threat and now a very interesting thing has happened. You see, I'm no longer a pariah, an outcast, a loner in the community. The powers that be in the community are now saying what I have been saying all these years. So not only does the congregation get a sort of *kvell* [Yiddish, meaning "feeling of pride"] out of the fact that their rabbi represents the thinking of the best of the community; they get a vicarious pleasure out of this now.

PAK: **What about in the early '50s?**

JMR: It was rough. I don't remember; I tend to suppress the unpleasant.

PAK: **You don't? Did you have any trouble with the board or your congregation in the '50s?**

JMR: Well, my wife remembers these things better than I do. You really should talk to her. There were a couple of times when there were stirrings in the congregation and meetings about the rabbi, but I do not believe that any of them was on the matter of integration, of civil rights. I got involved in the communist business, which is of no consequence here, but that created a stir, because I befriended a social worker employed by the Jewish community, you know the Jewish Federation [of] Social Service, who was accused of being a communist. This was in the height of the McCarthy era, and this created more stir than anything that I did in the civil rights business.

PAK: **Do you know of any incident where it was definitely some civil rights position in the early '50s . . . which caused a stir in your congregation?**

JMR: I can't think of one. Maybe I'm just naive. Maybe these things went on.

PAK: **What about national Jewish organizations, have they played any role in the civil rights movement in your area?**

JMR: Oh yes. Yeah we have a regional office of the ADL [Anti-Defamation League] and they are very helpful. We also have a regional office of the American Jewish Committee, and we use their personnel as a part of the Atlanta community. Today's national Jewish organizations have regional offices in Atlanta, and we co-opt them as part of the Jewish community, and they are members of our Community Relations Committee of the Jewish Community Council. By and large we have gotten along very well. That is, they understand that they can't take any unilateral action on local matters; that it all has to come through the Jewish Community Council. On the other hand, we use them. For example, when we recently were dealing with Negro housing, one of their men made the survey for us on Jewish ownership of slum property and this sort of thing. When we had a problem with prayers in the public schools, with teaching religion in the public schools, our contact with the public schools is the local director of the American

Jewish Committee [AJC], who has specialized in this, and has a relationship with the superintendent of schools. But he reports as a member of our
Community Relations Committee, you see—so we have a very good relationship with them.

PAK: Have they ever been detrimental to you in your work?

JMR: Well yes, one of the ADL directors who is no longer there, got into
some difficulty—a matter of anti-Semitism at Emory University in the dental school—and [the ADL director] was brought up short by the Jewish
Community Council and Community Relations Committee.

PAK: Not in the civil rights area?

JMR: Not in the civil rights; no, we pretty well agree on civil rights. The only
thing, the only conflict that I ever had within the area of civil rights was
after the Temple was bombed, where the ADL wanted to take over. You
know they were the great defense organization, and just one brief statement
had to be made to put them in their place, which I did.

PAK: What did they want to do?

JMR: Well, they wanted to run the public relations aspect of it and make the
releases and make—as a matter of fact they did do this, they became ex-
perts in it—I refused to make statements, you see. I wouldn't—not make
statements; of course I'd make statements—but national television wanted
me to appear, and I refused.

PAK: Why?

JMR: Well, for two reasons. First of all I was interested in making something valuable come out of this experience, and I felt very strongly—and it
turned out that I was right—that public exposure, for personal reasons or
whatever, was not the way to do it. The ADL needed it because they would
do anything to raise money. I mean, anything that happens that they can
get involved in, and show their value, helps them in their fundraising. I
wanted to play it much more quietly and smoothly than that. I made statements, constantly. I was on television, radio, and the local press and all this
sort of thing, but I didn't seek public exposure. I wouldn't go out of the city
to speak on the subject for six months after it happened, because I didn't
want to capitalize on it.

PAK: Do you think it would have hurt the atmosphere in your community?

JMR: I think that, yes. I think that it would have hurt what was happening in
Atlanta. We had the support of the political powers, of the power structure,
of the churches, and I wanted to solidify this and use it.

**PAK: If the history was to be written of civil rights activity, say fifty or a
hundred years from now, of your community, of the South as a whole,
what role do you think the rabbi—now in your community I guess it
would be yourself—but [also] in the South as a whole, from as much**

knowledge as you might have, [what role] would [the rabbi] play in the civil rights movement?

JMR: More than the ministers, but not enough. I have a feeling, and I've told this to my colleagues, I mean my Christian colleagues: the great tragedy of the civil rights movement is the abdication of the religious institutions. There was no strong, courageous leadership on the part of the churches, or their ministers, except in very rare cases. The challenge was not met in the religious area. This is one of the great tragedies of the whole thing, I think.

PAK: But you say rabbis would have played something of an important role?

JMR: Well I think that rabbis were not as bad as ministers.

PAK: What role would you say that they would play?

JMR: Historically, looking back historically?

PAK: Yes.

JMR: That's difficult to answer, and I'm hesitant to answer, because the role that they played was determined by the community in which they lived.

PAK: Let's take Atlanta then.

JMR: What I did in Atlanta, I did in Atlanta, and I cannot judge the actions or lack of actions of any of my colleagues in any other community. I don't know how that I would have acted.

PAK: What role do you think that you would have played in Atlanta in the long term?

JMR: Well, at the risk of being immodest, I think that I have played a very significant role. If only because my speaking out brought the subject into the open and made it possible for others to do so.

PAK: Do you believe that you have been more than a support to those who are making the real changes; do you think that you have actually initiated some of the changes?

JMR: I think that I have, in many areas, had the opportunity to lead the community in its change of thinking. I was involved in everything that happened. I was constantly speaking out.

PAK: Do . . . you have any general comments at this time?

JMR: No, I think that you have asked a lot of incisive questions, and I wish I could answer them better. I guess I'm not a historian really, because this whole thing is vague to me, and when I say that I was active in this I know that I was and yet, at this point, I can't really recall what I did. I know that I was on panel discussions on television and radio. I know that every time my name appeared in the paper with something, my children would come home and say, "What did you do now?" And I would say, "How do you know?" They would say, "Well the phone's been ringing constantly." This sort of thing, and I have been through the whole bit, with the threats and so forth, but I was never one to dramatize or to over dramatize this whole business. I sort of took it in stride, and this is the way it was, and that is all you can do with it.

PAK: What is your reaction to, in 1958 on Kol Nidre, Rabbi Emmet Frank in Alexandria, Virginia, preached a sermon. Are you familiar with it?

JMR: Yes, I am.

PAK: He equated "Byrdliness" with "Godlessness."²¹ What is your reaction to that approach?

JMR: Well you can look at the sermons and see what I did. I think you will find that I may never have been that specific but . . .

PAK: Do you think that that approach would have helped or hurt your position in the [civil rights work]?

JMR: I think it probably would have hurt, although I've spoken against politicians and their positions. But one of the things that makes the whole problem for us difficult is that you can't move too far ahead of your community. You have to handle this whole problem with a certain amount of *sechel* [Yiddish for "common sense"]. Otherwise you frustrate your own capacities. There was one period, for example, in Atlanta when all I did was preach and speak on the right to dissent, on the right to speak, because it was getting to be that you couldn't.

PAK: Was that in the early time or was that post-'54?

JMR: That was post-'54. Oh you could speak all you wanted before that.

PAK: How long did that continue until you were able—until '58?

JMR: I think probably after the bombing. Then you begin to say more and more, you see. I jotted down, I made a speech one time to a Rotary Club, and I just had notes. But I thought you might be interested in the kind of thing that I would say to the power structure, the upper echelon in business. You can turn it off right now.²²

PAK: Many rabbis have said that they don't consider Atlanta a southern community. Do you hold to that point of view right now?

JMR: Well, when they say that they don't consider it a southern community, it is true to the extent that it is not typical of the South, but it is not typical of the South because of what we were able to do in it that kept it from being typical of the South. As I told you before, not all of what we have done, of what the business people did, was motivated by the noblest idealism. Some of it was very practical. Most of it was. But the fact is that when I came to Atlanta twenty years ago, Atlanta and Birmingham were competing cities. They are no longer in the same class. Atlanta is different because Atlanta did meet this problem, face this problem, and to this extent it's not a southern city. Now it is also not a southern city because having faced this problem it attracted industry and business and people moved in. It sort of mushroomed you see, and it's true that Atlanta is an oasis in the South, and it's not a typical southern city.

PAK: What . . . do you think about the Freedom Riders? Are you in favor or against?

JMR: It depends upon when. There was a time when they were very important. There was a time when it was necessary to dramatize the Negro situation, and this was a way of doing it. Same thing with the sit-ins. At the moment I have a feeling that the Negro civil rights movement ought to concentrate on less dramatic but much more necessary and significant aspects of civil rights.

PAK: Were you in favor of them in '61 and '62?

JMR: Oh yes, I was.

6
Nathaniel Share

New Orleans, Louisiana, and Its Jewish Community

When Rabbi Jack Bemporad delivered a eulogy for his friend Rabbi Nathaniel Share, Bemporad referred to Nat as "one of those *Lamed Vuvniks* . . . those 36 men who were righteous and yet would be the last ones to claim that to be so, who are too humble and modest to claim anything for themselves. They are the righteous who redeem the world. Nathaniel Share was one of them." In Jewish tradition to be called a *Lamed Vuvnik* is the highest praise possible. As evident in the following transcript, Share had a passion for justice but also a sense of sorrow, because circumstances made it difficult for him to do more to help the cause of the downtrodden.

Nathaniel Share, the first of three children, was born on May 12, 1908, to Dora Levey Share and Moses Share. His parents were proprietors of a dress shop in Montreal, where he spent the first nine years of his life. In 1917 the Shares relocated to Columbus, Nebraska, where Dora and Moses opened a women's apparel establishment, The Style Shop, and Nathaniel completed public school. At age sixteen he enrolled simultaneously at the Hebrew Union College (HUC) and the University of Cincinnati (UC). Like many of his fellow students, Share attended secular classes in the mornings and Jewish classes during the afternoons. He earned Phi Beta Kappa honors at UC in his junior year while on his way to becoming, at twenty-three years old, one of the youngest people ever to be ordained at HUC. His first rabbinic position was at a small synagogue in Bluefield, West Virginia, but the congregation's inability to pay even his modest salary caused him to relocate to Syracuse, New York, where his parents had moved. He obtained a part-time position as an assistant to Rabbi Benjamin Friedman at the Temple Society of Concord, in Syracuse, New York, a stopgap measure until he found a full-time pulpit. New Orleans's Gates of Prayer welcomed him to its pulpit in 1934, only two years after ordination. Thirteen months after he moved to New Orleans, he married Isabelle Burr, his first cousin, with whom he had two children.

Founded as a traditional congregation in 1850 by Jews from Alsace and Lorraine, Gates of Prayer is the oldest continuously functioning congregation in New Orleans. It gradually adopted Reform practices during the last decades of

7. Rabbi Nathaniel Share, date unknown.
(Congregation Gates of Prayer, Metairie,
Louisiana). Used by permission of Rabbi Robert
Loewy. Photographer: Fred Kahn; photograph
used by permission of Catherine Kahn.

the nineteenth century but did not formally identify as a Reform temple until the hiring of Moise Bergman, a Hebrew Union College graduate, in 1904. Movement of the Jewish population into the suburbs and competition with two other Reform congregations lead the temple to relocate to Metairie in 1974. Share partook in the groundbreaking for the new building but died three months later.

Share had little reason to believe that New Orleans would remain his rabbinic home for his entire career. Rather than his preaching or charisma, Share's lengthy tenure resulted from his sincere interest in people, his ability to make each person feel important, and his pastoral presence. These traits, plus his humility and love of teaching, endeared him to many of his congregants, as evidenced by the grand retirement dinner with which they honored him at the end of his fourth decade of service.

Although he was a successful rabbi, Share might have been happier in another career. According to Jonathan, his son, Share wanted to devote his life to scholarship and teaching. "This was his true love, but under the influence of a strong mother who so dearly wanted a rabbi as a son, my dad complied and followed her wishes." While performing his rabbinic functions, Share earned a PhD in social work and marital counseling at Tulane University, where he also taught in the religious studies department. In addition, he played an active role in community affairs including a stint as the founding president of the Louisiana Association for Retarded Children. Share died on July 17, 1974, only a few months after his retirement. His congregants, ministerial colleagues, and the community at large experienced a great sense of loss.[1]

Editor's Introduction to the Interview

This book includes interviews with Nathaniel Share and Julian Feibelman, both rabbis who served congregations in New Orleans. Why two interviews for New Orleans and one for the other locations? New Orleans was one of the largest Jewish enclaves in the South and therefore had enough Jewish residents before and shortly after the Civil War to support several congregations, including more than one that either were started as or later became Reform. Only a few other locations in the region (including border cities such as Baltimore) underwent similar organizational development. In other places where only one Reform congregation existed during the nineteenth or early twentieth centuries, those cities tended to continue to support only one Reform congregation during the civil rights era even when the population could have supported additional temples. Atlanta's Temple, for example, had one thousand member families in 1957 and 1,200 a decade later. This was more than enough people to support multiple Reform congregations, but a single, permanent offshoot did not begin until 1968, with the founding of Temple Sinai. Typically, scions of old-time families remained with and newcomers joined the single temple with a dominant, long-tenured rabbi who served as the ambassador to the gentiles and surrogate Jew.

Logically, the presence of more than one Reform rabbi should have had an effect on their civil rights efforts. Feibelman and Share could work together and thereby avoid the isolation felt by the other rabbis. Theirs should not have been one voice or one leadership role. Their situation allowed them to divide responsibility and potentially lessen threat, yet that is not what occurred. As the Share and Feibelman interviews demonstrate, their positions and activities differed dramatically.

Synagogue membership throughout the South achieved a far higher percentage than that found in many northern cities, although the number was comparable with locations in which Jews comprised a small fragment of the total population. All of the rabbis served a tiny minority but, due to high affiliation rates, they also potentially reached a substantial portion of their group and spoke as the voice of the Jewish community.

Share indicates that approximately 20 percent of his congregation was of old-stock New Orleans lineage, but when he first arrived in 1934, this group constituted a far higher percentage. Share's statement reflects the major demographic shifts in most of the communities these rabbis served during and after World War II. The war brought soldiers from other parts of the country to the South. Some married southern women and/or located after the war where they saw economic opportunity. The process continued with the economic expansion fostered by tourism, the growth of educational and medical institutions, and other opportunities. Those with long ties to the South were more likely to acquiesce to Jim Crow and be more fearful of standing out against regional racial mores. Jews from elsewhere who did not have the same ties to the place and the place's ways provided something of a shield to the rabbis. Although some of the rabbis observed that the northerners could be as or more racist than their southern-born congregants, these newcomers were more likely to share their rabbi's views and support the independence of the pulpit.

Nonetheless, the picture is complex. Many scions of old-time families entered progressive ranks. In fact, Share indicates that none of the members of his synagogue could be classified as overt segregationists. Because they traced their roots in the city through generations and Jews had contributed to the economic, civic, cultural, and philanthropic life of the city, it made it difficult to classify Jews as outsiders. Their reputation and worth fortified the rabbis' status and their acceptance.

The rabbis willingly shared credit with the small group of Protestant ministers—often Episcopalians—and the far greater number of Catholic clergy who worked with them on behalf of civil rights. New Orleans boasted a large Catholic presence, and Catholics, like Jews, often experienced large amounts of religious prejudice in American history. In the interview, Share indicates specific steps the Catholic hierarchy took to appoint a black minister in a rural parish, install a black bishop in the area, and blunt any criticism with the threat and even implementation of excommunication. Synagogues and most Protestant churches followed congregational polity in that the members enjoyed the power to hire and fire their clergy. Thus many Protestant ministers in the region who spoke against segregation lost their pulpits. That far more rabbis did not meet the same fate reflected the different opinions of their congregants, and the different status the rabbis enjoyed. The hierarchical structure of the Catholic Church protected its clergy and facilitated desegregation from the top down. Within the Methodist Church, bishops also controlled local ministerial positions. However, the majority of Protestant clergy, including Methodists, either remained silent or openly supported the status quo. Their opinions both led and reflected those of their membership. Protestants held the overwhelming majority throughout the South. Had their clergy spoken and acted with the same vision as Jewish and Catholic clergy, desegregation in the South and the nation may have followed a far less confrontational and violent path.

In a manner that sets him apart from other interviewees, Share challenges the notion that rabbis exerted any influence on the civil rights movement. To him, seemingly nothing that they did or even could have done mattered. As far as he was concerned, the Jewish community was simply too weak and uninfluential to make a meaningful difference in the struggle for civil rights.

The actions of the interviewees ran the gamut from overt activism to acceptance of, or at least acquiescence to, the status quo. Share made his position in favor of black rights clear. Yet because of personal and family issues and what he perceived as total lack of support on the local and national level, he limited his actions even to the point of relinquishing his board membership on the Council on Human Relations and backing down on promoting civil rights in a sermon when one of his congregants complained. In his interview he neglects to record an incident that occurred in 1956 when bigots vandalized the Gates of Prayer cemetery, and the temple's board asked Share to limit his civil rights activism.[2]

Was Share's analysis of the ineffectiveness of Jewish activism correct, or might it have been a self-serving justification for what he perceived as his own inaction? Doubtless, as he indicates, African American protests, federal court actions, and laws passed by Congress acted as the determining factors in the ultimate success of the civil rights movement. Nonetheless, statements and actions by rabbis and other white clergy often did impact peaceful integration on the local level. Would integration have occurred without their efforts? Certainly, but the process likely would have been more conflict-ridden.

Perhaps the most boring of the interviews, Share often meanders in his answers and appears oblivious to the actions of other rabbis with the exception of Perry Nussbaum—and even with Nussbaum, he demonstrated only vague awareness. Ironically, he is one of the few rabbis who expressed support for civil rights marches and demonstrations. He also supported the controversial choice of Martin Luther King Jr. as speaker at the 1963 Union of American Hebrew Congregations (UAHC) convention. Yet, in a city of the almost possible and the example and presence of Julian Feibelman notwithstanding, like Eugene Blachschleger of Montgomery mentioned by other interviewees, Share basically chose a path of inaction. This seemingly meaningless interview may be highly representative of a significant, albeit undeterminable, portion of the clergy in the South.

—Mark K. Bauman

Nathaniel Share Interview

June 22, 1966

P. Allen Krause: What date would you consider to be the starting date of an intense civil rights activity in the South, and if this applies, in your area of the South?

Nathaniel Share: [*Thoughtfully*] I don't know how to answer that. I can't say.

PAK: Not a specific year possibly, is there a certain period?

NS: The schools' decision, of course, marks the beginning. I don't know about . . . and more than that . . .

PAK: Has there been an appreciable difference in your own city?

NS: Oh, sure, sure, sure—of course, but it's been by slow steps. Actually, in a way, the turning point came—I forget what year it was—when there were all these disturbances about the desegregation of the public schools. And the two schools that were closed, there was a demonstration, even rioting along the route—you must know something about that. That was really in a way the turning point in the city, because I think it frightened the business people and the important people, and they saw that something had to be done, and since that time everything has been handled in a much more orderly way. It's been slow, but we have had no real disturbances since then. That was the high point, or the low point for our city.

PAK: Was the school issue the central issue in your city?

NS: Well, it was a focus, an important focus, the major focus. Now, we have had, previous to that, at least two other kinds of desegregation. One had come so imperceptibly that many of us were not even aware it was happening and that was the desegregation of the public libraries. I can't even tell you when it took place but all of a sudden. . . . The second one was the desegregation of the public conveyances. This came after 1954, and this was done with a minimum of publicity. [It was about] the separation [on the street cars] . . . so on the very first night when the screens, that is what we called them at the time, they weren't screens, just little markers that said, "This Area for Colored," when that was taken out, some rowdies started to demonstrate on the street cars, and the police picked them up right away and rushed them off and nothing more happened after that. You see this was done quietly. The only thing was when the schools were desegregated, there were demonstrations by parents—and the mayor, in my opinion, showed real weakness in this case. He was a good man otherwise—that was Morrison, he was ultimately killed—he didn't act, he let it get out of hand.[3] The most the police did were to try to keep the street open, to try to keep the crowds, try to keep the people across the street from the school, that kind of thing. Instead of actually stopping, squashing this. So, this thing went on, until a couple years, the schools, these particular schools were closed, except that the few Negro children came and so on. After that, I can't think of anything since then that has really been of major importance. Rather, the other things have gone slowly, for example, lunch counters were desegregated, quietly; many of the stores downtown now employ some colored help. And this wasn't advertised—just quietly. The public service—

that is the transit company—employs Negroes now driving buses and the like. So, these things are coming slowly.

PAK: What's the reaction on the part of the non-Jewish white population to these changes that are taking place?

NS: Well, of course, there's no one reaction, as you know. Obviously, there's an acceptance—if there weren't, we'd have riots, demonstrations. I think, among the problems—this is strictly subjective—I would guess that a great majority of the people object, deplore, resent it, but they recognize it has to be. And, accepting it, they find that it's something that you can accept. What difference does it make if the guy you hand your dime to when you get on the bus is colored or white, what difference does it make?

PAK: So, there hasn't been a hard-core response?

NS: There is a hard core of protest, although, I think the Citizens' Council groups are diminishing in their influence. I think they're weakening. There have been very little hard-core protests left.

PAK: In New Orleans?

NS: In New Orleans, yes, but of course New Orleans is not the South; it's a different kind of city.

PAK: How old is your congregation?

NS: My congregation is 1850.

PAK: 1850—is the Jewish community there then pre-Civil War?

NS: Oh, yes. The Jewish community starts from 1828. The first congregation, as a matter of fact, goes back to still the Spanish period, when Judah Touro came down in 1803. By 1828 there were enough Jews to establish a small congregation. About that time they also established a cemetery. By 1850, there were several congregations, including mine.

PAK: You have a large congregation, do you not?

NS: About four hundred and sixty families.

PAK: What percentage of these people do you think, approximately, have been in the South more than, let's say, two generations?

NS: Well, when I first came here thirty years ago, a large percent, I would say. Now, I don't know, any kind of a figure I give you is simply a wild guess. Let me say, I'll say maybe 20 percent, one-fifth have their roots going way back.

PAK: You mean that, more than half of your congregation is made up of recent immigrants to the South?

NS: [*pause*] No, when I think of the children. . . . [*long pause*] Allen, I'm at a loss for what to say.

PAK: How much a part of the non-Jewish community is the Jewish community in New Orleans? How much do they share, in quotation marks, "the southern viewpoint," on, for example, the civil rights problem?

NS: To what extent does the Jewish community share that viewpoint? I think, my feeling is, they don't share it in the same way. They don't have the same feeling. I think there is a certain amount of, shall I say, social prejudice—"we wouldn't want to associate with the Negro"—in fact, you don't even think of it. It's not an area of the things you might do. But, they are not disposed to do anything to depress the Negro. They wouldn't take a stand against him. Partly, I think out of, you know, Jewish feelings, feelings for justice, and decency, and sympathy with the plight of the Negro. But, on the other hand, they're not going to stick their necks out for him.

PAK: How numerous are the real segregationists in your congregation?

NS: Oh, I have none.

PAK: You have none.

NS: Real segregationist—anybody who would come out publicly as a segregationist?

PAK: Right.

NS: I have none. I have a lot of people in my congregation who say we ought not get involved in this, we don't want to get mixed up in this. That's the feeling.

PAK: What is the economic level of the members of your congregation? What is their source of income?

NS: They are all middle, or upper–middle class people. Business, professional, we have some engineers with the space program down at NASA. They also have a few who are clerks, salesladies, salespersons, and so on, but mostly self-employed or professional people.

PAK: How susceptible would you say these people are to economic pressure put on by the non-Jewish community?

NS: They're afraid of it, especially those in the retail business are afraid of it. I don't know, certainly the professional people would not be too susceptible, because a doctor would hardly lose his practice because of that. But, they are afraid of it.

PAK: Do you think that is the major influence in why they do not speak out?

NS: No, no, no, no, no, I think this way, it's timidity, the old feeling of the Jew being exposed to the anti-Semites; "don't make yourself conspicuous," "don't speak up," "don't get involved," that's what they would say. Don't get involved. Why do we have to say anything? I think, at heart, I think most of my people, most of the Jews in New Orleans are at heart sympathetic to the Negro, but they don't want to get involved, and they don't want him to get too close to them either.

PAK: What percentage of the Jews in New Orleans . . . are affiliated with a congregation?

NS: Oh, a high percentage, the majority of Jews in New Orleans are affiliated.

PAK: Would you say over 75 percent?

NS: Yes.

PAK: Are affiliated in New Orleans.

NS: Yes. I think as conscious, as conscious identified Jews, we have some who have drifted away but most, the majority, are affiliated.

PAK: How many rabbis are there in your community now?

NS: There are now, one, two, three, six rabbis, and one at Hillel—if you want to count him, he's also a rabbi—and another is coming soon, and another congregation is trying to get one.

PAK: When the civil rights push began, did the ministers of the community take any active role in this? What was their response to it? Do the ministers have a liberal approach toward this whole affair or what?

NS: First of all, the ministers were almost completely conspicuous by their nonparticipation. I mean particularly the Protestants. The Catholic Church, which is, stronger, they're the largest; I think they have, I forget what percentage but it's a large percent of the population. The Catholic Church took a forthright stand. Some time ago, they desegregated the churches.

PAK: They have a Negro bishop now?

NS: Bishop, yes. But, that's, that's today, that's easy. But, some years back, a few years back, for example, a bishop, archbishop, appointed a Negro to serve a small church in a rural area and the people protested, and I think the bishop threatened to excommunicate them if they didn't subject, submit to the ministrations of this priest. There were other Catholics who were active in the segregationist White Citizens' Council, that kind of business, that protested. One of them was a very prominent man. He was a member of the school board, a lawyer, and a prominent man. And he was told that he would be excommunicated if he didn't shut up. I think he appealed to Rome, protested to Rome, and Rome sent back the answer to listen to the bishop. There were three and one of them was this Leander Perez, have you heard of him?[4]

PAK: Yes.

NS: He's from Plaquemines Parish. He's a *mamzer* [a Hebrew legal term, used here also with the derogatory behavioral connotation of "bastard"], a real *mamzer*. He and two others were excommunicated by the church, Leander Perez and two others; and they're still under excommunication. So, the church took a strong position, but it was more within the limits of the church's authority; they didn't go out into the community to crusade. The Protestants did almost nothing, with certain exceptions. First of all, we had a large number of Baptists and Methodists. And, they're not social crusaders to start with, and they had a lot of mixed feelings and so on. They did nothing. Now there was a small group organized, I forget who promoted it, but it was a voluntary group, white and Negro clergy, which met over a period of maybe a year, from time to time, to talk about these things, and to try to see what we could do. Once we even drew up together a statement, which was published in the press.

PAK: When did this group form?

NS: This was in the earlier years. I don't remember the date but it goes back, oh I guess before the trouble over the schools, between 1954 and within a few years after that. Other than that, there was an Episcopal priest, you see the Episcopalians have a lot of authority, a lot of influence, their priests are certainly much more free than the priests of the Catholic Church, I mean more autonomous. And, this man was active and influential in the group and there were some Negro clergy, but other than this Episcopal priest and the several rabbis who were in the group—and it was a very amorphous group, there was no hard and fast membership, but we just got together—except for the few of us, there was nobody who really amounted to anything in the community, you know, a minister of a small church and that kind of thing. This thing kind of petered out. I don't know what happened, but all of a sudden, after a while no one called a meeting and nothing more was done.

PAK: You mentioned that there were six rabbis in the community, what response did the rabbis have to all of this? This is Orthodox, Reform, and Conservative, right?

NS: Yes, yes, yes. Well, there was no Conservative rabbi, I think at the time, because their congregation is relatively young, maybe six, eight years, something like that.[5] In the early years, now this may have been even before '54, Julian Feibelman, represented, led a group of people that called on the school board, with a petition; it had to do with race in the schools. I don't remember what it was about now, whether it was to, I don't know if it was about desegregation, maybe it was; I don't really know. It had to do with some aspect of that; [he] presented the petition to the school board. He was the spokesman for the group. They were a group of socially important people, not economically important I think, but liberal people and not left wing either, radical left wing. This created, I think he got a lot of pressure from within his congregation. I think there was something else, I don't remember, he can tell you, something else that he did that again, was liberal, it was progressive, but again, he got a lot of pressure. There was nobody in the congregation to back him up, I believe. And, he came to, I assume he came to . . . anyhow, this is what he did. Leo Bergman tried to organize a council or reorganize a Council on Human Relations and nothing came of it. As far as I know, nothing else was done by the rabbis. We were in a position where we had absolutely no constituency; even the people who agreed with the way we felt, I believe, were not prepared to come out and say so. There were a few, there were a few, I know in my congregation, several, who would back me I think no matter what—but, two, three, four, a dozen, out of a thousand people in my congregation. That's the way we were—the whole community. There was no organized backing for the community, in the community.

PAK: Although your community might have agreed with your goals they would not have wanted you to take any part in . . .

NS: The feeling was, "Rabbi, why do we have to stick our necks out? Why get involved in this? It's not our problem."

PAK: What has been your personal response and your personal involvement in specific civil rights activities?

NS: Other than my being in that group of ministers that I referred to, I had no personal involvement. Actually, at this time, and I'm not saying this by way of excusing myself, but at this time I was going through some personal difficulties—I don't know if you know it but I've had a lot of trouble with my voice, psychic reasons—you can hear some strain in my voice now, and when you play this over you'll hear a lot more of it I think, and I was having difficulty with this and other difficulties in my family at the time, at this time. And I was not in a position to do anything which would jeopardize my standing, my position. If I lost my position, if I felt I had to leave that congregation, I couldn't get another job with the trouble I was having. And I knew damn well, the Union [of American Hebrew Congregations] would pat me on the back and say, "Gee, here's a guy you know . . . " and then I'd be out in the cold. I could not count on any backing; not only that, had I done anything, I'd have been a lone voice. If there were a group of liberal people in the community, which I could have joined and worked with, yes, but it meant sticking your neck out yourself. Actually there was no organized movement in the community at that time.

PAK: You said there were one or two attempts to try to start such a group?

NS: Well, I mean this ministers' group, which was really, actually, it wasn't an activist group, it was more which they got together and they talked. At one time, they did issue a statement. Twice, a couple of times, they issued statements which were published in the press, and the names of the participants were listed, alright. But, that's it. There wasn't anybody in the community at large. I'm talking about the business people, with the influence, and the others, the intelligent people in the community, who came out and said that we're not interested in the question of segregation; we want peace in our community, for example, that kind of thing. We want the law obeyed. We want order. It wasn't even that, until after all of this happened with the school, this went on for several weeks and there even was, at the beginning there was a demonstration, almost turned into a riot downtown. After all of that, finally a group of men, businessmen, Chamber of Commerce people, published a statement in the paper, took the whole page and listed their names and they said, "We want law and order." They got scared, they saw what was going to happen, and they saw what would happen to the city, how people would be scared away from traveling in our city.

PAK: Since that time have you been involved in these things or have any of the rabbis?

NS: No; you see now, it's in the hands of the courts. It's going through these things. The Supreme Court ordered, I think it was the Supreme Court, Federal Court ordered a year or two ago that they abolish the dual school system we had there and that is now, I mean this fall it's abolished. I think it's the Department of Health, Education, and Welfare has ordered that there must be Negro teachers in the white schools and so on, and we are going to have it. The opening of the lunch counters and the employment of Negroes in the stores and so on, these things have come about partly through pressure by the Negroes picketing the stores. Oh, there were no real demonstrations that way. And partly through, I guess through under-cover and background pressures. I think, I'm sure there has been a lot of quiet, undercover pressure. I think the leaders in the Negro community have been in touch with the business people, and they've gone about it in an effective way, I think, instead of making big demonstrations downtown. They pushed; there are Negro bus drivers now; they can come into the lunch counters; they're staying in the hotels.

PAK: Have you ever found it desirable to get involved with any of this pressure [on] yourself, on your own congregants, or on anybody in the community?

NS: I have not had, nothing has ever come up, nobody has ever asked me or appealed to me, no.

PAK: What about the pulpit? The actual pulpit—have you used that in any way?

NS: No, no. Very little, very little. It's been again—everybody knows where I stand and what my position is, I've made it clear, but I haven't preached on this, as such, necessarily.

PAK: Just for my purposes, what is the position that they know that you take?

NS: They know that I am a supporter of equal rights, civil rights, and so on. And the abolition of segregation and so on.

PAK: What's your response to something like the Freedom Rides? I don't think they ever got into your community that I know of; what's your response to that?[6]

NS: I've been sympathetic; I've been sympathetic with these demonstrations and so on, and the Selma[7] march, and now the march through Mississippi.[8] I felt, I felt that they're doing something. They're dramatizing it and so on.

PAK: **Do you think they actually have helped in the South to correct the problem?**

NS: Well, I don't know, you seem to qualify it in the South. They do help, because if, as a result of Selma, Congress passes a new civil rights law that provides for registering Negroes, it helps. And, I can't help but feel that Meredith's [actions], by marching in Mississippi and even his being shot, have done a lot to focus attention on Mississippi and to bring it to public attention so that the Mississippi people know the whole world is looking at them. So I think it's been helpful.

PAK: **What role do you think that national Jewish organizations have played in the civil rights movement in the South and in your area in particular?**

NS: I'm not aware of their having played any, and what they've done has not worked, done very much good. B'nai B'rith of course, B'nai B'rith, the ADL [Anti-Defamation League] has done a lot of quiet work. For example, the New Orleans man has done a lot of work in Mississippi, and has advised the Jews up there, things they could do and so on, because the anti-Semitic involvement with the Citizens' Council stunk. In the beginning, the statements—especially by B'nai B'rith—were resented strongly by the Jews in the South, especially in Mississippi and in Louisiana, too, they were, "what right do they have to mix in—they don't realize they're jeopardizing us" and in the earlier years, the people there were scared to death of economic boycott, by rights. So, there was a lot of resentment, I don't feel that anything actually, except possibly for the undercover work that ADL did, for example, and that the AJC [American Jewish Committee] was financing, I don't know. I don't feel that they helped very much at all. I'll tell you what helped; almost entirely it seems to me the federal power—the courts, and the congress—backed by the sentiment of the nation. These people saw, this is coming and you can't do anything about it, and you're going to have to give in.

PAK: **What about the resolutions of the CCAR [Central Conference of American Rabbis], do those have an effect? Some think they had either good or bad effect, or did they have no effect? Or let's take another situation: the UAHC in their convention in 1963 had Martin Luther King as their keynote speaker; what kind of response do you have to something like that?**

NS: Yes. The past president, the immediate past president of my congregation got exercised about that. And, he, I think he sent a telegram, or he got

the board, the board was meeting, got them to send a telegram protesting it. You know what happened; Eisendrath[9] met with the leaders from
the South . . . (I know one from Houston)[10] [who] led part of the attack
on Eisendrath. Then there was a big protest about it, and so one afternoon
was set aside, four o'clock in the afternoon we actually gathered with Eisendrath and talked about it. It was quite a number of people from the South
who were there. And, one of the rabbis who was from Houston, said it
was bad taste, it was a bad judgment, and so on and so on, and others protested, southern members, some of them from Mississippi, but, it was decided, Eisendrath went through with it, and I think quite a few of us there
were back of it. And of course, after we heard Martin Luther King, when
I came back and told people about having him there, I said, he made all of
you look foolish, he made us all look foolish protesting, because here was a
brilliant, brilliant address by a great man, no question about it. I got an insight into what the man was like that I couldn't have gotten any other way.
I know a few people you see, like this, like this crazy guy, ex-president of my
congregation, got excited and other people agreed, you see, so the board
sent a telegram. So what; it didn't mean anything.

PAK: **Would you say that the national Jewish organizations could play another type of a role, a better role in this at all?**

NS: I don't think so. I don't think that this has been a problem in which involvement of Jews, as Jews, has really had any effect. My feeling has been
that the power of the federal government, that's what's made the difference
and the general sentiment throughout the country, there it is.

PAK: **When this whole thing is analyzed, fifty years, a hundred years from
now, do you think that the role the rabbis played in your community
let's say, the group of rabbis, or in your state, or in the South, I mean,
one, two, three. Do you think they will be of any importance at all in the
overall picture?**

NS: I wouldn't even say nationally.

PAK: **You don't think so?**

NS: I don't think it is. Oh, rabbis have protested, they've spoken, they've identified themselves, but I don't think any rabbi has done anything that has
been in any way a turning point.

PAK: **Even in his own community?**

NS: That I can't say because I can't tell outside of New Orleans. In New Orleans, definitely. Now, I know, I know [Perry] Nussbaum, and I suppose
you're going to interview him, or you will, in Jackson, I'm sure he has done
some things because he was right on the hot spot there. I imagine there was
a position where his people had to back him up in certain respects, even if
they didn't want to, because they were on the griddle, too. In a way, he was

kind of their defender. Even if he did something it was to prevent something worse happening to them. In our community, we were not in that kind of a position. New Orleans is not South in that sense. And, our people felt detached, and they didn't want to get involved. They said, "Leave us be detached."

PAK: Have you ever in the course of your time that you've spent there in New Orleans, run into any opposition from any—from the board, from any official representatives of your congregation, or even from groups of individuals in the congregation—because of anything that you have done, or might have not done?

NS: Yeah, I had one such incident, well, two incidents that really amounted to more or less one thing. There was one man who was a judge, civil judge, and now he's on the Court of Appeals, which is a pretty high position, next to the Supreme Court. He is a timid man with a bullying—inside he's timid but he's a bully—and he's so scared about his chances of being elected and the good will of his fellow judges and so on that I was appointed to the board of this Council on Human Relations that I mentioned to you. And, he made an issue of it with our board. So as not to make any fuss about it, I wanted to withdraw from the board and just be a member. I could do as much as a member as on the board. All right, and so we left it at that. And the thing folded up—they didn't even meet after that, so nothing was done. Then later on, he made an issue again over my announcing a sermon which was about integration or segregation—what did we use to call it? Desegregation. This was right at the time where I felt like I was very vulnerable because of the other trouble I was having, and I had some support on the board, and if I had made a fight there could have been, I think I could have come through, but I didn't have the strength myself to fight with everything else I had to go through. And, I felt I would be fighting alone. So I didn't preach that sermon, and we just let the thing drop.

PAK: Do you know of any of the rabbis in the community other than—you said that Rabbi Feibelman had a situation similar to this earlier; did any of the other rabbis meet situations like this?

NS: Look, now please, in your [transcript] don't quote what I tell you about other rabbis.[11] I'll tell you this, any other rabbi, I'm sure, any of the rabbis did what they could, or what they felt they could, but none of us made himself the spearhead or got out on a limb and sawed himself off. The situation in New Orleans was that there was nobody who was going to stand with you, to back you up. You were going to be a leader without anybody to lead. None of us felt he could afford to put himself in that kind of a position. I think, I felt that way, and I assume the others felt that way.

PAK: Do you have any general comments or criticisms?

NS: No, except I might more or less reiterate what I said before, and that was that, I don't think that—and this isn't saying it to depreciate us in any way—I don't think any of our Jews, as Jews, had any even moderately decisive influence on events. I think the two things, I think the leadership in the Negro group, King and these people, the protests and these things. And, of course, the intervention of the courts and the congress, these have bought this about. If no Jew had opened his mouth, if no Jew had raised his voice, I don't think it would have changed, had any appreciable effect on what has happened. And I think if we had all hollered more, I don't think it would have hastened things, or made things any more effective.

7
William B. Silverman

Nashville, Tennessee, and Its Jewish Community

In 1717, the French began building fur trading posts along the banks of the Cumberland River in what later became western North Carolina. After glowing reports of the area's assets reached the eastern part of North Carolina, about sixty families from the British colony migrated in late 1779 and early 1780. They named their new fort Nashborough, after the North Carolina Revolutionary War hero, General Francis Nash. In 1784 North Carolina incorporated the settlement and renamed it the more English-sounding Nashville. Five years later North Carolina ceded its land west of the Allegheny Mountains to the federal government, and in 1796 Tennessee became the nation's sixteenth state.[1] In 1843 Nashville was named the state's permanent capital.

Prior to the Civil War, the Nashville & Chattanooga Railroad boosted the local economy, as did the increasing commercial use of the Cumberland River. The Cumberland intersects with the Ohio River, the largest tributary of the Mississippi River and an easy route to New Orleans and the Gulf of Mexico. By 1860 Nashville had emerged as a major shipping and distribution center for the South, with a growing number of affluent wholesale and retail merchants. The population expanded from 5,566 in 1830 to 16,988 by 1860.[2] The first public school opened in 1855.

The Union army targeted Nashville as a supply hub for the Confederacy. On February 23, 1862, General Ulysses S. Grant's troops marched into the city, making it the first Confederate state capital to fall. Union forces occupied the city for three years, maintaining control over its railroad and river access. Confederate forces tried to regain the city in December 1864 but the fifty thousand Union soldiers under General George Henry Thomas overwhelmed Confederate General John Bell Hood's 23,000 troops in this last major battle of the war.[3]

After Appomattox, commercial activity resumed, facilitated by the expansion of the Louisville & Nashville Railroad. In 1861 the company's only route took its trains between the two cities. After the war Memphis was added, and by 1881 L&N tracks extended to Pensacola and New Orleans in the South, and St. Louis and Cincinnati in the Midwest. Major industries developed in the city during the 1890s.[4]

Nashville enhanced its image as an educational center with the founding of four new institutions. Within months of the end of the Civil War, the northern American Missionary Association, supported by the United Church of Christ, established the Fisk Free Colored School. What became Fisk University grew into one of the premier African American colleges in the country. The northern Methodist Episcopal Church chartered the Central Tennessee College to educate freed slaves the following year. Nashville's Southern Methodist bishop Holland McTyeire persuaded his cousin by marriage, Commodore Cornelius Vanderbilt, to donate $1 million as an endowment for a new university. In the fall of 1875, Vanderbilt University began operating with approximately two hundred students. That same year, the five Meharry brothers, assisted by the Freedman's Aid Society of the northern branch of the Methodist Church, established the Meharry Medical College as an adjunct of Central Tennessee College. When the new century dawned, Nashville's thriving educational institutions earned it the title, "Athens of the South."[5]

Boasting almost eighty-one thousand residents in 1900, three decades later Nashville's population swelled to over 250,000. A Works Progress Administration (WPA) project opening in 1937, Nashville's first airport, Berry Field, sparked continued growth. In 1942 it became the base for the 4th Ferrying Command that transported American troops overseas. Consequently, the federal government quintupled its size. In 1946 the military returned the airfield to the city, which renamed it the Nashville International Airport.

In the post-war years, Nashville benefited from the new wave of technology, factory automation, and the growth of the recording industry. Building on the success of the Grand Old Opry that had opened a quarter century earlier, every major record company established its country music division in Nashville. The rise of the music industry resulted in increased tourism and convention business. By the time the civil rights movement began in earnest, Nashville was a thriving urban center of almost five hundred thousand people.[6]

When African Americans asserted themselves in the late 1950s, their history in the city, coupled with the presence and participation of prominent educational and other organizations, facilitated the transition to desegregation easier than in most southern metropolises. African Americans comprised approximately 20 percent of the city's early population. Although most of these were slaves, the freedmen among them hosted secret gatherings fostering a sense of strength generally not found in slave populations. In the 1830s, free black people including Alphonso Sumner and Daniel Wadkins organized clandestine schools for African American children and other supportive associations. During the Civil War many area slaves fought in Union ranks. At the war's end, most black congregations declared their independence from the white churches and, as previously noted, white northern missionaries helped establish institutions of higher learning for African Americans. In 1876 Fisk's Jubilee Hall became the first building in the United States constructed specifically for the higher education of African Americans. Fisk and Meharry Medical College benefitted from grants made by John D. Rockefeller's General Education Board and the Julius Rosenwald Fund. In 1895 twelve black physicians created the National Medical Association to protect African Americans in the medical profession and allied fields. Meharry's Dr. Robert F. Boyd served as founding president. The NMA grew into one of the major organizations for the promotion of black rights in the United States.[7]

In 1900 Booker T. Washington founded the National Negro Business League. Nashville's chapter, created in 1902, became one of the foremost in the country. The organization encouraged trade with black businesses in an effort to keep jobs and capital under black control. In 1904, a black Nashville entrepreneur founded the One Cent Savings Bank, the country's first African American–owned financial institution. By 1905 black citizens boycotted the city's newly segregated streetcars. Some black businesspeople supported the boycott by creating their own horse-drawn carriage line. Although the boycott ultimately failed, it demonstrated the resolve of African Americans not to be treated as second-class citizens. In 1911 George E. Haynes, head of Fisk University's social science department, presented the city government with a list of critical social and health service needs of the black community. Eight years later, a group of Nashville African Americans founded a branch of the National Association of the Advancement of Colored People (NAACP) in response to a wave of lynchings. That year the Nashville chapter marched on the governor's office, demanding protection from lynchers and the rights of black people as Tennessee citizens.[8]

By midcentury, then, many in Nashville's black community were already committed to equality. Within hours of the *Brown v. Board of Education of Topeka* decision, two African American representatives of the local NAACP chapter petitioned the board of education to immediately end segregation in the public schools. Z. Alexander Looby, the chief NAACP attorney in Tennessee, and his associate Avon N. Williams Jr. made the case and received an encouraging response from Mayor Ben West: "Our people are law-abiding citizens," he said. "We have no other thought except to conform to the law of the land." The mayor and school board requested time to analyze the intent of the Supreme Court order. Although West formed an integrated advisory Citizens Committee for Public Schools, months passed with little progress. The school board explained that it was waiting for further instructions from the courts. In September 1955, with no action on the horizon, Looby, Williams, and national NAACP attorney Thurgood Marshall filed suit on behalf of twenty-one African American children in *Kelley v. Board of Education*. In response, Federal District Court Judge William E. Miller gave the schools six months to draw up a plan in compliance with the Supreme Court's decisions. Subsequently, the school board presented a tentative plan that would begin desegregation in the first grade the following September.

At this point opposition began to solidify. The Ku Klux Klan and the newly formed White Citizens' Council (WCC) held well-publicized meetings in the city, and a group called the Tennessee Federation for Constitutional Government (TFCG) came to the fore. Its chairman, Donald Davidson, took refuge behind the veneer of "states' rights" and asserted that neither the school board nor the federal courts had legal authority to override Tennessee laws requiring segregation. The moderate Citizens Committee for Public Schools countered the TFCG but the school board requested and received an additional year to prepare for desegregation from the federal court. Meanwhile, the KKK, WCC, and TFCG had found a charismatic champion, Frederick John Kasper, "a tall, handsome, twenty-six-year-old firebrand whose drawl and dress (white shirt and tie, tan suit with matching Texas-style hat) concealed his evolving identity as a well-traveled professional agitator from New Jersey."[9] Kasper had previously stirred up trouble in Clinton and Oak Ridge, Tennessee, forcing Governor Frank Clement to send over six hundred National Guard troops to Clinton to take back the streets.

Nashville School Superintendent William Bass worked quietly with the school board to begin desegregation in the first grade in 1957, extended to all twelve grades by 1968. In an attempt to avoid violence, the plan that was delivered to Judge Miller in the spring of 1957 included a policy that allowed parents to transfer their children to other campuses. The NAACP attorneys were unhappy with the liberal transfer policy and the plan's lengthy implementation schedule. Nonetheless, Miller ordered the plan to be implemented in September 1957. When confronted by angry parents, the mayor informed them that his six-year-old son would enter the first grade at Ransom School, one of fifteen schools scheduled for integration that fall. As the school year approached, tensions rose, and city leaders feared violent confrontation. Although an estimated fourteen hundred black children were expected to enter first grade, only 126 were deemed to live closer to a white school than to a black one, and, of that number, only nineteen families had the courage to bring their children to a white school when school began on September 9.

The specter of school desegregation in the state's capital drew Kasper like a moth to a flame. He goaded his followers: "Blood will run in the streets of Nashville if nigra children go to school with whites! . . . Tomorrow is the day. Every blow that you strike will be a blow for freedom." Police Chief Douglas Hosse made it clear that disorderly conduct would not be tolerated anywhere near the schools and stressed that "all parents can be assured of their children's safety." He assigned nearly two-thirds of the city's police force to work twelve-hour shifts near the desegregating schools. Although scattered instances of violence occurred, none of the children or their parents was harmed. That night, however, a dynamite explosion destroyed a wing of Hattie Cotton Elementary School, where one black child had enrolled.

Nashville's residents cherished the city's image as the "Athens of the South," and the horror of that night broke the back of the pro-segregation movement. No further demonstrations ensued as desegregation proceeded. Nashville was one of the South's first cities to successfully implement a comprehensive school desegregation plan, and the only one to have done so with a strategy of building from the bottom up one grade at a time.[10]

A few months after the plan was implemented, Reverend Kelly Miller Smith Sr. of the First Baptist Church and divinity student C. T. Vivian formed the Nashville Christian Leadership Conference (NCLC), a branch of King's Southern Christian Leadership Conference (SCLC). James M. Lawson Jr., an African American minister and theology student at Vanderbilt University, recruited students from the four local black colleges and trained them in the SCLC's methods of passive resistance, thereby initiating the Nashville Student Movement. On February 12, 1960, about forty students staged a sit-in at Woolworth's. Although demonstrators were harassed and arrested, their numbers increased daily, and the sit-ins spread to Kress, McClellan, Grants, Walgreens, the Greyhound and Trailways bus depots, and other local department stores. Alexander Looby defended in court many of those arrested, and his home was bombed in retaliation on April 19, which in turn led to a protest march of thousands through Nashville to the steps of city hall. Once again, concerned with the city's image, Mayor West appointed a biracial committee. On May 10, the downtown lunch counters integrated.[11]

Along with the relatively moderate approach of the city's white leadership, the Nashville Student Movement succeeded because of support of black community leaders. Unlike Birmingham, Jackson, and similar locations, black clergy in Nashville stood solidly behind student activism. They also initiated and participated in ancillary civil rights actions. In March 1960, Kelly Miller Smith Sr. joined with Fisk University Professor Vivian Henderson in launching a "No Fashions for Easter" boycott of downtown businesses in opposition to the stores' discriminatory practices. Smith and other pastors also opened their churches to the student activists. When Martin Luther King Jr. visited Nashville, he told his Fisk University audience, "I came to Nashville not to bring inspiration but to gain inspiration from the great movement that has taken place in this community." King spoke the truth: the city was indeed the site of the most successful and sustained student-directed, sit-in campaigns of the civil rights movement. It also provided the training ground for individuals who later founded the Student Nonviolent Coordinating Committee (SNCC) and became key leaders in the civil rights movement: John Lewis, Diane Nash, C. T. Vivian, Marion Barry, and James Bevel.[12]

During the first fifty years of Nashville's existence, the only Jews in the city were transient peddlers, European immigrants eking out a living on the frontier. During the 1840s some including the Lande brothers (Aaron and Nathan) and the Powers brothers (Louis, Mike, and Sam) established small businesses. On the eve of the Civil War, the city's Jewish population numbered about 375, most of who owned clothing and dry goods stores. One of the most successful, Adolph Levy's men's store, established in 1855, continued into the twenty-first century. During the 1860s, however, Jacob Bloomstein could claim to be the city's most prominent Jewish merchant. He and his brother Louis, who had arrived from Poland in the early 1850s, began as cigar makers. They later opened grocery and dry goods stores that Jacob parlayed into extensive real estate holdings. In 1863 he was charged with surreptitiously feeding and clothing Confederate military prisoners working in a nearby quarry and imprisoned by the Union army. Three of his sons earned pharmacy degrees and opened the Bloomstein Pharmacy, a mainstay until 1920.[13]

David Weil, a Jewish immigrant from France who started out as a peddler in New Jersey, arrived in Nashville in 1863 and opened a wholesale business, supplying the many peddlers who passed through the city. By the late 1870s D. Weil & Company had grown into the largest and most lucrative wholesale house in the state capital. With the city still occupied by Union forces, new arrival Morris Loveman started a wholesale dry goods business, while one of his sons, David, took advantage of the popularity of the hoop skirt to build a dress manufacturing company. David later opened a dry goods store, D. Loveman's, which evolved into one of Nashville's most successful department stores. Jewish immigrants George and Louis Rosenheim opened a dry goods store in the late 1860s that grew into the largest retail store in Nashville, occupying an entire five-story building.[14]

Four of the city's Jewish merchants chose a less-traveled path. Nathan Cline and Louis Bernheim founded the country's first scrap iron business. Adolph Loveman, Morris's other son, and Simon Lieberman partnered with non-Jew Andrew O'Brien to open the Lieberman, Loveman & O'Brien Lumber Company.[15] Julius and Max Sax established the Nashville Savings Bank in 1863.[16] By 1870, sixty-three Nashville Jews owned retail businesses; eleven were clothiers; five ran wholesale companies; two served as bankers; two worked as shoemakers; twenty-nine were clerks; twenty remained peddlers; one taught school; and one, Prussian-born Gustavus Schiff, was a physician. Two rabbis and one Hebrew teacher rounded out the business directory list.[17]

Nashville's first rabbi, Alexander Iser, arrived in 1852 to serve congregation Mogen David (the Shield of David), that began a few years earlier as a minyan in the home of Isaac Garritson. Iser left Mogen David seven years later along with some discontented congregants to form Congregation Ohava Emes (Lovers of Truth). Jonah Heilbon next became Mogen David's spiritual leader. During the 1860s the city claimed slightly more than one hundred Jewish households. In 1864 Reform advocate Morris Fishel organized a third synagogue, B'nai Yeshurun (Children of Righteousness), and brought David Burgheim from Breslau as its first rabbi. Three years later, Ohava Emes merged back with Mogen David, under the name Ohavai Sholom (Lovers of Peace), and hired Burgheim as its rabbi. B'nai Yeshurun then hired Rabbi Labshiner, whose tenure, like most Nashville men who filled Jewish pulpits in the 1860s and '70s, lasted less than two years. On March 13, 1869, Labshiner's successor Judah Wechsler had good reason to say in his first sermon: "Nashville has the reputation among Jews all over the country as a hard place to labor for the cause of Judaism."

Meanwhile, Ohavai Sholom drifted away from Orthodoxy. Rabbi Isadore Kalisch came to the congregation in 1872 and accelerated the process. After the failure of B'nai Yeshurun, the congregation adopted a Reform prayer book in 1876, thereby completing the transition to Reform. In reaction, a small group that year created Adath Israel (Congregation of Israel) as a traditional synagogue. In 1897 Julius Loeb became its first rabbi. Adath Israel identified with the Conservative movement seven years later, which paved the way for the creation of Orthodox Sherith Israel (Remnant of Israel) in 1905.

While the 1860s and '70s were marked by high rabbinic turnover, the 1880s ushered in a period of pulpit stability. In 1876 Ohavai Sholom moved into an impressive new edifice on Vine Street and became known as the Vine Street Synagogue. Twelve years later the congregation hired Isidore Lewinthal, who had received his ordination from a moderate Reform advocate, Reverend James Gutheim of New Orleans. During his thirty-four-year tenure, Lewinthal played an active role in the religious and secular communities. Four years after Lewinthal retired, the members of the synagogue welcomed Julius Mark, who led the congregation from 1926 until he left to assume the prestigious pulpit of Temple Emanu-El in Manhattan in 1948. In 1950 Rabbi William Silverman began decades of service. Randall Falk succeeded him and led the congregation for the following twenty-six years.[18] Within the traditional community, Herman Saltzman served Sherith Israel for over thirty years, Abraham Chill for ten, and Zalman Posner for over five decades until his retirement in 2002. Only Adath Israel, which became known as the West End Synagogue, continued employing peripatetic rabbis, hiring nineteen from 1890 to the late 1960s.

The Jewish community of Nashville doubled in size during the last two decades of the nineteenth century, reaching an estimated 1,950. Although Jewish immigrants from Eastern Europe contributed greatly to the increase, over 60 percent were native born.[19] Wealth and influence also continued to increase. The Nashville Business Directory for 1901 lists 142 Jewish-owned retail establishments, two thirds of which were either dry goods or clothing stores. Thirty-three Jews worked as tailors, thirty-three as bookkeepers, eleven as shoemakers, six as insurance agents, nine as teachers, and four as lawyers. Five physicians, one dentist, and three pharmacists represented the medical profession. Twenty craftsmen, twenty-three salesmen, sixteen peddlers, and about 150 clerks and sales ladies joined the list.[20] One of the city's most successful businesses, Herman Brothers, Lindauer and Co., sold wholesale dry goods, boots, and shoes to the many drummers who used Nashville as their base. Jacob May, who began as one of these peddlers, won a state contract for prison labor. In 1908 he transformed this penitentiary-based enterprise into the May Hosiery Mill, which supplied socks to some of the finest department stores in the country.

Symbolic of their growing affluence, Jews joined political and civic organizations. Gustavus Schiff was the first Jewish member of the Nashville Medical Society and the Nashville Board of Education (1875–1877). He also served as an officer in the Masonic Germania Lodge and president of the German Relief Society. Dr. Samuel Bloomstein and attorney Nathan Cohn served on the board of education, while Simon Lieberman served as a school board member and its chair for several years. Benjamin Herman twice won election to the Nashville Board of Education and also served on the boards of the Masonic Widows and Orphans Home and the Nashville Chamber of Commerce. In 1926, Cohn High School was named for Corinne Cohn in recognition for her service on the school board. Ben Lindauer was on the Board of Parks, and served as president of the Nashville City Council in 1899. Louis Lebeck held office in the Retail Merchants Association while Jacob Levine, Joseph Wolf, and Adolph Loventhal served as Davidson County judges.[21] Lee J. Loventhal served on the city park commission for twenty-five years as well as on the boards of Vanderbilt and Fisk Universities. In 1925 he helped found the Community Chest, serving as its first president. During World War I he helped raise $2 million for the war effort.[22] Nashville Jews also made significant philanthropic contributions. Largely as a result of Jacob May's efforts, about two hundred and thirty Jewish families escaped the Holocaust. During World War II, Joe Werthan established the Joe Werthan Service Center, a 250-bed facility for servicemen in the area. Irwin Eskind, clinical professor of medicine at Vanderbilt University Medical School, endowed a biomedical library and a research chair in human development.

The 1960 United States census lists over 167,000 residents in greater Nashville. Although Jews comprised a miniscule .02 percent of the total, they played a visible role in the civil rights drama that unfolded in the city.[23] Dan May, Jacob May's son, played an important role in shaping a school desegregation plan for the city as chair of the board of education. Consequently, he received death threats and required police protection. On March 16, 1958, hundreds of anti-Semitic leaflets were distributed in the city. That same night a bomb went off at the entrance of the new Jewish Community Center. The response, similar to what occurred in Atlanta seven months hence, was the vocal support of city and state officials, the press, and the religious community. Some saw the blast as a response to the outspoken civil rights advocacy of William Silverman. If so, it proved totally ineffective. Harrison Salisbury's 1960 article on Nashville names only two clergy as leaders in the city's civil rights struggle: the Reverend Kelly Miller Smith and Rabbi William Silverman.[24] When Silverman left for Kansas City later that year, his successor, Randall Falk, also distinguished himself on the pulpit and the community with his vocal support of equal rights for all. In 1964, Falk led a human rights march with the pastor of a local Methodist Church. The following year he helped found the Nashville Human Relations Commission. Although over 60 percent of the heads of Jewish families were still business owners or managers and thus highly vulnerable to retaliation, they remained supportive of their rabbis; a reflection of the fact that Nashville had largely chosen the moderate path.[25]

William B. Silverman

William B. Silverman was born on June 4, 1913, in Altoona, Pennsylvania, the birthplace of his parents Simon and Rae (Friedland) Silverman. He graduated from Western Reserve University in 1935 and six years later received ordination at Hebrew Union College. At the beginning of his senior year at HUC he won election as student body president. Also in 1940 he married Pearl Biales. Silverman first served Temple Beth El (The House of God) in Battle Creek, Michigan, from 1941 through the summer of 1943 while simultaneously acting as the civilian chaplain at Fort Custer.

Two themes appear prominently throughout Silverman's career: his interest in explaining Judaism to non-Jews and protecting the welfare of children at risk. Both formed an integral part of his ministry in Gastonia, North Carolina, where, beginning in 1943, he served as rabbi of Temple Emanuel ("God is with us") and organized an advisory committee for the Gastonia Juvenile Court. In 1946 he moved to Temple Israel in Duluth, Minnesota, where he was appointed to the Minnesota Governor's Advisory Council on Youth Conservation and chaired that body's Committee on Parents and the Family. In 1950 Silverman became rabbi of Nashville's Vine Street Temple, one of the oldest and most prominent Reform congregations in the South. There he became known as the "Pistol-Packing Rabbi," because he was forced to carry a gun for protection as a result of threats in response to his outspoken support of desegregation. When his departure was announced in 1960, the *Nashville (TN) Observer* commented editorially that the rabbi's "religious statesmanship and wisdom" and his "almost solitary" stand against bigotry and violence would fill "a goodly chapter" in the history of Tennessee's capital city. That same year, Northland College in Ashland, Wisconsin, awarded Silverman an honorary doctor of divinity degree in recognition of his promotion of Christian-Jewish understanding and his "great influence for good" in civic affairs. The rabbi left Nashville for Kansas City, where he served

8. Rabbi William B. Silverman, 1954 (Annette
Levy Rankin Jewish Community Archives, Jewish
Federation of Nashville and Middle Tennessee).
Used by permission of Executive Director Mark
S. Freedman.

Congregation B'nai Jehudah (Children of Judah) until retiring in 1977. Kansas
City was known for the corrupt Pendergast political machine that quickly became a focal point for the rabbi's prophetic activism. Silverman also served on
the Missouri Health and Welfare and Juvenile Delinquency commissions.

Silverman's many publications include *The High Cost of Jewish Living* (1948);
Judaism and Christianity (1949); *The Still Small Voice* (1953); *The Still Small
Voice Today* (1957); *Rabbinic Stories for Christian Ministers and Teachers* (1958);
God Help Me!: From Kindergarten Religion to the Radical Faith (1961); *Religion
for Skeptics: A Theology for the Questioning Mind* (1967); *The Jewish Concept of
Man* (1967); *Judaism and Christianity: What We Believe* (1968); *Basic Reform
Judaism* (1969); *Kivie Kaplan: A Legend in His Own Time* (editor, 1981); and
When Mourning Comes: A Book of Comfort for the Grieving (coauthored with
Kenneth Cinnamon, 1981). When Silverman died in 2001, he bequeathed both a
record of fighting for the good and a literary legacy that kept alive the prophetic
tradition, the driving force of his rabbinate.[26]

Editor's Introduction to the Interview

Most rabbis could expect little Jewish influence in many of the communities in which they function. In Nashville, however, a Jew chaired the school board and oversaw the preparation of the plan for court ordered desegregation. William Silverman was far from the lone wolf Perry Nussbaum perceived himself to be. In a contrasting scenario discussed in the chapter on James Wax, a Jewish mayor presided over Memphis but took a decidedly negative position in relation to black civil rights.

One might expect violence against Jews in Jackson, Mississippi, as experienced by Perry Nussbaum and his congregation, yet Jews also faced it in more moderate locations such as Nashville and Atlanta. As a consequence of his outspoken support for integration, Silverman actually endured more direct violence then Charles Mantinband in Hattiesburg. He was subjected to repeated threats against his life, and his is the only case among these rabbis of actually being assaulted for a presentation. Having this occur within a white Methodist church made it even more dramatic and unusual. Silverman's young children were threatened as well, causing him to obtain a firearm that he kept with him when he accompanied his children to and from school each day.

The bombing of the Jewish Community Center in Nashville preceded the temple bombing in Atlanta but the communities in both cities abhorred the attacks on Jewish institutions and their reactions further reinforced the positions of their Jewish citizens. The bombings galvanized people to join together in support of desegregation and civil rights. Nonetheless, as the "Pistol-Packing Rabbi" learned, no place in the South was really safe.

In many southern congregations one activist rabbi followed another. In the case of Ohabai Sholom, earlier rabbis prepared the congregation for William Silverman's arrival, and Randall Falk, who became better known in the annals of civil rights, followed Silverman. In such cases, the succeeding rabbi walked into a more hospitable and easier environment in which to function.

—Mark K. Bauman

William B. Silverman Interview

June 23, 1966

P. Allen Krause: Rabbi Silverman, when you were in Nashville—what were the years that you were there, may I ask?
William B. Silverman: 1950 to 1960.
PAK: During that time is there any year, or two- or three-year period, when there was an intensification in . . . civil rights activity?
WBS: And how. 1957–58.

PAK: '57, '58, what was it that caused that, do you think?

WBS: Well what actually precipitated it was, as you know, that in 1954 you had the decision of the Supreme Court about the integration of the public schools. Nothing much was done about it in Nashville until 1957. They were going to integrate the first grade and several Negro children were to go into the first grade. Now this was the signal for the extreme rightist groups, the Klan, the Citizens Council, to start propaganda that they were not going to permit these Negro children to enroll. I assume that there was some excitement triggered by a character named John Kasper. I don't suppose you have heard much about him lately, but he came to Nashville and organized. He stirred up the hoodlum elements in the community, and they had to select a goat—and I was it. I was the goat, and they had the dynamiting of the Hattie Cotton School, which upset the community a great deal. After this time when some of the children, I think they were three little Negro girls— very formidable enemies—were being taken to school, crowds would gather on the school premises to hoot, to jeer, and to shout obscene remarks. I remember standing there at the Hattie Cotton School when the crowd was jeering, and Bill Bass was then the superintendent of the schools. I remember him speaking to a burly looking man and [saying], "John, the crowd's getting out of control, won't you help us?" John said, "Sure Bill. We'll help you. We'll go into that school and pull out those nigger brats and kick out their guts. That's the way we'll help you." With the crowd cheering, shouting, and making a great hero out of the man. Shortly after that the school was dynamited. Then the Clinton high school was dynamited. I remember that was in March 1957, that I was getting ready to go to a meeting that evening. I don't remember the exact date; it's on record. My wife came downstairs; we lived in a two-story house. She was very pale, and I said, "What's the matter dear?" [She said,] "you had the oddest phone call. A man called and asked for you, and I said that you were on your way out of the house. He said, 'Well, this is Captain Gordon of the Confederate Underground. We have just dynamited the Jewish Community Center, and we will dynamite the Jewish temple. We are going to shoot down Federal Judge William Miller in cold blood. Next will come your nigger-loving husband,' and then clicked the phone." Well, I called the Jewish Community Center and a police sergeant answered and I said, "What happened?" He said, "The Jewish Community Center has just been bombed." I went down there immediately, and by this time threats were coming in. Many of them for us. We had police guarding the house. They had announced through placards they were going to shoot me down, and they were going to shoot down William Miller. Why William Miller? Because Judge Miller had refused to accept the legal persuasion of the White Citizens' Council to prohibit these Negro children going to school, and he ruled them out of order. He said, "These children must be permitted to go to school on the basis of the decision of the Supreme Court." I had preached a sermon shortly before in which I had urged the people to follow "law and order," as they termed it, and to follow the American way and what was to me the Jewish way.

What followed was very much of a nightmare. You read about these things, and they seem quite unreal. But that whole night people were harassing us by telephone, and the report had gone over the radio and on television about the threats to my life and to Judge Miller's life. Well, all the FBI men were over guarding Judge Miller, and they had the county sheriff, [and] the police, [and] the governor sent men over to our home. They were throwing—how they got past some of these police I don't know—but they were throwing dead rats on the lawn and dead pigeons with little notes that said, "You are going to cart this dead pigeon away and Rabbi Silverman will be a dead pigeon until they cart him away." Members of the congregation became apprehensive. I had been speaking about this as a problem and saying that we Jews ought to be involved. Well, some of the members of my congregation said this is not a problem for Jews. I was telling them that it is a problem for Jews. And some of them said that even if it is a problem let's stay out of it and not have any trouble, because we are living in the South. To me it was a matter of maintaining the integrity of what we preach and the principles of Judaism and social justice. It's so easy to say *tzedek, tzedek, tirdof* ["justice, justice you shall pursue"][27]—everybody accepted that, but when you speak out on behalf of justice and you're becoming too specific— I was called a *nigger-loving rabbi*. That was the term used and I accepted it. I said, "Well, would I choose to use those words? Yes, I am a nigger lover. My religion teaches me to love those of every faith, and it doesn't make any difference the color of their skin or what their face is. I have been taught to love mankind. So I do not regard that as an insult. I don't like the term *nigger*, but being a lover of mankind is not an insult."

There was constant harassment against me, and I don't want to sound like a martyr; I'm just trying to reiterate what really happened. Unfortunately there wasn't a minister in town that came to my defense. Later on one man did, John Rustin,[28] of the Belmont Methodist Church, and he was soon removed from his post. They will never tell you that was the reason; [they'd tell you that] there was some other reason that he was removed. But, I think basically that he was the first white minister to come out and support the stand that I had taken, which was: we have talked long enough; these unruly forces will take over our community. They have defied city ordinances. The police have ignored them. It's about time for us to take action. I was in a Methodist church and was beaten up by four or five;

I choose to exaggerate it and say maybe ten or twelve. Some of the Methodists came to my defense, and I was pretty bruised and bloodied at the time.

PAK: When was this?

WBS: I'd say this was April '57.

PAK: Were you making a speech?

WBS: Um hum, and they caught me on my way out. There were threats, notes to desist, to be quiet. I think what really frightened us most . . . there was that time I received a phone call saying that "you have one son and he goes to Hillsboro High School, he takes this bus home, he walks up this street and goes to 418 Allendale Drive. We have been following him. Keep him home, because if you don't, we are going to put out his eyes. Your other boy goes to Parmer School.[29] He takes this bus. He walks up this street to 418 Allendale Drive. Keep him home or we are going to cut off his arms. We are not going to kill them; we are going to mutilate them. To show people what happens to the kids of a nigger-loving rabbi." This was quite a problem. There was fear, yes. I had a choice of keeping the boys at home. I remember I was deputized as a deputy sheriff, carried a gun. I carried one for six months. I went on television with a .38 snub nose, and I showed it and said, "I couldn't kill a bird, but I'm going to take my boys to school. This gun will either be there near me or it will be in a holster, and I don't want anybody coming near me when I'm driving my boys to or from school, because I will shoot first and ask questions later." They kidded me and called me the "Pistol-Packing Rabbi." I carried that gun with me to weddings and funerals and wherever I went, but my boys never missed a day of school. Now it would have been disastrous to their morale if they had been kept at home.

This became a cause célèbre in the community, about a rabbi being compelled to carry a gun to protect his children. Many of the decent citizens came to my assistance, at least expressed their sympathy. I remember that first night though, sitting home alone with my family with the police outside. We had guards for six months. Well we did organize a group, a community relations group made up of whites and blacks to work on this problem. And, in time we were able to drive out Kasper; we were able to drive out some of these forces. But you see what happened is that most of the anti-Semitic organizations gravitated to Nashville because here was a real meaty area. It's a border state and those in the Deep South probably figured, if they get away with it in Nashville they're coming here next, and let's teach them a lesson. Let's scare them off. It was a scare technique—letters, poison pen letters, telephone calls, threats—and of course I'll never forget the first Friday night after the dynamiting of the Jewish Community Center: they had threatened to dynamite the temple that night. I was urged by some of the board of trustees to call off services, and I said the services will not be called off. Anybody that is frightened need not attend services; there will be adequate police protection. I remember that as you came to services you had to be identified by the police, and you had to show some identification. Well, we had a packed temple, it was like Rosh Hashanah,[30] and I remember the exact title of my sermon. I think it's on record; perhaps it's in the archives there[31] but it was "We Will Not Yield." Here was the point, that they say, "Rabbi, stick to the Bible." It is in the Bible. This is what the Bible teaches. "Rabbi, stick to the Talmud."[32] This is what the Talmud teaches. "Rabbi, stick to Judaism." This is Judaism. And many a time when I would carry the gun I thought to myself, "Hey, what am I doing here carrying a gun? I'm not a gunslinger; I'm a rabbi. My job is to teach Judaism." And I said, "Damn it, this is Judaism. With its own principles and the fight for principles, and not to just talk about justice, but to actually work for it." I don't think I chose to be involved in this, really. I was catapulted into it by circumstance and by their doing me the dubious honor of selecting me as a victim. There were many marvelous and advantageous aspects of it. Namely that the board of trustees of the Vine Street Temple—later it was called Temple Ohabai Shalom, on Harding Road—met and gave me a unanimous vote of confidence. This was at a time of great pressure and great strain and outraged feelings. Even those who disagreed with me and my stand thought that it was important to sustain me, and the fact that I did receive a unanimous vote of confidence was of course heartening.

The fact that this just didn't end up with a rabbi carrying a gun, of being dislocated in terms of his work, or feelings of being frightened, but that it did result in community action, and the actual integration of the schools, the further integration with the second grade, third grade, fourth grade, and so on, that the community did organize, and it did resist the efforts of those who had converted it into a nightmare of hate, is, I think, something that I look back upon with genuine satisfaction.

PAK: Do you think the bombing was influential in speeding up the integration of the public school system there?

WBS: In a sense, but what I think the bombing did was that it compelled the people to choose sides. Before it was just a matter of, "Oh, let's be quiet and let's not have any outsiders tell us what to do. We can handle our own problems." And, "Let's scuttle into caves of silence and be quiet and everything will pass over and be forgotten." But they soon saw that it wasn't going to pass over and the people had to take action, and I was surprised by the number of people that I never felt would take action who did. Who joined the, I can't remember the title, the National Conference on Community Relations, or something of the sort—they were a biracial group, which in itself was an accomplishment. Here in Nashville, called the Athens of the South, you would never dream of this happening; with Vanderbilt University, with Fisk University, with the very outstanding cultural advantages. They were a marvelous cultural community. It was unheard of, unthinkable to believe that there would be mob violence, threats, and the like in Nashville.

We also had swastikas painted on the temple, black swastikas. Our home was daubed with swastikas. My car with swastikas. I was harassed. Several people let the air out of the tires of the car. This may be a human-interest aspect to you. They threatened to—what is the technical term when they rig your car so that when it starts, the starter blows up? I didn't know this for many years but until later, where my son, my older boy, Joe, used to get up at six o'clock in the morning. I didn't have a garage. I had a little place there with a shelter, and [he would] start the car. If anybody was going to be blown up, he was going to be blown up and not his dad. I never knew this for years. Here was a fifteen-year-old boy that would set an alarm and get up every morning and start the car and make sure that nobody got near it until I started it again and went off. There was always a comfortable feeling when you start a car and you hear that purr, and you know you haven't been blown to wherever you are going to blown to. It was a period of considerable tension and many urged me to leave. This was before the civil rights movements, the parades, [before] the [northern] rabbis' protesting went on. Because it was so new, so novel, it received international coverage. They sent reporters from New York to cover it. I don't know; there was somebody named Gail Green, I believe, a lady reporter. My wife didn't want any publicity about the kids, and she gave her the assurance there wouldn't be, and yet there was a feature story about the rabbi's wife and their children mentioned by name. All very unpleasant, the letters from all over the country both damning us and praising us. But I think this acted as a catalyst to precipitate the constructive and creative efforts to bring harmony into the community.

PAK: What was the majority response prior to 1957? The difference from trying to pretend that it wasn't there?

WBS: Well then the Jews didn't want to get involved, and most of the Christians didn't want to get involved. They wanted peace and harmony.

PAK: What was the majority response afterward? After 1957?

WBS: It's hard for me to assess the majority response, but I'll tell you what seemed to be the majority response was indignation—indignation, anger, and let's do something about it. And what happened, of course, in the Christian community is that [they realized that] if this could happen to the

Jews, and this could happen with a threat to a Jewish synagogue, the dyna-miting of a Jewish community center, and since this was done by profes-sionals, and it wasn't very long before Jacob Rothschild's temple in Atlanta was dynamited, I think by the same people. I know that my wife was given tapes to identify voices of the so-called Captain Gordon of the Confed-erate Underground, and no one was ever able to do anything. I believe that they had the people involved in Atlanta, but there was some sort of illegal federal bug machination so that these people got out of it.[33]

PAK: How many of the ministers of Nashville were visibly involved in the civil rights movement prior to 1957?

WBS: I don't know that any of us were really involved.

PAK: After 1957 were there any ministers as individuals or was there a min-isterial organization which formed?

WBS: I received telegrams of sympathy from the ministerial association. In fact it was John Rustin, a Methodist minister, who was the first. Others pri-vately, quietly expressed indignation. Rustin was the first to preach from his pulpit, but after Rustin left I understand that other ministers did preach. I left in 1960. By this time things were relatively quiet.

PAK: What about rabbis? How many other rabbis were in Nashville then?

WBS: Well there was a Conservative rabbi and an Orthodox rabbi, and I think Lou Silberman was there as the chair of [the department of] Jewish studies at Vanderbilt.[34]

PAK: Did any of these generally take part in any civil rights activity that you knew of?

WBS: Not to my knowledge.

PAK: Could I ask you a few questions about the Jewish community per se also? How long had your congregation been in existence by 1950?

WBS: Oh I would say about a hundred years. Although I'm not sure the exact time. Remember, I've been away from Nashville for six years. It was one of the congregations that Isaac Mayer Wise dedicated.[35]

PAK: What was the economic standing and the source of income for your congregants?

WBS: Most of them were merchants.

PAK: Middle class?

WBS: Middle class, some upper class.

PAK: Were they susceptible to economic pressures from the non-Jewish community?

WBS: You mean in relationship to this problem?

PAK: Right.

WBS: Yes.

PAK: Did they feel any pressure?

WBS: I don't think there was any real pressure. It was so momentary. We were going through a period of indifference for many years. Then the effort to bring these little Negro girls into the school, and this was going on over several months, enough to give us time. The ones who really felt it were the members of the congregation who lived in adjacent communities. Small towns where maybe there were two Jews or three Jews. I remember the story of one Jew, this may be interesting to you for your record because of the rabbinic teaching *al tadin et havercha ad sh'tagiya limkom* ["don't judge your fellow until you're in his place"].[36] There was one man in a little town outside of Nashville came and he said to me right after Yom Kippur, "I would like to make confession. I'm a member of the White Citizens' Council." I looked at him and I said, "Well I'm surprised." He said, "I am too." He said, "They came to me and asked me to join the White Citizens' Council and I refused. Then they put on the economic pressure. People refused to trade in my store and I thought I'd rather go bankrupt [than join the Council]. But when they started getting to my kids . . . my boy was beaten up in the schoolyard and my daughter wasn't getting invited anyplace, and my kids were hurt. I felt that if I wanted to live in the community, I'd better join. So I paid my dues. I don't do anything about it, but I want you to know that I feel lousy and I hate myself. I'm a member of the White Citizens' Council." Now others have told me that they did it for economic pressure. You are either with us or against us on integration, unless you want niggers in school with your kids, and do you want your son to marry a nigger or your daughter to marry a nigger and so on. The propaganda was pretty filthy. It was John Kasper who had literature which was really more than provocative. He urged people to get their guns, to protect themselves against the Jews and the niggers who were going to take over. Some of these lower-income groups in Nashville that became very agitated joined with him. Most of these were crackpots, and I really believe that many of them were imports; they came in from other areas.

PAK: **Do you think that a good number of Jews in your congregation, members of your congregation, hesitated to take part in civil rights activity or to simply join organizations or show physical support of the civil rights movement because of their economic . . .**

WBS: Some of them, yes.

PAK: **A large number?**

WBS: I don't think so. I don't really think so.

PAK: **How much a part of the non-Jewish community were the Jews in your community? . . . How many of them were "southern" in their orientation throughout the whole process?**

WBS: You're going to have to define what you mean by "southern."

PAK: By "southern" I mean accepted the southern position with regards to the Negro. . . . What we generally think of as the southern position.

WBS: I don't think there is very substantial ground on which the critic can answer. I would say that many of them did feel southern, but in the finer sense of the word. And the idea [is incorrect] that if you're southern you're reactionary or if you're southern you hate Negroes or something like that.

PAK: I'm talking just with regards to the civil rights movement in terms of the goals. Not necessarily the activities but the goals in it. How many?

WBS: You have your fringe or activists on both poles. Those who were reactionary and those who were liberal—those who really wanted to do something. The great percentage was the people well intentioned that didn't want to get involved. You say, "Rabbi, what was the relationship with the Christian community?" It was one of a very harmonious relationship that we had. The Jews were president of the Red Cross, president of the symphony orchestra, active in every facet of community and service. So these people really felt a part and still feel part of Nashville.

Back to what percentage of the people might have been vocally segregationists, my guess would be 3 to 5 percent. Although I would have to suspect that those who were not articulate, I would have to add perhaps another 20, 25 percent. But [these are] not segregationists in the ugly sense of the word. But they really believe it was better for the Negroes, and they give all the rationalizations that were generally given.

PAK: Could you go back to the early years of your time in Nashville and recall any specific events or activities which you might think to be in the area of the civil rights that you participated in?

WBS: Really, no. I don't think we used the term "civil rights" in 1950. I think we were involved in the Korean situation, were we not, about that time? Earlier there were the ordinary good-will movements and what not. There was a very fine relationship on the part of the Catholics, Protestants, and Jews there, except that the Catholic community could have used a little of Pope John's ecumenism. They had very little to do with the Jewish community except unofficially. And civil rights belonged to all the groups that were out to do good.

PAK: Such as?

WBS: Oh, the Red Cross, the National Conference of Christians and Jews. I was . . .

PAK: What about with regards to the Negroes? In 1954, after 1954 I would imagine you might have that the whole thing was called to the attention of people in the community if it was challenged. But prior to that were you involved in any way trying to get better job opportunities for the Negroes?

WBS: Yes, I was on the mayor's Commission on Human Rights, the governor's Commission on Human Relations, and we did work through various agencies to get Negroes placed on the police force, and we worked with the city council, the school board, departments. Trying to get them economic opportunities. I don't think we did enough. All I know is that piddling around the periphery we did some things, but there wasn't much pressure on us at the time.

PAK: **Were there any other areas that you were involved in other than . . .**

WBS: Yes, I was involved in mental health. Trying to organize a mental health unit, which we did. Well in terms of the Negro I would attend a lecture at Fisk University. I was on the boards of social agencies trying to help the Negro unwed mother. Provide job opportunities for Negroes.

PAK: **Were there ministers in any of these other things that you were doing?**

WBS: I believe so, but this was eminently respectable. This was very respectable and nobody protested because you were doing some social welfare, but the Negroes were still kept in their place basically.

PAK: **A paternalistic relationship?**

WBS: Yes, they were kept in their place, and you would throw them an ideological bone every once in a while. It was a good thing, and I think people smiled indulgently at the efforts of the rabbi or the priest or the minister to help.

PAK: **Did you ever speak on equality?**

WBS: I always spoke out on the question. I spoke very bluntly from my pulpit and some members of the congregation didn't like it, others loved it, but they—I must say this about the congregation in Nashville—at no time did anyone really try to stop me from speaking my mind. And in 1950, '51, '52, '53, '54, I did speak on the Negro question and rights for the Negro, and of course in 1954 I came out openly and blasted those who would not go along with the decision of the Supreme Court. There was no reason really to do anything about it because nobody had tried anything in Nashville. That wasn't until '57, an injunction in the courts for three years. They were going through all these legal battles and things didn't come to a head until '57.

PAK: **Were there any non-Jewish reactions from the community prior to 1957 in regards to what you had been doing?**

WBS: Most of everything was favorable.

PAK: **Were you quoted in the press very often?**

WBS: No, no. That's why I think it was favorable. What they heard was that the rabbi was speaking for Right. And it's all right if the minister, the rabbi, or the priest wants to talk; let them get it out of their system. It's okay as long as they don't take any actions or they don't interfere in our lives or don't hurt us economically. Nobody was really being hurt. There was "that rabbi who gives courageous sermons, and I think he talks too much" or "he's too blunt" or "he ought to go back north where he belongs," and something of that sort. But nobody took us too much to heart.

PAK: **It was that specific school integration issue which really brought problems . . .**

WBS: Exactly. What it meant was that children would be going to school, Negro children, and perhaps someday with their children. It meant head-lines in the paper about the rabbi. It meant the Jewish Community Center was dynamited. Although there was no cause and effect between any of my statements and the dynamiting of the Jewish Community Center. Then they became very agitated, but I was . . . I know people expect me to con-form to the stereotype. That is, to support and substantiate the stereotype they have about the typical southern community being opposed to the rabbi, fighting against the rabbi, being reactionary when the rabbi is being a liberal. This is not so; it is not so. These people didn't want trouble, but I found that I was being supported.

PAK: **Did you feel in the 1950s, in 1957 let's say, that these people actually felt good about you talking, because it made them feel that you were do-ing something that they couldn't?**

WBS: Well, that would be doing some psychological introspection that I'm not prepared to do. It would be quite normal for these people to be happy if their rabbi is doing something nice but not causing any trouble.

PAK: **Was there anybody in your congregation that you know of who was more of an activist in this area than you? Who wished you would go faster or farther?**

WBS: No. I remember there were some who thought I was going too fast.

PAK: **After 1957 were there any other specific involvements that you had?**

WBS: I was constantly involved with this ministers' group; I wish I could re-member their names. It was organized to work positively.

PAK: **How large a group was it?**

WBS: It was mostly representatives of groups, of the various [Christian] de-nominations, of the secular groups of the community, of the universities, a mayor representative, county represent[atives talking about] what could we do? How could we educate our people? How could we bring about the peaceful integration of schools? How could we help our people understand that this is inevitable? What does the Supreme Court mean by "all delib-erate speed"? And of course "all deliberate speed" meant *never* to some of the people in Nashville, as throughout the South. But many of them did act with a sort of resignation: this is inevitable, and we might as well accept the fact and see what we can do to effect the integration peacefully.

PAK: What about transportation in public facilities, things like that in Nashville?

WBS: Actually, following '57, Negroes were permitted to go on buses and did. Even in 1950 the Negroes were members of committees in which I served and would come in to meeting places, public meeting places as guests. Following '57 and following '60 and '61, you had sit-ins. The integration effort was no longer exciting. It was a matter of the sit-ins, pray-ins, the students of Fisk University. But I wasn't there; I understand that Rabbi Randall Falk, who is now the rabbi [at the temple], was very courageous in this effort to work on behalf of the civil rights, I mean involved in it. Although the dean at Fisk University told me that he really thought that the reason why Negroes were given the right to go into the ten-cent stores and the [*inaudible*] or what not, it wasn't because the community had become enlightened or educated but [because] the boycotts hurt. It hurt the pocketbooks, and then the people become a little more liberal and permitted the Negroes to visit the lunch counters.

There was one incident that I had to go through just before I left Nashville. I think this is very significant. I don't know whether you will find it so or not. It was more of a sermon than possibly material for your [research], but when our household items had been put on the truck it was shipped to, moved to Kansas City, my wife asked me [whether] I would like to have breakfast at the drugstore. I think that was a rhetorical question. So I went to the drugstore and I sat down at the counter and a man sat down and he really smelled. He was drunk, unkempt. Nobody paid much attention to him, though, except to move away from him. I must have had that symbol of what had happened or what was yet to come. A clean-cut looking Negro boy walked in wearing a uniform of the United States Army, and he started to sit down and the waitress had a conference with the manager and the manager says, "I'm sorry you can't sit here." Then he said, "Why not?" The manager said, "Because you are a Negro." "Well I'm hungry; I would like something to eat." "Well you can't sit here, but if you want some food we'll serve it to you." "Where will I eat it?" "You can sit on the curb." The manager said to the Negro boy, "What do you want?" He said, "I want two eggs up." Well the manager gave the instructions to the waitress to fry that boy two eggs. She did and she put the two eggs on a paper plate and slapped another paper plate on top of that, handed it to the boy upside down and he stood there with the egg yolk dripping all over the uniform. He looked at us and he asked this question: "What do you care?" I think those words burned themselves into my mind and heart—*what do you care*—because I knew that the slob was [an] unkempt, stinking man, and it was all right for him to sit there because of [the color of his] skin. Even with a black stubble of a beard [he] was [still] white, but this clean-cut boy, because he was a Negro, couldn't sit there. Anyone who calls themselves a religionist I believe would have to respond to the question, What do you care?

PAK: What did you have any [*inaudible*] communications with activist groups after the '57 [*inaudible*] in Nashville [*inaudible*]?

WBS: I was always a member of the NAACP [National Association for the Advancement of Colored People], even in the South. I'm trying to recall whether CORE [Congress of Racial Equality] was just becoming active at that time. I was a member. I supported CORE financially, still do. I'm a life member of the NAACP. I was then, and in the South, and encouraged people to join into the group. I can't think of too much action there. I was on the Social Action Commission. It was me and my group of congregations in the conference. Very active there. I was never successful in getting the congregation to organize a social action group, so we had people who did work unofficially who were for this, and those who were board members of the temple were. I'm trying to recall what organizations were, aside from the very respectable organization, attempted to improve the relations between the white[s] and the Negroes, and actually to push along the integration of schools peacefully.

PAK: I'm thinking of other areas of action.

WBS: At that time, I doubt whether there was too much.

PAK: Did you ever have . . . the opportunity as it arrived and you called up a person that you would say he was in the power structure in Nashville or somebody who might have been in the position to influence something and to push ahead civil rights in Nashville and use your own personal contact? Was there anybody in that position or anything like that [*inaudible*] to effect a change?

WBS: Yes, many times.

PAK: Such as.

WBS: Well, such as getting more Negro policemen on the force.

PAK: Who was your contact then?

WBS: Well, the mayor.

PAK: How did you know the mayor [*inaudible*]?

WBS: Well, through my contacts in the community. Governor Clement, who lived in Nashville, he was a very good friend and [I] was a colonel on his staff. A lot of it, I have to admit, was political fluff. They were just trying to avoid any act of commitment. It was a matter of palliative, but some good was being done. Some of the social agencies, getting more money or working to improve the schools, the Negro schools that were then operating. The Negro hospitals, getting more money for them. Doing greater social welfare and it still wasn't civil rights—this wasn't getting to the guts of the matter at all. I don't think we really did during the years that I had been in Nashville just as the guts of the matter, except to push along the integration of the schools.

PAK: What was the first time where you had integrated a function of any kind in your own congregation?

WBS: We had Negroes, it wasn't the first time; it was always from the time I got there.

PAK: Had it been prior to your arrival there?

WBS: I can't say. I believe Julius Mark was the rabbi there for twenty-two years. Julius Mark was also a former Chairman of the Commission on Justice of the Peace. I think that Julius took a very active part in promoting this sort of Negro-white relationship, so that he had done considerable work before I arrived. We had integrated services, Negroes, well . . . Dr. [Charles S.] Johnson was president of Fisk University, he preached from my pulpit. We invited the Negro community to oneg Shabbat [refreshments after Sabbath services]. We ate together, and we worshipped together. We had Negroes in our youth group.

PAK: Were any protestations [*inaudible*]?

WBS: Yeah, some of the people didn't like it but the board—I said, courageously—"You may not like it, but this is the right way and we are going to do it." And we did it.

PAK: Do you remember a time when the board seriously discussed it as a possibility of this being a serious matter, not a matter to be dismissed by just saying you don't like it?

WBS: Yes, the board did discuss it as a serious matter many times and letters [were] written. People came in to make their case before the board, or to protest against my permitting it or encouraging it. The board overruled these folks and supported me.

PAK: Was there ever a time when you got the feeling that the board might not support you?

WBS: No. . . . I could understand that the board was unhappy about the unpleasantness about the rabbi carrying a gun, about the threats that were being made. The dead rats, the dead pigeons, the police coverage, the notoriety in the newspapers, the television, the radio, the reporters. I don't think any board would like it particularly, but I don't believe that anybody held me responsible or blamed me. Nashville was marvelous to us. We spent ten years in Nashville. I have been invited back. I did not leave because of any altercations with the board. I was not asked to leave. I left in 1960. I could have remained on. I had a fine opportunity in Kansas City. I was invited there and accepted. I guess I should say what I usually did: it was a greater field of service, but it also had more salary and it was a bigger congregation and bigger prestige.

PAK: Just in passing does Kansas City seem to be quieter in the area of civil rights? More active in the area of civil rights?

WBS: More active and not quieter.

PAK: More problems [*inaudible*] in Nashville?

WBS: No, a different kind of problem. The past year, the president of the [*inaudible*] Kansas City Council on Religion and Race. One of our big projects this year was to initiate fair housing. The fair housing [initiative] saw about nineteen thousand people applying for a housing break.

PAK: This type of thing would not happen even now in Nashville, could it?

WBS: Yeah I think it could.

PAK: Fair housing?

WBS: I believe so. Although I don't want to speak [with] authority. . . .

PAK: Actually I want to go back to Nashville.

WBS: You just asked the question; . . . I have an unlisted phone right now . . . threats, harassment, and somebody had a record[ing] on [a] telephone . . . a fellow named Wayne Morris, where you dial victory, V-I-C-T-O-R-Y, and you would hear the words, "Now you will hear about the nigger-loving rabbi." Through our efforts the Negroes did move into what was formerly a really white neighborhood, and a lot of people are very unhappy with my leadership of this group, including someone within my congregation. Officially I am supported, as I was in Nashville.

PAK: In Nashville, could you reduce your methodological approach to this problem. . . .

WBS: Yes there were times when a method couldn't make any difference—and then you either fish or cut bait. You would come out and you would take a stand and you would stand by your stand. I think basically my position has been a religious position. Not economic, not social service or social action. I insist that as a rabbi, as a teacher of Judaism, that Judaism is a religion of action and I need not support that point of view. [From when I was] a rabbinical student . . . from the time now it says in Ishmael, "We will do and we will harken." That the pursuit of justice, activation of justice that has been basic to our faith. And if you want to argue with me, you have to refute my Judaism. This is not always an easy thing for a layman to do. You need to come up and say, "I, William Silverman, say this and believe this." I don't think [that's] a very tenable position. My position has always been the right side of the Lord God or the Bible or the Talmud or Judaism say this; therefore I must act in consonance with these teachings. Now don't argue with me. Go and argue with five thousand years of Judaism.

PAK: **What about related to non-Jewish communities? When you want to get something done, when you want to push this integration of schools et cetera, what was the methodology used to follow there?**

WBS: The methodology was the danger of spiritual or ideological isolationism. I will tell you an example that happened in Germany. When I was a student at the university and Hitler made his appearance and people would say, well, the Christians would say, "Too bad for the Jews." I said, "Oh wait a minute, friend, then they start with the Jews. Next they'll be after the Catholics and then the Protestants and then the universities and then democracy and then Christianity itself." So my argument to the Christian was—and I believe it; you have to use the argument of self-interest—whether or not you take action, you are going to be involved in this thing. Democracy is going to be involved. You aren't doing any great favor for the Negro and I still believe this. We think we are being so magnanimous when we help the Negro—we are helping ourselves; we're helping Judaism; we're helping democracy; we're helping the future. At least the moral future. So it's from a selfish point of view that we should help the Negro too. The approach was, I believe, first to identify here the specific approach. You become a part of the community. You join with the ministers and the ministerial association. You work with them. You become friends with them through the Rotary Club or the Kiwanis Club or some other group. When I talk of Rotary I regret that I had just one stomach to give to my congregation. Creamed gravies and all of that. Do I need it? Like a hole in my stomach, but you become friends with these people. You are on [a] first-name basis. You work with the governor. You become a name-dropper. Does this help? Yes, you can bet it helps. When you are able to go to an outstanding Christian minister on a first name basis and say to him, "Now John, let's get together and see what we can do about this situation." Once you have the Christian support you are not out on that limb all alone. You are going to be more effective with your own congregation.

PAK: **One rabbi said, "The only way you can be effective is when you put a gentile in front and you stay in the back."**

WBS: No sir, I don't agree. Either you have got to have a gentile at your side, it's helpful. If you can't have one at your side, do it alone.

PAK: **What is the climate of the mass media in Nashville? . . . .Was there newspaper coverage et cetera on the civil rights movement?**

WBS: You see you keep using the words "civil rights movement"; I don't think there was any. I don't think there really was a civil rights movement. I think a lot of it was sub rosa, was underground. It was concealed or hidden. The attitude of the radio, I think, was an awareness that something is about to happen. There was going to be a revolution of some sort. I think they were getting prepared for it. Once they had all the newsworthy items, I think it was just press to sell newspapers. It was exciting to television and radio.

PAK: [Was] it good press to print segregation as propaganda and then put it all over the press [*inaudible*]?

WBS: We had two newspapers in Nashville at the time: The *Nashville Tennessean* and the *Nashville Banner*. The *Nashville Tennessean* was a fairly liberal newspaper. The *Banner* was fairly reactionary. The *Tennessean* I think took a liberal point of view in editorials, feature articles, and the like. The *Banner* took a very safe and cautious point of view: "Now wait a minute, folks—let's not take this too fast. Let's not let outsiders interfere," but the attitude of the *Nashville Tennessean* I think was wholesome and helpful and progressive.

PAK: Was it helpful to you in your work?

WBS: Yes and no. It wasn't until the [*inaudible*] Pearson had a syndicated article in which he misquoted me as saying, "There isn't a single minister [*inaudible*] who is chained to the floor." Or something like that. Where he had taken it out of context. When this appeared many of the ministers were angry. That kind of publicity didn't help us, because I had made a statement to the effect of, "Not a single minister or clergyman has taken a stand in favor of integration." Not that they didn't come to the floor after this ad because many of them did and were sympathetic. But, well, the expression of shame, indignation, and shock on the part of the *Nashville Tennessean* and the *Banner*. It was very respectable to be shocked that an institution in Nashville had been dynamited, because there were little kids there just a while before. Somebody might have been killed. All you had to do was look at that demolished structure and realize that was a family or quasi-religious institution, and you had to be shocked to be respectable, and to be an American. So they were shocked when swastikas were painted on the temple. The *Nashville Tennessean* really tried conceptually to change attitude[s].

PAK: What role do you think the national Jewish organization played in Nashville when they found out with regard to the bettering of the position of the Negro?

WBS: Not much. We had all the organizations coming in. Of course all of them took credit for actions—the Anti-Defamation League and the Commission on Social Action and the American Jewish Committee and the American Jewish Congress and all the regional groups. They were sending representatives in and conferring and sending back reports, saying how they were endangered and the advice they gave—and the Jewish Community

Council of course. The local community was scared, didn't do much, re-
treated. "Let's be quiet. Let's not take any action. Let's be cautious." I don't
think they counted very much.

PAK: **Were they detrimental in any way to the goals?**

WBS: They were detrimental to the extent that their actions crystalized a certain resentment on the part of the good community of Nashville. Again
outside Jewish organizations, they learn to operate within their own group.

PAK: **Do you think that they could have played a better role? Or do you
think it was good enough?**

WBS: No. Oh now I think they could, because the climate would be more
amenable to them. At the time I don't think they meant very much.

PAK: **If in fifty years, let's say, from now somebody would want to do a history of the South and especially let's say a history of Nashville and analyze the, I'll say it in quotation marks, "The civil rights activities and
movements there." What role do you think would be placed with the
rabbi who is placed in that historical position [*inaudible*]?**

WBS: I think they will have a significant role, of greatest mark. And in my
quiet way, on an ideological level, I participated in those things and then
taking a stand and saying, "Well here I am and I will not retreat. I will not
surrender. This is right. Whether they dynamite or they don't dynamite.
Whether they threaten or they don't threaten. Whether you like what I am
saying or you don't like what I'm saying this is morally right." Emily [*inaudible*] and Randy Falk, I think, have carried on this work and this attitude
with purity. I think that the perspective of history will show [*inaudible*] . . .
not enough.

8
Malcolm Stern

Norfolk, Virginia, and Its Jewish Community

In 1736, fifty-six years after its establishment as a town on the Chesapeake Bay by an act of the Virginia Assembly in 1680, King George II formally granted a charter establishing Norfolk and its environs as a borough. According to a January 7, 1835, article in the *Norfolk (VA) Herald*, in prerevolutionary days the city was a "rare place indeed," its harbor being "filled with ships swallowing up cargoes of innumerable little schooners and sloops from adjoining rivers laden with tobacco, wheat, corn, lumber, etc."[1] In 1776, battles between British warships and the colonial army left it as the most devastated city in the colonies.

At the onset of the nineteenth century Norfolk emerged as the tenth largest city in the young republic, with slightly fewer than seven thousand inhabitants, including 2,724 African American slaves and 352 free persons of color.[2] Over the next hundred years, Norfolk grew modestly compared to many other cities. By 1900 it had fewer than forty-seven thousand inhabitants and ranked eightieth in the census list of the top one hundred US municipalities. But the country's entrance into World War I brought significant changes to Norfolk, mostly as a result of the construction of Hampton Roads Naval Air Force Station and the influx of families to operate that facility. This, plus the annexation of the bordering town of Berkley, almost doubled the population and jumped Norfolk up to the position of fifty-ninth largest city in the country. Growth continued with World War II as the Hampton Roads facility expanded into the world's largest naval station. By 1960 Norfolk's 305,872 inhabitants made it the forty-first largest municipality in the country and the largest in Virginia.

Although it boasted a cosmopolitan character as a port city with a major naval base, a number of factors determined that integration did not come easily to Norfolk. First, approximately 30 percent of its population at the time of the 1954 *Brown* decision had recently migrated from the Bible Belt section of the South. Second, the political leadership, in particular Sen. Harry F. Byrd and Gov. J. Lindsay Almond, militantly opposed integration with a program of massive resistance, a policy in total accord with the views of the majority of the white citizenry.

Education served as the primary battleground in the conflict over integration.

The average Norfolkian had no intention of complying with the wishes of the "Nine Old Men" on the Supreme Court. Although superintendent of schools John J. Brewbaker initially supported *Brown*, he and school board chairman Paul Schweitzer reflected their constituencies when they soon presented a solid front in opposition to integration.

As Malcolm Stern partly explains in the interview, Leola Pearl Beckett and other black parents filed suit in 1956 demanding that their children be admitted to all-white schools. On January 11, 1957, District Judge Walter E. Hoffman instructed the Norfolk School Board to integrate all of its junior and senior high schools as of August 15, 1957. On the day of Huffman's decision, the board rejected the applications of 151 African American children. When forced by the judge to reevaluate the applicants, the board affirmed that seventeen were qualified for admission to the city's six white junior and senior high schools. On September 27, 1958, however, rather than permit integration, the governor closed these schools to all students with the full support of the school board and the mayor, William F. Duckworth. In frustration, one of the city's councilmen complained, "We've got seventeen Negro children who are keeping 10,000 white children out of school."[3] The "Norfolk 17" failed to gain admission to the previously all-white schools until February 2, 1959.[4]

Two groups were energized in response to Norfolk's hard-line position. Shortly after World War II eight African American and eleven white women had gathered at Ohef Sholom Temple and created the Women's Council for Interracial Cooperation. In keeping with their mission statement, they focused on the school problem as early as 1955, almost three years before the schools were closed.[5] The Committee for Public Schools was formed during the summer of 1958 to keep the schools open. Unitarian minister James C. Brewer chaired its advisory board. Both groups distributed materials designed to influence the middle-class white electorate, met with politicians, and eventually filed briefs with the federal court.

In January 1956, the Norfolk Ministers Association issued a resolution that stated that opposition to the *Brown* decision was not only illegal but also "un-Christian." Although this exerted little impact at the time, it gave credence to anti-establishment speech. The real breakthrough came when parents realized that study groups were not a sufficient alternative to open schools, lacking, as they did, amenities such as chemistry labs, physical education, and music. Increasingly impatient with the closures, Norfolk's white parents of junior and senior high school students flip-flopped between November 1958 and January 1959 from 59 percent in favor of keeping the schools closed to the same number wanting them to reopen.[6] Simultaneously, rumblings emanated from the naval base concerning setting up its own schools and withdrawing their children from the public schools. Some even spoke about relocating the base itself, a potential economic disaster since it provided Norfolk's main source of income.[7]

Yet another impetus to desegregate came when CBS sent its muckraking re-porter Edward R. Murrow to Norfolk in preparation for a documentary, "The Lost Class of '59." The special program, broadcast on January 21, 1959, proved a great embarrassment to the city and especially its business community.[8] Shaken by the loss of federal dollars connected to falling school enrollment, petrified by the potential loss of the naval base (or, at least, its children), and mortified by the unfavorable national publicity, the business community finally supported the open school groups that it had previously ignored. On January 27, a full-page advertisement signed by one hundred business people appeared in the *Norfolk (VA) Virginian-Pilot* that stated, "While we would strongly prefer to have segregated schools, it is evident from the recent court decisions that our public schools must either be integrated to the extent fully required or must be abandoned. The abandonment of our public schools system is, in our opinion, unthinkable, as it would mean the denial of an adequate education to a majority of our children. Moreover, the consequences would be most damaging to our community. We, therefore, urge the Norfolk City Council to do everything within its power to open all public schools as promptly as possible."

While the moral argument of the clergy had gone unheeded, the business community's bread and butter argument carried the day. When the schools re-opened on February 2, 1959, integration added only seventeen African Americans to a mix of about ten thousand students. A year and a half later and after prodding, the number of black students inched up to fifty. Similar token increases occurred each year until 1971, when the courts imposed busing, and true integration was finally achieved. Yet even the impact of busing was short-lived, since, as in many cities, white flight to the suburbs quickly re-created de facto black-only schools in the inner city.

Despite this sad drama, Norfolk remained a part of the land of the almost possible, since people had the opportunity to speak out against the system without facing serious threats, and change came without violence. Rabbi Malcolm Stern operated within this milieu.

The Jewish connection with Norfolk is a very old one; yet in 1966, Stern believed that only about 10 percent of his congregants were "southern in their outlook" on the civil rights issue. The history of the community might lead one to expect a larger percentage in that category.

Norfolk's Jewish history dates from 1787, when Moses Myers arrived.[9] Myers established a mercantile house that flourished by selling products to the city's shipping industry. He served as a consular agent for the Netherlands, an agent of the French Republic, and Collector of the Port of Norfolk appointed by President John Quincy Adams upon petition of non-Jewish merchants in the city.[10]

By 1820, area Jews purchased land for a cemetery, although the first recorded Jewish worship service did not take place until twenty-four years later. In 1848

Jewish residents created Chevra B'nai Jacov (literally, "The Fellowship of the Sons of Jacob") or, as they called themselves, "House of Jacob." They rented two rooms for worship services and purchased a Torah scroll in Baltimore. The congregation quickly expanded its rental to an entire floor of the Odd Fellows Hall. Finally in 1859, the group purchased property on which they erected Norfolk's first synagogue building. In 1867, the congregation revived after a hiatus related to the Civil War as Ohef Sholom Temple ("Lovers of Peace"). The use of the term *temple* indicated identity with Reform Judaism. Three years hence, a schism resulted in the more traditionalists breaking off to form Beth El ("House of God"). Such divisions occurred typically during this era of transition in practice and worship.

Norfolk's Jewish community increased in population with the arrival of Eastern European Jewish immigrants and with influxes during the two world wars. By 1966 Ohef Sholom's membership included approximately one-eighth of the city's 7,750 Jews, who comprised about two-tenths of 1 percent of the total population.[11] Yet, even with the arrival of newcomers, Ohef Sholom was so anchored in its past that no one could be elected president unless he (women were ineligible) had grown up in the congregation.

The naval base drew many Jews. Consequently, unlike most southern communities, the vast majority of the Jewish heads of households did not work as merchants. Only 15 to 20 percent fit within the latter category with the remainder finding employment as doctors, lawyers, civil service employees, manufacturers' representatives, insurance salesmen, and other service professions. Although less dependent on white patronage to earn their living than their counterparts in other southern communities, most of Norfolk's Jews, nonetheless, remained hesitant to participate in the desegregation struggle and were overwhelmingly concerned with *mah yomru hagoyim* ("What will the non-Jews say?").

Their reluctance to support integration openly likely resulted from fear of other forms of reprisal. The night before the junior and senior high schools were to be integrated, fifteen thousand pieces of hate literature were hand-delivered throughout the city, including in the neighborhood where most Jews lived. This literature and other flyers and newspapers distributed prior to September 7, 1958, exhibited both racism and anti-Semitism. It typically described integration as a Jewish/communist plot meant to lead to miscegenation and the destruction of the American way of life. Yet according to Murray Friedman, this material failed to cause an appreciable rise in acts of anti-Semitism.[12] Thus the timidity of the Jewish community resulted more from fear of what might happen, rather than of actual events. Since they were largely upper-middle class and earned their money in ways not easily susceptible to boycotts, Stern expected more from them than what he got.[13]

Malcolm Stern

A third-generation American, Malcolm Henry Stern was born on January 29, 1915, to Arthur Kaufman and Henrietta Berkowitz Stern. His father was, in Stern's words, an "aesthete" who was not cut out for the family's hide and tallow business. Consequently when Malcolm was eight years old, the family relocated from Philadelphia to a small farm in Fox Chase, a northwest suburb. There his father dabbled in farming, playwriting, and painting, while his mother worked as a librarian in addition to owning and directing a Jewish summer camp for girls. His parents were sufficiently affluent to hire a live-in housekeeper, a descendant of slaves who was with them for thirty years and exerted an important influence on her young charges. His parents enrolled Malcolm and his younger brother as the only two Jews in the local public school, where their classmates, children of millworkers, traumatized them with anti-Semitic epithets. Subsequently, the boys attended private schools, including two years in Switzerland.

Stern graduated from the University of Pennsylvania in 1935. Two years hence he became the fifth member of his family ordained as a rabbi at Hebrew Union College. While a rabbinic student in Cincinnati, he conducted worship services in a number of Virginia towns and in West Point, Georgia, where he was disturbed by the "white only" signs and the obsequious behavior of the black servants in Jewish homes. Following ordination, he continued his studies and received a doctor of Hebrew letters degree from the seminary in 1941.

Stern's first full-time position was at Congregation Keneseth Israel in Philadelphia, where he assisted Dr. William H. Fineshriber, following Julian Feibelman, who had accepted a pulpit in New Orleans. Stern served in this capacity until 1943, when he enlisted in the Army Air Corps as a chaplain, serving eight months in Nashville and eleven in Montgomery. Although some Jews whom he met in Montgomery had Ivy League educations, Stern commented to his northern friends, "They hadn't had a thought since the Civil War."[14]

Stern returned from the army in 1947 and became the rabbi at Congregation Ohef Sholom in Norfolk, Virginia, which, like Keneseth Israel, traced its roots to the 1840s. It is probably not coincidental that Stern opted to go to a mid-nineteenth-century Virginia pulpit, given his lifelong interest in Jewish genealogy. While in Norfolk he researched and wrote *American Families of Jewish Descent*, the first genealogical survey of Jewish families settling in this country between 1654 and 1840. Published in 1960, the massive tome was hailed as the most valuable research tool in the field of American Jewish history in years. Stern later became one of the founders of the Jewish Genealogical Society (JGS) and founder of both the Jewish Historical Society of New York and the nonsectarian Genealogical Coordinating Committee (GCC), all of which he served as presi-

9. Malcolm Stern in front of the ark at
Ohef Sholom in Norfolk, Virginia, during
a rededication ceremony, October 1965
(Ohef Sholom Temple Archives). Used by
permission of President Edward G. Kaufman.

dent. In addition he served as the genealogist for the American Jewish Archives in Cincinnati. Reflecting his importance to the field, he was presented with the prestigious George Williams Award by the Federation of Genealogical Societies (FGS) for "outstanding contributions to the FGS and the genealogical community" and was inducted into the National Genealogical Society Hall of Fame. After his death a number of genealogical societies, including the GCC, established funds or scholarships named in his honor.

In 1964 Stern ended his affiliation with Ohef Sholom and moved to New York City to become the first Director of Rabbinic Placement for Reform Judaism, a sign of the esteem with which he was held by his colleagues. Stern retired from this position in 1980. The following year he joined the faculty of the New York campus of the Hebrew Union College–Jewish Institute of Religion, where he served as a counselor for student field work and an adjunct professor of Jewish history. His work contributed to making the American Jewish Archives in Cincinnati an internationally recognized institution. Malcolm Stern died on January 5, 1994, survived by his wife of over fifty years, Louise Steinhart Stern.[15]

Editor's Introduction to the Interview

Much has been written concerning rabbis in the South and civil rights, a subject expanded upon in this volume. Historians have discussed pressures exerted by congregations on their rabbis that in rare occasions led to nonrenewal of contracts, forced removal, or resignation. Yet, few rabbis lost their positions or bowed to calls for silence. However, along with many of his rabbinic colleagues, Malcolm Stern pointed to the loss of positions of their Protestant counterparts.

This issue begs for comparative research. The rabbis forced out tended to conflict with their congregations over other issues, lacked finesse, and/or failed to cement their positions with other activities and attributes that their congregants viewed favorably. Was this also the case with Protestant ministers? One senses that their civil rights activities alone led to their dismissal, an opinion shared by Stern and other rabbis. A far larger percentage of Protestant churches ardently supported segregation. Whereas a certain percentage of Jews in each congregation opposed integration, few espoused massive resistance, and even many of these recognized the correctness of the rabbis' moral and religious position.

A few of the interviewees point to Rabbi Eugene Blachschlager with special disdain, because they believed he did not speak out due to fear of losing his position. This was viewed quite differently than cases of those rabbis who remained silent to protect their congregants. Yet Stern depicts his friend with the understanding of the difficulties any rabbi would have to face in Montgomery, Alabama. Stern recognized that Blachschlager operated in an almost entirely different milieu.

Numerous interracial organizations operated within Norfolk before 1954 and even enjoyed integrated lunches. Stern worked with Episcopal ministers and integrated ministerial associations in a positive fashion to promote desegregation and interacted with key activists within the Jewish and general communities. At least one conservative rabbi acted as an early ally. Ultimately in his outspoken support for integration and civil rights, including voting, Stern enjoyed wide-scale support from his congregation, from the local Jewish organizations, from area rabbis, and from the general Jewish community. These factors marked Norfolk as different from most other cities in the South.

Somewhat surprisingly, Stern expressed ambivalence concerning Rabbi Emmet Frank of Alexandria, Virginia, who openly attacked longtime Virginia Senator Harry Byrd and his pro-segregation political machine. The activist rabbis including Stern tended to be pragmatic idealists. Frank had taken the principled stand, but they wondered if he had pushed Byrd further toward a reactionary stance with Frank's highly personal remarks.

While Allen Krause could count Norfolk as a city in the land of the almost possible, Virginia illustrated a state in the almost impossible category. The state government willingly closed all public schools rather than integrate. Thus the battle to integrate was tied to the battle to open the schools. Stern and his allies made the decision to support private schools and tutors so that the students would not lose time from school. Yet they argued that these measures were temporary and ineffective, that the public schools would have to open and on an integrated basis. They supported a court case for that purpose. Changes in department store policies and even voting came somewhat easier. The business community did not want to lose business, and Stern and his allies helped alter public opinion.

—Mark K. Bauman

Malcolm Stern Interview

June 24, 1966

P. Allen Krause: Rabbi Stern, in what year, during the course of your time in Norfolk, was there an intensification of civil rights activity in your area?

Malcolm Stern: Well, the Supreme Court decision in 1954, of course, precipitated a hardening of all kinds of lines. Prior to that time, I would say that while Norfolk was resistant to any kind of integration, major integration, there were interracial movements that were active and functioning. Then, once the Supreme Court decision came into being, those of us who were ardent for furthering integration began drawing our forces together working harder toward it. The initial response to the Supreme Court decision was: "A year from now, we'll be ready." But, then it became quite obvious that Norfolk and the whole state of Virginia was going to dig in for a long, hard siege.

PAK: What was the majority response—of the non-Jewish population?

MS: Yes, the general community was completely, was indignant at the Supreme Court decision.

PAK: There was not a feeling: "We'd rather have the status quo but since this is it, we might as well slowly work towards this?"

MS: No, they fought it. And the closer it got, by '57, when Negro parents began suing to have their children admitted to formerly white schools, by that time, the lines were drawn very tight. Senator [Harry] Byrd who runs the political machine in Virginia, or did run it, and the vestiges of the Byrd machine are still quite strong, enunciated his platform of massive resistance to integration.[16] And, this became the tone of the community. In the spring of 1957, there was a court order that the seventeen Negro children would be admitted to formerly all-white junior and senior high schools. And this is when the battle really broke out.

PAK: Was there a visible and vocal minority which we would consider to be moderate or liberal?

MS: Yes, yes, there were. There were groups, clergy groups, that spoke out, that tried to . . . I kept making shalom ["peace"] suggestions that would try to alleviate the situation. Norfolk itself is not a typically southern community; its chief industry is the Navy. So, it has some cosmopolite attitudes, so it was easier to find people who were sympathetic to a more moderate view-point in Norfolk than there would be outside in the rest of the [southern] states.[17]

PAK: What was the press and the mass media like?

MS: The press, the newspaper was under single ownership, but it adopted a very interesting policy. The morning paper was pro-integration, the evening paper was pro-segregation.[18] The editor of the morning paper won a Pulitzer Prize for his work on this subject, his editorials in defense of integration.[19]

PAK: And the other mass media, did they play any role at all in this, that you know? Did they editorialize on it?

MS: Not much, not much, because the tendency of the mass media there was not to editorialize, they stayed away from it.

PAK: What about your Jewish community itself? How long had your congregation been in existence?

MS: My congregation was organized in 1848. They went way back.

PAK: And the Jewish community?

MS: The first Jew to settle in Norfolk settled there in the 1790s,[20] and his home was preserved as a museum. The family is still there, they've been Episcopalian for four generations, but the organized Jewish community started in 1848.

PAK: With a Jewish community with such a long period of settlement in this area, what percentage of your people, do you think, have completely, adopted . . . "the southern" . . . ?

MS: The southern mores?

PAK: Yes.

MS: Certainly a good 10 percent of the congregation were southern in their outlook. Another 10 percent—no, maybe a slightly larger percent, 15 percent—I would say, were active liberals. And, the group in between, the other seventy-five percent, went whichever way the wind blew.

PAK: Do you think this 75 percent had an orientation: "We are for equality and would like to see it happen as long as it doesn't bother us and as long as everything is OK?"

MS: Exactly. Or, if it doesn't affect our pocketbook.

PAK: Is that different from the non-Jewish community, do you think?

MS: No, I would say that the percentage of liberals in the Jewish community was possibly higher, but we had liberals in the Christian community too.

PAK: You don't see any particular difference because of their being Jewish in the 75 percent, the majority of your congregation, in their approach . . . ?

MS: I would say their innate sympathies [were more moderate].[21] I could preach on integration, and did. I could bawl them out about integration, and did. And a few might murmur that we don't agree with you, a few of the hardcore ones might say that. Now my Christian liberal clergymen, a number of them were close personal friends, several of them were driven out of their pulpits entirely. Others lost members. None of this happened to me. The only thing that happened to me was that when I started making headlines on this subject, some of my membership got a little bit scared and then tried to have me silenced from public utterance but not from pulpit utterance.

PAK: What was the economic standing and the source of income of the members of your congregation?

MS: I would say that a large majority of my congregation were in comfortable circumstances. We had very little great wealth—Norfolk's not a manufacturing community, there's practically no industry there. I would say most of my people, maybe 15 to 20 percent, were storekeepers, which is rather small for a Jewish community of this size, a Jewish community of about ten thousand people. But the congregation was a community of about a thousand maybe, counting men, women, and children. We had about four hundred families in the congregation during this period. And most of my people, I would say, were in various services that served the community: we had some professionals—doctors and lawyers; a number of them were civil service employees, working in things related to the Navy. Some of them were traveling people who were manufacturers' representatives, these kinds of things; and insurance people, we had quite a number of insurance men, that sort of thing.

PAK: How susceptible do you think they were to economic pressures exerted by the non-Jewish community? Either potential or actual pressures?

MS: I think they were very [susceptible]. The whole attitude of the congregation when I came there, was *mah yomru hagoyim* ["What will the non-Jews say?"] They'd gone through an era of resort anti-Semitism; Virginia Beach nearby had restricted hotels;[22] there had been an active Ku Klux in the area, not in my day but prior to my coming, that lasted all through the '30s, and well down to World War II. There were vestiges of anti-Semitism: there still is a social club that doesn't admit Jews, this kind of thing. And, the old families in the congregation particularly were very sensitive to this sort of thing. Whatever the goyim [non-Jews, sometimes used in the pejorative sense] said, counted.

PAK: What percentage of the Jews in your community were affiliated with some sort of congregation?

MS: Almost a hundred percent, which is typical of the southern Jewish community. I'm sure you're getting that answer most places.

PAK: Yes, though sometimes it varies down to 60 percent.

MS: It depends: the larger the city [the lower the percentage]. But there is a great deal of pressure in a town like Norfolk. The children are asked by their playmates, which Sunday school do you go to? When a man is introduced on a speaker's platform, a gentile, they point to the fact that he's a teacher in the Sunday school at so-and-so church—this is part, an important part, of his biography.

PAK: **How many rabbis were there in the community while you were there?**

MS: We had one Conservative congregation which, off and on, had an assistant rabbi as well as a senior rabbi, [the] same senior rabbi.[23] Another Conservative congregation that was formed after I arrived in Norfolk and built very rapidly,[24] and we had one major Orthodox congregation which was a merger of three smaller ones.[25] We had four rabbis with the possibility of a fifth. Then, Virginia Beach had a rabbi;[26] we had a rabbinical association, with twelve to thirteen rabbis including the chaplains in the area.

PAK: **Virginia Beach is very close?**

MS: Now the entire county became the City of Virginia Beach,[27] but the actual town of Virginia Beach is twenty miles from downtown Norfolk.

PAK: **When intense civil rights activity broke out, let's say after the 1954 decision, where did the ministers stand in your community? What reaction did they have?**

MS: Well, we had had an Interracial Ministerial Association founded in 1948, which was originally designed to have eighteen white and eighteen Negro ministers. There were alternating presidents and then, gradually, the numbers didn't matter, and it became more or less just an integrated ministerial group that sat down and met periodically.

PAK: **Who started this?**

MS: It was started by a white Episcopal minister and his neighbor, a colored Baptist minister.[28] I was the only rabbi in it.

PAK: **At no time when you were there was there just a Protestant minister . . . ?**

MS: They had a Protestant Ministerial Association which eventually absorbed the colored ministers. The colored ministers had their own association.

PAK: **This was not just a token association, this one that was integrated, was it?**

MS: No, this was one that met purposely to work on interracial projects. And, as early as 1951, I remember we actually sponsored a service which I held in my temple, on Washington's birthday, [a] Brotherhood Week service, to which we brought as preacher the head of, the president of the Virginia Union University in Richmond,[29] which was a colored Negro school.

PAK: **Why did they only have thirty-six people in the beginning?**

MS: Actually, the meeting never consisted of thirty-six people, but they decided that they would start with that number.

PAK: Were there ministers that didn't want to have anything to do with this?
MS: Definitely.
PAK: Were they in the minority or the majority?
MS: I would say that they would be in the majority. This is Bible Belt country—they call Norfolk the largest city in North Carolina, which is the Piney Woods section of North Carolina. The state line was only seventeen miles south of us. And a lot of North Carolinians urbanized in Norfolk. Probably 30 percent of Norfolk's population were these Piney Woods, very fundamentalist Baptist and Methodist people. Their ministry almost universally was opposed to integration.
PAK: So what did they do in 1954 and after?
MS: What did our group do after 1954? We were less effective after 1954 than we were before.
PAK: So, you were talking about before then?
MS: Yes, what I was trying to mention, we had this interracial service, my membership was scared to death of it, the board bawled me out like mad because I contracted for it before asking the board's permission to do it. What saved my skin was the fact that it was done; and interestingly enough, the interracial ministers group, the Interracial Ministers' Fellowship as we called it, did not officially sponsor this service; they were afraid to. So, it was sponsored by a group of ministers of Norfolk. And, since one of the leading Episcopalian ministers was involved, this saved my skin, the fact that I could say, he was participating in the program, he's one of the sponsoring ministers involved, made it right with my congregation.
PAK: Did this actually come to a serious discussion at a board meeting?
MS: Yes, it did, and one of the members was delegated to sit down with me to discuss how wrong I was in doing this sort of thing, even though the man they picked was completely in sympathy with what I was trying to do.
PAK: What was your response to the response of the congregation and the board?
MS: My response was that they were fearful that bombs might be thrown or, this sort of thing. Why should the Jews take the leadership in this—all this sort of fear—and I tried to reassure them and told them that this was being done by responsible people, that it was a service of worship, it was announced as a service of worship. That our membership was not required to attend, it wasn't on Friday night, and that we were the logical people to do it, because if it were done on a Sunday, the ministers couldn't come, no one service could be the center of it. I even organized an interracial choir to sing for us.[30]
PAK: Did you make any commitment or state that you would make some changes in your methodology in the future?

MS: Not at that point, not at that point. I said, "Now we've done it, from here on in it's up to somebody else." Even prior to the Interracial Ministers' Fellowship there had been a Women's Council for Interracial Cooperation also, founded by Episcopal women—not by Jewish women, but in cooperation with Jewish women.[31] You see, the Episcopal Church in Virginia is the status church, the founding church; you know Virginia had an established church in colonial days, and there are vestiges of that in the social strata there. If—and the Jews always looked—when a Jew left Judaism in Virginia, he automatically embraced the Episcopal Church.[32]

PAK: **One rabbi said that his methodology—in doing anything in civil rights—was to put a Christian in front, and let him do what that rabbi really wanted to do, but the rabbi would stay in the background. Did you find that to be a logical approach, using an Episcopal minister, for example?**

MS: I wouldn't hesitate to do things, but I would be exonerated in the eyes of those in the congregation who opposed it if there were Episcopal ministers or [other] Christian clergy involved in it.

PAK: **Involved, but not necessarily in front?**

MS: No, not necessarily.

PAK: **What about the rabbis of the community? What was their response to this?**

MS: They were very late coming into the picture, and I'll allude to that later if we get into the school situation, that's where they came in.

PAK: **I'm afraid that I cut you off on your response to what the ministers did after 1954.**

MS: After '54? After '54, we kept meeting but we felt rather frustrated, we didn't know where to go, what to do, and until the schools became an issue—the possibility of closing the schools—all we did was kind of meet and inform ourselves on what was going on in interracial activity around the country, what progress was being made in integration, the Louisville story,[33] you know the gradual steps that ultimately led to integration throughout this country.

PAK: **Did you ever play a leadership role in this group?**

MS: Yes. I was president of the group one year.

PAK: **Which year, Rabbi?**

MS: I don't remember, I don't.

PAK: **Before 1954?**

MS: It would seem to me it was after. We had kind of a presidium, a steering committee—I was president of it. But, the function of the president was primarily to line up programs for the year. One other aspect of this was that we met in churches and synagogues for luncheons. Our meetings were luncheon meetings, and of course sitting down with a Negro at lunch was a unique experience in Virginia in those days. We had to get our women to put out a luncheon for us. I usually managed to do it about once every other year, get my women to do it. The way I would do it would be to go to a particular woman that I was close to and would say, "Would you mind arranging a luncheon for me for two dozen ministers who are coming?"[34]

PAK: What would be the normal way, if you were having a luncheon?

MS: Well, if I were having a luncheon there, I would ask the Sisterhood officially to do it.

PAK: Why couldn't you do that in this case?

MS: Because too many members of the Sisterhood would have fought the idea.

PAK: You think you probably could have had it, but it would have caused too much dissension?

MS: Yes. It could have been a very difficult thing to get across.

PAK: Rabbi, could you go into maybe two or three specific involvements on your part in specific civil rights programs, activities of various sorts in your community, and explain as you're doing so the participation of various members in your community, and your own methodology of action?

MS: Yes. Where I played the biggest role was when the schools were threatened with closing. As I mentioned, in the spring, in June of 1957, a federal court judge, who happened to be a personal friend,[35] ruled that the seventeen Negro children had to be admitted to formerly white junior and senior high schools. That was in June. It happened that the week after his decision was announced in the press, I was speaking at a Methodist church across the street from the temple,[36] and I said in that speech that if we didn't rise above our personal feelings of segregation versus integration, we'd have disintegration in the public schools. Nobody could believe that people would put their prejudices above having an education for their children. They just couldn't believe it. As I came out of the church, the federal judge happened to be the first guy that greeted me,[37] and I said, "I may be tarred and feathered for making a statement like this," even raising the issue in the pulpit,[38] because most of the clergy were ducking it by this point. There was a great deal of fear, the people were bewildered. I was active in the Rotary Club, and of course the Rotary was a bastion of the established community, the leaders, the business and professional leaders of the community, you didn't—nobody ever talked about integration publicly there, it just wasn't done. But, one of the men in the church who was a leading Rotarian and a man whom I knew and liked, and he liked me, came up to me afterwards and he said, "Can't we do something to reach some kind of a decision before this gets too far out of hand?" That gave me the idea of setting up a public meeting, a forum, at which there would be a panel discussion, where the clergy should act as ushers, [and where] people should present various programs and attitudes, and possibly try to work out a solution so that there could be some kind of integrated school without creating a ruckus. By this time, of course, Little Rock had already happened and everybody wanted to avoid the fracas that Little Rock had gone through. So I mimeographed this suggestion and mailed it to the mayor, to the members of the city council, to a number of my Rotary people, to people who knew me personally in the community who were part of the power structure of the community.[39] I was leaving to go to the CCAR [Central Conference of American Rabbis] [convention], which that year was in Chicago, and was heading on to the West Coast, so I said I would be back the first part of August, to set the thing up or to lend what hand I could, but, in the meantime, would they give it consideration? I didn't hear anything from Norfolk at all except [from] my very faithful organist, a Baptist, [who] kept sending me clippings from the newspaper. "Rabbi Stern proposes . . ."[40] and the whole thing was outlined, the morning paper came out . . . [saying that] was a good idea, and the evening paper came out with, "The Jews better shut up," or something like this, and I knew my people were running scared, you see, when this kind of stuff came out in the evening paper.[41] Nobody commented. Nobody. We had a lot of correspondence with Norfolk while we were on vacation but nobody mentioned any of it, so I knew that something had happened. It turns out that the mayor was quoted as saying that the idea wouldn't work; since the state law of massive resistance was on the books, no matter what came out of this forum, it would be illegal. I got back to Norfolk and found out that rumors had been running rampant that my suggesting this had taken the mayor off the hook, because he was being pressured to do something, and it gave him the opportunity to answer me in public this way, and all that sort of stuff. Came September and the schools—they kept postponing the opening date of school, trying to wrestle the thing through.

PAK: This forum never materialized?

MS: Never, no, the forum never materialized. Incidentally, this whole story is written up in . . . the [American Jewish] Archives, I wouldn't guarantee that it's there but I don't know if we have to take the whole tape to go into all the ramifications of it. But briefly, let me say this: that the schools didn't open, and the schools stayed closed. The clergy as a group, I mean our, the interested clergy as a group went to the next meeting of the city council. The council met every Tuesday—and the president of the ministerial association got up and said to the mayor, "Mr. Mayor, anything we clergy can do to get the schools reopened, please call on us." At which point, the mayor turned on us—and this was the first time anybody publicly knew where the mayor stood in the situation—and he said, "You tell those seven-teen niggers to go back where they came from, [and] we'll open the schools tomorrow." It really knocked the breath out of all of us when he said it, be-cause as I say, nobody had been aware of where he stood. Everybody knew where I stood, because I'd been making headlines on the subject, so I didn't speak at the meeting. But, this same Methodist minister who was president of the ministerial association got up later in the meeting and said, "Mr. Mayor, I can't leave here without letting you know that we are all shocked and dismayed at your remark, and, you can't stop progress." One of the Episcopal ministers got up, his name was Peyton Randolph Williams,[42] you know, old Virginia—first family of Virginia—got up, and he said, "If you send those seventeen children back, there'll be seventeen others to take their place tomorrow and so on. You just can't stop it." Well, the mayor turned out to be such a bigot that even his own associates disowned him and he was . . . he lost—well, he resigned before the next election, actually. He was pushed out.[43] But, it took the business community that whole first semester to wake up to the fact that they were losing business.

PAK: Did you, the clergy, have any other role in this?

MS: Yes, we had a tremendous role. It was about then that the other rabbis began getting into the picture, and taking a part. The Jewish Community Council quietly put up money to encourage things that would lead to the reopening of the schools, and naturally the integration involved.

PAK: Such as meetings or what?

MS: No, what actually happened was they contributed to a fund to engage a lawyer and persuaded twenty-three parents, Jewish and Christian, who brought suit in the Federal Courts, that their children's constitutional rights were being denied by not having public school.

PAK: Where'd the money come from for this lawyer, just from the Jewish community?

MS: No, it came from various sources, but some of it was Jewish money. That still wasn't known publicly, but that was what actually happened.

PAK: Did you have any role in that?

MS: No, that particular aspect, I did not. But, what happened was that the teachers, the public school teachers—incidentally, this only affected the white junior and senior high schools. The elementary schools were func-tioning, because the court order only affected the white junior and senior high schools. The Negro high school was functioning, but our junior and senior high school kids were out on the street officially. And, the teachers were under contract to teach so they were being paid whether they taught or not.[44] The parents went around hiring up the teachers to run tutoring groups for their children. And, when, after a couple of weeks of trying to organize tutoring groups in homes, they realized that no home could hold all of this, [and] they began badgering the churches and the temples to open their facilities. Originally I opposed it. I went to the board and fought and said, "We don't want to do anything that will encourage keeping the schools closed." But when it was obvious that the schools were going to stay closed, I capitulated along with others and said that we would open our facility.[45] Tutoring classes [were] not for our children specifically but for anybody who would sign up. One of my Sunday school teachers happened to be a Latin teacher, so she'd teach one period of Latin in our building, and then she'd take a taxi cab and go across town and teach another period. This was the way the high schoolers were getting an education. Some of the youngsters went out to another county where the schools were open, were bused or transported by their parents to other counties for schooling. Some were sent off to private schools—the local private schools were very heavily over taxed at this point. But, some children were lost to education forever. I mean we had teenage marriages resulting from this thing and so on. But, when the rabbis got together on this thing, we knew of only one Jewish child who was not getting an education somewhere. Well, the end of the semester was coming along and there was pressure to keep the tutoring groups going, and the argument went like this: "The teachers are so happy in this arrangement, they're teaching the children who really want an education" and so on. That was when the rabbis got busy. We started screaming, we went to mass meetings, talked to our own congregants, got the Christian clergy alerted and aware that this was no substitute for accredited high school education, that the youngsters couldn't get into college; they weren't getting any sciences. So on.

PAK: **Did you plan this out, or was it simply a matter of your talking over the phone with a couple of rabbis, and each talked . . .**

MS: Actually, we met; I don't remember the details of exactly how—you were constantly working with expedience, you know. There was no formal, organized, planned way of doing things. Somebody would get an idea and we'd call a meeting of anybody we could get that would be useful to the meeting and put them to work. That was the way we operated. And, then came the opening day of school. Oh, I'm ahead of my story. The court case of the twenty-three parents was adjudicated, and the court order ruled that their children's rights were being denied and the State of Virginia would have to reduce its massive resistance and open up the schools.

PAK: **This only took a few months?**

MS: It took—I think they brought their case in August, or September, it may not have been until October,[46] and by the end of January, they got a ruling. Based on the Supreme Court decision, you see. And, the governor of the state, [James] Lindsay Almond [Jr.] , on a Tuesday, the last Tuesday in January, announced on television, "We've only begun to fight," meaning, fighting this court order. The city council tried to pull a fast one by saying, "Okay, we'll reopen the schools, but we won't pay the teachers." And, on Saturday, the following Saturday, which was two days before the schools were to open, the governor went on television again, being a smart lawyer, capitulating. Senator Byrd never forgave him; he lost political status as a result of it.

PAK: Is that the beginning of the break between Almond and Byrd?

MS: Yes, yes. Almond was slated for a federal judgeship subsequently and Byrd didn't do anything to help him, and it delayed, and delayed, and delayed. Byrd was part of the committee that could have put a stamp [of approval] on it. He finally got it, but at great personal cost. Getting back to my participation, the first day of school came, all of us clergy volunteered to escort the Negro children to the opening of classes. The school authorities asked us not to, with a promise that there would be ample police protection.[47] One other thing that was done, this was done by one of my members[48] working with some of the Jewish Community Council, CRC [Community Relations Council] money, [he] got hold of the president of the Key Club, which was a Kiwanis-sponsored high school organization, and, got this lad—it was a Jewish boy, by the way, the leader[49]—to get all the Key Clubs together and put a full-page ad in both papers saying that the eyes of America were on Norfolk, and that they were calling on their fellow high schoolers and junior high schoolers, fellow teenagers, to show that they could open schools without incident. Because, we were worried, you know, what kind of crackpot might do some damage to these children.

PAK: This was the president of your congregation that talked to this . . . ?

MS: No, it was a man who was an officer of the congregation—I think at that time, he was the second vice-president of the congregation.

PAK: Did he come to you with that idea?

MS: He reported it to me, but he didn't consult me. One other thing that I did, in this last hectic week before school opened, I realized that there had to be a letting-off-steam period. I wrote the governor; I don't know that it had any effect, but I wrote the governor, even though at that point I didn't know he was going to capitulate, and suggested to him that the state set up in the Norfolk area, allot the funds for one school that would be for those who vehemently objected to sending their children to an integrated school.

PAK: Sounds like this would have meant everybody would [want to] go [to such a school]?

MS: Well, it would have been interesting to see what happened. As it turned out, the state took the idea—they probably didn't get it from me, but at

least I suggested it—and they agreed that every child who was staying out
of the integrated schools . . . [those children] would receive what it cost
the state per capita per child. So, they got a two hundred and eighty dollar
grant. Any parent whose child was not going to an integrated school, who
wanted to keep their child out of an integrated school, could collect two
hundred and eighty dollars a year from the state, for sending [the child]
to a private school. And there was a segregated school set up as a result of
this, with these funds which remained in existence for five or six years—I
think it's disappeared now. The majority of the community did not take advantage of it, showing that when the cards were down, and when the integration battle had been won, even a token integration, that the mass of the
population was not too upset.

The schools reopened. One of my girls[50] told me that the second day
of school, she was in a white high school of eight to ten thousand students . . . and [there was] this one Negro child assigned to that school, by
court order; and, she said, "I saw this girl standing all alone in the cafeteria
line, everybody giving her a wide berth, and I invited her to come over and
sit at our table." And I could have hugged her on the spot, and did; she said
a few people passed by and made remarks like, "nigger lover," and this kind
of thing. But, otherwise, this [reopening of the schools] passed without
incident.

PAK: This was a member of your congregation?

MS: One of my confirmands, yes.

**PAK: What were the repercussions from the non-Jewish community and
the Jewish community with regard to your participation?**

MS: My participation? One place along the line, I was personally attacked in
print by two or three writers, non-Jewish writers. I can't remember ever
having anything untoward done to me or happen to me as a result of it or
any reverberations. Once the battle lines had been completely drawn and
once the schools were closed, my own people were pretty solidly behind
what I was trying to do.

PAK: You didn't have, this time, some response from the board?

MS: No, no. No, the board never raised any objections to what we were trying to do. The business community finally capitulated just before school
was opened because [members of] the Navy were asking for transfers,
teachers were asking for transfers, they realized they were getting hit in their
pocketbook. So, a hundred of the leading businessmen, including some
of my members, ran a full-page ad in the paper urging that the schools be
reopened.[51]

After this was won the Negroes were beginning to win more and more
rights in the community; they won first the battle of the department

stores, and [then the battle of] the lunch counters, in which I played a very little role.

PAK: What was the role you did play?

MS: The Jewish department store owners talked to me about what they ought to do.

PAK: Did they contact you about this?

MS: Well, I'd meet them at social gatherings and they'd raise the question with me. They didn't seriously take my advice, but they were just more or less ventilating their own feelings on the subject and what they ultimately did was, a group of them got together, the Retail Merchants Association, which at that particular point had a Jewish president, they got together and they decided that, if you do it, I'll do it, we'll all do it at the same time. That's what actually happened. They did have one of them [who] closed his lunch room until the thing was settled among the four major department stores in town, this sort of thing, but [otherwise] they operated cooperatively. I didn't enter the picture. I merely got reports back from them about what had happened. I do remember that my wife and I were going to have—I think it was a leadership group of the Women's Interracial Council—a program planning group [to the house]. We said, "Let's have a meeting at our house." And, other people on the council who were Norfolkians, who had been positive hard workers, complete liberals, and hard workers for integration said, "We advise you against inviting Negroes into your home." I never did. I never did. We happened to live on a street that was one block long. We were, up to the last six, seven years of living there, the only Jews on the street. One other Jewish family, originally from New York, moved across the street from us, a dentist and his wife, who were members of the congregation. They never felt at ease with the rest of the block. We used to have block parties, Fourth of July, Memorial Day—we'd have a cookout with the whole block and so on. And, they never really felt at home or at ease, seldom participated, and if they did their participation was minimal. But, we had people on the block who were sending their children to the segregated white high school, the private school, when it got organized. We had definite bigotry on the street, not against Jews but against Negroes. And, in the interest of public relations with our neighbors, I never did, on the advice of these people, never did invite a Negro into my home.

PAK: Were there any other areas [of activity], Rabbi, in education or voting or anything like that?

MS: The voting issue was an interesting thing. Virginia had a "blank sheet" registration law, which was a successor to the Grandfather Law and the literacy test, and so on. You were supposed to memorize twelve rubrics: name, address, phone number, county in which you last voted, and so on—you had to memorize them in order, and fill out a blank sheet in the presence of the registrar. And, what happened was, and this our Interracial Ministers Group encouraged, they were conducting classes in the Negro churches on how to register. I never taught a class, but I got literature from the League of Women Voters and had it printed and was distributing it around the Negro community and even . . . our domestic servants, we always made them vote. We always taught them their responsibility about voting, both at the temple and at home. I remember the sexton of the Jewish cemetery, I was encouraging him to learn how to register and so on. This kind of thing.

PAK: Was there anything else you were involved with?

MS: I was a member of the Norfolk Symphony Board, and worked very hard to try to get the symphony integrated. The symphony had as an adjunct a chorale. We got the chorus integrated. The conductor of our symphony was most agreeable with engaging Negro musicians.[52] We got the board to approve it, [but] he couldn't find any qualified Negro musicians. This was legitimate, I mean it wasn't a question of [prejudice]—most of the Negroes who played instruments played jazz band instruments, not symphonic instruments.

PAK: What relationship did you have with so-called civil rights organizations or important individuals in these organizations?

MS: Very little. Actually, I'm sure, that many of the [southern] rabbis have told you that they were more disturbed by the civil rights organizations and their activities. The Freedom Rides and so on created more troubles for us living in the community than they contributed to the well-being of the community.

PAK: Even in Norfolk?

MS: Yes, the hit-and-run method of the Freedom Rides was, when rabbis came down on Freedom Rides, we had to be their *kapporah* [Hebrew for "sacrificial offering"].

PAK: Do you think in the long run that they were helpful?

MS: I think they definitely played a role in being helpful to the Negro community, no question of it, but they made our task harder.

PAK: Your goal would probably be for complete equality and for . . .

MS: Yes, equality of opportunity.

PAK: [Achievement of] the goals of the federal government, for example, in the civil rights law . . .

MS: Yes, yes. Right.

PAK: Do you think that the Freedom Rides helped that goal in your community?

MS: Yes, I think they did, no question of it. There were a number of things that I did which I didn't mention earlier. I brought in Fellowship House in Philadelphia—it was an early interracial, interreligious organization founded about 1941. When I first went to Philadelphia as an assistant, I had seen it, and I had been very active in its program. It's still functioning; it's a remarkable Quaker-sponsored, and very remarkable fellowship movement, of action.[53] I've conducted seders for them; I've helped build fellowship houses—we took an old wreck of a firehouse and we rebuilt it. They had a fellowship choir that went around the country putting on propaganda-type programs for integration, and I succeeded in having them come to Norfolk and put on a program in the high school auditorium. That took a battle.

PAK: How?

MS: We got the Interracial Ministerial Group to sponsor us, and since it was sponsored . . .

PAK: You said, "We."

MS: Well, this Interracial Ministerial Fellowship, I brought the suggestion to them, they agreed to it, then we went after the high school. And, fortunately, the superintendent of schools was a liberal. He subsequently retired, during all of this he reached the age of retirement, [and] he went to work for the Southern Regional Council[54] and he became their consultant on education. His name was John Brubaker, and he gave us permission to use the high school auditorium with the understanding that the public school system was not sponsoring it. There were some objections voiced in the community to letting the high school be used for an integrated program, but we got away with it.

PAK: That was in what year?

MS: I'd have to look it up, but my feeling was it was about in the spring of '57, before the schools actually closed, about February or March of '57.

PAK: What is your response to the national Jewish organizations with regard to the role that they may have played in the civil rights movement in your area?

MS: Well, NCRAC [National Jewish Community Relations Advisory Council][55] counseled with our local Jewish Community Council on methods and procedures, [and] . . . the American Jewish Committee, also; possibly the [American Jewish] Congress[56] and JWV [Jewish War Veterans]—I wasn't active with those organizations, so I don't know. But, through the Community Relations Council, which was the clearinghouse of the Jewish Community Council, we were getting information from all parts of the country through the national Jewish organizations. They served as an informative, information-giving, and sometimes advisory body.

PAK: Would you call them beneficial to the . . .

MS: Yes, they were helpful, they were, they did not enter into any actions that I know of, but they did lend aid.

PAK: Were they ever detrimental?

MS: I don't recall any instance of their being detrimental.

PAK: **Other than this Interfaith Council of Ministers, is there any other organization that you belonged to that you would consider to have been an important tool in the accomplishment of your goals in the civil rights movement?**

MS: Well, I constantly spoke to the Women's Council for Interracial Cooperation, I was on their program at least once a year, [or] once every other year. My Rotary contacts were very useful in, on a one-to-one basis, talking to people; the Symphony Board. Let's see, what else was I involved with? At one point, we had fifteen interracial things going. I remember at a CCAR meeting. I don't remember which one it was. I think it was in Asbury Park—we had a meeting of seven rabbis, just an ad hoc meeting called of southern rabbis.

PAK: **Is this the one that was a closed session?**

MS: Yes, yes.[57] Some of the others may have referred to it. But, there was a meeting of the southern rabbis to discuss pros and cons—I remember Julian Feibelman was talking about New Orleans and how difficult it was to work in the area of race relations in his area. And I said Norfolk was different, that we had fifteen projects going at that point in interracial activity. This was pre-1954.[58]

PAK: **If a history was to be written of Norfolk—let's say fifty years from now, and they were going to look at the civil rights movement in Norfolk first, but I'd also like you to address yourself to all of Virginia, and all of the South—what role did the rabbis of the community, of the state, and of the area play in the civil rights movement?**

MS: I would say it would have been a secondary role. It wouldn't have been a major role. I think that our very nature—the fact that our congregations were never in the forefront of it, were always waiting to see what the gentiles did first—prevented the rabbis from being the, the great outspoken leaders that some have been in other parts of the country.[59]

PAK: **Do you think the rabbis were instrumental in any way as, as beginners of some activity, giving impetus to something or, if they did anything, were they basically a support to something that was started by . . . ?**

MS: By others? Well, I tried to start things, as I've indicated. Without success. . . . One of the things that I suggested [spring 1958] when the whole talk was in the direction of integrating the schools—I made the suggestion that our local college department of education run a demonstration school that would be a top-notch educational institution using the latest techniques and integrated, as a kind of a pilot project in integration. Nothing came of that either.

PAK: Is it because you represented a small number of people, or is it because you didn't have the proper contacts, what was the reason?

MS: I would say that maybe I didn't lay my groundwork well enough; these were the ideas that I would dream up and then I'd sound off on them and perhaps if I had organized a body of opinion to back them, they might have come off. That may have been the weakness in it, from where I sat. But, also, I think the times weren't just right for it. I know Gabe Cohen from the *International Jewish Post*,[60] the editor in Indianapolis, came down to give a lecture at the Conservative congregation[61] in the middle of the school crisis, it was after the schools were closed, before we'd gone to work to convince people to reopen them. And he wrote an editorial in which he said the Norfolk rabbis were doing nothing to help the situation. I wrote him a stinging letter and said as a newspaper man, he should have investigated a little bit further,[62] and sent him copies of clippings with my name, and headlines, and this sort of thing, and I got pretty indignant about it. As I say, none of the Conservative or Orthodox rabbis took any kind of public stand. None of the Conservative or Orthodox rabbis got into the picture publicly until toward the end of the school crisis.

PAK: Do you think the national Jewish press was not understanding of the position that the rabbis . . . ?

MS: The *Philadelphia [PA] Jewish Exponent* wrote an article, quite a strong article, about what I had been trying to do. Prejudiced by the fact that the editor was a cousin of my wife's but, nonetheless, he did play up what my role had been, and that was picked up by the *Denver [CO] Intermountain Jewish News*, which copied the article from the *Exponent* with my permission.[63] The general Jewish press, I would say, was not too aware of what was going on in Norfolk. In the South generally, I would say they were rather condemnatory of the whole southern attitude, and in the [Central] Conference [of American Rabbis] there was a condemnation of the southern rabbi.

PAK: Rightly or wrongly?

MS: Well, you know it's easy to look at another guy, but until you're in his shoes, you can't recognize what he's doing, like the Montgomery and Selma crisis, and my late colleague Rabbi [Eugene] Blackschlager [who] was severely criticized. Well, Gene was the kind of docile rabbi who did what his board told him anyway, and in Montgomery, Alabama, he wasn't going to stand up and get his head chopped off. Norfolk was a little milder in climate, and I could say what I wanted to say without getting my head chopped off.

PAK: I'd like your response to what a rabbi [did] in the same state as you, in Alexandria—Rabbi [Emmet] Frank, who in 1958 preached a rather . . .

MS: [*interrupting*] nasty sermon about Byrd.

PAK: **What was your response to that sermon? Do you think that such a sermon was helpful or not helpful or what?**

MS: I think it enunciated quite clearly the disaffection of the Jewish community generally with Byrd.

PAK: **Do you think that was a good methodology in terms of accomplishing the goal of furthering the civil rights movement?**

MS: Hmmm . . . I think it may have stiffened the Byrd resistance. Byrd was, incidentally, a very charming man, a very shrewd operator, a very skilled politician. The Byrd machine stayed in office—it was absolutely without corruption; it was a clean machine—it has stayed in office for forty years, something like that, operating ethically. The way they would operate is, if [a man's] term was coming up, he would resign and the governor of the state, he was always a Byrd designate, would appoint somebody else to serve his unexpired term and then this guy would be up for election and generally got it, you see, and everything was done by the Byrd regime to inhibit voting. Not to prevent it, but to discourage it.

PAK: **So do you think that the sermon was not so helpful to the overall goals?**

MS: It's very hard to gauge. I would say at the time the Jews, my congregants, were highly critical of Rabbi Frank; only the extreme liberals applauded him, and I found myself being put on the defensive about it. But, at the time—you know, under the expediency of the situation—I wasn't sure that it was the right thing.

PAK: **You say that you had to be defensive about Frank with members of your congregation?**

MS: Right, right.

PAK: **Did you ever find that you had to defend your own role with members of the congregation because they felt you weren't doing enough?**

MS: No, nobody ever accused me of not doing enough, and when I left Norfolk, a number of the people who had been somewhat condemnatory of my role in the whole thing, spoke out very enthusiastically that in the height of the integration battle, our rabbi took a leadership role.

PAK: **When was the last time when you really faced a problem with this congregation because of civil rights activity?**

MS: Civil rights activity? At one point, I think it was just about the time of the school closing, five members of my board, wanted to call a special board meeting to have me muffled,[64] and, I had spoken my piece; I'd made my position very clearly enunciated in the press, and so on, in headlines, and this is what bothered them.

PAK: **This was the only time when this ever happened to you in your congregation?**

MS: No, they sat down with me after the interracial service back in '51. But in '58, in the fall of '58, after the schools closed and I had begun to make headlines too often, I agreed to consult with the president of the temple and with one liberal board member before I made any more public statements—and both men were liberals, so I wasn't afraid of them, and this satisfied them, and they called off the whole deal, and from then on I didn't have any major difficulties with the subject.

9
James A. Wax

Memphis, Tennessee, and Its Jewish Community

Few places in the South, indeed in all of North America, were more promising for settlement than the bluff south of the confluence of the Wolf and Mississippi rivers. Blessed with access to the Mississippi, the area was also the heart of one of the richest cotton-growing regions and extensive hardwood forests in the country. Inhabited originally by native nations, it served as the location of a French fort (1739), a Spanish fort (1795), and finally America's Fort Adams (1797). In 1818 the Chickasaw Nation ceded West Tennessee to the United States, which made it possible for John Overton, James Winchester, and future president Andrew Jackson to found Memphis on May 22, 1819. Natural resources notwithstanding, the city's growth was initially hampered by a national economic depression, a river sandbar, competition from other river ports, and the scourge of yellow fever. In 1840 fewer than two thousand people resided in Memphis but, partially due to the influx of central European immigrants, that number increased tenfold by the Civil War.[1]

David Hart, the first known Jewish resident, participated in that influx, arriving from the German states in 1838. Hart operated a combined inn and saloon in Memphis before moving to Indiana. The second documented Jewish Memphian, Joseph Andrews, arrived from Charleston, South Carolina, in 1840 and made his money in cotton, banking, and brokerage businesses. In 1847 he purchased land to be used as a Jewish cemetery that led to the creation of a Hebrew benevolent society three years later. The society organized High Holy Day services each year until area Jews established Congregation B'nai Israel (Children of Israel) in 1853. That same year the community received a $2,000 gift from New Orleans philanthropist Judah Touro that allowed it to lease and convert a building for use as a synagogue. The congregation hired Jacob Peres as cantor in December 1859. When he was caught opening his supper market on the Sabbath, the congregation ended his tenure in April 1860 with more than half a year left on his contract and refused to pay him the remainder of his salary. Peres successfully appealed to the civil courts for redress and thus received the balance of his wages.

A few months after firing Peres, B'nai Israel hired Simon Tuska, who had studied at the Rochester Theology Seminary and the famed Breslau Jewish Theological Seminary. Tuska was the first person to be sent and financed from the United States to be trained at a European Jewish seminary. Isaac Mayer Wise published Tuska's articles in his *Israelite* newspaper. The new rabbi turned out to be an excellent choice, so much so that the congregation's board of trustees extended his contract by ten years and raised his salary.

Nonetheless, the congregation continued to experience unrest. Although begun as a traditional synagogue, typical of acculturating German immigrants most of its members were not observant. With Tuska clearly on the side of the reformers, the tensions between them and the minority who preferred orthodoxy led to a group of about forty leaving to create congregation Beth El Emess (Emeth), ("The House of the God of Truth"). Yet B'nai Israel reabsorbed Beth El Emess a few years later.[2]

By 1857 Memphis boasted two railroad lines connecting it to Ohio and South Carolina. By 1861, the plantation owners and local merchants shipped sixty thousand bales of cotton annually.[3] With such a prosperous environment, several Jews cast their fate with the city, some of whom created successful businesses. The *City Directory* for 1855–56 notes that Jews were cotton buyers, bankers, grocers, auctioneers, and owners of more than half of Memphis's twenty-six clothing stores. Joseph Andrews, apparently the most affluent Jew during the antebellum period, accumulated property listed at close to $150,000 in the directory. By the end of the Civil War, J. H. Lowenstine and Brothers ran The Southern Palace, what the *Memphis (TN) Daily Bulletin* called a "splendid store" filled with dry goods, hosiery, boots, and shoes.[4] The Menkin brothers (J. S. and J. A.) had a comparable department store that ran large and frequent advertisements in the local press. Henry Seesel & Son parlayed a slaughterhouse into a grocery store chain. M. Boom provided meat to the city hospital, and Jacob Peres, the former cantor, brokered cotton, sugar, and groceries.[5] Jews also owned jewelry businesses. General Ulysses S. Grant's General Order No. 162 indicates that some of these Jews and others, fifteen in all, sold military goods in 1863.[6] According to a September 24, 1863, article in the *Daily Bulletin*, "The large Jewish element of Memphis was made manifest yesterday by the number of closed stores on Main Street. The Day of Atonement was very generally observed by those of Jewish faith."[7]

The success of Jewish Memphians is remarkable given the tragedy and trauma that the city endured. On four separate occasions beginning in 1867, Memphis was ravaged by yellow fever. Epidemics in 1873 and 1878 caused thousands of deaths, and as many as three-fourths of the city's residents fled, many permanently. Memphis had 2,100 Jews before the outbreaks but only three hundred afterward. Some, however, opted to stay in order to help those who had been stricken, many of whom were poor Irish who lived in the downtown area known as the "Pinch." One Jew who did so was Abraham E. Frankland, a partner in an auctioneer and commission merchant firm dealing in "real estate, negroes, merchandise, furniture, [and] groceries."[8] Frankland, a member of Congregation B'nai Israel and a leader in the Memphis lodge of B'nai B'rith, was president of the Hebrew Hospital Relief Association and the city's tax collector. He risked his life daily to help the sick during the epidemic of 1873. When the frost came ending the siege, Frankland penned a memoir, "History, Yellow Fever Epidemic Memphis, 1873,"[9] in which he expressed contempt for "the merchant princes [who] were afraid it [yellow fever] would kill trade," and who pled with the press "for God's sake do not publish anything [about the epidemic]—keep it out [of] the papers, or our trade is ruined. Say nothing about it, tis only a little sickness among the Irish in Pinch." Although a businessman himself, Frankland rhetorically asked, "What was the life of the poor to them compared to their money-making and money-getting?"[10] Frankland survived the epidemic but one of his sons succumbed.

Nathan Davis Menken, commander of General John Pope's Civil War bodyguard unit, provided funds to many Jews so that they could flee the city while he remained to care for the sick. Menken died on September 3, 1878, at the age of forty-four, one of the seventy-eight victims buried that year in B'nai Israel's cemetery.[11]

Max Samfield, rabbi of B'nai Israel, also remained behind only to experience the misfortune of having to bury his colleague, Rabbi Ferdinand Sarner of Beth El Emess. Samfield had come to Memphis only two years earlier, but his tenure lasted forty-four years. He became a significant actor in community affairs, helping to found the United Charities of Memphis and the Tennessee Society for the Prevention of Cruelty to Animals and Children. He participated in the establishment of the Young Men's Hebrew Association and the Hebrew Relief Association and founded, edited, and published the *Nashville (TN) Jewish Spectator*, the first Jewish weekly published in the South. In 1915 Samfield died in the city at age seventy-one.[12]

Yellow fever so devastated Memphis that the city failed to meet its financial obligations and lost its charter, a document not renewed until 1893. In the interim, the installation of proper drainage systems eliminated the outbreaks, and consequently the economy and population soared. By 1900 the city was home to over one hundred thousand people, a 60 percent increase since 1870. The Jewish community shared in the renaissance. Now, however, an influx of East European Jews fleeing oppression caused significant change in the community's make-up. These immigrants started as peddlers then opened stores and prospered, as had the earlier Central European Jews. These newcomers tended to live close together. Thus Memphis gained its first Jewish neighborhood when they supplanted the previous inhabitants of the Pinch who moved economically upward and geographically to other parts of the city. Uncomfortable with liberal Judaism, the new wave of Jewish immigrants founded small traditional shuls based on place of origin, but by the late nineteenth century these had mostly coalesced into a synagogue bearing the name of a famous Jewish philanthropist, Baron Maurice de Hirsch, and a smaller shul, Anshe S'fard, a Polish congregation that mixed Orthodoxy and Hassidic customs and practices. Within a short time Baron Hirsch Congregation had constructed a building, purchased a cemetery, and become the largest Orthodox synagogue in the country.

In 1901, anxious to help the new immigrants assimilate, leaders of the German Jewish community established the Jewish Neighborhood House in the Pinch, similar to the settlement houses created in cities throughout the country. Here the Eastern European immigrants took classes in hygiene, art, English, and citizenship. A federation of Jewish charities was established five years later to consolidate fundraising and make the delivery of services more "scientific."

The Memphis Jewish community shared in the post–World War I prosperity. Jews owned the four major department stores: Goldsmith's, Gerber's, Bry's, and Lowenstein's. Many newcomers also established businesses. One of their number, Philip Belz, arrived from Russia in 1910. In the midst of the Great Depression, he started a construction company that specialized in low-cost apartment buildings that eventually became one of the most successful real estate enterprises in the city. In 1975, Belz's son, Jack, purchased and refurbished the legendary Peabody Hotel.[13] Abe Plough started the Plough Chemical Company as a lad of sixteen in a room above his father's clothing and furnishings store. Beginning with Plough's Antiseptic Healing Oil, a "sure cure for any ill of man or beast," he entered the patent drug business, then the cosmetics business, and finally purchased the St. Joseph Company, famous for aspirin.[14] By 1960, Plough, Inc., had annual sales of about $500 million. Eleven years later he merged his business with the pharmaceutical company, Schering Corporation, and became chairman of both Plough, Inc., and Schering-Plough.

As Jews in Memphis benefitted from being part of the city, so also did the city benefit from their contributions. After the precipitous decline of the stock market on Black Tuesday, October 29, 1929, and the failure of a major Memphis bank, Plough personally advanced $175,000 and raised additional funds from friends to make good on the Christmas savings accounts of the bank's customers. He also added a hundred new employees and raised the salaries of those he already employed. From 1910 to 1914 Dr. Max Goltman, chief surgeon at Memphis General and Baptist Memorial Hospitals, served as superintendent of the city's Health Department and later established a scholarship fund for students at the University of Tennessee Medical School. Marcus Haase helped found the Memphis Council of Social Agencies in 1920 and served as its president several times. His brother Charles served as the Shelby County Food Administrator during World War I.[15] Morris ("M. A.") Lightman, founder of the Malco Theatre chain, raised money for many local nonprofits including the YMCA, the Crippled Adults Hospital, the Collins Chapel Hospital for Negroes, and for the tuberculosis, polio, and heart associations, in addition to serving as mid-South chair of the War Activities Committee during World War II.

By midcentury a new generation of Jews had risen to be counted among the most respected volunteers and philanthropists in the city. Rabbi James Wax of Temple Israel (B'nai Israel changed its name in 1943) twice served as president of the Memphis and Shelby County Mental Health Society. Attorney Benjamin Goodman Jr. presided over the Memphis chapter of the American Red Cross. Automobile-dealership owner Herbert Herff chaired the Memphis Symphony Society, and Morrie and Lillian Moss gave major gifts to Brooks Memorial Art Gallery.[16]

Civic commitment extended to the political process. William Goldman and Joseph Andrews won election as aldermen in the 1840s. In the 1860s Tobias Wolfe was elected wharfmaster; Henry Marks served on the police force; Paul Schuster and Dr. R. L. Laski were aldermen; and former spiritual leader Jacob Peres presided over the Board of Education on which A. E. Frankland and Henry Seesel Jr. served. Toward the end of the nineteenth century Joseph Gronauer won election as a delegate to the Republican National Convention, while Elias Lowenstein served on the committee to restore the city's charter and on the executive committee of the Board of Health. In the first three decades of the twentieth century, Eastern European Jewish immigrants became major players in city, county, and state politics. Israel Peres won election to the Tenth Chancery Division of the Circuit Court of Tennessee; Elias Gates presided over the Tennessee Bar Association; and Max Goltman superintended the Memphis Health Department. S. L. Kopald Jr. of Humko oil products won election as chairman of the Republican Party of Tennessee; Joseph Bearman held the office of assistant district attorney; Joseph Hanover became attorney general of Shelby County; and Eric Hirsch was elected president of the Memphis Cotton Exchange. In the 1940s Eugene Bearman, Marvin Brode, and J. Alan Hanover served in the state legislature; Abe Waldauer was appointed by Franklin Delano Roosevelt to be the Collector of Customs of the Board of Memphis, while Josephine Burson was named state Commissioner of Employment Security and Manpower and also headed Estes Kefauver's campaign for a United States Senate seat. Thus by the turbulent decades of the 1950s and '60s, Jews had become an integral part of the economic, philanthropic, and political life of their city and state.[17]

In contrast to the situation of the city's Jewish community, although many African Americans had access to the polls even during the 1950s, Memphis still entered the 1960s as a segregated city. A popular part of the local press was the "Hambone" cartoon depicting a lazy, uneducated black man. A float featuring

"Black Sambo" highlighted the annual Cotton Carnival parade. African Americans were allowed to visit the zoo, the main branch of the public library, and Brooks Memorial Art Gallery only one day per week, "Black Thursday." They also had one day to visit the summer Tri-State Fair and were constantly confronted by "Colored Only" signs designating their sections on buses, in theaters, at lunch counters, and at water fountains. More problematic was the unchecked brutality of the police, who justified their abuse by accusing blacks of "disorderly conduct" for little or no reason. As elsewhere in the Deep South, African Americans could live only in specific areas of the city, many of which were overcrowded. Anyone attempting to defy this restriction was subjected to arson, bodily harm, or both.

After the 1954 *Brown v. Board of Education* decision, a group of civic leaders organized the interracial Memphis Committee on Community Relations (MCCR). Six years later, spurred on by the sit-ins in Greensboro, North Carolina, and Nashville, Tennessee, eight black students held the first sit-in protest in Memphis on March 19, 1960, at the Cossitt branch of the public library. They were arrested, charged with vagrancy and loitering, and fined $51 each. Simultaneously, seven other black students took seats at the lunch counter in McLellan's department store, asking to be served. They received the same treatment from the city's police. That night about 4,500 black citizens gathered at Mt. Olive Colored Methodist Episcopal (CME) Church to listen to speakers who advocated nonviolent resistance to segregation. A plate was passed with the money earmarked for a freedom fund to help finance court litigation and bail bonds for protesters. The group also planned a massive drive to increase black voter registration to one hundred thousand.[18]

Subsequent to these demonstrations and the black community's show of support, a delegation from the MCCR held meetings with the city council and Mayor Henry Loeb Jr. (1960–1963, 1968–1971) requesting the end of segregation in public libraries, the city zoo, Brooks Memorial Art Gallery, the Pink Palace Museum, and Ellis Auditorium. During these discussions, students, following the advice of local branch of the National Association for the Advancement of Colored People (NAACP) attorneys including Benjamin Hooks, called a two-week protest moratorium. When the time passed without progress, the sit-ins and boycotts resumed. Occurring during the pre-Easter season, the boycotts were particularly effective and resulted in pressure on city government from the business sector. Finally, in the fall of 1960 the city council agreed to end segregation in buses, libraries, restaurants, parks, and the city zoo—an enormous victory achieved by the collaboration of black students and churches supported by the MCCR and the NAACP. Department store lunch counters took another seventeen months to desegregate and fifteen months after that for recreational facilities to end discriminatory practices.[19]

In 1967, A. W. Willis Jr. campaigned to become the city's first black mayor.

The idea proved premature, however, partly because many black Memphians did not believe that one of their own could be elected or, if elected, could govern effectively. Thus about two-thirds of them supported the white incumbent William B. Ingram (1963–1967), who, although patronizing, had been courteous and respectful to black citizens. With the African American vote split and Henry Loeb Jr. receiving 90 percent of the white vote, Loeb won a second term as mayor effective January 1968. Loeb's election set the stage for the tragic drama that unfolded.[20]

By the late 1960s African Americans could point to significant gains. Besides integration of several facilities, three blacks served on the nine-member city council, and the city had sent two black representatives to the ninety-nine-member Tennessee House of Representatives. Yet, considerable unrest continued as a result of the great disparity in income and employment opportunities between black and white Memphians. This was highlighted by the sanitation workers' strike of 1968, the first time that Memphis became a national, front-page civil rights story.

Unlike their white counterparts, black sanitation workers enjoyed no real prospects for promotion, lacked adequate health benefits and bathroom facilities, did not receive vacations or pay during inclement weather, and were paid lower wages than their white counterparts.

The straws that broke the camel's back began on January 30, 1968, when twenty-one black workers were sent home without pay because of rain. When the rain let up an hour later, white employees went back to work and received a full day's pay. Two days later, two black employees were crushed to death when their truck malfunctioned. Strike talk among the black workers became strife, spurred on by their union leaders. The workers presented demands to the mayor, including union recognition, a contract with the city, effective grievance procedures, union payroll deduction or dues check-off, merit promotion without regard to race, equal treatment in the retirement system, payment for overtime, and decent wages. Loeb responded that they had no right to strike, a position he held for the next sixty-five days even after the assassination of Dr. Martin Luther King Jr., who had come to Memphis in support of the almost 1,400 strikers.

The assassination of King and the violence that preceded it, the boycott of city businesses, pressure from the federal government, thousands marching in protest, and highly unfavorable national and international publicity failed to sway Loeb and the council. Indeed, not until Rabbi James Wax orchestrated a deal whereby Abe Plough would anonymously provide the city with enough money to give the strikers a raise in pay did the strike end on April 16, 1968. Memphis, known as a city of moderation, moved into the 1970s having committed what local historians now call the most egregious mistake in its history.[21]

Abe Plough was not the first member of the Jewish community to act on behalf of Memphis's African Americans. Over fifty years before the sanitation workers' strike, Rabbi William Fineshriber, who served Temple Israel from 1911 to 1924, denounced lynching. In 1936, attorney Herman Goldberger died in a suspicious accident en route to defending a black man in court. About that same time, David Asher Levy chaired the Board of Advisors of the Negro Council of Social Welfare Groups. Lew Weinberg's, established in 1939, was one of the first local stores to allow black customers to try on clothes. The Bornblum brothers hired African American salesmen for their men's store on Beale Street. M. A. Lightman, the founder and president of the Malco Theater chain, headed a 1945 fundraising drive to expand and upgrade the city's black hospital, while Abe Scharff, owner of a successful dry cleaning company, donated a house for use as a YMCA for blacks two years later. Lester Rosen served on the board of the Memphis Urban League in 1949. In the late fifties, Rosen braved the wrath of his fellow members of the segregated Summit Club when he brought an African American minister to dine with him. Rabbi Arie Becker of Beth Sholom, a Holocaust survivor, also took a stand as one of nineteen Conservative rabbis who answered Martin Luther King's call in 1963 to march to Birmingham. Moreover, a handful of Jewish department store owners organized meetings with other merchants to discuss the peaceful integration of their stores. Jack Goldsmith, owner of Goldsmith's, and Mel Grinspan, of the Shainberg's store chain, led this effort designed to have all stores integrate together so that none could be singled out for retribution. Subsequently, both Goldsmith's and Shainberg's stood up to threats from the Ku Klux Klan and hired black sales clerks.

These individual acts of courage were not the norm in the Jewish community. As elsewhere in the South, the majority of Memphis's Jews were hesitant to make waves. That being said, the number of Jews who did act to end discrimination was proportionally greater in Memphis than in most southern cities, possibly reflecting its more moderate atmosphere and rabbinical leadership.[22]

James A. Wax

James Aaron Wax was born in December 1912, two years after his parents, Morris and Rose Edlin Wax, had moved to Herculaneum, Missouri, a half-hour drive southwest of St. Louis and slightly over 250 miles north of Memphis. Herculaneum was an unlikely incubator for a rabbi, given its tiny size and the fact that the Waxes were the only Jews in town. Yet it proved to be a perfect place to shape the moral character that became a hallmark of Wax's rabbinic career.

Herculaneum was a company town largely under the de facto control of the St. Joseph Lead Company, at the time the largest lead smelter in the nation. Its inhabitants, especially those working in the factory, were so dependent on the company that they had no real choices in town elections or in gaining the protection provided by an effective union. This oppressive atmosphere nurtured a burning desire in young Jimmy Wax to make the world around him more just. "Even as a youngster," he told Joan Beifuss, an interviewer for the *Memphis (TN) Magazine*, "I was hoping to reform the world, be for the little guy." His father, who had fled Russian pogroms at the turn of the century and peddled before opening a dry goods store in Herculaneum, greatly influenced him. The people in town held the older Wax in high esteem because of his business ethics and devotion to civic improvement. They elected him to the school board, and he gained influence in the regional Democratic Party. "He used to hammer into my head two things," the rabbi told Beifuss: "You've got to be a good Jew, and by that he meant to live up to the moral principles, to be an honorable person. And you've got to be a good citizen."[23]

After high school, Wax attended Washington University in St. Louis. While there, he was exposed to the passionate sermons of Ferdinand Isserman, Temple Israel's rabbi, who was dedicated to social justice. This began the young man's realization that the rabbinate could be an ideal vehicle for his social justice objectives.

The Great Depression forced Wax to transfer to Southeast Missouri State College, in Cape Girardeau, Missouri, where he earned his BA in 1935. With little preparation he applied for admittance to the Hebrew Union College in Cincinnati where he graduated at the top of his class in 1939 with a bachelor of Hebrew letters degree. Two years later, Hebrew Union College granted Wax a master of Hebrew letters degree, and he returned to St. Louis where he served for two years as the assistant rabbi of the United Hebrew Congregation. After a brief period as the assistant rabbi of North Shore Congregation Israel in Glencoe, Illinois, Wax accepted the invitation to serve as assistant to Rabbi Harry Ettelson at Temple Israel in Memphis. It proved to be a good match, since Ettelson also was a man who believed that religion must speak to the issues of the day rather than confine itself to the spiritual realm. In 1954, after eight years in Memphis, Wax succeeded Ettelson as the congregation's senior rabbi, a position he held for over two decades.

Given the years he had already spent with them, it came as no surprise to the congregation that Wax supported the *Brown* decision. He made his position clear in an address to the National Federation of Temple Youth, "Despite the fact that eighty years have passed since the Negro was emancipated, he remains for all practical purposes a degraded and oppressed people and the task of conferring the rights to which he is legally and morally entitled rests upon us." Rabbis, he continued, were obligated to speak out "with vigor, with clarity, and if need be, with courage upon current social problems." On the Sabbath of his installation as senior rabbi, Wax reiterated a familiar message "This pulpit shall ever be concerned with the problems of life. . . . I shall make no distinction by virtue of religion, nationality, or race, for we are all children of one God."[24]

Wax became a crusader for those on the fringes of society—the mentally ill, the physically ill and handicapped, and African Americans. He helped found and presided over the Memphis Mental Health Association and served on the boards of the Tennessee Mental Health Commission, the United Cerebral Palsy Association, the Shelby County Tuberculosis Association, and the Mid-South Center Council for Comprehensive Health Planning. In addition, he helped obtain employment for the mentally and physically handicapped and was an early supporter of St. Jude Children's Research Hospital.[25]

Particularly significant was Wax's crucial role in the struggle for African American rights. In late 1958, Wax helped found the highly effective Memphis Committee on Community Relations but refused to chair the organization, thinking it best that a Protestant fill the post. Instead, he served as its treasurer until its demise in the 1970s. Wax also played an active role in the Tennessee Council on Human Relations, the West Tennessee chapter of the American Civil Liberties Union, and the Memphis Urban League—all viewed as communist front groups by many Memphians. Although substantially contributing to and through these groups, the role he played in the late 1960s after the interview when he presided over the Memphis Ministerial Association (MMA) drew the most attention. In 1967 the MMA made a bold statement when it elected a Jew as president and an African American, James W. Lawson Jr., as vice president. While presiding over the MMA, Wax strengthened its Social Action Committee and also appointed a biracial Committee on Race Relations.[26] Soon thereafter that committee drafted "An Appeal to Conscience," which appeared as a paid advertisement in Memphis newspapers on February 4, 1968. The ad asked Memphians to "purge their souls of every vestige of prejudice and intolerance" and concluded: "We are deeply concerned that the improved relationship between the races has been largely the result of legislation judicial decisions and executive order [sic] by government officials. . . . Race relations, like all human relations, ultimately must be regulated not by policies of secular agencies, but by principles of religions." The statement was published under the heading, "Have we not all one Father? Did not one God create us?" Wax indicated, "This will be the first time since the ministers association was formed early this century that it will make such a public appeal."[27] To no one's surprise the ad exerted little effect on the city's white population, especially on Loeb and the city council. The sanitation workers' strike commenced eight days later.

Four days into the strike, black ministers asked Wax for help to resolve the dispute. When his initial efforts failed,[28] Wax called for an April 3 joint strategy meeting of the interracial Memphis Ministerial Association (MMA) and the black Interdenominational Ministers' Alliance (IMA) where an unbridgeable rift

10. Rev. Henry Logan Starks (left) and Rabbi James Wax (right),
1968 (*Memphis Press-Scimitar* newspaper morgue. Preservation and
Special Collections, University Libraries, University of Memphis.)
Used by permission of Curator Gerald Chaudron.

surfaced. The MMA argued for a continuation of behind-the-scenes negotiation
but the IMA advocated direct action. After King's assassination, the latter approach won the day. Media throughout the nation covered the ensuing marches
and riots. Immediately following a Friday morning memorial service organized
by the MMA, approximately 250 clergymen headed by Wax and William A.
Dimmick, dean of St. Mary's Cathedral and later Episcopal bishop of Northern
Michigan, marched in black and white pairs to the mayor's office in city hall,
where the Rev. Bill Aldrich read an MMA statement urging Loeb to end the
strike, and the Rev. James A. Jordon, pastor of the Beale Street Baptist Church,

represented the black ministerial group with his impassioned discourse. Wax faced Loeb and told him: "We come here with a great deal of sorrow and frankly with a great deal of anger. What has happened in this city is a result of oppression and injustice, the inhumanity of man to man, and we have come to appeal to you for leadership in ending this strike. There are laws greater than the laws of Memphis and Tennessee and these are the laws of God. We fervently ask you not to hide any longer behind legal technicalities and slogans but to speak out at last in favor of human dignity."[29]

James Wax's moving statement was carried on local and national television, provoking mostly supportive responses from states outside the South, and mostly hate-filled ones from below the Mason-Dixon Line.

Wax had long laid the foundation for his positive interaction with African American ministers and the pivotal role he played during the strike. Rev. James W. Lawson Jr. of Centenary United Methodist Church and Rev. Dr. Henry Logan Starks of St. James African Methodist Episcopal Church were among those who opened their churches to nightly rallies for the striking garbage collectors. They participated with Wax in numerous rallies. As previously indicated, Lawson served as vice president of the MMA during Wax's presidency. The three were cofounders of Hope in Action: Metropolitan Interfaith Association. Starks was the first African American professor at the Cumberland Presbyterian Church's Memphis Theological Seminary; Wax served as an instructor of Hebrew there from 1972 to 1985.[30] These men enjoyed deep friendships and years of positive interaction and cooperation.

The majority of white Memphians and especially the business owners were dismayed by the violence that had struck their city and the negative publicity that it engendered. They applied pressure on elected officials to break the impasse. With Wax's intervention aided by Abe Plough, the city capitulated, and the strike ended thirteen days after King's death.

Although Wax's positions and actions were mostly unappreciated by Memphians during the turbulent 1960s, when he retired in 1978 he was widely praised for his significant role in doing what his father had asked of him when he was a child—working for the good of his city. Positive articles appeared in the local press, noting the many causes he had served with passion, and the board of trustees of his congregation, not always happy with his activism but generally supportive of it, adopted a formal resolution that read in part: "He has, by precept and example, demonstrated to us for 32 years the teachings which are the essence of prophetic Judaism. . . . We are especially grateful for the years we have had with our beloved Rabbi and his conscientious ministry to us and to our entire community. In sharing him with all the citizens of Memphis, we the congregational family of Temple Israel, recognize that he has fulfilled that sublime mandate spoken by the Almighty to Abraham, 'Be thou a blessing.'"

At Wax's death on October 17, 1989, Congressman Harold Ford, the first African American elected to the House of Representatives from Memphis, called Wax "the conscience of the city," while the editor of the Catholic diocesan newspaper spoke for many Memphians when he affirmed, "Memphis lost a great force for justice when Rabbi James Aaron Wax died last week."

Editor's Introduction to the Interview

Memphis sits at the upper border of the South. As in many similar locations, violence seemingly should have been avoidable. Even integration of the public schools progressed peacefully albeit under threat of impending court order. Yet negative and recalcitrant leadership tended to push the scales downward. In this case, the major culprit was a Jewish mayor and congregant of the key activist rabbi.[31] This created the unusual and dramatic specter of a Jew actually in power in confrontation with another Jew who condemned him with Prophetic wrath. But James Wax did not act in isolation. Jews assumed leadership roles in behalf of African American rights far greater than they did in most southern communities. Henry Loeb Jr. appears to have been somewhat of an anomaly until one counts people like attorney Charles Bloch in Georgia and Solomon Blatt, Speaker of the South Carolina House of Representatives.[32] These people provide illustrations of Jews who had power and openly advocated and even led efforts to resist desegregation. However, they were a tiny minority within the minority of Jews in the South.

Virtually all of the rabbis including Wax preferred to work through ministerial associations. They hoped to enlist the majority Protestant clergy, and the participation of these individuals offered them a shield against attack from the community and pressure from within their congregations. Masking social justice messages in Christological language added appeal. Typically the only Jewish members, they were asked to serve as officers and presidents. Sometimes the organizations were biracial. Some proved effective and others recalcitrant. Wax's experience was unusual in terms of the cooperation he received, having an African American vice present during his service as president, and the activism and effectiveness of the MMA. Yet even Wax believed that prominent Protestants should lead and provide the faces of action committees. In this spirit he rejected the presidency of the Memphis Committee on Human Relations.

The rabbis also tended to shun publicity. They believed that it hardened the positions of their opponents and hindered progress. Like his rabbinical colleagues, Wax was also skeptical of the efforts of external organizations to help implement

desegregation. From his perspective, these organizations were focused on dramatizing the problem and failed to take the interests of the local Jewish communities into account. In his interview, Wax places these issues and the preferred
methodology in a different light; in quiet diplomacy, "nobody loses." The local
strategies of these rabbis and thereby differed from Martin L. King Jr., for whom
confrontation and publicity served as primary means. Nonetheless, when faced
with recalcitrance, rabbis recognized the need for public actions and the spotlight that these generated.

For most rabbis, supporting black rights and opportunities was part of their
mission to help those in need. Many including Wax involved themselves in mental
health, medical, and social service work. They viewed their rabbinical roles and
responsibilities broadly. These efforts also cemented their positions within the
community and probably contributed to the acceptance of their civil rights stands.

—Mark K. Bauman

James A. Wax Interview

June 22, 1966

**P. Allen Krause: Rabbi Wax, what would you define as the legitimate scope
of a [work] like this?**
James A. Wax: I would say all states below the Mason-Dixon Line that are
normally referred to as southern.
**PAK: Would you include also the northern part of Florida, southern
Florida, or the entire state of Texas?**
JAW: Yes, on the basis of experience, even though the people of the southern
part of Florida haven't lived there as long, most of them have lived there
as long as they have in Mississippi or Alabama. I would still regard that as
southern.
PAK: And also Texas?
JAW: And also Texas. My experience has demonstrated that they have a southern mood.
**PAK: What are the aspects of the civil rights movement which, according
to your experience, might be covered in [my research]?**
JAW: I think what's important was the rabbi's role, his participation, and second, I think it's very important to try to ascertain, if it's possible, what is
the attitude of the Jews towards the desegregation process.
**PAK: In terms of actual civil rights actions, which ones would you suggest
that I look into? In your community, what were the aspects which might
be touched upon?**
JAW: I think all aspects of life are important here—I'm just thinking out
loud—certainly all public institutions supported by taxation would be one

category. Number two, privately owned institutions that catered to the
public, and by that I mean, a department store; the store is privately owned
but it's catering to the public. And in that category too would be restaurants—they're privately owned, but are serving the public. And there is a
third category, I frankly feel is beyond the reach of civil rights or integration: that's private social life. I think this is beyond the purview of our consideration. People have a right to associate with whom they want. I think
the country club has a right to restrict. One may not extol a club for excluding Jews, but if a group of people want to get together to play golf or
have dinner and so on, in a certain place, and they don't want Jews or anybody else, they have that right, it seems to me. It's not a noble idea but you
can't question their right.

**PAK: Have you had any Freedom Riders or similar type of activity in your
community?**

JAW: Freedom Riders came through Memphis some years ago; I cannot pinpoint it.[33] The purpose of desegregating at that time was bus stations, bus
terminals. I don't know for sure where they came from, but they were informed when they came to Memphis the bus terminals had already
been desegregated. In fact they had been for some time; they just didn't
know that.

**PAK: When would be the date when there was intense civil rights activity in
Memphis, such that you could see changes that took place after that time?**

JAW: We never had the demonstrations as they had in other southern cities.
After the Supreme Court decision of '54 there was a realization on the part
of civic leaders that changes were going to come, and also a number of civic
leaders were perceptive and realized that the '54 decision—which dealt only
with schools, you remember—that there would be other decisions and it
would be necessary to desegregate. So we organized in Memphis a committee of private citizens to study the race problem. We didn't use the word
race; we called it *human relations* or *community relations*. Our first committee didn't get very far; it didn't have the right people in it. Then I would
say about '56 or '57, we organized—I was one of the organizers—the Memphis Committee on Community Relations.[34] It's a membership organization that's controlled by an executive committee of either fifteen or seventeen men; it's biracial. I've been its secretary since it was organized [and I]
served on the nominating committee the first few years. There was a point
when I was asked to be president, and I frankly declined to be president on
the grounds that I didn't think it was helpful to the cause to have a member
of a minority group trying to advance the rights of a minority group. Those
who asked me readily appreciated this.

PAK: What is the composition of the group's membership?

JAW: It has in it businessmen, labor leaders, as I say, it's biracial—the president of the Negro college, LeMoyne, is on it.[35] He's been a big power in it. It has some lawyers. It's a reasonably representative group [but it] has no authority. What it's done is to mediate conflicts that have arisen or that could arise. One of the first problems we dealt with was the desegregation of the buses, that is, the local buses. That, you remember, was the big issue in Montgomery, and Martin Luther King emerged as the hero in that situation. Our committee is operated on the premise—it's been one of the major premises—[of] no publicity. And this has paid off in terms of progress that we have made and also eliminating needless friction. We've had little hostility, very few outbreaks. So far, nobody has ever lost their life because of the race question. I think I could say nobody's ever been injured as a result of our policy. You have to keep in mind that Memphis is on the border, literally the border of Mississippi, northern Mississippi and Arkansas; we have a lot of rural people in Memphis.

PAK: **What is the response of the non-Jewish population in Memphis—majority response and minority response—to this civil rights issue?**

JAW: What people feel in their hearts I can't say. I have a feeling there's still strong segregationist sentiment, but the so-called power structure in our community has gone along and effected these various changes. Frankly— and that's one of the things that interests me—the motivation of these men in the power structure was not necessarily noble; it was really rather selfish. These men would say, "Well, we don't want to happen in Memphis what happened in Little Rock and Montgomery. We don't want our community to get a bad image or have a bad reputation. Industry won't come here; it's going to hurt business," and so on. This was paramount in the thinking of a good many of our community leaders.

PAK: **Did the Christian clergy play any role in this [struggle for civil rights]?**

JAW: No, only one minister, Paul Tudor Jones of Idelwild Presbyterian, really took an active role, and he was president of the organization [MCCR] for awhile. But, no, the clergy was conspicuous by its absence.

PAK: **What goals would you say that you have for Memphis with regard to civil rights activity?**

JAW: I would hope there would be complete desegregation of all public institutions, whether publicly owned or privately owned, and that there would be an acceptance, in good spirit on the part of the people of the community. No one just giving in, but they would believe that it was the right, moral thing to do.

PAK: **What percentage of the Christian clergy would you say share this goal?**

JAW: I'm sorry to say that this would be a minority view among the Christian clergy, on the basis of their failure to perform.

PAK: How long has your congregation been in existence?

JAW: They were established in 1853, chartered in 1854; continuous since then. It's an old institution, highly respected in the community; it's the only Reform congregation. It's what we term a prestige institution.

PAK: What is the economic standing of the members of your congregation?

JAW: Most Jews are in the middle class economically or upper-middle class. Statements are that there are maybe twenty-five Jewish millionaires out of a population of about eighty-five hundred. Some of them have great wealth.

PAK: What is their source of income?

JAW: Well, they have stores; some of them have large real estate holdings, investments of one kind or another, mainly in business.

PAK: Would you say that they are highly susceptible or partially susceptible to economic pressure, if this was to be applied on them?

JAW: It could affect them—the Goldsmith Department Stores, which is now part of the Federated chain, headquarters in Cincinnati.[36] There was a boycott against them by the Negroes, though this was an unfair boycott, because the Goldsmith family, which then owned the store, are very charitable people and they gave their money away without consideration to race. When the store desegregated, what it amounted to was in the restaurant part. When the restaurants were desegregated a number of white people turned in their credit cards, or charge-a-plates, or whatever they're properly called. So, the store did sustain a loss there for a while, but it's been covered up by now; people have gotten over it.

PAK: Do you detect any fear of such a thing on the part of your congregants?

JAW: Not now. There may have been some apprehension that wasn't spoken about at the time when they were desegregating the restaurants, and so on.

PAK: When would that be?

JAW: That would have been, I guess in '57, or '60, '62; it's hard to know exactly.[37] The mood has changed very greatly.

PAK: Since 1957 or '54?

JAW: I'd say right along. It's hard to have an exact time; certainly not before 1954 and the Supreme Court decision, but these changes are taking place all the time.

PAK: How much a part of the non-Jewish community are the Jews in Memphis?

JAW: Jews stand very high. They're in every cause in the city; they're leaders.

PAK: Is there anything that you would say that would distinguish the Jewish community from the non-Jewish community in Memphis other than economic standing and the fact that they go to a synagogue instead of a church?

JAW: They're much more civic-minded than the non-Jews. They're much more generous; I don't just mean to Jewish causes. I'm speaking now of support of city causes. The Jews in Memphis have done much more than assume their obligations. If you take the Jews out of Memphis, so to speak, it would affect every phase of cultural life, civic life, and so on.

PAK: What about their outlook on civil rights activities?

JAW: We have some definite segregationists who were born in the South and reared there, and they have come to accept the values of the Old South. Then there are those who feel that segregation is wrong, I would say a goodly number. I would say that most Jews in Memphis feel that segregation is morally wrong, but they do not feel that they can do much about it, because the Jews are in an insecure position because of their minority status. I'm not sure I go along with that feeling, but they just don't want to stick their neck out as Jews.

PAK: How many rabbis are there in your community?

JAW: About five, I think. None have been involved in this except myself. Wait a minute; I take it back. The Conservative rabbi, Arie Becker, did participate in some demonstration that happened in Birmingham about three, four summers ago. He was very much criticized by his congregation for having participated with other Conservative rabbis; in fact, he was harassed. He and his family lived in somebody's house for a few days so he wouldn't be bothered by these phone calls. There was a strong feeling.

PAK: But he's still there, despite the strong feeling?

JAW: Yes.[38]

PAK: What has been your response and involvement in specific civil rights activities in Memphis?

JAW: Everybody knows; it's a matter of public record that I have been a charter member of our community relations group. I've been its secretary from the beginning, and I've had a hand in everything that's going on. As I said, I declined the presidency. I sat in on some of the arbitration committees, as time permitted; the one about having Negroes not just work on a truck that sells beer but to go in as a salesman to these places. Seems like a little thing to see Negroes on beverages service, it's called—not just beer, but Cokes and Pepsi-Cola. They could carry the cases into the store, but they never had the role of being a salesman. Well, quietly this was worked out that Negroes were made salesmen; they'd call on the customers. The same thing was true of the baking industry. They could deliver; they could carry the bread in; they couldn't serve as a salesman. In fact, I remember that distinctly. It was one of the easier ones to work out.

PAK: What about other areas, schools, for instance?

JAW: No, schools we actually had very little to do with—that was automatic;

it was a court order. We didn't ask the schools to do anything except obey the court order, and there was never any question about it.[39]

PAK: **Have you had any involvement in any other aspects of civil rights activity, let's say, integration of public facilities?**

JAW: No, they did close the swimming pools for a year but they were reopened, but what happened in the reopening of the swimming pools was all the Negroes went to one place and all the whites to the other. You can't force people to go to a swimming pool.

PAK: **Other than your work on this committee, have you found it necessary or desirable to participate in anything else or apply any types of pressure?**

JAW: No. This committee—which was a blue ribbon committee, so to speak—had the editors of both papers, and I think there was a bank president involved. It pretty much covered all that needed to be done. I make, I guess, as many speeches as anyone in the city, and, many of the speeches—they're not written out; some of them aren't even outlined—I've made frequent references to the race problem for church groups and other places.

PAK: **Have you been quoted in the newspapers on any occasion?**

JAW: Yes, I have. I don't use the words "Negro-white relations." I may not even use the words "race relations," but [I speak] in terms of human relations. There isn't any question. After all, our city's only a half million people, and I've been there twenty years. People know where I stand. There's been no equivocation on the matter. I've found that by approaching the subject from a moral point of view—I've often quoted Jesus saying, "Love you, one another"—this puts the onus not on the Jew; not on me. This is Jesus, and, to the Christian, this is the Savior. They have to quarrel with Jesus and what he said. And this has been an effective technique.

PAK: **I imagine there has been a time when you've spoken with individuals, maybe members of your congregation, on this subject?**

JAW: I've given a number of sermons on it. Some people don't like it. They don't like it because, for one, they are segregationists; number two, there are some who feel a rabbi should stick to what they call religion, just like they wouldn't want a rabbi to talk about the labor problem or Vietnam. On the other hand, as I view it in retrospect now, most of the people in our congregation, even though they didn't concur at the moment, are glad their rabbi took a stand on the race question, because I think that most of them deep down think that there is a moral issue involved here.

PAK: **You were in Memphis in 1954.**

JAW: Yes.

PAK: **How did you respond to the *Brown* decision? Did you do anything in 1954, '55, which you thought was necessary?**

JAW: Only to be a member of this group, one of its organizers. I've never been involved in activity on my own.

PAK: Who provided the impetus for the Memphis Committee on Community Relations?

JAW: The man who convened the meeting was a lawyer named Lucius Burch.[40] He was a very wealthy man, a native southerner; his family has lived in the South for a long, long time. He was an outspoken liberal, one of the sponsors of the late Estes Kefauver. He convened the meeting and called together people he thought might be interested and would be helpful. It was a heterogeneous group of everybody who was an integrationist. The editor of our morning paper, the *Memphis (TN) Commercial Appeal*, Frank Ahlgren, while he's a native of Minnesota, is a very, very conservative person. And a large number of readers are in Mississippi, so they weren't carrying any banner for integration, mostly with segregationist sentiments. Yet he was one of the leaders.

PAK: Were there any other clergy on the committee?

JAW: I was the only white minister at the time.[41]

PAK: What was your role then; you say you were its secretary?

JAW: Secretary, but unofficially, whoever was president, he always consulted with me—will we have a meeting, not have a meeting. When he wanted to appoint people on a subcommittee, we'd consult. I was on the nominating committee for two, three years in a row. We fixed up the slate of people whom we thought would be helpful. I had a hand in most of the decisions that were made. I had a consistent point of view; I'm not saying the others were not consistent, but I felt very deeply about this whole matter and the people in it, especially when ours was not a membership organization with a hundred people; it's a fifteen-man deal, something like that. They all knew where I stood and the time I gave to it.

PAK: One rabbi has said to me that the best approach to this problem on the part of a rabbi in the South is to put a gentile at the head and you get behind.

JAW: I would concur on that, yes. As a matter of fact, you strengthen the cause all the way around if you have a Christian or some others with you. Doing it yourself, you're limited in what you can achieve.

PAK: Have you ever used your own facilities, the temple machines, or anything like this in order to help the cause of this committee?

JAW: Since I am the secretary I keep the minutes, but what I do is to take minutes and dictate them. My secretary does the actual work; all notices for meetings are sent out from our office.

PAK: Has your congregation in any way gotten a stigma because of this?

JAW: No, I suppose among the thinking people—I'll use that word—they would expect Temple Israel to be a leader in this, not because Temple Israel is distinguished for its liberal [*inaudible*], but just that they would expect the temple to be involved.

PAK: What role have national Jewish organizations played in the civil rights movement in Memphis and in the South?

JAW: They played no role at all. I take a very dim view of national organizations' involvement. The Anti-Defamation League [ADL] wanted to come in to Memphis and have a symposium of ministers, sort of a ministers' institute on race relations; it didn't get anywhere. Some of the ministers were dubious about the whole thing and certainly the Jews in Memphis who knew about it didn't like it. The Anti-Defamation League, secondly, wanted to send a pamphlet to our six hundred policemen on the race question. I frankly was incensed about it. We have a very fine police commissioner. In fact, I think he is so outstanding that I took the initiative, and we had a civic dinner, a testimonial in his honor. The police commissioner is very important. If you recall, in Birmingham, for example, Bull Connor, and in other cities, the police commissioner, being a segregationist, created trouble rather than help solve problems. Our police commissioner is a fellow named Claude Armour. He is a southerner, he says so; I like his honesty, candor. I heard him say at a meeting, "I was born here in the South and I like the ways of the South. But when I became the commissioner I took an oath that I was going to uphold the law. Whether I like the law or not, is unimportant, or how they interpret it is unimportant; I want to see that we're gonna have law and order," and we've had it. The man has been eminently fair. Because of that we had this testimonial dinner for him, about a thousand people involved, and I took the initiative of organizing the thing. I bring this up because Commissioner Armour went before his policemen and he told them just what I said to you. He didn't like integration, or desegregation, but that's the law, it had to be carried out, it's going to be carried out. He said to the men on the police force, "If you all don't feel you can do it you can turn your badges in." Well, it seemed to me to be superfluous, totally unnecessary, for a defense agency or anybody else to come in and hand out pamphlets to our policemen. The job had been accomplished. They knew what they were supposed to do, and that was it.[42]

PAK: What about other national Jewish organizations? The UAHC [Union of American Hebrew Congregations], the CCAR [Central Conference of American Rabbis]?

JAW: No, I think perhaps a statement by the Social Action Committee [of the UAHC] may have annoyed some of our members but it was of no great consequence.

PAK: There was a rather vocal reaction on the part of the Mississippi rabbis

in 1963 when Martin Luther King was made the keynote speaker of the UAHC conference.

JAW: Yes, some of our people did not like it. But, our feeling was not as intense as it was in Mississippi. I remember they had a meeting of the members of the Southwest Council to which we belong, and Mississippi also, and I spoke at this meeting; Dr. [Maurice] Eisendrath[43] was there. I felt this was a case of poor judgment and that's what our people felt; it just wasn't a tactful thing to do. It was wrong.

PAK: Do you think this is detrimental to the accomplishment of your goals in your community in any way?

JAW: I don't know if it's detrimental but it sure doesn't help any. Our theory is that these problems can be worked out behind closed doors. I believe you have to be diplomatic in working out the race problem; it can be worked out to a large extent. But you have to avoid a situation in which there's a winner and a loser; nobody wants to be a loser. This has been the success of our Community Relations Committee; we work these things out behind closed doors. Nobody loses.

PAK: What role should the national Jewish organizations play, if any?

JAW: Oh, I think they have a responsibility to represe—no, I don't want to use the word "represent"—to make their point of view known where it counts, for example, in Washington. If we have lobbies for this industry and that business and so on, I think morality ought to have a lobby and present a moral point of view, where it counts, where legislation is being written and enacted. I think there they may have a place, but not to come into a local community.

PAK: Have you ever found yourself in uncomfortable situations in your congregation as a result of your civil rights activity?

JAW: No, never had that conflict of interest. The department store owners who felt the boycott that we mentioned earlier, they were glad that I was on the side that I was on.

PAK: Have there been any members of your congregation who have felt that you, on the whole, were not doing enough in this area?

JAW: No, no, I've never had that feeling. What I was criticized for [was that] once in a High Holiday sermon I had taken a potshot at Governor [Orville] Faubus, not by name, but people knew who I was talking about. One member who lives in West Memphis, Arkansas, across the river, a member of the temple, became very angry that I'd take a potshot at his governor. He was involved in politics, but we worked that out.

PAK: Do you remember the sermon given in 1958 by Rabbi Emmet Frank [of Alexandria, Virginia], a Kol Nidre [the eve of Yom Kippur, the Day of Atonement] sermon which created a big stir because he equated Byrd-liness with Godlessness?[44]

JAW: Oh, yes, yes I recall.

PAK: **What would your response be to something like that?**

JAW: I wouldn't do that.

PAK: **Why? Do you think it's too much publicity?**

JAW: It's negative; you don't get anywhere making a fellow mad. I might be wrong and very naive, but I think if you want something—if you want to settle a problem—you don't create more antagonism. Sit down and like Isaiah said, "Come and let us reason together."[45] Maybe this is a very naive point of view.

PAK: **How do you feel about the future in your community with regard to the whole area of civil rights?**

JAW: Oh, I think the climate will improve, more and more. A lot of the white people—I formerly thought it was only the southerner—but a lot of white people were literally frightened, [because] they thought the Negroes were going to take over the whole community [and] they would run the society. But they have learned that, gee, it isn't bad. The Negroes sit where they want on a bus; they go to school where they want; they go to the restaurants they want. These things aren't half as bad as they thought they were going to be. Negroes have become—though it may change now—when Negroes were unified, they became a strong political factor. In fact, in Memphis you couldn't be elected to public office during this past era, the last ten, twelve years, unless you had the Negro vote behind you. Now what's happening is, Negroes are not unified politically, and I think they're losing some of their political effectiveness, which is unfortunate. They still need to be a bloc. I'll put it this way: when Negroes were united, the candidates had to do their bidding. Now, since the Negroes are not united, there isn't the compulsion, the urgency, to represent the Negro point of view. They hurt themselves through their difference of opinion.

PAK: **If the history of civil rights during this period would be written fifty years from now, what role do you think that the rabbi would have played in the areas that you're familiar with in the South?**

JAW: Well, very frankly, although I don't know all the rabbis and everything they did or didn't do, I am of the opinion that the rabbis of the South did all that they could do to be helpful in the process of desegregation, which is of course different than integration. I think, for the most part, the rabbis did about all they could do. There's one rabbi that I think is a reprehensible character, and I don't mind being quoted, that's Ben Schultz of Clarksdale who made the statement—you'll find it quoted in Silver's book [*Mis-*

sissippi:] *The Closed Society*—that President Kennedy should have sent the troops to Cuba rather than to Mississippi. It was during the time of Meredith's admission to Ole Miss. But, aside from Schultz's involvement on the segregationist side, to my knowledge every rabbi did about everything he could do.[46]

PAK: Do you include all the rabbis—the Orthodox, Conservative, and Reform—or are you talking just Reform now?

JAW: That's a good question. Well, I wasn't thinking about the Orthodox when I made that statement. Frankly the Orthodox do not concern themselves, or the Conservative either, very much with community problems. That's not a criticism; I don't want to make a value judgment here, but they just have not been much interested, it seems to me, in community matters.

It's very hard. You're dealing with attitudes to a large extent. And that's hard to pinpoint. We had a Jew in Memphis named Will Gerber, who was a leader in the Crump organization—Mister Crump ruled the city, served as the state attorney for a while—[Gerber is] the past president of the Baron Hirsch Congregation in Memphis. That's Orthodox, a large Orthodox congregation. He had made some very strong segregationist statements. In fact, I think he realized what was happening, and that he was becoming allied with the White Citizens' Council. Though he was born in Russia, he could be very vitriolic. He was an outspoken segregationist. There was another segregationist in the South, he published a booklet, a little pamphlet on the race question, took a strong segregationist view—a lawyer named Bloch. These two names, I guess, ought to be preserved; not for honor, but they are a part of the record of the Jewish involvement, and unfortunately they were on the segregationist side. I don't know of any Jewish laymen who stood out on the integration side. Many were integrationist, but I don't know any who beat any drums for the cause.

II

In the Land of
the Almost Impossible

10
Milton L. Grafman

Birmingham, Alabama, and Its Jewish Community

Born in Washington, DC, in 1907, Milton ("Mickey") Louis Grafman grew up in Pittsburgh, Pennsylvania. He graduated from the University of Cincinnati in 1926, after which he enrolled in Hebrew Union College where he was ordained in 1933. From 1933 to 1941 he served a congregation in Lexington, Kentucky, and then filled the pulpit at Temple Emanu-El, Birmingham's oldest synagogue.

Birmingham, Alabama, proved to be one the most difficult arenas that the rabbis had to navigate during the civil rights era. Grafman received frequent threats, and someone attempted to dynamite the local Conservative congregation. When Grafman arrived, he was not included in the local ministerial association, the Protestant Pastors' Union. The group took nearly a decade to change its name and finally invite him to join. Even then at least one member acted with insensitivity. Like most rabbis in the South, Grafman believed that local, back-door efforts offered the best means to ensure peaceful desegregation. Like them also, he tended to work through local ministerial associations or groups of clergy. As part of one such group, Grafman signed a statement exhorting the Birmingham community to abide by the 1954 Supreme Court decision in *Brown v. Board of Education*.[1]

Grafman believed that efforts to change Birmingham's behavior from the outside did more harm than good. Birmingham was a city in transition during the early 1960s. Eugene "Bull" Connor was being removed as the city's police chief, and other changes were slowly taking place behind the scenes. It therefore frustrated Grafman that, regardless of the progress that Birmingham appeared to be making, in 1963 Martin Luther King Jr. decided to use the community as a staging ground for his nonviolent protest movement before Connor's replacement assumed office. King and the civil rights movement had not fared well in recent demonstrations in Albany, Georgia, and, as Grafman indicates, he needed confrontation to recapture the national spotlight. Connor, an outspoken segregationist, would almost certainly oblige him with a violent (and therefore newsworthy) response, whereas his more moderate replacement might be open to compromise. A group of eight white clergy, including Grafman, issued a statement pointing to the coming changes and requesting that outsiders exhibit patience and stay away so that the people of Birmingham would have time to resolve their problems themselves.

A pragmatic strategist, King came anyway. When sent to jail for demonstrating, he wrote the now-famous "Letter from the Birmingham Jail." The letter denounced the clergy who had signed the statement, Grafman included. To King, the problem was not recalcitrant advocates of massive resistance and violence like Connor, but moderates like Grafman, who fooled themselves into believing that gradualism would bring about substantive change. Unfortunately for the eight white clergy, King used them as symbols of an entire group, but it was they who were singled out in history. In his letter, King asked where the clergy had been when George Wallace stood in defiance at his 1963 inaugural and proclaimed, "segregation now; segregation forever." But Grafman in fact *had* spoken out, denouncing Wallace and church members who condoned racial injustice in a sermon on the Friday after the governor's pronouncement.

King's letter and Connor's use of brutality (including police dogs and fire hoses) both garnered the national publicity that King and his supporters craved. The Birmingham confrontation reinvigorated the civil rights movement. Nonetheless, Grafman's reputation, like those of the other seven clergy, remained tarnished regardless of the rabbi's activities on behalf of African American civil rights. With his behind-the-scenes work came grave risks. Grafman was subjected to death threats repeatedly during his years in Birmingham. Yet when reading Grafman's interview, one cannot help but conclude that perhaps the rabbi would have been satisfied with token desegregation and that he expressed far less empathy for the plight of African Americans and their desire for immediate change than he did for white racist angst.

Grafman argues in the interview that African Americans were ungrateful because they targeted Jewish businesses for sit-ins and demonstration, even though Jews in Birmingham had often been supportive of black causes and were more liberal than their white Christian counterparts. Yet he fails to realize that black leaders targeted Jewish firms purposefully because the African American leadership also believed that Jews were more progressive and thus would be more likely to initiate desegregation. The rabbi suggests an important new twist on the issue of boycotting Jewish businesses: Jewish merchants were more susceptible to black than to white economic pressure. Grafman did not believe that these Jewish merchants should be forced to suffer bankruptcy because of the potential loss of white customers if they succumbed to black demands to be the first to integrate their stores.

Grafman's is an enigmatic interview that raises many important questions. Was he equivocating on issue of civil rights? Were some of the parallels he alludes to truly moral equivalents? Did Grafman's individualistic, antiorganiza-

11. Rabbi Milton Grafman, date unknown (Goldring/
Woldenberg Institute of Southern Jewish Life).
Reprinted with permission from the Goldring/
Woldenberg Institute of Southern Jewish Life (ISJL).
For more selections from the ISJL's *Encyclopedia of
Southern Jewish Communities*: http://www.isjl.org
/encyclopedia-of-southern-jewish-communities.html.

tional perspective make sense? When questioned on his involvement in matters
of civil rights, Grafman was quick to clarify that he did the things because of his
sense of morality and not as a Jew. He was the only rabbi to indicate this. Why
did he attempt to separate his religion from his moral commitment? As a rabbi,
he was obviously viewed as a Jew and gained stature and entrée into various organizations as such. Did others separate his views and actions from his religion?
The rabbis that came closest to Grafman's opinions agreed with him that supporting black rights was not a Jewish issue. Others argued that fighting for the
rights of one minority translated into the support of the rights of everyone including Jews. Who was correct and who incorrect?

The rabbi did take the moral high ground in the important and symbolic incident at the University of Mississippi described in the interview and explained
in the accompanying citation, although, even in this, he sought to limit publicity and impact. He continued to pursue fair and equal treatment for African
Americans in the years after King's letter, so much so that an African American
leader asked him to speak at a memorial service when King was assassinated.
He chaired an interracial commission. Among its responsibilities was investigat-

ing the death of Bonita Carter, an African American who had been killed by a white police officer. In 1979, the city's first black mayor, Richard Arrington, renewed his appointment as chair of the committee. He spearheaded interfaith/ interracial conferences between his congregation and the Sixth Avenue Baptist Church. The rabbi retired in 1975 but remained in Birmingham where he passed away on May 28, 1995, remembered as a voice for positive change.

—Mark K. Bauman

Milton L. Grafman Interview

June 23, 1966

P. Allen Krause: What would you define as being the regional scope of this [research]? Would you include all of Texas and all of Florida or do you consider those to be "South"?

Milton L. Grafman: Well, I think I would include Texas for the simple reason that when we talk in terms of civil rights I presume you mean it for all peoples and all groups and all minorities. And the fact that there are minorities other than the Negro minorities, I think this comes to be overlooked. And thus, for example in Texas, you have quite a large population of Mexicans. I don't know what the situation is in Mexican Texas today, but I do know that in 1929, when I went out for the High Holy Days for the first time, and I went to Corpus Christi, Texas, for my High Holy Day pulpit,[2] and I toured the Rio Grande Valley for the Union [of American Hebrew Congregations],[3] organizing congregations, et cetera, and went down to the actual border [towns] of Laredo, Texas, Brownsville, Texas, Victoria, Texas, Harlingen, et cetera. I do know that the Mexicans, shall I say, were in an unenviable situation and were certainly looked down upon, et cetera. I don't know what the situation is today, but I would imagine that there are problems. Therefore, I would think that Texas could be involved. I feel quite certain that you have a very large Negro population in areas like Houston. I would say that you would take in certainly South Carolina and North Carolina, although North Carolina in many respects is a much [more] liberal state than any of the other southern states. Nevertheless, the Klan has been very, very active there and there've been quite a bit of problems as far as segregation is concerned, although the University of North Carolina is a very, very liberal institution. North Carolina, South Carolina, Georgia, Florida, perhaps outside of the Miami area, Alabama, Mississippi, Louisiana. You might even include Arkansas. I'm not so sure, though we've heard a couple of Florida rabbis say that the Miami area should not be included, but this is a different. I don't know what the situation is there now, but I do know that up until very recently, no Negro was permitted to spend the night on Miami Beach. He could work there, but he had to leave by sundown. I doubt, for example, that a Negro in Miami Beach would find it convenient to purchase a home; I doubt this very much.

PAK: In terms of scope, what date do you consider to be the beginning of intense civil rights activity in your area of the South?

MLG: Well, I would say in the entire South you would have to start with the Supreme Court decision in 1954, and you would have to start with 1954 because, for the first time, a decision was handed down by the Supreme Court, which, if implemented, was bound to cause—if not revolutionary— radical changes, and the South geared itself in 1954 against the implementation of this decision. I can remember, for example, that the general feeling among people in the South whom I came in contact with was that it would be years before this decision would be implemented, because there would have to be a suit in every school district. And of course, I forget the legal term where the justices decide that this is a law that fits all cases and not just the particular case, and this, of course, they did; the first, second, third case came up, [and the Court said that] this decision holds for all similar cases.[4] I think you have to start in 1954 in terms of what I think is the frame of reference of your [research]. Let's face it, the term, the phrase "civil rights"—I don't think was coined until after 1954. It's part of the linguistics of the American people today.

PAK: Can you see any noticeable changes in Birmingham since 1954?

MLG: Definitely. Oh yes. It was slow in coming, and what I think we have to understand and acknowledge from the very beginning is there's several factors that have to be taken into consideration if you're going to understand the resistance of the white people. See, I've lived in the South sufficiently long;[5] although I may not share the opinions, I can understand, though I don't condone, I can sympathize. Here you have a people who had been a master people and they not only are asked to accept people who were literally their slaves, accept them as their equals, but you cannot overlook the fact that the Reconstruction period, the post–Civil War period, was really a nightmare as far as the South was concerned. It was treated as an occupied territory. There were federal troops there; you did have your carpetbaggers; you did have local governments taken over by unscrupulous whites who used Negroes as a front in many instances. And in order to get around that, actually this is how the original Klan was formed, the original Klan. There were excesses—and this I'm not justifying—it is an historical fact. The Grandfather Clauses were a gimmick which lasted for well-nigh almost a hundred years, in order to strike back. You've got to understand the frustration of the people who, as like in Nazi Germany—a proud people— they believed, in Germany's case, that they were superior people; in this case they felt they were superior people. And suddenly they are a defeated people. This made possible a Hitler, made possible a reaction. The same thing is true as far as understanding the mentality and the psychology and the emotion and the sociology of this whole area. The interesting thing is that it is true that there was a paternalism on the part of the South. I can remember when I first moved to Lexington, Kentucky, a not-overly intelligent man, but an old-time southern Jew said to me that if he were a Negro, he would make it his business to see to it that at least one white man liked him so that he would be his protector. There are whites with this sort of paternalism. The interesting thing is that it is true that the southern whites liked the individual Negro but despised the Negro people as a group. Of course we've had this experience as Jews, too, where a person will say "There are individual Jews that I like, but I hate Jews." Well, this is the background; it's not a virtue, but you have to understand that this is part of the resistance.

PAK: What was the response of the non-Jewish white population in Birmingham to the activities after the *Brown* decision of 1954?

MLG: Well, nothing really happened for a long time, to begin with. There was a resentment against national organizations, both Jewish and Christian, that would come out with great *pronunciamentos* about civil rights; implementing the decision and so on. You had a resentment that somebody, an outsider—it's not sufficient that a court lay down an edict, a decision, but outsiders were telling them what they must do and how they must do it and how soon they must do it and so on. And I think that the reaction was really not too negative because the decision read that it should move to implement it with what is it, "with reasonable . . ."—I forget the phrase, but this was a phrase that could mean anything or it could mean nothing— deliberate speed or reasonable speed could mean fifty years very easily. So there wasn't any immediate reaction; there was a disgruntlement, a dislike, but there was no violent reaction.

PAK: What was the reaction five years later?

MLG: Well, that would be about 1959. I wouldn't think that, there wasn't too much reaction until, well, let's see, when was it? I guess in 1963 or 1962, when the federal government began applying pressure through court orders and so on to desegregate, and I believe it was 1963 that the schools were finally desegregated.[6]

PAK: Did you have a strong pro-segregation reaction at that time?

MLG: Yes, of course we did. Let me put it this way: there is a hardcore small minority that loathes, despises the Negro; for the most part, uneducated, lower–middle class, lower than lower-middle class on the social scale, who needs somebody to look down upon. That was the type that would join the Klan and similar organizations like the National States Rights Party—

that might even be willing to indulge in violence. The majority of the white people didn't favor integration. They don't favor it now; they don't want it now. The majority feel that there's nothing that you can do about it, and the thing to do is to rock with the punch. I'll give an illustration of this in just a little bit. I think that their cardinal sin was and is that though they would never dream of joining the Klan, and though they disapprove of killing people, they are not going to criticize anybody that is speaking up against or doing anything against the implementation of integration. They think it's horrible that anybody should be killed; they themselves wouldn't do it; they don't think anybody should be killed, but I think they sort of rationalized, well the victims asked for it or at least all these agitators and so on asked for it.

PAK: Can we move to the ministers in Birmingham? What is their response? What percentage of them would you say are or are not in accord with the federal government's position?

MLG: This is hard to tell, except that originally when things began coming to a crux during 1962, 1963, you couldn't discuss this question at the ministerial association meetings. You had very definite segregationist opinions that would be openly voiced if anybody tried to bring up anything related to the subject. It was almost better to steer clear of it than to bring it up because of these voices that would be raised. However, there were a number of ministers, and particularly among the younger men, who were very sympathetic and quite liberal; sympathetic to, I wouldn't say integration, but certainly desegregation, and this is very important. This is where I think you have the crux of this whole matter—there was a reaction and vehemence against them, on the part of so-called "nice people"; and frankly, this is my point of view, that I certainly feel that all our facilities should be desegregated, but I don't think that integration should be forced upon anyone. I don't believe that there has to be—has to be—a racially balanced school; I don't think there has to be a racially balanced neighborhood. I never felt this way as far as Jews are concerned, and this is contrary to our historic position. When prewar Poland had a *numerus clausus*, for example, and said that only 2 percent or whatever it was, 1 percent of the university, of the *gymnasium* student body could be Jewish, because this was their percentage of the population. We howled; we howled, and we didn't want our students to come under this sort of a religious or, from their point of view, racial balance or imbalance. I don't believe it's true that somehow or other you are psychologically, emotionally truncated if you do not have actual living experiences with people of other religions and of other creeds, other races, and so on. I have looked around here, for example, in Toronto, and I've seen two or three Negro faces; it seems strange to me, for example, not to see any Negroes on the streets, not to see any Negroes in this hotel. Actually [*laughing*] I don't know whether the northerners miss them, but I miss them. I played golf in Milwaukee two weeks ago. I find it difficult to adjust to the fact that there are no Negro kids that caddy for the same reason I found it difficult to adjust when I went South, and there were no white kids caddying. But I noticed that nobody here seems to be emotionally or psychologically harmed by the fact that they haven't forced "X" number of Negroes. . . . If this were true, then I think we would have to take this a step further, and maybe we will someday, I don't know—that the states of Wyoming, Maine, Idaho, Montana, Vermont—I could name you a whole list of states that have practically no Negro population—then perhaps, in order to have a normal population, psychologically and emotionally, we ought to uproot them. I'm not suggesting this but I'm saying that if you're going to carry this to its logical conclusion we will have to do what the ancient conquerors did when they captured countries—they uprooted the population—and do what the communists in Russia have done and are still doing, and which the Nazis did—literally uproot populations and say, "We are going to take 20 percent, 30 percent of the Negroes out of the South and divide them in these northern states."

PAK: What would you say would be your overall goal for the civil rights movement?

MLG: My overall goal, in my situation, from the very beginning has been this: that we must abide by the laws of the land. We must have law, and we must have order, or we shall have anarchy. We don't like all the laws that are passed. There are a lot of people that don't like to pay their income tax for whatever reason; ideological or because they're parsimonious, and they don't want to have to part with a nickel, let alone a dollar, let alone 20, 30, or 40 percent of their income. But they pay; they pay that tax nevertheless. There are a lot of laws that you and I don't like, but we obey them—we obey them. Some of them are traffic laws that we think that are unfair, but we obey them. I once got a ticket, didn't know why, and a policeman that walked by didn't know why. And I finally went, not to have the ticket canceled but to learn why I got this ticket. I discovered when I parked the rear bumper of my car was about fifteen inches in back of the yellow line that indicates this is where you're supposed to park and no further. I've never heard of getting a ticket like this. I paid it, and I was annoyed, furious; nobody could have parked in back of me because I was the last car on the block. This is the law. I didn't like it but I paid it. I think the same thing goes as far as desegregating the schools and the eating places where this is the law. But whatever goes for the general population—the white population—must go for the Negro population, too; they also must obey the law. I think that one of our problems today is there's a double standard of justice as far as implementation of laws: there has to be not only civil rights—there has to be civil responsibilities. And I don't think that two wrongs make a right. I don't think that, for example, when you have $100 million worth of damage done in Watts, or God knows how much damage there was to private-ownership stores. In Chicago last week or two weeks ago, they were seemingly protesting against police brutality.[7] Mr. Smith or Mr. Ginsburg who owned the store on the street where this violence took place and his storefront was smashed, his fixtures were destroyed; his stock was looted and he suffered a loss and maybe was put out of business. I don't think saying that the Puerto Ricans or the Negroes are frustrated justified this. I don't think when people are arrested for literal looting and vandalism in Watts, I don't think that they should be released because you say, "Well, they were frustrated," and I think that there should be, the Bible says, our Scripture says there should be one law for the home born and for the stranger. I think it should be for the home born, for the stranger, and whether they're white and whether they're black, whether Jew, Catholic, Protestant, period.

PAK: How long has your congregation been in existence?

MLG: Approximately, I think, eighty-three years. We were formed in 1882. Incidentally, the city of Birmingham was founded in 1871. The congregation was founded eleven years after. I understand that the first white child born in Birmingham was a Jew.

PAK: What is the economic standard and source of income of the Jewish community in your city?

MLG: I would say that mostly they are merchants. We have quite a number of professional men, a number of doctors—they're all excellent doctors, really. Outstanding lawyers. We have several members of the medical college—the University of Alabama medical school is located in Birmingham. We have quite a medical complex there, and both in the medical school and in the dental college they are on the faculty. I think we have some representation on the Extension Center of the University of Alabama in Birmingham.

PAK: What percentage of the group would be in the professions and what percentage approximately are merchants?

MLG: I'd have to double-check this, but I would say that overwhelmingly they would be in the merchant class. I should say merchants, restaurateurs, investment bankers; one of the banks in Birmingham, Steiner Bank, is Jewish-owned by members of my congregation. People in the insurance field, real estate.

PAK: How susceptible do you think your congregants are to economic pressure put on by the non-Jewish community?

MLG: They are susceptible, but they have been more susceptible to pressure from the Negroes than they have been from the Jews [*Editor's note: Grafman actually meant to say non-Jewish whites rather than "Jews."*] because the

Negroes have conducted boycotts, and this is where I have really felt a great deal of chagrin and have voiced this to my friends in the Negro community. For example, I was very much distressed when they had their first sit-in at a lunch counter. The first store which they sat in at was at the lunch counter of Pizitz. Now Pizitz was founded by a very unique individual: the late Louis Pizitz, an immigrant. I think he came to this country when he was twelve years old—never did learn how to speak English properly—but he was a mercantile genius and he really founded a mercantile empire, which has been carried on by his son and now by his three grandsons. And he was perhaps the greatest benefactor of the Negroes in Birmingham. Many of them, for example, worked in mines, and when the mines struck—it used to be that this was a major source of the economy of Birmingham—these people had no money, and he not only gave them credit, he helped feed them. He was responsible for the Negroes being able to have a YMCA. He was responsible for the Negroes having a hospital of their own, and whereas one may disapprove of a segregated YMCA or a segregated hospital, the fact remains that Negro doctors did have a place where they could be on a staff and where they could operate because, up until recently, a Negro doctor could treat a patient, but if that patient had to be hospitalized, he could not treat the patient in the hospital—he had to turn the patient over to a white doctor. He got two others—a Catholic and a Protestant—to go along with him. They were responsible for raising money but the idea was his. And then the hospital was turned over to some Catholic nursing order—I forget what order these nuns are who administer the hospital.[8] And it seems to me gross ingratitude, and I so mentioned that not just privately, but publicly, at biracial meetings, that I thought that in everybody's religion there was emphasis upon gratitude. And at least if this had been the second place [*chuckling*] that they had sat in—but the first! The answer was this was a new generation and they're not interested in what happened in the past.

PAK: Was this department store any more . . .

MLG: No, no.

PAK: Was not?

MLG: No. This was the thing. I would say, and I think it can be generally accepted, that the Negroes had no better friends than the Jews either locally or nationally. And yet, when they selected the store, the interesting thing is that they selected the store of a man who had been their benefactor: they picketed Parisian, and the president of Parisian, Emil Hess,[9] is one of our liberal young men. As a matter of fact, he has given employment to Negroes; he went out of his way; he came to me and asked me if I could recommend to him a Negro for a responsible job, which I did.

PAK: How did you know?

MLG: How did I know how to find such a Negro? The man has worked for me, and I thought he had greater capabilities than being a janitor. I thought he probably had the intelligence to do something better and more responsible, and he has worked out beautifully. I don't know exactly what the job is.

PAK: What role did you play in all this, particularly in integrating the department stores?

MLG: I played no role whatsoever. I played no role and not only that, I objected to it for this reason. You see I come back to this double standard of morality. When people talk about morality, I don't think that they are in an enviable position when they feel that the ends justify the means. I don't go along with it, or that the means justify the ends. Now the Negroes knew that the most vulnerable group to public pressure were the merchants; yet the merchants are not the power structure. If Negroes were going to break through in employment, it was not going to be in the department stores. So long as your banks, your insurance companies—the real power structure—did nothing, the merchants were in no position to do anything, unless they wanted to invite bankruptcy.[10] For example, after the demonstrations in 1963 and some sort of an agreement it seemed had been worked out by Martin Luther King and his associates, and not merely with the merchants, but with the industrial leaders and business leaders of the community, it was announced in the newspapers that within a period of two months Negroes would be hired as salespeople. Well immediately the stores began to have people calling to close their accounts. This one store, Parisian had, within I think two or three days, as many as three hundred people call to close their accounts. I think the vice president of this particular store told me that he took some of these calls, and he asked one woman why she was closing her account. He said, "We have not as yet desegregated or employed a Negro." She said, "But you're going to, and from now on I'm going to do all my shopping in Atlanta." He said, "But Atlanta is desegregated; they do have Negro salespeople." She said, "But that doesn't happen to be my city." Utterly stupid and irrational. There was quite a bit of this, and in this way they were affected economically. You see they were caught in a vice between the Negroes and the whites; they couldn't win for losing.

I pointed this out to Martin Luther King, incidentally, in a meeting that was held between fifteen white ministers and him and six of his associates. At this meeting he kept referring to the "merchants" and the role of the merchants. And I told him that in the city of Birmingham when you talk about merchants, you might just as well use the word "Jew," and that there was certainly implied anti-Semitism here by the use of the word "merchant." He kept harping on the radio, kept on harping in his talks and everything was quoted in the newspaper about the merchants, the merchants, the merchants. Birmingham, you talk about the merchants, you're talking about Jews.

PAK: And the Jews feel the pressure . . .

MLG: Yes, definitely.

PAK: How much a part of the non-Jewish community are these merchants—socially, culturally?

MLG: Well, they are very active in all facets of civic and cultural life. They are sponsors and generous supporters of the symphony orchestra, of the civic opera, the civic ballet, the library association; we have in the business field the Downtown Action Committee, et cetera.

PAK: How southern are they—and by this I mean—in the area of civil rights? If I took the group of Jews in Birmingham and put them side-by-side with a group of Protestants . . . ?

MLG: I would say that they are much more liberal and sympathetic and want to be as helpful as possible in changing the situation. But you've got to bear in mind that out of a metropolitan population of 630,000, shall I say, there are four thousand Jewish men, women, and children. This is a factor that can't be overlooked; they are very, very vulnerable.

PAK: Are you aware of any in your congregation who are really southerners in outlook in this area?

MLG: There are a few—but very few, very few.

PAK: Even the ones that have been in the South for two or three, four generations?

MLG: Right; they are not bigoted. I'm not saying that you won't find one here and there, but I'm saying taking the Jewish community as a whole, no, they are not.

Let's back up just a minute. Let me say they're realistic, and this I can understand and appreciate. I am not prepared to tell a man that he should commit economic suicide. It's very well at the [Central Conference of American Rabbis (CCAR)] conference for somebody that lives in New York or Detroit or in Oshkosh to say that Mr. Ginsburg or Mr. Cohen or whatever his name might be, should employ five Negroes or two Negroes or one Negro, no matter what the cost. If the cost means that he goes bankrupt, I'm not prepared to tell that man that he should go become bankrupt. And I feel very strongly on this issue, because my colleagues who have shouted the loudest have not been willing to take southern pulpits, period. And the main reason they haven't been willing to take southern pulpits, I think, is for economic reasons. They like their $15,000 and $20,000 pulpits. They like to think in terms of tenure and pension and economic security.

PAK: Is it different in the South? Do not most of the rabbis have tenure?

MLG: Yes, but my feeling is, if you are truly sincere about your prophetic Judaism, then you would not hesitate to give up a plush pulpit in the East or up North somewhere and take a pulpit in Gadsden, Alabama, for $9,000 a year, or maybe down in Vicksburg, Mississippi, for $11,000 a year, or at Selma, Alabama, for a pittance. This is what a prophet does; but he has no right to tell somebody else to commit economic suicide unless he's willing to make a sacrifice himself.

PAK: What was [the] response [of the ministers]?

MLG: Well, let me tell you to begin with, many ministers were caught in the vise also, because even those who wanted sincerely to take a stand—and this goes back a number of years, of course, prior to 1963—they really could not do so without splitting their congregations right down the middle. Again, it's very nice to tell somebody else to do this, but I could understand their reluctance to do this. However, more and more in the ministerial association the climate changed. We have had a number of ministers who have spoken very bluntly from their pulpit, and it might interest you to know that our ministerial association's been desegregated for at least two years, maybe three years. Now the number of Negro ministers who belong is not great; I don't know how many belong. I have never seen more than eight or nine present, but this doesn't mean anything, because I have seldom seen over a hundred ministers present in the ministerial association, maybe seventy or eighty might be a pretty good attendance, and bear in mind that we must have around four hundred churches. So this doesn't mean that more don't belong, but never more than eight or ten have showed up.

PAK: With that number of churches, with that many ministers, you would expect they might be a major force, at least a major religious force in the civil rights movement in Birmingham?

MLG: No, because to begin with, they have got their congregations that they were in danger of splitting—this is a problem I didn't have and that I didn't have to be concerned about; I never had a problem on this score whatsoever, which I think also answers your question. The implied question was whether or not, as you say, are they "typical southerners"—are they bigoted?—is what you mean by the question.

PAK: I'm going to get even more exact on my questions at the end concerning your relationship with your congregation.

MLG: Yeah. Now what happened—let me give you a concrete illustration. When the Freedom Riders came down to Birmingham in 1961, I forgot whether it was '61 . . .

PAK: It was '61.[11]

MLG: 'Cause I keep thinking in terms of '63 when we had the big demonstrations. And there was a bus came in from Anniston with these Freedom Riders—one bus had been burned on the way—and they came in a bus. Now the bus that had been burned was a Greyhound bus, as I recall; it was supposed to go to the Greyhound bus station. The interesting thing was that the television cameras were set up, the mics were set up, and everyone was all set, you know, to film all this; all these things are planned very carefully as you know. But the bus that they took, the second bus, didn't come to the Greyhound bus station; it went to the Trailways bus station. The journalists and television [and] so on finally found out, but in the meantime Bull Connor, who was then police commissioner, is reputed to have been at the city hall which overlooked that bus station, and watching what was happening, and when the bus rolled in these Freedom Riders were attacked and beaten up.[12] And the police were quite late in getting there; there was a great deal of indignation about this, and the *Birmingham (AL) News* came out with a great big headline, "Where Were the Police?" I think this happened on a Saturday[13]—you get foggy after these years, it's five years—but I do recall that Sunday morning I called David Cady Wright,[14] who's an Episcopal minister and who was at that time president of the ministerial association, and he was at an early service—they have a 7:30 service, and a nine o'clock service, and I couldn't get him out of there, but I left word he was to call me. I also put in a call for Bishop George Murray, who was the bishop coadjutor of the Alabama Episcopal Diocese,[15] who was quite liberal, and he was out of town. I called him first; then I called David Cady Wright. And I asked him what the ministerial association was going to do about this. And he said, "What do you want me to do?" I said, "What do you think ought to be done?" I said, "I think there ought to be an emergency meeting called of the ministerial association and a strong statement issued deploring and condemning the attack upon these Freedom Riders, condemning the fact that the police were not there." And he said, "I can't get a meeting this soon." I said, "Well, how about getting a meeting of the executive committee; get them together tomorrow," I said, "What are you waiting for? Are you waiting for the paper to come out with the headline 'Where Was the Clergy?' They've already come out with a headline, 'Where Were the Police?'" At any rate, we got a meeting the next day or maybe it was Tuesday, and I said to him, "If you don't mind, I'm not on the executive committee but I'd like to be present." And he said, "That's alright," and I said, "I would like Bishop [Joseph] Durick,"[16] because none of the Catholics belonged; they were free to belong but they just didn't; maybe now they'll join. "I would like Bishop Durick," who also was the auxiliary Catholic bishop; he's done a lot—now he's the Bishop of Nashville. And he said, "You can bring anybody you want to." There were about six or eight of us that had been meeting periodically, white ministers, sort of huddling together, trying to see what we could do. The ministerial association is unfortunately not a dynamic thing, so . . .

PAK: Tell me about this little group of ministers that were huddling together.

MLG: At the time it was a matter of meeting out of frustration, because we were trying to get something moving and we were just meeting with a stone wall.

PAK: When did this start?

MLG: We started this around 1960.

PAK: Did it come out of just a . . .

MLG: No, just kindred spirits, that's all.

PAK: Was anybody involved as the actual one who started it?

MLG: No. I remember walking out of a Rotary Club meeting and telling Ed Ramage,[17] who was the minister of a Presbyterian church, and the leadership had some very reactionary people among its leadership. And I said to him, "Ed," I said, "you know you get to feeling kind of lonely, and I don't think you have anybody to talk with even." He said, "Well, maybe we can get together." And just like that, we sat down and drew up a list of some names and we began having lunch. My purpose really was in trying to find somebody else with whom we could at least talk about this thing and try to explore ways and means of trying to improve the situation. And Ed was kind of lonely too. There were about six or eight of us that didn't get together at specific times, but we met every few weeks or so, sometimes it was once a month, and just talked. We'd talk about conditions from community to community; this is what you have to bear in mind, that the situation in no two communities is identical. For example, in the city of Atlanta you have an *Atlanta Constitution* and a Ralph McGill, a crusading newspaperman.[18] It makes a tremendous difference when you have the organ that really makes public opinion, speaking out. But when you have a press as we have, which really did nothing and whose editorial policy did not encourage any sort of action . . .

PAK: But they did come out condemning the police in the Freedom Rider incident?

MLG: Well yeah, but this is because violence had occurred. Violence had occurred, and this is more than they could take. And the *Birmingham News* has done since then an about face, although from time to time it swings back. Actually it has been wishy-washy, but it has improved, shall I say, in its news presentation, and also in its editorial policy.

PAK: Was 1961 the first time you started to get together?

MLG: Yes, 1961.

PAK: Had you tried doing this at any other time?

MLG: No, there was no need for it, seemingly. The issue had not come to a head; the issue came to a head with the Freedom Riders in 1961. We felt frustrated because, frankly, our ministerial association was, and still is for that matter, a rather pallid sort of an organization; it doesn't take very much action. Bear in mind that the ministerial association when I came there was called the Protestant Pastors' Union. It was not until after I'd been there about eight or nine years, maybe ten years, that the name was suddenly changed to the Ministers' Association of Greater Birmingham, and I was called and asked if I would like to join, and I said, "I understood this was the Protestant Pastors' Union." And he said, "No, its name has been changed; it's open to everybody and we'd like to have you be a member," and I joined.

PAK: What do you think brought about the change?

MLG: Well, I think what brought about the change is my Institute on Judaism for Christian Ministers. I've now had it for twenty-two years, and this was about eight or nine years after I started it, and I average around one hundred twenty, [one hundred and] twenty-five ministers, sometimes it drops down to a hundred attending this institute, and they look forward to it every year. The institute has become an institution; nobody ever told me this, but this is my feeling in the matter. Anyway, I thought that this was a good idea to belong, and I would go with a good degree of regularity. But this was in the early days of my membership, and I wasn't in a position to stand up and wave the flag. The truth of the matter is that in any community the Jews and the rabbi and the Jewish leadership cannot travel faster than the rest of the population, no matter what anybody says, because we have to live with these people day in and day out. A Freedom Rider comes down and a marcher and a demonstrator—he comes down and I don't know what he accomplishes, very frankly, except he goes back and he's a hero—and he doesn't have to live with these people, but we do, and our people have got to live with them. And the only way we can be effective is to work with the Christians who are willing to be active in any given program, and certainly in the field of civil rights. And unless you have this, and unless you have the press, you can't get very far. If you do your research, you will find out that this is true. At any rate, to get back to this other meeting; we had the meeting, and it was primarily at my insistence that we issued a statement; a statement was drawn up, and the committee appointed to draw up the statement was David Cady Wright, the president; Bishop Durick, the Catholic priest; and myself. And we drew up a statement—I've got the statement at home; I'd have to dig for it. There is a very interesting sidelight to this; I happen to type so I sat down at the typewriter, and before we got started

Bishop Durick said, "I think we should start by invoking Divine Guidance."
I said, "Frankly, I don't feel in this sort of a statement this is necessary because we're not issuing a theological pronouncement; we're issuing really
like a sociological statement; it's a civically responsible statement that we're
making here," but I yielded on the point. And I said, "Since it's your idea to
invoke Divine Guidance first, you give the format in which you would like
it." And he started out in the name of the Father, the Son, and the Holy
Ghost, and I said: "Bishop, before you go any further, [*chuckling*] you are
starting this with a theological dilemma for me. Even though you propose
something that I can sign, and we're preparing a statement that I'm going to want to sign, I will be unable to sign it if [*inaudible, but the sense is
he cannot sign it so long as reference is made in it to Jesus Christ, so they decided to omit reference to Jesus and simply use the word God*]. But then when
we got to the ministerial association meeting, which was called for the next
day, to approve the statement, we're about to vote when a minister gets up
and says, "Nowhere in this statement [*Grafman chuckling*] has the name
of deity been mentioned," et cetera, and he said, "no"; he said the name of
"Christ," because we did make a reference to God, you see, and God's help
and guiding us and so on, and he said, "I move that the name of Christ be
added," and somebody seconded the motion. At this point I arose and repeated my statement, at which point a number of the ministers jumped up
and moved an amendment to propose a substitute motion that the name
of Christ should come out. At which point I said that I would appreciate
if the original mover would withdraw his motion, because I don't want any
Christian minister to be placed in the position of voting against Christ
[*laughing*], anymore than I wanted to be signing this statement in the name
of Christ. You get the picture here—here we're dealing with violence, a
statement condemning violence, and this becomes a raging brouhaha on
the floor [*laughing*]. Fortunately, he withdrew his motion and everything
passed amicably. Well, I feel that, I know that I was greatly responsible for
that statement, not only for having the meeting called, but getting other
people who were not on the executive committee involved and add[ing]
their weight and also to help actually in the framing of the statement.[19]

PAK: How many other rabbis are there in Birmingham?
MLG: There are two other rabbis—one Orthodox; one Conservative.[20] We
have three congregations.
PAK: Did the other two rabbis play any part in this?
MLG: No.
PAK: Have they played any part in any civil rights activity?
MLG: No. To my knowledge, no.
PAK: Are they members of the ministerial association?

MLG: We have a new Conservative/Reform rabbi; he's been here about two years.[21] The predecessor of the present Conservative rabbi was there about twenty-six, twenty-eight years and he belonged but seldom came.[22] I think that they extended membership to him, but he seldom came. I happen to have a much closer relationship with the ministers than the other rabbis have ever had. The Orthodox rabbi just keeps to himself.[23]

PAK: Could you go on now to one or two other specific examples? What has been your response to and involvement in other specific civil rights activities in your area?

MLG: Let me point out to you that I am not an organization man for a lot of reasons. I do not belong to the NAACP [National Association for the Advancement of Colored People], never have, and I have no intention of so doing. I've never belonged to CORE [Congress of Racial Equality], certainly not to SNCC [Student Nonviolent Coordinating Committee]. I do whatever I do in accordance with the dictates of my conscience, with no desire for publicity, and I try to be as effective as I can. I feel that when I sit down with a group of ministers or a group of businessmen I can be much more effective than getting up and waving the flag, precisely because I represent less than 1 percent of the total population of the city of Birmingham; this makes a tremendous difference. Now let's get specific: we had these demonstrations in 1963. These demonstrations were in lunch counters, sit-ins, things like that. Many among us felt that in order to change the climate in Birmingham we would have to change our form of government. We had a city commission form of government. In that city commission form of government one commissioner scratches the back of the other, and each one has his department. Bull Connor was the Safety Commissioner and in charge of schools, also. Believe it or not, a group of citizens— I don't take any credit for this because there were lawyers and so on that dreamed up the idea, I wouldn't have thought of anything like that, or how you go about it or anything like that. But to the extent that it was possible to propagandize for it and so on, I did. Everybody knew what the issue was: the issue was not to change the government but to get rid of Bull Connor and [Mayor] Art Hanes and [Commissioner] Jabbo Waggoner—to get rid of the arch-reactionaries. When Martin Luther King picked on Birmingham, he knew what he was doing. He knew that if he acted a certain way, Bull Connor would react a certain way; and they had to get the reaction.[24] They knew that if they acted in a certain way with [Sheriff Jim] Clark in Selma, they would get a certain reaction from him. This is what's happening at the present time in Mississippi. What happened in Philadelphia yesterday is the reaction that was desired, because, if you get this kind of reaction—it's called nonviolence but you've got to get a violent reaction— then you can stir up the whole country.[25] This is what I object to: I object to provocation to violence all the while claiming that this is a nonviolent movement and nonviolent procedure. Well, believe it or not, we won that election, but before the election, the three commissioners instituted a suit; I don't know the exact basis for it, I don't know exactly what the suit was fought over, but there are two bills, there are two laws in the books of the state of Alabama with reference to the change of a city government. One law states that when a city changes its form of government the incumbents must fill out their term before another election can be held. But there was another law that said of the city of Birmingham that if it was to change its form of government that it could have an election immediately, and these two laws were in conflict. The election was on Tuesday and when we won the suit was filed; on Wednesday Martin Luther King started his demonstrations. He was begged not to start demonstrations at this time because it was going to take about three weeks before the Supreme Court of Alabama would rule on this question, and it was a moot question. Bear in mind that the judges of the Alabama Supreme Court were undoubted segregationists; they were at the time elected officials. It was a ticklish decision; this question could legally have been decided one way or the other. We felt that by him starting his demonstrations he was prejudicing the plausibility of the Alabama Supreme Court upholding the right to hold an immediate election. And so for five, six weeks, we were really in a power vacuum; we had no mayor. If my memory serves me correctly, at the time there was a lot of kidding about Birmingham having two governments: two mayors, two Kings (because one of the candidates for mayor was [also] a fellow by the name of King), and a parade every day. It was a terrible battle, and meanwhile the demonstrations were going on, and this is when the dogs were brought out and so on. The Supreme Court finally decided in favor of the immediate election, and this was the end of Bull Connor and Jabbo Waggoner and Art Hanes. We pleaded for an opportunity for this new city government to be able to do something; it never got the chance. And every time the city government tried to do something, there was always some sort of an incident came up. This is why Martin Luther King, you see, doesn't find great favor, because we felt that he just didn't care; he didn't want to give us a chance. He didn't see his purpose to give us a chance.

PAK: Who was the "we" that you're talking about?

MLG: I'm talking [about] like-minded people, the people that helped change the form of government, the people that wanted to change the climate of Birmingham. This was composed of businessmen and [*inaudible—possibly doctors*].

PAK: Who did the pleading with Martin Luther King?

MLG: I didn't. I did to this extent: when we had this meeting at the Carpenter House, which is the Episcopal diocese seat in Birmingham,[26] I brought this out. I brought out the fact that his continual harping about merchants was implied, if not actually anti-Semitism, because in the city of Birmingham everybody knew that the merchants were Jews. Then the first thing that the mayor[27] did was to appoint a citizens' committee of three hundred, and it was called the Community—I forget the name of the overall committee.[28] And then there were subcommittees under this big committee, and there was a committee on community affairs and I was on this committee. This was a biracial committee composed of sixteen whites I believe and either twelve or fourteen Negroes to approximate the ratio of Negroes and whites in the community.[29] This committee worked off and on; we met regularly every Friday afternoon, which was a terrible time for me; it was horrible. We used to meet at three o'clock on Friday afternoon. I'd get out of there sometimes at six o'clock and have to rush home in time to eat and get to temple. And this committee came under constant criticism from the bigots in the community, and even the nice people that would not go along with the Klan but didn't like what was going on. It came under criticism from not the local Negro leadership but from the outside Negro leadership. And despite this fact I feel that this committee was most helpful, because it was the one committee that met at city hall where Negroes and whites at the time, in a period of great tension, not only were meeting together but were trying to solve some problems and, if we didn't do anything else, we helped to clear the air quite a bit. As a result of this, among the other things that happened, was the desegregation of city hall, for example. The water fountains were desegregated and the washrooms were desegregated, and we did this quietly; there was no notice in the newspaper. The signs came down—period; that's all. Now there were those who thought that this was terrible; when I would mention this they'd come over and say, "It should be in the newspapers, you know." The point is, is it important to get in the newspapers or is it important to get the washrooms desegregated? Is it important to get a headline in the newspaper, or is it important to get a Negro working as a salesperson some place? Now this is the question. The question is whether how many jobs, for example, the headlines in the newspapers created, and how many jobs were secured by negotiation. We had some stormy sessions, except that it was very interesting how, when we had our first meeting, there was a stiltedness, you know; nobody really knew how to act. The Negroes were uncomfortable; the whites were uncomfortable. But after two or three meetings, they became relaxed and everybody spoke openly, bluntly, spoke his piece; criticized, condemned, but in a spirit of goodwill. This, it seems to me, was symptomatic of what was on the way. By the way, what I failed to say was before this happened, there was a group, and I don't know who called this group together except that

Bishop Murray was active in it, and there was a man by the name of Sidney Smyer[30] who was president of the Birmingham Realty Company, I believe. And at these meetings, which were held at the Carpenter House, there were Negroes and whites. And I can remember at one of these meetings—this is before the demonstrations—this Sidney Smyer, who is an arch-segregationist, saying, "Look, I was born on the farm. I was born in a segregated society; I believe in the separation of the races, but I believe every man should have an opportunity." And he said, "Furthermore, unless we do something about this, the federal government is going to throw the book at us. I don't propose to wait and I don't think we should wait until the federal government throws the book at us." Well, I had to admire him for his honesty if not for his approach to the whole problem from a position as to whether this was a moral thing to do or not, the right thing to do or not; but the truth of the matter is that I feel that the greatest instrument for de-segregation is economics. Here's a segregationist but he doesn't want his office buildings to be vacant. I don't admire the motive, but the net result is the same. We walked along for about two years or so; the schools were de-segregated. The lunatic fringe tried to create some violence. Much of it was blown up in the newspapers; for example, during the demonstrations of 1963, the whole story was not told. The Negroes were never depicted on the television, never shown taunting the whites. They were never shown taunting the white policemen. The Birmingham policemen were attacked for police brutality; this is an unfair and untrue statement. I admired their restraint. If anybody had any occasion to see what crap they took and what obscenities they took . . .

PAK: Was that after Bull Conner?

MLG: This was before Bull Connor, and after Bull Connor, too. I cannot say the same for the state police. When the Gaston Hotel was bombed, the state police moved in. As I recall the new administration was in office at that time, and they did not want the state police to come in but they did anyhow.[31] And probably I shouldn't say this, but the really rough stuff came from the state police, not from the local police. I read a tape of a radio program of a West Coast network about the Birmingham demonstrations. It just simply was not true. This girl, this young girl said that she had been arrested and she had been manhandled and she had been thrown into a sweat box, which she gave the dimensions; she said that sometimes you had to stand up and she'd not be able to do so. There is no such thing. It's not true.

PAK: You have seen the jail and . . . ?

MLG: Yeah, and it's just not true. Not only that but I happen to have connections with the police department and I know it's not true.

PAK: Can you give examples of your participation?

MLG: My participation, for example, was in meetings with the clergy, meetings with businessmen, and this community relations crowd, but I haven't tried to get newspaper clippings and so on. There was a paper, an independent paper got started, didn't last very long, I never did find out just what he was trying to prove or what a big parasite he was. But it took some snide swats at me; called me the bell cow of the Negroes or something like this. Let me say this; let's take my Institute on Judaism for Christian Ministers. About four years ago a minister said to me, that how come you don't invite the Negro ministers? I said the reason I don't invite the Negro ministers is because my invitation goes out to the members of the ministerial association. It's always been my policy from the beginning. And when the ministerial association is desegregated, my invitation will go to the Negro ministers who belong to the ministerial association. And this is what happened; when we desegregated the ministerial association they were invited. I might add this has been about three years, and never more than six have come. And when this happened I attended a temple board meeting and didn't ask my board's permission to invite these people, these Negro ministers; I simply told them that they are members of the ministerial association and that they were receiving an invitation, and I was simply notifying the board to this effect. And immediately when I made this statement somebody made a motion that the rabbi be commended for doing this.

PAK: Was this the first time that your congregation had Negroes as guests?

MLG: No, but this is the first time that they were officially invited. We have always had Negroes who would come. In previous years they would themselves go to the balcony. They, for example in, oh, about, either in '58 or '59, we had a program on "The Role of the Jew in the Confederacy." I have a member of my congregation, an investment banker very interested in history, and he is really quite an authority on Civil War history. We invited the general community. It was not one of these things where we went out to get five thousand people. We figured if we got seventy-five, a hundred people to come to this, it would be good. Well, we had about two hundred people that came, and there were some of those who were non-Jews, and before we got started, lo and behold, a Negro walked in. He sat eight rows behind the last filled row of chairs, so I went up to him, and said I was glad to see him, would he mind coming forward and joining the rest of the group; that the speaker did not speak very loud, which was true, and that I didn't have any amplification for the lecture and he could hear better. So he came forward. We've had Negroes who come to bar mitzvahs; they've come to weddings, and they sit wherever they want to sit. Now during the kneel-ins and the pray-ins and all this other stuff, I felt this way about it—that anybody that came to my temple that planned to worship was welcome, but anybody that came to my temple to use it as a fulcrum for political action or something, could come. But, very frankly, I would not feel happy about it because, my house, as it is engraved, "My house is a house of prayer for all people;"[32] this is engraved in stone. It's a house of prayer. These kneel-ins went on for about six or eight weeks and I instructed my ushers; but since we have different ushers every Friday night, I would go back to the entrance around 7:30, when the ushers got there, and I would remind them of what they had been instructed. That is if any Negroes were to come to our temple, because there were some churches that turned them down, that not only were they to be admitted, but they were to be asked where they would like to sit. They were not to be ushered to a seat announcing to them "won't you follow me," because I would never permit any Negro to walk out and say, "Yeah, we came but they put us on the right side where there's practically nobody sitting. They put us in a spot where nobody sits." "Would you like to sit up front? Would you like to sit on the right? In the center?" It so happens that we didn't have anybody come, but as long as those kneel-ins went on, the ushers got a personal instruction every Friday night.

PAK: **Why do you think that you didn't have anybody come?**

MLG: I don't know why, unless they felt that they wouldn't be turned away [*chuckling*]. This is very possible because the churches were turning them away, and I don't have to tell you they have made a terrible mistake—terrible.

PAK: **Did you have any involvement at all with the Freedom Riders?**

MLG: None whatsoever.

PAK: **I read here of Rabbi Nussbaum's correspondence . . .**

MLG: Yeah. I think that Rabbi Nussbaum was involved in this, just as I think Rabbi Lefkowitz is.[33] When they came down to Mississippi and came down to Jacksonville, they I think notified them in advance that they were coming, or they were arrested and Nussbaum . . . [*There was an accidental tape erasure here. The gist of Rabbi Grafman's remarks was that Rabbi Nussbaum was performing the duty of any Jewish chaplain ministering to the needs of Jewish individuals located in institutions in his area. Grafman was then asked if there were any other specific times that he was involved in civil rights activities.*]

MLG: I would have to go back to my files because when the years pass, you forget dates. I'm quite sure it was 1955. I had been invited by the Chautauqua Society to represent them at the University of Mississippi at a religious emphasis program.[34] I was to be there for five days, I think. Now, I had been to the University of Mississippi before and had enjoyed my visit. Very interestingly there was a forum on race relations—this must have been in 1952, prior to this visit, which was in 1955—and I attended this forum. And

I can remember that during the course of the discussion somebody turned
to me and asked me if I would be willing to express my opinion, which I
did. I remember that I received terrific applause when I finished with my
statement in which I pointed out that everyone is entitled to his rights, justice, and opportunity, et cetera, et cetera, and it was favorably received. So I
wasn't concerned about how the students were going to act at the University of Mississippi when the following incident developed. About ten days
before I was to go there, an Episcopalian minister from Miami, Ohio, I
can't think of his name right now,[35] was on the *$64,000 Question* program
with Hal March, and his field was jazz.... [*There was a break in the tape
here, but notes taken in 1966 reflect that Grafman stated that, about two
weeks prior to the University of Mississippi program, this minister won
$32,000, and he then said on air that he intended to give*] 1 percent or 2,
whatever it was to the NAACP. It so happened that this Episcopal priest
was one of the visiting clergymen for this Religious Emphasis Week program. Immediately a crisis developed in Oxford, Mississippi. State legisla-
tors demanded that President J. D. Williams, the chancellor, cancel this
Episcopal priest's invitation. The students did not want it canceled. I later
discovered, and the source of my information was somebody that was on
the faculty and in the administration position to know—at the time, I
wouldn't have quoted him because it would have jeopardized his position—told me that the chancellor had been told by certain influential legis-
lators [that] unless this man's invitation was canceled that they would with-
hold appropriations to the University of Mississippi. Pressure was brought
to bear, and Williams canceled the invitation. When it appeared in the
newspaper I got on the telephone and called whoever was—it may have
been Lebow [36] at the time, and it may have been his predecessor—and told
him the situation and said, "I don't feel like I can go there to speak. The
reason that I'm calling you is that I'm speaking under the auspices of the
Chautauqua Society. And if I don't go, I don't think that you will ever be
able to send a speaker to the University of Mississippi. So I don't want to
take the responsibility—I'm not a free agent here. I'd rather be a free agent,
because you're a subsidiary of the Brotherhoods, which is a subsidiary of
the Union of American Hebrew Congregations. But I think that before I
do anything that you better get clearance all the way up to the top." So Vorspan[37] called me back and he said, "You have our permission." So I said, "All
right." He said, "I think you should call these ministers." I said, "I'll be glad
to." We were in touch by telephone back and forth. So then I called all
these guys. One was a priest from New Orleans; another was a Presbyterian
minister from some place in Oklahoma; another one was a Methodist minister from New York. I forget, there was also a layman from Richmond,

Virginia. He refused to go along—he finally went. The others went along with me that unless this man [Kershaw] was invited to come and the cancelation canceled that we would not go.[38] We felt that we would state this on the basis of academic freedom, which was, of course, correct. I called back Vorspan and got the idea and talked to these fellas (and I paid for all these long distance phone calls myself incidentally; it ran about sixty-five dollars) that the most effective would be a trifaith statement. I talked to Vorspan; I said, "Look you have got a public relations department, why doesn't your public relations [department] draw up the statement and I'll see that it gets okayed." Which he did, and the statement was very good and very acceptable. Then Vorspan and Eisendrath[39] got in on the act somehow or other said that they wanted me to release the statement from Birmingham. They wanted me to give it to the *Birmingham News*, the *Birmingham (AL) Post-Herald*, the UP, the INS that was then in existence, the AP, and do it immediately and send the statement to Williams.[40] I refused to do it this way; I'm only doing what my conscience tells me to do. Besides, J. D. Williams was a friend of mine, an old friend. We were young men together in Lexington, Kentucky, when he was the head of the university school of the Department of Education in the University of Kentucky. He lived across the street from me; our kids, our little daughters played together. I had been his personal guest to speak at the University of Mississippi; I have been a guest in his house. I said, "I won't do it this way. I will get the agreement—in fact, I've got the agreement—of these men to put their names to this. I will send it to Chancellor Williams and we will not go." So I was asked, "Well what have you done in relation to the newspapers?" I said, "This is not my business. I'm not interested in newspapers. I'm only interested in doing what I'm supposed to—what my conscience tells me to do. Furthermore, how can you have a program announced for weeks, maybe months, that six men are coming to a Religious Emphasis Week program, and five men don't show up? Let him make the statement; let him tell why we didn't come; some explanation why must be forthcoming." This was not satisfactory. In the meantime I get an airmail special delivery from the Methodist minister in New York who'd been in consultation with Vorspan with regard to that. "I just thought I'd drop a note . . ." in which he gives me the specifics not only with regard to the [Birmingham] newspapers but the *Jackson (MS) Ledger*, the *Memphis (TN) Press-Scimitar*, the *New Orleans Times-Picayune*, "and then our people will take it up from there." I never knew who "our people" was. I don't work for "our people." I am doing what Milton Grafman tells Milton Grafman. So I called back and I said, "Unless it goes my way there will be no trifaith statement. We will each send our individual notifications to Chancellor Williams." And this is what happened, which was unfortunate because it was a good statement. So we each sent our individual requests. I sent a telegram. I eventually got back a cold letter from a man that was an old friend, and this terminated the friendship, and this was the end of it. The net result of that story was on Friday that I finally sent the thing in. Saturday, in the first edition of the *Birmingham News*—that's the afternoon paper that comes out about eleven o'clock—there was, I think, a front-page article, "Rabbi Refuses to Speak at Mississippi," or something like that. They called that the "Grafman edition," because the religion editor was running a series of profiles of ministers and their hobbies and this happens to be tape recorded, at that time it was wire recording; it was before tape recording. There was a picture of me on the church page sitting next to a wire recorder, and the front page was another one about the refusal to go to Mississippi. So I stepped off the pulpit Saturday at noon, I went to my study and there was a telephone call; this will give you another aspect of the climate at the time. The phone rang; it was for me and I answered the phone. The voice said, "Grafman?" I said, "Yes." He said, "Why the hell don't you haul your ass up north with all the other nigger lovers!" Bang. And with this there began a series of harassing calls. I didn't tell my wife, but it so happens I was staying at the temple rather late to do some reading and what not. I went to the hospital and came back to the temple. My wife called me terribly distressed. The gentile wife of one of the members of our congregation called her. It seems that she had gotten a call from somebody who told her anonymously that "we are going to get Rabbi Grafman." She gets hysterical and calls my wife. My wife gets upset about this thing, naturally. I said, "Don't worry; nothing's going to happen." So I went home. That night we had to go to an engagement reception. This will give you a picture of the atmosphere: the calls were coming in. My son was about fifteen at the time; my daughter was away at school. I said, "Son, I want you to go to this reception with me." He wouldn't do it. He said, "I'm going to stay home." I said, "Why don't you go to your friend's house?" No, he is fine. I said, "All right we will be gone a short time, nothing is going to happen, but in case there is anything suspicious—if there is a rock, if somebody rings the doorbell, whatever it is, you call me; you call the police chief in Mountain Brook, you call him. You call me at this place; we'll be back—we are only within five or ten minutes from you, or less than that."

I went and nothing happened, except that for months I received threatening calls during the middle of the night. I stay up very late, and so I was reading in the living room with the phone by my side. I developed a technique of kidding these people when they would call. They'd call me, and

I would talk back in Yiddish or throw in a little Hebrew. I even had teen-agers calling. One night at about eleven o'clock I had a teenager call and I replied, "Honey why don't you go to bed. You need your beauty sleep." You find with this type of mentality that if they find they are not irritating you, eventually they hang up. These were only harassments, and I have had these harassments off and on over the years, although not in the last couple of years. I had one threat to my life; a serious threat—so serious that the FBI and the local police had my house under surveillance for about two or three months. My wife didn't know about this, but she realized I had been threat-ened because unfortunately she answered the phone, she heard the guy's voice all the way across the room. She saw a police car cruising up and she said to me, "I noticed a police car goes up and down here periodically." I said, "Yeah they are just taking good care of your husband [*Grafman chuck-ling*]." I wasn't the only one that received these kinds of calls, but I had my share of them and as I say one serious threat. This goes back to this episode at the University of Mississippi, and I never was invited back, of course, and I got this cold letter from Chancellor Williams. We of course had the bomb scare over at the Conservative synagogue, which is a block up from our temple.

PAK: Why the Conservative synagogue?

MLG: Nobody knows because their rabbi, may his soul rest in peace, really had never been involved in anything.[41] I have felt that this was the reason, really, that over the years we have had a series of break-ins. They were very annoying, petty things: breaking the Coca-Cola machine, trying to find petty cash in the secretary's drawer, and so on. We were advised to keep night-lights on. They weren't brilliant lights; they were just lights, but they were better than darkness. I have always felt that if they had any intention of doing anything about our temple, that the reason they didn't was that there were these night-lights on. This was in '58 or '59. I think that the jani-tor of the Conservative synagogue found dynamite that turned out to be fifty-four sticks of dynamite.[42] It was enough to have ripped up a whole city block. If it had gone off hundreds of people could have been hurt and killed; every house within a radius of a half block I think would have been damaged. Fortunately the fuse stopped two inches before it reached the dy-namite. Of course this set off a flurry.

We had another incident like this that two guys drove up in a hearse and my janitor happened to come out and asked them what they wanted. They yelled something at him and they took off. We called the police im-mediately and there was dynamite in the car. Much to my chagrin they gave them a suspended sentence provided they left town immediately. I tell you this to give you a picture of how the climate has changed, you see. Then, of course, we had the National States Rights party headquartered there for about three years, and that is Dr. Edward Fields's group.

Now another episode was in September or October '64. The man who rents out space at the Alabama State Fair, which is held at the fairgrounds in Birmingham, rented space to the Ku Klux Klan at Shelton's Creek. Well, I didn't find out about it—I don't go to the state fair. Somehow it didn't trickle back to me until about Wednesday; the fair was over on Saturday. So the National Conference of Christians and Jews was having its monthly meeting Friday at noon, and the speaker was Dr. Sherman Raffel, who was a psychologist and was connected to the University of Alabama Medical Center.[43] He was speaking on the impact of prejudice upon children; he was a child psychologist. He called me Wednesday night. This was when I really found out about it because there was nothing in the newspapers about it. He said that he had prepared his talk and he was incensed about this and he was going to make a comment about it. He wanted to know whether or not he should, whether it was advisable. He said he weighed his words carefully, but now he wanted me to hear it. I listened to it and I said, "I very definitely would make this statement," which he did. When the meeting was over the chairman thanked him for his speech, and he said that if there is no further business the meeting will be concluded and at this point I said, "Mr. Chairman I think there is a little business." I said, "The National Conference of Christians and Jews always prides itself as an educational organization. It never takes any action, and it doesn't take any action because it says it is an educational organization. It seems to me that if we're involved with the education of our children as far as prejudice is concerned, it seems to me that there comes a time when even the National Conference of Christians and Jews has got to say something besides platitudes." Then in the course of my remarks I made reference to this exhibit by an organization that spews forth poison and the venom of hatred, you know et cetera, et cetera, and that I therefore moved that—bearing in mind that this was Friday and the fair came to an end on Saturday, and that it would be impossible to do anything between now and then— nevertheless I moved that something be done to prevent this from happening again, and that the president and the city call upon the officials of the Alabama State Fair to protest and demand this not happen again. Well this got into the newspapers, of course, that Rabbi Grafman of Temple Emanu-El with Dr. Sherman Raffel of the University of Alabama had instigated this.[44] Within the week I got a notice from the late Matt Murphy,[45] a court thing, notifying me that I was being sued for a million dollars [*chuckling*]. Although the attorneys told me not to laugh. I still laugh about it, because you can't laugh off any suit because you never can tell what will happen. I was named, Sherman Raffel was named, the temple was named, and the *Birmingham Post-Herald* was named. I don't think the *News* was named as a defendant. There is no such thing as group libel but in the complaint it said that I slandered Bobby Shelton the grand kleagle or whatever he is and other people.[46] We had a meeting of about ten attorneys to decide on who should represent us. Of course the newspaper has its own legal office of defense that was going to represent them. The lawyer said it would probably take about two years before the thing comes up. In the meantime Matt Murphy, the attorney for the Klan, was killed. Art Hanes[47] has become their attorney now, and I don't know what is going to happen. I just don't see how they've got a leg to stand on, but nevertheless it could be nasty, it could be expensive. Of course I immediately sent word by the grapevine that would reach the Klan that I welcomed the suit and the Justice Department welcomed the suit, because this would give us the opportunity and the Justice Department through us the opportunity to have certain questions asked of the Klan that we felt certain they didn't want to answer, but we would be delighted to force the answers out of them.

PAK: What is this "grapevine"? How did you do that?

MLG: Well I have contacts. Let me just put it this way.

PAK: Individuals who are themselves segregationists or not?

MLG: Yes, but I also have friends who are law enforcement officers who, off the record, were our stool pigeons. The Department of Justice admits that it has infiltrated the Klan. The Department of Justice is not the only law enforcement agency that has infiltrated the Klan, let's put it this way. I wouldn't want you to make reference to this. You better stop the recording. [*Pause in recording.*] For the suit, we're waiting to see what happens.

PAK: Have you ever used your personal offices, your contacts et cetera, to make a phone call, to put a little pressure on, to influence . . .

MLG: Oh yes, yes. You know these four kids were killed in the bombing of the 16th Street Baptist Church. Actually one of the hottest clues in this case walked into my office. This was a gentile man who had overheard a telephone conversation and was scared to death, scared to death. He was assured that his name would not even be used. The information was turned over to the proper authorities. Of course, nothing has happened because, in this case, the law enforcement agency pretty well knows as far as I've been informed who was responsible for that, but to be able to bring evidence into court that will stand up is another story. But this was an interesting thing to me that somebody would come in to . . .

PAK: Why did he come to you?

MLG: I asked him this and he said he just didn't feel like he could trust anybody and though he didn't know me, he just heard about me and he just felt that he could trust me for this.

PAK: **What was your response to the Selma to Montgomery march?**

MLG: What do you mean by response?

PAK: **Do you think that this was an error on the part of the . . .**

MLG: Yeah I do. See I have been opposed to demonstrations; I am opposed to demonstrations because I don't think two wrongs make a right.

PAK: **This would go back to what you said originally.**

MLG: Definitely, and not only that. I am convinced that all these demonstrations—I don't think that the American mind is capable of dreaming up these things, like the student revolts and so on. They are all following a pattern, and it is a pattern that was imported into this country, and I am very dubious and skeptical as to who is pulling the strings. Martin Luther [King] of course; one of the things that I didn't tell you about Martin Luther King is a matter of public record. When you say who asked Martin Luther King not to start the demonstrations in Birmingham, one of them was Father Foley.[48] Father Foley is the president of Spring Hill College in Mobile, which is a Catholic institution, which desegregated a long time ago, long before all this business came up. He is a great liberal; he's on the president's Civil Rights Commission, a commissioner for the state of Alabama. It was in the front pages of the *Birmingham News*, his statement that he had begged Martin Luther King not to start those demonstrations at the time. And it was an aide of Martin Luther King that told Father Foley [that] the Southern Christian Leadership movement's treasury was practically empty and they needed a demonstration in order to get the treasury built up again.

PAK: **Could you sum up in a couple-sentence statement the most effective methodology you use in implementing your goals?**

MLG: It depends once again on the community. I feel that the most effective way is to convince the local power structure that it has got to move in the direction of implementing the law of this land, and if it will not move for moral reasons it must move out of selfish self-interest because Birmingham has been painted, Alabama has been painted, has been given this image of being a dangerous area, a backward area. You know people come down to Birmingham and they are amazed when they come there to find out that there are actually nice people down there. Alabama has got 10 percent of the natural resources of this country. I don't know whether you know that or not. Birmingham has a unique situation of having coal, iron ore, and uh, uh . . .

PAK: **Steel?**[49]

MLG: Yeah, we had a subsidiary of the Tennessee Coal and Iron Company;[50]

it has three natural resources right there. There's every reason in the world for Birmingham to grow, develop, and to flourish and it's not going to so long as it continues to hold onto this image. Now let me say there has been progress and progress is being made daily.

PAK: And how do you go about influencing this power bloc? As an individual sometimes?

MLG: As an individual and also in these groups. Incidentally, I should mention this about my congregation; you were interested in what their reaction was.

PAK: Can I ask one question before you say that? What is your reaction to the statement that one of the rabbis made that the best approach for a southern rabbi is to put a Christian at the head of whatever he wants to do?

MLG: I agree, I agree with this.

PAK: But you sound like you have taken the lead?

MLG: Yeah, but I didn't really take the lead. I have worked with different people. Bishop Murray, I worked a great deal with, but the problem with Bishop Murray is that he was out of town a whole lot. He goes out of town; he has to visit the different churches and so on. The thing that I didn't tell you about, for example, when these kids were killed, these four kids, he and I went to the funeral. I'm not an organization man; I keep harping back on this. You know, I don't want to be critical, but some of my [rabbinic] colleagues, there is this kind of blind passion with them. Do you know what I mean? They have got to prove something to themselves. I don't know whether they are expiating the guilt they must feel because of the discrimination that exists in their local communities, about which they seem to be incapable of doing something or about which they turn their head[s] and refuse to recognize; or which they rationalize and justify. But they were put in a difficult position.

Let me back up a little bit. These kids were killed I guess on a Sunday and we had, I forget what day they were buried—they were buried at two o'clock Erev Rosh Hashanah,[51] with [our] services that night. Well it so happens there were about six or eight of us white ministers who were meeting; this was another group that was meeting with six or eight colored ministers. We had overlapping groups that were meeting up. It so happened that the minister of the church where three of these kids were going to be buried, where the funeral service was going to take place, was at this meeting,[52] and we said that we would like to attend the funeral and pay our respects and also by our presence indicate to his people and also to the white population where our sympathies lay. But we didn't want to come, knowing that his people would be there *en masse*, if we would be taking up seats;

the pews that they needed for their own people. He said, "No this will be perfectly all right. In fact," he said, "we will reserve seats for you." We decided we would meet at the Church of Our Lady-Fatima, which was a block away, and we would go together over from there. I got a phone call from Balfour Brickner the day before: "Mickey, we want you to be sure to go to that funeral for those three girls. We want you to represent the Union [of American Hebrew Congregations (UAHC)]. It is a terrible thing," he said, "our men cannot come down for the funeral." I said, "Balfour, I didn't need you to call me to tell me to attend this funeral; it so happens I'm going there. And I want you to know that when I go I'm going representing nobody but Milton Grafman. I'm not even representing Temple Emanu-El. I'm going there as a human being period, period."

Now I had suggested at this meeting with these ministers, we all decided there would be a reward fund, and we decided—I don't know who brought up what—that we should raise a fund to compensate the families of these children. There were several kids; one kid almost lost an eye and was hospitalized. The fund would pay the funeral expenses and also raise money to repair the church. I said that I felt that this money should not be raised throughout the country; no appeal should go forth, and I told the colored people, "I don't think that your civil rights organization should appeal to the country. I think that the white people of Birmingham should raise every dime as expiation for this sin." Well this made—I don't want to be taped on this [*pause in recording*].

We did start such a fund; however, the various civil rights groups all over the country started making appeals. Right away money started flowing into Birmingham and it flowed over to the church and it flowed over to individuals who were not connected to the church but who happened to be colored; the long and short of it was that this idea of mine that no money be raised anyplace but in Birmingham and that the white people pay for repairing the church et cetera just didn't get off the ground. Everybody wanted to send in money; they sent it over to the church, but there was no need for this money. So we didn't push this, this fund beyond a few days, because it was taken over, you might say. But with this money that we raised, we paid for the funeral expenses of all these kids; we paid for the hospital expenses of this one girl. We said we would pay expenses for anybody that was injured. Some white woman from Chicago was injured when the Gaston Motel was bombed; we paid. There was a white kid who evidently was from a segregationist family, that was knocked off of a bicycle by some colored kids—some colored kids shot at the white kid, and we wanted to pay; in fact, we started to pay the expenses, and they wouldn't let us pay it. I got a phone call at six thirty in the morning from an irate, I guess urban redneck, about us raising money to pay for this kid and that white people didn't want our money and all that sort of stuff. Well the long and short of it was that the money that we did raise, and I think it came to about ten thousand dollars. It was all divided in person. Also, my recommendation was that we should raise enough money to repair the church, put it in better shape than it was minus whatever they got from the insurance company, which was only fair. This was one of the things that threw a monkey wrench into the local interest in our doing this . . . [break in tape]

What else do you want to know? Oh yes, in conjunction with this bombing—did I tell you it was that the funeral was Erev Rosh Hashanah? That night, Rosh Hashanah Eve, when I recited Kaddish[53] I recited Kaddish for these four little kids, mentioning them by name, which is appropriate with a preliminary statement right before the Kaddish. I had a big struggle within myself since the kids were killed on Sunday morning and Rosh Hashanah was four days later, whatever, I guess it was Wednesday night. My sermons were prepared. I had two services at night and therefore I tried to keep my services to an hour, an hour and five minutes, which requires brevity of preaching; which I try to keep to eight to ten minutes believe it or not, and I do. I had a struggle within myself what to do, because I felt that I had to talk about this, and yet I didn't have any time to prepare, and I never go onto the pulpit unprepared. So I walked to the pulpit Rosh Hashanah morning—I only have one service Rosh Hashanah morning—and I took my sermon notes with me. I waited until the last minute, the Etz Chayim,[54] before I decided, and I told my congregation that something that they knew about me is that whether I preached well or poorly that I was always prepared. They might like or dislike the sermon, but it was a prepared sermon. When I had not been prepared, I had always told the congregation that I had been sick this week or that I had been out of town, and I therefore I want you to know that I am just going to ad lib for ten or fifteen minutes. I had done this occasionally, but never have I gone to the pulpit on the High Holy Days without being carefully prepared. I just felt that there were certain things that had to be said, and I felt that besides the fact Rosh Hashanah was no time to speak without the proper preparation. I hoped that they would indulge me if went beyond my usual discrete twenty minutes, because I was not going to speak from notes as I usually do; I was going to speak from my heart. Believe it or not, I spoke an hour and ten minutes. And one of the things that I didn't tell you was that at this meeting we set up a reward fund; we raised something like a hundred thousand dollars as a reward for the arrest and the conviction of these bombers. I made an appeal in the course of my remarks for our people to send in checks for this fund for the church, and I had already had cards mimeographed which I said the ushers would distribute, which they would sign saying how much they were willing to put up for the reward fund, if and when the killers were caught. I forget what the total was, but I want you to know that something like five thousand dollars rolled in, because I said, "I don't want you to send it to the temple, I want you to send it to me personally." I have a file of letters that came in in response to this Rosh Hashanah sermon, which I think will tell you more than anything else. Hundreds of letters—letters from kids.[55]

PAK: Is there any discrepancy between your response to and/or participation in civil rights activity and that of your congregants? Have you ever been criticized by your board or members of your synagogue for any . . .

MLG: Never, never once. I have been commended.

PAK: You've never had any moments of insecurity because of the ideals?

MLG: Never, never; not one moment.

PAK: What do you attribute that to?

MLG: I would say that from the early years when I made a comment about Negroes, and this goes back for about twenty-five years, I had members that got a little nervous, didn't think it was wise; but never a criticism. I was criticized severely for being a Zionist in the early days [*laughing*] and for having too much Hebrew in the service.

PAK: What do you attribute this to? Is it because there's a basic liberal tendency on their part?

MLG: I think that there's a basic Jewish sympathy for the underdog, for the oppressed.

PAK: Even on the part of your real segregationists, the few that you have in your congregation?

MLG: Yeah, never. Now wait a minute; let me back up. There is one young man by the way, one young man who is a merchant. I would say he is about thirty-two or thirty-three years old. He takes everything personally. I understand he blew his top to other people about my Rosh Hashanah sermon in '63. But I believe the reaction to him was one of writing it off and feeling it was ridiculous and so on. In my sermon, incidentally, I challenged the professional people and the people in real estate and other areas. I castigated the armchair liberals, among other things, who sit in their parlors and talk about what's wrong with Birmingham and how horrible the racial situation is, and they sit back and do nothing but wait for the merchants. And I said, "Can you doctors not employ a receptionist? A secretary? You lawyers you could not employ a bookkeeper? A secretary? If you can't find them—I'll find them for you." We have this guy who is merchant who was very perturbed.

PAK: Can you give me an explicit statement of what role you think national Jewish organizations have played in your area of the South?

MLG: The problem is, you've asked is what role they played in civil rights. When you use the words "civil rights," this is a phrase that refers to the [UAHC] social action committee, the NAACP. If you're talking in terms of this, I haven't played any role. I haven't played any role through any organization.

PAK: I think I understand the role that you have played. What role have national Jewish organizations played? ADL [Anti-Defamation League]? CCAR? UAHC?

MLG: Frankly, I don't think they have played any role that could not have been played by individual Jews through existing [local] organizations. We have talked about duplication, and there is not only tremendous duplication in the various Jewish organizations—every one of which has got to get in on the act—but it seems to me that if you want to work in the field of civil rights as a Jew, you should work as an American and you should join the NAACP, you should join CORE. There are people in every congregation who don't go along with various organizations, and I don't think that the synagogue should be the place to, um . . . let's stop this so I can . . . [*pause in recording*]

How should I put this? Take [Supreme Court Justice Louis] Brandeis, who was a great liberal as you know. Take [Samuel] Gompers, who was the founder of the American Federation of Labor. They were great liberals, and they achieved much and undoubtedly more than many of our people who have worked through organizations. Yet they did it on their own. They did it as Americans, not as Jews. I feel that this problem is not a Jewish problem; it is an American problem; and maybe I shouldn't say this but a lot of people feel that the synagogue is bankrupt. Some have even gotten to the point where they say God is dead, you know.[56] I think some reference was made last night in the president's message to this effect. So that social action is regarded as an opportunity to revitalize [the synagogue]; and yet, just a number of years ago customs and ceremonies [were] regarded as an opportunity to do this, just as Zionism was regarded as an opportunity to revitalize the synagogue. My feeling in the matter is that if the synagogue is dependent upon issues, if it has to look for issues to survive, it's in a bad situation.

PAK: Then you would not say that national Jewish organizations have been beneficial in any way to your work in Birmingham?

MLG: Do you mean in reference to the race question?

PAK: Yes.

MLG: I don't think that they are. I think that we would be better off if they hadn't been active as Jewish organizations.

PAK: Have they been detrimental at any times?

MLG: No; but I think what they have done is they have annoyed Jews in southern communities who have frequently been placed on the spot by their pronouncements.

PAK: Have they in any way spurred the Jews to become more involved in the right type of . . .

MLG: I have my doubts about this. I don't think they have affected Birmingham at all.

PAK: Do you think that if a history were to be written of the civil rights movement, let's say in fifty years, that the rabbi—let's take in Birmingham and then let's take throughout your whole state and then on a broader scene let's take the South—that the rabbi will have played any important part in it?

MLG: I think that individually, yes, but I don't think if a history is written that the history will reveal this because I think that most of our men, including myself, have worked quietly, have followed their conscience, and have not been interested in headlines. There are a few rabbis who will be mentioned, because they have been in situations where they were able to follow a more dynamic Christian leadership, had a more liberal press, had a milieu [that] was more amenable. In many communities in the South there has been an influx of northerners, which you really cannot therefore regard them as typical southern communities and where anybody working in the field of civil rights would find the task a lot simpler. Then, of course, there is the matter of temperament; one can get publicity if he wants it and one can shun it when he wants to. And so I think there are many men who have played a significant role. I consider mine a significant role. I've only done from time to time the things which my conscience called upon me to do— and, with a perfect willingness to accept whatever risk was involved. I happen to have lived through a tense period. When your life's threatened— when your family and you are harassed—you take a dim view of these people that tell you what to do a thousand miles from where you live. You know what you can do and what you can't do. Last night something, or was it today something was said about—I think it was Gittelsohn who said with reference to the discussion of that motion on Vietnam that the text was practically a retreat and so on, and Reform [Judaism] has always gone forward and so on.[57] Well, there are times where it is not heroic to go forward. If you are standing at the edge of a precipice, is it heroic to keep on marching forward, or does it make more sense to take a step back? There are times when you have to mark time; there are times when you have to take one step back in order to take two steps forward. This is realism.

PAK: Do you have any general comments or anything that you would add?

MLG: Well, I don't have any comments; I have concerns, shall I say. I dare say that there hasn't been too much variation in what you have been getting in your various interviews, right? There is a certain pattern that is emerging, wouldn't you say that?

PAK: Yes, only I don't think that you are as representative of the other interviews.

MLG: In what respect?

PAK: Well I think that you show more involvement even though you say it is a limited amount.

MLG: You see, well, how shall I put this? I don't consider myself a hero, and I know that I'm not. I don't feel like I have done anything spectacular. I feel that, in my quiet way, I have helped, and I've also felt that in my quiet way I have been a catalyst among certain people who were in a position to do something that I was not in a position to do. And the interesting thing is that I have the feeling that my colleagues feel that I have done very little, because they marched at St. Augustine. You see I came back from the conference—was it last year or two years ago—and I preached a sermon entitled "Why I Didn't Go to St. Augustine."[58] I may have that tape.[59] In fact, if you'd come to Birmingham I think some of the stuff I can put right in my hands. If you find an opportunity to come to Birmingham maybe I could clear a day and there is nothing that I like to do better than listen to tapes.

In the meantime I am going to try—I'm usually a very organized person. But when I moved my study things got all mixed up, and I found it difficult locating certain things in my files; yet I know they're there. So I am going to try to locate some of this stuff for you and use whatever you can. And there is certain stuff I will tell you can keep, and there is certain stuff that I want back. I think it really would be an education for you as far as the temper and attitude of the Jewish community of Birmingham. Though I think that I could speak for my congregation, had I spoken to the other two congregations I think their response would have been the same.

PAK: Were you going to say that there has been some sort of a pattern that has come out of these interviews?

MLG: My comment is that most of the men have worked quietly rather than march and demonstrate. You see the criterion [among my colleagues] of the ["real"] civil rights rabbi and the man that is "doing something" is the fellow that is going to go down to Mississippi today. My feeling in the matter is that by going to Mississippi they are helping to provoke violence, which finally got started yesterday; which the intelligent people of Mississippi don't want any more than the intelligent people of Alabama don't want.

PAK: You don't think that in the long run this works for a faster or better solution?

MLG: No, I do not, because in the long run, we have got to talk about the minuses that go along with this. We are developing a lawlessness among Negroes which we are condoning step by step. I have a great fear that there is going to be bloodshed; it has already started. I was not surprised at Syracuse, New York. It could happen in Harlem, but I think it could also happen in Chicago. This has been no surprise to me, and it was no surprise to me that there has been a yell for black power and for white blood this past April. The question that people have got to decide is: is this what they want also?

11
Moses M. Landau

Cleveland, Mississippi, and Its Jewish Community

Cleveland is a relative youngster among Mississippi cities. In 1884, the Louisville & Nashville Railroad completed an ambitious expansion passing through Coleman's Station and ultimately reaching Florida. Two years later the tiny hamlet's name changed to Cleveland. Strategically located twenty miles from the Mississippi River and on the rail line, Cleveland emerged as a timber center. People drawn by economic opportunity settled and began to clear the unfriendly swamp. In 1924, Delta State Teachers College came into existence. In 1955 the college morphed into Delta State College, a segregated institution until 1967, two years after it obtained university status.[1]

By 1960 Cleveland was home to ten thousand inhabitants, 39 percent of whom were African Americans. The median income was under $4,000, but 40 percent of its people, three-fourths of whom were people of color, earned 25 percent less. Almost 90 percent of the population had been born and raised in Mississippi, and the white majority wholeheartedly supported the Jim Crow system.

Cleveland resident Amzie Moore emerged as one of the most important African American civil rights activists of the 1960s. His home provided a haven and meeting place for key civil rights leaders including Bob Moses, Lawrence Guyot, Charles Cobbs, Thurgood Marshall, Ella Baker, and Fannie Lou Hamer. Cleveland remained an oasis of calm amid the typical violence in the Delta against African Americans. Nothing came of the many threats Moore received. The only recorded act of violence against blacks was the burning of the New Hope Baptist Church just beyond the city limits in retaliation for meetings Moore held in the facility as the president of the regional chapter of the National Association for the Advancement of Colored People (NAACP). By the mid-1960s about five hundred African Americans were allowed to vote in the general elections in Cleveland, but not in the primaries where virtually all elections were decided. The two high schools—one white, one black—remained segregated until 1969. The lack of overt violence notwithstanding, poverty, powerlessness, and racism continued to be overwhelming problems facing the black community.[2]

Cleveland's first Jews, European immigrants Leon and Rachel Kamien, arrived about the time the city obtained its new name. By 1892, they ran a general merchandise store. It prospered, and they opened a second store in 1904. The Kamiens donated land to the local Methodists and Baptists for building their churches. Ownership of the Kamiens' store passed from generation to generation, and in the 1960s the family remained one of the most respected in town.

Other Jews settled in Cleveland by the turn of the century. The Millers became merchants, while the Seelbinders developed a dairy farm. Solomon Seelbinder, a second-generation Clevelander, won election to the state Circuit Court in 1931, while Moses Hyman, M. J. Dattel, and Jacob Shaw became mayors of the nearby cities of Pace, Rosedale, and Shaw.

By the mid-1920s a critical mass of Jews led to the creation of congregation Adath Israel, which constructed its first permanent building in 1927 assisted by $4,000 in donations from Christian neighbors. The Reform synagogue served Cleveland and surrounding communities. The members of Adath Israel hired their first resident rabbi in 1928. This began a cycle of revolving rabbis averaging two-year tenures. During World War II and the two decades thereafter, the Jewish population of the city and its environs almost quintupled to 250, making it one of the largest Jewish enclaves in the state.[3] Most newcomers prospered as merchants on Main Street, and some owned car dealerships. Almost all of these approximately one hundred families joined Adath Israel, and the population of the congregation's religious school rose to seventy-five. In 1957 Moses Landau became the synagogue's rabbi in the midst of this prosperity and growth. He finally broke the cycle of rabbinical turnover.[4]

Moses M. Landau

Moses Maimonides Landau was born in Vienna, Austria, on July 1, 1907. The scion of a long line of rabbis, his great, great, grandfather, Ezekiel Landau (1713–1793) served as chief rabbi of Prague.[5] When his father died two years after Moses was born, he was sent to live with his aunt in the Carpathian Mountains section of his country. His family became refugees twice during World War I in 1914 and 1916. After the war Landau attended a local gymnasium, or university preparatory school. The family moved to Czechoslovakia for a year but then returned to Vienna. He completed his undergraduate degree in 1926 and earned a PhD in pedagogy from the University of Vienna. His education suggests that he came from a family of comfortable means. Landau studied in yeshivas in Czechoslovakia, Hungary, and Poland prior to being ordained at the Israelitische Theologische Lehreanstalt in Vienna in 1935.[6] His training thus mixed tradition and modernity. From 1935 to 1938 he taught Jewish religion at a gymnasium in Vienna. In 1937 the Austrian Ministry of Education appointed him professor. He served as spiritual leader of an Orthodox synagogue in Amstetten, Austria, prior to accepting a pulpit in Vienna in 1938.[7]

During that year's Nazi takeover of Austria (the *anschluss*), Landau was arrested at least twice before escaping to Brussels, Belgium, with the assistance of a woman in the Nazi party who was a friend and fellow teacher at the gymnasium. In Brussels the young rabbi helped organize refugee camps, serve as rabbi to thousands of refugees, and bring Jewish children from Germany. When Belgium's Minister of Justice declared that all of the refugees were communists, Landau appealed to the Cardinal Archbishop of Mecheln (Malines)/Brussels, the Primate of Belgium, to intercede. After four months in the country Landau obtained a German passport and crossed into France to board a ship for New York. An aunt who lived there sponsored him with immigration authorities. In escaping Europe, he became only one of three family members to survive the Shoah. His mother and sister, Chane and Klara Landau, fled to France after him but perished in Auschwitz.[8]

Arriving in New York in December 1938, like others in a similar situation, Landau began to learn English by going to movie theaters in the evenings. He obtained his first American rabbinic position that same month. Kansas City, Missouri's Congregation Beth Hamedrosh Hagadol was the only Orthodox synagogue he would serve in America. Three years later he became rabbi of Temple Judea, a Reform synagogue in Chicago, where he met and married Frances Stern.

With his thick German accent, academic orientation, and European background, Landau initially experienced limited success. After five years in Chicago, he accepted the pulpit at Mt. Sinai Congregation in Texarkana, Arkansas (1946–1950), ministered to Congregation Beth-El in San Pedro, California, for a year, and moved to Temple Beth David in nearby San Gabriel from September 1951 until mid-1954. He spent the next three years at the Moses Montefiore synagogue in Bloomington, Illinois, prior to accepting the position in Adath Israel in mid-1957. Thus in nineteen years Landau labored in six different congregations in the Midwest and West before settling in the small Delta community that became his home for over four decades.[9] The rabbi who could not keep a congregation and the congregation that could not keep a rabbi found an accommodation.

Although Cleveland was not a center of African American activism, its white citizens could not help but be aware of events transpiring around them, and they were almost entirely hostile to any changes to the status quo. This held true for Jews in Cleveland as well, whose acceptance in the community depended upon their loyalty to southern mores.

Consequently when Landau participated actively in an effort to rebuild African American churches that had been destroyed by bombs or fire, he did so with trepidation. He described his congregants to Rabbi Perry Nussbaum: "Some think alike as the goyim, and others are just 'nervous' whenever such a matter [advocating desegregation or supporting the African American community] comes up. . . . In my dealings with such a problem I have to consider these people whose

12. Rabbi Moses Landau, 1969. (Landau private collection.) Used by permission of Anne Landau.

rabbi I am and who will most certainly resign if any action is taken from my side to make them more 'nervous.' Then I would have no Congregation. The question would then be what I am going to accomplish. . . . At present, I feel that it is my duty to hold my congregation together, and this is the cause of my actions or my in-actions or trying to eliminate any publicity for any of my actions in this cause if possible." Regardless, Landau indicated that he had been "trying to persuade the leading ministers to take some action," had succeeded in getting the "leading Baptist, Methodist, and Presbyterian ministers on my side," and had been "holding some private meetings with some other ministers."[10]

Congregant Jon Levingston recalls that Landau was not "what people would call a warm and fuzzy fellow." Always wrapped in a cocoon of cigar smoke, he retained a heavy accent, gave sermons that were "not easy for the congregation to follow," and some found certain aspects of his personality "off-putting." And yet most Jews and many in the general community had "very great affection for him." Landau was grateful to the congregation that provided him a home and income, and arranged for him to be a professor of German and world literature at Delta State College/University. In contrast to his experiences in Europe, Cleveland replicated the Garden of Eden. According to Levingston, "There were a lot of people that appreciated, in the Jewish community, appreciated Rabbi Landau's absolute dedication to the community; his perseverance for many, many years providing service to this simple congregation. In those years when he was infirm, he would come and sit on a stool to lead services."[11]

The lessons Landau had learned in Europe colored almost everything that the rabbi said and did. He made every effort to ensure that Jews should never be victims again, and that they could position themselves politically and financially so that they would not suffer as they had suffered in the past. Thus to protect his people, Landau sought to establish warm relations with many of his Christian colleagues, service groups, and academia. His sermons and lectures frequently stressed geopolitical themes, particularly the relationship of Jews to the rest of the world and, as an important subtext, the survival of a strong Israel. Regardless of the failings evident in his previously peripatetic career, Landau's skills made him a great asset to Cleveland's Jewish community and made it possible for him to hold his position until just a month prior to his death at the Lieberman Home for Jewish Elderly in Skokie, Illinois, on May 18, 1990.

Editor's Introduction to the Interview

The situation in Cleveland differed somewhat from other locations in the South. The city was founded relatively late. The Jewish community failed to establish a congregation until the mid-1920s, a late date for a first congregation to begin in the Reform mode, and Adath Israel experienced high rabbinic turnover. When Moses Landau arrived in 1957, he came to a community lacking a strong rabbinical tradition or presence. Many congregations served satellite communities, but Cleveland stands out for its especially dispersed membership. This was one of a very few instances where congregants owned farms.

Landau's background also differed markedly from the other rabbis interviewed. Trained and ordained as an Orthodox rabbi, his first pulpits were in Orthodox congregations in Austria and then one in the United States. He experienced the hardships of refugee life during World War I, and the Nazis captured him twice before he fled prior to World War II.

One would expect that a person with his background would rise to leadership as an advocate of justice and the rights of African Americans. Yet Landau's accent, European background, and academic orientation made him ill-suited for many American pulpits. His poor experiences with six congregations prior to his arrival in Mississippi likely made him very cautious about taking action that he thought his congregants might view negatively. The persecution he had faced in Europe may have also inculcated another lesson: never to do anything that would jeopardize the people who welcomed him for four decades. According to his daughter, Anne, "My Dad's overwhelming concern was to protect the refugee Jews [in Brussels]. You might say he had the same mission in Cleveland during the late '60s."[12] Landau was also practical. He believed that if he lost his position he certainly would not be able to exert influence even behind the scenes. As a rabbi—a "different animal"—he could let his integrationist views be known in relative safety so long as his words were not followed by action. Had he agitated, Landau believed, neither he nor the Jewish community would have lasted in the state "for twenty-four hours." Experience and pragmatism thus informed Landau's behavior. He attempted to carve a middle road between Perry Nussbaum and Benjamin Schultz, even as he criticized both. In the case of Nussbaum, another rabbi who had trouble holding pulpits, Landau also bore the brunt of criticism.

Comparison and contrast between Landau and Nussbaum, and Cleveland and Jackson, offer additional insights. Both rabbis functioned within highly racist communities that were still quite different from each other. On one hand, Jackson housed an older, larger, and more established Jewish community than Cleveland. On the other, Cleveland was not the center of civil rights activities and confrontations as was Jackson. Growing up in Canada offered Nussbaum very different experiences than Landau's in Austria. As in so many of these cases, the environments in which the rabbis grew up and worked were important factors, but the variety of their reactions illustrate choices they made that preclude such determinism.

To some extent, Landau's views mirror those of Martin Hinchin. Landau believed that African Americans should be prepared economically and educationally prior to integration. He advocated a Marshall Plan akin to Lyndon Johnson's War on Poverty. Also like Hinchin, Landau remains an enigma amongst rabbis of his milieu. He denounced agitation, but praised the actions by presidents, Congress, and the federal courts that precipitated desegregation without recognizing any linkage between the two. He worked quietly for civil rights while remaining cognizant of how easily others patronized him and laughed at his ideas. He preached equality but did not believe that African Americans in his area were prepared for it. Many of his comments in the interview make it appear that he lived in a multilayered cocoon, seeing segregation and segregationists all around but hoping for and expecting integration.

—Mark K. Bauman

Moses M. Landau Interview

June 24, 1966

P. Allen Krause: What date would you consider to be the starting point of a more intense activity in civil rights in your area of the South?

Moses M. Landau: I believe that the dogs of Birmingham actually started the civil rights movement more or less.

PAK: Which would be that year?

MML: 1950? 1960? 1963, I believe?

PAK: Your community is Cleveland, Mississippi?

MML: Yes.

PAK: What reaction did Cleveland, Mississippi, have—and I realize there were many reactions—but the majority response to the decision of 1954, the Supreme Court decision?

MML: Negative. Vehemently negative.

PAK: Was there a minority response which was visibly moderate or even better than moderate?

MML: I wouldn't know. I don't think so.

PAK: How long has your temple been in existence there in Cleveland?

MML: About forty years.

PAK: How long has there been a Jewish community in Cleveland?

MML: Fifty years or so.

PAK: If I [were] to take your Jewish congregation and compare it with any Protestant congregation that there'd be a definite difference in attitude toward the civil rights movement?

MML: It depends on which class and congregation you refer to. There are varieties. I would say the Methodists are very moderate. The Jews, of course, are moderate. On the other side we have Episcopals [who] are scared. The majority Baptists are . . . [unclear tape recording]

PAK: What percentage of your congregation would you consider to be real segregationists at heart, in attitude?

MML: It would be hard to say; there are some. I would say the second or third generation Mississippians would be more the segregationists than those who are newcomers.

PAK: Does that make up as much as 25 percent of your people?

MML: I wouldn't know because this question has never been discussed. There was no discussion of segregation.

PAK: What is the economic position of your people, and what are the sources of their income in the community?

MML: Most, many of them are storekeepers, many are planters, and the group is spread over about twenty communities. They live in about four counties.

PAK: Would you say that they're middle class economically or not?

MML: Upper-middle class.

PAK: Now, you say that intense civil rights activity in your community really didn't start until almost nine years after the Supreme Court decision?

MML: I believe it begins with the Freedom Riders.

PAK: The Freedom Riders, which would be in the early 1960s?

MML: Yes.

PAK: What was the response of the Christian clergy to the Freedom Riders and to the intensification of so called civil rights activities?

MML: I would say negative.

PAK: Negative. Was there a minority that was positive and spoke out?
MML: I wouldn't know of any.
PAK: None. Are there any other rabbis in this community?
MML: No.
PAK: Has there ever been a time when you felt that it was desirable for you to become involved in any activity which we would label as leading to civil rights progress?
MML: Yes, but it would have been limited to twenty-four hours. Then I wouldn't be in the state anymore.
PAK: Could you explain more about that so that I can better understand?
MML: Let me put it this way: the majority of the people of Mississippi have been vehemently opposed to integration, including a great number of the Jewish community. The reason is because the Jewish community could not exist, could not exist if they had been in any way involved in the civil rights movement.
PAK: Have you ever spoken on the topic in any way from the pulpit?
MML: Yes. Oh, yes.
PAK: In what manner?
MML: For integration. Also, in civic clubs.
PAK: Would you tell me about a specific occasion? What have you said to the Rotary Club? How specific have you been able to become on this topic?
MML: [I have said] that we're in the middle of a world revolution in civil rights. We better get along with it and start working with it.
PAK: What was the response that you received from the non-Jewish community when you spoke like that?
MML: Oh, they consider the rabbi as a liberal. He's supposed to be somehow on the other side of the picture. They would be surprised if he would be on their side. And he's a kind of an animal. A kind of an animal who has the right to go his own way. It wasn't a hostile response, so long as there was no active participation.
PAK: You mean, so long as you didn't . . .
MML: . . . agitate.
PAK: . . . and speak with regard to a specific action in the community, for example, in favor of the Freedom Rides, when the Freedom Rides were going on.
MML: I personally was not in favor of the Freedom Riders. I don't think they accomplished anything. They were just plain hit-and-run people.[13]
PAK: Did you have any relationship with the Freedom Riders at all? Did they pass through your community?
MML: Not many. The Jews never came to temple, never asked for a rabbi.

Some of them were in jail, [in] Parchman, which is in our area, [but] they didn't ask for any rabbinical help or assistance or comfort. I suppose they were not that kind of people. And I don't think any rabbi that came down because he was called down to give them comfort that he told the truth, because they never asked for us.[14]

PAK: Rabbi, what has been the response of your own congregation to your sermons, to your talking in the community on occasion in regard to the area of civil rights?

MML: They realize that to be a Jew means to be absolutely, absolutely committed to the equality of man. They realize that. And so they could have no objection to my discussing the problem publicly.

PAK: Have you ever been faced with a situation in your congregation where the board or members of the congregation have raised objections to any of your activities in this area or maybe that you didn't act in a certain area and that this has become a serious problem in the congregation?

MML: As far as I know, even those of my people who are the rabid segregationists have great respect for the pulpit. They've never, never told me what to say and what not to say.

PAK: What about when you spoke to groups outside of the pulpit? Like the Rotary Club? How did the congregation react?

MML: The question's always been how you talk. Whether you deliver an agitating speech or reason, discuss problems. If you discuss problems, you could discuss any problems. But, if you are going to take sides and agitate, you accomplish nothing except the hostility of the people. So, I have always in my discussion with individuals and with the groups, just plainly discussed the problems as they are and how to solve them.

PAK: What are the mass media like in your community? What is their attitude toward this whole civil rights movement?

MML: Excessively negative.

PAK: Have you ever been quoted by name in any of the mass media with regards to statements that you made in favor of equality or civil rights?

MML: No. Unfortunately, I have a colleague about thirty-five miles north of me who has been often quoted by name in favor of segregation.[15] That man is coming from New York and having some kind of a reputation in the country and had his name and his picture in newspapers quite often. Because he tells the people what they want to hear. Those of us who tell the people what they don't like to hear don't get their names in newspapers.

PAK: Have you tried in any way to counteract his influence in the community?

MML: I don't think he has an influence, because even the segregationists, the harder segregationists, would be astonished if they hear a rabbi speaking their language.

PAK: Speaking what?

MML: Their language on segregation. Because they accept the rabbi as a man who has greater vision than to be a segregationist.

PAK: Do you belong to any organizations in your community or in the South?

MML: Rotary and the Southern, I believe, Association of Teachers of Modern Language in Colleges and Universities. I would say that's about it.

PAK: Do you belong to any other, to any ministerial associations?

MML: Yes.

PAK: The Ministerial Association in Cleveland is not just the Protestant white ministers?

MML: Segregated.

PAK: It's segregated. Does it include Catholics and Jews?

MML: Jews, yes. I am the Jew. But, no Catholic has ever attended.

PAK: Has this organization ever made any moves to help implement the civil rights act, [or] the civil rights decisions of the Supreme Court?

MML: It's a very difficult question to answer because you have to come down there to find out the situation. I don't know what you can do. What do you mean "civil rights"—it is a tremendous area.

PAK: Well, for example, did it come out after the Supreme Court decision of 1954 with a statement that we should accept that decision and not try to drag our feet? I remember an altogether different type of community, like Atlanta, and I realize that there's quite a difference in atmosphere there.

MML: Most certainly there is.

PAK: The ministers [in Atlanta] made a long statement and signed it back in 1956 or '57.[16]

MML: The local organization, which is a small, weak organization, could not come out. I was not there when the decision was made. I came much later then when the Supreme Court decision was made. I would most certainly say one thing: that is that I don't believe too much in statements. Like the resolutions of the Central Conference of American Rabbis (CCAR) after they have been passed and criticized and discussed for hours, still nobody ever pays attention to them. Excuse me for saying it. I've been too long here for me not to know. So resolutions don't mean anything. What counts are actions. Actions. I would say of the ministers of my area, and I'm only speaking of my area, they have done their best to help rebuild the burned down Negro churches. They have opposed, I believe my whole community opposed, the violence. I believe that we have very fine sheriffs, real gentlemen who are opposing any violence, protecting, whether it's Freedom Riders or civil rights workers, any area. I haven't seen any violence. I haven't seen any disturbance. I only saw once, a march around the courthouse, where the number of policemen and deputy sheriffs was much larger than the number of demonstrators.

PAK: Did you participate at all in this rebuilding of the Negro churches?

MML: Yes.

PAK: What was your role in that?

MML: Personally, I was not in favor of their rebuilding them. I felt that the church should not be rebuilt, but that integration should start right in the church. That is the place. No matter which Negro lost his church, he should be admitted to a white Baptist church. He has to pray. I don't think it was a good policy. However, publicity was given too much to a college professor and his students who built a $10,000 Methodist church some-where in [*unclear*], far away from us,[17] while no publicity was given to the local people who contributed hundreds of thousands of dollars to rebuild practically every church. They did it quietly, without any publicity till now. But again, personally I say that if integration is a good thing, it should start right in the church. The best way was—[with regard to] the churches that burned down—not to rebuild them, but to start integration right there.

PAK: Did you present that opinion to anybody in the Ministerial Association?

MML: Oh, yes, I did, not only to the Ministerial Association but to some very hard[line] segregationists who didn't want to contribute to the rebuilding of the churches. As a result of my opinion, they made big contributions.

PAK: Did you ever talk to any people whom you would consider to be in the power structure in your community in order to influence them to-wards integration of the churches?

MML: I don't think the power structure is in favor of integration. And I don't think that they would listen to anyone. As you know, the political leaders were those who were trying to interpose the state between the Federal gov-ernment and the people, [the ones] who favored continuous opposition to the Federal government decisions and the Supreme Court, prior to my ar-rival in the city, and it took a long time to overcome that.

PAK: And the response of the ministers when you made this suggestion to them was a negative response?

MML: What suggestion?

PAK: About not rebuilding the church but integrating their own.

MML: It was considered a joke.

PAK: A joke?

MML: Yes.

PAK: What's your reaction to the national Jewish organizations and the role that they played in the South and in your community?

MML: I would say the national Jewish organizations are sticking their necks out too much. They like to be in the driver's seat all the time. I don't think it's right, and we all resent it.

PAK: Have the national Jewish organizations ever been helpful to you?

MML: No way at all.

PAK: Have they ever been detrimental to you in terms of achieving your goals with regard to integration or desegregation?

MML: It is very hard to say, but no, I wouldn't say detrimental. They have not done anything to hurt us or to help us. I don't think that they're detrimental at all. My personal opinion about where to begin integration, where to begin civil rights, was not on the education, on the integration level. I believe it is on the economic level. And to make the Negro equal economically to the white man. To make them help themselves. To teach them to help themselves. To let them build themselves up economically. To make their contributions to this state. In other words, to live in clean homes, with all the necessary equipment, to dress themselves cleanly, to make enough money to buy enough clothes, good clothes. To build themselves up economically on an equal basis with the whites—[if this were done first,] I don't think there would be any problem with integration itself.

PAK: Has there been any activity in your community at all to bring about such an improvement in the economic condition of the Negro?

MML: It is extremely difficult to talk about activity. You need money for that. The state was for the white man. He pays all the taxes. And the Negro doesn't pay any because he doesn't have anything. And all the facilities that are available to people, like the good schools and so on, are built with white man's taxes. I think we need a good Marshall Plan to come in and help with the job.[18] I think, for instance, if enough money could be made available, maybe that there would be an economic improvement very, very fast. That it would be very helpful toward the equality which we all so aspire to.

PAK: Do the Negroes have the vote in your community?

MML: Yes.

PAK: Do many of them use it?

MML: No. Not many.

PAK: Are there any harassments or voting obstacles?

MML: The lady who is in charge—a very dear friend of mine, one of the finest ladies I've ever met—told me there's never been any harassment the last ten years.

PAK: Can you give us any area which I might have forgotten to ask about in which you've tried to exert your own influence on bringing about a more equitable type of arrangement in your community?

MML: I would like to say that, about two years ago, I believe, two Episcopal clergymen came down to our community and in contrast to some rabbi who came down and he broke the decision of the Conference [CCAR] that he should contact the local rabbi when he comes down;[19] he didn't contact me at all except for making problems in my communities. He was a kind of hit-and-run man. And I had to pick up the pieces thereafter. I was very sick at that time. I was just being brought home from the hospital, from Memphis, in an ambulance. But he did not pay me any visit. On the other side, the two Episcopal clergymen, when they came to town for the same purpose, were well received by the community. They were guests at Rotary. They were just trying to help, and I told them, the American society, especially the South, as far as I can see, is built on church and home and school. The Negroes have church buildings but no churches. They have no pastors of any education. Their homes, their families, their family life. The number of children who do not know their father is immense. And they come from homes, from shacks. And second is school, and the school question is, before you get a Negro child into a white school, how to get them into a Negro school. They are very beautiful buildings, built recently; I believe also a result of the Supreme Court decision, not voluntarily; I must assume not that they wanted to do so, but that they had to do it. I believe in my area alone, in my county especially, we built several very beautiful Negro school buildings costing millions of dollars, but, the attendance in school is very poor. How to get them to come? To attend school? If we have classes which are equal based—in other words, where Negro children of one grade know as much as the white children of the same grade— integration would be no problem. But, I want you to know at this moment, the schools in Cleveland are integrated, the college is integrated, anyone is admitted. We have no problem whatsoever, no fights, no demonstrations whatsoever. Integration across the county.

PAK: **What about these two Episcopal ministers?**

MML: This is what I told them, that the first three things [are] home, school, and church. They could be of help, if they [were to] adopt these things, to teach the Negro man responsibility for family.

PAK: **Has there been any results from this?**

MML: They agreed with me, but it was the same story all over; they went back and that was the end of it.

PAK: **That was the end of it?**

MML: I don't think that they come down to give help; they come down to make a name for themselves.

PAK: **Rabbi, what do you see as the future of your community in this area? Do you think that it's quite a ways off yet before there will be any real progress toward equality for the Negro?**

MML: I believe it's a national problem. It is not a southern problem; it's a national problem. If there is equality in the North there will be equality in the South. For instance, de facto segregation does not exist in the South. De facto segregation, in housing, does not exist in the South. The Negro man can have his own life next to a white man.

PAK: **Does he in fact do that?**

MML: It depends; some [do] because they are servants, helpers to a white man, who builds them a home right next door. It happens, but [in any case] we don't have the de facto segregation, which is the problem in the modern cities.

PAK: **Do you think the day will come in Cleveland when the atmosphere will have changed enough so that the rabbi and ministers will be able to take a more active role, I mean a visible role in specific projects?**

MML: A really active role, successful role, taken by any minister in the South, [needs to be] taken by southern ministers. I am sure that I'll get brickbats if I make this statement: I believe that the majority of those from the North who came down are just hit-and-run. Some came down to get their names in newspapers. I believe that everything can be done in a quiet way, and that the less agitation, the faster we shall accomplish it. I believe that the decisions, [which are] the law of the land, are acceptable to the South. I believe they'll learn to live with them. I believe the Congress, president, and the Supreme Court did a wonderful job in accomplishing what they have accomplished, and that is as much as anybody could do. I believe that the less agitation, the more success we're going to have.

PAK: **Has there been a time to date when there has been any kind of an integrated activity in your congregation or in any of the churches in the area?**

MML: You have to find first a Negro who is intelligent enough, or who's willing, or who has an educational background, [so that] you can talk to [him] in a civilized manner, but, I have not been able to find [one]. There are not too many. There are very few who are intelligent. But, they don't come out. I mean, in order to have an integrated school you must have two groups. Our group is here but their group doesn't exist.

PAK: **How large is the Jewish congregation that you have there?**

MML: We have about a hundred members.

12
Charles Mantinband

Hattiesburg, Mississippi, and Its Jewish Community

During the 1870s, William Harris Hardy built a railroad from Meridian, Mississippi, to New Orleans with a stop in a sleepy hamlet at the juncture of the Leaf and Boule rivers. Incorporated in 1884, the town was named after the attorney's second wife, Hattie. The lumber and turpentine industries and four railroads fueled Hattiesburg's economy. Settlers of Scottish, Irish, and English descent from Georgia and the Carolinas took advantage of the extensive lands opened for development at fifty cents to $1.50 an acre.[1] The town tripled in population by 1890 and rose to 4,175 by 1900. Growth accelerated with the establishment of the federal military post, Camp Shelby, south of the city.

The dwindling timber supply and dismantling of the army camp following World War I brought difficult times, although the population reached 18,600 by 1930. The nation's entry into World War II resuscitated Camp Shelby and helped turn the city into a mercantile, educational, and medical center for southern Mississippi. Hattiesburg entered the 1960s with a population just under thirty-five thousand, a city with a rosy future were it not for the civil rights crisis.

African American veterans returned from service during World War II and Korea no longer willing to passively accept the racial status quo. In 1959, one such veteran, Clyde Kennard, sought entrance into Hattiesburg's Southern College (later renamed the University of Southern Mississippi). The local chapter of the National Association for the Advancement of Colored People (NAACP) began to press for judicial remedies to the plight of the county's black citizens. The approach of the NAACP, however, was reserved compared to the Student Nonviolent Coordinating Committee (SNCC), which came to Hattiesburg in early 1962 to organize a voter registration campaign. Its work was complemented by the efforts of Victoria Jackson Gray, a resident who offered citizenship classes to members of her local African American community. In 1964 the Council of Federated Organizations (CFO), which included SNCC, the Congress of Racial Equality (CORE), the Southern Christian Leadership Conference (SCLC), and the Mississippi chapters of the NAACP, made Hattiesburg the headquarters of a state-wide voter registration drive known as Mississippi Freedom Summer.

The drive began on January 21, 1964, "Freedom Day," when one hundred local African Americans supported by student demonstrators and fifty northern clergy picketed the courthouse demanding to be registered. A few months later, Hattiesburg became the largest Freedom Summer site in Mississippi, with over ninety out-of-state volunteers, three thousand local participants, and about 675 Freedom School students. The state Freedom School director, Dr. Staughton Lynd, a Yale University history professor, called Hattiesburg "the Mecca of the Freedom School world."[2]

Local whites responded predictably with harassment, evictions, firings, arrests, beatings, and finally the 1966 assassination of Hattiesburg civil rights leader Vernon Dahmer. Anna Mantinband, in a memoir written after her husband's death, described a meeting of the Mississippi Council on Human Relations during which members of the White Citizens' Council "were busily checking our car licenses to identify those in attendance."[3] She continued, "The following day's [Jackson, MS] *Clarion Ledger . . .* printed a scurrilous and threatening report of the proceedings." Rabbi Charles Mantinband described the city's mood in the early 1960s as "ugly" and "defiant."

Maurice Dreyfus, Hattiesburg's first Jewish settler, did not arrive in the city until seventeen years after its incorporation. He had left his native Bavaria in 1866 when he took a steamer to New York, then made his way to New Orleans where he lived with his sister Marie and worked in the family business, Koch and Dreyfus Wholesale Jewelers. Two years later he traveled to California and in 1872 moved to Collins, Arkansas, where he entered the general merchandise business with a friend. After five years in Collins, Dreyfus settled in Brookhaven, Mississippi, where he and Emanuel Pfeifer opened a mercantile business. In Brookhaven, Dreyfus met and married Pauline Hirsch, with whom he had four sons: Theodore, Walter, Louis, and Edwin. In 1881 Pfeifer and Dreyfus built a lumber mill that operated until 1901 when they decided to move eighty-five miles southeast to Hattiesburg because of its timber and railroad lines. Dreyfus and Pfeifer prospered, as did many of the entrepreneurs in the young metropolis. In 1912 he bought out Pfeifer and brought his three oldest sons into the business. During the late 1920s, Dreyfus converted part of his saw mill operations into a naval stores business called Dixie Pine Products. After his death, his sons and grandsons continued both businesses until the sawmill closed in 1954, and they sold Dixie Pine twenty-two years later.[4]

The economic potential of the city drew many Jews, a high percentage of whom had recently emigrated from Eastern Europe. One of the new arrivals, twenty-two-year-old Frank Rubenstein, settled in the city in 1906 and opened a store called The Hub, borrowing the city's nickname. It grew into one of the city's largest department stores and was joined by other Jewish-owned businesses including Adler Dry Goods, The Globe, Fine Brothers-Matison, Vogue, L. Rubenstein, The Leader Family Outfitters, Louis Tailoring Company, and S & H Katz.[5] As was the case in so many southern cities and towns, stores owned by Jews occupied prominent positions in the city's main business district.

Informal services in Maurice Dreyfus's home led to the founding of Congregation B'nai Israel (Children of Israel) in 1915. Four years later the congregants purchased land at the corner of Hardy and West Pine Streets and completed their first house of worship in 1920. Members followed widely diverse approaches to Judaism. Those from Central Europe identified as Reform, while those from Eastern Europe tended to be more traditional. However, since the Jewish population was too small to support two synagogues, both groups made accommodations for the other. The congregation held Reform services on Friday nights and conducted Orthodox worship on Saturday mornings. This practice remained even after 1939, when the congregation voted to join the Reform movement's Union of American Hebrew Congregations (UAHC). Seven years later, the fifty-five member families began constructing a new temple on the corner of Mamie Street and South Twelfth Avenue, a structure that continues to house them today.

The Jewish community thus followed a pattern similar to other such enclaves. A small group of Jews from Central Europe arriving during the late nineteenth century lacked the numbers or means to create Jewish institutions prior to the influx of brethren from Eastern Europe. Then the creation of a congregation required compromise and cooperation. As the newer immigrants acculturated, became economically successful, and had children who moved into adulthood, the sole synagogue moved into the Reform camp but continued to accommodate the remaining traditionalists.[6]

Arthur Brodey, the congregation's first rabbi, served from 1935 to 1942. When Brodey left, the temple had difficulty finding a successor, given its size and small-town location. It finally hired Rabbi David Shor in the mid-1940s. Shor remained only until 1948, when he became the rabbi of Temple Albert in Albuquerque, New Mexico. Avery Grossfield filled the rabbinic position from 1949 to 1950—followed, after a short hiatus, by Charles Mantinband in 1951.

Although Jews comprised a miniscule percentage of Hattiesburg's population, they were prominent not only as merchants but also as civic leaders. Jerry Shemper, president of Ben Shemper and Sons, a scrap metal business, won election to the city council. Herbert Ginsberg, who served as a US Magistrate, had a law practice with Paul Johnson Jr. (Mississippi's governor from 1964 to 1968). Marvin Reuben became part owner, executive vice president, and general manager of NBC affiliate WDAM-TV, a position he held for almost three decades. Reuben gained notoriety during the 1950s and '60s for his editorials attacking the Ku Klux Klan and supporting compliance with the Supreme Court's *Brown* decision. In response to his editorials, the Klan threw acid on his wife's car, damaged the radio tower, and burned crosses in front of the station. In 1992 Reuben received the prestigious Hub Award that recognized Hattiesburg-area residents who had made outstanding contributions to the community. Today Reuben's legacy is remembered by a scholarship in his name awarded annually by the Department of Telecommunication and Film at the University of Southern Mississippi.

Their prominence as merchants and civic leaders, however, failed to provide members of the Jewish community with a sense of security when the civil rights movement hit their city. Jerry Shemper saw their fears to be a logical result of the murders of James Chaney, Michael Schwerner, Andrew Goodman, and other activists: "Imagine that coupled with . . . all the years of anti-Semitism, the second World War and Hitler and all the rest, it was not too hard to figure out why everybody was jumpy."[7] The fear was well justified. The most violent branch of the Ku Klux Klan, the White Knights, was based thirty-five miles away in Laurel, Mississippi. In addition, the Hattiesburg White Citizens' Council allegedly maintained a card file with information on the racial views of everyone in the city.

Another important factor had nothing to do with concern for bodily harm or the ability to make a good living. As a group, Jews in Hattiesburg had become acculturated to the southern way of life and racial mores. When Herbert Ginsberg was asked whether in the 1950s and '60s the members of B'nai Israel were any different in their support or opposition to desegregation than members of the city's white churches, he replied that they were not "rabid" about the subject. He continued: "I would say at that time most of the Jewish people in the community here were born and raised in the South and their background was the same. I don't think you could take the Jewish population here and the non-Jewish population and say this one was different from that. I think they're all pretty much . . . the same."[8] Maury Gurwitch, president of the congregation during Mantinband's tenure, and his wife, Shirley, supported Ginsburg's account. Shirley Gurwitch stated, "We had compassion for [African Americans] and we treated them well when they worked for us but we certainly didn't socialize with them." Maury Gurwitch added, "We were not looking to socialize with them. They all worked for us." When asked whether many in the Jewish community wished to integrate the schools, Maury Gurwitch responded in the negative. Regardless of their acceptance of the racial status quo, in contrast to their Protestant neighbors, few if any Jews joined the hate groups or resorted to violence or confrontation in support of segregation.[9]

Charles Mantinband

B'nai Israel's new rabbi arrived three years before the shock of *Brown v. Board of Education* swept through the South. Given the trepidations of most of Hattiesburg's Jews regarding the race issue, the differences over the issue it had with

Rabbi Grossfield leading to the rabbi's decision not to renew his contract (see chapter 12, note 27), and the extraordinary grapevine that existed among Jews in the South, it is difficult to understand why the congregation offered Mantinband its pulpit since he had previously participated in at least two civil rights-oriented organizations while in Alabama. On the other hand, he had a reputation as a fine man and a pastor, and it was not easy to attract a rabbi to fill their position. Clearly, Charles Mantinband and his congregation were not necessarily well matched, making his accomplishments in Hattiesburg all the more noteworthy.

Mantinband was born in New York City on April 2, 1895, to Samuel and Delia Gottlieb Mantinband. Charles's father had fled Poland when he was only thirteen and began a new life living with an uncle in New York. Shortly after Charles was born, the third of six siblings, his parents moved to Norfolk, Virginia, where relatives had previously settled. Educated in Virginia's public school system, he was a loyal southerner when he graduated from Maury High School in 1912.[10] He earned a bachelor of science degree from City College of New York in 1916 and a master of arts degree from Columbia University in 1918.[11] After graduation, he became the director of the Young Men's Hebrew Association (YMHA) in Memphis and, on April 14, 1918, married Anna Kest. The two had met the previous year at the East Side Settlement House, a gathering place for Jewish youth.

Six weeks after their modest wedding, the couple moved to Chickamauga, Georgia, a small hamlet where Mantinband had been sent by the Jewish Welfare Board to serve as a chaplain at Camp Forrest/Fort Oglethorpe. The next year he and Anna returned to New York, where he "took a stab in commerce,"[12] which proved not to be his life's calling. Instead, when Stephen S. Wise opened his Jewish Institute of Religion in 1920, Mantinband joined the first class. While at the seminary he directed the YMHA in New Brunswick, New Jersey, and, in the same year, the Mantinbands welcomed their first child, Carol. The Mantinbands had another child and in 1940 adopted two refugee orphans from Hitler's Europe.

Charles Mantinband served his first congregation, Vassar Temple in Poughkeepsie, New York, from 1923 until 1926. A brief article in the city's *Eagle-News* noted: "[Mantinband's] impending departure will deprive the community of one who has been very distinctly a force for liberality of thought, tolerance, and good feeling. . . . Rabbi Mantinband has been not only a religious leader, but a citizen in the best sense of the word. . . . He has spoken out courageously on a number of topics on which definite, sane pronouncements were desirable. Poughkeepsie will miss him."[13]

In 1926 Mantinband accepted the pulpit at Beth Ha-Shalom (House of Peace) in Williamsport, Pennsylvania. One of the highlights of his years at Beth Ha-Shalom was when the synagogue sponsored a debate between their rabbi and the well-known attorney and atheist Clarence Darrow on the topic "Is Religion

Necessary?" During his tenure, Mantinband wrote a weekly column for the *Williamsport (PA) Sun-Gazette* under the pseudonym of "Ben Adhem." The articles provide great insight into Mantinband's grasp of world literature and of his concern that every person should strive to be "a friend of man."[14]

Shortly after America's entry into World War II, Mantinband requested a leave of absence from his synagogue to work as a civilian chaplain in charge of the USO in Aberdeen, Maryland. In that capacity he provided pastoral services to Jewish personnel at Edgewood Arsenal, Perry Point Veterans' Hospital, Bainbridge Naval Training Station, and the Aberdeen Proving Grounds. On his departure in January 1946, the local paper praised him "for his warm personality," and for spreading "Christmas cheer" by annually dressing up as Santa Claus.[15]

Mantinband's three-year leave of absence from the Williamsport synagogue turned into a termination of his contractual agreement with the congregation. Thus, he requested that the Placement Commission of the Central Conference of American Rabbis (CCAR) locate him with a small congregation in the South. Anna Mantinband writes that a key reason for this request was that "our daughter had married a southerner . . . during the war," and they wanted to be closer to her. The request was granted when the Mantinbands moved to B'nai Israel (Children of Israel) congregation in Florence, Alabama, where he served the Florence, Sheffield, and Tuscumbia area. During his five years in this position, Mantinband established his first connection with the Southern Regional Council (SRC), an organization designed to bring about the end of the Jim Crow system through education. His active role in the Alabama Council on Human Relations reflected his remarkable transformation from a southerner who had walked out of a City College of New York classroom in protest when he was seated next to an African American student to a vocal proponent of integration and the equality of all. Although he received some criticism from his congregants, the Tri-Cities region was far removed from the Deep South. It served as a center of the Tennessee Valley Authority that attracted many nonsoutherners to jobs provided by the federal government. In 1952, his environment changed when he became rabbi of another B'nai Israel congregation—this one in Hattiesburg, Mississippi.

Mantinband's experience in Hattiesburg is covered in the transcript of the author's interview and will not be repeated here. However, one incident that did not come up in the interview begs for inclusion. Maury Gurwitch recalls a time when the rabbi was going to be away for a few days: "I remember once he told me, he said, 'I'll be gone this weekend.' I said, 'Where are you going?' He said. 'I'll be back in two or three days. Don't worry about it.' I was watching television and they had an NAACP convention in Miami, Florida, and I looked on the dais and there is Charles Mantinband sitting on the stage. I said, 'Nobody knows where our rabbi is and I'm looking at him.' Several times I told him I said, 'Rabbi you are scaring us.' I said, 'You know they could burn houses down. They

13. Rabbi Charles Mantinband, date unknown
(Goldring/Woldenberg Institute of Southern
Jewish Life). Reprinted with permission from the
Goldring/Woldenberg Institute of Southern Jewish
Life (ISJL). For more selections from the ISJL's
Encyclopedia of Southern Jewish Communities:
http://www.isjl.org/encyclopedia-of-southern
-jewish-communities.html.

could burn stores down. They could put us out of business and I really wish you would curtail these activities.' And he said, 'Maury I will not be muzzled. I am going to do what I am going to do.' So he really kind of scared us, but we never had any problems."[16]

Charles Mantinband remained the rabbi of Hattiesburg's B'nai Israel until 1963, when he resigned in order to take another small congregational position in Longview, Texas, a city located roughly halfway between where his daughter lived in Shreveport, Louisiana, and where his son, Bill, lived in Dallas, Texas. By the time he arrived in Longview he had long since lost his sight, but he never lost those qualities that made him beloved even in Hattiesburg. When he died on August 3, 1974, a local editorial author wrote, "Longview has been honored by his presence." He was "an inspiration to the community, a man of personal charm . . . a man of God, a man whose faith shines in action as well as in words, whose concern for his fellowman and his community is very real and warm-hearted."[17]

Editor's Introduction to the Interview

Charles Mantinband's peers considered him to be the most outspoken and courageous rabbi in the South in the arena of civil rights. No one worked in a more dangerous and unlikely environment. Mantinband illustrated what a courageous individual could accomplish in an area of the almost impossible. Raised in the South, he identified with the region even as he criticized it. It gives one pause to recognize that Mantinband, perhaps the most courageous and outspoken rabbi in the South, joined others in questioning the wisdom of northerners traveling to the region to march and demonstrate.

A number of rabbis, including Mantinband, socialized with African Americans in their homes—an extremely unusual occurrence in the South during their era and one that dramatically broke regional taboos. Rabbis also mention working with local African American clergy, a factor Mantinband illustrates when he describes mapping strategy with Medgar Evers and others beyond his local community over many years. Mantinband's refusal to join the NAACP until his move to Texas for tactical reasons reflects how his actions were calculated and rational. Mantinband foresaw changes in the movement unfolding from the South to the North and from cooperation between black and white allies to rejection of white involvement in certain quarters.

Allen Krause mentions Marvin Reuben, and Mantinband notes David Matison for their work in behalf of civil rights. Other rabbis identify the role of women in Save Our Schools (SOS)[18]-type organizations that opposed the closing of public schools as a means to avoid desegregation. The stories these and others on the grassroots level suggest that many rabbis did not work alone, a topic requiring further research.

Nonetheless, activist rabbis typically felt isolated within their Jewish communities. Mantinband's statements imply that he, too, felt alone among fellow rabbis. Other activist rabbis alluded to similar feelings. Mantinband also refused to inform his congregants of his efforts outside of Hattiesburg, much like Perry Nussbaum who perceived himself as a "lone wolf" in Jackson, Mississippi. The negative reactions of some of his congregants justified Mantinband's feelings and position. Yet perhaps the aura of the rabbi created a greater sense of individualism, self-sufficiency, and isolation than necessary, even as these factors empowered the rabbis to act. They viewed themselves and were viewed by others partly as scions of the biblical prophets with the strengths and limitations that the roles entailed.

Mantinband offers a very insightful account of his exchange with Harry Golden that partially contradicts his sense of isolation. He recognized the need to help and befriend people in the community, to act in a pastoral and social-welfare capacity, as a prerequisite to speaking out with less fear. To him, it was not enough to be a member of the clergy. One had to earn his stake in the society. Likewise, working with influential people behind the scenes to prevent the Klan from coming to town brought the rabbi at odds with the methods of the Anti-Defamation League (ADL) that emphasized prewritten newspaper editorials after the fact. Rabbis like Mantinband with southern pulpits understood local community dynamics from a different perspective.

Although Mantinband was a public figure in the civil rights movement, he makes it clear that he tried to avoid press coverage of his activities, believing such to be counterproductive. In the same way, he secretly became a life member of the NAACP and otherwise contributed to it but did not want to appear on its rolls. With Mantinband's interview, the impact of the Black Power phase of the civil rights movement also becomes apparent with his lack of positive interaction with the local NAACP chapter in Longview, Texas.

—Mark K. Bauman

Charles Mantinband Interview

June 24, 1966

Rabbi Mantinband began with the following opening statement:

> I delivered a paper on this theme two or three or four years ago, when we had the [CCAR] conference in Atlantic City,[19] and I called the paper "On the Horns of a Dilemma," and the reason I gave it that title was because at one time I was very dogmatic and I thought I knew what I knew and [that I] had commitment. Now I'm not quite so sure. I'm far more humble. I appreciate that there are many approaches, multiple approaches to this struggle, and all serve a purpose. Who am I to say that one method is better than the other? Circumstances determine what your approach will be and also your temperament. There's one fellow who can do one thing and another fellow who can do another and both perhaps are useful, and neither will bring in the millennium, if you get what I mean. So I refer you to that article if you care to look it up.

P. Allen Krause: What were the years, Rabbi, when you were involved in congregations in the South?

Charles Mantinband: The first five years after the war, I think that was '46 to '51, I was in Tri-Cities, Alabama—that is, Florence, Sheffield, Tuscumbia, Huntsville—and then I moved for eleven years, '51 to '62, to Hattiesburg,

Mississippi, and it was there that I was particularly involved with this difficulty. And because I stayed longer I had the opportunity to make my presence known and felt, as well to get more involved. I moved from Hattiesburg, Mississippi, to East Texas in 1962.[20] I've been in Longview, Texas, which is on the main line between Dallas, Texas, and Shreveport, Louisiana, for the last three and a half to four years.[21] And I think it ought to be said that most of my colleagues think I left because it was a good time to get out of Mississippi, and that my life was in danger, that he who fights and runs away will live to fight another day. But, actually, that is not the fact—I left under flying colors. I moved because of special circumstances of a personal nature. We were near our grandchildren and we were near our family, it was a new place, there was a brand new congregation that challenged me, and I still have close contact with Mississippi, even though I no longer live there.

PAK: In the years you were in the South prior to going to Texas, would you say there were any specific times when you noticed an intensification of civil rights activity in your area?

CM: Well, after the Supreme Court decision, the South was in an ugly mood, a mood of defiance. [There was] a feeling that they were not going to allow others—especially Yankees, especially the federal government—to determine for them what their way of living should be. And they discovered that there were certain legal obstructions that they could [use] that would somehow or other delay the implementation of equality. And so they did their best to confuse the issue and to make it difficult for enforcement. School segregation was the order of the day, and it remained that way. The authorities came by any kind of integration with great reluctance.[22]

PAK: Were the years after 1954 more intense in terms of civil rights activity?

CM: Yes, I think so, I think so. There was more hope, there was more promise, and of course it gave the Negro leadership—much can be said about that because it's a sorry state of affairs, the Negro leadership as I know it—it gave them a new lease on life. They could see daylight ahead. They began to sing with a great deal of fervor "We Shall Overcome," because no obstacle was now too great for them to be deterred from their onward march.

PAK: During this period post-1954, what was the response of the non-Jewish white community in the area in which you were living?

CM: Well, I am always hesitant about generalizing. By and large the mores of the community were such, as I explained before, that they would not in any way cooperate. They would not admit that change was inevitable. They used all the old clichés about "would you want your daughter to marry a Nigger?" and things like that. And they continued to obstruct as best as they knew how so that they could live unmolested. However, it wasn't very long before they knew that they didn't have a chance in the wide world ever to reverse this law. This was not only the great constitutional law, but it was also the great ethical and moral law, and slowly but surely they got to feel that they have to adjust to it. Now there were some people in every southern community who were liberals, some white people. For the most part they didn't become too articulate or too much in public notice because they could be hounded out; they could be ruined economically; pressure was brought to bear against them. From the very beginning I had to make up my mind to two things that I would do. The first was relatively easy. The second one was a little harder but I managed to do it. And remain. I didn't come in, do it, then run away. The first was that the pigmentation of a person's skin would make no difference to me and my relationship to him and my attitude toward him and my way of life with him. That we are all children of the living God and that this is a democracy; [that] I would judge a man—if I would judge him at all—in terms of his merits, his worth. That means that Negroes came to my home, through the front door, sat at my table all the time, and that was my private affair. That was not too difficult.

PAK: As early as when?

CM: Oh, I've always done this, but this was way back in '54 or even before. However, the second thing was much harder. I vowed that I would never sit in the presence of bigotry and hear it uttered or expressed; that I would . . . voice a contrary opinion and make my opposition felt and heard and known. I wouldn't be histrionic about it. I wouldn't be bravado about it. I wouldn't try to make a speech. I just would register the fact: This is what your church teaches you? Okay, I want you to know what my religion compels me to think and feel and be, and how it makes me behave. And when they would say to me, "God is a segregationist because the Bible is full of it," I always ripped out a Bible and I would open it to where [there was] the very opposite of what they would say. "Do you mean here? Or do you mean there? Or do you mean the other place?" And then they would say, "You're too smart for your pants." The fact was that the White Citizens' Council, the KKK, and a lot of individuals who were extremists had me tagged from the very beginning as a fresh guy and they loved to ask me, "Where do you come from?" And when I told them from Virginia and not from the Bronx it broke their hearts, because they just had made up their mind that nobody in the South could have this point of view. This was at the beginning. I'm happy to tell you that there are thousands of southerners who feel that way today, white southerners, and who say so—Jews and Christians.

PAK: What was the attitude of the mass media, including the newspapers, in the community at that time?

CM: Well, whenever the newspaper got hold of a story you may be sure it would be distorted and it caused a lot of mischief. I therefore avoided the newspaper at all costs. That was not only the local newspaper but the Jewish press, because they would blow it up. They were sensational. They wanted to sell papers. And very often the news items would inflame people with slanted headlines and slanted articles. So we frequently did things without reporting to the press, not because we were afraid or ashamed but because it just complicated life for us.

PAK: What was the editorial policy?

CM: Well, editorial policy has always been "too fast, too much, too early, too soon."[23] "The Negro isn't ready yet for the franchise," and many of them would [even] deny the fact that the Negro was discriminated against, that he didn't have equal opportunities, an education, or housing, or employment, or that he didn't have equal treatment and penalties under the law when he committed a crime. Now, when the average newspaper says that, it's bad enough, but when the United States senator, like Senator Eastland said that, as he did on *Meet the Press* and many other times and places, it was very sorry and, of course, very false.[24]

PAK: How long had your congregation been in existence in Hattiesburg?

CM: Well, I would judge as far as I know probably over half a century.

PAK: How long had there been a Jewish community there, per se?

CM: Well, I'm not sure about that, but I would say since the turn of the century. We didn't have, as they do in many parts of the East, a wave from Germany back in the 1840s, 1860s, but they started coming after the Russian excesses in 1880.[25]

PAK: What was the economic standing and the source of income of your people?

CM: They did pretty well. They worked hard; they began as peddlers, the peddlers became merchants, and the merchants became department store owners. And then the second and the third generation went off to college and became professional men or entered the field of communications. Radio or television outfits in many cases, including Hattiesburg and Laurel, which is the nearest town, were owned by Jewish people, and there was some manufacturing going on. But for the most part they were upper-middle class, I would say. They lived well.

PAK: Merchants?

CM: Most of them were merchants.

PAK: How susceptible were they to economic pressures from the community?

CM: Well, of course, constantly they wanted good will. They depended for their livelihood upon Negro trade, so they wanted all the Negro trade they could get. And on the other hand they were friends with the white power structure, and when they were asked to contribute to the White Citizens'

Council or to join it, it took a lot of doing to say, "I don't believe in it," or "Here's my money but don't tell anybody," or things like that. They were really trapped between these two pressures of these two extremes, and as time went on they were threatened and visited by boycotts, because once the Negroes realized what their economic power weapon was—which is the selective buying process, aided and abetted, if you please, by many of their leaders—the merchant was the one who suffered; in some towns, [he was] pretty well ruined, like in Tuskegee.

PAK: Were you against that method?

CM: No, on the contrary. I said to our Jewish people at the very beginning, "Don't underestimate the acumen of the Negro. He may not be as articulate as you like because he's frightened, but he knows who is his friend and he knows who is his enemy. He knows who is indifferent to his cause, and if you want to hold on to his good will and his trade, you better play honest and square with him. That means treat him with courtesy; let him have the same kind of good service that you pride yourself on giving your white customers. If he needs to use the restroom in your facility, make sure that there is a restroom for him. He won't like a segregated restroom, but he certainly will shudder at the thought of having no restroom at all. [And allow your Negro customer] to try out a dress or whatever the case may be. And if you don't do it, be prepared for a boycott."[26]

PAK: How did your people respond to these suggestions?

CM: Oh, they thought I was crazy. They thought I was way ahead of my time. They refused to believe it; they were certain that I was going to invite economic suicide for them, and they just would like to let the non-Jewish white man stick out his neck and be the pioneer.

PAK: If we were to compare your congregation with any [white] Protestant congregation, how would they compare with regard to their attitude in this whole area [of civil rights]?

CM: I can't be sure of this but my impression is, at the beginning, I would say that the Jewish congregation was ahead of the others. But in the last ten years I would say that the Catholics first and some of the white Protestant groups have forged to the front, and now we are lagging pretty sadly behind. And I think that times are changed for the better, [so that now] very often Jewish people say, "Well, it can't be so bad after all; look at what the Protestants, look at what the Catholics are doing. We can't afford to be too far behind them."[27]

PAK: Were there any other rabbis in the Hattiesburg area when you were there?

CM: Oh yes, we had a rabbi in Meridian, ninety miles north. We had a rabbi in Jackson, about eighty miles west. We had a Jewish chaplain in the army at Keesler Air Base, about seventy-five miles south, and then in other parts of the state and the Delta—I was the only rabbi in my immediate area. I would say that the others were rather quiet. Even my friend Perry Nussbaum, and he is my good friend, and he has done a great deal in this work, he was a sort of a Johnny-come-lately, if I may be pardoned for saying so. In the early days I used to appeal to him over and over again for help, and he said, "I'll be doing it. I know it's right; it's just a question of how wise it is. [I'll do it] when the right time comes." And perhaps he was justified in doing so. It takes a certain type of fearless patience to do this sort of thing, and perhaps Jackson, which wasn't always a liberal community, it is liberal today but it was very reactionary then, would have thrown him out.

PAK: What kind of help did you ask him for?

CM: Well, we had a Council on Human Relations. An organization that I'm very active in personally and have been for many, many years—I would judge about twenty years—is the Southern Regional Council (SRC).[28] This is the parent body of the Council on Human Relations. Its headquarters are in Atlanta, and we have a state body. I was its [Mississippi state] president, but in those early days I couldn't get Perry even to be a member, much less an active member. Which is not the case today, because he's very active in it today.

PAK: Was this organization definitely committed toward the Negro?

CM: Yes, it's a biracial group whose purpose was to work toward a better South, a new South, in which race relations, being a prime factor, would be improved.

PAK: What about the ministers in Hattiesburg, were they ever heard from with regard to the civil rights problem?

CM: Seldom. For the most part they were quiet, because they knew the climate of their community, and they hesitated therefore to use the pulpit for any such purpose. I think that has changed a little for the better. [This is] what I am able to see at a distance. And I know that in East Texas, where I am now, we move together—the Negro and the white ministers.

PAK: Did you ever reach that point in Hattiesburg?

CM: Not while I was there. The best we could do would be to have a Race Relations Sunday in February, a joint meeting at which time the Negroes would provide the program: do an old fashioned gospel service, sermon, and maybe sing some spirituals. It was a gesture, like a Brotherhood Week gesture, not very useful.

PAK: Can you take a few specific involvements that you might have had in civil rights activity and explain them to me?

CM: I had a member who owned a department store. He was the same fellow who also owned that radio station. He told me that he was interested in a certain Negro who showed great promise as a student, and after high school he helped him to go to the University of Chicago as a student to get his education. This fellow came back; he was a native of Hattiesburg, and he tried very hard to crash the segregation program of a local university, [the] state-supported University of Southern Mississippi, much as Meredith did a little bit later. And there was a frame-up, the details of which I don't have to give you, except to say the boy was arrested on two spurious charges, and he was found guilty, [and sentenced] to many years in prison. At his trial— the boy's name was Clyde Kennard, and he wasn't a boy, he was a man— both Dave Matison, this department store owner, and I, were character witnesses. That means that the whole public knew that we had gone to the courts publicly, in broad daylight, and said we knew this fellow and he was utterly incapable of stealing twenty-five dollars. He was a wealthy fellow who could borrow a thousand dollars with or without collateral any time he needed it. Or he was arrested for having whiskey in his car, when everybody knew he was an exemplary scout leader and never took a drink in his life—a Sunday school person. The fellow was found guilty, and he was sentenced to Parchman, to state prison. He was treated cruelly and ultimately he developed cancer and the prison authorities refused to give him the benefit of a doctor, and he died. And when he died, with great grandiloquent gesturing, the governor of the state gave him a pardon so he could die at home in peace.[29] This was about five years before Meredith. And when Meredith entered all this five years later, he was advised how to proceed on the basis of this sad experience. Whatever troubles he would have, they would be different from these, because we had learned [from the Kennard experience]. Well, that didn't make me very popular either in or out of my congregation.

PAK: **What exactly were the repercussions?**

CM: Well, [my congregants said] I was interfering; it was not the work of the rabbi; the rabbi ought to stick to religion; he ought to talk about God and Judaism. It never occurred to people that there should be the application of the ethical affirmations—the pronouncements, the imperatives— to everyday life. But we continued, and it wasn't very long before this was forgotten because there were other episodes. When I lived in Hattiesburg I occupied a residence that was owned by the congregation directly opposite the Temple, and it used to annoy our people that Negroes came and went to our place. I never made an issue of it, they just came and went like everybody else just came and went. But once at one of our board meetings a gentleman on the board said, "You must remember, Rabbi, this is our property." I said, "Yes, it is your house but it is my home. If you want your house back, I will give it to you back. But you can't tell me how to live my

personal, private life.[30] And who are these people who come to see me?
If they came into your store to buy a refrigerator, you would be delighted
to see them, or a suit of clothes. And why do they come to see me? Because we have things in common to talk about. It might be a minister, or it
might be a college president,[31] or it might be a laborer who is trying to be
a decent citizen and needs a word of encouragement and friendship. And
don't worry; your rabbi won't disgrace you." Well, the non-Jewish public
wasn't quite so pleasant about it. They would telephone with obscenities
over the wire and say, "You just tell that rabbi that if he's going to see any
of his nigger friends, we'll run him out of town. We won't have this kind
of radical, communist behavior." And so this thing went on and on and on
and on.

PAK: Was there ever a vote in the board with regard to this?

CM: The truth of the matter is that several times it came pretty nearly [to]
that way. I was once asked a question: did I think that my activity and involvement in the race question was so important that I would continue it
[even] if it meant a split in the congregation and perhaps the bankruptcy
of the congregation? I said candidly, "No, I didn't think so." I didn't think
the congregation ought to split or ought to break up; for the truth of the
matter is that I loved the congregation, and I wanted it to remain an integral whole and continue to function. But I said, "Remember, the only crime
of which I am guilty is that I take my religion seriously. I have more confidence in my neighbors. I have more confidence in the United States of
America. I don't believe that we'll be condemned for this process, [though]
we may be a little ahead of our time." Once, when the congregation was
very much annoyed with Rabbi Mantinband for the misbehavior that he
was doing, a Catholic priest with the rank of Monsignor[32] heard about it
and, uninvited, he came to our board meeting, apologized for his presence
there but said he had heard about this meeting. He wanted to tell them
they were in great error; that they had a rabbi who was a decent fellow,
with quiet courage; and every minister in that town felt the rabbi was right;
he just had more courage to articulate his notions then they did. They
would come around to it a little bit later, and let the congregation stand by
the rabbi and hold up his hand.

Another time, something else happened that was a little more dramatic.
At the very time when my members trembled, the Hattiesburg Ministerial Association of about seventy-five members, of which I was the only
Jew, elected me as its president, which was a lovely vote of confidence, and
which made our members feel that perhaps the rabbi is right after all. Yet
when I moved on after eleven years to Texas, I guess they were relieved and
I was relieved too, because in a way the hour-by-hour tensions disappeared.

Oh, we have our problems, naturally, in East Texas; [nevertheless], the fact
is it is nothing compared with what we had in Mississippi or in Alabama.

PAK: Even when you left in 1963?

CM: Yes, '62.

PAK: In 1962, the tensions were as great as . . . ?

CM: Oh yes. Matter of fact, shortly thereafter Arthur Lelyveld, who's one of
our most distinguished rabbis, as you know, of Cleveland [Ohio], went
down one summer and did some risky things which perhaps he shouldn't
have done, as part of the protest movement, and he was clubbed over the
head with a lead pipe and almost murdered.[33] And we had the three boys
in the Delta area,[34] not too far from Hattiesburg, two of whom were Jews
and one was a Negro, and they paid for their very innocent-behaviored
protest with their lives. They were martyrs to this cause. And my good
friend Medgar Evers, he was my good friend, who was the [state] head of
the NAACP, who was in my home many times; he was sniped at and shot
down at his own home not too many years ago.[35] And right at this very moment we have a protest march going on from Memphis to Jackson, Mississippi, with some of our rabbis, by the way, parading.[36] I'm not at the moment arguing for or against these marches, though I'm very dubious about
the wisdom of them. All I'm trying to point out is that the mood of the
South is still an ugly mood, still a defiant mood. I don't know what to expect tomorrow.

**PAK: Rabbi, could you talk about another specific instance in which from
the point of methodology you had a goal to accomplish, something in
your community possibly, in some area of civil rights?**

CM: Do you want me to stick to Mississippi?

PAK: Yes, I'd prefer it if you would stick to Hattiesburg.

CM: All right, then I won't say anything about Texas where I am now. I have
to recall what happened in Hattiesburg. We had in Hattiesburg an active
White Citizens' Council. As you know the program of the White Citizens'
Council was white supremacy, and by one means or another, by fair means
or foul, [their goal was] to interfere with, interrupt, [or] prevent any type
of so-called integration, which they called "mixing." It was not unusual for
some of their henchmen to go to the post office and to the banks and to
leave pamphlets around that presented their point of view. Quite periodically we had a group of people who went to the banks and to the post office and picked up these pamphlets and burned them or put them aside because, although there were plenty more where they came from, we felt that
that was one way of disposing of them. Well, one day I was walking down
the street, and I met a gentleman who was the president of this body. He
had been the mayor of the city, and as the mayor he had had a number of

interfaith committees from time to time, and I was always active in those
and we knew each other on a first name basis. He was a very respectable fellow, active in his Presbyterian church, and after the bombing of a synagogue
in Atlanta, he said to me, "I told my boys at the last Council meeting how
foolish it was to bomb a synagogue, which after all was lifeless, and which
was a house of God. I hope they would not do anything like that in our city
of Hattiesburg. If they want to know who the real mischief-maker was, his
name was Rabbi Mantinband." He says: "I know him; I know him well. I
know his personal habits. I know where he lives, and I can tell you how to
get at him if you decide that's what you need or want to do." Well, I could
not believe my ears because this was a threat of violence by a fellow who
was in dead earnest, and thought he would impress me. I had to do some
quick thinking; I don't scare easily. Usually I parry some of these efforts by
humor, but this was no laughing matter. So I took out a pen and a piece
of paper and I wrote something down. I noted the time, I noted the place,
and I noted exactly what he had said. "What are you doing?" said this
gentleman. I said, "I won't ask you to sign it because you'll probably refuse
to do that, and if I signed it, it would be your word against me, and there
would be some people who'd think you're the liar and some people who'd
think I'm the liar." [He responded,] "Well, what are you going to do with
that paper?" I said, "I'm going to take it to the FBI, and I'm going to take it
to the first five representative white Christians I meet in this town. I'm going to say to them, "Mr. so-and-so, president of the White Citizens' Council, threatened me in this fashion, and if ever in the next ten years anything
ever happens to me, I'm going to ask them to arrest you for creating the climate in which this type of thing would be possible." "Oh!" he says, "don't
do that; you know I was only trying to be funny. I was only joking; I didn't
really mean it that way." But I did go to the FBI and I did go to these five
people, and that fellow and I lived in that town and he never looked me in
the face again because I had called his hand.[37] It happened to work out that
way. But God help us it could have happened the other way too, as it happened to my friend Lelyveld. And if that isn't a problem, I don't know what
is. But, for the most part, I lived there for many years, and when I left I got
the key to the city and I had an open invitation from the two local colleges, and from the Chamber of Commerce, and from the ministerial group
to come back any time I wanted, and I've always been received with open
arms.[38] They knew my position. Harry Golden and I are good friends,[39] and
Golden and I once had an interesting discussion on how it was possible
for a rabbi to remain in the Deep South and be active in the civil rights
program, when the whole mores of the community are against it. He advanced one theory and I another. Said Golden: "Well, everything you say

stems out of your religious convictions and this is the Bible Belt; people are all church-going people. Your religion isn't the same as theirs, but, nevertheless, if you are sincere and humble in what you say and do [and these] result from your religious notions, then they will respect you for it even though they don't share it and they don't agree with it." I said, "Well that's fanciful and maybe that's so, but I don't think so." Actually if you live in a town long enough, you get to know everybody. If you get to know everybody, you're given the opportunity to befriend everybody, and if after ten years or more you have gotten this fellow a job, and this fellow you visited when he was in the hospital, and this person you were able to get a scholarship for his child, and this person you did him a favor and served on a committee with him and he learned how human you are, and all the rest of it, they'll say, "Well now, this fellow is out of step, and he's ahead of his times, and he's crazy, and we don't like what he says, but don't you touch him; he's my friend, and I like him." Whatever the case may be, I stayed a long time. I know there were people who might have wished me out of the way, but for the most part I survived.

PAK: You mentioned you were friends with Medgar Evers. Did this in any way influence you or result in civil rights activity [on your part]?

CM: You must remember, before I came to Mississippi I was active in the civil rights program in Alabama. I was a member of the Southern Regional Council; I was a member of the Alabama Council on Human Relations. And in the large cities of Alabama there are local councils on human relations, and I had visited Mississippi and spoken at their annual meeting, or the other way around—after I went to Mississippi I went back to Alabama and spoke at their annual meeting on a college campus or in a church—wherever they held that meeting. And I knew Medgar Evers as one of the workers there, the NAACP workers. It may interest you to know that while I lived in Mississippi and while I lived in Alabama, I was never a member of the NAACP, deliberately. Because I wanted to be able to look a fellow square in the eye and say, "I'm not an NAACP member." If I had been a member, certain doors would have been closed to me, and I knew that I helped the NAACP cause by contributing money now and again to their legal defense court work and things like that without getting my name on any membership blank. But, Kivie Kaplan,[40] who is the president now of the NAACP, will verify the fact that when I moved to Texas four years ago, I didn't wait to be solicited—I volunteered to become a lifetime member, because my heart was with that particular movement, even though I think they have their troubles and that there are other groups that are complicating their program for them. What I'm trying to say is that Medgar Evers and I knew each other at all these meetings on a state level. I would see him so often in Hattiesburg—during the Clyde Kennard trial he was very much in evidence there—and it was there that we planned certain strategy together. We labored together, alas, all in vain.

PAK: Were there times when you would make a phone call to a man such as Medgar Evers?

CM: I never hesitated to do so, [even though] I knew that in the first place every telephone wire was tapped. When you talk to [Rabbi] Marvin Reznikoff[41]—he is now fighting in one of these wiretapping situations in Baton Rouge in which he was involved, and he's trying to get some legal and monetary redress from certain power authorities for having interfered with his private life. I was told that in every bank and in every post office there were spies and informers. I never troubled to prove it or disprove it. I was also told that even if things weren't true, that they would fabricate them and they would make them up and falsify them. So I just proceeded as if nothing would happen and I took my chances. Certainly I would make these telephone calls.

PAK: Other than the NAACP, what other groups were there that you worked with?

CM: The other groups came later. The Urban League doesn't function very much except in large cities and industrial centers. I knew of their work, but I didn't have much contact with them, except from time to time at the annual meetings of the Southern Regional Council they would be represented. But CORE came into being, and Dr. Martin Luther King and his [Southern] Christian Leadership Council came into being; the student activity became a very vital thing—the SNCC. Especially when we had the Meredith uprisings and what followed, we had more and more people penetrating the interior of Mississippi from other parts of the country. And the long, hot, tough summer and we had much tragedy in its wake.[42] There came a time when Mississippi was no longer a battleground or a modified battleground. The general feeling is now that when the next riots break out, likelihood is they'll break out nearer to Montreal and Toronto and nearer to New York and Boston, nearer to Los Angeles; then they will [be nearer] to Jackson, Mississippi.

PAK: Were you quoted very often in the newspaper regarding the statements that you made?

CM: I think not. And that was largely because we tried to keep that quiet. I saw no particular purpose to doing it. It was a slow, painful, painstaking, day-by-day, hour-by-hour, up-hill fight in education. A newspaper wasn't likely to do very much good. For example, I have a volume called *The Bible and Segregation*[43] written by a Methodist seminary professor in Nashville, Tennessee. It was issued in hard back and paperback covers. I used to distribute that book a great deal and ask people to read it and tell me what they thought of it. When President Kennedy (of blessed memory) called a conference of two hundred church people in June of 1963, to Washington, in the White House, to talk over the race problem—which was bothering him a great deal—it was my privilege to be included in that company of about two hundred church people. About thirty were rabbis, and I was one of those rabbis. The Baptists of Texas and Mississippi who were there had their names and pictures in the newspapers. Although my congregation [in Longview] thought I ought to appear in the newspapers (because that was real news, for one thing, and also they were proud of it), my judgment was to the contrary. I withheld it from the newspaper, and I think my judgment was vindicated, because I had a job to do and I went ahead and did it. Publicity had no local application for the moment. On the other hand, we have an active NAACP in our city now, and I don't have very much to do with it—even though I'm a life member and I pay my dues to the national body every year—simply because not all Negroes trust white people any longer. Some of their leaders have said that the white liberal is their affliction, and they go ahead and do their own business their own way. Once in a while they have a demonstration, a dinner, or a public meeting and I might be present, but, for the most part, I'm not very active in the group due to no fault of my own. If I had a job to do, I perhaps would do it.

PAK: What role have national Jewish organizations played in Hattiesburg in the civil rights movement?

CM: As soon as the trouble began they were busy on the phones. The [*Indianapolis*] *National Jewish Post* wanted stories; I suddenly became a national figure. I got invitations to appear, speak everywhere, and all at once there was a very important meeting that never got into the press, sponsored by the American Jewish Committee. Golden and I were both sent down there as voices to be heard, and we went, and we were treated rather roughly by some of the frightened Jewish presidents of the South. The American Jewish Congress had me appear once at their national body in Florida and I went.

PAK: What role have they played in your community itself?

CM: We're too small to have more than a very nominal sort of program—they don't come down to get money or anything of that sort. I give them a little through our Welfare Fund. But the ADL is in perhaps the best circumstance to help us if we need help, because they're located in all these areas with regional offices, and they send their representative in to consult with us and to advise us.[44]

PAK: Have they ever helped you?

CM: I don't find their help too much to my liking. I don't belittle their efforts;

I don't even question their methods. It may be all right for the ADL, but it's not the way a rabbi usually works. A rabbi works quietly, behind the scenes—I'll give you an illustration. This was in Alabama: the KKK was coming to town; they were going to organize. The ADL got wind of it; they came down and said, "Let them come and when they come, here are editorials one, two, three, four, five already written down; take them up to the editor and ask him to print them." And since they [the members of the Jewish community] were advertisers, they knew the newspaper well, all this was arranged for. And if these things didn't deter them [the KKK], then we had editorials six, seven, eight, nine, ten, or paid ads A, B, C, D, to follow. This was their technique. I said, "Is that all you're going to do?" "What else is there to do? Do you have anything better?" I said, "Yes. That's not the way I would proceed. I'm not trying to pit my wisdom against yours, but before the KKK comes I'd like to visit—with you, if possible, without you if necessary—the ten leading white Christians in the community, lay people and church people, and say: 'The KKK is coming. We think this is evil; we think no good can come of it. We think it's the time to deal with this situation along preventive lines before the explosion rather than after. We may not succeed, but at least if you're out at the country club or you're at the Rotary or you're somewhere else where there's power structure and public influence, speak your piece.'" As sure as I'm talking to you, I say it with all humility and without bombast, the KKK never came to that town, because they found out in advance that people would not receive them kindly. On the other hand more recently in East Texas, the KKK announced a meeting and the newspaper refused to give them publicity, but they advertised in the Dallas paper and the Shreveport paper that they were coming to our town. Well, I had nothing to do with it because the [*inaudible*] was on a Friday night and I had my own [*inaudible*] take care of that particular topic, but a group of Negroes got wind of it, went out the night before, and burned down the little shanty in which the KKK meeting was to take place. Well, I didn't approve of that; I didn't like that, and that was also not recorded in the paper, but this is the mood of the Negro now. In defiance they're going to attempt violence against us. In a very literal sense, an eye for an eye and a tooth for a tooth.

PAK: This is a general question. As best as you can, Rabbi, can you tell me how often in the course of a year's preaching would you address yourself to this question?

CM: Seldom. I didn't feel that was a function of a sermon. I might do it by way of illustration. I might do it more easily at a forum or in a lecture or in an adult study class. I didn't want people to say that I used or abused the pulpit for a particular partisan purpose. Yet on the other hand there never was any doubt in anybody's mind as to where I stood. I felt of course that it was legitimate to be in the pulpit and sermon material. A man once said to me, "The reason I don't come to Temple, if you must know, is because you're always preaching on the race question." I put my hand in my inside pocket and I said, "Well, now, let's see. [These are] your rabbi's subjects for the last five months, as taken from our Temple bulletin. Check all [those times] where I spoke on the race question. You don't come so you don't know and you don't want to know." The truth of the matter is it just so happens that though I think I could with propriety deal with it, I just don't do it for other reasons, because I don't want to spend twenty minutes on discussing an issue that really ought to take two weeks to talk through, [giving people] the chance to explore and to ask questions. So I don't use the sermon for that purpose, because I think there are other and better ways.

PAK: So, where do you do your most effective work in the civil rights movement?

CM: There are a number of agencies through which you do it. I do it at the Rotary Club, of which I'm an active member. I do it at the ministerial association. I do it frequently when we have brotherhood and goodwill and interfaith activities, and I expand the notion of interfaith to interracial as well. When Race Relations Sunday comes around in February, and the CCAR issues a statement, I distribute those wholesale. I've had the privilege of writing occasionally this race relations message, and they're always anonymous. They're all in the name of the CCAR but they're written on a high level, and their appeal is not only to the broadest concept of patriotism and Americanism but also, if you please, to the highest concept of ethical religion. I do it whenever I can, because, as I told you before and I say it again, intolerance is rife everywhere and when you hear it, you have a chance to deal with it.

PAK: Rabbi, my final question would be this: If a history was to be written with regards to the civil rights movement many years from now about (let's say) Hattiesburg, Mississippi, and other parts of the South, what role do you think the rabbi—yourself with regard to Hattiesburg, and other rabbis with regard to the South—would have played in the civil rights movement?

CM: Well, I'm very sorry to say that the great disappointment for me has been the lack of a role of leadership on the part of the rabbi of the South. If you examine the tenure of office of the rabbis in the South you'll find that most of them have stayed a good long while. And most of them have played it safe. I think they've been opportunistic, and I think they have been lacking in the courage it takes to rise to the challenge of the present crisis. I'm not sitting in judgment on them. Perhaps if I were built differently, if I had a thinner skin, perhaps if I was twenty-five years younger, I might be a little more fearful myself. You mentioned before Rabbi [Jacob] Rothschild of Atlanta, Rabbi [Perry] Nussbaum of Jackson, Rabbi [Levi] Olan of Dallas, Rabbi [Marvin] Reznikoff of Baton Rouge, myself of Hattiesburg [and] northern Alabama, and I would say that there might be a half a dozen others like that.[45] Not to say that they [the other rabbis] don't do good work, wherever they live, but they haven't allowed their names to be seen or they haven't stood up to be counted, and they haven't struggled day in and day out with the problem of rabbis coming to the South to march and how to deal with it. They haven't joined the Council on Human Relations.

PAK: You're talking about the rabbis not mentioned by name?

CM: Yes. I say that the ones whom I have mentioned have all been very active, and there might be a few others whose names slip me for the moment. But I would be inclined to think that most rabbis play it safe, play it cozy—and it's not to my liking.

PAK: What role would you say that you have had in Hattiesburg in the civil rights movement?

CM: Others have praised me, but I'm not in a position to say. I would hope that on the whole it has been for good, and I would hope that it would reflect a luster upon the Jewish position, the Jewish heritage, the Jewish tradition as well as being helpful to the cause.

PAK: But overall in the South, you don't believe that the rabbi's role has been a significant one at all?

CM: Well, I could wish it were better; that's all I can say. In the Southern Regional Council where we have 120 members, all living in the South, and where we're not looking for money or membership—because we just got from a national foundation three quarters of a million dollars a year to spend on a better South and improved race relations—if we have five Jewish people, we have a lot. I've been on that nominating committee year in and year out and scanned the whole South for that purpose. Though there are individuals who are liberal, that are helpful, the fact remains that for the most part they just don't want to risk being identified with such a group.

13
Perry E. Nussbaum

Jackson, Mississippi, and Its Jewish Community

The land along the Natchez Trace offered abundant timber and close proximity to the navigable Pearl River, which snaked through Mississippi and Louisiana into the Gulf of Mexico. The state legislature designated LeFleur's Bluff, named for Louis LeFleur, a French Canadian who had operated a trading post there, as Mississippi's state capital in 1821, renaming it in honor of Maj. General Andrew Jackson, the hero of the 1815 Battle of New Orleans. In 1830, the Treaty of Dancing Rabbit Creek forced the resident Choctaw Nation to relocate west of the Mississippi, paving the way for nonnative American settlers. Unlike other cities that prospered from commerce along the Mississippi or with rail lines that reached the city during the 1840s, Jackson attracted only about 3,200 residents by the eve of the Civil War.

Nonetheless its strategic importance as a manufacturing center for the Confederacy drew General William Tecumseh Sherman, whose troops looted and burned the city after they captured it a second time in 1863. Jackson grew slowly after the war, and by 1930 its population remained less than 24,000. The discovery of nearby natural gas fields and the establishment of Hawkins Field, a major World War II airbase, pushed the population to over 98,000 by 1950. A decade later approximately 145,000 people, 40 percent of whom were African American, called Jackson home, making it the largest city in the state.[1]

The first Jews who migrated to Jackson peddled for a living. During the 1850s and '60s most of them originated in Alsace-Lorraine and the German states, while those who arrived in the 1880s and thereafter came largely from Eastern Europe.[2] Although few Jews lived in Jackson, they purchased land for a cemetery on the eve of the Civil War and founded Congregation Beth Israel (the House of Israel) the next year. The congregation hired a layman named Oberndorfer as *chazzan* (person who leads religious services; cantor). In 1867 the Jewish community erected the first synagogue structure built in Mississippi. When it burned down in 1874, the congregation replaced it with a brick edifice.

Jews quickly made their presence felt on Capitol Street, the main artery of the business district. John and Benjamin Hart (né Hertz) sold real estate, while

Isidore Lehman was the proprietor of the Jackson Steam Laundry. Relative new-comers Joseph Ascher ran a grocery store and Isadore Dreyfus founded an in-surance company before both succeeded in real estate sales and development. Harry Herman's men's store, called The Hub, and Lefkowitz's jewelry business were also prominent. In its heyday, the Vogue, owned by the Gordon family, boasted a higher sales volume per square foot than any store in Mississippi. Some of the businesses created by Jewish immigrants in the late nineteenth and early twentieth centuries endured for decades, including the Cohen Brothers' (Moise and Sam) clothing store and the Horowitz family's Mangel's clothing store. Like similar establishments elsewhere during the 1960s and '70s, competition from suburban malls pushed many of these out of business.[3]

As members of Beth Israel rose economically and the city's population shifted, most Jews moved to the suburbs. In 1940 Beth Israel followed with a new syna-gogue on Woodrow Wilson Drive in the Fondren neighborhood. The congre-gation moved to its present location on northeast Canton Road in 1967, the same year that members of the Ku Klux Klan bombed both the synagogue and the rabbi's house.

By the 1960s, Jackson's Jews had forged decades of positive involvement and good relations with their non-Jewish neighbors. While Aaron Lehman served on the school board during the Great Depression, he and his wife offered free breakfast to children who attended the school across from their home. The Leh-mans founded a home for elderly women in Jackson. Their son, Isidore, held the presidencies of the local school board, the Jackson Chamber of Commerce, the Hinds County Red Cross, and the Mississippi Chamber of Commerce. Depart-ment store owner Simon Seelig Marks served as the director of the Mississippi Merchants Association and vice president of the city Chamber of Commerce. At its 2001 Freedom Ball, the business club Jackson 2000 honored eighty-year-old Bea Gotthelf for her forty-plus years of leadership. Gotthelf helped found both the Concerned Women of Faith, an ecumenical group of black and white women that promoted racial understanding, and the Panel of American Women, which promoted peaceful integration of the city's public schools.[4]

Jackson's African Americans were restricted to the lowest-paying jobs and received barely a third of the income of the average white Jacksonian. The city served as a stronghold of the White Citizens' Council, and its mayor, Allen Thomp-son, was a rabid segregationist. As in many southern cities, a small group of blacks won favor from the white power structure, while the rest were kept in their place by the threat of loss of income, police brutality, and the Ku Klux Klan. Only the extraordinarily courageous threw in their lot with the "outside agitators" who came to Jackson after the *Brown* decision.

In the late nineteenth century, state law emanating from Jackson ensured that

African American freedmen were relegated to inferior status. In 1875, the Red Shirts, a military arm of the Democratic Party, was formed to reclaim political power from Republicans and make it all but impossible for African Americans to vote. Mississippi's constitutional convention in 1890 turned this effort into law through the subterfuges of poll taxes, residency requirements, and literacy tests. This "Mississippi Plan," ultimately followed by states across the region, set the legal framework for the political aspects of the "separate but equal" Jim Crow system that pervaded the South through the end of World War II. According to John R. Salter Jr., a professor at Tougaloo Southern Christian College, "Mississippi was functioning, in the . . . most cold-blooded sense . . . as a garrison state that viewed itself not only as being prepared for war but was . . . already fighting a war." Located on the northern border of Jackson, Tougaloo's student body was African American with the exception of two white girls, one of whom was the daughter of William Kunstler, a Jewish lawyer from New York and strong supporter of the National Association for the Advancement of Colored People (NAACP). Jacksonians who opposed segregation considered Tougaloo "the only comparatively 'free' island in the whole sovereign State of Mississippi"; the state that Salter labeled "the most repressively racist segregation complex in the United States."[5] The college and its president, A. D. "Dan" Beittel (who was white), faced constant attacks from members of the city government and the major newspapers, the *Jackson (MS) Daily News* and the *Jackson (MS) Clarion-Ledger*.

Within two years of the *Brown* decision, Mississippi created a State Sovereignty Commission with the sole purpose of preserving segregation. The commission quickly established a surveillance network that zealously monitored Mississippi citizens "whose utterances or actions indicate they should be watched." By 1974 the commission files included eighty-seven thousand names and over 250 organizations. The commission secretly funneled thousands of dollars each month to the White Citizens' Councils.[6]

The first dramatic challenge to the racial status quo occurred on March 27, 1961, when a group of nine Tougaloo College students entered the whites-only Jackson public library in an attempt to use its resources. Shortly after their arrival, the police answered the library's call and arrested the students for disturbing the peace. Beittel supported the "Tougaloo Nine" and refused to expel them even in the face of physical threats against him and the college. On the evening of the arrests, a group from Jackson State College, another local black institution, organized hundreds of people for a prayer vigil. That college's president, Jacob Reddix, a member of Jackson's conservative African American element that opposed activism, broke the vigil and expelled the four students who had planned it. Undeterred, on March 28, Jackson State students marched toward the jail where the Tougaloo Nine were held only to be dispersed by club-swinging policemen using tear gas and dogs. That night, over a thousand people attended a rally in support of the Tougaloo Nine.

About six weeks later, seven African Americans and six whites divided into two integrated groups and boarded buses in Washington, DC, in a test of the recent Supreme Court decision declaring unconstitutional segregation in interstate bus and rail stations. They were promptly arrested.[7] By summer's end, Jackson's police had arrested 306 civil rights activists, including forty-one Jacksonians who had joined the outsiders at one of the city's transportation terminals. Most of these prisoners were transferred to the infamous Parchman Penitentiary in the northwestern part of the state.

Emboldened by the protests, several Tougaloo College and high school students led by Salter resuscitated the Youth Council of the local NAACP chapter and boycotted the annual state fair, which only allowed African American attendance during its last three days. The boycott deprived fair concessioners of much of their normal income for those last days. This success, along with the integration of the University of Mississippi in Oxford in September 1962, encouraged black college and high school students to take the lead in an environment too risky for adults who were intimidated by the threat of violence and concerned with losing their jobs. The Youth Council published a mimeographed newsletter, the *North Jackson (MS) Action*, which they secretly distributed throughout the local black community. The next year it targeted the state fair in a more organized fashion. The council used the newsletter and a newly established phone tree to enlist students to intercept African Americans outside of the fairgrounds and make sure they were aware of the boycott. Consequently, virtually no blacks attended, causing the fair to close early.

This success led the Youth Council to organize a Christmas boycott of the downtown merchants unless they provided equality in hiring and promotion; ended segregated restrooms, water fountains, and lunch counters; used courtesy titles such as Miss, Mrs., and Mr. when addressing black customers; and served all customers equally. Boycotts proved to be the most viable method to involve black adults who only had to stop shopping at the selected stores. The loss of income from approximately seventy thousand black customers placed considerable pressure on the city's businesses to integrate.

Salter proposed picketing, sit-ins, and marches in support of the Christmas boycott, but these steps were abandoned once it became clear that they would necessitate bail for those arrested. Although the NAACP's Mississippi Field Director, Medgar Evers, agreed with Salter's approach, he could not persuade Roy Wilkins, the NAACP's national executive secretary, to provide funds. An appeal to Bill Kunstler resulted in the collection of a war chest of $3,000, sufficient to bail out only six people after their arrests.[8]

Members of the Youth Council clandestinely distributed fifteen thousand leaflets to African Americans in Jackson and surrounding counties in support of the Christmas boycott. In addition, they employed their phone tree and sent speakers to the area's African American churches. On December 11, Salter arranged for Kunstler to advise the New York media of a downtown civil rights demonstration. The advance publicity attracted both hoodlums and police but also ensured the full attendance of the national media. On the morning of December 12, Salter and five others began a demonstration at the Capital Street Woolworth's store. The national media coverage followed by the hysterical response of Mayor Allen Thompson ultimately created the "Jackson Movement." Nine days later, a bullet pierced the wall of Salter's home, barely missing his infant daughter.

Although Jackson's press labeled the boycott a failure, the city waived property taxes for affected businesses, a clear indication of the campaign's success. Simultaneously, the White Citizens' Council promised to foreclose mortgages, halt supplies, and mobilize a white boycott against any merchant who wavered in their support of segregation. Seventy percent of the African American population refused to patronize the boycotted stores during Easter. Again the pressure of the White Citizens' Council and state and local governments kept the merchants in line, turning the young peoples' successes into Pyrrhic victories, and police harassment and arrests of the activists continued.

During the spring of 1963, national coverage of the demonstrations in Birmingham offered Salter and the Youth Council a path to victory. Facing the national NAACP's opposition, the Youth Council publicized a sit-in at the Jackson Woolworth lunch counter on May 28, 1963. The small group of demonstrators found police chief Capt. J. L. Ray stationed with his troops outside the store and at least three hundred whites inside including almost certainly White Citizens' Council members. Demonstrators seated at the lunch counter were drenched with mustard and ketchup and bombarded by cries of "nigger lover," "communist," and other epithets. Some were sprayed with paint and beaten until almost unconscious. In the midst of the fray, Tougaloo College President Beittel entered the store and took a seat next to the demonstrators. When white hoodlums began ransacking the store everyone was finally forced out by the police, who hitherto had done nothing to quell the violence. The next night, a firebomb was thrown at Medgar Evers's home, an act the police termed a "prank" and refused to investigate.[9]

On May 31, hundreds of black high school and college students marched from the Farish Street Baptist Church, carrying American flags and singing freedom songs until the police, state highway patrolmen, and sheriff's deputies clubbed them and threw them into empty garbage trucks. About five hundred demonstrators were carried to stockades at the state fairground, where many remained incarcerated under oppressive conditions for weeks. That night, approximately fifteen hundred angry African Americans gathered at the church, although only about two hundred actually marched the next day. As before, fear and the lack of money to get people released from jail limited participation.

Medgar Evers told those assembled at an NAACP rally on June 7, 1963, "Freedom has never been free. . . . I love my children and I love my wife with all my heart. And I would die, and die gladly, if that would make a better life for them."[10] Five days later, Klansman Byron De La Beckwith murdered Evers with a shot in the back. Typical of Mississippi justice at the time, two all-white juries failed to convict Beckwith; he was not convicted until 1994.[11] On June 15, Nobel Laureate Ralph Bunche and Dr. Martin Luther King Jr. joined over five thousand people in a solemn funeral procession to honor the fallen NAACP leader. Police attacked with clubs and dogs some of those demonstrators who refused to stop at the end of the approved route. Enraged, some marchers retaliated by throwing rocks and bottles at the police. With the police about to fire into the crowd, President John F. Kennedy's envoy, Department of Justice attorney John Doar, stood between the opposing forces and, in so doing, averted a bloodbath. On June 19, 1963, the conservative leaders of Jackson's black community, including most of the city's African American clergy and the editor of the *Jackson (MS) Advocate*, announced that they had come to an agreement with Mayor Thompson. The agreement essentially maintained the status quo. Soon thereafter Salter left Tougaloo College to work for the Southern Educational Council, an independent organization that could not be paralyzed by the national office of the NAACP.[12]

With the passage on July 2 of the Civil Rights Act of 1964, the local business community finally turned a corner. The following day, the board of directors of the Jackson Chamber of Commerce issued a statement that read: "The Board of Directors of the Chamber, acting as the policy making body for this organization of business and professional people, officially opposed the Civil Rights Bill, and encouraged opposition to it during the period that it was under consideration in the Congress. Now that the bill has been passed, the Chamber Board recommends that businesses affected comply with the law, pending tests of its constitutionality in court. . . . We may not be in sympathy with all of the laws of the land, but we must maintain our standing as a community which abides by the law."[13]

The *Thunderbolt*,[14] a white-supremacist periodical based in Birmingham, immediately responded:

> In recent weeks our local newspapers have been carrying ads written and paid for by local businessmen and their Chamber of Commerce. They plead with the White people to obey the Civil Rights Laws, and to keep the peace and help quietly integrate all communities. They cannot stand the thought of losing a single dollar from any Negro boycott. . . . They are in a big rush to hire Negro clerks, cashiers, even white collar workers, place Negroes in

supervisory positions over White workers, just to appease the demands of Martin Luther King and his communist rabble. ... The rich businessmen know that they can afford to live in wealthy areas of a city where the Negro cannot move, they have their rich private country clubs and golf links and swimming pools and private schools. They are selfish and vicious in demanding that the white working class mix with black uncivilized animals just so that they may make money off their Negro customers! ... Speak up, white man, tell these sell-out traiors to either stand and fight with the white race or pack up their carpetbags and move in with the Negroes, because they are going to lose all their white trade. Since their principles are bankrupt, let their bank accounts also be bankrupt.

The Rev. Robert Tabscott, who arrived in the spring of 1964 to serve a Presbyterian church, recalled, "I had no idea what I was in for. It turned out to be hell. Hooded night riders, bombings, cross burnings, intimidations, murders, and terror. The FBI was not in command. The night belonged to the Klan. By summer's end in 1965, 44 black churches from Tupelo to Tunica, from Tumshuba to the Gulf Coast had been torched."[15] During Freedom Summer 1964, outsiders inundated Mississippi bent on helping the state's African Americans register to vote. Typical of the city's response, on July 12 a white man attacked a black woman at a Greyhound depot. After being treated for injuries, the woman was arrested for disturbing the peace. Her attacker was not charged.

These smaller incidents paled in comparison with the events of June 12, 1964, in Philadelphia, Mississippi, about eighty miles outside of Jackson. Three Freedom Summer volunteers, Michael Schwerner, James Chaney, and Andrew Goodman, disappeared, not to be discovered until their bodies were unearthed on August 4. On January 15, 1965, a federal grand jury indicted eighteen men, including Neshoba County Sheriff Lawrence Rainey and Deputy Sheriff Cecil Price, for the murders. Seven weeks later US District Judge Harold Cox dismissed the indictments, maintaining that the charges failed to make the case that a crime had been committed.[16]

Considering the labor and sacrifice that went into Freedom Summer, it is difficult to call it a success. The relatively few African Americans who had prepared still faced enormous hurdles to vote. Jackson moved just as slowly to desegregate the schools. In the fall of 1964 black parents from Jackson, Biloxi, and Leake County filed a lawsuit that led to the first court-ordered integration of Jackson's school system. Its back against the wall, the school board adopted what it called a "freedom of choice" plan, which allowed parents to send their children to either white or black schools. Between 1964 and 1969, black parents who chose a white school were pressured or fired by their employers, lost their housing, lost credit at the local bank, received threatening phone calls, had crosses burned on their lawns, and/or were victims of physical intimidation. Finally, in October 1969, the US Supreme Court issued *Alexander v. Holmes*, a landmark decision that involved thirty Mississippi school districts now ordered to replace the dual school systems with unified ones immediately.[17] Rabbi Perry Nussbaum functioned within this environment.

Perry E. Nussbaum

Of all the rabbis who served southern congregations in the late 1950s and '60s, Perry Nussbaum was probably the least appreciated and underrated by his southern contemporaries and the northern activists whom he helped at great risk. Unfortunately, the rabbi's abrasive personality often overshadowed his heroism and tarnished what should have been a stellar reputation.

Perry Edward Nussbaum was born on February 2, 1908, in Toronto, Ontario, to Galician-born Eisig and Adela Newman Nussbaum. Like many East European Jewish immigrants, his family attended a small Orthodox shul rather than a Reform temple. After graduation from Toronto's Central High School of Commerce, Nussbaum initially pursued a career as an accountant. When refused admission to the Chartered Accountants of Toronto (CAT), however, Nussbaum took a job at Holy Blossom Synagogue, one of the premier Reform congregations in North America. Holy Blossom needed a secretary for Rabbi Barnett R. Brickner, and Nussbaum, believing that CAT had rejected him because of anti-Semitism, applied for the job. Brickner suggested that he become a Reform rabbi and provided a recommendation for admission to the seminary. Thus in 1926 Nussbaum enrolled concurrently in the Hebrew Union College (HUC) and the University of Cincinnati.

It took Nussbaum five years to earn his bachelor of arts degree at the University of Cincinnati, and two additional years to receive ordination. HUC president Julian Morgenstern typically facilitated student placement in rabbinic positions, but because Morgenstern lacked confidence in Nussbaum's people skills, the young man was the last in his rabbinic class of twelve to find work, and, to do so, he had to make the long trek to Beth Israel Synagogue in Melbourne, Australia.[18] The young rabbi's experience in Melbourne was not positive, and the following year he again asked for Morgenstern's assistance in finding a position. At this point the latter suggested that Nussbaum consider another occupation. Nonetheless Nussbaum persisted and in 1934 was hired by Temple B'nai Israel, a small synagogue in Amarillo, Texas. While there, he met and married Arene Talpis, a schoolteacher from El Paso. Three years later, Nussbaum accepted a position at Temple Emanuel in Pueblo, Colorado.[19] In 1938, he earned a master's of arts degree from the University of Colorado. Three years later he moved to yet another small congregation, Temple Emanu-El in Wichita, Kansas. After having gone through four positions in ten years, Nussbaum entered the army chaplaincy in 1943. Discharged in 1946, he became associate to Rabbi Abraham Holtzberg at Har Sinai, a large congregation in Trenton, New Jersey.[20] With Nussbaum's history of problems dealing with superiors, this match was doomed from the start. He departed the city midway through his first year, while commenting: "Holtzberg didn't want an associate—he needed a secretary." Nussbaum next moved to Temple Emanu-El in Long Beach, New York. His three years in Long Beach were marred by repeated conflicts with the congregation's leaders that ultimately precipitated a decline in his wife's mental health and a move to Temple Anshe Amunim in Pittsfield, Massachusetts. Anshe Amunim added five years of bickering and tension to Nussbaum's troubled resume. By summer 1954, Perry and Arene Nussbaum wondered if there was any synagogue in which they could find a modicum of peace. Then came Jackson.[21]

While attending the annual meeting of the Central Conference of American Rabbis (CCAR) that summer, Nussbaum consulted with former classmate Rabbi Nathan Perilman who later wrote, "Perry, you have worked your head off.... You deserve a rest. I just talked at the banquet given in Jackson, Mississippi; in honor of the retirement of the rabbi there [Meyer Lovitt].... Now that man has survived twenty-five years in Jackson. There's no reason why you can't survive the rest of your career in Jackson.... You can go down to Mississippi now and take it easy and drink mint juleps and everything will be fine for you." In his memoirs, Nussbaum continues the story: "So I came down to Jackson, Mississippi, two months after the Supreme Court decision ... and I have had the roughest and toughest ... eleven years of my rabbinical career ever since."[22]

One of Nussbaum's first impressions of the Jackson Jewish community was its small size (only about one hundred families) and the vulnerability of its members. "I came into a section of the country where the Jews, even though they had lived for over a hundred years here, were still being regarded as a different kind of people." Some of their neighbors actually believed "that the Jews were still offering animal sacrifices."[23] The congregants' ignorance concerning Judaism, even in its Reform version, also dismayed him. Two of Nussbaum's primary objectives were to be an emissary to the non-Jews, educating them regarding Judaism,[24] while simultaneously educating his congregants about their religion and encouraging them to practice more ritual. In some respects, the first objective was the easier to achieve. Nussbaum's confrontational style and apparent total lack of diplomacy repeatedly undercut his efforts within his congregation. In his memoir, congregant Edward Cohen elucidates some of these difficulties. Cohen reminisces about Nussbaum's voice, which made everything he said both "unpalatable and inarguable. That voice was not southern." Cohen continues: "After the complacent Ike-like Rabbi Lovitt,[25] Nussbaum was as great a shock to the congregation as if we had all suddenly been sent to a Jewish military school.... In his words and deeds he took northern brusqueness, abraded it to a bludgeon and whetted it to a scalpel." Cohen relates an incident that occurred when he was nine years old, sitting with the Sunday school children so that they could rehearse Passover seder rituals. After explaining each of the edible symbols on the seder plate, Nussbaum told the children it was time to eat the hard-boiled egg. With a deep dislike of hard-boiled eggs, Cohen was the only child not to do so. "When the rabbi saw that my hard-boiled egg still sat on my plate he came and stood behind me [and said] 'eat the egg, Edward.'" When he refused, the rabbi told him, "If you don't eat the egg, you must leave the Passover seder." Cohen continues, "The rabbi stared at me, impatient, ready to continue, his detailed but . . . totally uncomprehended explanation of some arcane aspect of the service. I stared at the egg. The table grew quiet at the showdown. . . . The seder was the very symbol of welcome and Jewish inclusiveness; even relatives who were never spoken about or to were called home to share the seder. To cast a fellow Jew from the Passover table was unthinkable, especially if the excommunicant was a small child. The egg glistened, white as a slug under a rock. The look on the rabbi's face was superior, confident. . . . I stood and walked out. The rabbi stared after me. The battle line had been drawn for the rest of our years together."[26]

Another example of Nussbaum's lack of sensitivity and tact was when he "issued an ex cathedra directive that all Beth Israel children were to trick-or-treat for UNICEF" rather than for candy on Halloween. Cohen describes the predicament the children faced: "The United Nations was regarded in Mississippi as . . . the nesting place of Satan. If there could be anything more likely to rile my neighbors than liberal Yankees, it was one-worlders, who would subjugate Christian America to the heathen practices of all those unpronounceable nations whose delegates wore bathrobes in the street. Such was the political climate when I set out, wearing my mouse costume, into the heart of John Birch-era Mississippi . . . [carrying] a little cardboard box supplied by the rabbi and emblazoned in easily readable letters with . . . 'UN.'"[27]

Besides his personal challenges, Nussbaum faced the specter of forced desegregation that hung like the sword of Damocles over Jackson. In his memoir, Nussbaum notes that the first question asked by the congregational committee that met him at the airport was "Rabbi, what will you do about the Supreme Court decision?" He responded that he had never exposed any of his small congregations "to any kind of danger in the larger community."[28] Although that was his intent, Nussbaum found this difficult to manage in the capital city of the Deep South's most belligerent state. "It didn't take very long," he confessed, "before I realized that I could not divorce myself from this problem, as much as I knew that my congregation . . . would be happy if I did. . . . So I found myself more and more getting myself into various groups . . . trying to keep the moral values of this whole segregation issue alive." Cohen recalls, "From the first Friday night . . .

the congregation knew his tenure was not going to be a comfortable one. His abrasive personality was coupled with an integrity about principles that simply left no room for the niceties of public opinion. . . . Even before the first tremors of change were felt, Rabbi Nussbaum often used his sermon to chastise us about our complacency. When . . . the 'outside agitators' started to arrive . . . the rabbi's sermons became more pointed, contending that we Jews had been slaves, that Mississippi was a modern-day Egypt and that, no matter how few we were, it was our duty to march on the side of right. . . . My aversion to his insistent, abrasive *hoching* [nagging] was equaled, sometimes even surpassed, by my admiration for his courage."[29]

Ironically, while Nussbaum was making his position known, some northern colleagues criticized him for what they perceived as inaction. In January 1956, Nussbaum worried in a letter to Rabbi Jay Kaufman at the Union of American Hebrew Congregations' (UAHC) office in New York: "What disturbs me particularly is the reputation I may be getting in the 'East.' I hate to think that people are saying I've gone the way of the Citizens' Councils. On the contrary, one of these days I know I'll put my foot in my mouth—and then I'll be out of a job. I'm still waiting to get the reaction to my talk on the Ole Miss Campus this Wednesday. I gave them Amos and Social Justice—the YMCA man who is in charge of the Chapel talks . . . told me I was the first clergyman to face up to our current problems."[30]

As long as Nussbaum remained under the radar with his views, all went well. But when The Temple in Atlanta was bombed in October 1958, he could not help but write a column for his synagogue newsletter in which he warned, "If it can happen to the Atlanta congregation, it can happen . . . here." For these comments "there was hell to pay," since, in a small city like Jackson, Nussbaum's written words quickly spilled beyond the borders of the Jewish community.[31]

Nussbaum's interaction with the Jewish Freedom Riders provided defining moments in his rabbinical experience. Believing that a rabbi's job was to be a pastor to Jews in need, he visited these people first in the Jackson city jail, which was a very courageous act at the time, and then on a weekly basis in the notorious Parchman Penitentiary, 130 miles away. When he asked colleagues who lived closer to Parchman to take over for him, he was castigated by all of the state's rabbis with the exceptions of Robert Blinder in Vicksburg and Charles Mantinband in Hattiesburg, both of whom were farther away from Parchman than was he. Moses Landau in Cleveland, less than a thirty minute drive from Parchman, was particularly belligerent: "It is your privilege to be a martyr. . . ." wrote Landau. "I am paid by my Congregation, and as long as I eat their bread I shall not do anything that might harm any member of my Congregation without their consent."[32]

After visiting the Freedom Riders, Nussbaum sent a form letter to each of their families to assure them of their child's well-being. These letters were often the only communication parents had regarding the status of their children. The Nussbaum papers contain numerous grateful responses to these letters and provide powerful evidence of the importance of Nussbaum's work during the summer of 1961. Indeed, his actions during this chapter in his rabbinic career are sufficient to establish Nussbaum as one of the most courageous rabbis who served southern congregations during the 1960s.

In early 1965, despite the obvious danger, Nussbaum and two other clergy founded the Committee of Concern to raise funds to rebuild the forty-four black churches that had been bombed or burned the previous summer. Consequently his name was widely publicized in the southern and national press, again causing a stir within his congregation and local community.[33]

A dispute with another Mississippi rabbi gives additional insight into Nussbaum's willingness to stand up for his ideals. Rabbi Benjamin Schultz in Clarksdale made speeches that could have been written by Klansmen. In one delivered shortly after the University of Mississippi riots,[34] Schultz argued that "America needs more Mississippi" and that we should be sending troops to Cuba rather than to Oxford, Mississippi. Much of the the southern press praised the speech for months, and part of it was reprinted in the Jackson Citizens' Council's bulletin in October 1962. On February 1, 1963, both the *Greenville (MS) Delta Democrat-Times* and the *Jackson (MS) Clarion-Ledger* carried reports of another speech by Shultz in which he argued that the United States needed "more nationalism" and that the South needed better public relations. When Nazi killer Adolph Eichmann was tried, Schultz argued, he was afforded a defense; but the South obtained neither a defense, nor a defender.[35] Nussbaum beseeched Schultz, "Whether you intend it or not, you are portraying yourself as a defender of the South at a time when Mississippi . . . has defied every fundamental American legal, moral, and Jewish principle. You have been telling extremists what they want to hear. . . . You have become a fellow-traveler with those elements in the State to which I am absolutely opposed . . . because you refuse to see that your brand of political Conservatism is meat and drink for the fascists who are in control of Mississippi. . . . In such speeches you further the line of the unholy alliance in our State which panders to every latent human prejudice—in the name of decentralized government, states' rights, white supremacy, etc."[36]

Nussbaum and the Jewish community of Jackson paid a high price for his activism. The bombing of their synagogue on September 18, 1967, which destroyed much of the rabbi's office, was aimed at getting back at the man who had become too much of a troublemaker for the ardent segregationists.[37] The Klan followed two months later with a night bombing of his home, from which the family miraculously emerged with only minor cuts.[38] That night, Nussbaum asked a neighboring minister to call Douglas Hudgins, minister of the First Bap-

14. Arene and Rabbi Perry Nussbaum inspect their bombed home, 1967 (Goldring/Woldenberg Institute of Southern Jewish Life). Reprinted with permission from the Goldring/Woldenberg Institute of Southern Jewish Life (ISJL). For more selections from the ISJL's *Encyclopedia of Southern Jewish Communities*: http://www.isjl.org/encyclopedia-of -southern-jewish-communities.html.

tist Church, and ask him to come over. Hudgins's church, the most influential in the city, included the Hederman family, owners of the two local newspapers; arch-segregationist Tom Etheridge, the *Daily News*'s chief political columnist; and former governor Ross Barnett. Hutchins also served as chaplain of the Mississippi Highway Safety Patrol, director of the Jackson Chamber of Commerce, and president of the Jackson Rotary Club. According to Charles Marsh, Hudgins "was the premier theologian of the closed society. He articulated . . . an austere piety that remained impervious to the sufferings of black people, as well as to the repressive tactics of the guardians of [southern] orthodoxy."[39]

When Hudgins arrived with Governor Paul Johnson standing at his side, Nussbaum scolded the minister in front of national television cameras. Nussbaum waved his finger in Hudgins's face and shouted, "If you really want to show your sympathies, then tear up whatever you're preparing for your sermon next Sunday morning and speak to the people in the front pews about their culpability in everything that's happened not just to me . . . but to the blacks and their

churches over the years." When Hudgins offered his sympathy, Nussbaum continued, "Don't tell me now how sorry you are. Those sons-of-a-gun attacked me
and my family! They've attacked my house! I don't want to hear how sorry you
are!" As Marsh relates it, Hudgins was shocked, as was the governor, that Nussbaum would dare "deliver such an attack on Mississippi's most prominent religious figure." But Nussbaum had not finished. "Doug, if you're really sorry about
this," he said, "get on the pulpit Sunday and tell your people this is wrong. Talk
to those segregationists that fill up your church." On the Sunday morning after
the bombing, Nussbaum listened by radio to Hudgins's weekly broadcast of his
church's worship service. Typical of Hudgins's otherworldly piety, he regretted
that houses were bombed, but did not mention Nussbaum by name, nor that the
house bombed most recently had been the rabbi's. "The Lord works in mysteri-
ous ways," Hudgins concluded. Nussbaum found Hudgins's words "outrageous."[40]
Nussbaum delivered the same message to other prominent members of Jackson's
clergy, who two months earlier had marched to the synagogue after the bombing as an act of solidarity. He bluntly informed them that they were largely responsible for the climate that resulted in such acts of violence.[41]

Life for the Nussbaums was exceedingly difficult over the months and years
that followed. During the summer following the bombings, Nussbaum made a
concentrated effort to find another pulpit. He wrote to numerous congregations
and rabbis who were seeking associates, but the responses he received, although
often filled with praise for his courageous work, failed to include job offers.[42] His
was not an attractive resume. Here was a sixty-year-old rabbi not long from retirement who was known for a brusque personality and who had spent the last
fourteen years in a small southern community. Nussbaum remained in Jackson
five more years (until he was sixty-five) and then moved to Southern California
where he hoped to continue his activism while earning money by teaching and
giving lectures.

In August 1973, shortly before his retirement, the congregation arranged a
testimonial dinner for their controversial rabbi. Indicative of the new era, Gov.
William Waller praised Nussbaum: "His leadership helped me, and I believe he
brought encouragement to thousands of Mississippians who knew in their hearts
what they had to do to bring about certain changes, which were made and had
to be made." Mayor Russell Davis added, "He helped make it possible for ordinary men to walk in places they once had feared."[43] Nussbaum was named one of
one hundred "heroes" honored by Cincinnati's National Underground Railroad
Freedom Center, joining, among others, the Dalai Lama, Mohandas Gandhi,
Martin Luther King Jr., and Desmond Tutu. Along with Charles Mantinband in
Hattiesburg, Nussbaum's was a prophetic voice in a Deep South state during the
struggle for black civil rights. In this respect, Nussbaum was clearly a man who
walked in the footsteps of his hero, the biblical prophet Amos.[44]

Editor's Introduction to the Interview

Perry Nussbaum was vilified by both the right and the left. Conservatives such as Moses Landau believed he did too much, for example, in meeting with the imprisoned demonstrators in Parchman Prison, while liberals like Charles Mantinband considered him a Johnny-come-lately. A certain amount of baiting took place among the rabbis. Nussbaum started the Committee of Concern with two other clergy to raise funds to rebuild black churches destroyed by segregationists. In Landau's interview, he opposes these activities without mentioning Nussbaum. To appear more liberal, Landau suggested integrating the white churches instead of rebuilding since rebuilding only continued segregation. Local ministers ignored Landau's proposal as he should have expected, and his proposed solution, given the milieu, amounted to inaction.

On the other hand, although Nussbaum preached in favor of desegregation almost immediately on his arrival in Jackson, he did not become an outspoken advocate outside of his synagogue until the 1958 bombing of the Atlanta temple. Violence in Atlanta, the city that considered itself "too busy to hate," shocked Nussbaum and others into action. If it could happen there, it could happen anywhere in the South regardless of one's action or inaction. Still, Nussbaum starts his interview with a description of the supposed differences he had with Jacob Rothschild concerning the definition of the South. He notes the wide variations within the region concerning conditions in relation to the civil rights movement, a position that Rothschild could hardly contest.

Many rabbis serving southern congregations expressed mixed feelings, to say the least, about national Jewish organizations and their civil rights activities. Nussbaum goes beyond the usual criticisms concerning these organizations' methodologies, paternalism, and lack of knowledge and concern for the position of Jews living in the South. He attacks the motives of the national leaders who he believes took their stands in behalf of black civil rights in the region in order to gain financial support and prestige in the North for their organizations. According to Nussbaum, Jews in Mississippi were expendable because they could not contribute enough money. Conversely, national officials ignored issues facing their northern constituents because of fear of losing contributions.

Not many rabbis would have wanted to serve a small congregation in Jackson, Mississippi. For Nussbaum, however, this was perhaps his last chance. His personality and manner rankled congregants and contributed to discord in pulpit after pulpit. Some activist rabbis including Burton Padoll in Charleston fit the same mold. Typically these negative social attributes contributed to short tenures. Most of the activist rabbis in the South used diplomacy and pastoral commitments to assuage dissent and cement their positions. That Nussbaum failed to do so and still retained his position for over a decade speaks to his congregation's difficulty in obtaining a replacement. Yet Nussbaum attempted to accommodate to his congregation as much as possible without compromising his ideals and duty. This interview makes clear how he considered every tactic for a variety of audiences. This was a man under siege from multiple angles who felt totally alone. If not for the civil rights movement, Nussbaum likely would have left the rabbinate and his career would have been viewed as a failure. He fell into his destiny but rose to the challenge that defined his success as a rabbi and person.

Many rabbis would have conflicted with their congregants regardless of their civil rights activities. Several including Nussbaum were born into Eastern European families, typical of students at Hebrew Union College during the 1930s. They pushed the Reform movement toward more ritual, tradition, and Zionism. As Edward Cohen suggests, Nussbaum's introduction of more Passover ritual was actually a greater break from Classical Reform than his social activism. When Jacob Rothschild pressed for more ritual at Atlanta's Temple, several congregants considered breaking away to form an American Council for Judaism (ACJ) congregation. Nussbaum also confronted the ACJ element within his congregation for the same reasons. No other temple in the region considered a similar schism because of a rabbi's social activism.

—Mark K. Bauman

Perry E. Nussbaum Interview

June 21, 1966

P. Allen Krause: What would you define as the regional scope of this [research]? What is the South?

Perry E. Nussbaum: This is a very crucial point, from a Jewish point of view. I made this argument ten years ago, as a matter of fact, here in Toronto, Canada, to a Union [of American Hebrew Congregations] meeting, when I stood up and argued with [Jacob] Rothschild from Atlanta, and I made the point that there's no such thing as a solid South. But there's as much difference between Atlanta, Georgia, and Jackson, Mississippi, as there is between Jackson, Mississippi, and New York. Now, when it comes to the Jews, the difference between the Jews in the rural areas of Mississippi and Georgia is very decisive, and you can't compare their circumstances to the situation of a Jew in Atlanta, in Birmingham, in Memphis, in New Orleans.

PAK: Would you include all or part of Florida and all or part of Texas?

PEN: From a practical point of view, I think I would start with Mississippi, Louisiana, Georgia, Alabama, maybe Tennessee, maybe South Carolina, and then, if you have time, go into Florida. I wouldn't include Texas.

PAK: Not even the eastern part of Texas? Dallas and around there?

PEN: What we know as the Deep South are these states that I mentioned.

PAK: In terms of civil rights activity, what would you consider the areas that should be touched upon in [my work]?

PEN: By the local rabbi?

PAK: I want to know what role he [the local rabbi] played in civil rights activity. He might not have played any role in it; or he might have played a role against it.

PEN: Well, then you have to have a whole chapter on what is "civil rights" . . . and this is going to be very hard to define . . . really, I don't know how to answer that question. Maybe I can answer it this way: I came down to Jackson shortly after the Supreme Court decision of 1954. This was a decision which was concerned basically with the public schools, the integration of the public schools. For years the crisis developed as a result of that decision. The integration of the public schools was the kernel for every phase of human relations or civil rights.

PAK: Would that date then, 1954, be as good a time as any to start the [research]?

PEN: It depends, it depends. I'm not hedging here. For ten years, for fifteen years before '54 there were these movements in the South, but the Supreme Court decision would be as good as any for a cutoff date.

PAK: Did 1954 make a significant difference in your community, and, if so, what is the difference that it made?

PEN: The impact of that Supreme Court decision was felt in varying degrees in different parts of the South. In Jackson, Mississippi, an understanding in depth of the Supreme Court decision didn't come about for, oh three, four, five years after '54. This was "just another one of the encroachments of federal power on states' rights," and so on and so on. This is how it was interpreted; this was the propaganda line laid down by the writers and that type. It wasn't until half a dozen years later that people really became aware of the basic civil rights issues involved.

PAK: Has Jackson become a different place for the Negro since the beginning of the 1960s? Is it different in the 1960s than it was in 1950?

PEN: Sure, it's different. [In] 1954, nobody knew what it was all about; I didn't know what it was all about, the Supreme Court decision. I had an academic approach to it. It wasn't until the national Negro bodies organized and become aggressive, and they started stirring up sentiment to implement the Supreme Court decision. Now, as far as Mississippi goes, they left Mississippi to the lions; for years, I went around saying that they were leaving Mississippi to the lions. Mississippi doesn't arrive at its stage of crisis until James Meredith, until the integration of the University of Mississippi, which isn't more than four or five years ago. That's the first real crisis that we had. Admittedly we had other incidents, but this is when we got into national and international prominence, with the James Meredith business. Then we went from that to the assassination of Medgar Evers.[45] We had other incidents before these, but the emphasis of the civil rights activists in the South was away from Mississippi; they were concentrating on New Orleans; or, before they got to Mississippi, they were concentrating on Atlanta; they were concentrating on South Carolina. Much of their program depended on what native-born leadership they had in the state, in the communities. It isn't until a half a dozen years ago that you get the rise of such organizations as COFO, and the sending of hundreds of people into the states.[46]

PAK: Can I ask some quick shotgun questions about your Jewish community and then I will ask with regard to your personal involvement. Number one, how long has your congregation been in existence?

PEN: My congregation was founded in 1860.

PAK: Was there a Jewish community in Jackson dating back before then?

PEN: Well, 1860 is a pretty good cut off time for the settlement of many sections of the South. We're a pretty old community.

PAK: What's the economic standing and source of income of your Jewish community?

PEN: We're middle class—my people are mostly merchants. But your question isn't a good question, because Jackson is not a barometer of what has gone on in Mississippi. Not, in a very real sense, because the problem has been aggravated in the Delta part of Mississippi, where the Negro far outweighs the whites, in terms of population; where you have as high a ratio as 90 percent of the population of the community is Negro. Now, from a Jewish angle—and I think I wrote this in one of my articles years ago—scattered throughout the Delta, you have one or two Jewish merchants in little towns, and these merchants, from an economic standard, are pretty well off. Many of these merchants were already second generation, if not third generation, in terms of their settlement. But, they are part of the culture of the South. These Jews are no particular force.

PAK: Is there anything that distinguishes them from the non-Jewish whites in the South, other than the fact that they might go to synagogue and the non-Jew goes to church?

PEN: Not from the Jewish point of view. But for many of the goyim, the Jew is still something different; something strange.

PAK: I've read in certain places that the Jew in the South still is more liberal on the whole than the rest of the southern population.

PEN: It all depends what you mean by the Jew in the South. Here again you're generalizing.

PAK: Let's stick with Jackson.

PEN: Let's stick to Jackson. I've said that the Jews of Jackson did not have to join the [White] Citizens' Councils, and here's an illustration of what I'm driving at: Right after 1954, when the whites started organizing to preserve white power and white position, they organized the Citizens' Councils. The Citizens' Council was intended to be a substitute for the Ku Klux Klan, to be on a higher level, and it was very successful for a while. I said there was no need for the Jews of Jackson to join the Citizens' Councils in the first few years. I'm reasonably certain that during those first few years, Jews didn't join the Citizens' Councils. It had nothing to do with their intellectual level; we had enough Jews in Jackson so that we could maintain a front. But right in Jackson, I have members of my congregation who are native-born southerners—not Mississippians, native-born southerners, from Georgia, for instance—and they're as racist as any white non-Jew.

PAK: Is that a minority in the congregation?

PEN: This was the average Jew. It's so impossible to generalize here; I'd be interested to know what the other rabbis are saying about the kind of Jew who has migrated to the South in the last ten, fifteen years under the industrialization program of the various states of the South. We know that there's been a lot of industry that's come down from the North and this industry has come down to take advantage of the cheap labor and the anti-union conditions, et cetera, et cetera. I have in Jackson—and I would guess [it's the same] in other parts of the South—I've got northern Jews who, in my opinion, are more viciously segregationist than many of the native-born. Again, I say it's hard to generalize; these northern Jews, their approach to this whole problem of rights is that it is a purely economic problem. And it's a political problem, too. They're as bitter against the encroachment of federal domination and what Washington is doing to the states of the South as any of the native born. They came down because everything is cheap. And here's another point you see in talking about civil rights: You can't separate civil rights from what you call states' rights. You can't separate these so-called rights from the whole culture of the South. A culture that is so dominated by Bible Belt Christianity, which is by and large a Christianity founded on ignorance, on lack of intellectualism. And a Christianity which has no concept at all of social justice, which equates salvation with acceptance of Jesus and hoping to sleep in the arms of Jesus after you die, et cetera, et cetera, et cetera.

PAK: If that's the Christianity you have to cope with, are the ministers in your community generally of that order also?

PEN: Yes.

PAK: And have they been of that order with regards to the civil rights movement?

330 • Chapter 13

PEN: Now, talking *tachlis* [Yiddish for "getting to basics"] here, I said before—you can't generalize when it comes to the communities and the
rabbis. [Jacob] Rothschild in Atlanta, Jimmy Wax in Memphis, the rabbis
in New Orleans were in much more fortunate, much better situations than
the rabbi of Jackson, Mississippi. Because in Jackson, Mississippi, the Jewish community had no standing at all, was not part of any kind of power
structure. And the rabbi of the Jewish congregation in Jackson was—and,
in many respects, still is—a lone wolf in his operations. Now, I came down
here in '54, right after the Supreme Court decision. And there were two or
three Protestant ministers—primarily Methodist preachers—who could be
considered, by a stretch of the imagination, as liberal theologically. And, for
the first couple of years, the rabbi and these two or three men were quite
friendly. But as the situation worsened, as attacks were mounted generally,
and everybody got scared, and ran scared, and there were threats against
any minister who even dared to hint that segregation was "un-Christian,"
and a sin, and so on and so forth. When this atmosphere spread, the rabbi
definitely became a lone wolf, and the rabbi today is very much a lone wolf,
because I am the last—I'm the last of the [moderate] clergymen who were
in Jackson in 1954. I'm not counting the Catholic priest because that's a different story; I'm not counting the one or two Baptists, because that's a different story too, because the Baptists, their attitude toward this so-called
civil rights program, has been that it doesn't exist, which is part of their so-
called religious ideology, which has made the rabbi's problem, I think, a
much more aggravated problem than in the bigger cities of the South. Anything that I have had to do, anything that I have done, I did on my own;
and, in the process, I've created a lot of enemies. I've been the gadfly, and
there was a time when people were afraid even to be associated with me,
because they knew what I stood for; they knew what I was saying, and it
was dangerous. It's a game they play; it's a story in itself.

**PAK: What has been your response to and involvement in specific civil
rights activities in your area?**

PEN: OK, specifically. One of the things that I tried to do immediately was
to try to organize a group of clergy across the denominational lines, a
group which might be not necessarily the liberals advocating civil rights
but would be the buffer group between the extremists. This is what I
meant when I said before—I was a gadfly. Because I think I worked with
this thing for two or three years, and we had a meeting maybe; and then
we'd decide to meet again, and the second time we'd come together, half of
those who had shown up the first time didn't show up, and so on—it petered out—this is what happened, went on for years. This is one of the concrete things that I tried to do—organize a group. Another concrete thing

very definitely was the challenge to me when the Freedom Riders had their program in the summer of nineteen hundred and—I forget now, what was it five years ago?—I hadn't made up my mind what I was going to do, because in other parts of the South rabbis had rebuffed and rebuked them. I wasn't too sure what I was going to do. So I came back from a conference[47] to Jackson and the jails were filled with these Freedom Riders and most of them seemed to be Jews, and I made up my mind that, [in] all my life, I had never rejected my brethren. I'd been a chaplain all my life, in a variety of situations. So I forced my way into the jails of Jackson, and they thought I was nuts. The county sheriff told me to my face, "You're crazy. Why do you want to fool around with these nuts?" That was the first he'd seen anybody who had anything to do with the [effort on behalf of the] Negroes. But I insisted on my rights, and so for a summer, and I was scared stiff—and believe me I had reason to be scared stiff. I visited the inmates at the Parchman Penitentiary,[48] had a whole program organized. I got money from various parts of the country. I was the only contact with the outside world for many of them during the summer months. I didn't dare publicize it, because I didn't want my temple bombed and I didn't want to have any cross burned in front of my home.[49] There were elements that knew about it, and we went through a bad period there; Saturday nights people calling up on the phone cussing us out late at night—this was a regular program for weeks. So this was another very specific activity, and I never wrote up that story, because in those days had I written up that story, then it would have been the end of me in Jackson, Mississippi, as far as my congregation goes; no question about it. I didn't dare let them know.

PAK: **Did they know?**

PEN: No, no. One or two of them may have had some idea, but I operate on the axiom—and my congregation is operating on the axiom—that what they don't know won't hurt them.

PAK: **I noticed that a letter sent by one of the parents thanking you for keeping in contact was sent on a post card, an open post card. I was wondering how many of these you received?**[50]

PEN: Oh, now this is something else. I had "brother" [Rabbi Israel] Dresner today accuse me of being afraid.[51] I looked him in his face with [*inaudible*]. Dresner today asked me to give him the names of some people in Jackson; he's going up to Jackson this week with this demonstration—and I should give him names? I said to Dresner, "What do you want them for?" And he said, "Oh, to go around and talk to them." Now, he doesn't understand—I am fed up to the gills—and my people are fed up to the gills—with such men like Dresner coming and talking to us. We've been talked to enough. And I don't know why I should give him names; he could find his own names.

I said, "I don't want to. I'm not going to be there." So, he said, "Well, if you're scared. . . ." This is what I got burned up about, and gave him—I told him a few things. It hasn't got a thing to do with fear. I was scared stiff during that Freedom Rider summer, believe me, I was scared stiff, but it wasn't the kind of fear which prevented me from doing what I thought had to be done by a rabbi. And if you read that story, if you've read some of the business that was in the [American Jewish] Archives file, you'll know that right from the beginning that I just didn't apply myself to the Jews who were among the Freedom Riders. I took care of all of them and I don't even know if the archives even has this, because this is all that the whites, particularly the Citizens' Councils, needed to learn. I conducted the first integrated service in Mississippi, in Parchman. That's all they needed to know, and God knows what would have happened to me, to my family. Sure I was scared, but it wasn't the kind of fear that kept me from doing these things that I thought had to be done.

PAK: **Can I ask a question in terms of the methodology of it? I take it that you're in sympathy with at least some of the goals of the civil rights activity that has been taking place in the South. But you are not so much in sympathy with the methodology, at least, of the rabbis coming down from the North to come into your community?**

PEN: No, no. I've had too many experiences with the rabbis who have come down to Mississippi, who have come down, climbed on the bandwagon. I have had and I still have every sympathy in the world for the man who comes into Mississippi in the spirit of commitment—commitment—and I saw enough of these goyish preachers. If you understand what the word commitment means, they had to do it. This was fulfilling their conscience, fulfilling their religious being—this is commitment. And I saw some of them in the penitentiary; but I saw too many of my fellow Jews—and some of them were even rabbis —who were coming down to make the gesture— it was dramatic—and by the way, I never closed my door to any of them. Where other rabbis throughout the South would have nothing to do with them—nobody can accuse me of a cold shoulder, especially the rabbis. But—and I could see them, I could see them already while they were talking to me— composing articles that they're going to write, the speeches that they're going to deliver, how they came down to the South, and how they saved the South, that sort of stuff.[52]

PAK: **Do you think that they've helped the civil rights movement at all? Do you think their activity did?**

PEN: I don't know. I don't know. All I know is that, from what I read of the civil rights movement today, there are enough Negro leaders who are also fed up with the shilly-shallying of the Jews. They don't have any use any more for white leadership, and who are resentful of the patronizing attitude displayed by the whites. It's a fact that when you talk about the whites who have been in on the civil rights movement in my part of the country, a vast, vast percentage of them have been Jewish.[53] So, what the attitudes are towards the Jews today, I don't know; and whether the Negroes of today welcome the rabbis, I don't know. It's a dangerous thing even for me to suggest that this is a spontaneous thing on the part of Martin Luther King to have us send a delegation down to Jackson. Because a few years ago when this happened with St. Augustine, there were some who were pretty sure that the request first originated at the Central Conference meeting, and they asked Martin Luther King, "Do you want some of the Jewish men—Jewish rabbis?" So, which came first, the chicken or the egg, I don't know. I don't know if I answered your question or not.

PAK: Can I ask a further one with regards to specific instances of civil rights activity on your part?

PEN: Right from the beginning, right from the beginning.

PAK: Would you tell me the methodology?

PEN: I got involved. I came and found an existing state interracial organization, I forget the name of it.[54]

PAK: What methodology did you use? As a rabbi, did you use any certain type of methodology?

PEN: I don't know what you mean by methodology. I joined everything I could join when I first came here. It had nothing to do with race. I let people know that I was very interested in social problems—always have been interested in such problems. And in my first year there were still one or two interracial groups that were still kosher; by 1955, they'd all folded up. You've got to understand that it took a year or two for them to wake up to what was happening; and, within a year, any semblance of association between whites and Negroes disappeared. My first year we still had some kind of a juvenile organization, an agency for juveniles, whatever it was— that I got in on; it still had some Negroes. I think it met once or twice and that was the end of that. I joined everything I could, even at this Tougaloo College,[55] which back then was a small, struggling institution, Negro, very poor, and I met one or two people out at Tougaloo—they were all Negroes with one exception, a German refugee of Jewish origin.[56] So I started going out there—if you want to talk about methodology—for years, I was the only white clergyman in Jackson to go out on that campus.

PAK: You didn't fear any repercussions?

PEN: Of course I feared repercussions, because the extreme whites would take your license number whenever you got near these places. You never knew what was going to happen to you.[57] Now, I had some things in my favor. In the first place, I came down with a whole record of patriotism. I was a chaplain in the United States Army and Reserves, and I think in about six months I began to run the reserve chaplaincy program for the state of Mississippi. I was the senior chaplain, and that gave me status. And within six months [of arriving in Jackson], I was active in the American Legion.[58]

PAK: Did you do this because . . . ?

PEN: All was for public relations purposes; it turned my stomach to attend the American Legion meetings. I eventually became the state American Legion Chaplain; I eventually became the state chaplain for the Shrine. It would turn my stomach, but public relations-wise, it served a good purpose in terms of the rabbi in the Jewish community. And secondly, these were the organizations and the people who were at the heart of all of the extremism that was going on. While they would look at me askance because they would be hearing where I'd been, they had to [*inaudible; possibly* "look the other way"]. The state set up what they called a Sovereignty Commission, which is just another name for a Gestapo, with their files, and I know darn well that they have—they still have—my name in their files, with all of the things that I was doing. But, they couldn't very well touch me, because I have to my credit the super-patriotic affiliations and organizations. I played them, as I say, to the hilt for years. The best way I can describe this is that the editor of the *Washington [Jewish] Post*, who was making a survey—in those first half-a-dozen years, everybody made a survey of Mississippi—and most of them came to see the rabbi. This chap from the *Washington Jewish Post* came, and said that he has been told back in Washington, I think, or Atlanta, to go see Perry Nussbaum, because Perry Nussbaum was the head of the Fifth Column in Jackson. This is the image that I had built up in the community.

PAK: Did you ever attempt to influence any politicians in your community?

PEN: Yeah, now this is another story. It has nothing to do with civil rights. You see, you're bringing up something that is very important when you are talking about Jews and rabbis: the whole business of the attitudes to the Jews themselves, and the dissemination of anti-Semitic propaganda, and so on and so on. I think about the second year I was there I crossed swords with one of the Mississippi congressmen who inserted in the *Congressional Record* a whole *mishegas* [Yiddish for "craziness"] about the national conspiracy a la *The Protocols of [the Elders of] Zion.*[59] I don't know how much you know about that business—about the Israel Cohen canard—and this was put in by my district, in the northern part of Mississippi by Congressman Abernethy,[60] and I wrote him two or three letters and tried to get him to retract, and he wrote me nasty letters in reply; he was very bitter. The congressmen, in those days, and the senators were fighting the battle of segregation in Washington with no holds barred; and they were attempting all sorts of things—they would take for support anybody's tripe. That was number one. I didn't get anywhere with him.

A few years ago—it scared me stiff—there was an editor in the Gulf
Coast who was going to sue me for slander, because in my bulletin I called
the guy an anti-Semite.[61] I heard him make a speech in Jackson, and he told
a lot of so-called jokes that I didn't like. So I put in my bulletin an editorial about the guy, and sent copies of the bulletin not only to him, but to all
of my Rotarian friends who had brought him up to make the speech, who
saw his speech. I think he was going to really sue me for libel. The interesting thing to that is, when I asked the ADL [Anti-Defamation League]
and the American Jewish Committee if they were going to protect me,
their protection would have extended to becoming a "friend of the court"
if it went up to the Supreme Court of the United States. But up until that
point I would have had to fight this libel suit. Which brings me to something else I've forgotten here. When I first came down to Mississippi I realized immediately that one of the great weaknesses of the small Jewish community in all of Mississippi was the isolation of every congregation. There
wasn't a congregation in Mississippi that was larger than a hundred, a hundred and twenty-five members, and most of them were much smaller. There
were only about a dozen congregations, and none of them would have anything to do with the others. It was that sort of relationship. The rabbis who
had been in Mississippi had nothing to do with the others in the state. So I
set out to organize a Mississippi Assembly of Jewish Congregations, which
I did in 1955, I think it was, maybe '56.[62] The purpose of that Assembly was
to bring together the Jewish congregations of the state at least once or twice
a year. I used as a pretext [that] you need to have an annual teachers' training conference for all these congregations. United we stand, divided we fall;
a chain is as strong as its weakest link—and all that sort of stuff. In the process I made myself persona non grata to so many Jews in the state, because
they were so afraid that I was going to lead them down the road to integration. This is very significant. Trying to organize, trying to bring the Jewish congre[gations] . . . the Jews of the state together, immediately made me
suspect to so many of the Jews.

PAK: Was that in your mind at all?

PEN: Yeah. . . . I mean, I didn't say it—obviously, obviously—but there are
communities in the state where I can't go in.

PAK: Does this organization still exist?

PEN: No, it folded up. I kept it going for about four or five years. Then, when
I turned it over to lay people, it just fell by the wayside.

**PAK: I'm still not exactly clear, have you ever tried to influence political
action of any kind—let's say school integration or anything like that?**

PEN: Influence? Influence? No—I don't know what you mean by "influence."
In the first place, I was not going to do what the Christian power structure was not going to do. My own philosophy was that I would not be a

leader—I would be glad to be a vice-president, but not a president. I'd go along. I referred to myself as a gadfly before, and I was content to be a gad-fly, trying to get some of the Christian leadership to do a few things. But overt influencing? No, I wouldn't do it, because I would be doing it as a lone wolf—no support. I used to beg—and this went on for ten years—I would beg the Catholic bishop, the Episcopalian bishop, the Methodist bishop, I told them, let the three or four of us get together and we'll say something; we'll put things in the paper; we'll go to the mayor, we'll do this and do that. But as long as those boys found excuses not to go, I was not going to go by myself, because I knew what it meant; and my congregation, I knew, was much too small. The people that we'd go to for civil rights, whew—that's all we'd need. I have done this, I've gone when it comes to [*inaudible*] in the area of anti-defamation—I've gone, but not this. As I have said, this is a white Christian problem; damn it to everything, it wasn't Perry Nussbaum's problem, and the white Christians are going to have to do something.

PAK: What role have national Jewish organizations played in the civil rights movement in the South, specifically here in Jackson, and along these lines, how helpful have they been to you in aiding you in attaining your goals, or how detrimental have they been?

PEN: There is only one word that I can use, C-R-A-P, when you talk about the national bodies, because, from the beginning, they pulled the wool over the eyes of the Jews of the South. This isn't just true of Mississippi. When the Jews in the Deep South began to desert the B'nai B'rith lodges because they'd heard about the ADL's being an amicus curiae [a legal term meaning "friend of the court," referring to filing a brief in support of a particular position] of the Supreme Court decision, all that sort of stuff. This I think is from 1955 or '56. The president at that time of the B'nai B'rith made a tour of the South to pat everybody on the shoulder—"No, no, don't worry; we didn't mean it. Some of the things we're doing we can't help ourselves, but we are not going to do anything to expose any of the Jews in the South." A lot of attitude, and I knew damn well they didn't mean it; they went ahead with their own programs regardless of the attitudes of the Jews of the South. They issued their statements, and, you see, for Jews in Mississippi specifically, there are not enough Jews in Mississippi; there are not enough Jews with any kind of wealth to have any kind of influence in the national setups of any organizations. So they would go through the form of understanding the problem of the Jews in Mississippi, but they'd do anything, they'd say anything they'd want. I made a trip up to New York in the winter of 1956, I guess—they invited me to the National Community Relations Council, which was just beginning to be interested in this whole problem.[63]

I went up there and I tried to give them a picture of the Jews of Mississippi, and this is where I kept on insisting that you can't generalize about the whole of the South, and you can't generalize about the Jews in Mississippi. That the Jews in Mississippi had their own problems. I tried to get them to see that they ought to understand that there's a Jewish principle that even the least of us are entitled to consideration. I have never forgotten what one of the men there from one of the organizations, I forget which one it was, said very baldly: "Rabbi, we know that when the civil rights movement gets going in Mississippi, heads are going to roll; and I'm sorry, we know that Jewish heads are going to roll. But which is more important, Rabbi— Jewish heads in Mississippi or Jewish heads in Philadelphia, or Detroit, or Chicago?" In other words, they had to play ball with the Negroes in these big metropolitan centers, and [the southern] Jews who would be the scape-goats. Maurice Eisendrath, president of the Union of American Hebrew Congregations [UAHC], making these pompous statements and pictur-ing the Jew of the South as a—picturing the South in general—in the worst possible image. I'm not saying that it wasn't, but Eisendrath made such statements, and then, when he was charged [by representatives of the south-ern Jewish community] with making those statements, saying that he was misquoted. He wasn't misquoted; he knew what he was doing. The national organizations, in the main, consist of a setup of bureaucrats who aren't go-ing to survive very long and who aren't going to maintain their appeals and be successful in collecting their moneys unless there are crises, unless there are all sorts of sensational issues; the national Jewish bodies as far as I'm concerned—I'm talking about the national Jewish bodies—on a very prac-tical basis, they are not—I'm trying to pick my words here, obviously—the national Jewish bodies could have been much more sensitive to the position of the small isolated Jewish communities of the South. It isn't just a busi-ness of these Jews running away from their duty. It isn't just a business of these Jews being faithless to basic Jewish ideals. These Jews have very prac-tical problems. I took the position that I was not going to say to a Jew in a small town in Mississippi, "Don't join the Citizens' Council." If he wanted to take that position, okay; but he knew what the end result would be, be-cause if he said, "I will not join the Citizens' Council," he would be ostra-cized; his children would have no life; he would be run out of town. This was the atmosphere. I wasn't going to tell the Jews to do this. The national bodies expected it. One of the great ironies was this—I have never forgot-ten, I think I put it in one of my articles—when we were organizing the Mississippi Assembly of Jewish Congregations, one of the leaders from the Delta got up and said: "I don't understand it," he said. "All my life I con-sidered myself a good Jew." He said, "All my life these national Jewish bodies have treated me as if I were a good Jew. I have been president of my congregation; I have been president of this and done that, and I've contributed to all kinds of Jewish organizations. And I've got all kinds of letters of commendation from national Jewish bodies. Now, all of a sudden," he said, "I'm a lousy Jew according to the national Jewish bodies. Why? Because I'm not in the forefront of school integration."

PAK: Would you say that their actions were detrimental to your attaining your goals that you might have for Jackson?

PEN: You are asking a question that's hard for me to answer. In the first place I am not in the right Jewish power structure, nationally; never have been in it. I have seen these national Jewish bodies get themselves involved in the whole civil rights picture, and I have seen them be in the lead. Now, whether it is good for the Jews for the national Jewish bodies to be in the lead, I don't know. All I know is that these national Jewish bodies have had for years and years, and still have, enough areas of concern in other parts of the country. Areas of vital concern that they really could apply themselves to and not go way down into the Deep South. Did you see this article—I forget his name—you should read the article by the rabbi from around San Francisco—what's his name?

PAK: Gumbiner?

PEN: No, no—one of our boys. It was a sermon that he gave last Yom Kippur, and it was printed in *The Reconstructionist* about four or five months ago— in which he makes the point, after all these years—and this fellow was down in Mississippi—he makes the point, I think he was talking about Watts and the anti-Semitism that's come off this. He is making a point about the culpability of the Jews in perpetuating the plight of the Negro in the North. And how much has to be done by national Jewish agencies to . . .[64]

PAK: In the North?

PEN: In the North, yeah.

PAK: Well, in regard to the South, do you suggest a policy of silence, then?

PEN: No. You see, I have never been able to bring myself to say to these people from the North, "Don't come down into the South." I can't. I've never regarded myself as a god—I'm not too sure that I have the answer to any of these problems. I do resent the fact that people have come down from the North and they have all the answers, with that attitude. Some of it, to me, has been so unnecessary; it seems to me—things that they've done. I see some of these national [Jewish] bodies coming down into the South and trying to organize all kinds of programs. Why can't they leave it to some of the goyish bodies to do—why do they have to be the pioneers when they could devote their energies and their money to pioneering in

some of these other areas of human relations in their own northern communities? This is what I'm talking about.[65]

**PAK: Is there any discrepancy between your response to and or participa-
tion in civil rights activities, and that of your congregants?**

PEN: Look, I said that everything that I had to do had to be very sub-rosa for
many years. My congregation—I wasn't sure of any members of my congregation in terms of their support of me, or where their interests were in this
whole area—I wasn't sure of any of them until about the last three or four
years. It was the assassination of Medgar Evers, which, more than anything
else, pricked the consciences of a lot of people in the South. I was in town
all summer, and I used a large part of that summer to build up a following;
it wasn't organized, but I had a list of about maybe a dozen families who
were prepared to give some of these workers—these Jewish workers coming into the city[66]—prepared to give them meals and that sort of thing. Up
until the assassination of Medgar Evers everybody stayed away from helping. As we got going, it became—what word am I looking for here?—a
little safer, a little safer to be active in these things.

**PAK: Because the general non-Jewish community also was repulsed by this
Medgar Evers assault?**

PEN: Yes, yes. I had two or three of my younger families particularly who I
could count on to be involved in this, and they began attending some of
these sub-rosa meetings that we were having, especially at Tougaloo College. From that they were gravitating to other activities, so that by now I
have a nice element of civil rights workers. In fact, from my point of view
as a rabbi—again, it's the old story—I think some of them have gone too
far. You see, the Jew has to prove himself to be twice as good, or three times
as good as his *goyisheh* counterpart. I don't like the Jew with money making the contribution, darn it; that ought to come from the goy for some
of these things that are necessary. But I have got one of my younger men
who is in his thirties who is now a member of our [UAHC] Social Justice
Commission. I am not too sure, but I think he is the only Jew in the Deep
South who is a member of our Social Justice Commission. Now you may
not appreciate this, but just using that word down in Mississippi was *tamey*
["taboo"].

PAK: Did you call these meetings that you had?

PEN: No, no—I don't want to give a false impression here. I am not the leading light here. It depends on who you are talking to.

**PAK: Well how did these things get started then, or was it just a personal
talking to people type of thing?**

PEN: No, no. I may have given you a distorted picture. We had this campus,
this Tougaloo College campus, and the campus was the only place where it

was possible to have these meetings. Now it was just around this time the Negroes were developing some indigenous Negro leadership. Medgar Evers, who was assassinated, was a native-born Mississippian. It took a half-dozen years before you could find any Negro to assume any roles here, in this whole area. And these meetings would take place at Tougaloo; you couldn't have them anywhere else.

PAK: How did your congregants learn of them, to get involved in them?

PEN: Some of them would know. I would ask some of them. Those people I wanted to involve, I would ask them.

PAK: So you did this on a private, person-to-person basis?

PEN: Yes. Both one or another; you know these things aren't planned. But it was very pleasant for me to discover, oh, about three or four years ago. I think another reason was that I had two crises in my own congregation. One, after I was there about four years, I guess, maybe more than that—I forget the year when the Atlanta temple was bombed[67]—and I wrote an editorial in my bulletin in which I said that if it could happen in Atlanta it sure can happen here to the congregation in Jackson—the congregation being bombed. I had an element in my congregation which resented it terrifically, especially since copies of our bulletin fell into the hands of some of the goyim then.[68] The implication that the Jews in Jackson were in danger—that triggered the resentment of this whole element, and they passed around a petition to amend the constitution of the congregation so that anything that I wanted to say or do in public would have to be okayed by the board of trustees. I forget whether a special congregational meeting was called, or whether this was the annual meeting when this whole thing was hashed out. If that thing had passed, I would have had to have resigned; I couldn't have stayed. But I beat them.[69]

PAK: Who prevented it from passing?

PEN: Well, I had an element there who valued me—who valued me—for keeping the congregation on an even keel. You asked me before about some of my methodology. All along here I am not watering down my sermons.[70] I think I was the one that coined, right in the beginning, a slogan; I saw it repeated elsewhere, but I think I was the one that coined it. I said early in my career in Jackson from the pulpit, I said it enough times that they understood me: "I know what our problem is as Jews in Jackson, and I am going to do my best not to expose the Jews of Jackson. We are a little community, and I think my responsibility as the rabbi is primarily to the Jewish community of Jackson. That is why I am a rabbi. But I will never let a member of my congregation tell me, the rabbi, what Judaism means and says about social justice." Well, that naturally rubbed and rubs a lot of people the wrong way. We've done a lot of things in our congregation. In the early

years, the world would have collapsed on us if we had a Negro come into
our services; and I thanked God that a Negro didn't come in, because if he
had come in, I know there would have been some who would have thrown
him out physically, and I would have had to stand in the pulpit and tell
my people what I thought of them. Here's something else you ought to
consider—you're not a rabbi yet, and you're going to learn the hard way—I
hope it isn't going to be as hard as some of us—what it means to want security in the rabbinate. You won't have to go through the things that some of
us have had to go through.

We had, in 1955, I think, or '56, at the conference—the Pittsburgh
one—we had an executive meeting of all the rabbis of the South.[71] This
was the first and the last time we got together—the rabbis in the South
got together—to compare notes, and, of course, everybody was a big *ma-
cher* [Yiddish for a "big shot"]. I've never forgotten what one of the rabbis
in the South said—Gene Blachschleger from Montgomery, *alav ha-shalom*
[Hebrew for "may he rest in peace"], who died a couple of years ago. Montgomery, Alabama, was the capital of the Confederacy and has all its traditions. He got up and he said his only interest is surviving. He had about
seven or eight or nine years to go until his retirement, and that's his only
interest. Well, Gene, poor fellow, that was his policy. And Gene didn't say
anything; he didn't do anything to disturb that future. So he had a heart attack anyway, and died. But I'm at that point: my basic interest after years
of it—I had opportunities to get out of Jackson during those first three or
four years. It was very tempting to get out of Jackson those first three or
four years. If I had known what I was getting into I would have never gone
into Jackson. But I just couldn't, in those first years, I just couldn't give up.
I couldn't, because I said, here was a congregation—isolated, small—and
damn it, they needed some organization. They needed some revitalization.
I couldn't bring myself to leave. But then as things got worse and worse,
and I wanted to get out, I couldn't get out. I'm now at the point where I
know I can't get out; the only thing I could get out to would be to things
that I don't want to go to, not at my age. So I'm pulling a Gene Blachschleger here. I still have not backtracked on anything that I have said or
done in my congregation. I've played with fire all the time, and I wonder
sometimes that I have gotten away with some of the things that I've said or
done. I don't know the answer to that.

PAK: If you had the choice now, would you have gone to Jackson in the
first place?

PEN: If I had known in 1954 what I was going into I wouldn't have gone into it.

PAK: That's how the situation is for a rabbi in the South?

PEN: Not in the South—in Jackson, Mississippi. I'm a nobody; I don't like this business of being a lone wolf. The only reason why I went down to Jackson, Mississippi, was because I had spent my post-war years in organizing congregations, and I was worn out. They said, "Go down to Jackson now. Go down and drink mint juleps." I went and I found a congregation—it was nothing, it was a tiny congregation—and I had to start from scratch, which I hadn't minded, because I have always loved that kind of challenge. But when you combine that with all these other factors—when I say to you that the Methodist minister, the minister of the biggest Methodist church in Mississippi, in Jackson, was there eighteen years—eighteen years—got thrown out on his ears two years ago.[72]

PAK: **Because of his civil rights activities?**

PEN: Not civil rights; not civil rights. He was one of these boys, who in the first ten years any time I would try to get him to come to a meeting would say "Oh why stir up things," said he; and it was too late for him when he decided to apply his Christianity over the issue of whether they'd let Negroes go to services.

PAK: **Was that the issue?**

PEN: Yeah. When he did it, it was too late, you see. Too late he was saying to his congregation, "If you're a real Christian, you don't discriminate." By that time their attitudes had been so hardened that he was out on his ears, and the man who succeeded him for the last three years, he's out on his ears. That's all the precedent that my people need, a big congregation; so even though I have been there twelve years, there is no guarantee that I am going to last there until retirement.

PAK: **When was the second time which you talked about?**

PEN: Well, so help me, I don't remember—I mean there are so many of these things that have happened. The second time was about three or four years later, and I had another crisis situation and this was when I demanded— oh, this wasn't so much the civil rights, I guess, as I went out to fight the battle of the country club—I set out to expose the cultural anti-Semitism, and there were some people who resented it, and they brought it up to the congregational meeting. Well, they reelected me; but this time there were a significant number of abstainers. That was three or four years ago, so you never know. For your information, to show you the power of the rabbinate: I have a small Jewish community of maybe a hundred and fifty families—I'm serving less than five hundred souls. I have had four of the oldest, wealthiest families inside my congregation. They were unhappy because I'm too orthodox, which brings in another element. You want to know the problems of a rabbi, and you can't separate them. I walked into Jackson, Mississippi, and found an American Council for Judaism chapter in Jackson and I had to fight them.[73] I had to say to them three months after I was there, when I heard they were bringing in a speaker, that when they brought this speaker into town I'd walk out of town. I was new enough for them to be afraid to take me up on that dare. So my first half-dozen years was fighting the American Council-ites, and in my part of the country nothing could be any more vicious, because they were stupid, ignorant, didn't know anything at all about Judaism. Out of this group of American Council-ites you get a certain kind; you get the conservative element, the back-spearing element. They would cross into the racist picture. You have all these people and you can't set up any hard, well-defined categories to capture all the problems.

PAK: Do you have any hope or optimism with regard to Jackson, Mississippi?

PEN: Yes, sure; it will come. I mean it is not going to happen overnight, and a lot of it depends on the tactics of the civil rights organizations. I think there is still going to be bloodshed. I don't know; I'm being very honest; I don't know whether the kind of march that they're having now[74] is good or bad for the civil rights movement; I don't know, as I know that this token integration that has been going on isn't the answer either. The South has been getting away with murder, literally as well as figuratively, because the South is saying the problem is all because of the politicians from the North, including President Johnson. We have two of the most powerful politicians in the country who come out of Mississippi, one who controls the Judiciary Committee[75] and what not, and Senator Eastland,[76] who is the second man in the military committee of the Senate. They are two of the most powerful men in Washington, so that some of the shenanigans that have gone on are preposterous. So I don't know whether the status quo now is the answer, because it's really only tokenism. But give it time, give it time—give it twenty years, thirty years—before accepting whether this kind of aggravated pressure and demonstrations (which can only lead to physical violence, which can only lead to killings) is of value. I don't know if that's the answer either. I know the civil rights organizations need these dramatic things now, but I don't think anybody knows the answer.

PAK: Rabbi, would you care to make any comments or say anything at the end of this interview?

PEN: I wouldn't know what to tell you. As I said, I have been trying to give you a background picture that the problem of the rabbi of Jackson, Mississippi, has been one hell of a problem. Maybe you ought to ask Professor Jake Marcus[77] what he thinks about the problems of the rabbi of Jackson, Mississippi. There have been some people, I think, some rabbis who have been very understanding of my problems and sympathetic and have helped. There have been others—and this I have got to say—some of the men in the real seats of power in our Reform movement, have shown no regard at all for Nussbaum in Mississippi. The reason why they have done that, the reason why they don't show any regard—oh, there have been times when damn it all, all they had to do was to write me a letter when I've made the press over some sort of crisis. All they had to do is to write me a letter, that sort of thing. But the reason why I haven't got anything from them, they treat me as nonexistent, because my community has nothing financial to offer, is what it boils down to. If I had one Jew who would be able to give to the national bodies a five thousand dollar check, we would get more attention than we do. We are expendable. I think that is about the best way to put it. The New Orleans Jewish community is expendable, Memphis is, Birmingham is, in some respect, are expendable.

Notes

Preface

1. Krause, "Rabbis and Negro Rights in the South, 1954–1967," *American Jewish Archives* 21 (April 1969), also available in *Jews in the South*, ed. Leonard Dinnerstein and Mary Dale Palsson (Baton Rouge: Louisiana State University Press, 1973), 360–85; Krause, "The Southern Rabbi and Civil Rights" (rabbinic thesis, Hebrew Union College-Jewish Institute of Religion, 1967).

2. Bauman and Berkley Kalin, eds., *The Quiet Voices: Southern Rabbis and Black Civil Rights, 1880s to 1990s* (Tuscaloosa: University of Alabama Press, 1997).

3. OC Human Relations, "Past Human Relations Award Recipients," accessed January 8, 2016, http://www.ochumanrelations.org/human-relations-award-recipients/awards-40-recipients/.

4. Krause, "Charleston Jewry, Black Civil Rights, and Rabbi Burton Padoll," *Southern Jewish History* 11 (2008): 65–122.

5. Krause, "Rabbi Benjamin Schultz and the American Jewish League Against Communism: From McCarthy to Mississippi," *Southern Jewish History* 13 (2010): 153–210.

Author's Introduction

1. I was particularly influenced by Professor Donald Meyer, a brilliant American social-intellectual historian, and by two of the books he assigned: Ralph Henry Gabriel, *The Course of American Democratic Thought* (New York: Ronald Press Company, 1956) and Gilbert Murray, *Five Stages of Greek Religion* (Boston: Beacon Press, 1951). The fourth chapter of Murray's book is entitled "The Failure of Nerve."

2. CORE was founded in Chicago in 1942 by James L. Farmer Jr., George Houser, James R. Robinson, and Bernice Fisher. As early as 1947, they sent an integrated group of sixteen men on a trip through the border states to test segregation in interstate travel, a tactic that Farmer called a "Freedom Ride." By 1961, fifty-three CORE chapters spread throughout the United States. One of my tasks as a CORE member was to go with a young white woman to apply to rent an apartment shortly after the manager had told an African American couple that the apartment was no longer available. If the manager offered us, two white people, the apartment, CORE would take the manager to court for racial discrimination.

3. In time, I deeply regretted my amateurish approach. Interviewing men, some of whom had heavy accents, in public settings with high levels of ambient noise, with poor-quality tapes in a tape recorder that failed to warn me when the batteries were running

short on power, left me decades later with recordings that were often difficult to hear or clearly understand. Thankfully a friend who worked for the FBI recommended a forensic specialist, who, underwritten by a grant from the Southern Jewish Historical Society, was able to make even the most difficult tapes largely intelligible.

4. Harold Fleming, director of the Southern Regional Council; Arthur Levin, southeast regional director of the Anti-Defamation League; Seymour Samet, southeast regional director of the American Jewish Committee; and Rabbi Richard Hirsch, director of the Reform movement's Religious Action Center in Washington, DC. Shuttlesworth was the African American civil rights activist responsible for bringing Martin Luther King Jr. and the Southern Christian Leadership Conference to Birmingham in 1963. In 2005 and 2009, I interviewed individuals who were active congregants in the rabbis' congregations in the 1960s as well as Charles Wittenstein, who also served as a southeast regional director for the American Jewish Committee during the civil rights era. On Shuttlesworth see Andrew M. Manis, *A Fire You Can't Put Out: The Civil Rights Life of Birmingham's Reverend Fred Shuttlesworth* (Tuscaloosa: University of Alabama Press, 1999); Marjorie White, *A Walk to Freedom: The Reverend Fred Shuttlesworth and the Alabama Christian Movement for Human Rights* (Birmingham: Birmingham Historical Society, 1998); White and Andrew Manis, eds. *Birmingham Revolutionaries: The Reverend Fred Shuttlesworth and the Alabama Christian Movement for Human Rights* (Macon: Mercer University Press, 2000).

5. While doing research for *The Provincials: A Personal History of the Jews of the South* (New York: Atheneum, 1973), Evans read my work. He wrote, "Apparently the rabbis had enough confidence in you to open up with penetrating comments." Eli Evans to Allen Krause, undated, in author's possession.

6. Mark K. Bauman and Berkley Kalin, eds., *The Quiet Voices: Southern Rabbis and Black Civil Rights, 1880s to the 1990s* (Tuscaloosa: University of Alabama Press, 1997); Melissa Fay Greene, *The Temple Bombing* (New York: Perseus Books, 1996); Marc Dollinger, *Quest for Inclusion: Jews and Liberalism in Modern America* (Princeton, NJ: Princeton University Press, 2000).

7. Quoted in Morris Schappes, "From Mississippi to Harlem," *Jewish Currents* XVIII (September 1964), 4.

8. James A. Wax, "The Attitudes of the Jews in the South toward Integration," *CCAR. Journal*, XXVI (June 1959), 14.

9. 42 percent, 34.8 percent, 31.9 percent, 30 percent, and 28.5 percent, respectively. Donald B. Dodd, comp. *Historical Statistics of the States of the United States: Two Centuries of the Census, 1790–1990.* (Westport, CT: Greenwood Press, 1993) 3, 9, 21, 23, 36. 38, 42, 50, 66, 68, 72, 82, 86, 88, 94, 98, 104. [Editor's note: Although South Carolina fits this profile, the author did not interview a rabbi from that state for this study, and thus it is not included. For insights into one rabbi's experiences in South Carolina, see Allen Krause, "Charleston Jewry, Black Civil Rights, and Rabbi Burton Padoll," *Southern Jewish History* 11 (2008): 65–122.] A Southern Regional Council (SRC) document dated August 7, 1960, notes that twenty-eight southern cities and counties now had integrated lunch counters, but none were integrated in Alabama, Georgia, Louisiana, Mississippi, or South Carolina. See Julian Feibelman Collection #94, Box 29, Folder 5, Jacob Rader Marcus Cener of the American Jewish Archives (AJA).

10. Beginning July 1964 in Harlem, New York, until August 1967 in Washington, DC, the nation was beset by a spate of riots or urban insurrections in many major cities.

In response President Lyndon B. Johnson appointed what became known as the Kerner Commission to assess the causes of the violence. The report, released in early 1968, concluded that the violence was the result of black frustration over a lack of economic opportunity.

11. See comments by Rabbi Charles Mantinband in "Mississippi, the Magnolia State," 1961, Nearprint file, AJA. For an exception from the Orthodox experience, see Mary Stanton, "At One with the Majority," *Southern Jewish History* 9 (2006): 141–99; Stanton, *The Hand of Esau: Montgomery's Jewish Community and the Bus Boycott* (Montgomery: River Publishing, 2006).

12. I coin the phrases "in the land of the somewhat possible" and "in the land of the almost impossible" to denote the relative nature of what could or could not be accomplished on the grassroots level in the South. In locations including Columbus and Atlanta, Georgia; New Orleans, Louisiana; and Mobile, Alabama, for example, outside pressure was often the catalyst, but many individuals recognized the possibility of peaceful change relative to the far lesser likelihood of change without dramatic confrontation in places like Jackson or Meridian, Mississippi, or Selma or Birmingham, Alabama.

13. Additional important secondary works include Hollace Ava Weiner, *Jewish Stars in Texas: Rabbis and Their Work* (College Station: Texas A&M University Press, 1999); S. Jonathan Bass, *Blessed are the Peacemakers: Martin Luther King, Jr., Eight Religious Leaders, and the "Letters from the Birmingham Jail"* (Baton Rouge: Louisiana University Press, 2001); Raymond A. Mohl, *South of the South: Jewish Activists and the Civil Rights Movement in Miami, 1945–1960* (Gainesville: University Press of Florida, 2004); Adam Mendelsohn, "Two Far South: Rabbinical Responses to Apartheid and Segregation in South Africa and the American South," *Southern Jewish History* 6 (2003); James L. Moses, "'The Law of Life is the Law of Service': Rabbi Ira Sanders and the Quest for Racial and Social Justice in Arkansas, 1926–1963," *Southern Jewish History* 10 (2007); Janice Rothschild Blumberg, *One Voice: Rabbi Jack Rothschild and the Troubled South* (Macon, GA: Mercer University Press, 1985); Eric Goldstein, *The Price of Whiteness: Jews, Race, and American Identity* (Princeton, NJ: Princeton University Press, 2006); Cheryl Greenberg, *Troubling the Waters: Black-Jewish Relations in the American Century* (Princeton, NJ: Princeton University Press, 2006); Jack Nelson, *Terror in the Night: The Klan's Campaign against the Jews* (Jackson: University of Mississippi Press, 1996); Clive Webb, *Fight against Fear: Southern Jews and Civil Rights* (Athens: University of Georgia Press, 2001); Webb, *The Rabble Rousers: The American Far Right and the Civil Rights Movement* (Athens: University of Georgia Press, 2010).

Editor's Introduction

1. Ezekiel "Zeke" Palnick, an activist rabbi in Alabama and Arkansas, also hailed from Canada. Although beyond the scope of this book, the roles of Canadian-born rabbis and possible influences of that national cultural background is a topic worthy of future research.

2. Greenberg, *Troubling the Waters: Black-Jewish Relations in the American Century* (Princeton, NJ: Princeton University Press, 2006).

3. When I gave a presentation outlining the themes in this introduction at the 2013 Southern Jewish Historical Society conference in Birmingham, Alabama, Irene Palnick commented that her late husband, Rabbi Ezekiel "Zeke" Palnick, welcomed major civil

rights protests in his Arkansas community so that after the outside protestors departed, his position favoring integration and civil rights would appear to be more moderate and acceptable.

4. Krause, "Rabbis and Negro Rights," 385.

Chapter 1

1. This account relies heavily on P. Irving Bloom, "School Desegregation in Mobile, Alabama," (MA thesis, University of Cincinnati, 1964).

2. *Mobile (AL) Register*, April 3, 1963, 1A.

3. Ibid., June 26, 1964, 4A.

4. *Mobile (AL) Press*, May 2, 1964, cited by Bloom, "School Desegregation in Mobile," 96.

5. Bloom, "School Desegregation in Mobile," 68.

6. John LeFlore was the most significant African American involved in the struggle for black equality in Mobile. When a branch of the NAACP was organized in Mobile in 1926 LeFlore served as its executive secretary until 1956 when Alabama's government and courts halted all NAACP activities in the state, at which point LeFlore and others in Mobile shifted their civil rights work to the Non-Partisan Voters League. LeFlore directed the organization's casework program. As a result of his activism, LeFlore's home was bombed in 1967. Eight years later he became the first African American elected to the state legislature from Mobile since Reconstruction. Although in 2010 Bloom did not recall any meetings with LeFlore, interaction likely did take place in that Bloom wrote of informal contact with "select individuals" in the African American community "from time to time." See LeFlore interview, Oral History section, University of South Alabama archives, accessed April 17, 2010, http://www.southalabama.edu/archives/html/manuscript/oralhist/oralhist3.htm.

7. For the history of Jews of Mobile see Bertram W. Korn, *The Jews of Mobile, Alabama, 1763–1841* (Cincinnati: Hebrew Union College Press, 1970); Robert J. Zietz, *The Gates of Heaven: Congregation Sha'arai Shomayim—The First 150 Years—Mobile, Alabama, 1844–1994* (Mobile: Congregation Sha'arai Shomayim, 1994); Rita Whitlock, *A Family Album: The Family of Congregation Ahavas Chesed: 1894–1994/5655–5755* (Mobile: privately printed, 1994); Steven Leonard Jacobs, "Mobile's Jewish Community," *Encyclopedia of Alabama*, 2010, accessed March 22, 2010, http://www.encyclopediaofalabama.org/face/Article.jsp?id=h-1878; Stuart Rockoff, "Mobile, Alabama," *Encyclopedia of Southern Jewish Communities*, The Goldring/Woldenberg Institute of Southern Jewish Life, accessed March 22, 2010, http://www.isjl.org/alabama-mobile-encyclopedia.html. For the Mordecai family, see Emily Bingham, *Mordecai: An Intimate Portrait of a Jewish American Family* (New York: Hill and Wang, 2003); Myron Berman, *The Last of the Jews?* (Lanham, MD: University Press of America, 1998); on Phillips see David T. Morgan, "Philip Phillips, Jurist and Statesman," in *Jews of the South*, ed. Samuel Proctor and Louis Schmier with Malcolm Stern (Macon, GA: Mercer University Press, 1984): 107–20.

8. About 200 CE, Judah ha-Nasi compiled and elaborated on rabbinical traditions to compose the Mishnah. The book expands upon and systematizes the Torah and creates the framework for Jewish practices. Rabbis in Jerusalem and Babylon later offered commentary and analysis of this major literary and religious manuscript that are called the Gemara. The Mishnah and Gemara are collectively known as the Talmud.

9. Correspondence between Bloom and the author, April–May 2010, in author's possession, for most of this biographical information.

10. On March 27, 1963, the Non-Partisan Voters League initiated the Mobile County Public School Desegregation suit, which became the cornerstone of the league's school desegregation efforts. The case, submitted on behalf of Birdie Mae Davis, called for a preliminary injunction, directing defendants to present for approval of the court, within a period to be determined by the court, a plan for the reorganization of the entire school system of Mobile County, Alabama, into a unitary, nonracial system. Jack Greenberg served as lead attorney in the case. During the 1960s and '70s he worked on some of the most important civil rights cases in the South, including defending Martin Luther King Jr. On June 11, 1963, after President Kennedy federalized the Alabama National Guard, two African Americans (Vivian Malone and James A. Hood) successfully registered at the University of Alabama, despite Governor George Wallace's headline-grabbing "stand in the schoolhouse door" posturing. Due to constant attempts to obstruct court rulings in the Davis case in favor of the plaintiffs, the litigation did not end until the late 1970s.

11. Bloom, "School Desegregation in Mobile."

12. Charles S. White-Spunner served as the US Attorney for the Southern District of Alabama. He headed the team of lawyers who defended Birdie Mae Davis, et al., in the counter-suit brought by the State of Alabama in June 1970. In 1960 he served as a delegate to the Republican National Convention.

13. Rabbi Solomon E. Cherniak (1911–1960) served Shaarai Shomayim Congregation from 1949 until shortly before his death.

14. Reference is to Joseph N. Langan (1912–2004). Langan served as a city commissioner from 1953 to 1969, including a number of terms as mayor (the city was governed by a three-member commission at that time). In a eulogy entered into the records of the Alabama legislature, November 17, 2004, Rep. Jo Bonner writes:

> During his time in both local and State government, Mayor Langan developed a strong reputation as a leader who felt duty-bound to do his part in the strengthening of relations between the black and white communities in Mobile and throughout the State of Alabama. In spite of progressive policies that led to strong public outrage and the end of his careers in both the State legislature and city hall, Mayor Langan dedicated himself to assisting the members of the African American community in their efforts to advance their causes. During his tenure in the State legislature, he argued for equal pay for both black and white public school teachers. Additionally, during his service as mayor, Mayor Langan was an important part of keeping the community calm at a time when racial riots and crimes were tearing apart Alabama and much of the South. His strong and enduring relationship with Alabama civil rights activist John LeFlore was crucial to maintaining this calm.

15. Teko Thames-Wiseman, wife of neonatologist Dr. Hollis Wiseman, had a long history of civic activism in Mobile. One of the founders of ABLE, her activism extended into the twenty-first century. In 2003, the Baldwin County Trailblazers presented her with the Stewardship Award for her dedicated work on behalf of the environment, and Mobile United granted her a Green Award for her "long commitment to environmental excellence."

16. The Elementary and Secondary Education Act (ESEA) is the federal govern-

ment's largest investment in K–12 education. Title I of the law provides financial assistance to schools educating low-income students, but officially segregated schools were not eligible for Title I funds.

17. On April 3, 1944, in *Smith v. Allwright*, the US Supreme Court declared white-only primary elections to be unconstitutional. As a result, African American citizens in Mobile and throughout the country began to push for the right to vote in primary elections. The so-called "Boswell Amendment," passed by the Alabama legislature in 1945 and subsequently ratified by the Alabama electorate in 1946, was one reaction. This amendment permitted any registrar to disqualify a prospective voter if he or she could not "read and write, understand and explain any article of the Constitution of the United States." As a consequence of its selective use, this became a blatant device for excluding black voters. When, as a result of the efforts of Voters and Veterans, a group closely associated with the NAACP, the Supreme Court voided the amendment in 1951, the legislature maneuvered to pass an alternative, the so-called "Little Boswell Amendment." State Senator Joseph Langan led an effort of four or five senators to stop the passage of this legislation, and, through the use of filibuster, succeeded. Nonetheless, it was passed by means of a statewide referendum in 1952. John LeFlore notes in an interview that this courageous stand by Langan was the key factor in his defeat for reelection. The Mobile-based, Non-Partisan Voters League fought this new roadblock and, with the support of Gov. Jim Folsom (1947–1951, 1955–1959), successfully increased the numbers of African Americans registered in Mobile. A great setback occurred with the election first of John Patterson (1959–1963) and then his protégée, George Wallace (1963–1967, 1971–1979, 1983–1987), to the gubernatorial office. Requirements for registration were now imposed, less or more difficult at the discretion of the local registrar, with the result being a drastic decrease in the number of black voters. This situation remained the same until the passage of the federal Voting Rights Act of 1965. See interviews of John LeFlore and Joseph Langan, McLaurin Oral History Project, USA Archives, University of South Alabama, Mobile. "Landmark: *Smith v. Allwright*" LDF (NAACP Legal Defense and Education Fund, accessed January 26, 2016, http://www.naacpldf.org/case/smith-v-allwright; Scotty E. Kirkland, "Boswell Amendment," August 2015, *Encyclopedia of Alabama*, accessed January 26, 2016, http://www.encyclopediaofalabama.org/article/h-3085; Kirkland, "Mobile and the Boswell Amendment," *Alabama Review* 65 (July 2012): 205–49.

18. The Reverend James J. Reeb, a thirty-six-year-old graduate of Princeton Seminary, had served as a Presbyterian chaplain and Unitarian Universalist assistant pastor before settling as a Quaker working in a low-income housing project in Boston. He responded to the call for support from Martin Luther King Jr. and arrived in Selma on March 8, 1965. On March 9, his first day as a volunteer, he was savagely bludgeoned by a group of white thugs. He died two days later. Although President Lyndon Johnson invited King to be present in Washington, DC, on March 13 when the president's Voting Rights Act was transmitted to Congress, King chose instead to deliver Reeb's eulogy. King began with a quote from Shakespeare's *Romeo and Juliet*, "And if he should die, take his body and cut it into little stars. He will make the face of heaven so fine, that all the world will be in love with night," and spoke sadly of how Reeb's death was at least partly the result of "the indifference of every minister of the gospel who has remained silent behind the safe security of stained glass windows." The eulogy, "A Witness to the Truth," is published in *inSpire* 6, no. 2 (winter 2002); Laura Anderson, "James Reeb," *Encyclopedia of Alabama*, July 13, 2015, accessed January 26, 2016, http://www.encyclopediaofalabama.org/article/h-2054.

19. Author's email to Superintendent, United Methodist Church, Mobile, AL, May 21, 2005.

20. The Mobile Municipal Auditorium opened in 1964.

21. Reference is to Albert Sidney Foley Jr. Foley was ordained in 1942, and from 1944 through 1947 taught religion, speech, and sociology at Spring Hill College. Foley was assigned to teach "Migration, Immigration, and Race." The volumes he read and the studies he conducted in preparation for the course made him realize how illogical prejudice was and how much injustice segregation caused. Consequently, Foley organized a Mobile Student Interracial Union at the college and conducted surveys among black Catholics and his students concerning racial opinions and treatment. These actions earned him the censure of his church superior, Archbishop Thomas Toolen, and he was shortly reassigned. In 1946, the organizing meeting of a provincial Institute of Social Order took place. At that meeting a group of nearly two dozen Jesuit priests established a subcommittee on interracial relations and selected Foley as its leader. In 1947 Foley, while at St. Louis University pursuing an MS in sociology, joined the Midwest Clergy Conference on Negro Welfare and the Catholic Committee of the South. During the 1950s he became a member of the Commission on Interracial Cooperation, forerunner of the Southern Regional Council, an interreligious and interfaith organization dedicated to educating people concerning the issue of race. He was reassigned to Spring Hill College in 1953. That year the college determined to implement desegregation, a process the board of trustees had discussed for several years. In 1955 Foley became a founding member of the Alabama Council on Human Relations, the state branch of the Southern Regional Council. By 1960 he had established the Human Relations Institute at Spring Hill College. From this venue, he held small group workshops in race relations, police/community relations, executive development, and other areas. Around 1961 he was also appointed to the Alabama Advisory Committee to the US Civil Rights Commission. From 1965 through 1968 he conducted workshops on school desegregation in Mobile and Birmingham designed to change attitudes and bring about integration. For the last seventeen years of his life, Foley worked through federal grants with the Job Training Partnership Act and the Head Start Program, among other things. He continued to teach at Spring Hill until retiring as professor emeritus in 1979, and continued his work with the Human Relations Institute until his death in 1990. See Carol A. Ellis, "The Tragedy of the White Moderate: Father Albert Foley and Alabama Civil Rights, 1963–1967" (MA thesis, University of Alabama, 2002).

22. Joseph Langan.

Chapter 2

1. Donald McNabb and Louis E. Madère Jr., *A History of New Orleans* (New Orleans: privately printed, 2003), chapters 1 and 2; see also John G. Clark, *New Orleans, 1718–1812: An Economic History* (Baton Rouge: Louisiana State University Press, 1970).

2. McNabb and Madère, *History of New Orleans*, chapter 3; Clark, *New Orleans, 1718–1812*, 181–359.

3. Lawrence H. Larsen, "New Orleans and the River Trade: Reinterpreting the Role of the Business Community," *Wisconsin Magazine of History* 61:2 (Winter, 1977–1978), 112–15.

4. Eli N. Evans, *Judah P. Benjamin: The Jewish Confederate* (New York: Simon & Schuster, 1988).

5. US Census, "Population of the 100 Largest Urban Places: 1860," accessed November 15, 2010, http://www.census.gov/population/www/documentation/twps0027/tab09.txt; and "Population of the 100 Largest Urban Places: 1900," accessed November 15, 2010, http://www.census.gov/population/www/documentation/twps0027/tab13.txt; Larsen, "New Orleans and the River Trade," 120–24.

6. Alecia P. Long, *The Great Southern Babylon: Sex, Race, and Respectability in New Orleans, 1865–1920* (Baton Rouge: Louisiana State University Press, 2004); Anthony J. Stanonis, *Creating the Big Easy: New Orleans and the Emergence of Modern Tourism, 1918–1945* (Athens: University of Georgia Press, 2006); Mark Souther, *New Orleans on Parade: Tourism and the Transformation of the Crescent City* (Baton Rouge: Louisiana State University Press, 2006).

7. Sarah Lolley, "WWII Museum Continues to Expand in New Orleans," *Pittsburgh Post-Gazette*, November 8, 2009, http://www.post-gazette.com/pg/09312/1011168-37.stm; "Andrew Jackson Higgins, Founder of Higins Industries, New Orleans, LA," Higgins Classic Boats Association, accessed January 26, 2016, http://higginsclassicboats.org/Web_Studio_Higgins_Website/History.html.

8. Robert Lewis, "World War II Manufacturing and the Postwar Southern Economy," *Journal of Southern History* 73–74 (November, 2007): 837–66; Tai Deckner Kreidler, "The Offshore Petroleum Industry: The Formative Years, 1945–1962," (PhD dissertation, Texas Tech University, 1997), accessed November 24, 2010, http://etd.lib.ttu.edu/theses/available/etd-10272008-31295012202502/unrestricted/31295012202502.pdf.

9. Leonard Reissman, "The New Orleans Jewish Community," *Jewish Journal of Sociology* IV (June 1962): 112–13. See also Irwin Lachoff and Catherine C. Kahn, *The Jewish Community of New Orleans* (Charleston, SC: Arcadia, 2005). Catherine Kahn graciously read this chapter and made comments, several of which prevented errors. For an earlier New Orleans rabbi and civil rights account, see Bobbie S. Malone, *Rabbi Max Heller: Reformer, Zionist, Southerner, 1860–1929* (Tuscaloosa: University of Alabama Press, 1997). Further information in this section was derived from "New Orleans, Louisiana," *Encyclopedia of Southern Jewish Communities*, Goldring Woldenburg Institute of Southern Jewish Life (ISJL), accessed January 26, 2016, http://www.isjl.org/louisiana-new-orleans-encyclopedia.html; "Reform Congregations—New Orleans," ISJL, accessed January 26, 2016, http://www.isjl.org/louisiana-new-orleans-reform-congregations-encyclopedia.html.

10. Reissman, "New Orleans Jewish Community," 111.

11. Alfred O. Hero Jr., *The Southerner and World Affairs* (Baton Rouge: Louisiana State University Press, 1965), 490.

12. Louis Lomax, *The Negro Revolt* (New York: Harper and Row, 1962), 76.

13. George McKenna, "Throwing Open the Windows—Again," *Human Life Review* XXX, 3 (Summer 2004).

14. Julian Beck Feibelman interview conducted by Orley B. Caudill, Center for Oral History and Cultural Heritage, University of Southern Mississippi, March 16, 1974 (hereafter cited as Feibelman/Caudill interview).

15. Ibid.

16. Ibid.

17. Berkley Kalin, "A Plea for Tolerance: Fineshriber in Memphis," in *The Quiet Voices: Southern Rabbis and Civil Rights*, ed. Mark K. Bauman and Berkley Kalin (Tuscaloosa: University of Alabama Press, 1997): 50–66.

18. Feibelman/Caudill interview.

19. Julian B. Feibelman, *The Making of a Rabbi* (New York: Vantage Press, 1980), 240.

20. Ibid., 334.

21. Kristen Hannum, "Father Albert Foley: How One Priest Took On the KKK," *US Catholic* 79 No. 11 (Nov. 2013): 47–48, in *US Catholic Faith in Real Life*, accessed January 22, 2016, http://www.uscatholic.org/articles/201311/father-albert-foley-how-one -priest-took-kkk-28118; "Spring Hill Jesuit Fought the KKK, Worked for Civil Rights in Alabama," *Jesuits News Detail*, accessed January 22, 2016, http://www.jesuits.org/news -detail?TN=NEWS-20140116013636.

22. Feibelman, *The Making of a Rabbi*, 446.

23. Reference is to the *Brown v. the Board of Education of Topeka*, May 17, 1954, in which the Supreme Court ruled that the so-called "separate but equal" system of school segregation as practiced principally in the South was unconstitutional. "*Brown v. Board of Education of Topeka, Kansas*, 347 US 483 (1954)," Justia: US Supreme Court, accessed January 26, 2016, https://supreme.justia.com/cases/federal/us/347/483/case.html.

24. Feibelman appeared before the Orleans Parish School Board on September 12, 1955. He spoke on behalf of the approximately 180 people who signed a petition asking the board not to "offer defiant resistance" to what was now "the law of the land." On November 17, 1955, he received a letter from Eula Brown, president of the New Orleans' Teachers Association, in which she thanked him for his "christian, democratic stand in spearheading and being spokesman for the committee of citizens . . . in presenting to the Orleans Parish School Board a petition asking immediate compliance with the United States Supreme Courts' decision rendering separate public schools for American children unconstitutional." Feibelman Collection, #94, Box 29, Folder 5, Jacob Rader Marcus Center of the American Jewish Archives (AJA).

25. During this period, Feibelman kept his home phone off the hook and finally had to get a second phone line installed in the house. In addition his front door was spattered twice with eggs and tomatoes. His family was so frightened they would not let him go out at night. Julian Feibelman interview, November 7, 1978, Amistad Library Oral History Archives, Tulane University.

26. The Southern Conference Educational Fund (SCEF) was established in 1946 as the educational arm of the Southern Conference for Human Welfare (SCHW). Methodist minister James A. Dombrowski served as an administrator of the SCHW until he left in 1947 to become the Executive Director of the SCEF. The SCEF became a completely separate organization the following year and based most of its activities out of its New Orleans office. Dombrowski and Aubrey Williams became the most visible figures in SCEF during the 1950s and helped establish the organization as a leading proponent of integration and civil rights in the South. Dombrowski was widely considered to be a communist sympathizer, so that any group with which he associated was tainted as a communist front organization. Thomas A. Krueger, *And Promises to Keep: The Southern Conference for Human Welfare, 1938–1948* (Nashville: Vanderbilt University Press, 1967); Frank T. Adams, *James A. Dombrowski: An American Heretic, 1897–1983* (Knoxville: University of Tennessee Press, 1992).

27. In 1948 Bunche received appointment as the United Nations representative to negotiate an end to the hostilities between Israel and its Arab neighbors. He won the Nobel Peace Prize in Oslo in 1950 in recognition of his work.

28. An undated flyer is suggestive of the type of material that might have been distributed for this event. It reads: "Welcome Negroes to Jewish Community Center 5342

St. Charles Avenue All Recreational Facilities Are Open To You Free. Free Refreshments. The Swimming Pool is Now Open Come and Bring the Entire Family. Temple Sinai is located at 6227 St. Charles Avenue." Feibelman Collection, #94, Box 29, Folder 5, AJA.

29. For his description of Operation Understanding, see Feibelman, *Making of a Rabbi*, 480.

30. As noted previously, Feibelman had already received mean-spirited calls and threatening letters. Shortly after his September 12, 1955, appearance before the school board, he found one hand written over a copy of the *New Orleans (LA) Times-Picayune* article, "School Board Studies Plea to End Segregation." The article described "a group of delegates led by Rabbi Julian B. Feibelman." The note, signed "K.K.K.," read, "It takes a damn Jew to advocate mixing these burr headed apes with whites. Your Communistic wish to lower us to nigger levels will bring disaster to all—even Jews. Hitler was right." Feibelman Collection, #94, Box 30, Folder 3, AJA. Another letter writer asked: "'Rabbi' Feibelman: Why do you have to take upon yourself to tell Superintendent Redmond . . . what to do about the 'negroes'—why don't you let them go to *your church*? Why don't you invite them to your home for tea—let your children have 'dates' with negroes?" Other letters included the following: "If you think a pogram [sic] in the land of democracy cannot happen wait a few years you misbegotten son of an Arabian ass. . . . Get out your petitions. We'll burn you with them later." "One who is for Segregation forever" wrote, "You can well accept Integration, because you know there will never be any Negroes in your Synagogues. Christ was a Jew, but did the Lord place male and female of the negro in the Ark? Was there any negroes when Christ made his sermon of the mount?" An undated letter from Paulsen Spence of Baton Rouge, written on the letterhead of the *Jeffersonian Republican Democrats*, states, "On account of my friendship with certain Jews, I dislike very much to bring the subject up but I personally think the American Jew is making a fool of himself and if he does not change his way, he is setting himself up for the same treatment afforded the German Jews." Feibelman Collection, #94, Box 29, Folder 5, AJA.

31. Clive Webb, *Rabble Roussers: The American Far Right in the Civil Rights Era* (Athens: University of Georgia Press, 2010).

32. The reference is to Leander Perez, who is discussed previously in this chapter.

33. An anti-Semite, on more than one occasion Perez expressed views similar to the following: "The Jews are leading the Negroes. They'll resent it and I say they are unadulterated damn liars because I do resent any Goddam Jew trying to destroy our country and our rights and that's what they are doing, and they are using the Negro for it." Reese Cleghorn, "The Segs," *Esquire*, January, 1964, 72, as quoted in Harry Golden, *Mr. Kennedy and the Negroes* (Cleveland: World Publishing Company, 1964), 213.

34. Save Our Schools (SOS) was a nonprofit organization incorporated in 1960 by concerned white parents and citizens of New Orleans with the objective of maintaining free and public education during the critical period of school desegregation. John Pettit Nelson Jr. acted as a principal founder. On Nelson, see Cheryl V. Cunningham, "The Desegregation of Tulane University," (MA thesis, University of New Orleans, 1982).

35. Feibelman is listed on the letterhead as one of the three cochairs of the organization along with a Catholic priest and Protestant minister. An editorial in the *Shreveport (LA) Journal* (December 6, 1960) indicates that the SOS organization in New Orleans was led by individuals active in communist front organizations. Examples given of such organizations included the SCEF and the ACLU. The writer devoted a paragraph to Feibelman's connection to SOS. Feibelman Collection, #94, Box 29, Folder 5, AJA.

36. Rosenwald's daughter in question is Edith Rosenwald Stern. Feibelman aided the

wealthy and politically influential Zemurray on the death of his son during World War II. See Rich Cohen, *The Fish That Ate the Whale: The Life and Times of America's Banana King* (New York: Farrar, Straus and Giroux, 2012).

37. A letter from congregant Stanley Diefenthal, dated September 15, 1955, makes it clear that the congregation did have at least one segregationist.

> I question the wisdom ... of your undertaking leadership ... on such a controversial thing as public school integration, especially in view of your position as spiritual leader of such a large portion of our Jewish population. I am confident that your view of this matter does not coincide with a majority of your congregation, and I sincerely hope it does not represent the opinion of the Board of Temple Sinai although I fear that a rather large number of newspaper readers are now convinced that it does. I, personally, am opposed to integration ... and [am] very strongly opposed to the idea of Jewish community and religious leaders taking [an] active part in public discussions of the question of whether we shall accept or reject it. ... Therefore, much as it pains me to write you this letter ... I feel it is my duty to go on record as asking you on behalf of all Jews in New Orleans ... to refrain from pursuing this course of action.

He also received a letter apparently from a student at Tulane University, who signed his name in rather primitive Hebrew (Y. Moshe ben David) in order to protect himself "against the well-known amount of influence that you have here at Tulane." The writer claims that he is a member of the White Citizens' Council of New Orleans along with other Jews, and that "we have been fairly successful in keeping anti-Semetism [*sic*] down to a minimum, in contrast to the Klans of your day." He expresses upset with Feibelman's "unwarranted political announcement in the newspaper today ... asking the Citizens of New Orleans to keep the schools open" and finds the SOS group less than honest in their statement that they do not propose to argue the merits of segregation or desegregation. "This hypocrisy and mockery can best be exemplified by your own speeches that I heard myself in your own Temple." On the other hand, Feibelman received a number of complimentary and supportive letters from rabbinic colleagues around the country, and about two times as many commendatory than condemning messages from local writers. Feibelman Collection, #94, Box 29, Folder 5, AJA.

38. Theodore G. Bilbo served as governor and then senator from Mississippi during a political career begun in 1908 that spanned four decades. A consummate demagogue, he made good use of racism and anti-Semitism. He advocated the deportation of blacks to Africa, called Congresswoman Claire Booth Luce a "nigger lover," and in 1938 praised Adolf Hitler on the floor of the US Senate. Chester M. Morgan, *Redneck Liberal: Theodore G. Bilbo and the New Deal* (Baton Rouge: Louisiana State University Press, 1985); Stephen Cresswell, *Rednecks, Redeemers, and Race: Mississippi after Reconstruction, 1877–1917* (Jackson: University Press of Mississippi, 2006).

39. Sociologist Leonard Reissman noted about the Jews of New Orleans that their "attitudes towards race are not unrestrainedly equalitarian but sometimes are hedged by some of the elaborate rationale that Southerners of conscience have evolved to justify segregation." Reissman, "New Orleans Jewish Community," 111.

40. The two-page statement on race relations issued on May 20, 1958, included the assertion "We favor the laws that ... guarantee full privileges of citizenship to each American regardless of race or creed. We deplore attempts to circumvent and to defy the court

decisions, which are made for the protection and benefit of all . . . people." Thirteen Christian clergymen along with Feibelman and Rabbi Leo Bergman of Sinai Temple signed the statement. Feibelman Collection, #94, Box 29, Folder 5, AJA.

41. Feibelman asked one "very successful" minister how he stood on the issue of integration. Feibelman said that the minister's response ("I really haven't made up my mind") was "incomprehensible to me." Julian Feibelman interview conducted by Kim Lacy Rogers, November 7, 1978, Amistad Library Oral History Archives, Tulane University. Rogers cites the Feibelman interview as a source for her "Humanity and Desire," (PhD dissertation, University of Minnesota, 1982) but not for her book *Righteous Lives: Narratives of the New Orleans Civil Rights Movement* (New York: New York University Press, 1993).

42. Feibelman served Temple Sinai from 1936 until his retirement in 1967. Leo Bergman served Touro Synagogue from 1948 until 1978. Nathaniel Share filled the pulpit of Congregation Gates of Prayer from 1934 until his death in 1974.

43. Victor H. Schiro served as mayor from 1961 to 1969.

44. Feibelman refers to Rabbi Arthur Lelyveld, then Senior Rabbi of Fairmount Temple in Cleveland. Lelyveld was badly beaten in Hattiesburg, Mississippi, on July 1964 during his participation in the Freedom Rides. Lawrence Van Gelder, "Rabbi Arthur J. Levyveld, 83, Rights Crusader," *The New York Times*, April 16, 1969.

45. First appointed to the city council in 1974, two years later the Rev. A. L. Davis Jr. became the first African American elected to the New Orleans City Council since Reconstruction. See "New Orleans Minister First Black Elected to Council," *Jet* 51, no. 7 (November 4, 1976), 20.

46. He apparently refers to Nathaniel Share.

Chapter 3

1. Sources for this section include John S. Lupold, "Columbus," August 26, 2013, *The New Georgia Encyclopedia*, accessed January 26, 2016, http://www.georgiaencyclopedia .org/articles/counties-cities-neighborhoods/columbus ; "History of Columbus, Georgia," accessed April 25, 2010, http://www.columbusga.org/history/.

2. Raphael Jacob Moses, *Last Order of the Lost Cause: The True Story of a Jewish Family in the "Old South,"* comp., ed., and exp. Mel Young (Lanham, MD: University Press of America, 1995); Robert N. Rosen, *The Jewish Confederates* (Columbia: University of South Carolina Press, 2000).

3. See Lynn Willoughby, *Judge Aaron Cohen: Memoirs of a First Generation American* (n.p.: privately printed, 2008).

4. Information for this section was derived from sources in note 1: "History of Temple of Israel," Temple Israel, accessed January 26, 2016, http://www.templeisrael.org/history .htm; Encyclopedia of Southern Jewish Communities, Columbus, Georgia," Goldring/ Woldenberg Institute of Southern Jewish Life, accessed April 24, 2010, http://www.isjl .org/georgia-columbus-encyclopedia.html.

5. Richard Hyatt, "A Culture of Violence," *Columbus (GA) Ledger-Enquirer*, May 2007, accessed April 10, 2010, http://lemedia.com/series/race_series_pdf/050407_race _series_6_A6.pdf.

6. "Carson's Hometown of Columbus, Georgia," *Oprah's Book Club*, April 21, 2004, accessed May 2, 2010, http://www.oprah.com/oprahsbookclub/Novel-Carsons-Hometown -of-Columbus-Georgia.

7. Craig Lloyd, "Thomas Brewer (1894–1956)," December 12, 2013, *The New Geor-*

gia Encyclopedia, January 26, 2016, http://www.georgiaencyclopedia.org/articles/history-archaeology/thomas-brewer-1894-1956; Lloyd, "Primus E. King (1900-1986)," *The New Georgia Encyclopedia*, accessed January 26, 2016, http://www.georgiaencyclopedia.org/articles/history-archaeology/primus-e-king-1900-1986; "Breaking the White Primary: The Primus King Case," accessed January 26, 2016, https://library.columbusstate.edu/displays/Primus.php; Andrew Billingsley, *Mighty Like a River: The Black Church and Social Reform* (New York: Oxford University Press, 1999), 53–54; Hyatt, "Culture of Violence."

8. In 1930 R. W. Page, owner of the afternoon *Columbus Ledger* (founded 1886) purchased the morning *Columbus Enquirer* (founded 1828). The latter had received a Pulitzer Prize in 1926 for Public Service "for the service which it rendered in its brave and energetic fight against the Ku Klux Klan; against the enactment of a law barring the teaching of evolution; against dishonest and incompetent public officials and for justice to the Negro and against lynching." Each Sunday a single paper, the *Columbus (GA) Ledger-Enquirer* was distributed, although the two papers did not fully merge until 1988. "Ledger-Enquirer," The McLatchey Company, accessed January 22, 2016, http://www.mcclatchy.com/2006/06/09/353/ledger-enquirer.html.

9. Richard Hyatt, "Do We Know Each Other," *Columbus (GA) Ledger-Enquirer*, May 7, 2007, accessed April 26, 2010, http://l-emedia.com/series/race_series_pdf/050607_race_series a6.pdf.

10. Richard Hyatt, "The Right to Fight," *Columbus (GA) Ledger-Enquirer*, May 6, 2007, accessed April 26, 2010, http://l-emedia.com/series/race_series_pdf/050407_race_series_6_A6.pdf.

11. Michael B. Friedland, *Lift Up Your Voice Like a Trumpet: White Clergy and the Civil Rights and Antiwar Movements, 1954–1973* (Chapel Hill: University of North Carolina Press, 1998), 44–45; Richard Hyatt, "Different Gospels: Two Ministers Fought on Moral Battlefield," *Columbus Ledger-Enquirer*, May 3, 2007, accessed April 26, 2010, http://l-emedia.com/series/race_series_pdf/050307_race_series_5; see also *Stevens Point (WI) Daily Journal*, June 8, 1959, 5; *Corpus Christi (TX) Times*, June 8, 1959, 1; *Modesto (CA) Bee and News-Herald*, June 11, 1959, 10; *Kansas City (MO) Star*, June 10, 1959, 23.

12. Richard Hyatt, "From Two Worlds to One: Slowly, Leaders in Black Columbus become Leaders in Columbus," *Columbus (GA) Ledger-Enquirer*, May 3, 2007, accessed April 26, 2010, http://l-emedia.com/series/race_series_pdf/050307_race_series_5.

13. The text of this resolution can be found in a tribute book published by Temple Israel after Goodman's death. Regina Satlof Block, an active synagogue member and wife of the congregation president, graciously sent a copy of this resolution to the author.

14. Ibid.

15. Priscilla Black Duncan, "'Awesome': That's Rabbi Goodman," *Columbus (GA) Enquirer*, December 2, 1985; "Rabbi Goodman: A Lively 36 Years," *Columbus (GA) Ledger*, September 4, 1986. I am grateful to Anita Satlof Lawson and Regina Satlof Block for the two articles.

16. For Presbyterian minister Robert McNeill, see the introductory material for chapter 3.

17. During the 1950s and '60s Shearith Israel employed rabbis Kassel Abelson (1956), Seymour Panitz (1957–1960), Morris Silberman (1960–1961), Leonard Borstein (1962–1967), and Joseph Renov (1967–1968). I am grateful to Sandra Berman, an archivist at the William Breman Jewish Heritage Museum in Atlanta, for this information.

18. According to Christopher Allen Huff, "In 1960 Governor Ernest Vandiver Jr.,

forced to decide between closing Georgia's public schools or complying with a federal order to desegregate them, tapped state representative George Busbee to introduce legislation creating the General Assembly Committee on Schools. Commonly known as the Sibley Commission, the committee was charged with gathering state residents' sentiments regarding desegregation and reporting back to the governor. The report issued by the Sibley Commission laid the foundation for the end of massive resistance to desegregation in the state and helped avoid a showdown between Vandiver and the federal government." Busbee later served as governor (1975–1983). Huff, "Sibley Commission," November 5, 2015, *The New Georgia Encyclopedia*, accessed January 26, 2016, http://www.georgiaencyclopedia.org/nge/Article.jsp?id=h-2617.

19. His involvement with school desegregation thus appears to have begun a short time after the *Brown v. Board of Education* decision of the Supreme Court on May 17, 1954.

20. Arthur Levin served as the ADL southern regional director from 1948 to 1962. The district included Georgia. Adolph "B" Botnick worked in the ADL Atlanta office from 1961 to 1964 and then served as the regional director from 1964 to 1992 at the New Orleans office.

21. The resolution against the Vietnam War was passed at the UAHC biennial conference in November 1965.

22. Reference is apparently to Rabbi Joseph Freedman of Temple B'nai Israel (the "Hebrew Congregation") in Albany, Georgia, who replaced Martin Hinchin in 1958. Freedman stayed until he retired in 1973. Concerning his Albany congregation, Hinchin told the author, "They took a strictly southern view." Albany is about eighty miles south of Columbus. In one of the many ironies, Ezekiel Palnick, an activist rabbi when he served in Little Rock, Arkansas, succeeded Freedman in Albany. See Caroline Gray LeMaster, *A Corner of the Tapestry: The History of the Jewish Experience in Arkansas, 1820s–1990s* (Fayetteville: University of Arkansas Press, 1994); LeMaster, "Civil and Social Rights Efforts of Arkansas Jewry," in *The Quiet Voices: Southern Rabbis and Civil Rights*, ed. Mark K. Bauman and Berkley Kalin (Tuscaloosa: University of Alabama Press, 1997), 95–120.

Chapter 4

1. Martin I. Hinchin, *Fourscore and Eleven: A History of the Jews of Rapides Parish, 1828–1919* (Alexandria, LA: privately published, 1984); "Rapides Parish Timeline," LaGenWeb, accessed January 26, 2016, http://rapidesgenealogy.org/.

2. "The History of Alexandria, Louisiana," Alexandria–Louisiana.com, accessed January 22, 2016, http://www.alexandria-louisiana.com/alexandria-louisiana-history.htm; "Alexandria History," City of Alexandria, accessed January 26, 2016, https://www.cityofalexandriala.com/history.

3. Information from this section is derived from *The Encyclopedia of Southern Jewish Communities* "Alexandria, Louisiana," Goldring/Woldenberg *Institute of Southern Jewish Life (ISJL)*, accessed January 26, 2016, http://www.isjl.org/louisiana-alexandria-encyclopedia.html, among other sources; "Congregations–Alexandria, Louisiana," ISJL, accessed January 26, 2016, http://www.isjl.org/louisiana-alexandria-congregations-encyclopedia.html; "History," Congregation Gemiluth Chassodim; The Jewish Temple of Alexandria, Louisiana, accessed January 26, 2016, http://jewishtemple.org/history.html. Benjamin's family had also been involved in the Reformed Society of Israelites, and he, too, worked as an attorney in New Orleans. See Gary Phillip Zola, *Isaac Harby of Charleston, 1788–1828* (Tuscaloosa: University of Alabama Press, 1994).

4. Elliott Ashkenazi, *The Business of Jews in Louisiana, 1840–1875* (Tuscaloosa: University of Alabama Press, 1988), 134.

5. "Alexandria, Louisiana," *ISJL*.

6. Between 1873 and 1900, seven rabbis served the congregation: Marx Klein, L. Meyer, Joseph H. M. Chumaceiro, S. Saft, I. Heineberg, J. Schreiber, Alexander Rosenspitz, and Jacob S. Raisin. "History"; "Alexandria, Louisiana," *The Jewish Encyclopedia*, accessed July 15, 2010, http://www.jewishencyclopedia.com/view.jsp?artid=1173&letter =A&search=alexandria Louisiana. Chumaceiro had previously filled a New Orleans pulpit as Raisin had done in Charleston, SC.

7. See sources in notes 2 and 3 (chapter 4). Lee Shai Weissbach, "East European Immigrants and the Image of Jews in the Small-Town South," *American Jewish History* 85:3, (1997): 231–62; Scott Marler, "Merchants in the Transition to a New South: Central Louisiana, 1840–1880," *Louisiana History* 42:2 (spring 2001): 165–92.

8. Fairclough, *Race and Democracy: The Civil Rights Struggle in Louisiana, 1915–1972* (Athens: University of Georgia Press, 1999). Adam Fairclough email to author, June 24, 2009.

9. Judith Rollins, *All Is Never Said: The Narrative of Odette Harper Hines* (Philadelphia: Temple University Press, 1995), 165–66.

10. Ibid., 202. This comment was also applicable to the Jewish-owned businesses.

11. "Negroes Sing at Jail in Gadsden," *New York Times*, August 5, 1963, 20.

12. For this section, see also Greta de Jong, *A Different Day: African American Struggles for Justice in Rural Louisiana, 1900–1970* (Chapel Hill: The University of North Carolina Press, 2002).

13. Much of Hinchin's biographical information comes from his correspondence with the author, April 23, 2010.

14. Hinchin may refer to the ruling of the Court in *Shelley v. Kraemer* (1948) that declared real estate restrictive covenants unconstitutional. In February 1948 the Civil Rights Commission concluded that blacks were being treated as second-class citizens. In response to President Harry S. Truman's Ten Point Program, the Federal Fair Employment Practices Act was proposed and legislation was brought before Congress that would protect the right to vote, do away with poll taxes, and take strong action to prevent lynching. However, Republicans sided with Southern Democrats to block most of these reforms. Simultaneously, the NAACP's Thurgood Marshall and other attorneys argued several cases before the Supreme Court that resulted, among other things, in declaring unconstitutional segregation in interstate transportation. "*Shelley v. Kraemer*, 334 U.S. 1 (1948)," Justia: US Supreme Court, accessed January 26, 2016, https://supreme.justia .com/cases/federal/us/334/1/case.html.

15. As is apparent at the end of the interview, this also represented Hinchin's view.

16. Temple B'nai Israel in Albany was incorporation in early 1854. Congregation Gemiluth Chassodim was founded five years later. Edmund A. Landau, "The Jew in Albany," Thronateeska chapter, Daughters of the American Revolution, *History and Reminiscences of Dougherty County, Georgia* (Albany, GA: privately printed, 1924); Martin Hinchin, *Fourscore and Eleven: A History of the Jews of Rapides Parish, 1828–1919* (Alexandria, LA: privately printed, 1984).

17. The Albany Movement, begun in the fall of 1961 and ended in the summer of 1962, was the first mass movement in the modern civil rights era to have as its goal the desegregation of an entire community. It resulted in the jailing of more than one thousand African Americans in Albany and surrounding rural counties. Martin Luther King Jr. was drawn into the movement in December 1961. Hundreds of black protesters, King

included, were arrested in one week, but eight months later King left Albany admitting that he had failed to accomplish the movement's goals. When told as a chapter in the history of the national civil rights movement, Albany was important because of King's involvement and because of the lessons he learned that he applied in Birmingham. Out of Albany's failure came Birmingham's success. Lee Formwalt, "Albany Movement," December 12, 2015, *The New Georgia Encyclopedia*, accessed January 26, 2016, http://www .georgiaencyclopedia.org/articles/history-archaeology/albany-movement; "Albany Movement," Stanford University, accessed January 26, 2016, http://kingencyclopedia.stanford .edu/encyclopedia/encyclopedia/enc_albany_movement/.

18. Gillis William Long, a member of Louisiana's "Long Dynasty," served as congressman for the Alexandria-based Eighth District between 1963 and 1965 and from 1973 until his death in 1984. In 1965 he accepted the position of assistant secretary of the Office of Economic Opportunity and thus became a key part of President Lyndon Johnson's "War on Poverty." The committee that Hinchin refers to is likely an outgrowth of Johnson's initiative.

19. During the summer of 1961, one group of St. Louis–based Freedom Riders ended their journey in Shreveport, 113 miles northwest of Alexandria.

20. On June 5, 1966, University of Mississippi graduate James Meredith, accompanied by a few supporters, began a march from Memphis, Tennessee, to Jackson, Mississippi, designed to encourage black voter registration. The following day Meredith was shot and wounded in Hernando, Mississippi. The next day leaders of SNCC, the Southern Christian Leadership Conference, and the CRE called upon all freedom-loving people in the country to join them in Hernando. On June 22, 1966, the marchers arrived in Philadelphia, Mississippi, where they conducted a memorial service for civil rights martyrs James Chaney, Andrew Goodman, and Michael Schwerner. Violence broke out during which African American marchers were beaten and one local white man was shot. For the next two weeks, from two hundred to two thousand people marched, reaching Jackson on June 26, four days after this interview was conducted in Toronto. Fifteen thousand people joined together in Jackson to celebrate the completion of the march and affirm the right and the importance of the ballot. Aram Goudsouzian, *Down to the Crossroads: Civil Rights, Black Power, and the Meredith March against Fear* (New York: Farrar, Straus & Giroux, 2014); Charles W. Eagles, *The Price of Defiance: James Meredith and the Integration of Ole Miss* (Chapel Hill: University of North Carolina, 2009).

21. On November 14, 1960, three black first graders enrolled in a whites-only elementary school, McDonough 19, in New Orleans. At the same time six-year-old Ruby Bridges arrived at all-white William Frantz Elementary School, escorted by US Marshals. Token integration came to Alexandria in September 1964, at the urging of leaders of CORE.

22. Founded in New York in 1843, the B'nai B'rith served as a social organization that welcomed Jews of every persuasion (Reform, Orthodox, and nonreligious). It filled another important need by providing life insurance. In 1913 it created the Anti-Defamation League, a Jewish defense agency to combat anti-Semitism. The Central Conference of American Rabbis (CCAR), founded in 1889 by Rabbi Isaac Mayer Wise, is the professional organization for Reform rabbis. The 1954 convention of the CCAR hailed the *Brown* decision "as a profound victory of our prophetic tradition and as an eloquent expression of the faith of all Americans in the basic justice of our democratic system" and called upon "our colleagues and the congregations they serve to assist in the swift and harmonious implementation of this decision which reaffirms America's position as leader in the free world." In 1961 the conference praised the Freedom Riders, who have "sub-

jected themselves to discomfort and danger in the name of a great ethical principle." It reaffirmed this position in 1965 with a resolution "supporting volunteer civil rights workers" in the South and asking "that their safety be ensured by law enforcement authorities, and that if necessary by Federal intervention when local enforcement has broken down." *Central Conference of American Rabbis Yearbook* (New York: CCAR, (1954) LXIV, 106; (1961) LXXI, 66; (1965) LXXV, 65).

23. The CCAR plenum affirmed its "moral distress concerning the war in Vietnam and a will for a cessation of the conflict as expressed in the resolution ... adopted in November by the Biennial Convention of the Union of American Hebrew Congregations." *CCAR Yearbook* (New York: CCAR, 1966), LXXVI, 52–53.

Chapter 5

Allen Krause did not compile his introductions to this interview or that of Rabbi Milton L. Grafman before his untimely death. Yet the backgrounds for Atlanta and Birmingham, Rothschild and Grafman have been sufficiently documented in works noted in my subsequent citations. Therefore I did not deem it necessary to add the material here.

1. For Rothschild, see Janice Rothschild Blumberg, "Jacob M. Rothschild: His Legacy Twenty Years After," in *Quiet Voices*, ed. Bauman and Kalin, 261–85; Blumberg, *One Voice: Rabbi Jacob M. Rothschild and the Troubled South* (Macon, GA: Mercer University Press, 1985); Melissa Fay Greene, *The Temple Bombing* (New York: Addison-Wesley, 1996); Clive Webb, *Fight Against Fear* (Athens: University of Georgia Press, 2001); on the Temple see Blumberg, *As But a Day to One Hundred and Twenty, 1867–1987* (Atlanta: Hebrew Benevolent Congregation, 1987).

2. Harold Martin, *Ralph McGill: Reporter* (Boston: Little Brown, 1973); John T. Kneebone, *Southern Liberal Journalists and the Issue of Race, 1920–1944* (Chapel Hill: University of North Carolina Press, 1985).

3. In his interview, Rothschild discounts the integrated services and other events held at the Temple, including meals, a highly unusual and charged practice even in Atlanta, although it did not result in a substantial increase in African American membership in his synagogue.

4. The African American institutions of higher learning in Atlanta in the 1960s were Atlanta University, Morris Brown College, Clark College, Gammon Theological Seminary, the Atlanta School of Social Work, Spelman College, Turner Theological Seminary, Phillips College, and Morehouse College. In 1929 a confederation of Morehouse and Spelman took place with Atlanta University handling post-graduate studies; Morehouse, men's undergraduate programs; and Spellman, women's undergraduate programs. Similarly, in the mid-1960s, the theological schools (Gammon, Turner, Phillips, and Morehouse) came together under the umbrella of the Interdenominational Theological Center. See Glenn Sisk, "The Negro Colleges of Atlanta," *Journal of Negro Education* 33:4 (autumn 1964), 404–8.

5. William B. Hartsfield was mayor from 1937 to 1941 and from 1942 to 1962. Louis Sullivan, "William B. Hartsfield (1890–1971)," January 6, 2016, *The New Georgia Encyclopedia*, accessed January 26, 2016, http://www.georgiaencyclopedia.org/articles/government-politics/william-b-hartsfield-1890-1971.

6. Herbert T. Jenkins was chief of police from 1947 to 1971.

7. As early as February 1954 the Atlanta Board of Education (ABE) passed a resolution to begin preparations for the *Brown v. Board of Education of Topeka* decision. On

January 1, 1958, a suit was filed in federal court (*Calhoun v. Latimer*) seeking redress in that the ABE had not yet complied with the Supreme Court's ruling that public schools must be integrated. On June 16, 1959, Judge Frank Hooper ruled that the Atlanta public schools were still segregated and ordered that the ABE had to file a desegregation plan "within a reasonable time." On December 1 of that year, the board complied by filing a token desegregation plan. After having received an extension by the court, the ABE finally permitted nine African American students to attend one of four different, all-white high schools. Token desegregation thus began on August 30, 1961. "*Calhoun v. Latimer*," 377 US. 263 (1964)," Justia: US Supreme Court, accessed January 26, 2016, https://supreme.justia.com/cases/federal/us/377/263/case.html.

8. The Sibley Commission was named for the chairperson, John Sibley.

9. The Atlanta Manifesto was first published on November 3, 1957. It consisted of a preamble followed by six paragraphs. The first paragraph declared, "Freedom of speech must at all costs be preserved"; the second insisted that "as Americans and as Christians we have an obligation to obey the law" with specific reference to the 1954 *Brown* decision; and the third affirmed that "the public school system must not be destroyed . . . in order to avoid obedience to the decree of the Supreme Court." The next three paragraphs declared that "Hatred and scorn for those of another race, or for those who hold a position different from our own, can never be justified"; "communication between responsible leaders of the races must be maintained," and the last addressed the need to turn to God for guidance in that "our difficulties cannot be solved in our own strength or in human wisdom." *Theology Today* 15:2 (July, 1958), 165–67.

10. Ahavath Achim (Rabbi Harry Epstein) was the Conservative synagogue and Shearith Israel (Rabbi Tobias Geffen), Or VeSholom (Rabbi I. Joseph Cohen), Anshe S'fard (Rabbi Nathan Katz), and Beth Jacob (Rabbi Emanuel Feldman) were the Orthodox synagogues.

11. Janice Rothschild, *As But a Day: The First Hundred Years, 1867–1967* (Atlanta: The Temple, 1967).

12. Dr. Benjamin Elijah Mays served as the president of Morehouse College from 1940 to 1967. Randal M. Jelks, *Benjamin Elijah Mays: Schoolmaster of the Movement, A Biography* (Chapel Hill: University of North Carolina Press, 2012).

13. This referred to the October 23 meeting of the Mississippi rabbis to draft a letter to Maurice Eisendrath, president of the UAHC. However, the letter was never sent, because Allan Schwartzman (Greenville) refused to sign any letter that would also bear the signature of Benjamin Schultz (Clarksdale). See P. Allen Krause, "Rabbi Benjamin Schultz and the American Jewish League against Communism: From McCarthy to Mississippi," *Southern Jewish History* 13 (October, 2010).

14. Hollowell was a legendary Atlanta attorney who litigated landmark civil rights cases in the city and across Georgia. He represented Charlene Hunter and Hamilton Holmes in their successful case to desegregate the University of Georgia. He also served as the lead attorney for *Calhoun v. Lattimer*, which led to [token] desegregation of the Atlanta's public schools. He later became the Regional Director of the Equal Employment Opportunity Commission. Maurice C. Daniel, *Saving the Soul of Georgia: Donald L. Hollowell and the Struggle for Civil Rights* (Athens: University of Georgia Press, 2013).

15. In November 1963, a coalition of nine African American organizations in Atlanta issued a report calling for an "open occupancy proclamation" from the mayor, among other things.

16. The attacks on Jewish institutions began on November 11, 1957, when an attempt

was made to bomb Temple Beth El in Charlotte, North Carolina. On February 9, 1958, Temple Emanuel in Gastonia, North Carolina, was bombed. Both Temple Beth-El in Miami and the Nashville Jewish Community Center were bombed on March 16. In late April, within a little more than twenty-four hours, Congregation Beth El in Birmingham and the Jewish Community Center in Jacksonville, Florida, experienced similar assaults. Atlanta was thus the seventh such bombing of a Jewish institution within less than a year. It was followed two days later by the bombing of Anshei Emeth synagogue in Peoria, Illinois. See Clive Webb, "Counterblast: How the Atlanta Temple Bombing Strengthened the Civil Rights Cause," *Southern Spaces* (June 22, 2009) http://www.southernspaces.org /contents/2009/webb/1a.htm.

17. Ivan Allen Jr. became mayor in 1962 and held the office for the next eight years. According to Tammy H. Galloway, he was the only southern elected official to testify before Congress in support of the public accommodations section of President John F. Kennedy's proposed civil rights bill. Galloway also observes that Allen "spearheaded a banquet of Atlanta's black and white leaders to honor King after he received the Nobel Peace Prize in 1964," Tammy H. Galloway, "Ivan Allen Jr (1911-2003)," *The New Georgia Encyclopedia*, accessed January 23, 2016, http://www.georgiaencyclopedia.org/articles /government-politics/ivan-allen-jr.

18. The individual was J. Paul Austin, president of Coca-Cola.

19. Influenced by the growing Black Power movement and discouraged by low employment, the inability to move into white neighborhoods, and police brutality, inner city residents rose up during the summer of 1965 and their rioting made Atlanta's motto, "The City Too Busy To Hate," seem like a Potemkin village. By this time the African American community had grown disenchanted with Mayor Allen, making his last few years more difficult and possibly causing him not to seek a third term. Stephen Tuck, "Civil Rights Movement," September 9, 2004, *The New Georgia Encyclopedia*, accessed March 9, 2010, http://www.georgiaencyclopedia.org/nge/Article.jsp?id=h-2716. SNCC'S Atlantic Project, headed by Bill Ware, took advantage of this discontent to push an agenda of Pan-Africanism and complete separation from the whites, even those who had worked with them on civil rights issues. This approach was even unacceptable to the national office of SNCC, which in due time would be taken over by the anti-white philosophy that it initially rejected. See Clarissa Myrick-Harris and Norman Harris, "Atlanta in the Civil Rights Movement, 1966–1970: The Quest for Black Power," Atlanta Regional Council for Higher Education, accessed March 9, 2010, http://www.atlantahighered.org/civilrights /essay_detail.asp?phase=4.

20. Located in Towson, Maryland, Goucher College was a women's college when Rothschild was interviewed, though it has subsequently gone coed. Contrary to Rothschild's implication, Goucher was never an HBCU.

21. Krause refers to behavior negatively associated with Sen. Harry F. Byrd (D-VA) that Frank equated with "Godlessness."

22. Rothschild wanted the microphone turned off at this point in the conversation so he would be off the record.

Chapter 6

New Orleans is the only city for which Allen Krause interviewed two Reform rabbis. In his original organizational scheme, the interviews of Julian Feibelman and Nathaniel Share appeared in the same chapter. This logically allowed one introduction to the city's history for both interviews. Yet the two men and their experiences and ideas were so divergent that I have chosen to separate the two while allowing the introduction to the Feibelman interview also to serve this chapter.

1. Sources for this biographical sketch include a lengthy family memoir written by Share's sister, Betty Share Banner, correspondence with Jonathan (Jonnie) Share, and the text of Rabbi Jack Bemporad's eulogy; "Brief History of Congregation Gates of Prayer," *Gates of Prayer*, accessed January 26, 2016, http://gatesofprayer.org/index.php/about-us /our-history.

2. Emily Ford and Barry Stiefel, *The Jews of New Orleans and the Mississippi Delta* (Charleston, SC: History Press, 2012), 100–101.

3. Reference is to DeLesseps Story "Chep" Morrison Sr., the mayor from April 1946 to July 1961. Voted into office to clean up the corruption of the Huey Long machine, his many reforms earned him easy reelection in 1950, 1954, and 1958. His support for a new suburban-style community for African Americans and his willingness to put money into improving infrastructure and recreational facilities in other black neighborhoods, joined with his support of hiring blacks for the New Orleans police force, earned him the disfavor of many white people. Nevertheless he was a staunch defender of segregation and was known to make derogatory statements about African Americans in private settings. When a handful of blacks were admitted to white schools in September 1960, leading to mobs throwing both racial slurs and bottles, Morrison did nothing to stop the violence. He showed the same indifference when sit-in demonstrations followed. He ended up disliked by both sides: by the blacks, who felt betrayed, and by the segregationists, who wanted him to take an active role in combating integration. After leaving office he unsuccessfully campaigned to become governor three times. See Edward F. Haas, *DeLesseps S. Morrison and the Image of Reform: New Orleans Politics, 1946–60* (Baton Rouge: Louisiana State University Press, 1974); Glen R. Conrad, "DeLesseps Morrison Story," *A Dictionary of Louisiana Biography* (New Orleans: Louisiana Historical Association, 1988), 585.

4. For additional information on Perez, see introduction to Feibelman interview.

5. Reference is to the Conservative Congregation (established 1960). This congregation subsequently changed its name to Tikvat Shalom in 1976 before moving to Metairie, Louisiana, the following year. In 1999 it unified with Chevra Thilim (1875), originally an Orthodox congregation, to form congregation Shir Chadash. See Catherine Kahn and Irwin Lachoff, *The Jews of New Orleans* (New Orleans: Acadia Press, 2005).

6. Freedom Riders left Washington, DC, on May 4, 1961, intent on reaching New Orleans. However, violence and imprisonment awaited them in Anniston, Birmingham, and Montgomery, Alabama; and their experiences in Jackson, Mississippi, prevented them from reaching Louisiana.

7. On February 18, 1965, an Alabama state trooper shot a young African American, Jimmie Lee Jackson, in a Selma cafe while he attempted to protect his mother and grandfather. Martin Luther King Jr. subsequently called for a march from Selma to Montgomery, where the demonstrators petitioned Governor George Wallace to protect blacks that were attempting to exercise the right to vote. Two weeks later a group of approximately six hundred people left Selma, answering King's call. The marchers traveled only six blocks when state troopers and members of the Dallas County Sheriff's Department brutalized them with billy clubs, tear gas, and bullwhips. In response to a national appeal by King, about 2,500 people set out from Selma two days later (March 9), but a federal judge intervened with a restraining order. Thus King led the marchers only a short

distance to the Edmund Pettus Bridge, where he held a brief prayer service prior to the group disbanding. On the same day, James Reeb, a minister from Boston, was attacked and killed in Selma. One week later the same judge issued a restraining order against the troopers and police, forbidding them to interfere with the right of the people to peacefully march. On March 20, thousands set out once again, reaching Montgomery on March 25. Consequently, on August 6, President Lyndon Johnson signed the Voting Rights Act of 1965. "Jackson, Jimmie Lee (1938-1965)," Stanford University, accessed January 26, 2016, http://kingencyclopedia.stanford.edu/encyclopedia/encyclopedia/enc_jackson_jimmie _lee_1938196/.

8. On June 5, 1966, University of Mississippi graduate James Meredith, accompanied by a few supporters, began a march from Memphis, Tennessee, to Jackson, Mississippi, designed to encourage black voter registration. The following day Meredith was shot and wounded in Hernando, Mississippi. The next day leaders of SNCC, the Southern Christian Leadership Conference, and the CRE called upon all freedom-loving people in the country to join them in Hernando. On June 22, 1966, the marchers arrived in Philadelphia, Mississippi, where they conducted a memorial service for civil rights martyrs James Chaney, Andrew Goodman, and Michael Schwerner. Violence broke out during which African American marchers were beaten and one local white man was shot. For the next two weeks, from two hundred to two thousand people marched, reaching Jackson on June 26, four days after this interview was conducted in Toronto. Fifteen thousand people joined together in Jackson to celebrate the completion of the march and affirm the right and the importance of the ballot. Aram Goudsouzian, *Down to the Crossroads: Civil Rights, Black Power, and the Meredith March against Fear* (New York: Farrar, Straus & Giroux, 2014); Charles W. Eagles, *The Price of Defiance: James Meredith and the Integration of Ole Miss* (Chapel Hill: University of North Carolina, 2009).

9. Rabbi Maurice Eisendrath served as executive secretary/president of the UAHC from 1943 until his death in 1973. He was an outspoken, dedicated champion of civil rights for African Americans. Everett Gendler, "MLK Jr. and Maurice Eisendrath," April 5, 2013, Rav.Blog, CCAR, accessed January 26, 2016, http://ravblog.ccarnet.org/2013/04 /recalling-mlk-jr-and-maurice-eisendrath-2/ (includes picture of Eisendrath holding a Torah while marching with King).

10. This incident occurred in 1963.

11. A few lines here are deleted because of repetition and not because of comments concerning other rabbis.

Chapter 7

1. Anita Shafer Goodstein, *Nashville, 1780–1860: From Frontier to City* (Gainesville: University of Florida Press, 1989); Jan Duke, "Nashville 1800–1850—Its Beginnings and Early Times," accessed July 21, 2010, http://nashville.about.com/od/historyandsites/a /NashHistXline1.htm; "Nashville History," Nashville Convention and Visitors Bureau, accessed July 21, 2010, http://www.visitmusiccity.com/visitors/nashvillehistory; "Nashville/ Davidson County Time Line," Nashville Public Library, accessed July 21, 2010, http:// www.library.nashville.org/research/res_nash_history_timeline.asp; "Nashville: Introduction," City-Data.com, accessed July 31, 2010, http://www.city-data.com/us-cities/The -South/Nashville-History.html.

2. "Population of the 90 Urban Places: 1830," US Bureau of the Census, accessed March 26, 2010, http://www.census.gov/population/www/documentation/twps0027

/tabo6.txt; "Population of the 100 Largest Urban Places: 1860," US Bureau of the Census, accessed March 26, 2010, http://www.census.gov/population/www/documentation /twps0027/tabo9.txt.

3. "The Age of Jackson," accessed July 31, 2010, City-Data.com, http://www.city-data .com/us-cities/The-South/Nashville-History.html; Larry H. Whiteaker, "Civil War Essay," *Tennessee Encyclopedia of History and Culture*, 1998, accessed August 1, 2010, http:// tennesseeencyclopedia.net/imagegallery.php?EntryID=C097; Cathy Wentz Eisenstadt, "Battle of Nashville," *Civil War Major Battle Accounts*, Ancestry.com, accessed August 1, 2010, http://freepages.genealogy.rootsweb.ancestry.com/~footprintsfromthepast/military _cw_battles.htm#NASHVILLE; "Nashville, Davidson County, Tennessee, December 15- 16, 1864," Civil War Trust, accessed January 27, 2016, http://www.civilwar.org/battlefields /nashville.html.

4. Charles B. Castner, "*A Brief History of The Louisville & Nashville Railroad*," accessed August 1, 2010, http://www.lnrr.org/history.html.

5. "Fisk University," accessed January 23, 2016, http://www.fisk.edu/about/history; "History of Vanderbilt University, accessed January 23, 2016, http://www.vanderbilt.edu /about/history/; Meharry Medical College, "Early History," accessed January 23, 2016, http://www.mmc.edu/education/som/aboutus/somhistory.html.

6. "Berry Field National Guard Base, Nashville International Airport," GlobalSecurity .org, accessed August 2, 2010, http://www.globalsecurity.org/military/facility/nashville .htm; "Development during Twentieth Century and Twenty-First Century," City-Data. com, accessed July 31, 2010, http://www.city-data.com/us-cities/The-South/Nashville -History.html; "The Story of Music City," Nashville Visitors and Convention Corp., accessed July 21, 2010, http://www.visitmusiccity.com/visitors/nashvillehistory.

7. Bobby L. Lovett, "Nashville: Civic, Literary, and Mutual Aid Associations," in *Organizing Black America: An Encyclopedia of African American Associations*, ed. Nina Mjagkij (New York: Garland Publishing, 2001), 351–52, 242–44; "Story of Music City"; Kimberly E. Nichols, "National Medical Association," in *Organizing Black America*, 468.

8. Lovett, "Nashville," 353.

9. Kasper, a white supremacist and anti-Semite, subsequently continued as a rabble-rouser in other southern locations where desegregation was imminent. He served prison terms for incitement to riot, was a suspect in the school bombing in Nashville and a number of synagogue bombings, and in 1964 ran as the presidential candidate for the National States' Rights Party. For this and the following paragraphs, see Clive Webb, *Rabble Roussers: The American Far Right in the Civil Rights Era* (Athens: University of Georgia Press, 2010); John Egerton, "Walking into History: The Beginning of School Desegregation in Nashville," in *Southern Spaces*, accessed July 21, 2010, http://www.southernspaces .org/contents/2009/egerton/1a.htm; Jerry Shattuck, "The Desegregation of Clinton High School," in *The History of Jim Crow*, accessed November 18, 2008, http://www .jimcrowhistory.org/resources/narratives/Jerry_Shattuck.htm; US Slave, "The Desegregation of Clinton, Tennessee," usslaveblogspot.com, October 17, 2011, accessed January 27, 2016, http://usslave.blogspot.com/2011/10/desegregation-of-clinton-tennessee.html; Robert S. Griffin, "The Tale of John Kasper," accessed November 18, 2008, http://www .robertsgriffin.com/TaleKasper.pdf. Although a white supremacist, Griffin's comments about Kasper appear to be accurate.

10. Egerton, "Walking into History"; E. Thomas Wood, "Nashville Now and Then: An Explosive Moment," September 7, 2007, *Nashville Post.com*, accessed November 18, 2008, http://www.nashvillepost.com/news/2007/9/7/nashville_now_and_then_an _explosive_moment.

11. In sharp contrast to Harrison Salisbury's blistering article on Birmingham, Alabama, published in the *New York Times* on April 12, 1960, his April 18 article notes the progress in race relations that had occurred very quietly in the Tennessee capital: desegregation of Vanderbilt; African Americans serving on the city council, board of education, and police force; and the integration of religious, civic, social, and professional gatherings. Salisbury's article ends on a hopeful note, giving the reader the sense that Nashville's mostly moderate population would find a way to bridge the racial gap and emerge whole without violence.

12. Bobby L. Lovett, "Nashville Student Movement (1960–1964)," *Civil Rights Movement Veterans*, accessed July 30, 2010, http://www.crmvet.org/tim/timhis60.htm #1960nsm; James Ralph, "Nashville Student Movement," in *Organizing Black America*, 354–55; Nishani Frazier, "Many Minds, One Heart: SNCC's Dream for a New America," *Journal of African American History*, 93:4 (2008), 590. Between 1961 and 1963 protesters targeted movie theaters, fair employment practices, hotels, and other areas of discrimination. The SNCC's "full-scale assault" on Jim Crow did much to destroy the system by the end of 1963. "Economic Boycotts and Protests," *Encyclopedia of African American Business* 1, ed. Jessie Carney Smith (Santa Barbara: Greenwood Press, 2006), 261–62.

13. All of the information on Nashville's Jewish history is taken from the following sources unless otherwise noted: Fedora Small Frank, *Five Families and Eight Young Men: Nashville and Her Jewry, 1850–1861* (Nashville: Tennessee Book Company, 1962); Frank, *Beginnings on Market Street: Nashville and Her Jewry, 1861–1901* (Nashville: Jewish Community of Nashville and Middle Tennessee, 1976), 104–6; *Encyclopedia of Southern Jewish Communities*, "Nashville, Tennessee," The Goldring/Woldenberg Institute of Southern Jewish Life (hereafter cited as ISJL), accessed July 21, 2010, http://www.isjl.org/tennessee -nashville-encyclopedia.html; Jean Roseman, *Shalom Nashville: A Jewish History* (Nashville: Eveready, 2010); Rob Spinney, "The Jewish Community in Nashville, 1939–1949," *Tennessee Historical Quarterly* 52 (1993): 225–41.

14. Frank, *Beginnings on Market Street*, 104.

15. The Gale Group, "Secondary Smelting and Refining of Nonferrous Metals," High Beam Business, accessed August 29, 2010, http://business.highbeam.com/industry-reports /metal/secondary-smelting-refining-of-nonferrous-metals. The lumber company became the A. M. Loveman Lumber & Box Company, Inc.

16. When the bank failed thirty years later, the Sax brothers relocated to New York.

17. E. Douglas King, *King's Nashville City Directory* (Nashville: E. Doulas King, 1870); Frank, *Beginnings on Market Street*, 154.

18. When it relocated to Harding Road, the congregation officially changed its name to "The Temple, Ohabai Sholom."

19. Frank, *Beginnings on Market Street*, 156.

20. Ibid., 88.

21. Ibid., 110, 107, 124, 121, 78–79; "Nashville, Tennessee," ISJL.

22. For this and following, see *Encyclopedia of Southern Jewish Communities* "Nashville, Tennessee," Goldring/Woldenberg Institute of Southern Jewish Life (ISJL), accessed February 3, 2016, http://www.isjl.org/tennessee-nashville-encyclopedia.html.

23. The estimated Jewish population in 1960 was 3,200. "Cities of 25,000 Inhabitants or More, April 1, 1960," 8, accessed August 31, 2010, http://www2.census.gov/prod2 /decennial/documents/41983291.pdf; Morris Fine and Milton Himmelfarb, eds., *American Jewish Year Book 1961* 62 (New York: American Jewish Committee, 1961), 60.

24. "Jewish Center Blasted," *Nashville Tennessean*, March 17, 1958, 1; "Nashville Issue Is Full Equality," *New York Times*, April 18, 1960, 1.

25. Ibid.

26. The main sources for this biographical sketch and the history of the congregation are David J. Meyer's excellent article, "Fighting Segregation, Threats, and Dynamite: Rabbi William B. Silverman's Nashville Battle," *American Jewish Archives Journal* LX: 1, 2 (2008), 99-113; "Silverman, William B.," *Who's Who in World Jewish History* (New York: Pitman Publishing Corporation, 1972), 844; Annette Levy Ratkin, "The History of The Temple Social Action/Justice Committee," in "The History of Congregation Ohabai Sholom," accessed January 27, 2016, http://www.templenashville.org/_content/6_beit_tikkum_olam/social_action_programs/The%20History%20of%20Social%20Action.pdf; Fedora S. Frank, "A Short History of Congregation Ohabai Sholom," ed Gwen Moore, The Temple: Congregation Ohabai Sholom, accessed January 27, 2016, http://www.templenashville.org/index.php?id=8.

27. Deuteronomy 16:20, one of scripture's most forceful statements on the importance of just behavior.

28. John W. Rustin served the Belmont Methodist Church from 1950 to 1959 before moving to the Broad Street Church in Kingsport, Tennessee. Rustin indicated that he made the move because the Broad Street Church is "made up of intelligent, progressive people who expect a progressive program from their minister. "Kingsport is City on Tiptoes says New Broad Street Pastor," *Kingsport Times*, July 6, 1959, 8.

29. Parmer Elementary School was located at the corner of Parmer Avenue and Leake Avenue, less than a mile from the Silverman home.

30. The Jewish New Year, one of the holiest days of the Jewish calendar and a holiday on which a large percentage of Jews attend worship services.

31. American Jewish Archives, Cincinnati, Ohio.

32. The Talmud is an encyclopedia-length compilation of rabbinic discussions and decisions compiled over almost a thousand years. In its effort to understand the commandments given in scripture, it largely shaped what became the Jewish religion.

33. After the jury returned its verdict, the prosecuting attorney in the trial in Atlanta, Tom Luck, remarked, "Possibly we went to trial too quickly, before enough evidence could be gathered. There was incredible pressure in the press, from the city, from the community, to find the guilty men and get convictions as soon as possible. We simply proceeded before we had enough evidence. I feel certain that these were the guilty parties, but we had a very weak, circumstantial case." Melissa Fay Greene, *The Temple Bombing* (Reading, MA: Perseus Publishing, 1996), 269–373.

34. The rabbis of the Conservative West End Synagogue during this era were Arthur Hertzberg (1947–1951, 1953–1957), Harold Stern (1951–1953), Jossef Kratzenstein (1957–1959), and Jerome Kestenbaum (1959–1970); the rabbi of Orthodox Congregation Sherith Israel from 1949–2002 was Zalman Posner. Lou H. Silberman taught at Vanderbilt from 1951 to 1980. In 1955 he was named Hillel Professor of Jewish Literature, and from 1970 to 1976 he served as chair of the religious studies department. Prior to coming to Nashville he served as rabbi of Temple Israel of Omaha, Nebraska, for seven years. Silberman was one of the Vanderbilt professors who submitted his resignation in 1960 when James Lawson, a graduate student in the Vanderbilt Divinity School, was expelled for participation in a sit-in. On Silberman see "Biographical Sketch: Lou H. Silberman," "A Finding Aid to the Lou H. Silberman Papers, 1934–2005, Manuscript Collection No. 103," The Jacob Rader Marcus Center of the American Jewish Archives, accessed January 27, 2016, http://collections.americanjewisharchives.org/ms/ms0103/ms0103.html.

35. Isaac Mayer Wise, considered the institution builder of American Reform Judaism, served as rabbi of Congregation Bene Jeshurun in Cincinnati from 1854 until his death in 1900.

36. This was one of the teachings attributed to the first century BCE scholar Hillel. From the Talmud, Avot 2:4.

Chapter 8

1. George Holbert Tucker, *Norfolk Highlights 1584–1881* (Norfolk, VA: Norfolk Historical Society, 1972), chapter 11.

2. US Census, accessed March 25, 2010, http://www.census.gov/population/www /documentation/twps0027/tab03.txt; Norfolk Historical Society, "Norfolk Census," accessed March 25, 2010, http://norfolkhistorical.org/links/census.html.

3. Benjamin Muse, *Virginia's Massive Resistance* (Bloomington: Indiana University Press, 1961), 186–87.

4. Antonio T. Bly, "Thunder during the Storm—School Desegregation in Norfolk, Virginia, 1957–1959: A Local History," *Journal of Negro Education* (spring 1998): 106–14.

5. See interview and note 31 (chapter 8).

6. Ernest Q. Campbell, *When a City Closes Its Schools* (Chapel Hill: University of North Carolina Press, 1960), 52, 140.

7. Navy children comprised 40 percent of those in the public schools. "What 'Massive Resistance' Costs Norfolk and Its Businessmen: How Shutdown of Schools Hits an Energetic City," *Business Week*, October 4, 1958, 32; Richard M. Mansfield, "Schools Sought for Navy," Norfolk *Virginian-Pilot*, January 22, 1959, 1.

8. Luther J. Carter, "School Crisis Bared Before Nation on TV," *Virginian-Pilot*, January 22, 1959, 5; Carter, "The 'Lost Class' and Its Dilemma," Ibid., January 23, 1959, 6.

9. Tucker, *Norfolk Highlights*, chapter 9.

10. Lee Shai Weissbach, "East European Immigrants and the Image of Jews in the Small-Town South." *American Jewish History* 85:3 (1997): 257–78; Tucker, *Norfolk Highlights*, chapter 50. Tucker apparently relied on the writings of Stern for much of his information.

11. *American Jewish Yearbook* 61 (New York: American Jewish Committee and Jewish Publication Society, 1966), 8. In his interview, Stern estimates that his congregation numbered approximately four hundred families or one thousand people and that the total Jewish population came to ten thousand; the latter figure differs from the AJY estimate.

12. Murray Friedman, *What Went Wrong?: The Creation and Collapse of the Black-Jewish Alliance* (New York: Free Press, 1994).

13. Malcolm Stern, "The Year They Closed the Schools: The Norfolk Story," in *The Quiet Voices: Southern Rabbis and Black Civil Rights, 1880s to 1990s*, ed. Mark K. Bauman and Berkley Kalin (Tuscaloosa: University of Alabama Press, 1997), 288, 293–94; Murray Friedman, "Virginia Jewry in the School Crisis: Anti-Semitism and Desegregation," in *Jews in the South*, ed. Leonard Dinnerstein and Mary Dale Palsson (Baton Rouge: Louisiana State University Press, 1973), 344–45.

14. Stern, "Year They Closed the Schools," 288.

15. Sources for this biographical sketch include the introduction to the Malcolm H. Stern Letters, Manuscript Collection 626, Jacob Rader Marcus Center of the American Jewish Archives (AJA), http://www.americanjewisharchives.org/aja/FindingAids/stern .htm, accessed March 24, 2010; Wolfgang Saxon, "Malcolm Stern, 78, Dies: Historian of

Judaism in the U.S.," *New York Times*, January 7, 1994, accessed March 24, 2010, http://www.nytimes.com/1994/01/07/obituaries/rabbi-malcolm-stern-78-dies-historian-of-judaism-in-the-us.html?pagewanted=1; Stern, "Year They Closed the Schools," 286–87.

16. James J. Kilpatrick, editor of the *Richmond (VA) News Leader*, coined the phrase "massive resistance." In 1964 he began a conservative column syndicated in approximately five hundred newspapers. The phrase is a throwback to the eighteenth century controversy over state's rights. See Virginius Dabney, *Virginia: The New Dominion* (Charlottesville: University Press of Virginia, 1971), 536; Richard Goldstein, "James J. Kirkpatrick: Conservative Voice in Print and on TV, Dies at 89," *New York Times*, August 16, 2010, accessed January 27, 2016, http://www.nytimes.com/2010/08/17/us/17kilpatrick.html?_r=1.

17. In addition, Norfolk lacked the large black population found in most other cities in Virginia and throughout the South.

18. The evening *Norfolk (VA) Ledger-Star* was absorbed by the morning *Virginian Pilot* in August 1995.

19. Lenoir Chambers won the award in 1960. See Alexander S. Leidholdt, *Standing Before the Shouting Mob: Lenoir Chambers and Virginia's Massive Resistance to Public School Integration* (Tuscaloosa: University of Alabama Press, 1997).

20. On Moses Myers (1753–1835), see Melvin I. Urofsky, *Commonwealth and Community: The Jewish Experience in Virginia* (Richmond: Virginia Historical Society, 1997).

21. Morton J. Gaba, Executive Director of the Jewish Community Council of Norfolk, wrote immediately after the *Brown* decision that there was an "overwhelming acceptance of the Supreme Court decision by the total Jewish community" that is "at variance with the point of view of the community at large" where the majority of the "white Christian community find the . . . decision deeply objectionable." However, he adds, within the Jewish community "the matter is not regarded as an issue about which Jews need become exercised. . . . No sermons have been preached" and when the Community Relations Committee met at his request "to consider the whole problem of the Jewish stake in the implementation of the Supreme Court decision, the initial reactions were, 'What does this have to do with the Jewish community?'" He continues: "Jews find themselves in a dilemma. Should they speak up . . . and brand themselves as dissenters . . . or should they keep quiet . . . and go along with their Christian neighbors, disbelieving, but silent? The second choice is the unanimous one." With a reference almost certainly to Stern, Gaba concludes: "This may be an unkind analysis. . . . It overlooks the reservoir of good will created by one of our rabbis through his personal participation in intergroup relations." Gaba, "Segregation and a Southern Jewish Community," *Jewish Frontier* XXI, No. 10 (October, 1954): 12–15. Similarly, in an October 2, 1958, letter to Albert Vorspan, director of the Commission on Social Action of Reform Judaism, Stern wrote: "The overwhelming majority of Norfolk Jews have whole-heartedly supported in every feasible way the local attempts by the School Board and others to comply with the Supreme Court decision. They have given no support to the pronouncedly segregationist Tidewater Educational Foundation." See Malcolm Stern Papers, MS #626, Box 4, Folder 28, AJA.

22. In the late 1940s, the Martha Washington Hotel in Virginia Beach had highway billboard signs proclaiming that it had a "Christian clientele." See Malcolm Stern, "Living the Norfolk Story," first prepared as a sermon delivered at Congregation Rodef Shalom in Philadelphia on February 27, 1959. Malcolm Stern Papers, MS #626, Box 4, Folder 28, AJA.

23. Rabbi Paul Reich served Congregation Beth El from 1934 to 1967.

24. Rabbi Joseph Goldman served Temple Israel from 1954 to 1982.

25. Rabbi Israel Bornstein served B'nai Israel Congregation as assistant rabbi/cantor from 1949 to 1961 and as senior rabbi from 1961 to 1988.

26. Temple Emanuel, a Conservative synagogue founded after World War II, was served by rabbis Myron Kahn (1953); Azriel Weissman (1954–1957), Phillip Rabinowitz (1957–1962), and Philip Pincus (1962–1976).

27. In 1963 Princess Anne County merged with Virginia Beach, so that Norfolk and Newport News became part of the newly created City of Virginia Beach.

28. Rev. Moultrie Guerry, Rector of St. Paul's Episcopal Church, and Rev. Richard Martin of Grace Church. See Moultrie Guerry interview, Perry Library, Old Dominion University. When in 1954 a black family's home was firebombed after they moved into a white neighborhood, Guerry went into the area and established interracial dialogue meetings. A Study Committee on Housing emerged from this in which Stern participated. This led to Stern sending a letter on August 20, 1956, to presidential candidate, Adlai E. Stevenson, urging that "within the framework of Democratic [Party] politics there might be developed a free-enterprise credit program, with government underwriting, that would assure to would-be developers of Negro real estate such funds as would be needed to set up apartment projects and private homes for sale or rent to Negroes." Stern Papers, Box 4, Folder 28.

29. In "Living the Norfolk Story," Stern identifies the person as Dr. Samuel Proctor. Proctor served as president, however, from 1955 to 1960. Dr. John Marcus Ellison, the first African American president of Virginia Union, served in that office from 1941–1955. Stern has either mixed up Proctor for Ellison or the service took place after 1954. Given the response that would have been heightened after the *Brown* decision, the latter was most likely the case.

30. Stern was an accomplished musician. In his interview, Guerry states, "One day . . . we had the Jewish Rabbi play the organ at a communion service that we had for the ministers. He didn't participate in the communion, but he certainly made his contribution with the music." Guerry Interview.

31. All of the women who created the committee on April 17, 1945, were active in civic organizations. The council had an office and met for years at the Norfolk YWCA. In the mid- to late 1950s, however, due to pressure from the Norfolk Community Fund board, they were evicted from the YWCA. They then surreptitiously met in various homes and religious institutions, including the Norfolk Jewish Community Center. Mrs. H. M. Silverman served as president of the organization from 1955 to 1957. See the Women's Council for Interracial Cooperation Papers, MG #54, Perry Library, Old Dominion University.

32. During the colonial era, the Anglican Church, or Church of England, acted as the established church of Virginia. After the American Revolution, the church broke affiliation with the English parent body and became the Episcopal Church.

33. A *Time* magazine article dated September 24, 1956, begins, "While unmarked police cars stood inconspicuously by, more than 2,000 Negro students filed into 54 previously segregated elementary and secondary schools in Louisville, Ky. last week. They were received without protest or excitement. 'The Negro and white youngsters sat down together and started studying together, and that was that,' said one school official. Louisville's quiet achievement in integration drew admiring comment from editorial writers the country over and from President Eisenhower at his weekly press conference." Louisville was perceived of as a community that achieved school integration with much less angst than elsewhere in the South.

34. According to Guerry, the fellowship group "didn't always meet at St. Paul's. After awhile other people got up the nerve to invite us. One or two ministers got into a little trouble about it, but we could go to a black congregation or a white congregation. And it was one of the finest things we ever did." Guerry interview.

35. Judge Walter E. Hoffman. On Hoffman, see Michael Payne, "Integration and Interests: The Forgotten Role of Judge Walter Hoffman in Ending Massive Resistance in Virginia," Washington Undergraduate Law Review (spring 2014) 7 no. 3, accessed January 27, 2016, http://students.washington.edu/wulr/integration-and-interests-the-forgotten -role-of-judge-walter-hoffman-in-ending-massive-resistance-in-virginia/.

36. The service took place on June 8, 1958, at Ghent Methodist Church.

37. Hoffman served as an elder of Ghent Methodist Church.

38. Hoffman had been dealing with late night phone threats and harassment. His response to Stern's comment was "If it's any consolation, I'll be ahead of you." Stern, "Living the Norfolk Story," 5.

39. The letter was mailed in June 1958. In the newspaper articles that resulted, the mayor is quoted as saying that "state laws made the plan impracticable." On June 13, 1958, before the mayor's response became known, Stern sent a copy of his letter to other local clergy, noting that private schools have reached their capacity and cannot meet the needs of all children if the public school system is shut down; that the ability for graduating twelfth graders to gain college admission is being endangered; and that families will be broken up if children are sent to live with relatives or out of state so that they can go to a public school. He asked his colleagues "in pulpit, in social conversation, and by any other means at your disposal" to "encourage people to speak up for keeping our schools open." Stern Papers, Box 4, Folder 28.

40. A back page headline in the June 24, 1958, *Virginian-Pilot* reads, "Public Forum on Schools Proposal Sent Council." That same day the pro-segregationist *Ledger-Star* ran the headline, "Mayor Turns Down Proposal for Open Forum."

41. On June 25 articles appeared in the *Richmond News-Leader*, "Rabbi Asks Referendum on School Issue in Norfolk" and in the *New York Post*, "Rabbi Seeks to Save Norfolk Integrated Schools." On June 26 the editorial in the *Virginian-Pilot* expressed skepticism that, although Stern was a "citizen of good-will," his plan was impractical, because in such a forum the extreme partisans on both sides would likely drown out the voices of the moderates. The editorial ended by quoting Stern's prophecy of the disintegration of Norfolk's public schools.

42. Williams's ancestor Peyton Randolph (c. 1721–1775), a personal friend of George Washington, headed the Virginia conventions of 1774 and 1775 and was the first president of the Continental Congress. Stern explains that Williams was "of old Virginia stock." Stern, "Living the Norfolk Story," 10.

43. Mayor W. F. "Fred" Duckworth served from September 1950 to September 1962.

44. According to Stern, the openly segregationist Tidewater Educational Foundation was unsuccessful in getting the vast majority of teachers to teach in their newly created schools. The Presbyterian, Episcopal, and Baptist churches also rebuffed the TEF when they were asked for the use of their facilities. The parents who did not wish to send their children to a TEF school created tutoring groups. Stern, "Living the Norfolk Story," 9.

45. In the process of reaching this decision, Stern approached "a pro-integrationist assistant superintendent of schools" for his opinion and was advised that extending hospitality to these tutoring groups would prevent the growth of the TEF schools. Stern, "Living the Norfolk Story," 9.

46. For a detailed timeline see Bly, "Thunder during the Storm."

47. Only adults who had official reasons to be at the schools were allowed past the police who stood twenty-four-hour guard at each campus. Stern, "Living the Norfolk Story," 15.

48. Albert Hofheimer.

49. Ronnie King.

50. Jane Whitehill, a junior at Granby High School.

51. The advertisement reads, "Although we prefer segregation, the best interests of the community will be served by reopening the public schools." Stern "Living the Norfolk Story," 13.

52. Some would disagree with Stern's reading of Edgar Schenkman, who was the conductor of the symphony from 1948 to 1965. According to Mark Mobley,

The orchestra and its audience were not integrated until the appointment of Russell Stanger as music director in 1966. Schenkman resigned that year, retaining his Richmond Symphony post. Stanger, a young Massachusetts native, came to town insisting on open auditions. James M. Reeves was the orchestra's first black member, entering at the back of the double basses. "I had tried out under Edgar Schenkman," Reeves said. He said, "You play all right, but you don't play head and shoulders above everyone in the orchestra, so I can't justify taking a black into the orchestra." [Reeves replied,] "I play tuba, too. Can I try out on that?" He said, "Yeah! You're good on tuba, too! But I don't need but one." . . . Reeves worked his way up to principal before resigning in 1981. Today's auditions are held behind a screen, so the race and gender of an applicant are not known until the final round.

Mobley, *Virginian-Pilot*, September 8, 1994, E1.

53. Fellowship House grew out of the Philadelphia Friends' Young People's Inter-Racial Fellowship Committee on Race Relations that Marjorie Penney (1908–1983), a Baptist, had been directing since 1932. Penney opened the first Fellowship House in 1941 to provide an everyday-life setting where people of all colors and creeds could meet, cook, eat, play, pray, and study together. For the Philadelphia community, Penney and her staff created and conducted lecture series and courses that emphasized learning about and understanding differences and encouraged cooperation and inclusiveness. They also acted on the larger city, state, and national levels on such concerns as a federal anti-lynching law, anti-Semitism, integrated recreational facilities, and open housing. Fellowship House/Farm Acc. 723, Urban Archives, Samuel Paley Library, Temple University.

54. Founded in 1919 as the Commission on Interracial Cooperation, the SRC engaged Southern communities on issues of democracy and race. One of the most effective regional civil rights organizations, it promoted an end to all-white primaries in the 1940s, established state human relations councils to help desegregate southern schools in the 1950s, and founded the Voter Education Project that registered more than two million African Americans in the 1960s.

55. A voluntary association of Jewish community relations agencies, the National Jewish Community Relations Advisory Council, founded in 1944 by the Council of Jewish Federations, is the instrument through which its constituency of national and community Jewish agencies jointly determine the issues of concern, the positions they should take on them, and how they can most effectively carry out those positions.

56. The mission statements of the American Jewish Committee and the American

Jewish Congress emphasize combating anti-Semitism and other forms of bigotry and protecting human rights.

57. Stern refers to the meeting that took place on June 25, 1956.

58. Unless there was an earlier meeting, which is doubtful, Stern does not remember the date of the meeting correctly.

59. Stern later wrote: "Probably the bravest of all [southern rabbis] was Rabbi Charles Mantinband, a quiet, self-effacing individual whose fervent belief in the equality of mankind led him, as the rabbi of Hattiesburg, Mississippi, to take the presidency of that state's Council on Human Relations and a leadership role in the Southern Regional Council and to otherwise publicly proclaim his creed. Despite the understandable qualms of his congregation, the very threats on his life led them to rally to his support even though most did not agree with his views." Stern, "The Role of the Rabbi in the South" in *Turn to the South: Essays on Southern Jewry* ed. Nathan M. Kaganoff and Melvin I. Urofsky (Charlottesville: University Press of Virginia, 1979), 31.

60. Cohen's publication was called the New York *National Jewish Post* from 1945 to 1957. In 1957, it merged with another periodical and became known as the *National Jewish Post and Opinion*.

61. Temple Israel.

62. Stern wrote that Cohen had interviewed two Conservative rabbis "who had not opened their mouths on the issue of closed schools," and, on the basis of those interviews, he editorialized that "the rabbinate of Norfolk was doing nothing in the battle for integration." Stern wrote to Cohen, "At least two of Norfolk's rabbis, Dr. Paul Reich [of the Conservative Beth El synagogue] and myself have been in the forefront of interracial cooperative activities through the years." Stern Papers, Box 4, Folder 28. In "Living the Norfolk Story," 13, Stern notes that the only rabbi Cohen interviewed was Joseph Goldman, then president of the Tidewater Rabbinical Association. It is possible that Cohen's article served as an impetus for Goldman to call local rabbis, ministers, and educators together in an effort to get the public schools reopened. The widely circulated statement that resulted from this meeting, written largely by Stern, warned parents that the teachers' salaries would end in June, and that subsequently they would probably seek jobs elsewhere. In addition, the statement noted that applied sciences were not being taught in the tutoring groups, which would make the students ineligible for college admission, and that local church and synagogue facilities were simply not sufficient to deal with the numbers involved.

63. "Virginia Rabbi Fights Segregation Despite Mounting Anti-Semitism," *Denver (CO) Intermountain Jewish News*, October 10, 1958.

64. This meeting took place in October or November 1958. The petition of the five members was a direct result of Stern's participation in the meeting of the city council when the Interracial Ministerial Association had the confrontation with Mayor Duckworth discussed earlier in chapter 8.

Chapter 9

1. Sources for this historical sketch of Memphis and its Jews include John E. Harkins, "Memphis," *Tennessee Encyclopedia of History and Culture*, accessed April 15, 2010, http://tennesseeencyclopedia.net/imagegallery.php?EntryID=M069; "Memphis History," accessed April 11, 2010, http://www.memphishistory.com/; "History of Memphis," Memphis Public Library & Information Center, accessed April 15, 2010, http://www

.memphislibrary.lib.tn.us/history/memphis2.htm; Selma S. Lewis, *A Biblical People in the Bible Belt: The Jewish Community of Memphis, Tennessee, 1840s–1960s* (Macon, GA: Mercer University Press, 1999); Abraham J. Karp, "Simon Tuska Becomes a Rabbi," *American Jewish Historical Quarterly* 50:2 (December 1960): 79–97; James A. Wax, "The History of the Jews of Memphis: 1860–1865," *West Tennessee Historical Society Papers* 3 (1949): 41–48; *Encyclopedia of Southern Jewish Communities*, "Memphis, Tennessee," The Goldring/Woldenberg Institute of Southern Jewish Life, (ISJL), accessed July 8, 2009, http://www.isjl.org/tennessee-memphis-encyclopedia.html; "Temple Israel, Memphis, Tennessee," ISJL, accessed July 8, 2009, http://www.isjl.org/tennessee-memphis-temple-israel-encyclopedia.html; *The Encyclopedia of Southern Jewish Communities*, "Beth Sholom, Memphis, Tennessee," ISJL, accessed July 8, 2009, http://www.isjl.org/tennessee-memphis-beth-sholom-encyclopedia.html; *The Encyclopedia of Southern Jewish Communities*, "History of the Orthodox Congregations of Memphis," ISJL, accessed July 8, 2009, http://www.isjl.org/history-of-orthodox-congregations-of-memphis.html; Cyrus Adler and Max Samfield, "Memphis," *Jewish Encyclopedia.com*, accessed April 11, 2010, http://www.jewishencyclopedia.com/view.jsp?artid=398&letter=M; Cyrus Adler and Frederick T. Haneman, "Samfield, Max," *Jewish Encyclopedia.com*, accessed April 11, 2010, http://www.jewishencyclopedia.com/view.jsp?artid=118&letter=S&Tu=SAMFIELD; Richard Gottheil and Peter Wiernik, "Jewish Spectator," *Jewish Encyclopedia.com*, accessed April 11, 2010, http://www.jewishencyclopedia.com/view.jsp?artid=296&letter=J&search= JEWISH SPECTATOR.

2. Wax argues that only a few members left and that the synagogue was founded by a group of about fifty immigrants from Eastern Europe who had not been associated with B'nai Israel. Wax, "History of the Jews."

3. Lewis, *Biblical People*, 14.

4. Wax, "History of the Jews," 56–57.

5. Ibid., 60–61. Other successful cotton brokers included A. Genzburger, S. Isaacs, L. Helman, S. Lewin and H. L. Peres (Jacob's brother).

6. Ibid., 60.

7. Ibid., 64.

8. An advertisement quoted in Lewis, *Biblical People*, 35; Alan M. Kraut, "A. E. Frankland's History of the 1873 Yellow Fever Epidemic in Memphis, Tennessee," *American Jewish Archives Journal* LIX Number: 1 & 2 (2007): 89–98.

9. Frankland, "History, Yellow Fever Epidemic, Memphis 1873" (Memphis, 1874), handwritten manuscript, Abraham E. Frankland Papers, MS 464, Jacob Rader Marcus Center of the American Jewish Archives (AJA).

10. Frankland, "History, Yellow Fever Epidemic," 19–22.

11. Cyrus Adler and Elvira N. Solis, "Menkin, Nathan D.," *Jewish Encyclopedia.com*, accessed April 16, 2010, http://www.jewishencyclopedia.com/view.jsp?artid=464& letter=M.

12. Cyrus Adler and Frederick T. Haneman, "Samfield, Max," *Jewish Encyclopedia.com*, accessed April 16, 2010, http://www.jewishencyclopedia.com/view.jsp?artid=118&letter= S&search=SAMFIELD.

13. As quoted in William E. Schmidt "Memphis's Grand Hotel," *New York Times*, October 3, 1986, http://www.nytimes.com/1986/10/05/travel/memphis-s-grand-hotel .html?&pagewanted=1.

14. In 1870 Leopold Gerstle, a Bavarian Jew who had arrived in the United States five years earlier, founded the St. Joseph Corporation of Chattanooga, Tennessee. The com-

pany was particularly known for its orange-colored chewable pain reliever. However it was not until after Plough bought St. Joseph that the signature aspirin became a staple in American households. Charles Barnette, "L. Gerstle/Bluff City, Tenn.," accessed January 24, 2016, http://www.bristol-tenn-va-bottles.com/id24.html.

15. Lewis, *Biblical People*, 92–93, 96–98; "Marcus Haase Obituary," *Journal of the American Medical Association* 11 no. 2 (February 1, 1925), at JAMA Dermatology, accessed April 18, 2010, http://archderm.ama-assn.org/cgi/reprint/11/2/NP.pdf.

16. Lewis, *Biblical People*, 182. There was one Jew, however, whose civic-mindedness resulted in a $10 fine, as noted in the *Memphis (TN) Daily Bulletin*, August 19, 1862. Jacob Greensburg committed "a nuisance by throwing eggs on a house kept by Rebecca Shell for infamous purposes." Wax, "History of the Jews," 71.

17. Lewis, *Biblical People*, 61, 106, 114, 129, 133, 138, 149.

18. Sharon D. Wright, *Race, Power and Political Emergence in Memphis* (New York: Garland, 2000), 57.

19. Ibid., 58–59.

20. Ibid., 60–65.

21. Ibid., 65–71; Lewis, *Biblical People*, 185–91; "Teaching with Documents: Court Documents Related to Martin Luther King Jr. and Memphis Sanitation Workers," National Archies and Records Center, accessed January 24, 2016, http://www.archives.gov/education/lessons/memphis-v-mlk/; "Memphis Sanitation Workers Strike (1968)," accessed January 24, 2016, http://kingencyclopedia.stanford.edu/encyclopedia/encyclopedia/enc_memphis_sanitation_workers_strike_1968/.

22. Lewis, *Biblical People*, 88, 109, 133–34, 138, 143, 150, 180, 187, 189; "Memphis, Tennessee," accessed April 22, 2010, http://www.isjl.org/history/archive/tn/memphis.html.

23. Joan Beifuss, "Profile: Rabbi James Wax," *Memphis Magazine*, February 1981, 39.

24. James A. Wax, "Social Justice," address to the National Federation of Temple Youth, Hebrew Union College, Cincinnati, OH, March 2, 1946; Wax Collection, Box 4, Folder 1. Scrapbook 4, Memphis Shelby County Public Library & Information Center, Memphis, Tennessee; *Memphis (TN) Commercial Appeal*, April 2, 1954.

25. This account of Wax is based on Patricia M. LaPointe, "The Prophetic Voice: Rabbi James A. Wax" in *The Quiet Voices: Southern Rabbis and Black Civil Rights, 1880s to 1990s*, ed. Mark K. Bauman and Berkley Kalin (Tuscaloosa: University of Alabama Press, 1997), 152–67; Beifuss, "Profile." Temple Israel's Rabbi Micah Greenstein and its chief archivist, Margie Kerstine, assisted by Harriet Stern, provided additional information.

26. At the time 111 white and thirty-five black clergy comprised the MMA membership. H. Scott Prosterman, "Rabbi James Wax: A Forgotten Hero," accessed July 2, 2010, http://www.g21.net/daily051305.htm; Prosterman, "Fulfilling the Dream: Completing the Undone Work of Martin Luther King, Jr.," April 4, 2011, KOS Media, accessed January 24, 2016, http://www.dailykos.com/story/2011/04/04/963345/-Fulfilling-the-Dream-Completing-the-Undone-Work-of-Martin-Luther-King-Jr.

27. *Joplin News Herald*, February 1, 1968, 6; *Kokomo (IN) Tribune*, February 4, 1968, 41.

28. As president of the MMA, Wax mediated between the city and American Federation of State, County, and Municipal Employees (AFSCME) that sought to represent the sanitation workers. Because the city refused to recognize the union, all communications were directed through Wax even when both parties were present. Wax forced four key issues: recognition of the union with a contract, a check-off dues system, a grievance procedure, and higher wages. Prosterman, "Rabbi James Wax."

29. One of the clergy present, the Rev. Brooks Ramsey, past president of the MMA,

called Wax's statement "one of the most powerful statements of justice and equality of our time." Prosterman, "Rabbi James Wax."

30. Dr. Rosalyn Nichols (coordinator of the Rev. Henry Starks Dinner, Memphis Theological Seminary) telephone interview with editor, July 8, 2015. On the strike and the roles of these clergy in it, see Michael K. Honey, *Going Down Jericho Road: The Memphis Strike, Martin Luther King's Last Campaign* (New York: W. W. Norton Company, 2007). For a famous picture of the confrontation between Wax and Loeb published in the *Memphis Commercial Appeal*, see Bauman and Kalin, eds., *Quiet Voices*, 164. Starks is the tall minister standing immediately behind Wax.

31. Although Loeb had intermarried and joined the Episcopal Church, he had been a member of Wax's synagogue.

32. Clive Webb, *Fight against Fear: Southern Jews and Black Civil Rights* (Athens: University of Georgia Press, 2001).

33. The Freedom Riders that came to Memphis left Newark, New Jersey, on their way to Little Rock on June 13, 1961.

34. The Memphis Committee on Community Relations (MCCR) was established in January 1959 to avoid violence and demonstrations while promoting equality through quiet diplomacy. Wax served on the organization's first board along with leading clergy and the local newspaper editors. During Wax's presidency, the Memphis Ministerial Association created a Race Relations Committee to work with the MCCR. Selma Lewis, "Diversity and Unity: 1968–1988," in "Our History," Metropolitan Inter-Faith Association, accessed January 27, 2016, http://www.mifa.org/diversificationandunity. See also Lewis, *Biblical People*.

35. During the 1960s Hollis Price served as president. LeMoyne traces its roots to before the Civil War.

36. Brothers Isaac and Jacob Goldsmith founded the store in 1870. The Federated Department Store chain purchased what were then four stores in 1959. See Kenneth T. Jackson, "Memphis Tennessee: The Rise and Fall of Main Street," in *American Places: Encounters with History A Celebration of Sheldon Meyer*, ed. William E. Leuchtenburg (New York: Oxford University Press, 2002), 174–75.

37. Seven Owen College students conducted the first sit-in on March 18, 1960. In 1968 Owen merged with LeMoyne to form LeMoyne-Owen College. Lemoyne Owen College, "History," accessed January 28, 2016, http://www.loc.edu/about-loc/history.asp; Perre Maness, "LeMoyne Owen College," *Tennessee Encyclopedia of History and Culture*, accessed January 28, 2016, http://tennesseeencyclopedia.net/entry.php?rec=778.

38. Becker came to Congregation Beth Sholom in 1959. On the synagogue's website he is referred to as "our beloved Rabbi Arie Becker." "Our History" Beth Shalom Synagogue of Memphis, accessed January 24, 2016, http://www.bsholom.org. Along with eighteen other rabbis, Becker flew to Birmingham on May 7, 1963, from the Rabbinical Assembly conference in New York and participated in demonstrations. Lewis, *Biblical People*, 191; Harriet Stern, "A Southern Rabbi in Martin Luther King's Court," *Southern Jewish Heritage* (winter 1995): 3–4, 7, 9.

39. Six years after *Brown v. Board of Education of Topeka* not a single African American child was enrolled in a white school in Memphis. However, the Memphis Board of Education, anticipating the circuit court's ruling, quietly enrolled thirteen black children in previously all-white schools in September 1961. As a result of the pressure of business people and practical politicians, even Mayor Loeb quietly acquiesced. The *Memphis (TN) Commercial-Appeal* editor Frank Ahlgren, by no means a liberal, agreed to keep the news

out of his paper, admitting that it would be a means of defusing tension. Police Commissioner Claude Armour assigned 160 officers to guard the schools and arrest "anyone who gets out of line—I don't care who it is." Roger Biles, "A Bittersweet Victory: Public School Desegregation in Memphis," *Journal of Negro Education* 55:4 (autumn, 1986), 474–75.

40. Lucius E. Burch Jr. was a litigator, amateur pilot, environmentalist, philanthropist, and key player in state and city politics. Shirley Caldwell-Patterson et al., *Lucius: Writings of Lucius Burch* (Brentwood, TN: Cold Tree Press, 2003); J. Morgan Kousser, *Colorblind Injustice: Minority Voting Rights and the Undoing of the Second Reconstruction* (Chapel Hill: University of North Carolina Press, 1999).

41. Selma Lewis's list of the Initial Board of Directors of the Metropolitan Inter-Faith Association contains at least two white clergy, Merlin Kearney and Msgr. Joseph Leppert. Possibly they were added to the board at a later time or Wax's memory was inaccurate. Lewis, "Diversity and Unity."

42. In "The Other South," the author wrote, "Police Commissioner Claude Armour of Memphis, a city with an excellent integration record, puts it this way: 'I had to face the decision whether we were to have fear, strife and bloodshed, or whether we were to enforce the law. I decided we would enforce the law and have peace, and that's what we have done.'" *Time*, May 7, 1965.

43. Rabbi Maurice Eisendrath served as executive secretary/president of the UAHC from 1943 until his death in 1973. He was an outspoken, dedicated champion of civil rights for African Americans. Everett Gendler, "MLK Jr. and Maurice Eisendrath," April 5, 2013, Rav.Blog, CCAR, accessed January 26, 2016, http://ravblog.ccarnet.org/2013/04/recalling-mlk-jr-and-maurice-eisendrath-2/ (includes picture of Eisendrath holding a Torah while marching with King).

44. Krause refers to behavior negatively associated with Sen. Harry F. Byrd (D-VA) that Frank equated with "Godlessness."

45. Isaiah 1:18.

46. Benjamin Schultz, a fervid anticommunist, defended the South because he believed liberals were unable to poison the minds of southerners. Although his comments were also racist, he was more concerned about the communist threat than with segregation and black rights. Indeed, when the city of Clarksdale held a memorial service following the death of Martin Luther King Jr., Schultz was given the honor of providing the eulogy, which contained many favorable comments about King and his cause. P. Allen Krause, "Rabbi Benjamin Schultz and the American Jewish League against Communism: From McCarthy to Mississippi," *Southern Jewish History* 13 (2010): 153–213; James Silver, *Mississippi: The Closed Society* (Jackson: University Press of Mississippi, 1964).

Chapter 10

Allen Krause did not compile his introductions to this interview or that of Rabbi Jacob Rothschild before his untimely death. Because the backgrounds of both cases have been sufficiently documented in works noted in my citations, I did not deem it necessary to add the material here.

1. On Grafman, see Terry Barr, "Rabbi Grafman and Birmingham's Civil Rights Era," in *The Quiet Voices: Southern Rabbis and Black Civil Rights, 1880s to 1990s*, ed. Mark Bauman and Berkley Kalin (Tuscaloosa: University Alabama Press, 1997): 168–89; S. Jonathan Bass, *Blessed Are the Peacemakers: Martin Luther King, Jr., Eight White*

Religious Leaders, and Letters from the Birmingham Jail (Baton Rouge: Louisiana State University Press, 2001); Clive Webb, *Fight against Fear* (Athens: University of Georgia Press, 2001); Michael J. Klarman, "How *Brown* Changed Race Relations: The Backlash Thesis," *Journal of American History* 81 (1994): 81–118; Klarman, *Brown versus Board of Education and the Civil Rights Movement* (New York: Oxford University Press, 2007).

2. The rabbinic seminary students are assigned to serve as student rabbis in small communities on the High Holy Days as a common practice.

3. The umbrella organization for North American Reform synagogues.

4. In 1947, some black parents in Clarendon County, SC, unhappy with the lack of school buses for their children, brought suit in US District Court (*Levi Pearson v. County Board of Education*) asking for equal treatment for black children by the school district. Although their case was dismissed on a technicality, Judge J. Waties Waring urged the young NAACP attorney Thurgood Marshall to seek not equality of schools but rather total integration. That case (*Briggs v. Elliot*) was filed in 1950. When the Supreme Court was asked to decide *Brown v. Board of Education of Topeka*, it bundled with that case three others, including the Clarendon County one. "Pearson v. Clarendon County and Briggs v. Elliott," July 2014, South Carolina African American History Calendar, accessed January 28, 2016, http://scafricanamerican.com/honorees/pearson-v-clarendon-county-and-briggs-v-elliott/.

5. Grafman's first pulpit was in Lexington, Kentucky, where he served from 1933 to 1941. He began his year tenure at Temple Emanu-El in Birmingham on December 8, 1941.

6. In 1957, James Armstrong joined eight other black parents in filing a class action lawsuit against the Birmingham Board of Education to desegregate the public schools. *Armstrong v. Birmingham Board of Education* moved slowly through the courts until the summer of 1963, when the US Fifth Circuit Court of Appeals ordered that Birmingham's schools be desegregated. The process began that fall when Armstrong enrolled his two sons in Graymont Elementary School, but Alabama Governor George Wallace tried to close the schools and issued an executive order prohibiting their integration. Angry white parents protested, and the Ku Klux Klan bombed the home of NAACP attorney Arthur Shores as well as the 16th Street Baptist Church, killing four young girls. "*Dwight Armstrong . . . v. the Board of Education of the City of Birmingham, Jefferson County, Alabama, et. al appellees*, 333 F.2d 47 (5th Cir. 1964)" Justia: US Law, accessed January 28, 2016, http://law.justia.com/cases/federal/appellate-courts/F2/333/47/14504/.

7. In 1964 urban riots/insurrections took place in New York (Harlem, Bedford-Stuyvesant, and Rochester), New Jersey (Jersey City, Patterson, and Elizabeth), Chicago, and Philadelphia. In the summer of 1965 the Watts district in Los Angeles erupted, and in 1966 Watts, Chicago, Cleveland, and Omaha all experienced violence in their ghetto areas.

8. The Sisters of Charity of Nazareth ran Holy Family Hospital, built in 1946. The George W. Hubbard Hospital, constructed across the street from Meharry Medical School and established to treat African Americans, had been in existence since 1910. In 1994 Hubbard merged with Nashville's Metro General Hospital. See Hulda M. Lyttle, "A School for Negro Nurses," *The American Journal of Nursing* 39, 2 (February, 1939): 133–38; David Hefner, "Breathing New Life into Meharry," July 19, 2001, *Diverse Issues in Higher Education*, accessed August 19, 2010, http://diverseeducation.com/article/1521/.

9. The Parisian Dry Goods and Millinery Company, founded in 1877, was acquired from the original owners in the 1920s by Carl Hess, a German immigrant. The store barely survived the Great Depression, but Carl's son, Emil, applied his Wharton MBA to its

management in the 1950s and reinvigorated it into one of the premier department stores in Alabama. Hess, who had a reputation as a philanthropist and a civic-minded member of the community, was part of the group that was working to improve the plight of the city's African American population, which was derailed when Martin Luther King Jr. and Fred Shuttlesworth organized the sit-ins and boycotts. After this difficult period, Hess and his partner decided to open a second store in the suburbs to serve a different clientele. Expansion continued during the 1960s and 1970s until, by 1983, the company had stores throughout Alabama. In 1998 the chain was bought out by Saks, which then sold it in 2006 to Belk, Inc. At that date, it included thirty-eight stores situated from Detroit, Michigan, to Jacksonville, Florida. Kathy Campbell Bowers, "Parisian Department Stores," *Encyclopedia of Alabama*, accessed January 28, 2016, http://www.encyclopediaofalabama .org/article/h-1779?printable=true.

10. The so-called "Big Mules," whom Diane McWhorter characterized as "the local directors of the iron and steel industry and related businesses" and as the city's "elite industrialists, bankers, and attorneys," held the real power in Birmingham. McWhorter, *Carry Me Home: Birmingham, Alabama, The Climactic Battle of the Civil Rights Revolution* (New York: Simon and Schuster, 2002), 167–68.

11. This is the group that set out from Washington, DC, on May 4, 1961, arriving in Birmingham about 4:30 P.M. on Mother's Day, Sunday, May 14. The Freedom Riders on the Greyhound bus were taken to an Anniston hospital after being beaten by the mob. That night about 2 a.m. the Rev. Fred Shuttlesworth sent a small caravan of cars to rescue those in the hospital. They were brought to Birmingham where they were housed in African American homes. Meanwhile Shuttlesworth cared for those who were beaten after the Trailways bus arrived in Birmingham. See McWhorter, *Carry Me Home*, 155–64; Andrew M. Manis, *A Fire You Can't Put Out: The Civil Rights Life of Birmingham's Reverend Fred Shuttlesworth* (Tuscaloosa: University of Alabama Press, 1999), 263–67.

12. The Greyhound bus terminal was across the street from city hall. The Trailways station was four blocks away.

13. The Monday morning after the attack on the Freedom Riders, the *Birmingham (AL) Post-Herald*'s coverage focused on the fact that a *Post-Herald* photographer, Tommy Langston, had been beaten by the mob, asking "Where Were the Police?" The afternoon *Birmingham (AL) News* repeated the same headline over an editorial that inferred that "Bull" Connor was responsible for the city's bad press: "We fell, this city of Birmingham, into the trap, like a stupid beast falls into a pit in the jungle." McWhorter, *Carry Me Home*, 203–15. Given the chronology, it appears that Grafman's calls to Wright and Murray took place on Sunday, May 21, one week after the attack.

14. David Cady Wright was rector of the prestigious St. Mary's on the Highlands Episcopal Church. Wright went with five other Birminghamians including lawyer Mayer Newfield, son of the late Rabbi Morris Newfield, Grafman's predecessor, to meet with Connor on January 9, 1962, carrying a petition asking that the city parks be reopened. The group was treated so rudely by Connor that Diane McWhorter wrote, "The long adolescence of the [moderate white] power structure . . . had come to an end in a single hour on January 9, 1962." *Carry Me Home*, 258.

15. Murray was bishop suffragan of Alabama from 1953 to 1959. He then served as bishop coadjutor of Alabama from 1959 to 1969 and became Alabama's bishop in 1970. The bishop coadjutor was the elected and ordained bishop who was to succeed the sitting diocesan bishop after his retirement or resignation. The diocesan bishop stood as the primary bishop of the diocese, meaning that all other bishops in the diocese were respon-

sible to him. Mary Frances Schjonberg, "Two Retired Bishops Die: Services Planned for Bennett J. Sims and George M. Murray," July 18, 2006, accessed January 28, 2016, http://archive.episcopalchurch.org/3577_76773_ENG_HTM.htm.

16. In 1955 the forty-one-year-old Durick became the youngest bishop in the United States when he was appointed the auxiliary bishop in the Mobile-Birmingham diocese. In December 1963 he was appointed bishop coadjutor of the Tennessee diocese, where he introduced Project Equality, an ecumenical program designed to gain equal employment opportunities for black Tennesseans. Six years later when he was elevated to the position of bishop of the diocese, he initiated a program seeking full human dignity for all, regardless of race, and became an outspoken opponent of the Vietnam War and of capital punishment. Wolfgang Saxon, "Bishop Joseph Durick, 79, Civil Rights Advocate," *New York Times*, June 28, 1944, accessed January 28, 2016, http://www.nytimes.com/1994/06/28/obituaries/bishop-joseph-durick-79-civil-rights-advocate.html.

17. Edward Vandiver Ramage became pastor of the First Presbyterian Church of Birmingham in 1946. On Easter Sunday 1961, after two black women walked down the aisle and sat in the front row, Ramage greeted them at the end of the service and invited them to return. Death threats and acts of intimidation followed, but, even after he was branded a "communist" by members of his flock, Ramage remained. It was thus a great disappointment to the pastor, much as it was to Grafman and the other clergy, when he was classified as an obstruction to integration as a result of King's *Letter from Birmingham Jail* in 1963. Bass, *Blessed Are the Peacemakers*.

18. Widely known for his courageous attack on segregation, Ralph McGill won a Pulitzer Prize in 1959 for editorial writing. The Pulitzer committee specifically cited his article on the bombings of the Temple in Atlanta and Birmingham's 16th Street Baptist Church. He served as editor-in-chief of the *Atlanta Constitution* from 1942 until 1960, when he became its publisher. Harold Martin, *Ralph McGill, Reporter* (Boston: Little, Brown, 1973).

19. A *New York Times* article published the day after the meeting indicates that a group of white ministers met and pledged themselves to "make efforts to re-establish better communications between the races in Birmingham." These clergy "issued a statement urging that the Greater Birmingham Ministers Association appoint a committee to cooperate with other groups" to facilitate this process. The group also asked that all churches in the city declare next Sunday "a solemn day of prayer for all people," and "in an obvious reference to an outbreak of racial violence here May 14" the ministers' statement said "no one of us is free from guilt. We confess to God our father our failures to say and do that which is right." The article concludes, "Representatives of Protestant, Roman Catholic, Greek Orthodox and Jewish faiths attended the meeting." The article seems to be a report only of the small meeting described by Grafman that preceded the meeting in which the larger group approved their resolution. "Ministers in the South Ask Racial Accord," *New York Times*, May 26, 1961, 20.

20. The rabbis who served Congregation Beth El (Conservative) during these years were Abraham Mesch (1935–1962), Morton A. Wallach (1965–1967), Philip Silverstein (1967–1968), and Mark A. Elovitz (1969–1976). Apparently Cantor Akiva Ostrovsky filled in during the hiatus between Mesch's death and the hiring of Wallach. Mark H. Elovitz, *A Century of Jewish Life in Dixie: The Birmingham Experience* (University: The University of Alabama Press, 1974), 169.

21. Morton A. Wallach.

22. Abraham Mesch.

23. The rabbis who served Knesseth Israel Congregation (Orthodox) during this period were Seymour Atlas (1959 to 1962), Nahum Ben-Natan (1963–1967), and Moshe Stern (1968–1981). Atlas had served Congregation Agudath Israel in Montgomery, Alabama, from 1946 until 1956. When the Montgomery Bus Boycott began in late 1955, he picked up his maid and took her home, which resulted in very nasty things being written on his car, including "nigger-lover." As a result he was given a license to carry a gun in his car. In early 1956 he was asked to join with a Roman Catholic priest and Reverend Ralph Abernathy for an interfaith Brotherhood Week program to be broadcast on the local African American radio station. Abernathy had just been arrested for his participation in the Montgomery bus boycott, and a photograph of the three clergy, titled "Talking Tolerance," appeared in *Life* magazine alongside a story about the boycott. The board of trustees of the synagogue ordered the Rabbi to demand a "retraction" from *Life*. He was told to explain to the magazine that the Brotherhood Week had been purely coincidental, that it had nothing to do with Negroes, Reverend Abernathy, Supreme Court decisions, or with the Montgomery bus strike. Atlas refused, and, at the very next Sabbath service, offered a prayer for the success of the bus strike. Facing increasing pressure from the board, Atlas resigned and headed for a small synagogue in Bristol, Virginia. Following Atlas's resignation, Harry Golden, well-known newspaper publisher and author, wrote an article, "A Rabbi in Montgomery," in which he took the congregation to task for pushing out their rabbi because of his civil rights activism. (See *Congress Weekly* 24 [May 13, 1957]: 8–9.) A rebuttal appeared in the next addition of *Congress Weekly*, sent by Irving London, former president of the Montgomery Congregation Agudath Israel. Addressing Golden, London wrote: "I am deeply upset over this distorted account of the dismissal here in Montgomery and I cannot help but feel that you have been victimized as an innocent bystander in an attempt to build up a rabbi who rode the coattails of a 'good cause' to cover up his own failings." Golden's sarcastic answer was, "If you do not believe I have given a true picture of the general attitude towards this problem prevailing now in the Jewish communities of the deep South, then perhaps I have been living on the planet Mars these last few years." (*Congress Weekly* 24 [June 17, 1957]: 14). On Atlas and the Montgomery situation, see Mary Stanton, "At One with the Majority," *Southern Jewish History* 9 (2006): 141–99.

Almost seven years later, when Golden was working on a manuscript to be called *Mr. Kennedy and the Negroes* (New York: World Publishing Company, 1964), he asked Rabbi Charles Mantinband for an appraisal of the rabbis in the South. In a letter dated December 19, 1963, Mantinband included a comment about Atlas: "He was silent" during the bus boycott and Martin Luther King's activity, but, once he knew he was leaving "he became vocal and articulate." Charles Mantinband Papers, Amistad Research Center, Tulane University, Box 2, 1963. Atlas's memoir, *The Rabbi with the Southern Twang: True Stories from a Life of Leadership within the Orthodox Jewish Congregations of the South* (Bloomington, IN: Trafford Publishing, 2007), tends to agree with Mantinband's evaluation, which was inferred in the comments of Mr. London.

24. Theophilus Eugene "Bull" Connor was a salesman who had gained fame in Birmingham as a radio announcer for the city's minor league baseball team. He acquired the nickname "Bull" because of his ability to provide irrelevant chatter during lulls in the broadcasts. In 1937 he was elected to the three-member city commission as an opponent of labor unions and federal housing, and because of his inflexible opposition to making any concessions to the city's black population. As police commissioner he turned the local police force into his private militia, even using it as a means to finance his 1941 po-

litical campaign. He gained international notoriety for turning high powered streams of water and vicious dogs loose on demonstrators, many of whom were children. President John F. Kennedy said of him: "The Civil Rights movement should thank God for Bull Connor. He's helped it as much as Abraham Lincoln." William A. Nunnelley, *Bull Connor* (Tuscaloosa: University of Alabama Press, 1991), 4, 12, 25–28, 164.

25. On June 5, 1966, University of Mississippi graduate James Meredith, accompanied by a few supporters, began a march from Memphis, Tennessee, to Jackson, Mississippi, designed to encourage black voter registration. The following day Meredith was shot and wounded in Hernando, Mississippi. The next day leaders of SNCC, the Southern Christian Leadership Conference, and the CRE called upon all freedom-loving people in the country to join them in Hernando. On June 22, 1966, the marchers arrived in Philadelphia, Mississippi, where they conducted a memorial service for civil rights martyrs James Chaney, Andrew Goodman, and Michael Schwerner. Violence broke out during which African American marchers were beaten and one local white man was shot. For the next two weeks, from two hundred to two thousand people marched, reaching Jackson on June 26, four days after this interview was conducted in Toronto. Fifteen thousand people joined together in Jackson to celebrate the completion of the march and affirm the right and the importance of the ballot. Aram Goudsouzian, *Down to the Crossroads: Civil Rights, Black Power, and the Meredith March against Fear* (New York: Farrar, Straus & Giroux, 2014); Charles W. Eagles, *The Price of Defiance: James Meredith and the Integration of Ole Miss* (Chapel Hill: University of North Carolina Press, 2009).

On June 23, the day of this interview, Mayor Clayton Lewis dismissed the violence: "There isn't anything to it—it's just those rabble-rousers, a bunch of foreigners that came in here." Police Chief Bruce Latimer added that things would be fine once the agitators left: "We got good nigger people here. . . . We don't push our niggers." *New York Times*, June 23, 1966, 22.

26. Charles C. J. Carpenter was one of the eight clergy signing the letter to King. Consecrated as bishop of the Episcopal Church in Alabama, he was the chair of the interracial committee on community affairs. He became a controversial figure when he came out against the National Council of the Episcopal Church's advisory document, issued at the end of March 1960, which expressed "general sympathy" with the sit-in movement. Carpenter argued that the document had no official standing and was an "inadequate presentation of the sit-in situation." *Anniston (AL) Star*, June 29, 1969, 1–2; Bass, *Blessed Are the Peacemakers*.

27. Mayor Albert Boutwell took office on April 15, but the Alabama Supreme Court did not confirm his election until May 23. By this time Birmingham's businessmen, including the "Big Mules," joined the racial "moderates" like Boutwell, Police Chief Jamie Moore, Sheriff Melvin Bailey, and real estate mogul Sydney Smyer in working to reach an accommodation with King, Shuttlesworth, and the other leaders of the civil rights movement in Birmingham. "Alabama Lieutenant Governors: Albert Boutwell, Lieutenant Governor: 1959–1963," Alabama Department of Archives and History, accessed January 28, 2016, http://archives.state.al.us/conoff/Boutwell.html.

28. It was called the Jefferson County Coordinating Council of Social Forces.

29. In 1960 there were approximately 350,000 residents of the city of Birmingham, of which about 65 percent were white and 35 percent African American. US Census of Population and Housing, 1990: Population and Housing Unit Counts: United States. Washington: US Dept. of Commerce, Bureau of the Census, 1993; Table 46: Population Rank of Incorporated Places of 100,000 Population or More, 1990; Population, 1790 to

1990; Housing Units: 1940 to 1990; (C 3.223/5: 1990 CPH-2–1), accessed April 25, 2008, http://www.bplonline.org/locations/central/gov/BirminghamsPopulation1880–2000.asp.

30. On a 1963 business trip to Japan, while incoming Birmingham Chamber of Commerce president Sidney Smyer Sr. was attending the Rotary International meeting, he encountered in a newspaper a wire photo of the attack of a police German shepherd on a black teenager in Birmingham. He apparently shook his head and muttered, "something's got to give." Once a Dixiecrat and leader in the state's massive resistance movement, Smyer had already begun to convert to racial moderation in the wake of such negative publicity following Birmingham's earlier brutal reception of the Freedom Riders. He had an important power base, since his business interests in the Birmingham Realty Company made him an honorary "Big Mule." Historian Glenn T. Eskew writes: "local real estate executive Sidney W. Smyer . . . realized the need for race reform after Birmingham received negative publicity following the vigilante violence that greeted the Freedom Riders in 1961. With young lawyers, small businessmen, and liberal reformers, Smyer orchestrated a change in city government to ease racial tensions in Birmingham. In doing so he challenged the civic leadership of the iron and steel interests that defended the race wage and segregation. A split in the white power structure developed between those people willing to concede desegregation and those who refused to integrate. In spring 1963, the civil rights demonstrations exacerbated the division. Smyer advocated adjustments with the black community to prevent further erosion of Birmingham's national reputation." Nunnelley, *Bull Connor*, 109; Eskew, *But for Birmingham: The Local and National Movements in the Civil Rights Struggle* (Chapel Hill: University of North Carolina Press, 1997), 13.

31. On November 6, 1962, by a 700-vote majority (out of 37,176 votes cast), the citizens of Birmingham voted in the new mayor/council form of city government. Albert Boutwell then defeated Bull Connor in the mayoral election of April 2, 1963. The Gaston Hotel was bombed on May 11, 1963.

32. Isaiah 56:7.

33. Perry Nussbaum of Jackson, Mississippi, visited Freedom Riders incarcerated in the Jackson city jail and in Parchman Penitentiary. During Sidney Lefkowitz's illustrious World War II career as an army chaplain, he was awarded a Bronze Star and seven battle stars. He served Temple Ahavath Chesed in Jacksonville, Florida, from 1946 until retirement in 1973, where he openly supported the civil rights movement. On Lefkowitz, see "One of the Greates [*sic*]: Glimpses of History," *Florida Times-Union*, February 12, 2008; Charlotte Bonelli, "History: The Jewish Service Heard around the World," winter 2009, accessed January 28, 2016, http://rjmag.org/Articles/index.cfm?id=1539.

34. The Jewish Chautauqua Society was founded in 1893 in Philadelphia to help teach non-Jews tolerance and understanding of Judaism. One of its more important programs is bringing rabbis to college campuses to teach. It was sponsored by the Reform movement's North American Federation of Temple Brotherhoods (now Men of Reform Judaism). The invitation was extended in 1955 for the program scheduled for early 1956. Men of Reform Judaism (MJR), "MRJ Jewish Chautauqua Society," Accessed January 28, 2016, http://www.menrj.org/mrj-jewish-chautauqua-society.

35. Rev. Alvin Kershaw, a native of Louisville, Kentucky, was a professor of philosophy at Miami University in Ohio and the part-time rector of the local Episcopal Church. The invitation came as a result of Rev. Will Campbell, who, in August 1954, became the director of religious life at the Oxford campus. He was supported by the Committee of One Hundred, a voluntary group funded by private donations. The committee, consisting of representatives from the student body, faculty, and community, brought to the university

religious leaders who presented monthly public lectures. The committee's and Campbell's agenda was clearly to have race relations discussed, but, for practical reasons, decided to publicize the conference as one dealing with "religion and human relations." In addition to Kershaw, Campbell invited the Rev. Joseph Fichter, SJ, sociologist at Loyola University of the South at New Orleans; Rev. George Chauncey, pastor of the First Presbyterian Church, Monticello, Arkansas; Rev. Joe Earl Elmore of New York City, former director of Methodist student work at the University of Mississippi; and Francis Pickens Miller of Charlottesville, Virginia, a retired colonel and anti-Harry Byrd leader in his home state. According to correspondence found in the Campbell papers, Grafman was a substitution for Ralph McGill, the editor of the *Atlanta Constitution* who withdrew after the controversy erupted because he thought he would be too controversial due to his recent comments on the Emmett Till case and integrated athletics. See Charles W. Eagles, "The Closing of Mississippi Society: Will Campbell, the $64,000 Question, and Religious Emphasis Week at the University of Mississippi," *Journal of Southern History* 67: 2, (2001), 331; "Ministers Quit Emphasis Week," *Salisbury (MD) Times*, February 11, 1956, 1; "Ralph McGill to Will D. Campbell," December 16, 1955, Will D. Campbell Papers, Collection No. M341, McCain Library, University of Southern Mississippi.

36. Sylvan Lebow was executive director of the National Federation of Temple Brotherhoods.

37. Albert Vorspan served for many years as the senior vice president of the Union of American Hebrew Congregations and as codirector of the UAHC Commission on Social Action. For some of Vorspan's views on issues including the civil rights movement, see Larry Yudelson, "Al Vorspan: 'Shrill' and Proud," *New Jersey Jewish Standard*, April 20, 2012, accessed January 28, 2016, http://jstandard.com/content/tag/albert+vorspan.

38. The sources are not clear as to which of the invited speakers initiated the process of rejecting the invitation. The AP release, published in papers around the country, states: "First to withdraw was the Rev. Joseph Fichter, SJ, sociologist at Loyola University of the South at New Orleans. Joining him Friday were: the Rev. George Chauncey, pastor of the First Presbyterian Church, Monticello, Ark., The Rev. Joe Earl Elmore of New York City, former director of Methodist student work at the University of Mississippi. Rabbi Milton Grafman, Temple Emanu-El at Birmingham, Ala." See, for example, *Frederick (MD) Post*, February 13, 1956, 10. Five decades later, Will Campbell remembered it this way: "By Wednesday night the wheels were in motion. Elmore, my friend in New York, had read the cancelation in the *New York Times* and sent a long telegram to me as we had planned. With no prompting, Joseph Fichter, a well-known Jesuit sociologist, wired that he could not appear on a program in such an atmosphere of blatant suppression of free speech, adding that he, too, was a long-time member of the NAACP and supporter of its goals. One by one the telegrams came. By Friday evening the last speaker had withdrawn." Will D. Campbell, "Religious Emphasis Week, Ole Miss, 1956," *Southern Quarterly* (Winter 2008); Charles Eagles, *Price of Defiance: James Meredith and Integration of Old Miss* (Chapel Hill: University of North Carolina Press, 2009); Eagles, "Closing of Mississippi."

39. Rabbi Maurice Eisendrath served as executive secretary/president of the UAHC from 1943 until his death in 1973. He was an outspoken, dedicated champion of civil rights for African Americans. Everett Gendler, "MLK Jr. and Maurice Eisendrath," April 5, 2013, Rav.Blog, CCAR, http://ravblog.ccarnet.org/2013/04/recalling-mlk-jr-and-maurice-eisendrath-2/ (includes picture of Eisendrath holding a Torah while marching with King).

40. The INS (International News Service) was a US-based news agency (newswire) founded in 1909 by newspaper publisher William Randolph Hearst. Its main competitors were the much larger AP (Associated Press), a news cooperative formed in the spring of 1846 by five daily newspapers in New York City, and the UP (United Press) agency, whose principal founder in 1907 was newspaper publisher Edward W. Scripps. In 1958 the INS combined with the UP to become the UPI (United Press International).

41. Abraham Mesch.

42. On April 28, 1958, a blue bag loaded with 54 sticks of dynamite was discovered in a basement window well of Temple Beth El, the fuse having burned out only a minute before detonation. This elicited a response from Bull Connor, who said that the "attempted bombing of Temple Beth El is one of the most outrageous acts that has been perpetrated in our community." At the time of the bombing, Beth El, located down the street from Emanu-El, was by far the largest congregation in Alabama with over 650 families. Elovitz, *A Century of Jewish Life in Dixie*, 169.

43. Raffel was president of the Alabama Psychological Association.

44. The article states that Raffel "made the protest in speaking to the National Conference of Christians and Jews, Alabama Region, board of directors" and that "the action came on a motion by Rabbi Milton Grafman, Temple Emanu-El, who said it was an exhibit 'by an organization devoted and dedicated to spreading hate.'" Leonard Chamblee, "At State Fair—Klan Booth Is Protested," *Birmingham Post-Herald*, October 10, 1964, 12.

45. Birmingham attorney Murphy, the "Imperial Klonsel" (general counsel) of the United Klans of America, had successfully defended the three men accused of bombing the 16th Street Baptist Church and three of the four men accused of killing civil rights worker Viola Gregg Liuzzo. Murphy died in an automobile accident a short time after the Liuzzo trial.

46. Based in Montgomery, Shelton was the Imperial Wizard of the Alabama Knights of the Ku Klux Klan. Gary May, *The Informant: The FBI, the Ku Klux Klan, and the Murder of Viola Liuzzo* (New Haven, CT: Yale University Press, 2005).

47. Arthur Hanes was the mayor of Birmingham whom Grafman had opposed in 1963.

48. The reference is to Albert Sidney Foley Jr. Foley was ordained in 1942, and from 1944 through 1947 taught religion, speech, and sociology at Spring Hill College. Foley was assigned to teach "Migration, Immigration, and Race." The volumes he read and the studies he conducted in preparation for the course made him realize how illogical prejudice was and how much injustice segregation caused. Consequently, Foley organized a Mobile Student Interracial Union at the college and conducted surveys among black Catholics and his students concerning racial opinions and treatment. These actions earned him the censure of his church superior, Archbishop Thomas Toolen, and he was shortly reassigned. In 1946, the organizing meeting of a provincial Institute of Social Order took place. At that meeting a group of nearly two dozen Jesuit priests established a subcommittee on interracial relations and selected Foley as its leader. In 1947 Foley, while at St. Louis University pursuing an MS in sociology, joined the Midwest Clergy Conference on Negro Welfare and the Catholic Committee of the South. During the 1950s he became a member of the Commission on Interracial Cooperation, forerunner of the Southern Regional Council, an interreligious and interfaith organization dedicated to educating people concerning the issue of race. He was reassigned to Spring Hill College in 1953. That year the college determined to implement desegregation, a process that the board of trustees had discussed for several years. In 1955 Foley became

a founding member of the Alabama Council on Human Relations, the state branch of the Southern Regional Council. By 1960 he had established the Human Relations Institute at Spring Hill College. From this venue, he held small group workshops in race relations, police/community relations, executive development, and other areas. Around 1961 he was also appointed to the Alabama Advisory Committee to the US Civil Rights Commission. From 1965 through 1968 he conducted workshops on school desegregation in Mobile and Birmingham designed to change attitudes and bring about integration. For the last seventeen years of his life, Foley worked through federal grants with the Job Training Partnership Act and the Head Start Program, among other things. He continued to teach at Spring Hill until retiring as professor emeritus in 1979, and continued his work with the Human Relations Institute until his death in 1990. See Carol A. Ellis, "The Tragedy of the White Moderate: Father Albert Foley and Alabama Civil Rights, 1963–1967" (MA thesis, University of Alabama, 2002).

49. I believe Grafman meant to say limestone here. It took a combination of coal, iron ore, and limestone to produce steel.

50. Banker and tycoon J. P. Morgan and his recently formed conglomerate, the United States Steel Company, exploited the financial Panic of 1907 in order to take control of the Tennessee Coal and Iron Company, then US Steel's major competitor. By the 1950s TCI/USS had long been the force that decided the economic fate of Birmingham by means of union-busting, support of the governmental status quo (the city commission system), the Jim Crow system, and strong opposition to the development of other industries in the area. TCI/USS was thus one of the most important causative factors for the economic and social problems Birmingham faced during the civil rights era.

51. Literally, the eve of the New Year. The opening services for the Jewish New Year would begin that evening.

52. The funeral service for three of the children, Addie Mae Collins, Carol Denise McNair, and Cynthia Diane Wesley, was conducted in the Sixth Avenue Baptist Church on September 18. Press reports listed as many as eight thousand people including many white attendees present to hear Martin Luther King Jr. give an impassioned eulogy. The service for Carole Robertson had taken place separately at St. John AME Church the day before. John Porter served as the minister of Sixth Avenue Baptist from 1962 to 2000. Eskew, *But for Birmingham*.

53. The prayer said in remembrance of those who have recently died or on or near the anniversary of their death.

54. The name of the prayer that is usually recited just before the sermon is delivered.

55. Audio excerpts from the sermon are available at American Jewish Archives.

56. Jacob J. Weinstein's opening address to the plenum was an eloquent response to the Christian "God is Dead" movement and to the danger of social action being disconnected from the God-centered approach of the ancient Hebrew prophets. Sidney L. Regner, ed., *Central Conference of American Rabbis Year Book* LXXVI (New York: CCAR, 1966), 4–11.

57. Roland Gittelsohn (1910–1995), one of the leading Reform clergy of the twentieth century, served from 1953 to 1977 as rabbi of Temple Israel of Boston. A Marine Corps chaplain, he was awarded three combat ribbons and on March 26, 1945, preached a memorable eulogy at the dedication of the Marine Corps cemetery on Iwo Jima. President Harry S. Truman appointed him to an ad hoc committee studying civil rights issues. In the discussion of the war in Vietnam, Gittlesohn's report noted, "We know . . . that pride in our country and concern for its prestige make it well-nigh impossible for us to

admit error—'to back down' is American parlance for the very same psychic mechanism that Orientals call 'to lose face.'" Ibid., 63.

58. At the June 1964 CCAR convention in Atlantic City, a group of sixteen rabbis responded to Martin Luther King Jr.'s request and flew to St. Augustine to participate in demonstrations to integrate public facilities in the city.

59. Grafman had his sermons taped regularly.

Chapter 11

1. CityTownInfo, "Cleveland History," accessed January 19, 2016; http://www.citytowninfo.com/places/mississippi/cleveland; Delta State University, "History" accessed January 19, 2016, http://delta.stateuniversity.com/.

2. Lucy Hutton-Seaberry-Moore interview, F341.5 .M57 vol. 748, pt. 1, University of Southern Mississippi. Center for Oral History and Cultural Heritage, accessed July 9, 2009, http://www.deltastate.edu/pages/1291.asp; Amzie Moore interview, University of Southern Mississippi. Center for Oral History and Cultural Heritage, accessed July 9, 2009, http://anna.lib.usm.edu/~spcol/crda/oh/ohmooreap.html.

3. About twenty small communities and four counties provided congregants, including Alligator, Benoit, Beulah, Boyle, Deeson, Duncan, Gunnison, Hushpeckena, Marigold, Mound Bayou, Pace, Renova, Rosedale, Shaw, Shelby, Winstonville, and Zumbro in Bolivar County and, within ten- to thirty-minute drive from Cleveland, Cottondale, Dockery, Drew, and Ruleville, in Sunflower County.

4. The following account of the history of Jews in Cleveland and the Congregation Adath Israel relies heavily on *Encyclopedia of Southern Jewish Communities*, "Cleveland, Mississippi," Goldring/Woldenberg Institute of Southern Jewish Life (ISJL), accessed January 28, 2016, http://www.isjl.org/mississippi-cleveland-encyclopedia.html.

5. His rabbinical lineage by generation: Ezekiel Landau, Israel Landau, Moses Landau, Joshua Landau followed by the Moses Landau in this chapter. Anne Landau (Sullivan), Moses Landau's daughter, email to Bauman, June 12, 2015. "Landau," Jewishencyclopedia.com, Gotthard, Deutch, et al., *Jewish Encyclopedia* (1906), accessed January 28, 2016, http://jewishencyclopedia.com/articles/9608-landau.

6. He later said he received ordination from the "Jewish Theological Seminary of Vienna."

7. For this biographical data, see Moses M. Landau letter, May 1984 (copy graciously provided by Anne Landau); *Chicago (IL) Daily Tribune*, August 17, 1941, W2, and November 30, 1941, W9; Jim Garrett, Landau obituary, *Bolivar (MS) Commercial*, May 20, 1999, accessed November 14, 2007, http://www.bolivarcom.com/NF/omf/bolivar/archive_display.html?[rkey=0002218+[cr=gdn; "Landau, Moses Maimonides," *Who's Who in World Jewry* (New York: Pittman Publishing Corporation, 1972), 514.

8. Anne Landau email to Bauman. One of the arrests came as a result of his support for Austrian Chancellor Kurt von Schusshnigg whom Hitler replaced with an Austrian Nazi party leader. Moses Landau to Cardinal Jozef-Ernest Von Roey, October 10, 1938 (copy graciously provided by Anne Landau).

9. I am grateful to Rabbi Larry Goldmark for researching CCAR Yearbooks to ascertain the synagogues Landau served.

10. Nussbaum, one of four clergy who created the Committee of Concern to raise money, solicited his Mississippi colleagues to join in the effort. See Landau to Nussbaum, January 5 and January 15, 1965, Nussbaum papers, MS Collection 430, Box 2, File 6, AJA.

11. Levingston, born in Landau's second year at Adath Israel, knew Landau as a child and then as an adult after he returned to Cleveland in 1983. Levingston managed his family's furniture business, served as president of Radio Cleveland Corporation, and chaired the boards of directors of the Mississippi Development Bank and the Mississippi Democratic Party, among other positions. The rabbi frequented the Levingston's home as a guest.

12. Anne Landau email to Bauman.

13. In September 1964, Landau wrote in his congregational newsletter:

> The first phase of the "invasion" of Mississippi is over. . . . Those who came here uninvited to help us to prepare our "ground" could have done better if they had stayed home and helped prepare their own "ground." Their "ground" needs as much preparation as ours if not more. One incident is a point in the case. A colleague of your rabbi from Rochester, New York, spent a few weeks in our area. He did not show any courtesy to your rabbi by informing him of his presence. . . . He finally succeeded in getting himself arrested. It is to be assumed that without an arrest in Mississippi he could not face his Congregation and justify his presence here. He and his kind come and go. They become "experts" over night. When they are gone, it is left for us to pick up the pieces. . . . In the "good old times" when a rabbi was preparing a sermon, he looked for material in the Bible, Talmud, Midrash. . . . As all these books are available now in English translation, and we assume that rabbis can, at least, read English, it is difficult to understand why they have to come here to look for material for their sermons and annoy, bore and weary their congregations. . . . To be sure: Their accomplishments are nil, and the damage they [have] done to race relations is great. Let them stay home and take care of their own and we will take care of our problems.

14. Cf. the Perry Nussbaum interview, chapter 13. Photojournalist Bill Steber writes, "Parchman penitentiary is located on 20,000 acres in the heart of the Delta and since the turn of the century it has remained one of the most feared institutions in the state. . . . William Faulkner called Parchman 'destination doom,' and author David Oshinsky described it as 'the quintessential penal farm, the closest thing to slavery that survived the civil war.'" Bill Steber, "Parchman Penitentiary, Parchman, MS, 1977," Houston Institute for Culture, accessed January 24, 2016, http://www.houstonculture.org/artist/steber10 .html.

15. Landau refers to Rabbi Benjamin Schultz, who served Congregation Beth Israel in Clarksdale, Mississippi, from 1962 until his death in 1978.

16. On November 3, 1957, a statement signed by eighty clergy that became known as the "Atlanta Manifesto" was published. A second statement, "Out of Conviction," signed by 312 clergy of Greater Atlanta, was published on November 22, 1958.

17. Possibly Landau is referring to Oberlin College students and faculty who, in December 1964, traveled to Antioch and Ripley, Mississippi, to rebuild churches burned down by the Ku Klux Klan.

18. On June 5, 1947, Secretary of State George C. Marshall outlined what became known as the Marshall Plan. Between 1947 and 1953, the United States pumped $13 billion into the economies of several European Countries, helping them to climb out of postwar economic devastation and thereby counteract communist expansion.

19. It is generally considered unethical for a rabbi to visit a colleague's community

in order to perform any rabbinic function without first informing the colleague that you are coming.

Chapter 12

1. "Hattiesburg—The Beginning," Hattiesburg Area Historical Society, accessed January 24, 2016, http://hahsmuseum.org/history.html?History=History.

2. Bobs M. Tusa, "A Brief History of the Civil Rights Movement in Hattiesburg, Mississippi," August 1999, McCain Library and Archives, University of Southern Mississippi, Historical Manuscripts, accessed May 30, 2010, http://www.lib.usm.edu/legacy/archives /crsitdoc.htm; William Harris Hardy, *No Compromise With Principle* (New York: American Book, 1946); Benjamin Morris, *Hattiesburg, Mississippi: A History of the Hub City* (Charleston, SC: The History Press, 2014).

3. Anna Kest Mantinband, *Time for Remembering* (n.p.: privately published, 1979), 71.

4. "History," B'nai Israel—Hattiesburg, MS, accessed December 22, 2012, www .hattiesburgsynagogue.org/wordpress/history/. The author is grateful to Terry Schwartz and Robert Dreyfus for additional information about Maurice Dreyfus.

5. The following is largely derived from "B'nai Israel—Hattiesburg, Mississppi," accessed December 22, 2012, www.hattiesburgsynagogue.org/wordpress/history/; *Encyclopedia of Southern Jewish Communities*, "Hattiesburg, Mississippi," Goldring/Woldenberg Institute of Southern Jewish Life (ISJL), accessed December 22, 2012, http://www.isjl .org/mississippi-hattiesburg-encyclopedia.html; *Encyclopedia of Southern Jewish Communities*, "B'nai Israel—Hattiesburg, Mississippi," ISJL, accessed January 29, 2016, http:// www.isjl.org/mississippi-hattiesburg-encyclopedia.html. Alhough these were called department stores, several would more accurately be described as specialty stores. Waldoff's specialized in men's and women's wear; Fine Brothers–Matison in men's, women's, and children's items; and Vogue's in women's goods. Milton Waldoff e-mail to author, March 1, 2010.

6. Lee Shai Weissbach, *Jewish Life in Small Town America: A History* (New Haven, CT: Yale University Press, 2005); Leonard Rogoff, *Down Home: Jewish Life in North Carolina* (Chapel Hill: University of North Carolina Press, 2010).

7. Jerry Shemper interview conducted by author, July 26, 2005; Clive Webb reinforces this point in "Big Struggle in a Small Town: Charles Mantinband of Hattiesburg, Mississippi," in *The Quiet Voices: Southern Rabbis and Black Civil Rights, 1880s to 1990s*, ed. Mark K. Bauman and Berkley Kalin (Tuscaloosa: University of Alabama Press, 1997), 213.

8. Herbert Ginsberg interview conducted by author, January 3, 2005.

9. Maury and Shirley Gurwitch interview conducted by author, January 27, 2005.

10. This was reflected in an annual sermon he preached in January throughout his rabbinate that paid tribute to General Robert E. Lee. Mantinband, *Time for Remembering*, 3.

11. He also earned a PhD from Burton College and Seminary in Colorado Springs, Colorado (1958), and an Honorary Doctorate from Lincoln University in Chester County, Pennsylvania, whose alumni include Langston Hughes and Thurgood Marshall.

12. Mantinband, *Time for Remembering*, 11.

13. Clipping found in Mantinband, *Time for Remembering*, 19.

14. Although most of his readers probably did not understand the point of the pseudonym, those familiar with Leigh Hunt's poem "Abou Ben Adhem" would have greater insight into the intent of the writer. The poem reads:

Abou Ben Adhem (may his tribe increase)
Awoke one night from a dream of peace
And saw within the moonlight in his room,
An angel writing in a book of gold.

Exceeding peace had made Ben Adhem bold;
And to the presence in the room he said,
"What writest thou?" The vision raised its head,
And, with a look made of all sweet accord,
Answered, "The names of those who love the Lord."

"And is mine one" said Abou. "Nay, not so,"
Replied the angel. Abou spoke more low,
But cheerily still; and said, "I pray thee, then,
Write me as one that loves his fellow-men."

The angel wrote, and vanished. The next night
It came again, with a great and wakening light,
And showed the names whom love of God had blessed;
And, lo! Ben Adhem's name led all the rest.

15. "Rabbi Mantinband Leaves USO; Known To All Faiths As Friend," *The Flaming Bomb*, January 17, 1946, clipping found in Mantinband, *Time for Remembering*, 54.

16. Shirley and Maury Gurwitch interview.

17. "A Citizen of Distinction," *Longview (TX) Morning Journal*, August 5, 1974, 4- A.

18. The use of the abbreviation SOS reflected awareness of the military utilization of the same initials during World War II to designate an emergency situation.

19. The paper was delivered in June 1964.

20. He actually moved to Longview on March 1, 1963.

21. Mantinband had such poor vision that he did not drive an automobile. He and his wife frequently used trains for transportation—thus his reference to Longview being "on the main line."

22. In their annual New Year's letter mailed to family and friends in December 1954, Anna Mantinband wrote: "We should say a word about the South and the impact of the Supreme Court Decision last May: Black Monday, it is now labelled [*sic*] and stigmatized. Die-hards persist in maintaining the status quo and obstructing, shouting 'Defend southern tradition,' 'Beware mixed marriages and mongrelization.' They have organized so-called Citizens' Committees to enforce segregation at all costs." Rabbi Charles Mantinband Papers, McCain Library, University of Southern Mississippi, MS 327, Box 2, Folder 6.

23. Although the *Hattiesburg (MS) American* opposed integration, when Leonard Lowrey became its managing editor in 1962 its editorial policy became less inflammatory than that of most other newspapers in the state. Its response to James Meredith's intention to enroll at the University of Mississippi reflects this: "Along with most other Mississippians, we are anxious to see segregation maintained in the schools of our state from the University of Mississippi, on down, if it's at all possible," Lowrey wrote. "Grave concern has been expressed by some that the university will be closed or that it will lose its accreditation as a result of the Meredith matter. No matter what else, Ole Miss, and all of our other state institutions of higher learning, should be kept open and in good standing."

Lowrey, "The Long View," *Hattiesburg American*, September 27, 1962, 1, quoted in Susan Weil, *In a Madhouse's Din: Civil Rights Coverage by Mississippi's Daily Press, 1948–1968* (Westport, CT: Praeger, 2002), 84. Since Mantinband left Hattiesburg in early 1963, he was probably referring to the paper's policy under the previous editor, Andrews Harmon.

24. Senator James O. Eastland (1904–1986) represented Mississippi in the Senate in 1941 and from 1943 until 1978. His seniority gave him considerable power. He served as President Pro Tem of the Senate from 1972 to 1978 and as chair of the Judiciary Committee from 1956 to 1978.

25. Following the assassination of Tsar Alexander II in 1881, government-sponsored pogroms and laws against the Jews of Russia started a mass exodus of Jews from Russia to the United States.

26. On July 18, 1967, the Hattiesburg chapter of the NAACP initiated a boycott of downtown businesses including Fine Brothers-Matison Company, which had refused to replace white cashiers with African Americans. *OpenJurist*, "411 F.2d 181—*Smith v. Grady*," No. 25351, United States Court of Appeals Fifth Circuit, May 15, 1969, accessed February 26, 2010, http://openjurist.org/411/f2d/181/smith-v-e-grady.

27. This impression would have seemed somewhat charitable to Avery Grossfield, Mantinband's predecessor in the Hattiesburg pulpit, who wrote, "After a lengthy correspondence with the President of the Hattiesburg, Mississippi, congregation—during which no mention whatsoever was made of the Negro problem—I accepted their pulpit. As soon as we arrived—on May 1, 1949—the President said to me: 'We don't speak on the "nigger" problem here.' I asked him why he did not discuss this subject with me during our correspondence; that, had I known this earlier, I would never have agreed to come. Further, the Negro question was not the main issue now—the main issue was Freedom of Speech and Freedom of the Pulpit. I told him that I would speak on the subject whenever I saw fit—and that I did not intend to remain in Hattiesburg after the expiration of my contract on August 31, 1950." Grossfield to author, June 14, 1966.

28. Founded in 1919 as the Commission on Interracial Cooperation, the SRC engaged Southern communities on issues of democracy and race. One of the most effective regional civil rights organizations, it promoted an end to all-white primaries in the 1940s, established state human relations councils to help desegregate southern schools in the 1950s, and founded the Voter Education Project that registered more than two million African Americans in the 1960s. In their annual New Year's letter to family and friends (December 1954), Anna Mantinband wrote,

> A movement close to our hearts is the Southern Regional Council, devoted to attaining, through research and action, the ideals and practices of equal opportunity for all people in the South. Its membership is limited to people within the South. It fights shy of the political arena; prefers to engage in educational endeavor. SRC beats no tom-toms but carries on its work quietly, without fanfare. Some who oppose it call it "pink" or "subversive." The fact remains that the movement has received two tremendous votes of confidence. The Fund for the Republic (Ford Foundation) voted it $240,000 for intensive field and research activity. And Uncle Sam, through the Department of State, now officially turns to the headquarters office in Atlanta to enlighten foreign visitors on the true story of the South and race relations. Rabbi remains chairman of the Mississippi Division.

Mantinband served as chairman of the Mississippi division from 1953 until 1956. Mantinband Papers, Box 2, Folder 6.

29. Mantinband's deep involvement in the Kennard case is reflected in his considerable correspondence on the matter. In a letter to the rabbi dated April 16, 1963, Medgar Evers suggested, "Clyde Kennard is on the mend and is living with his sister, presently in Chicago, 6045 South Ada Street. I am sure he would be delighted to hear from you, as well as others who have his interest at heart." Six days later, Mantinband wrote to Kennard, "Dear Clyde: After many attempts to locate you, and inquire about your well-being, I finally got your address in Chicago. I am sure that your sister is taking good care of you, and perhaps mother is with you also. The news that your health has improved and the outlook favorable, is indeed very welcome. Did you know that, after eleven years in Hattiesburg, we moved to East Texas, March 1st? Life here is altogether different. The tensions have lifted for us, though we continue our contact with friends in the Magnolia State. . . . [A] copy of this note is going to Dr. James Silver of the University of Mississippi faculty, who has great interest in your experience. You would do well to be in touch with him. Please let us hear from you. How is the book coming? . . . With every good wish for your continued improvement, in which my wife joins me, and cordial regards to your family, I am, Yours Faithfully, Charles Mantinband." On August 1, 1963, University of Southern Mississippi professor F. A. Varrelman forwarded to Mantinband a handwritten note from Kennard's mother, Leona Smith, advising him of Clyde's hospitalization and his subsequent death on July 4. Mantinband wrote to Mrs. Smith: "We extend our deepest sympathy to you in your sorrow. As you know, your fine son Clyde was our good friend, and a frequent visitor at our home. We did our best to advise him all along the way. . . . Some day, when the history of the race trouble in Mississippi will be documented and written, the name of Clyde Kennard will be high on the list of heroes and martyrs. . . . Please accept the enclosed, and use it in any way you think best." Charles Mantinband Papers, Amistad Research Center, Tulane University, Box 2, 1963; Timothy J. Minchin and John A. Slamond, "Clyde Kennard: A Little-Known Civil Rights Pioneer," *Mississippi History Now*, Mississippi Historical Society, September 2010, accessed January 29, 2016, http://mshistory.k12.ms.us/articles/349/clyde-kennard-a-little-known-civil-rights-pioneer; John Dittmer, *Local People: The Struggle for Civil Rights in Mississippi* (Urbana: University of Illinois Press, 1995).

30. Anna Mantinband tells of a night when she answered the phone and a lady warned, "Mrs. Mantinband, you tell the rabbi he'd better be careful whom he entertains in his home. All of Hattiesburg is aroused about him." Mrs Mantinband writes that their house was under constant surveillance by men sitting on the bus stop bench across the street. One day when she boarded the bus the "watcher on the bench" also did so and, although the bus was not half full, he sat next to her and said: "I see the reverend is taking a trip. I seed him get in a car with a New York license yesterday. I got a little book; I knows every move the reverend makes." In addition, the Mantinbands found that their mail was routinely opened when they picked it up at the post office. Mantinband, *Time for Remembering*, 72.

31. Reference is probably to Dr. Lawrence C. Jones, who founded the Piney Woods Country Life School (Jackson, Mississippi) in 1909 and remained its president until 1974, or possibly to Jonas Edward Johnson, founding president (1907) of the Prentiss Normal Industrial Institute, one of the schools funded by the Julius Rosenwald Fund. When Johnson died in 1953, his wife, Bertha LaBranche Johnson, replaced him and served as president until 1971. Prentiss is about forty-five miles northwest of Hattiesburg. The school closed in 1989. Although Mantinband also visited Tougaloo College in the Jackson area, its presidents were Caucasian until George Owens (1964–1965). Bruce G. Posner, "Joining the Mainstream: Tougaloo Debates Its Course," *Change* 7:10 (winter, 1975/1976),

14; Blackpast.org, "Piney Woods School (1909–)," in *Online Reference Guide to African American History*, accessed January 29, 2016, http://www.blackpast.org/aah/piney-woods-school-1909; HBCUConnect.com, "Prentiss Institue Junior College: College History," accessed January 29, 2016, http://hbcuconnect.com/colleges/117/prentiss-institute-jr-college.

32. This occurred in early May 1962. The "uninvited visitor" was Monsignor John T. Martin, pastor of Sacred Heart Catholic Church from 1953 to 1967.

33. Rabbi Arthur Lelyveld, then Senior Rabbi of Fairmount Temple in Cleveland. Lelyveld was badly beaten in Hattiesburg, Mississippi, on July 10, 1964, during his participation in the Freedom Rides. Lawrence Van Gelder, "Rabbi Arthur J. Levyveld, 83, Rights Crusader," *New York Times*, April 16, 1969.

34. The bodies of James Earl Chaney, Andrew Goodman, and Michael Schwerner were found in Philadelphia, Mississippi, on August 24, 1964.

35. On September 2, 1960, Evers wrote to Mantinband, "I was delighted to see your note of August 23. . . . I would very much appreciate the opportunity of stopping in, talking with you when I'm in the Hattiesburg area. . . . Likewise we would extend the same invitation to you when you're in our city, either in my home . . . or in my office. Best wishes to your family." Mantinband Papers, Amistad Research Center, Box 2, 1960–1961. In 1954 Medgar Evers was appointed to the new position of field secretary for the Mississippi branch of the NAACP. He was assassinated on June 12, 1963, three weeks short of his thirty-eighth birthday. On June 26, 1963, Mantinband wrote to his widow, "Dear Friend: No words of mine are adequate to express our sense of loss in the tragic circumstances of the past month. I knew Medgar well, and esteemed him for the fine person he was. More than once he crossed the threshold of our home when we lived in Hattiesburg. Before me as I write is a personal note from him dated April 16th of this year. Please accept our deepest sympathy and also the enclosed check in the amount of $25 to add to your family Education Fund. May God bless you and keep you. Yours Faithfully, Charles Mantinband," Mantinband Papers, Amistad Research Center, Box 2, 1963.

36. On June 5, 1966, University of Mississippi graduate James Meredith, accompanied by a few supporters, began a march from Memphis, Tennessee, to Jackson, Mississippi, designed to encourage black voter registration. The following day Meredith was shot and wounded in Hernando, Mississippi. The next day leaders of SNCC, the Southern Christian Leadership Conference, and the CRE called upon all freedom-loving people in the country to join them in Hernando. On June 22, 1966, the marchers arrived in Philadelphia, Mississippi, where they conducted a memorial service for civil rights martyrs James Chaney, Andrew Goodman, and Michael Schwerner. Violence broke out during which African American marchers were beaten and one local white man was shot. For the next two weeks, from two hundred to two thousand people marched, reaching Jackson on June 26, four days after this interview was conducted in Toronto. Fifteen thousand people joined together in Jackson to celebrate the completion of the march and affirm the right and the importance of the ballot. Aram Goudsouzian, *Down to the Crossroads: Civil Rights, Black Power, and the Meredith March against Fear* (New York: Farrar, Straus & Giroux, 2014); Charles W. Eagles, *The Price of Defiance: James Meredith and the Integration of Ole Miss* (Chapel Hill: University of North Carolina Press, 2009).

37. The Temple was bombed on October 12, 1958. Melissa Faye Green, *The Temple Bombing* (Reading, MA: Addison-Wesley, 1996); Janice Rothschild Blumberg, "The Bomb That Healed—A Retrospect," *CCAR Journal* (1983); Blumberg, "Jacob M. Rothschild: His Legacy Twenty Years After," in *Quiet Voices*, ed. Bauman and Kalin. In Blum-

berg's telling of this story, Anna Mantinband avers that it was the mayor "who had just gone out of office" who accosted her husband. Moran M. Pope served as mayor of Hattiesburg from 1953 to 1957. Anna Mantinband's version varies slightly in that she writes that her husband responded to the ex-mayor, "I'm writing verbatim what you just said and I'm turning it over to my attorney so that if anything happens to me they will know the source." Mantinband, *Time for Remembering*, 73.

38. The author of a newspaper article titled "Rabbi Honored at Inter-Faith Dinner" wrote that about sevety-five men representing "the Jewish, Catholic and Protestant faiths; local government, business and civic leaders; the city's two institutions of higher learning and the Hattiesburg Ministerial Association" were present. Those paying tribute to Mantinband stressed his "dedication to his work, his willingness to accept responsibilities and his success in achieving an attitude of mutual respect and cooperation among all faiths." The speakers included the president of William Carey College, the dean of the University of Southern Mississippi, the pastor of Court Street Methodist Church, an attorney representing the business community, a representative of nearby Jewish communities, President Abe Pevsner of B'nai Israel, and Mayor Claude Pittman Jr. The article continues, "Mayor Pittman handed Rabbi Mantinband a key to the city and Pevsner presented him with a gift on behalf of the congregation." Clipping with notation "Feb 1963," Mantinband, *Time for Remembering*, 79.

39. On August 2, 1957, author and newspaper publisher Harry Golden wrote to Mantinband, "Dear Rabbi: You are a real doll, about writing me from time to time. I hope to see you soon, but in the meantime I would like to write a little article about you for the *Congress Weekly*. I have had it in mind for a long time. I have a different idea of why you could uphold our tradition of social justice and why others fail under the ax of the Trustees. I start a regular article with the American Jewish Congress [publishers of *Congress Weekly*] in September and I would like to get it in and then reprint it in the *Carolina Israelite*. Confidentially give me as many insights as you possibly can and please do not be modest about yourself. I am proud of you. Cordially yours, Harry." Mantinband Papers, Amistad Research Center, Box 2, 1963. For Golden, see Leonard Rogoff, "Harry Golden, New Yorker," *Southern Jewish History* 11 (2008): 41–64; Stephen J. Whitfield, "The 'Golden' Era of Civil Rights: Consequences of the Carolina Israelite." *Southern Cultures* 14 (2008): 26–51; Kimberly Marlowe Hartnett, *Carolina Israelite: How Harry Golden Made Us Care about Jews, the South, and Civil Rights* (Chapel Hill: University of North Carolina Press, 2015).

40. Kivie Kaplan (1904–1975), a member of the Executive Committee of the Union of American Hebrew Congregations, served as president of the NAACP from 1966 to 1975. He was an enthusiastic fan and supporter of Mantinband and others who were serving on the front lines in the struggle for black civil rights. For Kaplan, see Edward Kaplan, "Two Civil Rights Testimonies," *Southern Jewish History* 17 (2014): 181–215.

41. Reznikoff served as rabbi of Congregation B'nai Israel in Baton Rouge, Louisiana, in 1954 and again from 1957 to 1975. In 1961 the Louisiana House Un-American Activities Committee tapped his phone.

42. Reference is to the 1964 Freedom Summer.

43. Christina R. Dickey, *The Bible and Segregation* (Haverhill, MA: Destiny, 1958).

44. The closest regional office of the B'nai B'rith Anti-Defamation League was in New Orleans.

45. In a December 15, 1960, letter to Aubrey Brown Jr., editor of the *Richmond (VA) Presbyterian Outlook*, responding to a request asking for names of rabbis in the South who

"have worked and spoken constructively and courageously in the South on the race issue," Mantinband listed Rothschild, Julian Feibelman (New Orleans), and Emmet Frank (Alexandria, VA). Toward the end of 1963, while working on a manuscript to be called *Mr. Kennedy and the Negroes* (New York: World Publishing Company, 1964), Harry Golden asked Mantinband for an appraisal of the rabbis in the South. In a letter dated December 19, 1963, Mantinband responded: "To be sure, I do not know them all well, and they may be forthright and outspoken in a manner unknown to me. But, for the most part, I suspect, that they comfort themselves by feeling they are influential and useful behind the scenes, and play it safe and cozy. Lillian Smith [an outspoken southern critic of segregation, author of a number of books that dealt with the problem] refers to a 'conspiracy of silence' on the part of church leaders. I feel that the sins of these colleagues of mine are the sins of omission rather than of commission, and more than once [I] have urged that if the spiritual leaders, so-called, do not set the example and lead, then the courageous, God-fearing lay people in the Jewish community should stand up and be counted." He continues that Marvin Reznikoff (Baton Rouge) is "an unsung hero in our profession" who helped integrate his ministerial alliance and who defied the Louisiana legislature. Consequently, his phone was "tapped by the Sovereignty Commission and the White Citizens' Council." Mantinband wrote that Nussbaum has "in more recent years taken a public and heroic stand on the side of truth and justice, both in and out of his pulpit." As for Seymour Atlas in Montgomery, "he was silent" during the bus boycott and Martin Luther King's activity, but, once he knew he was leaving "he became vocal and articulate." "On the negative side," he continues, "there is the Benjamin Schultz . . . who would have Washington and the world learn from the noble example set by the Magnolia State. Sorry spectacles are Eugene Blachschleger of Montgomery and Milton Grafman of Birmingham, who are both in hot spots, but realize that they have as much chance against the tide of public opinion as a toothpick against Niagara. Once Blachschleger said to me: 'If Martin Luther King passed me on the street, I would not recognize him. We have never spoken to each other.' Grafman, who is deeply concerned with anti-Semitism, once said publicly—I did not hear him, but it was reported to me—'Better a hundred Negroes be hurt than that harm come to the head of a single Jew.' A number of B'nai B'rith officials, attending this ADL session, scored him for this unwarranted attitude." Mantinband Papers, Amistad Research Center, Box 2, 160–61, 163; Terry Barr, "Rabbi Grafman and Birmingham's Civil Rights Era," in *Quiet Voices*, ed. Bauman and Kalin; S. Jonathan Bass, *Blessed Are the Peacemakers: Martin Luther King Jr., Eight White Religious Leaders, and the "Letters from Birmingham Jail"* (Baton Rouge: Louisiana State University Press, 2001).

Chapter 13

1. Sources for this sketch include Joel Spring, *The Cultural Transformation of a Native American Family and Its Tribe, 1763–1995: A Basket of Apples* (Mahwah, NJ: Lawrence Erlbaum Associates, 1996), 38–41; Westley F. Busbee, *Mississippi: A History* (Wheeling, IL: Harlan Davidson, 2005); Richard Aubrey McLemore, ed., *A History of Mississippi*, 2 vols. (Hattiesburg: University and College Press of Mississippi, 1973); Jackson County, Mississippi, "History of Jackson County," accessed January 25, 2016, http://www.co.jackson.ms.us/about/history/; "Jackson, Mississippi," in Dunbar Rowland, *History of Mississippi: The Heart of the South*, 4 vols. (Chicago, IL, and Jackson, MS: S. J. Clarke Publishing Company, 1925); Mary Ann Wells, *Native Land: Mississippi, 1540–1798* (Jackson:

University Press of Mississippi, 1994); Jackson Convention & Visitors Bureau, "Vibrant Jackson History," accessed June 15, 2010, http://www.visitjackson.com/About-Jackson /Jackson-History; John K. Bettersworth, *Mississippi: A History* (Austin, TX: Steck Company, 1959); James Taylor Carson, *Searching for the Bright Path: The Mississippi Choctaws from Prehistory to Removal* (Lincoln: University of Nebraska Press, 1999).

2. Except where otherwise noted, this section is based on *Encyclopedia of Southern Jewish Communities*, "Beth Israel—Jackson, Mississippi," Goldring/Woldenberg Institute of Southern Jewish Life (ISJL), accessed July 19, 2010, http://www.isjl.org/mississippi -jackson-beth-israel-encyclopedia.html; Beth Israel Congregation, "Temple History," accessed January 29, 2016, http://bethisraelms.org/.

3. "Arrival of Buyers," *New York Times*, March 7, 1939, 41, October 30, 1945, 35, September 18, 1951, 50, July 18, 1967, 45; Kelly Ingebretsen, "At the Center of it All: Changing Face of Downtown Jackson," *Mississippi Business Journal*, 26:48, August 1, 2005, S18; "Banquet for Negro Ag. Leaders Given By Chain Stores," *Greenville (MS) Delta Democrat-Times*, December 5, 1952, 12; "For Sale: Display Materials," *Greenville (MS) Delta Democrat-Times*, May 23, 1977, 10.

4. Jerry Mitchell, "Perkins, Gotthelf Honored for Work," *Jackson (MS) Clarion-Ledger*, March 4, 2001, 1.

5. John R. Salter Jr., *Jackson, Mississippi: An American Chronicle of Struggle and Schism* (Malabar, FL: Robert E. Krieger Publishing Company, 1987), 8 (first quotation), 2–3 (second quotation); David J. Langum, *William M. Kunstler: The Most Hated Lawyer in America* (New York: New York University Press, 1999).

6. Charles Marsh, *The Last Days: A Son's Story of Sin and Segregation at the Dawn of a New South* (New York: Basic Books, 2001) 85; Salter, *Jackson*, 13.

7. US Supreme Court decision *Boynton v. Virginia* took effect on November 1, 1960. "The Freedom Rides," accessed June 15, 2010, http://www.core-online.org/History/freedom %20rides.htm; "*Boynton v. Virginia* 364 U.S. 454 (1960)," Justia: US Supreme Court, accessed January 25, 2016, https://supreme.justia.com/cases/federal/us/364/454/case .html; Christina Vignone, "Uncovering Yonkers: *Boynton v. Virginia (1960)*," Fordham University, accessed January 25, 2016, http://www.uncoveringyonkers.com/boynton-v -virginia-1960.html.

8. Salter, *Jackson*, 48–57.

9. Ibid., 58–69.

10. Juan Williams, *Eyes on the Prize: America's Civil Rights Years, 1954–1965* (New York: Viking Penguin, 1987), 44.

11. "Jackson MS, Boycotts (winter–spring)," *Civil Rights Movement Veterans*, accessed July 4, 2010, http://www.crmvet.org/tim/timhis62.htm#1962jackson; "Jackson Sit-in & Protests (May–June)," *Civil Rights Movement Veterans*, accessed July 4, 2010, http://www .crmvet.org/tim/timhis63.htm#1963woolworth; Salter, *Jackson*, 40–80. The response of the white people of Jackson to the assassination of President John F. Kennedy on November 23 was symptomatic of the mood. Edward Cohen wrote in his memoir that when the principal of Murrah School announced the death of the president over the public address system, "the response of virtually all my fellow students was immediate jubilant cheering." *The Peddler's Grandson: Growing Up Jewish in Mississippi* (Jackson: University Press of Mississippi, 1999), 67.

12. Salter, *Jackson*, 227–38.

13. Robert Zelle, "Mississippi Civil Rights—One Man, One Story," accessed June 15, 2010, http://robertezelle.blogspot.com/. Zelle introduces his blog with the following

statement: "My father, Robert L. Zelle Jr., fit the description of 'the right man in the right place' during the turbulent 1960s and 1970s. As a white businessman working behind the scenes to promote Civil Rights in Mississippi, his story has basically been forgotten. Maybe this blog will help keep his story alive, and to remind people that there were others like him who have been forgotten by the history books." Complete Chamber of Commerce statement, accessed July 5, 2010, http://mdah.state.ms.us/arrec/digital_archives /sovcom/result.php?image=/data/sov_commission/images/png/cd04/030256.png& otherstuff=2|72|3|47|1|1|1|29716|.

14. This hate periodical was published in Birmingham, Alabama, by National States Rights Party member Edward Fields from 1958 until the late 1980s. See Clive Webb, *The Rabble Rousers: The American Far Right and the Civil Rights Movement* (Athens: University of Georgia Press, 2010).

15. Robert Tabscott, "Fighting Evil in the Night," *St. Louis (MO) Post—Dispatch*, August 2, 1996, 7B.

16. Jerry Mitchell, "Journey to Justice," 13, 2010, http://blogs.clarionledger.com/ jmitchell/2010/06/28/atmosphere-of-violence-in-1960s/. Mitchell's article includes a photograph of Rainey and Price laughing during their trial.

17. HighBeam Research, Charles Bolton, "A Look at How Far We've Come: School Desegregation in Mississippi," *Jackson Advocate*, January 15–January 21, 2009, accessed January 29, 2016, https://www.highbeam.com/doc/1P3-1644618271.html; The Mississippi Truth Project, "The Civil Rights Movement in Mississippi," accessed June 16, 2010, http:// www.mississippitruth.org/pages/CRMtimeline.htm; infoplease, "Civil Rights Time Line," accessed January 25, 2016, http://www.infoplease.com/spot/civilrightstimeline1.html; University of Southern Mississippi, "Civil Rights in Mississippi Digital Archive" accessed January 25, 2016, http://digilib.usm.edu/crmda_timeline.php; "Timelines of History: Timeline Mississippi," accessed June 16, 2010, http://timelines.ws/states/MISSISSIPPI .HTML.

18. Milton Grafman graduated with Nussbaum. [Atlanta] *Southern Israelite*, May 31, 1933, 17.

19. The biographical sketch in *Who's Who* places Nussbaum in Amarillo from 1934–1935 and in Pueblo from 1935–1941: "Nussbaum, Perry E.," *Who's Who in World Jewry: A Biographical Dictionary of Outstanding Jews* ed. I. J. Karpman (New York: Pitman Publishing, 1972), 662.

20. Nussbaum's *Guide for Service to Jewish Soldiers* was published in 1945 by the Jewish Chaplains' Council of the National Jewish Welfare Board, which published pocket-sized prayer books and scriptures for Jewish servicemen beginning in World War I.

21. See Gary P. Zola, "What Price Amos? Perry Nussbaum's Career in Jackson, Mississippi," in *The Quiet Voices: Southern Rabbis and Black Civil Rights, 1880s to 1990s*, ed. Mark K. Bauman and Berkley Kalin (Tuscaloosa: University of Alabama Press, 1997), 233.

22. Perilman chaired the CCAR placement committee. Perry Nussbaum interview, August 5, 1965, Nussbaum papers, Ms. Coll. #430, Box 4, Folder 6, Jacob Rader Marcus Center of the American Jewish Archives, 2 (hereafter cited as Nussbaum memoir). Although the interviewer is unidentified, the text reads like a memoir, with only 14 brief interjections in the 45 typewritten pages available. It will thus be treated as such.

23. Nussbaum memoir, 7–8.

24. During his years in Jackson, Nussbaum served as president of the Mississippi Association of Mental Health, as founding president of the Greater Jackson Clergy Alliance, as a founder and secretary of the Mississippi Religious Leadership Conference, as

state chaplain for the American Legion and the Reserve Officers Association (he held the rank of colonel when he retired from the military), and as an active member of various community service groups. Nussbaum papers, Box 1, Folder 1.

25. With the phrase "the complacent Ike-like Rabbi Lovitt," Cohen is comparing Rabbi Lovitt's complacency to that of Dwight D. "Ike" Eisenhower, who, by Cohen's reasoning, was a relatively inactive president. From Cohen's perspective, Lovitt had done little to encourage religious observance among his congregations whereas Nussbaum applied substantial pressure to do so.

26. Cohen, *Peddler's Grandson*, 108–10.

27. Ibid., 110–11.

28. Nussbaum memoir, 5–6.

29. Cohen, *Peddler's Grandson*, 155–56.

30. Nussbaum to Jay Kaufman, January 20, 1956, Nussbaum papers, Box 1, Folder 8.

31. Temple Beth Israel *Newsletter* (October, 1958), 17–18.

32. Nussbaum papers, Box 1, Folder 7.

33. See, e.g., "Churches: Beauty for Ashes," *Time*, 85, February 5, 1965, 61, http://content.time.com/time/magazine/article/0,9171,839238,00.html; "Fund for Negro Churches," *Jackson (MS) Clarion-Ledger*, January 10, 1965, A14. The article includes a picture showing Nussbaum handing a batch of checks to Dr. William P. Davis, the committee's chairman.

34. The first week of October 1962.

35. *Greenville (MS) Delta Democrat-Times*, February 1, 1963, 2; *Jackson (MS) Clarion-Ledger*, February 1, 1963 (unpaginated clipping), Nussbaum papers.

36. Nussbaum to Schultz, October 25, 1962, as cited in P. Allen Krause, "Rabbi Benjamin Schultz and the American Jewish League against Communism: From McCarthy to Mississippi," *Southern Jewish History* 13 (2010): 153–213.

37. The bomb was planted near his office and went off at a time in the evening when Nussbaum usually sat working at his desk.

38. "Synagogue Hit By Explosion," *Jackson (MS) Daily News*, September 19, 1967; "Rabbi Asks Reward of $100,000," *Jackson (MS) Clarion-Ledger*, November 23, 1967, 1A.

39. Marsh, *God's Long Summer*, 89–90; Jack Nelson, *Terror in the Night: The Klan's Campaign against the Jews* (Jackson: University Press of Mississippi, 1993), 70–72.

40. Marsh, *God's Long Summer*, 104–5.

41. "Clergy Walk to Synagogue," *Jackson (MS) Clarion-Ledger*, September 21, 1967.

42. On June 5, 1969, he wrote to Rabbi Malcolm Stern, director of the Reform movement's Rabbinic Placement Commission, "Arene and I have reached the limits of our emotional resources. Since the bombings in 1967 I have developed gout and high cholesterol, and have been unable to keep them within safe limits. My doctor tells me I must become less tense. My poor wife hasn't slept properly within months." Among others he wrote to Rabbi Arthur Lelyveld in Cleveland, Ohio; Rabbi Morris Graff in Miami, Florida; and Rabbi Levi Olan in Dallas, Texas. Nussbaum papers, Box 1, Folder 4

43. Nussbaum papers, box 1, folder 4. Life remained difficult for liberal clergy. For example, Nussbaum received a letter from the Rev. Perry H. Biddle Jr., minister of Jackson's First Presbyterian Church, who had "been voted out of my church 203–195 after almost three years. Race is behind it all." Biddle concluded, "I enjoyed working with you on the Miss. Rel. Leadership Conference and count it a privilege to have known a true prophet of Israel." Nussbaum papers, Box 1, Folder 3.

44. *Cincinnati Enquirer*, "*Hall of Heroes*," August 1, 2004, http://www2.cincinnati.com/freetime/nurfc/J12_hallofheroes.html.

45. In 1954 Medgar Evers was appointed to the new position of field secretary for the Mississippi branch of the NAACP. He was assassinated on June 12, 1963, three weeks short of his thirty-eighth birthday.

46. In August 1962, representatives from the National Association for the Advancement of Colored People (NAACP), the Congress of Racial Equality (CORE), the Southern Christian Leadership Conference (SCLC), and the Student Nonviolent Coordinating Committee (SNCC) met in Clarksdale, Mississippi, where they agreed to participate in an umbrella organization that they named the Council of Federated Organizations (COFO). The NAACP's state president, Aaron Henry, was elected president, but the moving force was Robert Moses, SNCC's field secretary, who was selected as project director of Freedom Summer to begin in June 1964. Over a thousand volunteers descended on Mississippi, mainly to register black voters, the responsibility of SNCC and CORE. SCLC conducted "Citizenship Schools" meant to prepare African Americans for voter registration, while the NAACP handled legal issues. Within ten weeks, thirty-seven churches and thirty homes or businesses were burned or bombed, a thousand local and out-of-state volunteers were arrested, eighty beaten, four critically wounded, and four murdered. Doug McAdam, *Freedom Summer* (New York: Oxford University Press, 1990); Raymond Arsenault, *Freedom Riders: 1961 and the Struggle for Racial Justice* (New York: Oxford University Press, 2006).

47. Nussbaum refers to the Central Conference of American Rabbis convention in New York City. The conferees adopted a resolution praising the Freedom Riders and passed a second resolution to underwrite the cost of the fines levied on CCAR members Martin Freedman and Israel Dresner who were among the ten clergy Freedom Riders arrested in Tallahassee, Florida, nine days earlier. Dresner was one of sixteen rabbis who marched and was later arrested in St. Augustine in 1964 when trying to integrate a restaurant along with, among others, Reverends Martin Luther King Jr. and Fred Shuttlesworth. Dresner worked closely with King and was the central figure in the anti-segregationist Supreme Court case, *Dresner v. Tallahassee*. He was arrested four times for his civil rights activism in Florida and Georgia. *Dressner v. City of Tallahassee* 375 US 136 (1963), Justia: US Supreme Court, accessed January 29, 2016, https://supreme.justia.com/cases/federal/us/375/136/case.html.

48. Parchman is about twenty-five miles northeast of Cleveland and twenty-five miles southeast of Clarksdale.

49. As previously noted, this turned out to be prophetic. Nussbaum's synagogue was bombed fifteen months after this interview and his home dynamited two months after that.

50. Nussbaum had already donated some of his papers including ones related to the Freedom Riders to the American Jewish Archives.

51. The confrontation between Nussbaum and Dresner took place June 21, 1966, at the Toronto convention of the CCAR.

52. When arrested in St. Augustine, Dresner and Freedman actually did not opt to pay the $500 fine. Instead they returned to Florida in August 1964 in order to serve a sixty-day jail sentence. To their surprise, they and eight other clergy arrested with them were released from prison after serving only four days. Michael Abrams, "Freedom Rider Rabbi Remembers His Arrest in Tallahassee Airport 50 Years Ago," *Tallahassee (FL) News*, January 30, 2012, http://thetallahasseenews.com/index.php/site/article/freedom_rider_rabbi_remembers_his_arrest_in_tallahassee_airport_50_years_ago; Eric Hersch-

thal, "The Rabbi Was a Freedom Rider," *New York Jewish Weekly*, accessed January 29, 2016, http://www.thejewishweek.com/arts/film/rabbi_was_freedom_rider.

53. His reference is to Jews who are not southerners but who went into the South as part of the various attempts to end segregation.

54. The Mississippi Council on Human Relations, a branch of the Southern Regional Council. Nussbaum became so active in the group that in 1965 he headed the search committee that hired Kenneth Dean to be its executive director. Kenneth Dean interview conducted by Betsy Nash, June 9, 1992, John C. Stennis Oral History Project, Department of History, Mississippi State University, accessed January 29, 2016, http://digital .library.msstate.edu/cdm/singleitem/collection/jcs1/id/881/rec/1.

55. For Tougaloo College, see Yasuhiro Katagiri, *The Mississippi State Sovereignty Commission: Civil Rights and States' Rights* (Jackson: University Press of Mississippi, 2001) 152–58. Its president from 1960–1964, Dr. A. D. "Dan" Beittel, was succeeded by Dr. George A. Owens (1964–1984). "Our History," Tougaloo College, accessed January 25, 2016, https://www.tougaloo.edu/about-tougaloo-college/our-history. Beittel, who was white, was a close friend of Charles Mantinband, who frequently spoke at Beittel's previous institution, Talladega College in Alabama, and at Tougaloo. In a letter to the college's board of trustees dated May 4, 1964, Nussbaum, Fr. Bernard Law, and the Rev. Duncan M. Gray Jr. expressed their dismay that Beittel had resigned his position. They praised him for his "unhesitating expressions of courageous insight . . . on the campus and in public" and for "his display of moral integrity without regard to personal cost." They observed that under his leadership Tougaloo "has become the sole institution in the State where freedom of expression is the rule" and concluded with the request that "you use your good offices to ensure Dr. Beittel's reconsideration of a resignation which we believe was forced upon him." Their request went unanswered. Beittel left Tougaloo but remained in Mississippi on the staff of the American Friends Service Committee. Nussbaum papers, Box 4, Folder 7.

56. His reference is to faculty members. The Jewish refugee scholar may have been Ernst Borinski. See Gabrielle S. Edgcomb, *From Swastika to Jim Crow: Refugee Scholars at Black Colleges* (Malabar, FL: Krieger, 1993).

57. See, for example, this excerpt a segregationist periodical distributed throughout the South: "This journal reported in its November 15, 1964 issue . . . the activities of the communist-front [*sic*] Mississippi Council on Human Relations. It also named a number of people . . . who attended its November meeting. . . . The following people . . . were also in attendance at the meeting in Galloway of the Interfaith Group: Mrs. S. W. Moore, Don Thompson, Power Hearn, Rabbi Nussbaum, Helen Rodriduez [*sic*], and Father [Bernard] Law." *Southern Review*, clipping, no date or page number, Nussbaum papers, Box 4, Folder 7.

58. Nussbaum left the Army as a colonel in the Chaplain Corps after twenty-five years of service. "Perry E. Nussbaum, 79, Rights Figure in South," *New York Times*, April 4, 1987, 2:32.

59. The *Protocols of the Elders of Zion* is a forgery made in Russia for the Okhrana (secret police) that blamed the Jews for the country's ills. It was privately printed in 1897 and made public in 1905. Copied from elements of both Maurice Joly's *The Dialogue in Hell Between Machiavelli and Montesquieu* (a political satire unconnected to Jews or anti-Semitism) and Hermann Goedsche's 1868 anti-Semitic 1868 novel, *Biarritz*, it claims that a secret Jewish cabal is plotting to take over the world ("Protocols of the Elders of Zion:

Timeline," *Holocaust Encyclopedia*. United States Holocaust Memorial Museum, Washington, DC. https://www.ushmm.org/wlc/en/article.php?ModuleId=10007244). The *Protocols* was exposed as a forgery by Lucien Wolf in *The Jewish Bogey and the Forged Protocols of the Learned Elders of Zion* (London: Press Committee of the Jewish Board of Deputies, 1920). Nonetheless, Henry Ford republished it in 1920 in the *Dearborn (MI) Independent* after it had been discredited. Adolf Hitler later used the *Protocols* to justify his anti-Semitic policies. American-Israeli Cooperative Enterprise, "Anti-Semitism: History of the *Protocols of the Elders of Zion*," Jewish Virtual Library, accessed January 29, 2016, http://www.jewishvirtuallibrary.org/jsource/anti-semitism/protocols.html.

60. Thomas G. Abernethy, who served in the United States House of Representatives from 1942 to 1973, was a racist and anti-Semite who inserted into the *Congressional Record* (Vol. 103, p. 8559, June 7, 1957) an excerpt from the fictional *A Racial Program for the Twentieth Century*, allegedly written by a Jew named Israel Cohen. The Nussbaum papers are somewhat confusing on this issue. They contain a copy of a letter addressed to an ardent segregationist representative, John Bell Williams, dated October 7, 1957. Nussbaum cites a *Jackson (MS) Clarion-Ledger* article (October 3, 1957) in which columnist Charles Hills quotes the fictional "Israel Cohen." Nussbaum maintains that the paper's editor, archsegregationist Tom Hederman Jr., advised him that Williams had inserted the Cohen material into the *Congressional Record*. By mid-October Nussbaum had realized that Abernethy was the guilty party, so he sent Abernethy a letter on October 14. On March 26, 1958, Nussbaum found an article in the Jackson press describing a talk given in Little Rock by the head of the women's division of the Mississippi Citizens' Councils "in which she mentions a plan by the communists in the early 1900's which makes me wonder if she is not using the authority of the *Congressional Record* account." Nussbaum wrote to Abernethy that same day that he could not "believe that you intentionally lent yourself to the perpetuation of a canard. . . . In a spirit of fairplay and with a view of keeping religious prejudices out of the serious issues of integration versus segregation . . . I am again respectfully . . . urging you to put some statement into the Record acknowledging the lack of historical substance to the Cohen story." Again, the Nussbaum papers do not include a response. Years later another article in the *Jackson (MS) Clarion-Ledger* prompted Nussbaum to write to Williams again. Although this letter is not extant, Williams responded to Nussbaum (September 5, 1961) that he registers "shock" at "the insinuations made in your letter of August 30, concerning a *Congressional Record* insertion by me under date of August 18." Williams had apparently inserted an editorial attack on the NAACP made by an African American newspaperman, J. W. Jones, then editor of the semi-monthly, black-owned *Community Citizen*. See "Negro Education Leader Urges Equal Schools," *Tupelo (MS) Daily Journal*, August 30, 1954, 1; "Negro Leader Appeals to Race," *Greenwood (MS) Commonwealth*, August 23, 1954, 1; "Negro Says Mixing Ole Miss Won't Help Us," AP, *Greenwood (MS) Commonwealth*, September 19, 1962, 1. In the article Jones accepts the segregationist position that the NAACP is a communist front organization. Nussbaum's point is that, in the mind of many southerners, the NAACP was created by Jews (Joel and Arthur Spingarn among others) and was being run by Jews like Kivie Kaplan. Williams responded, "I took the liberty of showing this article to three Members of Congress who are very prominent members of your faith. . . . [And] all of these gentlemen . . . stated that, in their opinions, nothing in the article could be interpreted as Anti-Semitic even by the farthest stretch of the imagination." Nussbaum replied on September 12, "I do apologize for assuming that you inserted the Jones editorial as it appeared in our local paper," but, he adds, "In a most friendly manner" "that neither you

nor the three Members of Congress of the Jewish faith whom you consulted faced up to the problem of anti-Semitism in terms of *Congressional Record* Insertions." Nussbaum continues, "I have regretted for years that the defenders of Segregation do not understand in depth the effects of an alliance, even though it be unconscious, with the professional bigots. . . . To quote, for example, *The Cross and the Flag* is to dignify a publication which is notoriously antisemitic." Nussbaum papers, Box 4, Folder 1.

61. Reference here is to Clayton Rand, owner of the *Neshoba (MS) Democrat, DeKalb (MS) Democrat,* and the *Tunica (MS) Times,* as well as the *Gulfport (MS) Dixie Press.* He wrote a syndicated column, *Crossroads Scribe,* and a number of books. Mississippi State University Libraries, Special Collections Department, Manuscript Division, "Clayton Rand papers MSS.91," accessed January 29, 2016, http://library.msstate.edu/FindingAid /Clayton_Rand_papers_finding_aid_MSS.91.pdf.

62. On Sunday, May 15, 1955, twenty-five delegates responded to Nussbaum's invitation and gathered in Jackson to form the organization.

63. A voluntary association of Jewish community relations agencies, the National Community Relations Advisory Council, founded in 1944 by the Council of Jewish Federations, is the instrument through which its constituent national and community Jewish agencies jointly determine the issues of concern, what positions they should take, how they can most effectively carry out those positions, and which of the issues should be given priority attention in the coming year.

64. Allen Krause's question refers to "Taking a Stand in Dixie" (*The Reconstructionist* 27 no. 18 [January 12, 1962]: 7-14; 27 no. 19 [January 26, 1962] 18–22) by Rabbi Joseph H. Gumbiner. Gumbiner had served Temple Mishkan Israel in Selma, Alabama, during the 1930s. Gumbiner became the Hillel director at the University of California, Berkeley. On July 18, 1961 he joined a group of about thirty people from various parts of the country to attend a conference of religious leaders at Tougaloo College. At the conclusion of the conference, he and eight others, including African Americans, "decided to have coffee together at the restaurant in the airport before leaving for home." They were arrested, tried, and convicted of "breach-of-the-peace," and placed in cells in the Jackson City Jail. The next day CORE posted Gumbiner's bail, and he returned to California. Shortly thereafter, he wrote the article that is a detailed description of this experience. Nussbaum refers to one paragraph in which Gumbiner wrote, "But I knew that the dimensions of this problem are not southern. We who live in carefully zoned neighborhoods in the North must not be self-righteous about the South. The problem confronts all men of good will in American and throughout the shrinking world." "Purim in the Selma Jail: Jewish Activists in 1965," *Southern Jewish Life Magazine* (SJLM), accessed January 29, 2016, http://www.sjlmag.com/2015/03/purim-in-selma-jail-jewish-activists-in.html; see also "Scottsboro: A Southern Tragedy, a Jewish Controversy," SJLM, accessed January 29, 2016, http://www.sjlmag.com/2011/03/remembering-scottsboro-boys-case-its.html. Yet Nussbaum indicates the article he is referring to was written by a rabbi from Mississippi. Alan LaPayover, director of the Reconstructionist Rabbinical College Library, graciously identified and forwarded a copy of the Gumbiner article, but the closest other article in description he was able to locate was written by Albert Hoschander Friedlander ("We Went to Selma," *The Reconstructionist* 31, no. 6 [April 30, 1965]): 24–27. Although he graduated from high school in Mississippi, Friedlander filled the pulpit of a congregation in Wilkes-Barre, Pennsylvania, when he wrote this article, and this does not appear to be the one to which Nussbaum refers. Nussbaum must have been mistaken in either the author of the article or, more likely, the journal in which it appeared.

65. In a letter to Charles Mantinband in response to the question whether demonstrations serve a good and useful purpose, Nussbaum wrote, "They do not down here. They have hardened the die-hards" and "they have led most of the 'good' people to renewed rationalization about 'keeping the peace.'" Nussbaum papers, Box 4, Folder 5, April 17, 1964.

66. Reference is to Jews coming to support integration and black voter registration.

67. The Hebrew Benevolent Congregation ("The Temple") was bombed on October 12, 1958.

68. The problem was compounded when a reporter for the local newspaper obtained a copy of the bulletin. The next day his column bore the heading: "Rabbi Says It Will Happen"; Zola, "What Price Amos?" 412.

69. The board proposed three amendments to the synagogue constitution to be voted on at the November 2, 1958, annual congregational meeting. The first amendment would require a secret ballot passed by at least two-thirds of the members to enter into any contract involving more than $2,000, an obvious threat to Nussbaum's tenure. The second amendment would bar the rabbi from attending board meetings unless invited, and the third would require the rabbi to have board approval to speak in public on any subject that might be of concern to the board. Even though the amendments failed, Nussbaum considered it a Pyrrhic victory, since 20 percent of the congregants present voted in favor of the provisions and thus against him.

70. For examples of these sermons, see the Nussbaum papers. As early as Rosh Hashanah 1955, he preached a powerful sermon titled "Classified Ads," based on the pretext of his finding an unsigned ad in the personals section of the newspaper. The sermon read in part, "I believe in God, but who will help me maintain my belief in my fellow men?" Nussbaum challenged the congregants not to go along with the majority: "We will not climb on any bandwagon of prejudice and inflammatory speeches. We will not echo arguments that seem to be founded on the premise that the Negro was ordained by the Lord ever to stay on a lower level of human society because . . . he doesn't deserve anything better. This is not Judaism."

71. The 1956 conference took place in Atlantic City, New Jersey. The conference program has the following entry for Monday, June 25, from 2:00–4:30 PM:

MEETING FOR THE SOUTHERN RABBIS IN PRIVATE SESSION
To take counsel together on those aspects of desegregation peculiar to their section of the country.

Sidney Regner, ed, *CCAR Yearbook* LXVI, (Philadelphia: Maurice Jacobs Press, 1957), xxi.

72. W. B. Selah, pastor of Jackson's Galloway Memorial Methodist Church, the largest and most prestigious Methodist church in Mississippi, was one of the twenty-eight Methodist clergy in the state who signed the "Born of Conviction" statement in January 1963. On Sunday morning, June 2, 1963, two days before the murder of Medgar Evers, Evers and five Tougaloo College students attempted to gain entrance to Galloway to worship with the congregation and were turned away. Noticing this, Selah cut short his sermon and made a brief statement in which he affirmed his affection for his parishioners but declared that he could not serve in a congregation where any one was turned away based on the color of their skin. He thus announced that after eighteen years at Galloway he would seek another appointment. W. J. Cunningham, *Agony at Galloway: Our Church's Struggle with Social Change* (Jackson: University Press of Mississippi, 1980), 7;

Taylor Branch, *Pillar of Fire: America in the King Years* (New York: Touchstone, 1998), 121; Marsh: *God's Long Summer*.

73. The American Council for Judaism was founded in 1942. It affirms the unique experience of Judaism in the United States, and, in so doing, takes a strong anti-Zionist position. Supporting the Classical Reform mode of Judaism, the group also opposes the Reform movement's trend toward Jewish tradition and ritual observance.

74. On June 5, 1966, University of Mississippi graduate James Meredith, accompanied by a few supporters, began a march from Memphis, Tennessee, to Jackson, Mississippi, designed to encourage black voter registration. The following day Meredith was shot and wounded in Hernando, Mississippi. The next day leaders of SNCC, the Southern Christian Leadership Conference, and the CRE called upon all freedom-loving people in the country to join them in Hernando. On June 22, 1966, the marchers arrived in Philadelphia, Mississippi, where they conducted a memorial service for civil rights martyrs James Chaney, Andrew Goodman, and Michael Schwerner. Violence broke out during which African American marchers were beaten and one local white man was shot. For the next two weeks, from two hundred to two thousand people marched, reaching Jackson on June 26, four days after this interview was conducted in Toronto. Fifteen thousand people joined together in Jackson to celebrate the completion of the march and affirm the right and the importance of the ballot. Aram Goudsouzian, *Down to the Crossroads: Civil Rights, Black Power, and the Meredith March against Fear* (New York: Farrar, Straus & Giroux, 2014); Charles W. Eagles, *The Price of Defiance: James Meredith and the Integration of Ole Miss* (Chapel Hill: University of North Carolina Press, 2009).

75. Senator James O. Eastland, who served in the Senate in 1941 and then from 1943 until 1978, acted as President Pro Tem of the Senate from 1972 to 1978 and chaired the Judiciary Committee from 1956 to 1978.

76. Nussbaum meant John C. Stennis, who served in the Senate from 1947 until 1989. He was Chairman of the Armed Services Committee from 1969 to 1981 and President Pro Tem from 1987 to 1989. During the 1950s and '60s he staunchly opposed integration, while Eastland was perceived by many as one of the most powerful and malicious racists in Mississippi.

77. Dr. Jacob Rader Marcus was a distinguished historian, professor of American Jewish history at Hebrew Union College—Jewish Institute of Religion, and founding director of the American Jewish Archives.

Bibliographic Essay

1. For complete bibliographies, see Mark K. Bauman and Berkley Kalin, eds., *The Quiet Voices: Southern Rabbis and Black Civil Rights, 1880s to 1990s* (Tuscaloosa: University of Alabama Press, 1997), 4; P. Allen Krause's research and article was published in *American Jewish Archives* XXI (April 1969); Leonard Dinnerstein and Mary Dale Palsson, eds, *Jews in the South* (Baton Rouge: Louisiana State University Press, 1973); Clive Webb, *Fight Against Fear: Southern Jews and Black Civil Rights* (Athens: University of Georgia Press, 2001); Lavender's *A Coat of Many Colors: Jewish Subcommunities in the United States* (Westport, CT: Greenwood Press, 1977); See also Jack Nelson, *Terror in the Knight: The Klan's Campaign against the Jews* (Jackson: University Press of Mississippi, 1993).

2. Golden, *Our Southern Landsmen* (New York: G.P. Putnam's Sons, 1974); Golden, *Jewish Roots in the Carolinas* (Greensboro, NC: Deal Print Company, 1955). Evans, *The*

Provincials (Chapel Hill: University of North Carolina Press, 2005; orig. published 1973). See also Nathan M. Kaganoff and Melvin I. Urofsky, eds., *Turn to the South: Essays on Southern Jewry* (Charlottesville: University Press of Virginia, 1979); Samuel Proctor and Louis Schmier with Malcolm Stern, eds., *Jews of the South: Selected Essays for the Southern Jewish Historical Society* (Macon, GA: Mercer University Press, 1984); Ferris and Greenberg, eds., *Jewish Roots in Southern Soil* (Waltham, MA: Brandeis University Press, 2006).

3. See, for examples, the following articles in *Southern Jewish History*; Adam Mendelsohn, "Two Far South: Rabbinical Responses to Apartheid and Segregation in South Africa and the American South," 6 (2003); Mary Stanton, "At One with the Majority," 9 (2006); James L. Moses, "'The Law of Life is the Law of Service': Rabbi Ira Sanders and the Quest for Racial and Social Justice in Arkansas, 1926–1963," 10 (2007); P. Allen Krause, "Charleston Jewry, Black Civil Rights, and Rabbi Burton Padoll," 11 (2008); Krause, "Rabbi Benjamin Schultz and the American Jewish League Against Communism: From McCarthyism to Mississippi," 13 (2010); as well as Mary Stanton, *The Hand of Esau: Montgomery's Jewish Community and the Bus Boycott* (Montgomery: Rover Publishing, 2006); Raymond A. Mohl with Mathilda "Bobbi" Graff and Shirley M. Zoloff, *South of the South: Jewish Activists and the Civil Rights Movement in Miami, 1945–1950* (Gainesville: University Press of Florida, 2003); S. Jonathan Bass, *Blessed are the Peacemakers: Martin Luther King, Jr., Eight White Religious Leaders, and the "Letters from Birmingham Jail"* (Baton Rouge: Louisiana State University Press, 2001); Hollace A. Weiner, *Jewish Stars of Texas: Rabbis and Their Work* (College Station: Texas A&M University Press, 2006); Leonard Rogoff, *Homelands: Southern Jewish Identity in Durham-Chapel Hill, North Carolina* (Tuscaloosa: University of Alabama Press, 2001); Deborah Weiner, *Coalfield Jews: An Appalachian History* (Urbana: University of Illinois Press, 2006); Henry A. Green, *Gesher Vakesher, Bridges and Bonds: The Life of Leon Kronish* (Tampa: University of South Florida, 1996); Mark K. Bauman, *Harry H. Epstein and the Rabbinate as Conduit to Change* (Cranbury, NJ: Associated University Presses, 1994).

4. Cheryl Greenberg, *Troubling the Waters: Black-Jewish Relations in the American Century* (Princeton, NJ: Princeton University Press, 2010).

5. See, for examples, Weissbach, "Kentucky's Jewish History in National Perspective: The Era of Mass Migration," *Filson Club Historical Quarterly* 69 (1995); Weissbach, "Stability and Mobility in the Small Jewish Community: Examples from Kentucky History," *American Jewish History* 79 (spring 1990); Bauman, *The Southerner as American: Jewish Style* (Cincinnati: American Jewish Archives, 1996); Bauman, *Dixie Diaspora: An Anthology of Southern Jewish History* (Tuscaloosa: University of Alabama Press, 2006).

6. See, for examples, Jacobson, *Whiteness of a Different Color: European Immigrants and the Alchemy of Race* (Cambridge, MA: Harvard University Press, 1998); Brodkin, *How Jews Became White Folks and What That Says about Race in America* (New Brunswick, NJ: Rutgers University Press, 1998); Roediger, *The Wages of Whiteness: Race and the Making of the American Working Class* (London: Verso, 1991). A more recent example of this very extensive literature is Eric L. Goldstein, *The Price of Whiteness: Jews, Race, and American Identity* (Princeton, NJ: Princeton University Press, 2006).

Bibliographic Essay

As I wrote in *The Quiet Voices: Southern Rabbis and Black Civil Rights* (Tuscaloosa: University of Alabama Press, 1997), studies of this subject began with P. Allen Krause's research and article published in *American Jewish Archives*, XXI (April 1969). A series of articles followed on the Reform rabbis and southern Jews in general that continued and expanded on Krause's findings. The trend of thought can be found in *Jews in the South* edited by Leonard Dinnerstein and Mary Dale Palsson (Baton Rouge: Louisiana State University Press, 1973) (which reprinted Krause's article), Abraham Lavender's collection *A Coat of Many Colors: Jewish Subcommunities in the United States* (Westport, CT: Greenwood Press, 1977) and several journal articles.[1]

This literature identified only about ten or twelve Reform rabbis in the South who acted in any significant fashion beyond things like presenting sermons in favor of civil rights for African Americans. As a school of thought, these historians argued that Jews in the South had largely acculturated and accepted southern mores while simultaneously fearing for their safety and positions in civil and economic society if they or their rabbis spoke out in favor of black rights. Thus congregations silenced or even fired their rabbis over the issue.

These arguments fit well within the reigning literature on southern Jewry that emphasized then and continues to do so now that southern Jewish history is clearly distinctive from the history of Jews elsewhere in the country. Jews in the South were largely accepted, the argument goes, but the conditions of that acceptance were acculturation to southern racial and other mores and remaining silent on controversial issues. This literature began during the 1970s with Harry Golden's *Our Southern Landsmen* (New York: G. P. Putnam's Sons, 1974), his *Jewish Roots in the Carolinas: A Pattern of Philo-Semitism* (Greensboro, NC: Deal Print Company, 1955), and the best-known book on Southern Jewish history, Eli N. Evans's *The Provincials: A Personal History of the Jews in the South* (Chapel Hill: University of North Carolina Press, 2005; orig. published 1973). Another anthology expanding on this line of thought is *Jewish Roots in Southern Soil: A New History* (Waltham, MA: Brandeis University Press, 2006), edited by Marcie Cohen Ferris and Mark I. Greenberg.[2]

During the mid-1990s, far more information appeared about numerous rab-

bis and Jewish laypeople in the South who had spoken out in favor of rights for
African Americans. Much of this was brought to light in *The Quiet Voices* and
Clive Webb's *Fight against Fear: Southern Jews and Civil Rights* (Athens: University of Georgia Press, 2001). Several articles published in *Southern Jewish History* (including two by Krause) as well as several books expand on this trend.[3]

This new historiography demonstrates that numerous Reform rabbis acted
positively on behalf of the modern civil rights movement for African Americans
and that their participation was disproportionate in relation to the number of
Jews and Jewish clergy in the region. It also recognizes the actions of a very few
Conservative and Orthodox rabbis, but far more research is required in these
areas.

This literature tends to stress the long view of the civil rights movement. It
demonstrates that earlier activists typically preceded the activist rabbis of the
1950s and '60s in the same pulpits. Furthermore, the actions of the rabbis during
the height of the civil rights movement were often another dimension of their
advocacy on behalf of other social issues. Frequently, congregations attempted to
silence these individuals in the face of violence and intimidation, but the rabbis
avowed freedom of the pulpit. Although many felt pressure, few lost their positions solely or even largely because of their role as civil rights activists. Unlike
Jewish and non-Jewish activists from elsewhere in the country, they preferred to
work behind the scenes and with Protestant and Catholic clergy, often through
ministerial associations. They made friendships with but also conflicted with Reform rabbis from the North who did march and demonstrate as well as with colleagues in the South who acted more or less than they in support of desegregation. Although some welcomed the stances of national Jewish organizations that
supported the civil rights movement and even held positions in them, tensions
existed between the national groups and their southern brethren.

Cheryl Greenberg's outstanding *Troubling the Waters: Black-Jewish Relations
in the American Century* (Princeton, NJ: Princeton University Press, 2010) tells
the larger story of Jewish-black relations from an organizational perspective.[4]
Hers is perhaps the best treatment of the rise and fall of a black-Jewish "alliance"
or "coalition." Nonetheless, her institutional sources give short shrift to the positions of Jews in the South. Although unintentional, to some extent Krause's
interviews with the southern rabbis provide an antidote to this viewpoint biased
toward the southern Jewish perspective.

Be that as it may, *To Stand Aside or Stand Alone: Southern Reform Rabbis and
the Civil Rights Movement* fits within the revisionist camp, goes far beyond it,
and provides new answers and questions. Here still more activist rabbis are identified and their actions explained. The rabbis' responses to Krause's queries expli-
cate their thinking on numerous issues. His research into their backgrounds pro-

vides the data for generalizations concerning the influences that bore on them and their communities.

Yet this book breaks equally or more important new ground in relation to the ideas and roles of less activist, gradualist rabbis. Previous historians have only touched on these individuals in passim and with derision. The interviews in this volume give voice to their rationale and delineate their actions. They appear to have agreed on theories, methods, and the nature of their circumstances as much if not more than their more active colleagues.

As the earlier works on southern Jews and civil rights fit into a larger school of Southern Jewish historiography, so too does this later body of work, although several of the contributors would waver between the two or find greater common ground with the distinctiveness perspective. Beginning in the 1990s, several historians led by Lee Shai Weissbach and me raised questions about the distinctiveness of many of the experiences and actions of Jews in the South.[5] *To Stand Aside or Stand Alone* and the revisionist works that preceded it demonstrate that in several ways southern Jews including the activists did differ in thoughts and methodology from their counterparts elsewhere. Nonetheless, the numerous rabbis that did advocate and act in behalf of civil rights for African Americans refused to accept southern racial mores and institutionalized racism. They did stand up and did stand out. A minority of Jewish lay people joined them. Yet even the majority of Jews in the South differed from the majority of their white Protestant peers. Whereas numerous Protestant clergy lost their positions explicitly because of their civil rights advocacy, most southern Jews seemed to recognize the moral correctness of their rabbis' positions. They pressured their rabbis based on real fear but virtually never couched their arguments as support for continued segregation—even if they personally welcomed the status quo.

Another body of literature that touches on the subject of this book had not yet appeared when Krause conducted his interviews. During the last two decades, the controversial field of "whiteness studies," led by Matthew Frye Jacobson, Karen Brodkin, David R. Roediger, and others, has stormed the historical arena of immigrant groups and their relationship to the white Protestant majority and people of color.[6]

To Stand Aside or Stand Alone does not confront this aspect of historiography directly, yet it implicitly reflects on it. Jews in the South, however much they benefited from racism against African Americans, acculturated, and rose economically and in civic affairs, remained within a racialized borderland. Although they did not suffer from segregation, like African Americans they faced exclusion from elite social clubs and certain neighborhoods. They were viewed as different from white Protestants and recognized this. The fear they lived with through the civil rights movement was not paranoia; it was based on actual events. Although

Jews in the South illustrated characteristics associated with whiteness, throughout the civil rights movement they remained a marginalized other.

Certainly African Americans and other minorities experienced far more prejudice and discrimination than Jews did, and the negative treatment of these other minorities and particularly African Americans in the South did shield Jews from the strident anti-Semitism prevalent in much of European history. Yet the times of the greatest discrimination against African Americans tended to coincide with the highest tides of anti-Semitism in the United States. The era of the modern civil rights movement provides evidence of this relationship. Jews in the South thus followed a variety of paths through what they perceived as the perilous maze of the civil rights movement.

Index

Touro, Judah, 123, 187

Touro Synagogue, New Orleans, Louisiana, 334n42

Townsend, John, 61

transportation. *See* desegregation

Trenton, New Jersey, 297

Tri–State Fair, 192

Tulane University, 41, 45, 51, 119

Tuska, Simon, 188

UNICEF, 298

Union of American Hebrew Congregations (UAHC), 34, 73, 81, 89–90, 101, 121, 127, 216, 237, 244, 247, 267, 299, 304, 315, 317

Union Theological Seminary, 60

Unitarian, 31, 162, 328

United Church of Christ, 134

United Hebrew Congregation, St. Louis, Missouri, 195

University of Alabama, 221, 240

University of Cincinnati, 20, 23, 117, 296

University of Chicago, 279

University of Georgia, 340n14

University of Judaism, 81

University of Mississippi, 40, 210, 215, 235, 238–39, 292, 299–300, 305, 362–63n35, 363n38, 369–70n23

University of Pennsylvania, 41, 165

University of Southern Mississippi, 265, 279

University of Vienna, 252

Urban League, 41, 194, 196, 284

Valdosta, Georgia, 61

Vanderbilt, Cornelius, 134

Vanderbilt University, 134, 137, 140, 148, 149, 345n11, 346n34; Vanderbilt University Medical School, 140

Vandiver, Ernest, Jr., 335–36n18

Vassar Temple, Poughkeepsie, New York, 269

Vicksburg, Mississippi, 225, 299

Vidalia, Georgia, 19–20

Vietnam War, 6, 73, 83, 89, 205, 248, 336n21, 339n23, 359n16, 365n57

Virginia Beach, Virginia, 171

Virginia Union University, 171

Vivian, C. T., 137

Vorspan, Albert, 236, 237, 348n21, 363n37

Voter Education Project, 351n54

Votings Rights Act (1965), 343n7

Wadkins, Daniel, 134

Waggoner, Jabbo, 230, 231

Waldauer, Abe, 191

Walker, Mardon, 108–9

Wallace, George, 17, 27, 214, 327n10, 328n17, 342n7, 357n6

Wallach, Morton A., 330, 359n20, 21

Waller, William, 302

Washington, Booker T., 135

Washington University, St. Louis, 195

Wax, James, 6, 8, 11, 143, 187, 191, 193–210, 308, 353n2, 354n25, 354–55nn28–31, 355n34, 356n41

Wax, Morris, 194–95

Wax, Rose Edlin, 194

Wechsler, Judah, 139

Weil, David, 138

Weinberg, Lew, 194

Werthan, Joe, 140

West, Ben, 135, 137

Western Reserve University. *See* Case Western Reserve University

West Point, Georgia, 165

White–Spunner, Charles S., 24, 327n12

White Citizens' Council, 17–18, 21, 27, 33–34, 39, 48–9, 96, 123, 125, 129, 136, 144, 150, 210, 266, 268, 275–77, 281–2, 290–1, 293, 299–300, 307, 310, 315

Whitehill, Jane, 179, 351n50

Wichita, Kansas, 296

Wilkins, Roy, 292

Williams, Avon N., Jr., 135

Williams, J. D., 237–9

Williams, Peyton Randolph, 176

Williams, Sam, 106–8

Williamsport, Pennsylvania, 269

Willis, A. W., Jr., 192

Wilson, James, 57

Winchester, James, 187

Wise, Isaac Mayer, 149, 188, 338n22, 347n35

Wise, Stephen S., 269

Wiseman, Hollis, 327n15

Wiseman, Mrs. Hollis. *See* Thames–Wiseman, Teko

Wolf, Joseph, 140